NINE DAYS IN MAY

NINE DAYS IN MAY

THE BATTLES OF THE 4TH INFANTRY DIVISION ON THE CAMBODIAN BORDER, 1967

WARREN K. WILKINS

University of Oklahoma Press : Norman

Library of Congress Cataloging-in-Publication Data

Name: Wilkins, Warren, author.
Title: Nine days in May : the battles of the 4th Infantry Division on the Cambodian border, 1967 / Warren K. Wilkins.
Description: Norman : University of Oklahoma Press, [2017] | Includes bibliographical references and index.
Identifiers: LCCN 2016043361 | ISBN 978-0-8061-5715-3 (hardcover : alk. paper)
Subjects: LCSH: Vietnam War, 1961–1975—Campaigns—Cambodia. | United States. Army. Infantry Division, 4th—History—20th century.
Classification: LCC DS557.8.C3 W55 2017 | DDC 959.704/3422095977—dc23
LC record available at https://lccn.loc.gov/2016043361

The paper in this book meets the guidelines for permanence and durability of the Committee on Production Guidelines for Book Longevity of the Council on Library Resources, Inc. ∞

1 2 3 4 5 6 7 8 9 10

For those who were there

CONTENTS

ILLUSTRATIONS

FIGURES

MAPS

ACKNOWLEDGMENTS

Cherished for her legendary wit, the estimable Dorothy Parker once observed, famously, "I hate writing, I love having written." Indeed, as I was once again reminded, few endeavors are as frustrating, exhausting, or rewarding.

I am profoundly grateful for the extraordinary support and assistance I received from the larger "Nine Days in May" community of veterans, family, and friends. If materials gleaned from archives and other official repositories served as the *skeleton* of the "Nine Days" narrative, the stories and experiences of the participants themselves added some much needed meat to those dry, historical bones. With few exceptions, these remarkable men patiently endured hours of interviews, shared personal photos and other critical documents, and encouraged reluctant comrades to come forward.

That so many would agree to relive those fateful days in a faraway land remains a debt I can never repay. In particular, I would like to thank John Barclay, Landis Bargatze, Oliver Butler, Hank Fischer, Bob Gamboa, Mike Hamer, Mike Horan, Richard Jackson, Larry Jumper, Billy Lomnicki, Branko Marinovich, Bill May, Steve Pestikas, Tom Radke, Don Rawlinson, Victor Renza, Larry Rodabaugh, Cliff Rountree, Michael Scott, Robert Sholly, and Erin Stroh. Robert Childers, Sharon Mills, Garza Molnar, and Dan Wilkins ensured that the bravery and sacrifice of their deceased loved ones did not escape my attention. Sadly, a handful of veterans and relatives who assisted in this project, including Mary Wheeler, Gilbert Nash, and Doyle Volkmer, have since passed away.

For nearly a decade, I have been exposed to some of the finest historians and scholars of the Vietnam War, and in that time my work has benefited accordingly. Andrew Birtle and Erik Villard of the Center of Military History, for example, granted me access to a veritable treasure trove of files related to the 4th Infantry Division. Erik, moreover, enhanced my understanding of the relationship between the production and distribution of rice in Vietnam and the rhythm of Communist military operations in the Central Highlands and along the populated coast. Col. (ret.) Gregory Daddis and Jay Veith, meanwhile, critiqued an early draft and provided much needed perspective. As always, the indomitable Merle Pribbenow furnished Communist documents, histories, and other materials used in this study.

Similarly, Martin Gedra at the National Archives and Records Administration and James Tobias of the Center of Military History dutifully retrieved essential documents. Bob Babcock, Jim Stapleton and Marissa Sestito deserve my thanks as well. Nor can I forget the yeomanlike efforts of my editor at the University of Oklahoma Press, Adam Kane.

Finally, I would like to thank God and my family, especially my mother and sister, Andrea.

ABBREVIATIONS AND ACRONYMS

(-) denotes a company operating without all of its organic elements

AAR after action report

ADC assistant division commander

AF Air Force

AIT Advanced Infantry Training

AO area of operations

AP Associated Press

APC armored personnel carriers

ARVN Army of the Republic of Vietnam

B3 Central Highlands

C&C Command and Control

CBU cluster bomb unit

CIB Combat Infantryman's Badge

CIDG Civilian Irregular Defense Group

CMH U.S. Army Center of Military History

CO commanding officer

COSVN Central Office for South Vietnam

CP command post

CTZ Corps Tactical Zone

DEFCON defensive concentration (artillery fire)

DSJ Daily Staff Journal

EPO Enemy Proselytizing Office

FAC forward air controller

FDC fire direction center

FNG fucking new guy

FO forward observer

FSB fire support base

FSC fire support coordinator

FWMAF Free World Military Assistance Forces

G1 personnel officer or section at division or corps level

G2 intelligence officer or section at division or corps level

G3 operations officer or section at division or corps level

GVN Government of Vietnam (South Vietnamese government)

HE high explosive
IFFV First Field Force, Vietnam
JGS Joint General Staff
KIA killed in action
KP kitchen police
LAW light anti-tank assault weapon
LNO liaison officer
LP listening post
LRRP long-range reconnaissance patrols
LZ landing zone
MACV Military Assistance Command, Vietnam
Mech Mechanized (infantry)
MOS Military Occupational Specialty
MP Military Police
NCO noncommissioned officer
NDP night defensive position
NVA North Vietnamese Army
OCS Officer Candidate School
OSS Office of Strategic Studies
PROVN A Program for the Pacification and Long-Term Development of South Vietnam
PTL platoon leader
RA Regular Army
RPD *Ruchnoy Pulemyot Degtyaryova* (Degtyaryov light machine gun)
RPG rocket-propelled grenade
R&R rest and recuperation
RTO radio/telephone operator
S1 personnel officer or section at battalion or brigade level
S2 intelligence officer or section at battalion or brigade level
S3 operations officer or section at battalion or brigade level
S4 logistics officer or section at battalion or brigade level
SITREP situation report
TAOR tactical area of operational responsibility
TOC Tactical Operations Center
TOT time on target
USMA United States Military Academy
VC Viet Cong
VHS Vietnam Helicopter Syndrome
WIA wounded in action
WO1 warrant officer
XO executive officer

NINE DAYS IN MAY

INTRODUCTION

From the outset, Gen. William C. Westmoreland, the commander of Military Assistance Command, Vietnam (MACV), envisioned waging and winning the war in Vietnam in phases. The objective of the first was to arrest "the 'losing trend' by the end of 1965" and establish the logistical infrastructure required to sustain an expected influx of American forces.[1] Success in the Ia Drang Valley and in battles north of Saigon brought the "losing trend" to a resounding halt by year's end, and the establishment of bases and other logistical facilities to accommodate an expanded American military presence in South Vietnam continued apace. Contemplating his next phase, in which "U.S. and allied forces would mount major offensive actions to seize the initiative in order to destroy both the guerilla and organized enemy forces," Westmoreland appreciated that he did not immediately possess the forces necessary to conduct it. Amassing and deploying such forces, moreover, would take time. The problem, however, was determining how to safeguard critical areas of the country while keeping Viet Cong (VC) and North Vietnamese Army (NVA) forces off balance long enough for U.S. forces to transition to a third and final phase aimed at destroying the enemy's "guerilla structure and main force units remaining in remote base areas."[2] Defeating the enemy's main force units, Westmoreland reasoned, would provide the time and space required to conduct the types of pacification programs he believed were central to securing a politically viable, non-Communist South Vietnam.

Released in December 1965 with the imprimatur of MACV and the South Vietnamese Joint General Staff, the "Combined Campaign Plan for Military Operations in the Republic of Vietnam, 1966" outlined allied intentions for the forthcoming year. Foremost amongst the articulated objectives was the clearing and securing of the populous areas around Saigon, in the Mekong Delta, and in certain coastal regions of I and II Corps. The Combined Campaign Plan also prescribed defending

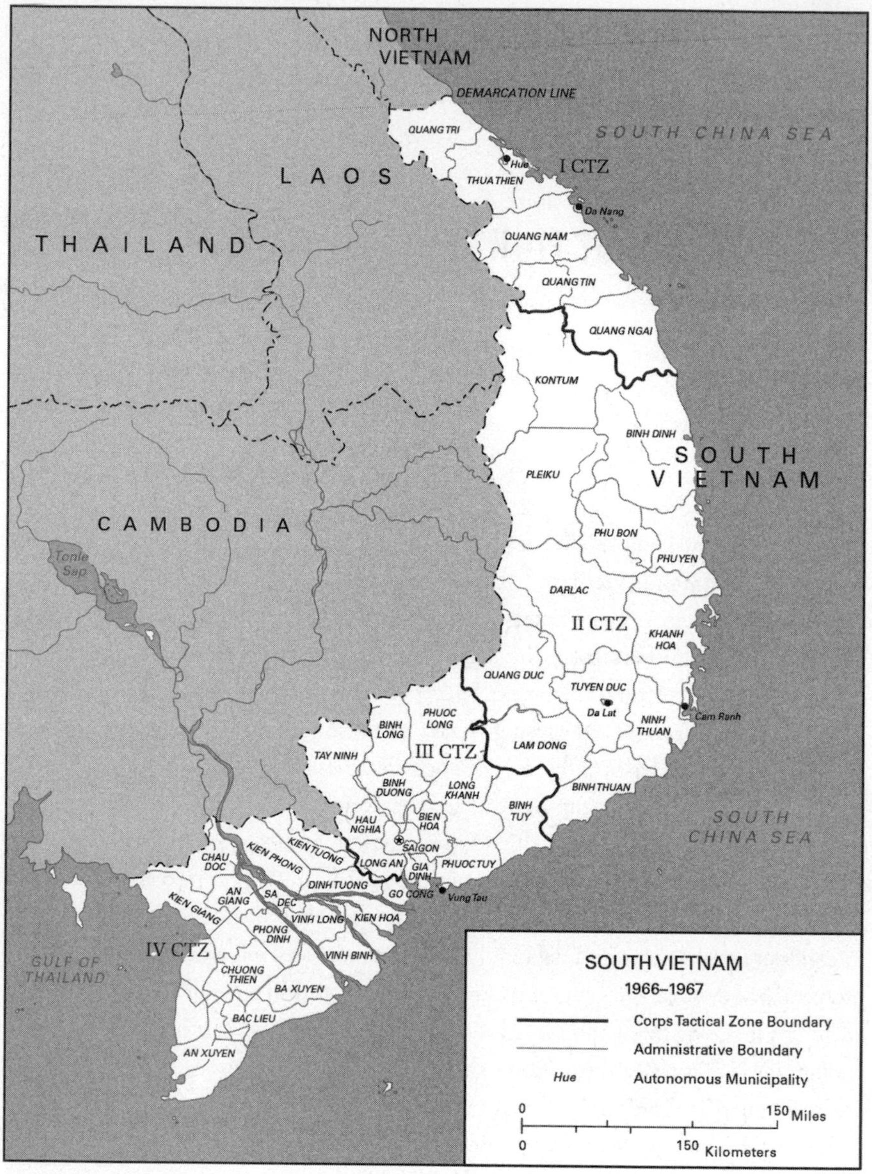

South Vietnam, 1966–1967. *Courtesy the U.S. Army Center of Military History.*

important government and civilian locations beyond the specified strategic areas, as well as offensive action against significant Viet Cong and North Vietnamese forces.[3]

Not surprisingly, the plan's principal geographic focus reflected the wisdom of the top American commander in the country. General Westmoreland had determined "that the critical regions requiring first attention were the populated area around Saigon

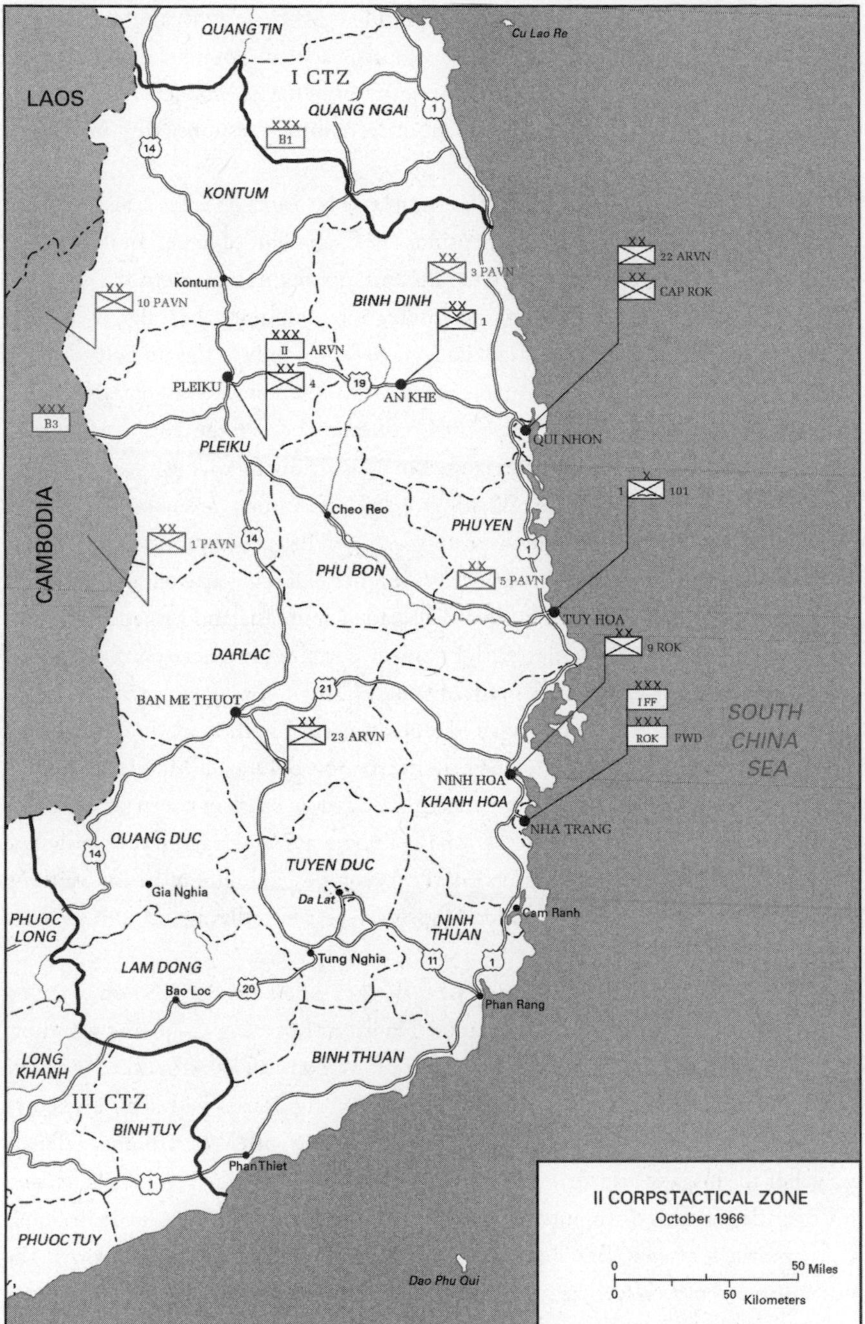

II Corps Tactical Zone, October 1966. *Courtesy the U.S. Army Center of Military History.*

in the III Corps and the coastal lowlands in the I and II Corps." Westmoreland then added that "the more important of these regions was that around the capital city."[4] Further, by "mutual agreement," South Vietnamese forces "concentrated on area security" while American and other allied units assumed responsibility for "major offensives" against the NVA and Viet Cong.[5]

Elsewhere in South Vietnam, as Westmoreland himself conceded, the American command applied the age-old military principle of "economy of force." In the Central Highlands, a remote, forested stretch of hills and mountains in western II Corps, the chore of monitoring North Vietnamese infiltration and, more generally, of holding down the fort in that strategically crucial region, fell initially to the 3rd Brigade, 25th Infantry Division. Then, in July 1966, as American forces in the Highlands labored through Operation Paul Revere I near the Cambodian border, the Advance Planning Group of the 4th Infantry Division landed in Nha Trang following a lengthy flight from McChord Air Force Base in Washington State. Planning Group personnel then flew on to Pleiku Province and the base camp of the 3rd Brigade, 25th Infantry Division. An advance party from the 2nd Brigade, 4th Infantry Division arrived soon after and settled into an interim site within the 3rd Brigade camp. The 2nd Brigade party was then expected to join the division's 4th Engineer Battalion in a new, permanent base camp approximately seven miles south of Pleiku City.[6]

Docking in Qui Nhon on July 29, the organic 4th Engineer Battalion splashed ashore and was airlifted to Pleiku. There, in the shadow of Dragon Mountain, a broad flat peak to the northwest, the battalion began the arduous task of constructing a base camp for the 4th Infantry Division. Formally known as the "Dragon Mountain base camp," the base was renamed Camp Enari in May 1967 in honor of 1st Lt. Mark N. Enari, who was posthumously awarded the Silver Star for rallying his pinned-down platoon in late 1966.[7]

On the morning of August 6, the USS *Walker* sailed into Qui Nhon carrying troops from the 2nd Brigade, 4th Infantry Division. Boarding C-130 aircraft, more than two thousand 2nd Brigade soldiers were flown up to Pleiku by the end of the day.[8] However, since certain civilian and military dignitaries had been invited to welcome Col. Judson F. Miller and his 2nd Brigade to South Vietnam, the "official" arrival of the brigade was delayed until Sunday, August 7. That October the 1st and 3rd Brigades of the 4th Infantry Division joined Colonel Miller's brigade in South Vietnam, the former at Tuy Hoa in Phu Yen Province on the coast of II Corps. The 3rd Brigade, deployed farther south in III Corps, set up near Saigon.

Thoroughly transformed after a frenetic period of expansion and reorganization, the 4th Infantry Division on the cusp of combat in Vietnam would look markedly different than the one that had served stateside in June of 1965. Then the 4th had been composed of five infantry battalions, two mechanized infantry battalions, and two armored battalions (along with the usual contingent of supporting elements). The division fielded the 5-2-2 alignment until November of 1965, when the Army announced that the number of infantry battalions in the 4th and 25th Infantry Divisions would increase to eight.[9] Accordingly the 4th was reorganized to comport with the 1-8-1 "maneuver mix" found in the 25th by subtracting an armored battalion, adding two infantry battalions, and converting one mechanized infantry battalion into a standard infantry battalion. Six thousand new recruits were then sent to flesh out the division.[10]

Reorganized and, in part, rebuilt, the 4th was alerted in the second half of 1965 and warned of an impending deployment to South Vietnam. To prepare for the rigors of a combat assignment, the division embarked on a grueling regimen of individual and unit training at Fort Lewis, Washington. The 4th also assisted in the activation of a training center at Fort Lewis, and it aided some forty-seven non-divisional units that were also preparing to deploy.[11]

Overseeing the war in II Corps as the commander of First Field Force, Vietnam (IFFV), Lt. Gen. Stanley "Swede" Larsen concluded that he would have to defeat the enemy's main force units before "true pacification" could begin. Larsen, a veteran of the bloody battle for Guadalcanal and a former assistant commandant of the U.S. Army Infantry School, planned to "destroy the NVA units first, destroy the hard core [VC] next, and finally root out the infrastructure."[12] Accordingly he advised the commander of the newly arrived 4th Infantry Division, Maj. Gen. Arthur Collins Jr., to "hit the enemy early." Whenever possible, Collins was to use spoiling attacks to keep the North Vietnamese off balance. "If you ever let him get set," warned Larsen, "you're going to pay hell getting him out."[13]

Larsen's warning reflected the pitched struggle both sides were waging for control of the Central Highlands. Strategically speaking the Highlands held great significance for Communist war managers in Hanoi. "As the Highlands stand on high ground and in the middle of the country, our armed forces operating from the region can easily move north or south or advance to the lowlands and the coast," declared a prominent Communist history of the war waged in the Highlands. "The Central Highlands had been likened to the 'roof' of South Vietnam, the 'backrest' of Zone 5, and the 'gateway' to Saigon and Nam Bo. The Highlands was also a corridor linking the great rear of socialist North Vietnam with the great front of heroic South Vietnam."[14] Allied commanders, consequently, were compelled by these exigencies to compete for control of the Central Highlands, even if it meant divesting troops and firepower from the resource-intensive pacification campaign on the insurgency-plagued coastal plain.

Hanoi, meanwhile, understood that with the Highlands safely in hand, heavily armed and capably led North Vietnamese regiments could march out of the mountains and down to the coastal plain to assist the local forces there. Such unfettered access to the populated lowlands of II Corps would disrupt vital allied pacification programs and the annual rice harvests. Alternatively, if North Vietnamese regulars could keep American mobile units tied down in the rugged Central Highlands, the Communist military-political movement in the cities and along the coast stood a better chance of obtaining the rice and recruits it needed to upend the South Vietnamese state.[15]

Set against this strategic backdrop, Hanoi created the B3 (Central Highlands) Front on May 1, 1964, to control Communist military operations in the Highlands.[16] Gen. Chu Huy Man, a native of Nghe An Province in North Vietnam and a veteran of the First Indochina War, was in command of the Front when the 4th Infantry Division arrived in South Vietnam. Man had commanded a regiment in the war against the French, and he later served as the political commissar of the 316th Division during the battle of Dien Bien Phu. When the First Indochina War concluded in 1954, he remained in the military, serving as the commander of a Vietnamese detachment in Laos and as the political commissar for the Communist Military Region 4. Subsequently reassigned, Man infiltrated into South Vietnam in 1964. The following year he was transferred to the Highlands, where he assumed command of the B3 Front.[17]

Officially established on December 20, 1965, the 1st NVA Division was arguably the preeminent fighting formation in the B3 Front.[18] Composed initially of the 32nd, 33rd, and 66th NVA Regiments, the division was under the command of General Man's able deputy, Col. Nguyen Huu An. A career soldier, An had enlisted in the Viet Minh "armed resistance" in 1945, rising from the rank of private to regimental commander during the war with the French. An served thereafter on the staff of the 316th NVA Division and eventually was promoted to the post of deputy chief of staff of the Northwestern Military Region. Resourceful, tenacious, and utterly committed to the Communist cause, An had also commanded North Vietnamese forces, alongside General Man, during the historic Ia Drang Valley campaign in the fall of 1965.

Fighting throughout the spring and summer of 1966, the B3 Front regrouped that fall and began preparing for a major dry season (October–May) offensive. The objectives for the proposed offensive clearly reflected the strategic relationship between the ongoing war in the Highlands and the struggle for control of the more populated coastal plain: "Annihilate and wear down part of the U.S. strength to aid the local movement to destroy strategic hamlets and wrest back the people; draw the U.S. forces to the Highlands and pin them down and keep them in the jungle-and-mountain area, thereby creating favorable conditions for the lowland theater to go on the offensive and contributing to the efforts of the entire South Vietnam in defeating the enemy's second dry-season strategic counteroffensive."[19] Colonel An's battle-tested 1st NVA Division, now composed of the 32nd, 66th, and 88th NVA Regiments, was to play a critical role in the upcoming offensive.

Heeding General Larsen's advice, General Collins launched Operation Paul Revere IV in October 1966 and eventually pushed two brigades up the Plei Trap Valley in western Pleiku Province.[20] The North Vietnamese counterattacked elements of Collins's 2nd Brigade near the Cambodian border. "The 2nd Brigade has been fighting real honest to goodness battles," Collins would write candidly in a letter to a fellow general at the end of November. "After scouting the area around PLEI ME, the IA DRANG VALLEY, and the CHU PHONG [*sic*], which were the favorite entry points for the NVA three times in the past year, we began to have indications that the enemy was in the rugged mountainous terrain west of the SE SAN River. . . . I won't go into all the details of the operations as you probably read about them in various reports that are submitted except to say that we were soon in contact with three regiments and knew we had a full division in front of us. We used a lot of artillery and B-52 strikes to dislodge him from the fine base he had established in the mountains, and he withdrew west toward the Cambodian border."[21]

The first major offensive conducted by the 4th Infantry Division in the Central Highlands, Paul Revere IV, concluded the following month. Successful if not decisive, the operation also underscored the dangers of fighting the Highland war so close to Cambodia. "The Cambodian sanctuary afforded major tactical and strategic benefits to the enemy," observed a divisional report. "The availability of the sanctuary enabled the enemy to stockpile large quantities of supplies well forward with no risk of destruction, to withdraw into the sanctuary when his forces became threatened, and to maintain significant forces in complete safety which could be employed at will to reinforce units in contact or to conduct attacks against U.S. forces. Operations against the enemy in the vicinity of the border were difficult for U.S. forces in that maneuver room was limited and it was difficult to interdict enemy routes of withdrawal, reinforcement, and resupply *without a border violation.*"[22]

Concerned about expanding the ground war beyond South Vietnam's borders, President Lyndon Johnson prohibited MACV from conducting cross-border raids against the enemy and the bases that sustained him. American ground units *could* operate temporarily in Cambodia for the purposes of self-defense, provided that they did not "widen" the war in any way. As a result, at the strategic level, the 4th Infantry Division would fight a largely defensive war in the Central Highlands.

By the late spring of 1967, the battle for Highland supremacy had shifted to the Ia Tchar Valley, a remote and forebodingly untamed area nestled between the Cambodian border and the Chu Goungot Mountains in Pleiku Province. Dashed by successive American offensive operations and the arrival of the 4th Infantry Division in 1966, Hanoi's hopes for liberating the Highlands had evolved instead into a grinding war of attrition predicated on drawing American units into the rugged uplands and away from the populated coastal plain. Such was the strategic mandate of North Vietnamese forces as they prepared that spring for the upcoming rainy season offensive. Meanwhile, Maj. Gen. William R. Peers, Collins's successor as commander of the venerable 4th, initiated Operation Francis Marion and eventually dispatched two of his battalions to the Ia Tchar to search for the North Vietnamese and preempt a potential enemy offensive in western Pleiku.

Tramping through the dense undergrowth and along narrow ridges overlooking steep ravines, troopers from the 1st of the 8th Infantry, many of whom were draftees, searched initially without much success. And then the tempo changed. On the morning of May 18, while pushing deeper into the valley, a company observed North Vietnamese soldiers strolling down a well-worn trail not far from the Cambodian border. The enemy soldiers appeared oblivious to their surroundings. Shouts and gunshots soon followed, and the North Vietnamese fled in haste, leaving four rucksacks and some blood behind. The company commander, a young lieutenant, sent a platoon after them. Pursuing cautiously at first, the troops were still making their way west down the trail when suddenly the jungle erupted in gunfire. Outnumbered and hopelessly surrounded, the young grunts would fight frantically to escape the deadly trap.

Fought in a tangled notch near the Cambodian border, the desperate fight waged by the encircled platoon marked the beginning of an epic nine-day, five-battle struggle the grunts would soon call "the Nine Days in May border battles." And when the guns finally fell silent, an unheralded American brigade would emerge battered but unbowed, its service memorialized with a Presidential Unit Citation and *three* Medals of Honor for extraordinary acts of gallantry. Tragically, the bloody battles in the Ia Tchar Valley–Chu Goungot Mountains were fought and won within the context of a broader and seemingly intractable strategic stalemate.

Formally established in November of 1917, the 4th Infantry Division or Ivy Division, an appellation derived from the four green ivy leaves in its insignia, fought valiantly in several historically significant actions in World War I, including the Aisne-Marne Campaign of 1918. Twenty-six years later, after months of training on Slapton Sands in England, the 4th splashed ashore at Utah Beach in Normandy, liberated Paris with the French 2nd Armored Division, and eventually became the first Allied ground unit to enter Nazi Germany. Few divisions have enjoyed a more storied history. And yet, in the nearly half-century since the 4th debarked in the now defunct Republic of Vietnam (South Vietnam), very little has been written about its service in that divisive conflict. The violent battles in the Highlands in May 1967 are no exception.

Long forgotten, the story of the "Nine Days in May" bears recounting, not merely to preserve the history of a proud division, but to remember the service and sacrifice of the men who lived it.

AUTHOR'S NOTE

As is typical for this type of battle history, quoted material derived from the author's interviews with *Nine Days in May* veterans is not individually cited. A complete list of interview subjects and dates can be found in the bibliography.

1 STEADFAST AND LOYAL

Gen. William C. Westmoreland, the self-assured "inevitable general," did not mince words. "During the period 1 November 1966 to 1 May 1967—the Northeast Monsoon Season—we will maintain and increase the momentum of our operations," he explained in August 1966. "Our strategy will be one for a general offensive with maximum practical support to area and population security in further support of Revolutionary Development."[1] Indeed, unlike in previous years when Westmoreland had to "stem the tide" or build up his troop strength for future offensive action, 1967 was to be the "year of the offensive."[2]

In November of 1966 MACV and the South Vietnamese Joint General Staff released the "Combined Campaign Plan for Military Operations in the Republic of Vietnam, 1967." Broadly defined, the mission of the Combined Campaign Plan was unambiguous: defeat the VC/NVA and extend South Vietnamese government control throughout South Vietnam. Citing the initiative the allies had gained in 1966, the 1967 plan stressed the importance of maintaining it "through a strategic and tactical offensive conducted in consonance with political, economic, and sociological programs of GVN [Government of Vietnam] and US/FW agencies." Additionally the Plan established "National Priority Areas" and "Areas for Priority of Military Offensive Operations" in South Vietnam's four Corps Tactical Zones (CTZs I, II, III, and IV).

Within "National Priority Areas," which consisted of population centers and other areas of national import, the South Vietnamese were primarily responsible for providing security and lending support to "Revolutionary Development activities," or those activities typically associated with pacification. The Americans, meanwhile, would tackle the VC and NVA in the generally less populated and harder to reach "Areas for Priority of Military Offensive Operations." Specifically American forces were to destroy the enemy and his bases or, short of that, push him into "sparsely populated" areas with insufficient food resources.[3] Interestingly enough, although the Plan expressly forbade a division of labor between the various allied nations, it very obviously implied that the South Vietnamese were to concentrate mainly on pacification, while the Americans and Free World Military Assistance Forces were to focus on the main force war and major VC and NVA elements.[4]

Outside of the National Priority Areas and the "Areas for Priority of Military Offensive Operations," the Combined Campaign Plan recommended using spoiling attacks to frustrate the enemy's designs and intentions.[5] In the II Corps Tactical Zone, the military region of South Vietnam that contained the Central Highlands and General Larsen's First Field Force, Vietnam (IFFV), the priority areas were located along the coast and to the east of the mountains. Operations in the Highlands were therefore something of a secondary concern. Much of the 1967 strategy for the region, in fact, mirrored the economy-of-force approach General Westmoreland had subscribed to in 1966. "In the Central Highlands we intended to screen the Cambodian border with light forces and send reinforcements to the area only when North Vietnamese regiments undertook to cross the border and mount offensive operations," the MACV commander wrote. "This saved us troops for more important tasks."[6] Westmoreland, it should be noted, did not discount the threat posed by Communist forces in the Highlands. Rather his immediate concerns were simply elsewhere in the opening months of 1967.

Although the principal operational mandate of the 4th Infantry Division in the Central Highlands remained largely unchanged—meet and defeat the North Vietnamese whenever they slipped across the Cambodian border in strength—the leadership at the top of the division did not. On January 3, 1967, General Collins relinquished command of the division to General Peers.[7] Peers was born in Iowa on June 14, 1914. A Midwesterner by birth, he grew up in Southern California and graduated from the University of California, Los Angeles (UCLA). In 1938, after serving for a period of time on "extended active duty," he received a commission in the Regular Army. Peers then served with the 1st Infantry Regiment in Wyoming, first as a platoon leader, and then as the commander of a "heavy weapons" company. While attending the Infantry Officer Course in 1942, he received word from Capt. John Coughlin, a longtime friend and a member of the recently formed Office of Strategic Studies (OSS) Detachment 101, about a new assignment in the Pacific. Peers, then a young and precocious first lieutenant, accepted the offer and was eventually assigned to Detachment 101, which went on to operate in Japanese-occupied Burma from 1942 to 1945.[8]

Assuming command of Detachment 101 in late 1943, Peers increased the recruitment and training of Kachin tribesmen. Under his supervision the outfit organized approximately ten thousand of these indigenous troops into ten battalions.[9] Peers was subsequently promoted to colonel in February of 1945, and he continued to command the detachment until its deactivation in July of 1945. Appropriately Detachment 101 received a Presidential Distinguished Unit Citation in 1946 for its valorous wartime service in the Allied campaign against the Japanese in Burma. Peers was awarded the Army Distinguished Service Medal.

Following the campaign in Burma, Peers served in China as the deputy strategic services officer for the entire country. With the war and his clandestine work with the OSS behind him, Peers returned to the United States in 1946 and was assigned to the operations section (G3) of the 6th Army in California. In 1949, after serving on the intelligence faculty at the Command and General Staff College at Fort Leavenworth, Kansas, he received a transfer to the Central Intelligence Agency. Returning to the Army in 1951, he attended the Army War College in 1952 and thereafter served in a variety of assignments, including as commander of the 1st Battle Group in Germany in the late 1950s and later, in 1961, with the Joint Chiefs of Staff. Interestingly Peers also spent time with the 4th Infantry Division at Fort Lewis, serving as an assistant division commander (ADC) from September 1963 to July 1964.[10]

Tough but fair-minded, General Peers enjoyed the respect of his contemporaries and those that served under him. "We all jokingly referred to him as 'Willie Ray,'" said Bob Quinn, a captain and an assistant brigade S3 in the 4th Infantry Division. "He was a hell of a nice guy and a good commander. He was sort of a down-to-earth guy, and you could talk to him. He had fought in Burma in World War II, and apparently he was a boxer because the first time that I looked at his face, all I could think about was Carmen Basilio! His nose was wrapped around his face, and there were more twists and turns in it than the Burma Road! He had been in some fights—I can guarantee you!"

Most, in fact, judged the general a fighter, and Peers acknowledged that he had to "defeat and/or eliminate the NVA/VC main forces," if the United States were to succeed in Vietnam. The North Vietnamese regulars in the Highlands, he maintained, employed tactics "akin to those used by the Japanese forces in World War II." The Highland war, moreover, was something of a conventional jungle war , and Peers was quick to recognize that it differed greatly from the war in the southernmost provinces of II Corps Tactical Zone (II CTZ).[11] Regardless of the challenges, however, he expected his brigades to serve with distinction, and to embody the simple yet eloquent motto of the 4th Infantry Division: Steadfast and Loyal.

On January 1, 1967, two days before Peers succeeded General Collins as commanding officer (CO), the 4th Infantry Division began Operation Paul Revere V, later renamed Sam Houston. Conducted in the same general area as Paul Revere IV, Sam Houston was in essence an extension of earlier border surveillance–NVA interdiction operations. The 4th was to monitor the Cambodian border, detect and interdict infiltrating NVA units, and provide security for logistical facilities and engineer construction within the area of operations (AO). As with Paul Revere IV, Sam Houston also included a civic action component designed to promote pacification and revolutionary development activities. Accordingly, that February, Peers oversaw the implementation of the "Good Neighbor Program," an ambitious civic action initiative designed to improve living conditions in local Montagnard villages.

General Larsen expected Peers to respond aggressively to the enemy's cross-border incursions. Larsen, in short, wanted the 4th Infantry Division to hit the enemy as soon as he entered South Vietnam. "My job," Peers recalled, "was to sound the alarm when the enemy (B3 Front) moved east from Cambodia."[12] Thereafter he was to prevent the enemy from overrunning U.S. Special Forces camps and key government-population centers in the western Highlands.

Settling in to his new post, Peers had to conduct Sam Houston, at least to start, with little more than a brigade headquarters (2nd, 4th Infantry Div), four infantry battalions, an organic armored cavalry squadron, and a tank battalion.[13] His 1st Brigade was still at Tuy Hoa in Phu Yen Province, under the operational control of IFFV as it had been since December 1966. Similarly the 3rd Brigade, 25th Infantry Division was also unavailable, having departed the Highlands for operations in Binh Dinh Province.[14] Help arrived at the end of January, however, when General Larsen released the 1st of the 8th Infantry for operations in the Highlands. Commanded by Lt. Col. Harold H. Lee, the battalion was airlifted into the 4th's AO on January 26, 1967, and eventually deployed near Duc Co. The remaining two battalions of the 1st Brigade, the 3rd of the 8th Infantry and the 3rd of the 12th Infantry, continued to operate on the coast.

While handing over the reins of the 4th Infantry Division, General Collins warned Peers that the North Vietnamese were constructing a base area in the Plei Trap Valley. Weeks passed with little to confirm Collins's suspicions, but by February aerial reconnaissance had detected enemy activity west of the Nam Sathay River near the Cambodian border. Signs of digging, extensive trail activity, and evidence of fortifications stirred the American command into hitting the border area with a B-52 strike. Long-range reconnaissance patrols (LRRPs) and communications intelligence also uncovered signs of enemy activity. The NVA, it appeared, had reentered the Plei Trap Valley.[15] Mindful of the desire at IFFV to strike the enemy as soon as he entered South Vietnam, Peers decided that February to send two battalions of the 2nd Brigade across the Nam Sathay. With any luck his forces would finish the job that Collins had started.

Hanoi, however, had other ideas. Since the wholesale introduction of American combat troops in 1965, policymakers in the North had grappled with a vexing strategic quandary: how should the military-political campaign to crush South Vietnam proceed in the face of American military intervention? Convening at the Twelfth Plenum in December 1965, the North Vietnamese Central Committee elected to confront the challenge head-on. North Vietnam, the Committee decided, would match the American troop buildup in the South, and the VC/NVA would continue to fight a big-unit war complemented by guerrilla war in pursuit of a quick and decisive victory.[16]

Throughout 1966, as casualties mounted and the prospects of a quick victory over South Vietnam began to recede, opposition to the existing strategy increased within the North Vietnamese military-political establishment. In early 1967, and perhaps in response to this dissent, the Central Committee approved Resolution 13, which reemphasized the importance of the "diplomatic struggle" and opened the door to negotiations with the United States. Simultaneously the measure directed the VC/NVA to fight big-unit battles, in concert with low-intensity guerilla war, with the goal of delivering the "decisive victory" Communist diplomats needed to broker a favorable settlement at the negotiating table.[17]

For guidance in conducting the "fight" facet of this new "talk-fight" strategy, Front commanders like Gen. Chu Huy Man were expected to follow the plan the NVA Combat Operations Department had proposed for the 1966–67 winter-spring campaign. Presented to a select group of North Vietnamese military and political officials in June of 1966, the plan advised utilizing "four 'blocs' of main force units to attack the enemy on four different battlefields: Eastern Cochin China, the Central Highlands, Region 5, and Tri Thien." These attacks, according to the plan, were to occur in combination "with attacks and insurrections in three large cities—Saigon, Da Nang, and Hue—to destroy and shatter the puppet main force army and inflict heavy losses on U.S. forces in order to win a decisive victory on the South Vietnamese battlefield in 1967."[18]

In the Central Highlands, General Man and Col. Nguyen Huu An, commander of the 1st NVA Division, had learned how to fight the Americans by *fighting Americans*. "Since we have no experience in fighting American troops, we will resolve to learn as we fight," Man had remarked before the battles in the Ia Drang Valley in 1965. "We'll fight them and see what happens."[19] The Americans, they had learned, possessed superior firepower and mobility, but experience had taught the two Communist commanders that their troops could partially offset those advantages by getting as close to the Americans as possible and "grabbing the enemy's belt to fight him." Without their "heavy firepower," An averred, the Americans were not "much different than" the South Vietnamese. Some of An's soldiers had even claimed that the Americans were afraid of close-quarters combat.[20]

Man and An were also familiar with the 4th Infantry Division, their principal opponent in the spring of 1967. An, in fact, would later boast that, during the 1966 dry season offensive, the main force units of the Central Highlands "had tested their strength against another type of U.S. soldier—the 4th Infantry Division—and had brought him to his knees."[21]

For the upcoming 1966–67 winter-spring offensive, Man planned to launch attacks west of the Nam Sathay River to counter the 4th Infantry Division. Man hoped that these attacks would disrupt Operation Sam Houston and prevent the enemy from destroying the Front's rear areas and supply caches.[22]

General Peers, after basing his 2nd Brigade at 3 TANGO between Pleiku and the Plei Trap Valley, commenced his two-battalion thrust across the Nam Sathay River on February 12. By nightfall on the sixteenth, Col. James Adamson's brigade had encountered elements of two of the three regiments that composed the 1st NVA Division. In response Peers requested and received his 1st Brigade, excluding the 3-12 Infantry, from Phu Yen Province. Released from IFFV control, the 1st Brigade headquarters and the 3-8 Infantry completed the move to New Plei Djereng by the twenty-first. Peers then assigned responsibility for the area between the Nam Sathay and the Se San Rivers to Col. Charles A. Jackson, now in command of the 1st Brigade. Adamson, meanwhile, would continue working west of the Nam Sathay to the Cambodian border.[23]

Over the next couple of weeks, the two brigades continued to make contact with North Vietnamese forces. On March 2 a company from the 1st of the 22nd Infantry skirmished with elements of the 32nd NVA Regiment near the Cambodia border, suggesting that the enemy formation was west of the Nam Sathay and in the midst of withdrawing from the Plei Trap Valley. Peers, thinking that the North Vietnamese were exiting the valley, shifted his attention to the Plei Doc, an area along the border west of the Chu Goungot Mountains. Troops from the 1st of the 12th Infantry landed first, touching down north of Duc Co on March 16. Set up in a wood line around the landing zone, an estimated platoon of North Vietnamese opened fire and detonated mines, destroying one incoming slick and damaging seven others.[24] The Americans brought in air and artillery strikes, and the entire battalion was eventually airlifted into the landing zone (LZ). Stubbornly, the NVA refused to disengage until the next day.

Unlike the previous fall, however, when they had assaulted defensive perimeters and in one instance a battalion firebase, the North Vietnamese switched from attacking dug-in or prepared positions to ambushing American companies while they were still on the move. Striking at a time and place of their choosing, the enemy assault troops, supported by mortars and rocket-propelled grenades (RPGs), closed quickly and "hugged" the startled grunts to reduce the effects of American supporting arms. This change in the enemy's tactics would make Sam Houston considerably more costly than Paul Revere IV.[25]

Less than a week after the attack on the 1-12 Infantry, the 2nd Brigade lost contact with a LRRP team working an area near the Cambodian border. Throughout Operation Sam Houston, the 4th Infantry Division relied on reconnaissance patrols, particularly the LRRPs, for intelligence collection. LRRP teams, as the forward eyes and ears of the division, performed a host of duties, including screening the front or flanks of an ongoing operation. Adamson could scarcely brook the loss of such a valued intelligence-gathering asset without a response. Accordingly he tapped Lt. Col. Harold H. Lee's 1-8 Infantry to retrieve the missing team. Lee in turn dispatched two companies, A and B Companies, 1-8 Infantry, on the morning of March 22. What followed was the last significant engagement of Operation Sam Houston and the first major battle the battalion would fight in the Central Highlands.

Debarking at Nha Trang on October 5, 1966, the 1-8 Infantry trundled off the USS *Gordon* and onto trucks and C-130s bound for Tuy Hoa, a picturesque coastal town on the South China Sea. The battalion would remain in the fertile lowlands of Phu Yen Province, far from the jagged peaks and forested draws of the Central Highlands, until January of 1967. "That," said 1st Lt. Howard Brooks, executive officer of A Company, 1-8 Infantry, "was the good times." Most, in hindsight, agreed with Lieutenant Brooks. Situated south of Tuy Hoa, the battalion base camp was a short jaunt to the beach and it was not unheard of for detail-weary troopers to frolic and bathe in the cool blue waters of the South China Sea.[26] "Tuy Hoa was a tropical paradise on the coast of the South China Sea," said Pfc. Tom Carty, a radio/telephone operator (RTO) with A Company, 1-8 Infantry. "The land was lush in the many colors [*sic*] of green. The South China Sea was as blue as blue could be."[27] Rice paddies and hamlets dotted much of the surrounding countryside, making search-and-destroy operations on the coast generally less onerous than comparable humps in the Highlands.

The nature of the conflict also changed when the 1-8 Infantry left for the Central Highlands in January 1967. Lieutenant Brooks likened the struggle in the Tuy Hoa area to a "classic guerilla war" that involved some "sniper fire and some modest actions." Brooks hastened to add that during Operation Adams, a brigade-level search-and-destroy operation in Phu Yen Province in the fall of 1966, the battalion was primarily opposed by local Viet Cong.[28] In the Highlands, the battalion faced the North Vietnamese Army, not poorly trained guerillas brandishing outdated weapons. Stalking the jungle-covered uplands in regimental strength, the NVA could strike suddenly and with devastating effect. "Our lives changed when we went to Pleiku," said Spc4 Victor Renza, a machine gunner in B Company. "Before that, the VC would fire shots at us and we would chase them. But it was nothing you couldn't live with." The Highlands, however, had few of the moral ambiguities associated with conducting a counterinsurgency campaign along the populated coast. Here it was kill or be killed. "We had fairly simple rules of engagement," said 1st Lt. Larry Rodabaugh, a platoon leader in B Company. "If it moved, shoot it."

Capt. William D. Sands III, CO of A Company, 1-8 Infantry, preferred that kind of a straightforward fight. A graduate of the Citadel, Sands had served as the commander of B Company, 1-8 Infantry during basic training and Advanced Infantry Training

(AIT) at Fort Lewis, Washington, in 1965 before transferring to the 101st Airborne Division. A career-minded officer, he was eventually reunited with the 4th in South Vietnam and assumed command of A Company, 1-8 Infantry in late 1966. Sands was a short-timer by March 1967, but he voluntarily extended his tour in Vietnam to command A Company as it prepared, along with B Company, 1-8 Infantry, to search for the missing LRRP team.

Sands met with Capt. Robert Sholly, the bespectacled commander of B Company, on the afternoon of March 21 to coordinate the rescue mission Lieutenant Colonel Lee had ordered for the following day. The two men were already well acquainted. "William (Bid) Sands and I were good friends and had been working together for several months as the respective company commanders of Alpha and Bravo Companies," Sholly would later write. "Bid and I had not had much time to discuss the operation prior to our companies being launched late on the afternoon of March 21st, so we had a short session on the LZ." As the pair parted ways, each agreed to come to the aid of the other in the event of enemy contact. Sands, following the meeting, moved out on a southwesterly axis while B Company, according to Sholly, advanced "in a southeasterly direction in order to put some distance between our two organizations."[29]

Sholly and Sands, incidentally, commanded companies composed largely of originals. "An original was a guy who was assigned to the 4th Infantry Division, was stationed at Fort Lewis, Washington, and then deployed with the division when it went to Vietnam in the summer and fall of 1966," said Spc4 Victor Renza. "A lot of us were drafted together in 1965. We trained for ten months together at Fort Lewis, and then we went to Vietnam together. We were the best of friends, and the relationships started back in the barracks. While we were at Fort Lewis, it was almost like being on a college campus for us. We trained during the week, and then we did things nineteen-year-olds do on the weekends—we partied, we drank beers, and we chased girls." Ron Snyder, a sergeant and squad leader in A Company, believes that the rigors of Vietnam strengthened the bonds the originals had forged at Fort Lewis. "The stuff we went through [in Vietnam], it wasn't just fighting Communists every day," he recalled. "We had to fight off ants, deal with sleeping on the ground, shivering in the soaking rain, and humping through jungle. Our rucksacks were so heavy sometimes that guys had to help each other get off the ground. We had to deal with a whole lot together."

Heading out on the morning of March 22, Sergeant Snyder and A Company, flanked to the south by B Company, moved west-southwest along a ridgeline. Negotiating the thick vegetation and uneven terrain near the Cambodian border, the company did not get far before Captain Sands suddenly halted the four-platoon column. Sands, as the column clattered to a standstill, ordered his First Platoon to move up and flank the Second Platoon on the left. Farther back the Third and Fourth Platoons pulled up the rear.

Slipping out of the column formation, the First Platoon, with Sgt. George Olsen's 3rd Squad in the lead, maneuvered forward and to the left of Second Platoon. Olsen was accustomed to running point with his squad, and he placed Pfc. Jacob Horn up front. Stepping through the underbrush, Olsen stole a glance at his watch. It was around 7:30 A.M. Moments later Horn was shot and knocked to the ground next to a tree. Cut down in the opening volley of North Vietnamese fire, Horn had descended into a uniquely excruciating hell, the kind of hell all soldiers privately feared. He had been hit in the groin by an enemy round. "Oh God, let me die," Horn wailed in anguish. "They got me in the balls!" Wedged up against the tree, the Kentucky native offered an inviting target to the NVA who, from time to time, would pump a round into his near lifeless body. Tragically none of the soldiers in the platoon could reach Horn and the young private eventually died of his wounds.

Off to the right, Sergeant Snyder and Spc4 Kermit Coleman heard the flurry of NVA fire and immediately hit the ground. Snyder had been instructed to take his squad and run point for Second Platoon, and he had selected Coleman, a well-respected black soldier from the projects, as his point man. Coleman objected but Snyder, an original from Erie, Pennsylvania, persuaded his reluctant charge to follow orders. Snyder could certainly empathize with Coleman's lack of enthusiasm. Gutsy but hardly gung-ho, Snyder had contemplated dodging the draft and emigrating to Canada, but the very notion of being thought of as a coward was so distasteful to him that he decided instead to honor his draft notice and serve in the Army. More importantly he had a bad feeling that the NVA were out there, somewhere, just waiting to strike. "Coleman, we are definitely going to run into some gooks out here," he told his point man rather sternly that morning. "You've got to straighten up." Listening to the roar of gunfire off to his left in front of First Platoon, he now realized how prophetic his instincts had been.

Lying in wait, a large NVA force had cut the lead elements of the First and Second Platoons to pieces and was probing aggressively to flank and fragment the entire company. Captain Sands instantly appreciated the gravity of the situation. Trailing behind the Second Platoon with his command group, he requested artillery support and attempted to organize something of a cohesive defensive perimeter. Sands, suspecting that he would also need reinforcements, raised B Company on the battalion net and reported that his company was under assault. In the interim, the NVA fire continued unabated. "You got to get down here," Sands shouted over the radio to Sgt. Dick Surface, Sholly's RTO, shortly after the first appeal for help. "We are taking heavy casualties and don't know how long we can hold out."[30] Nearby a North Vietnamese soldier armed with an RPG pulled the trigger. Wobbling as it left the tube, the warhead streaked across the jungle and slammed into the A Company command group, killing Captain Sands.

Lt. Col. Harold H. Lee, CO of the 1-8 Infantry, had been monitoring the ongoing battle over the radio and, after speaking with Captain Sands first, directed Captain Sholly to assist A Company. Sholly, however, was already en route. An outstanding officer with ranger and airborne qualifications, Sholly had heard gunfire to the west that morning and immediately attempted to contact Sands on the radio. When his counterpart failed to respond, Sholly promptly halted the two-column formation his company had been moving in and positioned all four platoons on line, facing west. Swiftly realigned, B Company then began advancing toward the sound of the guns. Sholly, meanwhile, informed Lee that B Company was on the way.

Ushered along by Sholly, B Company pushed west-northwest through the jungle. Dense in spots, the tropical vegetation made it difficult for the four platoons to remain abreast of one another. Some soldiers had to crouch while making their way through the thick undergrowth and overhanging bamboo shoots. As the platoons advanced steadily westward the sounds of battle grew louder. Suddenly the Fourth Platoon began receiving fire. Pinned down in a bamboo field, the platoon returned fire but it began taking casualties and could not silence two well-placed North Vietnamese machine guns in front of it. Tree-borne enemy snipers produced additional casualties among the grunts and further restricted the platoon's movement. The North Vietnamese, it appeared, had maneuvered a sizable force in between A and B Companies. Sholly, realizing that he had to intercede quickly if he hoped to reach Captain Sands's embattled company before it was too late, summoned the Second Platoon, then on the far right of the formation, and ordered it to mount a flanking movement to ease enemy pressure on the Fourth.

Spc4 Victor Renza was an M-60 machine gunner in the Second Platoon. Brash, outspoken, and uncommonly independent-minded for a young draftee, Renza bristled at military discipline and resented the regimentation inherent in Army life. He quite frankly had no interest in soldiering. Renza, in fact, had attended a vocational high school in New York State and had aspirations of becoming a hairdresser. "I heard it all," Renza said of his fellow soldiers' initial reactions to his preferred career choice. "Before I was in the Army, I remember guys saying to me, 'I wish I was a hairdresser. You can get all the broads.' [But] I heard all kinds of shit about it when it when I was at basic, how I was a *fag* and all that." No one, though, questioned Renza's manhood in the field or in a firefight. Indeed, when the chips were down, not many would dispute that the sharp-tongued New Yorker was a straight-up, barrels down *motherfucker* on the M-60.

Specialist 4th Class Renza, along with other members of the Second Platoon, swept forward and into a dry creek bed approximately five feet wide and four feet deep. As they paused briefly before scrambling out of the bed and into the jungle on the other side, the NVA, hidden in the bush on the opposite bank, opened up with heavy automatic weapons fire. From out of the creek bed a chorus of voices exclaimed, excitedly, "There's gooks to the front, gooks to the front!" and in an instant the men of the Second Platoon were laying down a curtain of return fire.

Hunched over in the creek bed, Renza and his assistant machine gunner feverishly set up their M-60 and prepared to fire. Seconds later a single rifle shot whistled by Renza's ear with an audible crack. Renza felt his legs give out underneath him, and he dropped out of sight. The color drained from his face. Recognizing that his present location was no longer tenable, he reached up and grabbed the M-60 and, together with his assistant gunner, crawled in a southerly direction until the banks of the creek bed leveled off and offered some cover.

Second Platoon, much like the Fourth, had also become bogged down. Stalled on the flanks, Captain Sholly tried to press ahead with the two platoons situated in the center, but heavy enemy fire halted their advance as well. B Company, despite fighting well, could not push through the North Vietnamese. "We were in the middle of a bamboo field with brush and the enemy had snipers in the trees from which they could fire down into our area," Sholly recounted. "We could not see out of the brush and bamboo, so we were at a disadvantage. We set up a fire into the trees but could not break the tie."[31] Sholly subsequently pulled his command post (CP) group back to work on the NVA with supporting arms.

Lacking air and artillery support in the chaotic opening moments of the battle, the lead elements of A Company had suffered a number of casualties. Among the injured were several severely wounded men, whose desperate cries of "Medic, medic!" rose up from the battlefield. Sgt. John "Doc" Bockover, a medic with the Second Platoon, heard the cries and began running toward the front lines. Bockover, his medical supplies in tow, raced into a dry creek bed where, in almost comedic fashion, he crashed headlong into a tree overhanging the bed. The spectacle was not an altogether incongruous portrait of the quirky original from Indiana. Bockover enlisted in the Army in November of 1965, a little more than a month before his eighteenth birthday. Training did not come naturally to him, and though he tried his best, he was scarcely an exemplary soldier. Indeed he might never have graduated from basic training, poor as his vision was in his right eye, if his platoon sergeant had not qualified for him on the rifle range. Surprisingly, however, no combat medic in the battalion would perform more gallantly in the battle.[32]

Stunned momentarily by the tree, Bockover regained his equilibrium and resumed moving to the front. Inching forward he reached an injured RTO and tended to his wound despite the crack of AK-47 rounds all around. Bockover and Sgt. Jim Peirce, a hardnosed squad leader in the Fourth Platoon, then approached Spc4 John Mott, a replacement who had arrived in Vietnam only two weeks before. Mott was propped up against a tree and covered in blood. Hunks of flesh and bone had been blown from his face, and he was having difficulty breathing. Bockover, without panicking, sliced Mott's throat cleanly and precisely and inserted the end of a pen in the incision to enable the wounded man to breathe. Mott gazed up at Peirce. "Sergeant Peirce," he whispered, "did I get my CIB?" Peirce's heart sank. Mott had asked him repeatedly about earning the highly coveted Combat Infantryman's Badge, which recognized combat service. Hiding his grief, Peirce looked down at Mott and said proudly, "Yes, John, you sure did!"[33] Mott inhaled one final time and died.

A Company had been split into two separate perimeters.[34] North Vietnamese troops, moreover, were maneuvering on the flanks, past pockets of pinned-down grunts, in an attempt to envelop the entire company. But as the NVA swept around the First Platoon, toward the rear of the company, they bumped into the Third Platoon, which was moving forward to link up with the First and piece together a defensive perimeter. A violent, close-quarters scrum erupted. Machine gunners fired frantically at the NVA from the hip. Others, including Sgt. Ross Rembert, a gung-ho squad leader in the Third, opened up on the enemy with their M-16s.

Despite the determined stand by Rembert and the Third Platoon, A Company was not receiving enough close-in artillery support to loosen the enemy's grip. 1st Sgt. David McNerney, upon learning that Captain Sands had been killed, assumed command of the company and immediately adjusted the incoming artillery fire to within twenty meters of friendly positions. The effects of that fire were devastating. "Shrapnel was hitting everyone and cutting vegetation like a weed eater," wrote Pfc. Tom Carty. "It didn't seem like the artillery would ever stop."[35] Gunships and fighter-bombers followed, easing North Vietnamese pressure on the hard-pressed company.

Shortly thereafter, McNerney dashed over to a nearby tree and, braving a welter of NVA fire, climbed to the top and tied an identification panel to the highest branches he could find. Converging on the battle in an overloaded UH-1 Huey, WO1 Don Rawlinson of the organic 4th Aviation Battalion had requested a visual aid for assistance in aligning his approach. The chopper carried supplies A Company desperately needed to survive on the ground. Rawlinson, gazing down into the thick jungle canopy, instantly recognized the panel McNerney had lashed to a tree branch. "My God," he exclaimed to his co-pilot as the chopper cruised on in, "can you believe someone climbed up there in that tree and did that?" For that and other acts of extraordinary gallantry that day, Sergeant McNerney would receive the Medal of Honor.[36]

Captain Sholly, from his ad hoc CP on a small incline, was also harnessing all manner of fire support to destroy or disperse the North Vietnamese force lodged between the two companies. Few had a better facility with firepower. "Sholly was an excellent commander, and he was a master at orchestrating artillery and air support," said Pfc. Cliff Rountree, an adventurous Californian and a member of Sholly's Fourth Platoon. "There just wasn't anybody better than him, as far as I am concerned." Sholly hit the NVA with 105-mm, 155-mm, and 175-mm artillery fire along with gunships and napalm strikes, the latter delivered by A-1E Sky Raiders.

Bolstered by this support, and the actions of a few key individuals, B Company managed to consolidate south of A Company. In the Fourth Platoon sector, Sfc. Bruce Grandstaff helped organize the troops into a defensive formation and he personally silenced a number of NVA positions. Grandstaff also carried a wounded man to safety in spite of the intense enemy fire and was awarded the Silver Star. Meanwhile, on the opposite flank, SSgt. Frankie Molnar, a squad leader in the Second Platoon, acted as a base of fire—and in the process drew a sharp enemy response—so that his men could knock out an NVA position. Molnar later attempted to return his squad to the company perimeter but ran into heavy North Vietnamese fire. Placing his squad on-line, he repeatedly exposed himself to enemy fire in order to distribute ammo, earning a Bronze Star in the process, and never stopped encouraging the young troopers under his command.

The cumulative effect of concentrated American firepower eventually dislodged the North Vietnamese, and by early afternoon B Company was marching west-northwest again, its dead and wounded carried along in ponchos. The firing soon tapered off, as the North Vietnamese, buffeted by supporting arms fire and fought to a veritable standstill by the separated platoons of A Company, withdrew from the battlefield. A Company had held its ground, albeit at significant cost.

Marking slow but steady progress, B Company finally reached the battlefield later that afternoon. Captain Sholly, realizing that a joint position would have to be established before nightfall, quickly organized a perimeter large enough to accommodate both companies. Sgt. McNerney and the battered A Company platoons then moved into the center of the enlarged perimeter.[37] For the remainder of the day, the two companies evacuated the dead and wounded and dug fighting positions.

Waged at close range, the battle in the Plei Doc on March 22 cost the 1-8 Infantry twenty-seven KIA and forty-eight WIA, with A Company suffering the lion's share of the losses.[38] Colonel Adamson, the 2nd Brigade Commander, praised the performance of his two companies. Adamson was less sanguine about the number of NVA killed, however. "That evening at about 2300, General Peers asked me for an enemy body count. I said I had no idea," Adamson admitted. "He said Saigon wanted to know. Later I received a call from Swede Larsen by secure radio asking the same question. I was to provide a number. I said '150.' The next day we found about forty-five bodies and had the body count previously given withdrawn and '45' reported in its place."[39] Officially the division reported a final tally of 136 North Vietnamese KIA.[40]

Whatever the final tally—and it was doubtlessly greater than forty-five given the North Vietnamese practice of dragging their dead from the battlefield—the 1-8 Infantry, the aptly named Bullets, had passed its first Highland test.

2 OPERATION FRANCIS MARION

Operation Francis Marion opened on April 6, 1967, the day after Operation Sam Houston ended and just a few short weeks before the approaching southwest monsoon, which typically lasted from May to October, gripped the Central Highlands. The 4th Infantry Division, as in Sam Houston, was expected to monitor the border for North Vietnamese infiltration, conduct spoiling attacks to prevent the enemy from building up its forces in the western Highlands, and provide security for engineering-improvement projects, logistical facilities, and the major roadways in the area. To promote pacification, the new operation called for a "continuing Civic Action Program consisting of short range, high impact projects in the forward areas and long range, nation building projects." That April, General Peers expanded the Good Neighbor Program, the division's principal civic action program in the Central Highlands, and extended the existing TAOR (Tactical Area of Operational Responsibility) around Dragon Mountain. The 4th, moreover, was to assist South Vietnamese pacification initiatives, including the Revolutionary Development and Refugee Resettlement Programs.[1]

General Peers viewed Francis Marion as a continuation of the border surveillance–enemy interdiction mission the 4th Infantry Division had performed in Pleiku Province since its arrival in the Highlands. What distinguished the operation from its immediate predecessor, however, was his decision to establish a defense in depth. "General Larsen wanted the enemy hit the moment he stepped into Vietnam," Peers noted. "General Collins was partially successful (Paul Revere IV) in the Plei Trap. I went in with the intention of completing the job—cleaning the enemy out. After Sam Houston, I began to shy away from the border."[2] Deploying his forces accordingly, Peers positioned the 1st Brigade in an arc that ran along Route 14B from New Plei Djereng Special Forces Camp in the north to Plei Me Special Forces Camp in the south. Beyond the arc, divisional LRRPs, Special Forces teams, and indigenous Civilian Irregular Defense Group (CIDG) units would monitor the border and report any sign of enemy activity. Colonel Adamson's 2nd Brigade, meanwhile, was to operate *behind* the arc and serve as a general reserve.[3] So while Peers fully intended to monitor the Cambodian border and interdict North Vietnamese infiltration routes into the Highlands, routes that included passageways through the Chu Goungot–Chu Yam Mountains, he also planned to let the NVA venture farther into South Vietnam before he countered their incursions.

Substantial Army aviation and artillery assets were also committed to Francis Marion, ensuring that the infantry brigades would not fight alone. For the most part, the organic 4th Aviation Battalion was tasked with supporting the 2nd Brigade, while the 52nd Combat Aviation Battalion was assigned to the 1st Brigade. Nevertheless the two aviation battalions were expected to provide support to whichever brigade needed it. The 179th Assault Support Helicopter Company of the 52nd Combat Aviation Battalion, for example, furnished CH-47 helicopters for both brigades.[4] The two brigades could also call on fighter-bombers from the U.S. 7th Air Force for close air support. Divisional planners, moreover, allocated the organic 4th of the 42nd Artillery to the 2nd Brigade and the organic 6th of the 29th Artillery to the 1st Brigade to ensure that each brigade received sufficient artillery support during the operation. Additional guns were available as well.[5] The division's 4th Medical Battalion, meanwhile, assigned a medical company to each brigade.

Col. Charles A. Jackson, a proud South Carolinian who mischievously selected the radio call sign "Stonewall," commanded the 1st Brigade. Replacing Col. John D. Austin in February, Jackson claimed that he had learned of the brigade's "high level of professional ability, drive, and force" while serving stateside in the Pentagon.[6] Jackson's comments, ironically, were similar to the characteristics many had ascribed to him. Commissioned as a second lieutenant after graduating from the Citadel, Jackson fought in both North Africa and Italy in World War II. Discharged after the war, he was subsequently recalled to duty and served with the 40th Infantry Division during the Korean War. Jackson taught at the Infantry School following Korea and was eventually assigned to the United States Army, Europe. Later he commanded an armored rifle battalion in the 4th Armored Division in Europe.[7]

A 1960 graduate of the Armed Forces Staff College, Colonel Jackson demonstrated, in just a few short months, the ability to command a brigade and coexist with his battalion commanders. "I was fortunate enough to have a wise brigade commander in Colonel Jackson," said Lt. Col. John P. Vollmer, CO of the 3-12 Infantry, "and I had a hell of a lot of respect for him." Lt. Col. Tom Lynch, commander of the 3-8 Infantry, agreed with Vollmer. "He [Jackson] was a good man," noted Lynch. "I don't think he was a tactician, [but] he let me command the battalion. A lot of brigade commanders try to relive their experiences as battalion commanders, and they decide that they know what's best. But he didn't do that with me. He let me command the battalion. The risks that I took were mine, and he supported me all the way."

Jackson located his brigade CP in a building damaged by NVA shellfire in the Highland village of Le Thanh. Ideally situated for a brigade base camp, the village sat astride Route 14B north of Highway 19, well to the west of the 2nd Brigade base at OASIS. In honor of its CO, the 1st Brigade base at Le Thanh was christened "Jackson Hole."[8]

West of Jackson Hole, in his headquarters across the border in Cambodia, the commander of the B3 Front, Gen. Chu Huy Man, waited for the southwest monsoon to begin. The heavy rains usually slowed the pace of operations in the spring and summer, but with Colonel An's 1st NVA Division, three independent regiments, and an array of supporting units available, Man was expected to draw American forces away from the populated lowlands and into the rugged Central Highlands, where he could inflict heavy casualties on them in short, sharp battles along the border.[9] Man knew, however, that he would have to strike somewhere that spring-summer if he wanted to lure the Americans out of their bases in the Highlands and on the coast. With that in mind, Man sent elements of the 1st NVA Division, which had been regrouping in Cambodian Base Areas 701 and 702, back into South Vietnam to help "light the fuse" in western Pleiku Province.

Colonel Jackson's 1st Brigade spent the first few weeks of Francis Marion scouring the jungles and grasslands of western Pleiku Province in search of the NVA and their principal infiltration corridors. The brigade mounted search-and-destroy operations north of Highway 19, to the southwest of New Plei Djereng, and in the Ia Drang Valley.[10] Slow to start, enemy activity increased in the closing weeks of April, as did the number of contacts between brigade elements and North Vietnamese troops. Meanwhile, in Darlac Province to the south, U.S. Special Forces troops ran into an NVA battalion, and a few days later two Viet Cong companies were reported in the vicinity of the Buon Blech Special Forces Camp. South Vietnamese and CIDG forces in the province had also made frequent contact with both VC and NVA units throughout the month of April.[11] Concerned, General Peers dispatched a task force organized around the 3-8 Infantry to northern Darlac on April 24. Colonel Jackson's remaining battalions, the 1-8 Infantry and the 3-12 Infantry, stayed behind to continue operations in Pleiku Province.[12]

Peers also repositioned his 2nd Brigade. Maneuvering on-line with the 1st Brigade, Colonel Adamson's three battalions set up south of Highway 19 and to the west of Plei Me.[13] The redeployment produced almost immediate results. On the thirtieth of April, while patrolling north of Plei Me, a dismounted platoon from A Company, 2nd of the

8th Infantry (Mechanized) ambushed a small North Vietnamese force and chased the retreating survivors back to a bunker line defended by machine guns. The Americans pounded the bunker complex with air strikes and artillery fire and were soon joined by two armored personnel carriers from the battalion scout platoon. Two air strikes and steady shellfire, however, failed to dislodge the stubborn defenders. Falling back for the night, the Americans requested armored personnel carriers (APCs) and tanks.[14]

Late the next morning, A Company, supported by APCs and two tanks from the 1st Squadron, 10th Cavalry, assembled for a renewed assault. Mounting up and moving out, the company advanced through the battle area but encountered little opposition. The North Vietnamese had seemingly taken flight the previous night. Rolling along, the Americans rumbled through enemy flanking fire and into a hidden NVA base camp. Heavy enemy fire greeted the American mechanized force, and as the shooting match intensified, desperate North Vietnamese soldiers scurried out of well-concealed bunkers and attempted to toss grenades inside the tanks and under the tracks of the APCs. The tankers, meeting the frenzied enemy infantry head-on, responded with machine-gun fire and canister rounds. Delivered at close range, the shotgun-like effect of the canister rounds wiped out dozens of would-be attackers. Some of the NVA managed to approach the tanks, only to be crushed and reduced to pulp beneath their churning tracks when they drew too close. Others stumbled into APCs and were gunned down by .50-caliber machine-gun fire. American infantry, jostling about inside the clanking APCs, dismounted from to time to eliminate some of the NVA bunkers with hand grenades.[15]

Routed, the North Vietnamese fled in panic. That night A Company withdrew and supporting arms pounded the battlefield. Remarkably the two-day fight (April 30–May 1) resulted in only three American KIAs. Searching the area the next day, American troops found 138 enemy bodies on the battlefield along with a number of weapons and documents. The hard-hit enemy unit had been a battalion of the 95th NVA Regiment.[16] The following day, May 3, the Americans found a notebook that probably belonged to an officer from the 95th, and though incomplete, the handwritten entries detailed the mission and goals of the enemy's rainy season offensive:

> The US was planning to pull out his force from the Western Highland to reinforce lowland. . . . Try by every possible means to lure the enemy out [of his bases] in order to destroy him, force him to fight on our own terms. B3 will coordinate its actions with all battlefields of *mien* [Region]. . . . For our part we should participate in the battles of B3. Force the enemy to divide his forces, then engage him. Attack his rear and his front. Harass him violently everywhere to the extent that he is compelled to disperse his forces for defense. Prevent him from massing his troops for offensive

> action. Try to win over the enemy troops, and have [as many as possible] come over to our side so as to create conditions for the other units to destroy F. Prevent him from pulling out from the Western Highland to reinforce the low land. Instead lure more enemy troops to the Western Highland so that the units of the low land can destroy several F. In our part we should try to lure F out and deal F several blows [Author's note: F apparently refers to American units or forces].[17]

The notebook mentioned the U.S. Special Forces camps at Duc Co, Plei Me, and New Plei Djereng, the 2nd Brigade base at Oasis, and the South Vietnamese district headquarters at Than An as potential targets for the coming offensive.[18] Meanwhile, on May 1, before elements of the 2-8 Infantry (Mech) rolled into action north of Plei Me, a company from Lt. Col. John P. Vollmer's 3-12 Infantry tangled with a large NVA force northwest of Duc Co. While policing up the battlefield the following day, the Americans captured a North Vietnamese prisoner, who disclosed that two battalions from his unit, the 66th NVA Regiment, had crossed the border and were building base camps in the area. According to the prisoner, the 66th intended to attack Duc Co in early June before pushing on to Plei Me. Colonel Adamson's 2nd Brigade, moreover, found an NVA complex with a radio typically used in a battalion headquarters, and had multiple contacts with enemy reconnaissance teams south of Duc Co. The North Vietnamese, it seemed, were preparing for a major attack.[19]

General Peers decided to strike first. Calling in the Air Force, Peers blasted the bush southwest of Duc Co with four B-52 raids. Next, he sent Lt. Col. Tim Gannon's 1-8 Infantry, then under the command of Adamson's 2nd Brigade, to search the area.[20] Colonel Adamson generally opposed sending ground troops to investigate B-52 strikes and on occasion refused to do it.[21] Reluctantly, Adamson dispatched the 1-8 Infantry to search the areas hit by the big bombers. "I was not privy to the rationale for the early May mission," recalled Lieutenant Colonel Gannon. "[In] late April and early May, we had small but continuous contact with NVA reconnaissance teams south of Duc Co. We captured a Chinese radio—looked like SCR 300, had a telephone attached—and we captured a prisoner. I was told to conduct a post-strike recon southwest of Duc Co (B-52 targets). My people reported a body count of one bird. Nothing more in that area." A subsequent sweep on May 11, this time to the west of Duc Co, once again found little in the way of enemy activity, and on the thirteenth the battalion rejoined Colonel Jackson's 1st Brigade.[22]

That same day, Jackson instructed Gannon to investigate the site of a fifth B-52 strike, which had been conducted some fifteen kilometers northwest of Duc Co, with two of his companies. After a thorough probe of the area, the two companies were to then head east and return to Jackson Hole. Jackson also ordered a second battalion,

Lt. Col. John P. Vollmer's 3-12 Infantry, to move within supporting range of Gannon. Line companies from the same battalion were generally expected to operate within one to three hours of each other at all times.[23]

Previously, the 1-8 Infantry had conducted search-and-destroy operations along the Ia Drang Valley. Traipsing through the tall grass, the battalion operated along the valley for nearly three weeks in early April, screening and interdicting potential enemy infiltration routes. The troops failed to locate any large NVA units but had several skirmishes with small enemy elements. Staying in the field, the battalion then began working the Cambodian border north of the Ia Drang River on April 23. A few days later, the battalion was placed under the operational control of Colonel Adamson's 2nd Brigade.[24]

Sweeps and skirmishes in the Ia Drang kept the troops of the 1-8 Infantry sharp and allowed their new commander, Lieutenant Colonel Gannon, to gain valuable experience. Gannon had assumed command of the battalion on March 29, 1967, following a stint as the executive officer of the 3rd Brigade, 25th Infantry Division. Gannon's military career began when he joined the Army in February 1951 as an enlisted man. The even-keeled Nebraskan showed promise and was quickly recommended for Officer Candidate School (OCS) at Fort Benning, Georgia. In March 1952, he graduated from OCS and received a commission as a second lieutenant of Infantry. Appropriately, Gannon chose the word "Mustang"—a term used to describe an officer who began his military career as an enlisted man—as his radio call sign in Vietnam.

Gannon, unlike some battalion commanders in Vietnam, possessed a temperament that meshed well with his new assignment. "Gannon kept track of what was going on in the battalion, had the instincts of the professional combat officer, and knew how to get the most out of his troops without a lot of bluster or by being a blowhard," said Capt. Robert Sholly, CO of B Company. "He was a professional officer in all contexts. He could be friendly, yet there was no question about who was in charge. He wanted your input, but he made his decisions based on factors of which you may not have been aware. He had a calm manner and never seemed to get flustered. He would admit he did not know the correct thing to do in a particular situation, but he never dithered in making up his mind on what to do once he knew the options."

On May 13, Lieutenant Colonel Gannon established a firebase on a small knoll west of Duc Co and dispatched A and B Companies, 1-8 Infantry to begin sweeping to the west-northwest, toward the site of the fifth B-52 strike. "Each unit carried three days' rations—we would resupply them with three days more," Gannon explained. "[The] plan was to check B-52 target and then move east toward mountain [*sic*] and eventually reach Jackson Hole."[25] A Battery, 6-29 Artillery, was airlifted into the

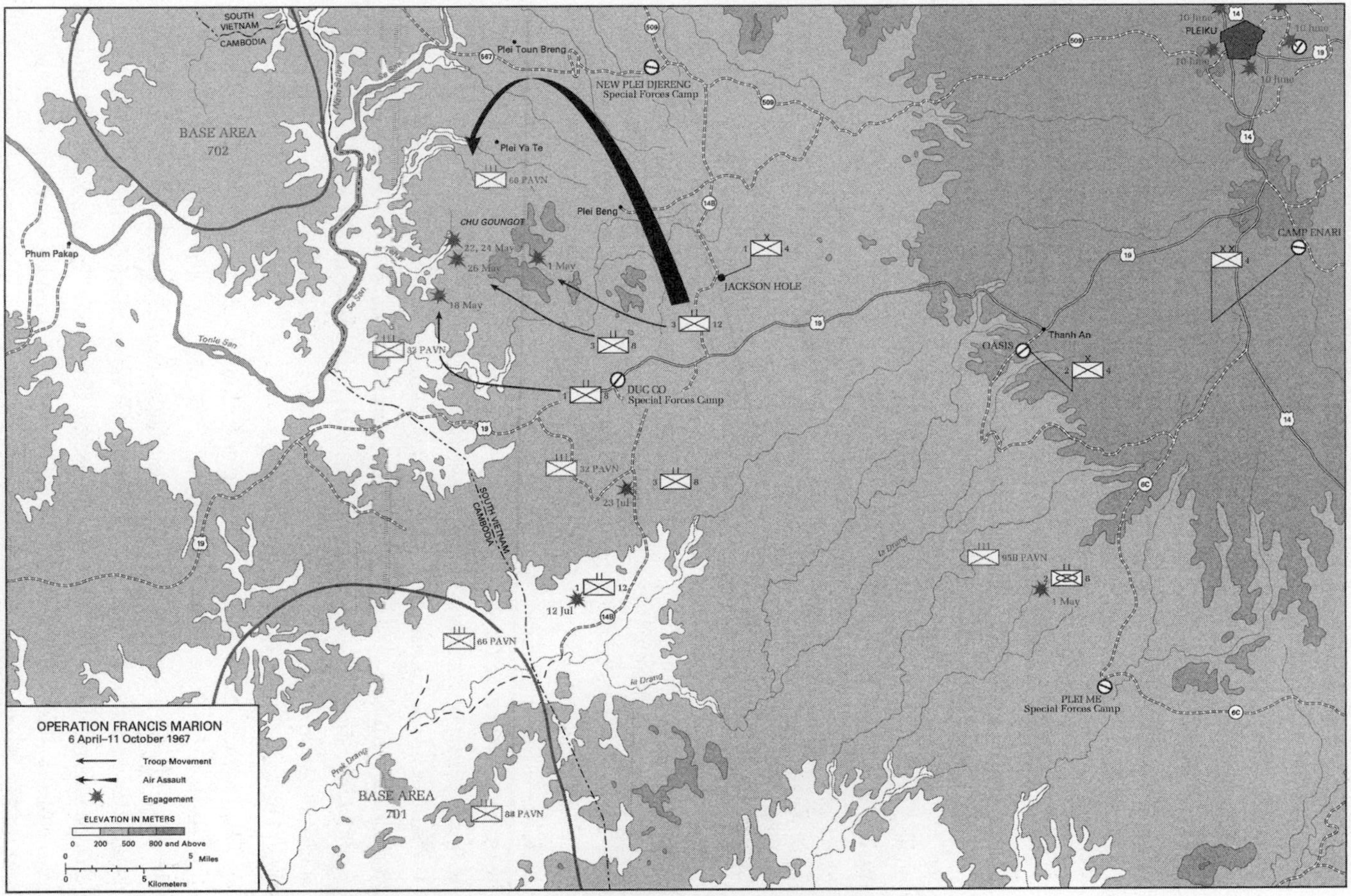

Operation Francis Marion, April 6–October 11, 1967. *Courtesy the U.S. Army Center of Military History.*

battalion firebase for direct support. C Company, meanwhile, was to provide security for the base while A and B Companies probed the bomb site.

The thirteenth passed uneventfully. On the fourteenth, however, Gannon lost his most experienced company commander. Scheduled to leave the field for R&R at the end of May, Captain Sholly was in the bush that afternoon with B Company, investigating a dry lake bed, when he stumbled down an embankment and wrenched an ankle. A medic immediately rushed to his aid and treated him, mistakenly, for heatstroke. Embarrassed, the young medic quickly corrected the misdiagnosis and got his ailing CO walking again, albeit gingerly. Ignoring the pain, Sholly limped another two hundred meters or so before concluding that he was jeopardizing the pace of the company and would have to request a helicopter for a medical evacuation (medevac) from the field. Sholly then selected his senior platoon leader, 1st Lt. Cary Allen, to command the company in his absence, and a short time later he boarded a chopper bound for Oasis. Sholly's departure left Gannon with a lieutenant in charge of B Company and Capt. Walter Williamson, who had succeeded Captain Sands back in March, at the helm of A Company as the battalion pushed on toward the Ia Tchar Valley.

Forbiddingly remote, the little-known Ia Tchar Valley was a relatively flat tract of jungle between the Cambodian border, marked in that area by the Se San River, and the rugged Chu Goungot Mountains. Double-canopy jungle covered much of the valley floor and the narrow ridges that lined it, making it difficult to observe artillery fire or air strikes from the ground or the air.[26] If, as General Peers believed, the terrain had "favored the enemy and U.S. firepower could not be employed to its full advantage" during Operation Sam Houston, similar conditions prevailed in the Ia Tchar.[27] The month of May, moreover, welcomed the southwest monsoon and with it the drenching tropical downpours and notoriously low cloud ceilings that had hampered American air mobility and close air support in the past. The North Vietnamese also maintained several *binh trams*—large, efficiently organized logistical complexes consisting of storage and training areas, rudimentary medical and R&R facilities, and rice farms—right across the border in Cambodia. These jungle supply stations supported enemy units operating in the Highlands and ensured that they would be well armed and outfitted for combat.

Despite these disadvantages, Lieutenant Colonel Gannon's 1-8 Infantry pushed into the lower Ia Tchar. The fifteenth and sixteenth passed without incident, and on the seventeenth, following yet another day of fruitless searching, the battalion bedded down in the valley within range of the Cambodian border. Five days had now elapsed since Colonel Jackson had ordered the battalion to investigate the location of the fifth B-52 strike. For the exhausted troopers of A and B Companies, however, the coming darkness meant another restless night in the bush, tossing and turning in weather-beaten ponchos.

Back at the battalion firebase, Pfc. Leslie Bellrichard, a profoundly religious draftee serving with C Company, wrote a letter to his brother Mark. Mark and his wife had mailed a photograph of their children, and Bellrichard wanted to respond to his younger brother. "They sure are beautiful," the twenty-five-year-old from Wisconsin crowed proudly in the letter. "I'm real happy for you both." Previously he had written to his brother from Vietnam and declared, ominously, that "this whole country is hostile. Everything wants your blood—leeches, mosquitoes, flesh-eating ants, thorns that even Texas can't grow . . . and then there's the North Vietnamese Army and the local Viet Cong." Never removed from his thoughts for very long, however, the faith that had sustained him and the deep, abiding affection he had for his fellow soldiers poured out onto the page. "Ever since I've been in this battalion," he wrote, "it's been my prayer that God will protect the men and bring the power of his holy spirit to bear here and save these men's souls."[28]

That night the sky opened up, soaking the valley below.

PART I

1-8 Infantry

THE BULLETS

3 TOWARD THE SOUND OF THE GUNS

The morning of May 18, 1967 dawned cool and damp in the southern Ia Tchar Valley. It had been raining steadily since about midnight, but now with the advent of dawn the torrential downpours and blustery gales so typical of the southwest monsoon had given way to a light drizzle. Shivering in the early morning air, Spc4 Victor Renza rubbed the sleep from his eyes and gazed around the B Company perimeter from the confines of a shallow foxhole. Small fires peeked back at him through the mist, and ill-defined shapes were beginning to stir. Observed with almost ritualistic devotion, the morning routine was well under way as men used snippets of C4 explosive to boil water for a cup of coffee and munched on C-rations. Others stretched their limbs and made small talk.

Sipping from a canteen cup filled with coffee, Specialist 4th Class Renza savored the warmth of the heated metal in his hands as the stimulating effects of the caffeine slowly sharpened his senses. A lot had changed since the fight in the Plei Doc on March 22, some of it for the better. Renza, with the high mortality rate of machine gunners in mind, had pleaded with Captain Sholly to get off the M-60. Normally a full-strength rifle platoon contained two machine guns, and he had manned one of them from his very first days in-country. Machine gunners, much like radio telephone operators, were routinely targeted by the NVA in battle and many did not last long as a result. Sholly finally relented and Renza handed the M-60 over to a new guy, Pfc. Joe DeLong, in April.

Renza was delighted to hand the M-60 off to some unsuspecting FNG (fucking new guy), but he had mixed emotions about transferring out of the Second Platoon and into the Fourth Platoon following the battle on March 22. He was, on the one hand, thrilled to reunite with his buddy Sgt. Bob Sanzone, an original and a fellow New Yorker he had met and befriended while on a train bound for the induction facility at Fort Jackson, South Carolina, back in 1965. On the other hand, he was not especially enthused about the prospect of serving in a platoon with Plt. Sgt. Bruce Grandstaff, a brusque, hard-charging career soldier with an appetite for action. Officers and career NCOs (noncommissioned officers) in the company admired Grandstaff for his indomitable courage and unwavering dedication to the craft of soldiering; in the opinion of many of the draftees who served under him, however, he was the embodiment of a lifer and what some would call a "John Wayne, gung-ho, motherfucker."[1]

Formerly the standing platoon sergeant for the Fourth Platoon, Grandstaff had stepped in as the acting platoon leader when Lt. Bernardo Bosch, who normally commanded the Fourth, was reassigned to the Exploitation Response Force back at Camp Enari. "We're going to find ourselves a fight," Grandstaff would boast to his young charges even before the promotion. Some in the platoon, particularly the more gung-ho types, swore by him. Others, including Renza who, like most draftees, fought tenaciously when he had to but who generally preferred a quiet day in the bush to an afternoon of pitched battle, found his outspoken bravado a little alarming. As the leader of the platoon, however, Grandstaff had more authority to act on that bravado and actually *find* a fight.

Renza finished his coffee and watched as Grandstaff walked over to the CP group in the center of the company perimeter. 1st Lt. Cary Allen, the acting B Company commander, had summoned his four platoon leaders to the CP for a quick briefing on the operations and activities planned for the day. Platoon leaders were then expected to return to their respective platoons and brief their squad leaders, who in turn would relay the information to their awaiting squads. Addressing his platoon leaders, Allen explained that the company would continue sweeping in a northerly direction that morning and he wanted the Fourth Platoon to begin on point. The four platoons were to proceed, at least initially, in a column formation.

Professionally capable, Allen, as the senior platoon leader in the company, had been the logical choice to succeed Captain Sholly in the event of an emergency. Allen, moreover, had performed superbly in command of the First Platoon and would even earn a Silver Star for his actions during a firefight in late April. Nonetheless he was not, strictly speaking, an infantryman by trade. "He wasn't infantry. He was a Regular Army guy who needed to spend two years with a combat branch before he went into his logistics role," said Sholly. "When you got a Regular Army commission in those days, and you were a quartermaster or something else in logistics or transportation, you would spend your first two years in a combat arms unit before they let you go into the support unit field. So he was spending his first two years in the infantry, and when he came to Vietnam he was assigned to us as part of that two-year assignment." Allen had received intense training at the infantry advanced course at Fort Benning, Georgia, prior to Vietnam, but he had earned Sholly's trust by demonstrating first and foremost that he was a quick study in the field.

Specialist 4th Class Renza sighed as the word came down to saddle up. B Company was breaking camp and moving out. Packing up his rucksack, Renza prayed the sun would poke through the dismal overcast and dry the sopping wet fatigues clinging to his slender frame. Ordinarily his pack tipped the scales at fifty or sixty pounds, but he reckoned that the rain from the night before had added another ten pounds in water weight to the load. Groaning slightly, Renza slipped inside the straps of his rucksack and waited for the company to form up. As he stood there, wincing under the weight of his water-logged pack, a figure tramped across the soggy perimeter toward him. Renza followed the movement through the mist and fog with mild apprehension until he caught a glimpse of the face beneath the approaching helmet.

"Hi, Rob!" Renza chirped cheerfully. "Did you get any sleep?"

"Are you crazy?" snapped Sgt. Bob Sanzone as he squished to a stop. "I haven't gotten a full night's sleep since I've been in the fucking Army!"[2]

Sanzone despised Army life in general and did not particularly relish serving as the acting platoon sergeant, a position he had assumed when Sergeant Grandstaff had taken command of the Fourth Platoon. Gifted mathematically, Sanzone had been studying engineering at a college in Kansas, and was waiting to return to school to resume his studies following a brief hiatus, when the draft intervened in the fall of 1965. He reported for duty and despite his distaste for the Army excelled as a soldier, reaching the rank of sergeant long before most of the kids he had been drafted with. Rank certainly had its privileges, but it also put him in league with *them*—the stick-up-their-ass NCOs and the ticket-punching career officers the draftees presumed were running the Army. Renza and Spc4 Charlie Ranello chided Sanzone relentlessly for becoming one of *them*, and while nothing more than good-natured ribbing, the jabs occasionally touched a nerve. On the morning of the eighteenth, however, Sanzone sounded more like a disgruntled draftee than a member of the company cadre with stripes on his sleeve.

"Renza, we have to get out of this motherfucker," he exclaimed, his voice betraying a hint of restless desperation. "We have to get out of here."

Specialist 4th Class Renza smiled nervously. "I know Rob—only one hundred and twenty days left and we'll be out."

"I know. I count every hour of every day," Sanzone replied. "I got a letter from Toni yesterday, and she really misses me. I just got to get home to see her."

"You will, Rob, you will."

Sanzone removed the letter from his helmet and held it in his hands. He had been dating Toni for a few years and had proposed to her before leaving for Vietnam. She accepted, and the engaged couple planned to marry as soon as he returned to the States. Renza looked at the neatly creased letter as his best friend spoke about his fiancée and how much he needed to get home. Outwardly Renza projected confidence, each word a cheerful reminder that all would be well. Privately, though, he had his doubts. And each day that they spent beating the bushes, in the heart of "Indian country," only intensified those anxieties to the point where he feared that neither one of them would make it out of Vietnam in one piece.

Renza and Sanzone were still talking when a flinch-inducing shout interrupted their conversation. "Ok, Fourth Platoon, let's move out," barked Sgt. Bruce Grandstaff, strutting out of the morning mist. "We've got point." The two young New Yorkers exchanged anxious glances. "I'll see you later," Sanzone murmured. Renza nodded and turned away.

By midmorning, B Company had been moving on foot for over an hour. The route travelled had taken the company through thick tropical rain forest, across a sparsely vegetated stretch of gently rolling hills and easily traversed valleys, and then back into dense jungle. Bands of brilliant sunlight nudged through the overhead canopy and, as the sun moved higher in the sky, the heat and humidity in which the troops were plodding bordered on the unbearable.

Advancing cautiously on an azimuth of 350 degrees, the company observed a lone North Vietnamese soldier at approximately 10:40 A.M. Clothed in a khaki uniform, the enemy soldier was armed, yet when fired upon, fled north along a high-speed trail. A sweep of the area was then conducted, after which the company continued moving north in a column formation led by the Fourth Platoon on the left and the Second Platoon, commanded by 1st Lt. Larry Rodabaugh, on the right. The First Platoon fell in behind the Second, while the Third Platoon brought up the left rear behind the Fourth.[3]

Lieutenant Rodabaugh trudged along through the tangled undergrowth in silence. A keen and conscientious twenty-five-year-old platoon leader from Indianapolis, Indiana, Rodabaugh had attended Butler University, and later the University of Southern Illinois, before landing in Nyack, New York. Painting and the odd drywall job here and there paid the bills, but he yearned for something more and then one afternoon, in the fall of 1964, he found himself sitting alone at a bar. *What the hell am I doing*, he thought to himself as he sat, drink in hand, staring out the window. And then it hit him. Peering out into the early autumn afternoon, he saw an Army recruiting office across the street. Rodabaugh set his glass down and marched out of the bar and straight into the office. "What do you have for me?" he asked the startled recruiter bluntly. Promised a clerk position in Germany, Rodabaugh enlisted in early 1965, passed a few written exams, and in March of 1966 graduated from Officer's Candidate School at Fort Benning, Georgia.

Up ahead his three-man point team had given the signal to halt. Something had aroused their attention. Crouching down, Rodabaugh maneuvered forward through the brush, his hushed movements unaffected by the quiet trepidation stirring within. Rodabaugh's unease with what awaited him was not entirely unfounded. He knew that the company was dangerously close to the Cambodian border, and he suspected that if the NVA wanted to fight they would do so somewhere near it.

Rodabaugh reached his point team and, gazing downward, discovered the cause of the holdup. Scanning the jungle floor with his eyes, Rodabaugh traced what appeared to be a trail running perpendicular to B Company's northerly axis of advance. In addition to its west-to-east bearing out of Cambodia, the trail was approximately two to three feet wide and, judging by the conspicuous lack of vegetation on it, exceedingly well travelled. *Well, this sure as shit can't be good*, Rodabaugh thought to himself as he motioned for his remaining squads to move on line and take up positions parallel to the trail. Muddy, high-speed trails coming out of Cambodia were usually indicative of an NVA presence, often a very large one, in a given area.

Suddenly Rodabaugh observed three North Vietnamese soldiers, AK-47s slung casually over their shoulders, walking east along the trail around 10:55 A.M.[4] Attired in khaki-colored uniforms, the three were overheard whispering to one another and giggling, evidently oblivious to the American platoon nearby. Rodabaugh gestured for his RTO and got Lieutenant Allen on the horn. "Six, I've got a high-speed trail running west to east, and I've got a couple of dinks on it," he explained evenly. "What do you want me to do?" Allen thought it over briefly and then instructed Rodabaugh to capture one of the North Vietnamese soldiers strolling down the trail.

Allen's order was scarcely controversial. Higher headquarters had counseled units in the field to capture enemy soldiers whenever possible, because prisoners frequently yielded intelligence. Timely tactical intelligence could then impart where the enemy was and in what strength, and that information—if disseminated properly—could help avert disaster or at the very least alert an American unit moving through a particular area to the possibility of enemy contact. A scrawny, barefooted North Vietnamese soldier of no particular account, after all, had warned Lt. Col. Hal Moore and his cavalry troopers in the Ia Drang Valley in '65 that there were three NVA battalions located nearby. Those battalions, the prisoner warned, wanted to "kill Americans." Years later Moore called that hapless NVA soldier a "godsend."[5]Allen, though inexperienced as a company commander, had led a platoon in the field long enough to understand the value of actionable intelligence.

Obeying Allen's orders, Lieutenant Rodabaugh sized up the three NVA soldiers on the trail and, from the jungle adjacent to the trail, hollered over to them in passable Vietnamese, "Lai day, lai day"! (Come here, come here!) Startled, the North Vietnamese soldiers jettisoned their packs and dashed off into the bush to the north. Rodabaugh and his men opened fire, but the three managed to escape. It was now after eleven o'clock in the morning. Rodabaugh cautiously approached the four abandoned packs and noticed blood on the ground but no sign of the enemy soldiers. Summoning his RTO, he radioed Allen again and apprised him of the situation.[6]

Initially Allen ordered Rodabaugh to pursue the fleeing NVA with his Second Platoon. Rodabaugh, however, needed time to consolidate his dispersed squads, so Allen decided to dispatch Sgt. Bruce Grandstaff's Fourth Platoon down the east-west trail instead. Grandstaff received orders to move west-northwest and investigate the trail in that direction. Allen then sent the First Platoon on a similar mission down the segment of trail running east-southeast. Both platoons received explicit instructions to advance no farther than two hundred meters from the main body of the company. In the interim, the Second and Third Platoons were to remain behind, establish a perimeter, and begin cutting an LZ for the evacuation of the captured North Vietnamese packs.[7]

Grandstaff listened to Allen and then reiterated the order to his Fourth Platoon squad leaders. "Second and Third Platoons are going to stay here in the perimeter," he told them gruffly. "First Platoon is going to recon to the south about fifty meters, and we are going to recon to the west. First squad, you take point. 2nd and 3rd fall in behind them. And 4th squad, you take up the rear. Leave your rucksacks here at the perimeter. Just take web gear and ammo."[8] A short while later, the Fourth Platoon began moving west, down the high-speed trail.

As the Fourth followed the trail westward, the old hands in the platoon took note of the thick underbrush and the towering overhead canopy. Spc4 Victor Renza was among them. A respected original, he began to have grave reservations about the wisdom of the mission. *Where the hell are we going*, he wondered to himself while trooping warily along near the back of the platoon column. *We're on a high-speed trail coming from Cambodia, and we're getting farther and farther away from the rest of the company. This is a bad situation.*

Renza bit his tongue and continued walking. Four months, one hundred and twenty days or so and a wakeup, and he would be out of the bush and back in the world. Soon, though, the growing unease he felt about Sergeant Grandstaff and the mission got the better of him and he turned and faced his buddy, Sgt. Bob Sanzone, and asked, "Where the hell is he going?" Sanzone shrugged. "I don't know, but I'm ready to go back to the company!"[9]

Rummaging through the packs the North Vietnamese had discarded, 1st Lt. Larry Rodabaugh was surprised to find an unopened box of Crest toothpaste and the latest issue of *Hot Rod* magazine. Rodabaugh also found what appeared to be documents, so he sent the packs back to the company CP group. Lieutenant Allen, after reviewing the contents of the packs, radioed the Tactical Operations Center (TOC) at the 1-8 Infantry fire support base and briefed the battalion S3. Arrangements were then made to evacuate the packs to the TOC for additional analysis. Allen, furthermore, informed the S3 that he had dispatched his First and Fourth Platoons to reconnoiter stretches of the east-west trail his Second Platoon had discovered.

While the Fourth Platoon ventured west, Plt. Sgt. Clifford Johnson's First Platoon probed cautiously to the east-southeast. The jungle there seemed unusually still, almost serene. Pfc. John Barclay, an eighteen-year-old replacement from Chicago, tightened the grip on his M-16 with every stride. Barclay had volunteered for the draft in 1966, hoping to see action in a straight-leg infantry outfit. A knot now formed in his belly. *This is it*, he thought, *we're going to get hit*. Barclay stole a glance at his buddy, Pfc. Ken Brosseau, off to his right. Drafted in September 1966 at the ripe old age of twenty-five, Brosseau had trained with Barclay at Fort Polk, Louisiana, and later at Fort Knox, Kentucky, and the pair had arrived in Vietnam together in April of 1967. Though their eyes met momentarily, neither man uttered a word.

First Platoon continued patrolling southeast along the trail. Contrary to expectation, however, the platoon did not find any sign of the enemy and Lieutenant Allen ordered Johnson to return to the company after he and his men had travelled a distance of approximately two hundred and fifty meters. Turning around, the platoon quietly retraced its steps, and a short while later, it reunited with the Second and Third Platoons in the company perimeter. Pfc. John Barclay walked into the perimeter and promptly removed his helmet. His heart had finally ceased hammering away inside his chest. Sitting down atop his helmet, he cracked open a can of peaches and breathed a deep sigh of relief before hungrily consuming the soft, sweet fruit inside.

Around 11:30 A.M. the lead elements of the Fourth Platoon spotted a North Vietnamese soldier wearing a green uniform and carrying a rucksack. *Bang!* The lone NVA brazenly squeezed off a shot and then vanished in the bush. The platoon hit the dirt, while Sergeant Grandstaff, who was near the head of the column, contacted Lieutenant Allen's RTO, Sgt. Dick Surface, and informed him that he intended to pursue the enemy soldier. Surface in turn relayed the SITREP (situation report) to Allen. Meanwhile, toward the rear of the platoon, Spc4 Victor Renza had crawled over to Sgt. Bob Sanzone and his RTO, Pfc. Charlie Reed, in time to overhear Grandstaff talking to Surface over the radio. "What the fuck is he doing?" Renza asked angrily, referring to Grandstaff. "That asshole." Sanzone, though, remained silent.[10]

Soon the four squads of the Fourth Platoon were upright and on the move again. Resuming the chase, the platoon eventually branched off the main east-west trail and began following a secondary trail that ran to the northwest. Down the trail a short ways the Americans ran into a handful of NVA. *Bang! Bang! Bang! Bang!* The sound of gunfire reverberated across the jungle. No more than four or five in number, the North Vietnamese appeared long enough to potshot the Americans before disappearing once again into the bush. Instinctively the platoon went to ground, but a few soldiers in the point squad managed to return fire.

Lieutenant Allen had been attending to company affairs back in the CP group when the gunfire erupted. Shortly thereafter, the radio began to crackle and on the other end was Sergeant Grandstaff, calling in an update from the Fourth Platoon. Allen asked if the platoon required any assistance. "I instructed PSG [Platoon Sergeant] Grandstaff to move the Weapons Platoon to the west. After a short time, PSG Grandstaff called me stating that his platoon had spotted one NVA, and they were trying to capture him," Allen later wrote. "Approximately ten minutes later, PSG Grandstaff called again saying that four or five more NVA had been sighted. I asked him if he needed any help and he replied, 'negative.'"[11]

Allen also advised Grandstaff to rejoin the company, though the acting company commander stopped short of outright insisting that he return. Flush with adrenaline and unwilling to suspend the hunt just yet, Grandstaff reported that his platoon had encountered four or five NVA and that he was still in position to eliminate them. Critically the chain of command then lapsed into a momentary state of impasse—Grandstaff wanted to continue the chase, Allen favored consolidating the company —and in the ensuing uncertainty, the Fourth Platoon continued its pursuit of the NVA.

In and out the fleeing North Vietnamese weaved, drawing the Fourth Platoon deeper and deeper into the jungle. Numbering only four or five before, the enemy grew suddenly in strength as a group of ten to fifteen NVA appeared out of nowhere and engaged the platoon in a brief exchange of fire around 12:00 P.M. The Americans, despite the confusion, reported that the enemy fire originated from the north-northeast as well as the west. Artillery was fired in support of the platoon and gunships were requested.[12] The North Vietnamese fire slackened somewhat, and an uneasy silence soon settled over the jungle. Sergeant Grandstaff, sensing that the odds had changed, got on the horn with Lieutenant Allen and requested help. Allen ordered Grandstaff to return with the Fourth at once.

Operating one of the company radios that day, Sgt. Dick Surface recalled the conversations between Grandstaff and Allen in vivid detail. "When Grandstaff went down there to the west, we heard a couple of shots. We talked to Grandstaff, and he said that there were some NVA zigzagging—not moving straight down it, but zigzagging—down there on that trail," Surface said. "At that point, Allen told him to come back. Grandstaff said that he thought he could still get them. The next time Allen talked to him, he affirmed the order to come back. Allen was pretty firm." Grandstaff accepted the order without objection and then asked if the company would fire a single rifle shot so that his platoon could shoot an azimuth and find its way back to the perimeter. Allen agreed and a shot was fired.

Set up near the point squad of the Fourth Platoon, Grandstaff had his RTO get on the radio and call for Sergeant Sanzone to come forward immediately. Sanzone listened glumly and then took off his radio headset. Specialist 4th Class Renza, his buddy from basic training, was staring at him. Both men were lying in a prone position alongside the trail. "Tell him to get us the hell out of here!" Renza growled, expressing a sentiment many in the platoon shared. Visibly frightened, Sanzone seemed incapable of mustering a response. Instead he scooped up his M-16 and scrambled to his feet. Hunched over at the waist, Sanzone, with his RTO following close behind, began moving down the trail toward the front of the platoon.

Sgt. Dick Surface *felt* the roar as much he heard it. "When the firing started, it was horrendous," he remembered. "It was kind of like being at the rifle range multiplied by about fifty." Originating somewhere off to the west, in the vicinity of the Fourth Platoon, the sudden roar of gunfire reverberated across the jungle with earsplitting intensity. Surface, as an RTO, had been privy to all communications over the company net, including those of Sergeant Grandstaff, and he knew instantly that the Fourth Platoon was in trouble. A short distance away, Lieutenant Rodabaugh had been reorganizing his Second Platoon when the tumult started. "We knew right away, from the firing that could be heard and from what Grandstaff was saying over the radio, that Fourth Platoon was in big trouble," Rodabaugh said. The only question, Rodabaugh thought to himself, was *how* big.

Soon the B Company perimeter was bustling with activity as soldiers from the three remaining platoons, some of whom were milling around and eating only moments before, began dropping their rucksacks and grabbing their rifles. "Let's go!" squad and fire team leaders shouted. "Mount up, mount up!" Lieutenant Allen, bringing a measure of order to the commotion, directed Lieutenant Rodabaugh and 1st Lt. Charles E. Aronhalt Jr., platoon leader (PTL) of the Third Platoon, to assemble their respective platoons quickly.[13] Placing the Second and Third Platoons side by side at the front of the company formation, Allen moved his CP group in behind the two lead platoons and ordered the First Platoon, under the command of Plt. Sgt. Clifford Johnson, to pull up the rear. All three platoons then headed west, toward the Fourth Platoon.

Paced by the Second Platoon on the right and the Third Platoon on the left, B Company entered a shallow ravine less than fifty meters from its jump-off point. The Second and Third were advancing in a fairly standard formation—three-man point team and accompanying machine-gun crew, a squad containing the platoon leader close behind, the remaining squads following in trace—when the lead elements of both platoons crossed the ravine and started up the other side. Suddenly the jungle erupted in a nerve-shattering squall of automatic weapons fire, turning the narrow little gully into which the Americans had descended into a violent tempest. Bullets snapped off branches and twigs and raked the advance elements of both platoons. Some of the grunts screamed out in agony, others stared numbly at the bodies of their friends lying on the slope ahead.

Concealed in the thick jungle on the opposite side of the ravine, the North Vietnamese annihilated the forward elements of the Second and Third Platoons in a single, devastating volley. "They were waiting for us, and they just cut up the front of my platoon and Chuck's [Lieutenant Aronhalt] platoon," said Rodabaugh. "They hit us hard almost as soon as Chuck and I started moving." Halted by the intense incoming fire, the two platoons hugged the dirt, called for artillery support, and opened up with M-16s. Spc4 Charlie Ranello of Pittsburgh, Pennsylvania, and Pfc. Randy Lewis were both near the front of the Second Platoon. Close friends of Spc4 Victor Renza, the two were marching through the jungle to rescue him when the NVA salvo cut Ranello down.

Months before, while still in the Tuy Hoa area, Ranello envisioned a frightful ending for the men of B Company. "Charlie walked over [that night] to talk," wrote Spc4 Bill May, a fellow Second Platoon trooper. "During the day, one of the platoons had killed a VC. The VC had stood his ground against a full platoon. He never had a chance. He carried an old French carbine that was so rusty that the bolt had to be forced forward to chamber a round. As we set up that night, Gun Two's [machine gun] position overlooked the ongoing construction of the base. It was an impressive display of American might to say the least. But Charlie said, 'May—we're all going to die here, they're going to kill us all.' Surprised, I asked him what he was talking about. He then said, 'You know that gook they killed today?' I told him that I had heard about it and had heard it had been easy. Charlie then said, 'Look down there. He could see what we can see and he wasn't afraid of us. They're going to kill us all.' At the time I laughed it off as Charlie just being himself but he was right. They weren't afraid of us. Charlie died on May 18 charging toward the action. He wasn't afraid of them, either."

Ranello's death deprived Second Platoon of an experienced, courageous machine gunner and, if no one else retrieved it, a fully functioning M-60, a weapon whose firepower the platoon desperately needed if it hoped to punch through the North Vietnamese and rescue the Fourth Platoon. Unwilling to leave an M-60 or a fallen comrade behind, Spc4 Joseph Mancuso, twenty-one, of North Bellmore, New York, moved out with several other soldiers to fetch Ranello and the gun.

To the left of the Second Platoon, Lt. Chuck Aronhalt attempted to pull his Third Platoon back but the sheer intensity of the North Vietnamese fire precluded movement in any direction. Aronhalt remained calm, however. Educated at Johns

Hopkins University, he had studied engineering in college and was trained to think analytically. Consequently, when the NVA prevented him from pulling his troops back safely, frustrating his attempts to reposition his platoon, he changed course and brought up his M-60 machine guns. Aronhalt then tried, unsuccessfully, to organize a perimeter. A push to get the platoon moving forward to retrieve some of the wounded failed as well. More and more of his men, meanwhile, were being killed and wounded. Subjected to a withering barrage of enemy fire, the Third Platoon could neither advance nor withdraw.

Unable to maneuver his platoon effectively, Aronhalt concentrated for a time on rescuing the wounded, and he personally carried some of his men back to less exposed positions. On one trip forward, however, his M-16 jammed, so he grabbed a discarded M-60 machine gun and laid the weapon over the top of a large anthill, exposing his head and shoulders to enemy fire. Lt. Larry Rodabaugh, huddled off to the right, had been directing his Second Platoon when he turned to the left and saw Aronhalt pumping out rounds on the M-60.[14] "Chuck, get your goddamn head down," Rodabaugh cried out anxiously, hoping his friend would hear him over the noise of battle. Aronhalt glanced over at Rodabaugh, but before he could speak, a round pierced the left side of his head and rapidly exited the right, killing him instantly. "I saw the round go right through his head, clean through," Rodabaugh recalled. "It went straight through, and I watched his brains actually dribbling out of his head." Aronhalt was posthumously awarded the Distinguished Service Cross for his extraordinary valor that day.

For a moment Lieutenant Rodabaugh stared at the limp figure crumpled down beside the anthill to his left. *The sons of bitches got Chuck*, he thought angrily. Rodabaugh knew, though, that he had to put the death of his friend behind him and concentrate on his own platoon, which had also run aground in the shallow ravine west of the temporary B Company perimeter. The NVA, it seemed, had been waiting for them. "The minute they [NVA] encountered Grandstaff, they started firing and they began maneuvering to encircle him," said Rodabaugh. "So by the time Chuck and I began to move, the NVA had had time to jam a force in there between us and Grandstaff."

Their best chance, Rodabaugh concluded, was to abandon the frontal assaults—the standard straight right—and instead throw a right *hook*. Drawing on his training, he rounded up a machine-gun crew and an RTO and started moving through the jungle to the right to outflank the NVA positioned along the ridge of the ravine. The maneuver, while doctrinally sound, was also fraught with risk. If Rodabaugh failed to lead what amounted to a fire team far enough out to the right before turning left to sweep around and then behind the NVA on the ridge, he and his men could stumble, with potentially fatal consequences, onto a hidden enemy machine gun or a small army of enemy soldiers.

Lieutenant Rodabaugh daringly led his team to the right, away from the rest of the platoon, until he felt reasonably certain that he could begin bending back to the left and into the rear of the North Vietnamese line. Unbeknownst to Rodabaugh, however, a North Vietnamese soldier dressed in khaki and wearing a sun helmet had snuck up behind them. Spraying the Americans with his AK-47, the NVA killed the machine-gun crew and wounded the RTO, Pfc. Kurt Arens. Rodabaugh, who was hunched over and dashing through the brush when the shooting started, was also struck when a bullet penetrated his extended left arm and continued upward, toward the shoulder, just beneath the surface of his skin. Astonishingly the high-velocity round, apart from peeling the flesh back on his upper arm like a banana, caused little structural damage.

Wounded but not incapacitated, Rodabaugh whirled around and spotted the shooter standing, rifle at the ready, no more than forty feet away. Reflexively Rodabaugh aimed "center mass" and before he knew it he had emptied half of the twenty-round magazine in his CAR-15. Hopelessly riddled, the NVA staggered backward and then collapsed in a bloody heap. Rodabaugh exhaled and turned his attention to his fallen comrades. Thinking, mistakenly, that they were all dead, he scooped up the radio and hustled back to the main battle area of the Second Platoon, where he promptly slid in behind a downed tree. Sgt. Esteban Colon-Motas, a squad leader in the Second, suddenly raced past him and picked up Sgt. John Ingoglia. "As he was returning, I saw enemy rounds burst through Colon-Motas's body as he was hit multiple times, still carrying his buddy," said Rodabaugh. "When he got to a log in back of me, he threw Ingoglia behind the log then fell over the log and died."[15] Colon-Motas, twenty-nine, received the Bronze Star for saving Ingoglia's life.

Meanwhile Sfc. Alhandro Yuson, Rodabaugh's platoon sergeant in the Second, directed a small group of soldiers to provide covering fire while others helped pull back some of the wounded. Yuson spotted and killed several NVA soldiers attempting to infiltrate the platoon from the rear and then personally helped recover the bodies of several wounded men. Yuson, at one point, suffered a head wound from a chunk of flying shrapnel but he refused to leave the line, ensuring that the Second remained well organized throughout the battle. The feisty veteran was later awarded the Silver Star for his heroism under fire.

Eerily quiet that morning, the jungle surrounding the four understrength platoons of Bravo Company, 1-8 Infantry, was alive and teeming with North Vietnamese by early afternoon, so much so that the company CP group, trailing along behind the Second and Third Platoons, was soon engaged and pinned down by heavy enemy fire. That fire, ominously enough, suggested that the NVA, an army trained in and lethally adept at fire and maneuver, had already halted the forward momentum of the two lead platoons and were now maneuvering along the flanks to envelop the entire company. "As the enemy started to circle around the Fourth Platoon," said Sgt. Dick Surface, an RTO with the headquarters element of B Company, "we ran into their fire. They were fanning out on our right flank. We tried to call the 'Three-Three' [S3 officer at the battalion TOC] to let them know that we were under fire, too, but we couldn't communicate with them down there at the bottom of that hill."

Surface surmised that if he could not get the radio to cooperate, he would have to hike, under heavy fire, back up the slope and out of the ravine in order to get the reception he needed to communicate with the battalion TOC. Dreading the prospect of having to abandon the relative safety of the ravine to run back up the slope, Surface fiddled stubbornly with the radio a while longer but it would neither transmit nor receive communications. He had to get to higher ground. Resigned to his fate, he snatched the radio and scampered up the slope with Sgt. Don Hunter, a communications NCO in the company, amid the crack and hum of enemy automatic rifle fire. The two, after reaching the top, found an opening in the bamboo and settled down in it. Surface handled the radio, and right away he recognized the calm yet commanding voice on the other end.

"I want to speak to your 'six,'" said Lt. Col. Tim Gannon, CO of the 1-8 Infantry, impatiently.

Surface paused. His "six," or unit commander, was 1st Lt. Cary Allen and Allen was still down in the ravine, commanding the company and coordinating fire support. "I'm not at his location. We had to move up here to communicate."

"I'm up in the air now," Gannon replied curtly, "so get back with your 'six' so that I can talk to him."

Gannon, Surface now knew, was airborne in his Command and Control (C&C) chopper and would soon be orbiting over the battlefield. Anxious to rejoin Lieutenant Allen and the CP group, Surface began easing back down the incline leading into the ravine as soon as the brief exchange with Gannon ended. Along the way he became ensnared in a snarl of vines and as he wriggled about, twisting this way and that, Sergeant Hunter yanked the radio from his back and dashed down the slope. Jerking free, Surface hurried after Hunter and eventually wound up flat on his belly alongside Sgt. William Brown Jr. in the Second Platoon sector. Rounds were ricocheting off the trees nearby, and he pressed his chest and abdomen further into the ground. Brown, meanwhile, was putting bursts of M-16 fire into the bushes.

Surface lifted his head up slightly and looked around. Seeing nothing but jungle, he lowered his eyes momentarily and immediately cringed. "Looking up, you really couldn't see much of anything, but if you looked down you could see their feet," Surface remembered. "Down there by the roots, you could definitely see their feet and there were a lot of feet moving back and forth. Some of them had those sandal-thong things made out of truck tires, and some of them were wearing boots." North Vietnamese troops, it suddenly occurred to him, were converging on the rest of the company.

Closing fast, the NVA drew to within ten meters of Sergeants Brown and Surface. Surface, aiming the barrel of his M-16 at a point in the bushes where he imagined an enemy torso might be, blasted the vegetation out in front of his position. Faceless flashes of color and motion, the fleeting shapes in the jungle before him began to stumble and fall, knocked askew and then dropped by the crackling fire of M-16s on automatic. Surface was unsure whether he or Sergeant Brown, or someone else entirely for that matter, had delivered the kill shots. Either way, it didn't make much difference to him. Popping another magazine into his M-16, Surface continued to fire into the area all around his position, including in the trees. Tracer rounds streaked across the jungle as the two sides slugged it out in the bush.

Too distracted to notice the roar of battle only moments before, Surface began to hear the anguished wails of his comrades lying wounded close by. Hauntingly shrill, their shrieks were such that he feared he would never forget the sound.

In command of the company for less than a week, 1st Lt. Cary Allen lacked the experience and, it may be said, the gravitas frequently associated with more seasoned company commanders. Critical judgments still had to be made, however, and orders based on those judgments had to be issued in a timely enough fashion to influence events on the ground. Uncertain as to the exact size, strength, and dispositions of the NVA, Allen had to decide, for example, where to commit his trailing First Platoon. He could reinforce the Second and Third Platoon sectors and maybe punch through the NVA blocking force, or he could flank the First out to the right or left. The company to that point had been unable to maneuver on either its right or left flank. Allen, perhaps in response to enemy pressure on his right (northern) flank, ordered Plt. Sgt. Clifford Johnson, the acting commander of the First, to send elements of his platoon out to the right.

Sergeant Johnson personally led the flanking effort. Married and something of an Army "lifer," the Pittsburgh, Pennsylvania, native prosecuted his duties as a senior NCO capably but without the gung-ho bluster that made some draftees roll their eyes. "We respected him," said SSgt. Jim Buckmaster, an original drafted in 1965. "Although he wasn't a 'rah-rah' or 'gung-ho' guy necessarily, he got the job done." About a week before, in fact, Johnson had confided to one of his soldiers that he did not want to die in Vietnam, but if he did his body was to be returned to the United States.

Running into NVA flanking fire, Johnson called back and ordered Sgt. John McKeever to bring up his M-60. McKeever covered the twenty-five or thirty yards of jungle separating the two as quickly he could and crawled to within fifty to seventy-five feet of Johnson. Both men were now lying on the ground in the prone position.

"Where do you want me to shoot?" McKeever asked, readying the gun for action.

"Spray the trees," Johnson answered firmly. "Just keep spraying the trees."

On cue Sergeant McKeever raked the trees with machine-gun fire. McKeever, like Sergeant Buckmaster, was a draftee and a well-thought-of original who had certainly seen his share of firefights. Some fights were unavoidable, that much he would readily concede, but experience had also taught him to recognize those situations in which discretion *was* the better part of valor. Heedlessly chasing the North Vietnamese through the jungle, as the Fourth Platoon had done, seemed like a recipe for trouble. The NVA had wanted a fight, and now the entire company was obliged to give them one.

Yelling loud enough to be heard over the gunfire, Sergeant Johnson, in between bursts of fire from his M-16, ordered McKeever to move the machine gun up closer to his position. The dense foliage in the immediate area slowed McKeever, but he eventually squirmed forward and caught sight of his platoon leader. Spray the trees, Johnson barked again. Thumping away with the M-60, McKeever burned through belts of ammo, chopping off branches and turning leaves into mulch. All the while Johnson kept shooting and shouting, oblivious to the enemy fire snapping through the bush.

Suddenly the machine gun behind Sergeant Johnson fell silent. After laying down a curtain of suppressive fire, Sergeant McKeever had expended the last of his M-60 ammunition. With the firefight still ongoing, and with the possibility of additional NVA joining the fray, McKeever knew he could not afford to let the gun remain silent for long. He had to find ammo. Luckily, his ammo bearers were not far behind, and they tossed several 100-round belts of ammo up to him. Grateful, McKeever scooped up the belts and quickly resumed firing.

The NVA fire slackened somewhat, and during the ensuing lull McKeever could hear other troops in the platoon flanking element yelling. Their shouts, from what he could tell, were directed at Sergeant Johnson. Johnson, however, never responded. *Why isn't he answering them*? McKeever wondered, fearing the worst. Soon afterward his M-60 jammed. Isolated and in a vulnerable location, McKeever quietly gathered up his gun and moved back to the First Platoon section of the developing B Company perimeter.

Lieutenant Allen's decision to flare elements of the First Platoon out to the right to protect his exposed right flank and rear proved exceedingly wise. Boiling out of the steamy jungle in strength, the NVA had encircled the Fourth Platoon and had intercepted the Second and Third Platoons before they could reach the Fourth, effectively blocking their advance in a shallow ravine. Pressure had also begun to build on the right (northern) flank of B Company (-) in what was likely an attempt by the NVA to outflank and encircle the entire company.[16]

Pfc. Ken Brosseau, an older if untested replacement in the First Platoon, was watching and waiting when the jungle started to stir on the flank of the company. "I saw them trying to go around us. I saw probably fifteen or twenty NVA out there, and then I basically fired one or two magazines out into that area," said Brosseau . "I think we probably surprised them. We were just trying to stop them from trying to get around us." That the company would inevitably run into a large group of NVA at some point that afternoon came as no surprise to him, however. "The first time I saw that trail, I knew we were in an area with a whole lot of NVA," Brosseau stated. "A company of our guys marching down it could never have tramped down a trail that much."

The gunfire in the area of the First Platoon gradually increased, and as the two sides pawed blindly at one another in the jungle, the battle threatened to engulf the entire company. In the midst of the firing, Spc4 Larry Gerken, a drafted original from Pittsburgh and a self-effacing Silver Star recipient, sought refuge behind a large tree. Spc4 John Richey, Gerken quickly discovered, was on the other side of the tree. The two were not alone. Silently lurking in the undergrowth nearby, a North Vietnamese soldier poked his head up and then ducked back down. Emboldened, the NVA waited a moment and then popped his head back up again, unaware that he had been spotted by Gerken and Richey. A second, maybe two, elapsed before a bright red clot exploded from the back of the NVA's head in a violent spasm of blood and tissue. With M-16s shouldered and gazes fixed, Gerken and Richey had waited patiently for the NVA to pop his head up again, and when he did, the two young Americans did not miss.

Sometime thereafter an NVA soldier emerged from the bush and exploded a grenade near Specialist 4th Class Richey, injuring two members of his squad. Richey, who escaped the blast unharmed, gunned down the enemy soldier and carried the wounded men to safety. Later on in the afternoon, while crawling forward to knock out an apparent NVA emplacement, Richey noticed an enemy grenade bouncing toward him. Startled, Richey scooped up the grenade and tossed it back at the emplacement. The explosion silenced the enemy position, allowing Richey to lay down suppressive fires for the rest of his squad. In October of that year, the Army awarded Specialist 4th Class Richey a Silver Star for his gallantry in action.[17]

SSgt. James "Rock" Smothers, a muscular African American NCO in the First Platoon, paid class and color no mind, even in a troubled age of social unrest and racial injustice. "It was not necessarily uncommon for black soldiers to be unfriendly over there in Vietnam, with everything going on in the country with the civil rights movement and race relations," said Pfc. John Barclay. "I think, understandably, that a lot of black soldiers thought that their fight was back home. I can respect that, but honestly Smothers seemed like the type of guy that only saw one color over there—green." Smothers, moreover, was a first-rate NCO with a feel for combat, a trait admired by soldiers of every race and creed.

Surveying the surrounding foliage, Smothers suddenly detected movement to his front. "The motherfuckers are behind the Y-shaped tree," he screamed, warning the other grunts nearby. Ten to twelve feet to Smothers's right, Specialist 4th Class Richey had swapped M-16s with his friend, Pfc. John Barclay, and was firing furiously in the general direction of the NVA. Richey and Barclay were both behind the same tree, and while Richey blazed away with Barclay's M-16, Barclay tried desperately to fix Richey's jammed rifle, but to no avail. Neither one of them had an ideal angle from which to shoot at the Y-shaped tree, so it—and presumably the enemy soldiers Smothers spotted hiding around and behind it—remained relatively untouched despite the intense back-and-forth fire.

Frustrated, Smothers called over to Barclay and asked, his tone betraying a hint of disgust, "Don't you see it?"

"No," Barclay confessed.

"I'll mark it."

Loading his CAR-15 with a fresh magazine, Sergeant Smothers locked in and laced the Y-shaped tree with a ribbon of red tracer rounds. Pfc. Barclay poked his head around the tree that he and Specialist 4th Class Richey had crowded behind and easily traced the slender ribbon of red from Smothers's rifle to the intended target. *Got it*, he mused privately, forgetting for a moment that even a modestly observant set of eyes could follow the same tracer trail right back to Smothers's position.

As expected, the NVA traced the red ribbon back to Sergeant Smothers and immediately unleashed a volley of heavy automatic rifle fire. Smothers was struck in the arm. "I'm hit, I'm hit!" he yelped excitedly. "The blood is squirting!" Fumbling through his personal effects, Smothers found a bandage and began wrapping his arm to staunch the bleeding. Private First Class Barclay had considered rushing over to assist Smothers, but the continuous chatter of AK-47 fire and the conspicuous lack of decent cover between the two of them argued in favor of him staying put. Barclay glanced over at Smothers. The wound, from what he could see, did not appear particularly serious and Smothers seemed to have the situation under control.

Relieved, Barclay slid back against the tree and listened to the fateful sound of bullets slamming into the trunk on the other side of him. *They're still out there*, he mumbled under his breath. Barclay then remembered that he was carrying an M-72 LAW along with his M-16. Short for light anti-tank weapon, the LAW was a shoulder-fired, high-explosive rocket that grunts in Vietnam employed primarily against NVA bunkers and other defensive redoubts. Barclay readied the rocket and swallowed hard. He would only have one shot at that Y-shaped tree.

In seemingly one fluid motion, Barclay wheeled around the tree and fired the LAW. A loud explosion rocked the jungle. The 66-mm rocket had detonated on impact, splintering the Y-shaped tree into kindling. Slipping back around the tree, Barclay lowered the spent rocket launcher and exhaled. *Got you, you motherfuckers*, he thought satisfyingly. The NVA behind and around that Y-shaped tree had shot Sergeant Smothers, and now they were almost certainly dead. Barclay had no time to celebrate, however. Friendly artillery fire was beginning to explode throughout the area, and the First Platoon was pulling back to tighten up its perimeter.

Lieutenant Allen's counterstroke and his use of supporting arms had thwarted, for the time being, an apparent attempt to outflank the company. "Lieutenant Allen saved us from having the whole company overrun," said Spc4 Larry Gerken. "I have nothing against him, and as a matter of fact I think he was a pretty good officer. He called in and adjusted air and artillery strikes and that probably saved our ass."

Sergeant Smothers had played a pivotal role as well. Smothers assumed command of the First Platoon when acting platoon leader Sgt. Clifford Johnson failed to return to the company perimeter. The plainspoken career soldier adjusted artillery fire, rallied his shaken troopers, and directed the platoon throughout the battle. Smothers would later earn a Bronze Star for his courage and leadership on the eighteenth.[18]

On the sixteenth of May, the 4th Infantry Division issued a temporary restriction on the use of artillery fire in support of its maneuver elements in the field. Friendly units, according to the new self-imposed restraint, were to "develop the situation" first before requesting artillery fire. The measure was designed to conserve ammunition and promote the use of maneuver against enemy forces.[19] "About forty-eight hours before, [the] Division Arty Commander published instructions that were to be strictly adhered to [so] that artillery fire was not to be used until troops on the ground had attempted to outmaneuver the enemy—it was a memo to conserve artillery ammunition," noted Lieutenant Colonel Gannon. "The inference was [that] 'it better be fully justified' or commanders would be taken to task."[20]

Such restrictions were not entirely unheard of. Capt. Ray Harton, an artillery officer with the 6-29 Artillery, admitted that "there were times we were directed by higher headquarters to restrict firing to save ammo. The firing batteries knew they were not to fire without approval. The artillery liaison officer (LNO) had to clear the firing. For a few days prior to May 18, 1967, we had been restricted from firing artillery unless we had people in contact. We were not allowed to recon by fire."[21] Once authorized, however, the artillery was expected to make the jungle bounce.

Returning to the Second Platoon, Lt. Larry Rodabaugh would soon do just that, but only after he finished dragging Pfc. Claire Johnson, Lieutenant Aronhalt's wounded

RTO, back to a clearing in the jungle where 1st Lt. Cary Allen had established the company CP and a medical collection point. Scattered with bamboo and grass, the clearing was approximately one hundred feet by three hundred feet and was capable of accommodating one helicopter. "It was like a hole in the jungle," said Rodabaugh, "and it was the only hole we had." Conferring briefly with his Second Platoon leader in the clearing, Allen ordered Rodabaugh to direct air and artillery strikes on the NVA wedged between the Fourth Platoon and the remainder of the company. Allen then explained that he would handle the fire support required to interdict and isolate the battlefield.

Rodabaugh, taking Private First Class Johnson's radio, left the clearing and found a relatively secure spot with his Second Platoon. "I called in artillery support and I got some asshole at an artillery base where the heavy stuff was like the eight-inch, one-seventy fives [175-mm], and one-five-fives [155-mm]," said Rodabaugh. "First, they asked me if I was sure that I was in contact, because they didn't have a lot of ammunition there. So I told them that if they wanted to check it out, they could come out and join me."

Allen, according to Rodabaugh, intervened and "finally convinced them that we needed a lot of fire support." Shortly thereafter the boom of artillery fire heralded an approaching avalanche of steel as harried batteries belted out 105-mm, 155-mm, and 175-mm rounds. "I can say that I controlled the artillery fires in the AO," said Capt. Ray Harton. "Once that platoon was in contact there was no, and I mean *no*, firing denied by anyone that I controlled. My call sign was 'Twenty.' I do not believe that anyone would say that they did not know who I was. They may not have known me personally, but they knew the call sign 'Twenty.'" Later on the eighteenth the temporary restriction on artillery fire was lifted.

With calls of "up, down" and "right, left," Rodabaugh adjusted the abundance of incoming artillery fire via the radio, carefully directing much of it onto the ravine ridge in front of the Second and Third Platoons. *Please God*, he prayed, *don't let me hit any of my guys out there.*

The fate of the Fourth Platoon to the west, however, was out of his hands.

4 THE LOST PLATOON

Plt. Sgt. Bruce Alan Grandstaff, the acting commander of the Fourth Platoon, waited for Sgt. Bob Sanzone to join him near the front of the platoon. Moments before, Lieutenant Allen had ordered Grandstaff to return immediately to the B Company perimeter. The jungle, following a series of small cat-and-mouse clashes with the NVA, the latest involving a group of some ten to fifteen around 12:00 P.M., was now unexpectedly still.

Respected if not beloved, Grandstaff was born in Spokane, Washington, on June 2, 1934. Athletic, Grandstaff was a multi-sport standout as a youngster, though later, while at North Central High School, he unveiled a musical side as well, playing—perhaps to the surprise of some of his former gridiron teammates—a mean trumpet in the school band. Grandstaff attended Eastern State University for a year after high school and then enlisted in the Army, returning to Spokane in 1956 following a two-year hitch. Starting anew, he landed a sales job with a grocery outlet and resumed his studies in military science at Eastern State. Grandstaff married in 1958 and became the proud father of two beautiful little girls, Heather and Tami, shortly thereafter. Heather, the Grandstaffs' oldest daughter, was only four months old, however, when she was diagnosed with cancer. "It was one of the most severe forms of cancer known to man—neuroblastoma of the kidney," recalled Tami Grandstaff. "She had surgery and cobalt radiation therapy but she survived, against all the odds. My dad became strong in his faith as a result, although he had no prior religious training. He had Heather baptized twice." Profoundly affected by the experience, Grandstaff was awarded full custody of the girls after the couple divorced, and he eventually rejoined the Army.[1]

In July of 1965, after a stint with the 2nd Infantry Division in Korea, Grandstaff was assigned to the 4th Infantry Division at Fort Lewis, Washington. That fall, as thousands of new recruits flooded into Fort Lewis to replenish and expand the ranks of the division, Grandstaff served as a basic training drill instructor in B Company, 1-8 Infantry. A barrel-chested fitness enthusiast, he exhausted his young charges mentally and physically during training, but more than a few expressed a begrudging admiration for the squared-away sergeant. "He had like a 52-inch chest and a 30-inch waist," said Spc4 Victor Renza. "He worked out with weights long before it was fashionable, and he was a tough bastard. I remember thinking, *Man, I want to be like this guy. He's never going to get it* [i.e., get killed]. He was certainly a good soldier, no doubt about that." Tough, demanding, and full of fight, Grandstaff, who would earn a Silver Star for the battle in March 1967, talked the "talk" in the barracks but could back it up on the battlefield.

Summoned to the front of the Fourth Platoon, Sergeant Sanzone hurried forward, up the strung-out line of grunts beside the trail, and crept over to Grandstaff and his RTO, Pfc. Mike Sessa. Grandstaff respected Sanzone, and he trusted him to respond candidly regardless of the situation. Sanzone, moreover, was arguably the most intelligent soldier in the company, irrespective of rank. Theirs would be a meeting of the minds, not a one-sided exchange that usually occurred between a superior and his subordinate.

"I don't like this," Grandstaff whispered softly. "What do you think, Bob?"

Sanzone was about to reply, when suddenly the rumble of assault rifles and machine guns merged into one continuous roar. Surprisingly savage, the North Vietnamese onslaught hit the Fourth Platoon initially from the north and west, scattering the lead elements of the platoon and those closest to it. Slicing through the jungle like a scythe, the rounds sheared off branches and clumps of leaves and cleaved saplings. Some of the rounds struck flesh with a sickening *slap*. Men fell, clutching wounds and howling as if rendered instantly mad. Others were killed instantly.

Desperately seeking cover, Platoon Sergeant Grandstaff and Private First Class Sessa, a PRC-25 radio hanging conspicuously from his back, scrambled behind a tree. Nearby Sgt. Bob Sanzone and Spc4 Tom Sears, nineteen, from upstate New York, gained cover behind a pair of trees no more than ten to fifteen meters apart. Grandstaff, ignoring the chaos and confusion all around them, directed the rear of the platoon to move forward and link up with the lead elements of the column.

Tucked away in the middle of the column, Pfc. Cliff Rountree, a gung-ho replacement who had joined the battalion the previous December, started moving forward as instructed when he suddenly bumped into frightened grunts sprinting back from the front of the platoon. "Get back! Get back!" they screamed in panic. "There's a whole bunch of gooks online!" *Oh shit*, thought Rountree, *the gooks are assaulting the front of the platoon*! Farther back, toward the rear of the platoon, Spc4 Victor Renza ran into the same human traffic jam. "I crawled about twenty-five meters toward the front with the rest of the 4th Squad, all of us now well off the main trail and moving through very thick underbrush," Renza said, recalling the muddle. "Suddenly I saw the guys from the 1st and 2nd Squads crawling towards us yelling, 'Pull back, pull back!' At this point it seemed like no one knew what direction to move in. We were just like thirty little ants, scattered in the grass, running in circles."[2]

Off to the side, no more than fifteen to twenty meters away, Renza spied a dry creek bed and slithered through the grass and assorted vegetation until he reached the edge of it. Sliding in, he righted himself quickly and then squatted down, joining one other soldier in the bed, with his back pressed firmly against the east wall of the north-south creek. Six or seven of his fellow troopers clambered in after him, some tumbling awkwardly over the bank and into the dirt below. The rest of the platoon dispersed in haste. Murderous North Vietnamese rifle and machine-gun fire, meanwhile, opened up on the Fourth from the northeast, southeast, and east, adding to the fire coming from the north and west.[3] The enemy was now between the platoon and the rest of the company.

Pfc. Gilbert Nash was pulling up the rear of the platoon, just one man from the end of the column, when the commotion began upfront. A married, twenty-year-old African American draftee from Harlem, New York, Nash was an aspiring actor who had left high school early to pursue a career in film. As a child he had dreamed of someday making it big in Hollywood or on Broadway, not humping the boonies near the Cambodian border as an FNG—fucking new guy—with a veteran cast of hardbitten lifers and game but cynical draftees.

Nash considered B Company, 1-8 Infantry a marked improvement over his original assignment with the 4th Infantry Division. Finishing up AIT (Advanced Infantry Training) in March 1967, Nash was sent to Vietnam as a replacement and assigned to C Company, 1-8 Infantry. While processing in, however, he stumbled upon a disturbing sight in a room just beyond the company clerk's office back in Pleiku. "I saw the biggest rebel flag I have ever seen hanging on the wall to my left," Nash remembered. "It was the first time I had ever seen the rebel flag before, and it scared the shit out of me. That flag had to have been eight feet in diameter [*sic*]. I knew right then where I was." The flag incident and subsequent events, including an episode in which Nash claims he was forgotten during an ambush exercise and left alone overnight, unnerved the young New Yorker and prompted his request for a transfer out of the company.[4] Granted his walking papers, Nash joined B Company in the field on May 16 and immediately fit in. "B Company had black guys, white guys—everybody was in there," said Nash. "I just felt more at home. In C Company, I just felt like I didn't belong."

Nash flew out to B Company in an overloaded resupply helicopter, and he met Sergeant Grandstaff shortly after arriving. "Nash, your job is to keep the back door open," Grandstaff told him bluntly. "I don't want the gooks closing up an ambush on us." For nearly two days Nash had kept his eyes peeled and his ears attuned to the sound of every snapped twig and rustled leaf, half expecting the entire North Vietnamese Army to appear on the other side of every bush. New to the unit, he had no intention of letting the NVA close up an ambush on the Fourth Platoon if he could help it. But now, with the jungle erupting in gunfire at the front of the platoon, he worried that he was about to be put to the test.

Lunging into the brush off to the side of the trail, Nash rolled into a prone position and scanned the jungle for muzzle flashes and any sign of movement. The sudden roar of gunfire had frightened him, yet as he peered out from beneath his helmet, he saw nothing but a sea of green and earthen brown. Whatever was happening upfront, he was comforted by the fact that the North Vietnamese were, for the moment, nowhere in sight. Catching his breath, he checked his M-16 and surveyed the jungle again. As his eyes swept warily over the landscape, he was jolted by an eruption of RPG (rocket-propelled grenade), machine-gun, and automatic weapons fire to the east. *They're hitting the shit out of the rest of B Company*, he realized instantly. Soon afterward Nash heard someone screaming, "Bring up the rear, bring up the rear!" The voice, stern and unyielding, belonged to Sgt. Bruce Grandstaff.

Private First Class Nash rose to his feet—just how long he had been lying there, squinting at every break or opening in the bush for a glimpse of the enemy, he could not be certain—and advanced in a crouch toward the front of the platoon. Along the way Nash spotted a knife on the jungle floor and, absentmindedly, decided to bend over and pick it up. At precisely that moment a tremendous volley of NVA fire roared across the jungle, inches above his bowed back. "I could *feel* it, man," Nash later shivered. "If I had been standing up, I would have been killed."

The soldier to Nash's left had not been so lucky. "Help me! Help me!" the man cried out in agony, his torso torn open by the same thunderous volley that Nash had inadvertently avoided. Nash, noticing that the man had remained upright despite his wounds, yelled to him, "Get down! Get down!" Slipping into shock, the man instead continued to stand until he finally collapsed onto the jungle floor. Nash witnessed the final, fleeting moments of the man's life in stunned silence, wondering if there was anything more he could have done.

Anxious to avoid the same fate, Nash scampered up a small knoll and assumed a prone position facing the dry creek bed to the west. To his right, another soldier had already been shot and killed. Two guys—two guys that he *knew* of, that is—had already been killed, and he had only narrowly averted death himself. The NVA, despite his best efforts, had indeed slammed the back door shut on the Fourth Platoon.

Chest deep and approximately five feet wide, the dry creek bed turned sharply to the right and left of Spc4 Victor Renza. Reluctant to leave either bend unattended, Renza told the soldier beside him to cover the one on the left while he took the one to his right. Just as they were about to move, Pfc. Cliff Rountree observed a muzzle flash on the west bank of the creek bed and hollered, "Machine gun! Get the fuck out of the ditch!" Rountree then clambered out of the bed and into the surrounding vegetation.

Renza, however, never heard the warning. "At that point it seemed like the whole other side of the streambed opened up with automatic weapons fire," he recalled. "The bullets started to my right, smashing into the streambed wall, and were working their way toward us. A bullet tore into the leg of the guy to my right, missed me, and continued up the streambed wall to my left. He grabbed his leg with both hands and screamed as loud as he could. I looked down and saw bright red blood pouring out of his thigh and through his fingers onto the ground."[5] Cleverly located in a small clearing overlooking the creek bed to the northwest, an enemy machine gun had cut loose on the helpless Americans, wounding the man to Renza's right and slaying with ruthless efficiency a half dozen more.

Raising his M-16, Renza cranked some rounds off into the tree line to the west and climbed out of the creek bed. The NVA machine gun then ceased firing, allowing Renza to reach down into the creek and drag the wounded man out. "My leg, my leg!" the man squealed as he staggered forward into Renza, knocking the two of them to the ground.[6] Short-lived, the pause in the enemy machine-gun fire ended moments later, and high-velocity slugs were soon clipping the undergrowth all around them. Heavy enemy rifle and automatic weapons fire ripped through the area from the north and south as well.

Renza, realizing that the only viable option was to turn around and head east, the direction from whence the platoon had come, gestured in that direction and screamed, "C'mon, follow me." Inexplicably, however, the wounded man stared blankly into his eyes, as if incapable of comprehending the meaning of the words, and then skidded off in the opposite direction, clutching his M-16 in one hand and his bloody leg in the other. "I don't know if the guy understood me or not," said Renza. "He looked dazed, sort of out of it. He was obviously in a great deal of pain." Flabbergasted, Renza put his head down and began sliding eastward across the jungle floor, toward a log about ten meters away.

Slowed by the extraordinarily intense enemy fire, Renza slinked along, inch by inch, until the log was finally within reach. About the same time a bullet sliced through the back of his boot and snapped his foot violently to one side. He immediately wriggled his foot. Miraculously, the round had missed both his heel and his ankle. "The fire was so intense that if you lifted yourself up more than twelve to fourteen inches, you got cut down," Renza stated. "I don't believe a person can put into words how intense that fire was." Lying perpendicular to the creek bed, the log was just about large enough in diameter to shield him from the intense grazing fire *if* he could somehow crawl over it without drawing even more enemy fire in the process. With nowhere else to hide, he decided to avail himself of the only cover in the immediate area.

Sidling up beside the log, Renza flung his left hand and leg over the top of it and, with his remaining limbs, propelled himself upward onto the fallen tree trunk. He had made it halfway over the log when a round tore into the left side of his back, inches from his spine. Packed with kinetic energy, the round pitched Renza over the other side of the log and sent his M-16 hurtling out of his hand. "I'm hit," he moaned, waiting for someone—*anyone*—to answer.

"Help me, help me!"

"Lay still, lay still! Don't move!"

Spc4 Kenneth Barker pleaded with the wounded man to remain motionless, but his pleas seemed to be falling on deaf ears. A recent replacement from Illinois, Barker had been in the middle of the Fourth Platoon column, wondering about the wisdom of marching west down a trail near the Cambodian border, and had curled up behind a slender tree at the first sign of trouble. While there, and in between the bursts of M-16 fire he let loose on the NVA west of the creek bed, Barker, barely twenty years old and new to the war, watched with morbid fascination as the wounded man wiggled slowly toward his position. Now a mere eight to ten meters away, the man got hit again and squealed out in agony. Yet every time the man squirmed in pain, the NVA would key in on his movement and shoot him again. Over and over again the vicious cycle repeated itself.

Barker watched helplessly for several more minutes, all the while hoping that the North Vietnamese would put the dying man out of his misery. Shockingly, in that short period of time, the man was shot six or seven times and his blood-curdling screams rattled Barker to the bone. "Just let him die, for God's sake, just let the poor bastard die," Barker whispered under his breath. Eventually the screaming stopped. Hauled out of the dry creek bed by Victor Renza, the young soldier in the newish-looking jungle fatigues had finally succumbed to his wounds.

Up front, not far from Sergeant Grandstaff, Spc4 Tom Sears blazed away with his M-16. Smallish in stature, the flaxen-haired replacement had joined the 4th Infantry Division in the fall of 1966, arriving in-country some four to six weeks after the originals. Sears had started his tour as an RTO and had served as a radio operator for Sergeant Grandstaff before passing the radio and all the responsibilities that went with it to Private First Class Sessa, an original who had transferred into the Fourth

Platoon from A Company, 1-8 Infantry. Earlier in the day he and Sessa had exchanged rucksacks—burdening Sears with the radio once again—following an injury to Sessa's ankle. Sessa eventually felt better, and the two were able to swap back prior to moving out as a platoon down the east-west trail. Sears welcomed the switch, and as he traded lead with the NVA that afternoon, he breathed a sigh of relief knowing that, if nothing else, he didn't have to worry about a long, conspicuous radio antenna betraying his position behind a small tree.

Apparently unseen, Sears poured rifle fire on the North Vietnamese who were attacking what had been the lead elements of the Fourth Platoon. Much to his surprise, however, the volume of enemy fire in his area never subsided completely. At times the noise became overwhelming as rifle, machine-gun, and B-40 rocket rounds punched through the dense undergrowth around him, killing and maiming his friends at an alarming rate. Sooner or later the NVA would draw a bead on his position and that would be that, but until then he intended to fight.

Surrounded by scores of North Vietnamese, and with one of its radios knocked out of commission, the outnumbered and outgunned Fourth Platoon to a man refused to roll over and play dead. Pulling back into a ravine to the west, the platoon managed to consolidate and establish—despite the loss of all but two of the men who had entered the dry creek bed—a hastily thrown together perimeter approximately fifteen to twenty meters in diameter.[7] The men, moreover, were returning fire and functioning remarkably well given the circumstances. Near the center of that perimeter, Sergeant Grandstaff was back on the radio requesting air and artillery support to ease the mounting pressure on his embattled platoon. Whether the Fourth could hold on with the help of supporting arms was still very much in doubt, however.

Meanwhile, back in the tactical operations center at the battalion firebase, a disturbing picture of the B Company battle was beginning to take shape. A large, well-armed North Vietnamese force had maneuvered around and behind the Fourth Platoon, separating the platoon from the rest of the company, and was chewing up its pinned-down squads with devastating machine-gun, rifle, and RPG fire from the west, northwest, northeast, and southeast. Two hundred meters or so to the east, the three remaining platoons of the company had curled into a defensive perimeter following an aborted attempt to rescue the Fourth. Intact but still heavily engaged, the rest of the company reported receiving automatic weapons fire from the north and west, as well as sniper and rocket fire from the east and southeast.[8]

Climbing aboard his command and control chopper early that afternoon, Lieutenant Colonel Gannon, accompanied by Captain Sholly and Captain Harton, a field artillery officer with the 6-29 Artillery, instructed his pilot to fly out to the scene of

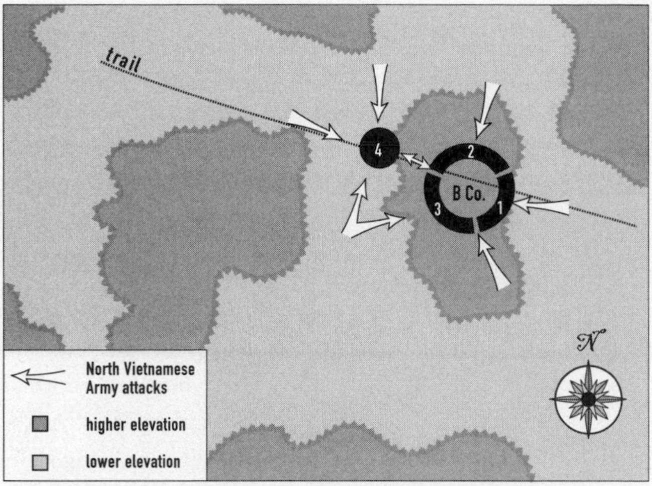

B Company, 1-8 Infantry, May 18, 1967. Situation at 1:00 P.M.
Map by Charles Grear, adapted from original drawn by S. L. Dowdy, in Robert Sholly, Young Soldiers, Amazing Warriors.

the action. The flight was brief and uneventful, and as the chopper circled over the battlefield, Gannon communicated with B Company via the radio. Fourth Platoon had stirred up a hornet's nest, and the company's three remaining platoons had run into a gauntlet of enemy fire trying to rescue it. Allen, the acting company commander, appeared poised and in control but, up against unfavorable odds in an adverse tactical environment, was in dire need of more fire support and some reinforcements. Gannon moved immediately to provide the latter. Perched inside his cramped C&C chopper, he ordered Capt. Walter Williamson, CO of A Company, 1-8 Infantry, to close on Allen from the northeast. At the time of the order, somewhere around 1:30 that afternoon, Williamson's four platoons were operating in rugged terrain east of B Company, ostensibly within mutually supporting range of Allen.

Sergeant Grandstaff could not stand idly by and wait for A Company to arrive, however. Grandstaff desperately needed artillery support—as many tubes as he could possibly get, in fact—but he was having trouble raising Lieutenant Allen on the company net. Switching frequencies on his remaining radio, Grandstaff reestablished communications with the company CP via the battalion command net and promptly relayed his fire commands over the new frequency.[9] "Heads up!" a loud voice announced shortly after the commands went through. "There's a spotter round coming in!" Pfc. Gilbert Nash, facing the dry creek bed to the west of Grandstaff, ducked his head and waited. A round then whistled in and exploded off in the distance. "Drop!" exclaimed another voice, before it was drowned out by the rattle of rifle fire.

Nash, in the noise and confusion, did not hear whether the voice wanted the round "dropped" by a little or a lot, nor did he immediately recognize either of the two voices. But what he learned from the brief exchange comforted him. Artillery fire had been requested and since the spotter round had landed too far away, it was presently in the process of being adjusted so that subsequent rounds would fall closer to the platoon perimeter. If the voice, for example, had requested that the artillery "drop fifty," the big guns would begin putting shells fifty meters closer to the perimeter.

Distant to start, the rumble of exploding shellfire drew perilously near as Grandstaff, with input from Sgt. Bob Sanzone and assistance from Lieutenant Colonel Gannon's C&C chopper orbiting overhead, walked the artillery in toward the Fourth Platoon. Calling in the necessary corrections over the radio, Grandstaff adjusted the fire to within forty-five meters of the platoon perimeter.[10] West of the creek bed the explosions pitted the landscape and sent shards of blisteringly hot metal flying through the air. Some of the shells, however, landed too close to the perimeter. On the opposite side of the creek bed, for example, shrapnel from an errant shell pierced the left leg of Pfc. Gilbert Nash. Fortunately the wound was not severe. Nonetheless such trade-offs were inevitable when an entire platoon depended on close-in artillery support for its survival.

Skillfully adjusted, the artillery fire kept enemy heads down and suppressed some of the incoming small-arms and automatic weapons fire. Grandstaff, though, knew that the respite would not last for long. Trained to "hug" American infantry to minimize the effects of American supporting arms, the North Vietnamese would eventually move forward, further shortening the distance between the combatants, and take up positions inside the protective umbrella provided by the artillery. An infantry assault would likely follow, and the platoon would be overrun.

Concerned but still composed, Grandstaff fired up the radio again and reached 1st Lt. Larry Rodabaugh, PTL of the Second Platoon. "Where are you guys?" he asked Rodabaugh pointedly. "You've got to get up here to us." Wounded and working the radio for his own pinned-down platoon, Rodabaugh offered few assurances. "We're trying, but we've lost a lot of men." Remarkably, Grandstaff remained undaunted. Shouting above the din of battle to his hard-pressed troopers, he exhorted each and every one of them to make the NVA pay for the deadly ambush they had sprung on the Fourth Platoon. "Listen up, men—Stand your ground! We're going to kill all of these motherfuckers for what they've done!"

Spc4 Victor Renza, wounded and unable to fight, pawed at the hole in his back and cried out, "I'm hit!" Drowned out by the chorus of rocket blasts, machine-gun bursts, and artillery explosions, his frantic plea went unanswered. Renza called out for Grandstaff but could hear little over the *sssss . . . BOOM . . . sssss . . . BOOM* refrain of artillery shells crashing through the canopy and exploding with a thunderous report on the jungle floor. *No one is going to be able to hear me over this shit*, thought Renza.

Discouraged, he curled up closer to the log and rested his right cheek on the jungle floor. Unarmed and alone, Renza decided against lifting his head up. He also resisted the urge to pull his right arm out from under his upper body. *Sit tight, just sit tight and it'll be alright*, he told himself.

For a while it was. Scarcely more than one-hundred and twenty five pounds, Renza discovered that the log afforded his painfully thin six-foot frame ample protection from North Vietnamese fire. "I was so goddamn skinny that I wasn't any higher than the log when I was lying down behind it," Renza recalled. "It wasn't a big log either. It may have been—oh, I don't know, maybe twelve inches in diameter—but that was enough because I was just so skinny. I was skin and bones." Ironically, had Renza been more stoutly put together, he would not have been able to hide behind the log and escape the savage gunfire sweeping the Fourth Platoon.

In time two other soldiers crawled over to the log, bringing the number of men hiding behind it to three. One of them was Sgt. Leland Thompson, an artillery forward observer attached to B Company. The three men were now lying head-to-toe, one behind the other, up against the log. Since Renza could not actually *see* Thompson or the other man, he did not know who the men were but he appreciated their comforting words all the same. "Don't worry," they told him reassuringly, "we are going to get you out of here. You're going to be OK." Tired, thirsty, and in considerable pain, Renza wanted very much to believe them. They were all he had, other than his own unconvincing assurances, to hang on to.

Pruning the trees and shrubs nearby, the relentless enemy fire scattered leaves and bits of branch over the bodies of the three prone soldiers. Renza, his right arm growing numb from the weight of his upper body pressing down on top of it, suddenly tasted blood. His heart skipped a beat. *Well, that's it*, he told himself. *One of those rounds must have gotten me in the lungs, and when the lungs fill up, you're as good as dead*. Renza dragged his left hand slowly across the ground toward his face. Gently inserting his left index finger into his mouth, he curled his lips around it briefly then pulled it back out. His finger felt sticky, and it was wet with red saliva. Renza, looking at his crimson-colored finger, exclaimed, "Hey you guys, I am bleeding from my mouth and I need a medic."Neither man responded, however. Confused Renza tried again. "Are you guys still there? I *need* a medic."[11]

Helicopter gunships eventually arrived on station to support the surrounded Americans. Figuring that the pilots would have difficulty locating his platoon in the dense jungle, Sergeant Grandstaff scooped up two smoke grenades and crawled among the small trees and ant hills in the area to a slight clearing thirty meters southwest of the platoon perimeter. Grandstaff reached the clearing unscathed and quickly popped the first grenade. Drifting slowly skyward, the smoke failed to penetrate the overhead canopy and was seen, not by the pilots orbiting above the platoon as Grandstaff had intended, but by the North Vietnamese, who then raked the clearing with heavy fire. Unfazed, Grandstaff crept another twenty meters to the west and lobbed his final grenade. Out of grenades, he turned around and headed back to the platoon perimeter.

1st Lt. Cary Allen had been following the action from a patch of elephant grass well to the east of the Fourth Platoon. "During the succeeding action, while monitoring the radio, I heard PSG Grandstaff maintain constant contact with the artillery and gunships at his location," Allen wrote. "In attempting to pinpoint his position for the gunships, he must have been shot, as he said something to me to the effect that he needed a medic. From what I could ascertain, the pilots were unable to indentify his smoke due to the triple canopy of jungle forest in the location."[12] Allen then left the radio briefly to assist other troopers under fire.

Shot in the leg while returning to the platoon perimeter, Grandstaff had hoped the smoke from the first two grenades would mark his platoon's position for the gunships. The smoke, he discovered, never made it through the canopy, so he asked around for some more smoke grenades. Without a visual, the pilots would likely hold off on the rocket and strafing run he had requested. No one in the platoon, however, had any smoke grenades left. Improvising, Grandstaff collected seven magazines of tracer ammunition—the pilots could see tracers just as easily as smoke, he figured—and inched out of the platoon perimeter. Small-arms fire sliced through the bushes above him as he wriggled slowly across the jungle floor. Finally, after covering a distance of about thirty meters, he stopped and fired up through the jungle canopy, knowing that the bright red tracer rounds would also mark his position. A hail of NVA fire quickly followed, and he was hit in the other leg. Pulling himself back inside the platoon perimeter, both legs now bleeding profusely, Grandstaff slid over to the radio and contacted the gunships. The trick worked. The pilots had spotted the tracers and were forming up over the target area.

The assault swept across the jungle from the west. Moving swiftly through the undergrowth, a small wave of North Vietnamese, many in khaki uniforms, attacked across the dry creek bed and up the embankment on the eastern side of the creek. Pfc. Gilbert Nash fetched two fresh magazines from his pocket and was lying, his right finger lightly tapping the trigger of his M-16, on the embankment above the creek bed. Nash figured that the NVA would come for him at some point, and he decided that he would be ready when they did. Studying the jungle below, he quickly noticed two North Vietnamese soldiers to his right.

Wearing floppy bush hats and sandals, the NVA had crept to within twenty-five yards of his position and were looking around, half-hidden in the grass. Nash flipped his M-16 to semi-automatic and aimed for the torso of the nearest enemy soldier. *BANG!* The slug hit the NVA square on, knocking him backward. Then, without thinking, Nash swiveled the barrel of his M-16 and squeezed off another round. *BANG!* Struck in the upper body, the second North Vietnamese soldier tumbled out of sight. Minutes later, Nash saw a North Vietnamese soldier in a bush hat poke his head up from behind the body of a dead American soldier. Nash hesitated at first as the NVA dropped back down behind the dead American. Quietly flipping his M-16 back to full auto, Nash fired a quick burst into the shoulder of the dead American soldier lying on his side. "When I fired that dead GI's body rolled over and exposed the gook, and I fired a short burst into that motherfucker," Nash recalled. "I didn't want to tell anybody about it. I didn't even want to talk about it. But I know that GI was dead. I saw him hit the ground with a hard *thump.* I knew how bad he had been hit. I would *never* have shot one of our guys that might have still been alive. It still bothers me that I had to do it, though." Short but deadly, the burst killed the NVA soldier and sent his floppy hat flying.

Not far from Nash, Pfc. Cliff Rountree reached back for his M-72 LAW. An NVA machine gun across the dry creek bed was spitting lead, and someone had to knock it out before the enemy crew spotted more survivors. Immersed in the rugged outdoorsmen-veteran culture of rural northern California, Rountree had grown up around guns and had admired the warrior ethos of his forebears. It was simply in his blood. "My father had served in the war [World War II], and so had a lot of other guys in the community," said Rountree. "I wanted to be part of that warrior tradition. I wanted to be respected, and I wanted to be afforded the respect and admiration of the men who I grew up around who had fought in World War II."

Rountree, while attending junior college in California, had toyed with the idea of enlisting in the Army for its microwave technology training, but he grew tired of waiting for a slot to open up and decided to volunteer for the draft instead. In Vietnam he repeatedly demonstrated extraordinary courage in battle, most notably when he braved heavy enemy fire to administer to the wounded men in his unit during a sharp firefight. That action, which occurred in April 1967, would earn Rountree a Bronze Star. "Rountree was a *hell* of a soldier," said Victor Renza. "He had *big balls.*"

Hoisting the LAW onto his shoulder, Rountree shifted his eyes back to the North Vietnamese machine gunner set up behind a tree on the opposite side of the creek bed. Steadying himself, Rountree aimed for the tree and then fired. In an instant the round was across the creek bed and through the tree, vaporizing the NVA gunner in the process. Incredibly, only a knocked-out machine gun and a tattered set of black pajamas remained after the blast. More North Vietnamese, however, scrambled into the dry creek bed and up the embankment on the eastern side of the creek. Five or six NVA had nearly crested the sloped incline when Private First Class Nash heard the enemy soldiers grunting and firing on the way up. Nash lined up the small group and cut them down in a hail of bullets. A second wave of NVA followed the first and advanced straight toward the young private. Nash hurriedly slid a full magazine into the receiver of his M-16 and "put the whole magazine into those motherfuckers." Bunched together, the North Vietnamese were wiped out in the flurry of fire.

Nash was in the middle of reloading and preparing for the next NVA infantry assault when he heard a strange *thump, thump* sound. Looking around, he noticed a stick grenade with smoke emanating from one end. Nash, knowing that the grenade was not American, grabbed it and threw it back into the dry creek bed, setting off a loud explosion. Someone yelled "Nice throw!" but Nash was too busy to respond. Nash was finishing loading his M-16 with a fresh magazine when he heard the *thump, thump* of another North Vietnamese grenade. "What the fuck?" he blurted out loud. Incredulous, he picked up the enemy grenade and tossed it back at the NVA.

Nash listened silently for another *thump.* While he waited, convinced that the NVA would almost certainly try to overrun his position again, an enemy round crashed into the right side of his head, about three inches above his ear. Furrowing along the surface of his scalp, the bullet shattered his equilibrium and left his body in convulsive fits. "I could feel my left hand bouncing up and down uncontrollably, but I was going in and out," Nash said. "When that bullet hit me in the head, I had no control over my body. I could feel my hand bouncing around back there near my waist. I think I was probably semi-conscious." Incapable of controlling his bodily movements, Nash stared impassively into the jungle, conscious but uncomprehending, as the sounds of battle slowly faded away.

The NVA, meanwhile, hurled more grenades up the embankment, determined to overwhelm the outnumbered American defenders on the east bank of the creek bed. One landed near the crest of the embankment, exploded, and injured a soldier immediately to the right of Pfc. Cliff Rountree. *They're still in the dry creek bed,* thought Rountree, groping at his web gear for a grenade of his own to lob. Rountree had already taken a bullet fragment in his left calf and shrapnel in his right arm.

Shrugging off the pain, the feisty twenty-year-old grabbed a grenade and cocked back his arm. The NVA were down below him, in the dry creek bed, and the only way to root them out was with grenades. Rountree, grimacing as his injured right arm moved painfully forward, hurled the grenade down the embankment. Moments later the grenade exploded in the creek bed. Figuring that he must have done *some* damage with the first grenade, Rountree tossed in some more for good measure. Several explosions shuddered up the embankment. "Throwing grenades back at them into the creek bed helped repel that NVA assault," Rountree later noted, "but it bothers me because there may have been wounded Americans down there. I wasn't in a position to get off any kind of a shot, and I am not sure what other choice I had." Gradually the

NVA assault from the west across the dry creek bed petered out. Beaten back, thanks in no small part to the actions of Nash and Rountree, the NVA paused to regroup.

Nearby, Sgt. Bob Sanzone hollered impatiently to Spc4 Tom Sears. "Sears, get over here! Sears!" Sanzone had been shot in the leg sometime before—possibly by the NVA machine gunner Cliff Rountree had all but vaporized with the LAW—but, unlike Sears, he still possessed a functioning M-16 rifle. Sears had been firing away with his own when a round slammed into it while he was in the act of shooting, jamming the rifle. Startled, Sears began jabbing at the weapon with his bayonet but it refused to fire.

Tossing aside his damaged M-16, Sears snaked across the jungle floor and closed up next to Sanzone. Paired up, the two men were now lying side by side on the slope of a small hill, approximately thirty meters east of the dry creek bed.

"Are you OK?" Sears asked, not noticing the leg wound Sanzone had suffered earlier in the battle.

"I'm OK," Sanzone replied, "but I'm hit in the leg."

Painful but apparently not life-threatening, the wound had prevented Sanzone from scrambling over to Sears. Still lucid, Sanzone then suggested that they share his M-16 until Sears could find another weapon. Sears agreed and it was decided, by mutual agreement, that Sanzone, who was laying slightly upslope and to the right, would scan the jungle to their right, or north, while Sears kept an eye on their left or southern flank. Both men would watch the area to their front.

A short while later the NVA assaulted the perimeter again, this time from the north-northwest. Facing the dry creek bed to the west, Sears and Sanzone were scanning the jungle looking for targets when a wave of North Vietnamese raced toward the platoon perimeter. Sears, stunned by the sheer velocity of the enemy assault, watched dozens of khaki-colored figures zigzagging through the undergrowth and immediately asked for the M-16. Sanzone handed the rifle to Sears.

Carefully picking his shots, Sears dropped one NVA soldier and then another, the location of the hill making it difficult for the enemy to return fire accurately. Sears shifted the barrel to his right and opened fire again on semi-automatic. *Bang! Bang! Bang!* Shot dead, several more NVA collapsed in the bush beyond the dry creek bed. Sears then handed the rifle back to Sanzone, who quickly added to the tally of bodies piling up in the jungle to the right of the hill. The NVA eventually located the two and returned fire. Sanzone took a round in his other leg, Sears two in the back, but together the two men killed or wounded a staggering number of North Vietnamese while sharing Sanzone's M-16.

The second NVA assault soon stalled. Gallantly, the surviving Americans had met the assault head-on and repulsed the attackers. Surrounded by a vastly superior force and running low on ammunition, the able-bodied survivors of the Fourth Platoon, battered but unbowed, had defeated the first two North Vietnamese attempts to overrun the platoon perimeter. Shortly thereafter, at approximately 1:37 P.M., Sergeant Grandstaff temporarily suspended the artillery fire supporting the platoon so that the gunships could begin working the area west of the dry creek bed.[13]

Outfitted with machine guns and tube-launched rockets, the gunships swooped in after the artillery and unloaded on the jungle below. "They were coming in at treetop level," recalled Spc4 Victor Renza. "I remember looking up and seeing them screaming overhead, and then another group would make a pass over me. I could see the rockets coming out of the tubes right over my head! They were just unloading these rockets through the trees." Low on fuel and ammo after numerous passes, the gunships departed and the artillery resumed firing at 2:04 P.M.[14] Some thought the gunships were not as effective as Grandstaff had hoped. "I think the fire was a little too far out, a little too far to the west," Renza stated flatly. "I'm not saying that it was entirely ineffective. I'm saying that, from where I was, it looked as if those rocket rounds were landing fifty meters or so away. It didn't suppress a lot of that NVA fire from the other side of the creek. They [NVA] were just too tight in on us for some of the fire to be effective."

Grandstaff, from his battered CP group near the center of the tiny Fourth Platoon perimeter, worked the remaining radio by himself. His RTO, Pfc. Michael Sessa, had been shot and killed and there was no one nearby to take his place. Sessa was not alone. Skilled marksmen, the North Vietnamese had picked off a number of grunts during and after the wave assaults. Pfc. Tom Sears, from his position on the hill east of the creek bed, couldn't see the entire perimeter but the moans of the wounded and, more conspicuously, the discernible decline in M-16 fire testified to the toll the battle had taken on the platoon.

Fierce firefights between small groups of NVA and the increasingly desperate survivors of the shrinking Fourth Platoon perimeter raged on. Wriggling forward on his forearms, Sergeant Sanzone leaned on Specialist 4th Class Sears for balance at one point while Sears, who was smaller in stature, waited patiently for him to pull the trigger. Suddenly Sanzone exhaled as if the wind had been knocked from his body. Seconds later, Sears felt a dull thud and what seemed like the full weight of Sanzone's body pressing down on top him. For a brief moment time seemed to stand still. Sgt. Robert Benjamin Sanzone, the pride of Levittown, New York, and an accomplished soldier despite his aversion to the Army, lay motionless on top of the body of his friend. From somewhere off to their right, an NVA soldier had killed Sanzone instantly with a through-and-through head shot.

Pinned beneath his dead buddy, Sears pulled himself together and wriggled free. *Whoever shot Bob*, he muttered under his breath, *probably has a line on me, too.* Sears snatched the M-16 and headed west, toward the dry creek bed, in a low crawl. An enemy round then smashed into his pelvis, stopping him after he had only moved a short distance. The wound throbbed unmercifully, but Sears knew he had to get moving again.

Artillery, gunships, and the frantic resistance of men fighting for their very existence had failed to prevent the North Vietnamese from slowly tightening the noose around the encircled Fourth Platoon. As the clock approached 3 P.M. Sergeant Grandstaff, growing increasingly desperate, adjusted the artillery fire north of the platoon perimeter to within twenty-five meters of friendly positions. "They've got us from all sides," he shouted into the radio, hoping he would be heard over the thunderclap of exploding artillery shells. Lieutenant Allen, now back with his RTO, was listening in. "How many effectives have you got?" he asked. Grandstaff replied that he had ten, maybe eleven left.[15] His men had not been outfought, but they were on the verge of being overrun. It was no longer a question of *if* but rather of *when*. The enemy was simply too numerous and too fanatically determined to think otherwise.

The blow, when it finally came, fell swiftly and severely. Pushing forward, the NVA advanced on the Fourth Platoon perimeter just before 3 P.M. More violent than the previous assaults, the attack brushed aside the worn-out defenders and surged onward toward the center of the rapidly crumbling platoon. Back at the B Company CP, the radio crackled in Lieutenant Allen's ear. "We're being overrun," Sergeant Grandstaff barked angrily. "Place the artillery fire on top of me. I've only got eight men left!"

Moments later the Fourth Platoon radio went dead.

5 AN INDECENT INTERLUDE

Injured in a fall on May 14, Captain Sholly, his swollen ankle wrapped in an Ace bandage, hitched a ride on a resupply bird and flew out to B Company on the afternoon of the sixteenth. Sholly visited with Lieutenant Allen and some of the troops and quickly concluded that the company was in good shape. Allen had done a fine job in his absence, as had Sergeant Grandstaff. Strangely, Sholly felt safer in the field with his company than he ever did back at the battalion firebase.

As he circled over the Fourth Platoon on the eighteenth, Sholly exchanged worried glances with Lieutenant Colonel Gannon. Sholly, Gannon, and Capt. Ray Harton had all heard Sergeant Grandstaff request artillery fire on top of his embattled platoon over the radio. Given the gravity of the request, Gannon, understandably, turned to Sholly—the company commander to whom Grandstaff normally answered—before deciding whether to approve the request. Sholly supported Grandstaff. "He's the guy on the ground," the B Company captain told Gannon. "He's the guy you've got to trust." Gannon nodded and tapped Harton, the artillery liaison officer, on the shoulder. "Do it."

Reluctantly Captain Harton dialed up a battery of 155-mm howitzers from divisional artillery. "That day is one of my nightmares," Harton wrote after the war. "I actually gave the order for the artillery unit to fire upon our troops as requested by Grandstaff. He requested the artillery. Lieutenant Colonel Gannon and Captain Sholly agreed and made the decision. I had a unit of 155-mm howitzers cocked and ready when Lieutenant Colonel Gannon said give it to him. I asked more than once, 'Are you sure'? The answer was, 'Yes.'" Harton alerted C Battery, 5th of the 16th Artillery, and the big guns opened fire. "I immediately made the correction for C, 5-16th and fired many rounds of 155-mm artillery on top of the platoon," he added. "Lieutenant Colonel Gannon made the decision. I made the correction and ordered the firing."[1]

The decision to bring artillery fire down on the Fourth Platoon weighed most heavily on Captain Sholly, the injured B Company commander and the officer to whom Lieutenant Colonel Gannon had tacitly deferred. Bespectacled and rather unassuming in appearance, Sholly was born in 1938 in Santa Fe, New Mexico. The son of a park ranger, he grew up in a series of national parks, including Big Bend National Park in Texas, and as a child lived quite austerely compared to other boys his age. His boyhood accommodations in Big Bend lacked basic amenities like electricity and a telephone, and he was homeschooled until the eighth grade because the park did not have enough children on hand to justify the expense of hiring a professional teacher. Later on, however, he moved in with his grandparents in Fresno, California, to attend a local high school. College bound, Sholly graduated from high school in Fresno and returned to Texas to enroll at Texas A&M University.

Afflicted with a virulent strain of the flu during his sophomore year at A&M, Sholly spent weeks convalescing and eventually fell behind in his school work. Unable to catch up, he withdrew from school and enlisted in the Army in 1958, where he served for a time as an MP (Military Police). Sholly later applied to the Officer Candidate School at Fort Benning and earned a commission as a second lieutenant, finishing his tour as a young officer in the 2nd Armored Division. Life as a soldier had come naturally to him. "The fact that I was raised in national parks, with an independence that not many people have as children, gave me far more outdoor experience for the Army than most other people," he noted. "I have always credited my land navigation skills and being comfortable in the outdoors under all kinds of circumstances with how easy it was for me to fit into an infantryman's life." Eager to continue his career in the Army, Sholly joined the National Guard and resumed his classes at A&M.

In early 1966, Sholly, then a captain in the Texas National Guard, petitioned the Army to return to active duty. The war in Vietnam was heating up, and the professional soldier in him longed for a part in it. Whatever had animated other young American men to dodge the draft and flee to Canada, the opposite had taken hold of Sholly and would not let go. The Army, needing good officers at the time, granted his wish. That August he was assigned to the 4th Infantry Division stationed at Fort Lewis, Washington, and shortly thereafter flew to South Vietnam with the rear detachment element of the division. Sholly then served in a series of successive staff positions—with the G1 Section of the division, on the 1st Brigade staff in Tuy Hoa, as the S1 of the 1-8 Infantry in October—but it was not until a meeting in December 1966 with Lt. Col. Harold Lee, the battalion CO at the time, that he finally received the combat command he so desperately desired.[2] "B Company is on its ass," Lee had told him at the meeting, "and I want you to get them off of it."

Sholly stayed intimately involved with the affairs of his company, even while recuperating from his ankle injury at the battalion firebase. On May 16, just two days before the battle, he noted in his journal that Lieutenant Allen had been handling the company quite competently in his absence. Allen's performance was of small consolation to him on the afternoon of the eighteenth, however. That morning he awoke, learned of the battle brewing with B Company, and recorded the following entry in his journal: "Got up this morning—about 12:30, got word that company was in contact. Still fighting. Looks like heavy friendly casualties. My men. Feeling guilty as hell."

Afterward, when Lieutenant Colonel Gannon arranged a flight out to the battle in his command chopper, Sholly insisted on joining him. "I imagine we were there before 1300," Sholly recalled. "In the air it was not a long distance. We flew over the unit while all the shooting was going on initially. Harton was throwing artillery fire, and we had aircraft and all kinds of stuff. It [the jungle below] looks like broccoli when you're up above it. There was a lot of smoke coming up through the canopy. The platoon had lost radio contact with Allen and the rest of the company, and we could barely hear them. We switched the radio to a different net, and we could hear Grandstaff shouting and bringing in artillery fire. And we could hear sounds in the background, the shooting and everything else." Progressively dire, the radio transmissions eventually culminated in Grandstaff asking for an artillery strike on the remnants of his shattered platoon.

Ahead of the impending artillery strike, the cramped C&C chopper carrying Lieutenant Colonel Gannon, Captain Sholly, and Capt. Ray Harton banked hard and departed the air space over the Fourth Platoon. Sholly, casting a final downward glance at the smoky jungle as the chopper sped away, stirred softly in his seat. Protocol dictated that in circumstances such as these the commander in the air should respectfully defer to the more informed judgment of the commander on the ground. Grandstaff, moreover, had earned Sholly's trust. Sholly, in fact, had already recommended Grandstaff for a direct commission. "I trusted Grandstaff implicitly. He was a very, very good soldier," said Sholly. "He made some tactical errors in judgment [earlier in the battle], I guess, but none of us were on the ground." Procedurally, Sholly knew he had played it by the book. Nonetheless it was still *his* company and they were still *his* men, and the feeling that somehow, someway he should have been down there on the ground with them gnawed at him all the way back to the firebase.

Preceded by a short, distinctive whistle, the round crashed through the canopy and exploded in the shell-denuded jungle beyond the Fourth Platoon perimeter. Another round fell, and then another. Clouds of thick white smoke billowed up from the ground. Trees were uprooted and thrown violently asunder. The artillery barrage had begun. Bugle blasts, meanwhile, resounded over the shrill whistle of incoming artillery, imploring scores of khaki-clad North Vietnamese to push onward, through the storm of American steel. All around them the earth pitched and heaved as round after round of heavy artillery blew chunks of earth and debris into the air.

Lucid, though bleeding profusely from his leg wounds, Sergeant Grandstaff realized that the end was finally at hand. His courageous platoon was all but doomed. Expecting no quarter, Grandstaff resolved in those final fleeting moments to take as many of the North Vietnamese with him as he possibly could.

"Come and get us, you bastards," he taunted the NVA defiantly. "C'mon, you motherfuckers! Come and get us!"

"Come and get *us*, GI," mocked a hidden North Vietnamese soldier.

Sometime thereafter an RPG exploded near the Fourth Platoon CP. The blast killed Sergeant Grandstaff instantly. Grandstaff, remarried and the proud father of two little girls, had been awaiting the birth of his third child back in the States. "Hi Mom and Dad. Well, I suppose you are all over to our house now and my new son or daughter has been born," he wrote in a letter dated May 2, 1967. "Sure do wish I knew what I've got—a son or a daughter. I have received three letters today. One from you, one from Claudia, and one from [John] Tuft. Yes, I've been counting the days too. Sure wish they were going faster."[3]

The following day, May 19, Sgt. Dick Surface, while sorting through the company's mail after a Huey resupply run, happened upon a letter addressed to Grandstaff. Sealed tight, the envelope in which it came was inscribed with the message "It's a girl" on the front. Jeanne Grandstaff, the youngest daughter of Claudia and Bruce Grandstaff, was born on Monday, May 15, three days before the death of her father.

The two men lying behind the fallen log with Spc4 Victor Renza were also dead. Sgt. Leland Thompson, the reassuring twenty-one-year-old forward observer from Portland, Oregon, had not squirmed noiselessly away in search of a medic, as Renza had hoped, nor had the third soldier lying with them. They had been killed by the murderous NVA fire shredding the shattered platoon. Renza winced as salty streams of sweat seeped into the open wounds on his back, unaware that Thompson and the other man were still behind him but now dead. He began to wonder if the two men had deserted him. Had the entire Fourth Platoon, for that matter? *Maybe they pulled back with the platoon and forgot me*, he thought fretfully. *Fuck it. I'll just turn my head around and take a look and then I'll know one way or the other if those guys are still behind me*. Something stopped him, however, and the urge eventually passed.

Settling back down on his right arm, his right cheek once again planted firmly in the dirt, Renza lay motionless, surrounded by the ever-present sound and fury of battle, for what seemed like an eternity. A wry smile, the sort of impish grin the cat that had eaten the canary might wear after the deed had been done, suddenly creased his cheeks, and the tension ebbed unexpectedly from his bruised and bloodied body. *What the fuck?* he asked himself, half smirking. *Why do these people want to kill me? What did I ever do to them?* Renza chuckled at the absurdity of it all, at how a skirt-chasing, politically indifferent twenty-year-old from New York could end up fighting in the jungles of Southeast Asia in some grand geostrategic crusade he could scarcely even articulate.

"C'mon, you motherfuckers. Come and get us!"

"Come and get us, GI!"

Renza listened to the exchange in stunned silence. Defiant to the bitter end, Grandstaff had spent his final moments on earth taunting the NVA and they had taunted him right back, in English. *Man, those gooks have big balls*, Renza thought to himself. But so did Grandstaff, and when the artillery fire he had requested started raining down on top of the Fourth Platoon, their world was suddenly turned upside down. "When the rounds were coming in and landing, I was being lifted off the ground. Trees were being ripped right out of the ground. Artillery was tearing that whole area to pieces," Renza remembered. "It probably lifted me a couple of inches right off of the ground, and then I would slam back down. My body would go right up and then go right back down. Everything became a blur. It was like in a movie when they show a camera and then shake it so that everything blurs, or when they show an earthquake or an explosion and all of a sudden the dust on the floor starts to dance. The dust would stir, or whatever was loose on the jungle floor, when these explosions went off."

One round landed on the other side of the log he was lying behind, shearing a medium-size tree in half. Snapped in two, the tree fell over the log and covered the prone body of the wounded American. Shell-shocked, Renza gazed out through the branches of the downed tree. *Will it never end?* he asked silently, trembling in fear.

Up on the incline above the dry creek bed, a short distance away from Renza, Pfc. Cliff Rountree ducked his head and listened to the rounds coming in. Rountree had agreed with the decision to bring artillery fire down on top of the platoon, as did the rest of the Fourth Platoon survivors. "Yeah, fuck those motherfuckers," they had told Sergeant Grandstaff before the first shell burst inside the perimeter. "Bring that shit in." Grandstaff, it is therefore worth noting, did not act without the express support of the few remaining men under his command.[4] Jostled by the exploding artillery rounds, Rountree felt reasonably certain that he would make it if he could just survive the blizzard of hot steel and debris that was about to obliterate the platoon perimeter.

The crisis had passed. Curled into a defensible perimeter, and supported by artillery, air strikes, and helicopter gunships, the three remaining platoons of B Company, 1-8 Infantry were in no immediate danger of being overrun. Indeed, the near-constant artillery fire, although a welcome barrier between the company and the North Vietnamese, had frightened some of the grunts holding the line. "If you've been in a combat zone and have seen the big 155-mm, 175-mm, and eight-inch rounds start flying in, it's horrifying," said Pfc. Ken Brosseau of the First Platoon. "They come whistling in and fires flare up, trees buckle and get cut right in half, and that's what was happening. They were just unloading artillery all around us." Much of that support had been capably coordinated by Lieutenant Allen who, after a somewhat rocky start, had proven a steady hand at the company helm.

North Vietnamese mortar and RPG rounds, however, continued to slam into the company perimeter on and off throughout the afternoon. One round, most likely from a shoulder-fired RPG, exploded violently to the left of SSgt. Paul Burk, then a squad leader in the Second Platoon. Kicking up debris, the explosion wounded three soldiers. Burk, in an action that would ultimately result in a Silver Star commendation, raced to the aid of his wounded comrades and carried them, one by one, to safety. A heavy exchange of fire then ensued, injuring several more Second Platoon soldiers. Burk, spotting one of the wounded men, moved forward to rescue the man when suddenly, out of nowhere, a North Vietnamese soldier appeared. Startled momentarily, the Pennsylvania native tossed a grenade in the direction of the enemy soldier. The blast killed the NVA and cleared the area. Burk then grabbed hold of the wounded man and hauled him back to the rear.

Off to the west, however, beyond the Second and Third Platoons, Sergeant Grandstaff and the Fourth Platoon remained out of reach. Lieutenant Rodabaugh, still in command of the Second, was directing air and artillery strikes on the NVA between Grandstaff and the rest of the company, but neither he nor Allen had had consistent contact with Grandstaff prior to his last-ditch request for artillery fire on top of his position. Ominously, neither had been able to raise Grandstaff on the radio following that request. Allen later recounted the muddled state of communications in a lengthy written statement:

> I didn't have any contact with PSG Grandstaff for a while after this [Grandstaff's decision to call off the gunships and resume artillery fire earlier in the battle], because I moved from my position to aid some of my men who were pinned down by automatic weapons fire. When I moved back to the command position, my RTO said that PSG Grandstaff had stated that they were still pinned down and under very intense fire from all sides. Our radio contact was becoming very weak at this time, and it was hard to understand PSG Grandstaff's messages. He told me earlier that one radio had been put out of commission. We were unable to maintain clear reception because his one radio had bad batteries, and they were

> losing strength fast. Again I didn't have contact with PSG Grandstaff for approximately 30 minutes. When he did call me again, he stated that the NVA had attempted to overrun them a couple of times but had failed. I asked him how many men he had left, and he said something about 10 or 11. It was about this time that he adjusted the artillery fire closer to his position. In my last contact with PSG Grandstaff, he said, "We're being overrun. Place the artillery fire on top of me. I've only 8 men left."[5]

Allen had other concerns as well. Engaged in fierce, close-quarters combat with a numerically superior North Vietnamese force, the three platoons under his immediate control had suffered a number of dead and wounded, including a growing list of seriously injured men that required immediate medical evacuation. Allen had set up his CP and a medical collection point in a clearing east of the Second and Third Platoons, but without an LZ he had no means of evacuating the seriously wounded. Efforts to clear a one-bird LZ were already under way—Company 1st Sgt. Victor Lopez, a no-nonsense Mexican American NCO, had corralled a few able bodies and put them to work on it—but the job was far from complete.[6] In the interim, the wounded waited, many moaning in abject agony, for the machete-wielding detail to hurry up and finish.

Sgt. Dick Surface, dispatched to help clear the proposed landing zone, chopped away at the thick bamboo jutting out of the ground, sweat dripping from his brow. "We need to get a medevac in here," Sergeant Lopez had said. "We need to get an LZ cut." Surface had been nearby at the time and got picked to pitch in. Previously, after expending a few magazines firing at the NVA alongside Sergeant Brown in the Second Platoon, Surface had dashed over to an anthill close to where Lopez and the RTOs from the company headquarters section were lying. Lopez, Spc4 Henry Kuntzler, and Sgt. Donald Hunter, the communications NCO with whom Surface had ambled out of the ravine to get better radio reception, were firing up into the trees. Surface began firing into the trees, too, when Kuntzler, lying at the time next to Sergeant Hunter, raised his upper body, much like a man performing a push-up, to observe the NVA. Kuntzler was promptly shot in the arm, leaving Surface to bandage what looked more like a mess of "blood and flesh and muscle" than a human arm. Fortunately the hastily applied field dressing saved Kuntzler's mangled limb from a subsequent amputation. A short while later Lopez ordered Surface to start clearing an LZ.

Surface watched in dismay as the blade of his machete bounced harmlessly off a thick, jointed stalk of bamboo sticking out of the ground in front of him. Steadying the bamboo with his free hand, he swung again and sliced through the woody exterior of the plant. Surface cast the hewed piece aside and sized up another stalk. A bullet suddenly crackled past. "You can't really get work done on your belly, so basically you're standing up and the bullets come winging through there," said Surface. "At that point in time your adrenaline is running so much that the only thing you're attempting to do is to get an LZ in so that the helicopters could get the guys that were wounded out and get some more ammunition in." Occasionally a rifle round would pass so close to his face that he could feel the heat from the round on his skin. *Get down and stay down,* a voice inside his head told him, but he could never quite bring himself to do it.

Every now and then he thought about the Fourth Platoon. Periodically throughout the battle, he had kept an ear to the west, marking the different sounds—rifle or machine gun, AK-47 or M-16—in an attempt to determine how the Fourth Platoon was faring. And as long as he could hear the sound of M-16s firing away, he could cling just a little bit longer to the notion that his best friend, Sgt. James Foreman, was still alive and kicking. As the day dragged on, however, the volume of small-arms fire off to the west declined precipitately. "When I first started chopping down that LZ, I could hear the Fourth Platoon firing and the enemy firing—plus what was cracking through the bamboo where I was at," Surface stated. "But the firing down there became substantially less. You couldn't hear the M-16s firing as much."

Angry, Surface chopped down on a strip of bamboo. Surface had trained with the Fourth Platoon back at Fort Lewis. Most of the guys in the platoon were friends of his. But Jim Foreman was his best friend. Foreman was from the same small town in Indiana, and the two of them had been drafted on the same day in 1965. Surface squeezed the handle of his machete. *If my friends are out there dying,* he thought to himself, *then the rest of us here need to be trying a lot harder to get to them.*

Silence fell softly over the tangled clutch of downed trees and shell-sheared branches that made up much of what had been the Fourth Platoon perimeter. The 155-mm howitzers had done their worst. Victor Renza smelled gunpowder in the air and wrinkled his nose. Renza had weathered a portion of the artillery barrage on his belly, hidden in the branches of a fallen tree, but even there, with his right cheek pressed against the ground, he could not escape the pungent aroma. "It was quiet," remembered Renza, "but the place reeked of gunpowder. The air was heavy with that smell." The artillery fire had stopped, and the jungle was silent once again. The nightmare, it seemed, was finally over.

Time passed slowly, the hours measured not by the hands of a clock but in the length of the shadows creeping across the jungle floor. Suddenly a single shot rang out, and then another. The artillery barrage had only halted the North Vietnamese temporarily. Firing on the move, the NVA emerged shortly after the artillery fire ended to advance, in a line formation, through the smoking ruins of the Fourth

Platoon from the east. A second wave of North Vietnamese advanced on the platoon perimeter from the northwest a few minutes later.[7] Fourth Platoon, despite all of the shellfire and a spirited last stand, was now at the mercy of the enemy.

The bushes around Spc4 Victor Renza started rustling and he soon heard the sound of voices. Clearing his throat, he was about to yell out when a group of four North Vietnamese soldiers, each carrying an AK-47, stepped gingerly through the brush in a pronounced crouch. The four had come from the direction of the dry creek bed and were moving east on-line. Renza, his heart racing, sized up the enemy soldiers a scant twenty-five feet away. Small in stature, the men were wearing khaki uniforms, somewhat soiled but in otherwise excellent condition, and close-fitting sun helmets. The men also wore boots, not sandals, on their feet but what impressed Renza the most was their deliberate, purposeful gait. *Man, look at how these guys come through the jungle*, he thought to himself as he lay shrouded in the branches of the downed tree. *We come bobbing along all upright and nonchalant. No wonder they're winning!*

Soon after, another group of North Vietnamese soldiers, advancing in the same easterly direction as the first, stepped over the fallen tree, shaking some of the branches next to Renza's head. Seven or eight NVA, four of whom Renza could see distinctly, were now standing within twenty feet of him. Paralyzed with fright, he exhaled haltingly. "I was taking the most shallow [*sic*] breaths I could possibly take, trying my best to play dead," said Renza. "I had already heard sporadic single shots. I would hear a shot, and then thirty seconds later there would be another one. It was obvious that they were shooting wounded guys."

Conversing with his comrades in whispered tones, one of the North Vietnamese soldiers pointed offhandedly to the east, as if gesturing toward the rest of B Company. None of the other soldiers spoke, and the group continued tiptoeing eastward through the brush and debris. Then, without warning, the group circled around and began walking back toward the fallen log. The NVA had noticed the three Americans lying behind it. Terrified, Renza glimpsed the approaching enemy soldiers and then closed his eyes.

Bang! Bang! Bang! Bang! Bang! Bang!

Two of the six rounds the NVA fired slammed into the log inches above Renza's head. Remarkably the wisecracking New Yorker never flinched. "My guess is that they saw the three of us lying there, and they just pumped six rounds—two, I guess, for each of us—out," Renza stated. "They just missed me. The branches of that fallen tree were hanging over me, and I think that probably kept them from getting real close to me. To get to me, they would have had to have crawled into those branches and I think they got a little lazy. That NVA must have just assumed that he had hit me. I pretty much looked dead at that point anyway. I wasn't moving, I was barely breathing, and my shirt was covered in blood." Satisfied that the three Americans were dead, the NVA turned around and walked away.

While Renza played dead, the small group of NVA sat down and ate lunch a short distance away to the east. The soldiers, AK-47s slung over their shoulders, noshed on rice and chatted casually. Several of them ate with their backs to him. Slowly opening his eyes, Renza glanced at the NVA and then at his M-16 lying on the ground beneath the branches of the downed tree. Three, maybe four feet away, the weapon was just out of reach. "I could see the stock of my weapon and I would look back at the NVA," said Renza. "And I am thinking that if I eased over a little bit, I could get my weapon and take those guys out. I kept asking myself—can I get to my M-16 and take them out before they could turn around and take me out? But even if I could get to it, I had no idea how many rounds I had left. Before I jumped out of that creek, I fired into the opposite tree line and I know it suppressed some of their [NVA] fire. I don't care how much of a badass you think you are, when someone's shooting at you, you get down. So I started to think—what if I get to my M-16 without them noticing, and then I open up on them and I only have two rounds left?"

Changing his mind from one minute to the next, Renza agonized over what to do about the enemy soldiers sitting less than a stone's throw away. He could do nothing—and let the bastard that had just tried to kill him get away—or he could make a move for his M-16. Finally, after one last round of internal deliberation, Renza decided against making a move for his rifle. Discretion, he figured, was indeed the better part of valor.

More often than not, the encounters began innocuously enough, as it had with Spc4 Victor Renza. A faint rustle in a nearby bush, the muffled snap of a broken twig. Scouring the underbrush, the advancing NVA stopped whenever they came upon the body of a Fourth Platoon trooper. What happened next depended entirely on the individuals involved. One North Vietnamese soldier, for example, was observed kicking the bodies of fallen Americans in an apparent attempt to determine if the men were still alive. If the men moved, they were liable to be shot.

Beads of sweat glistening on the surface of his skin, his uniform damp with perspiration, Spc4 Tom Sears was crawling west on his belly when the North Vietnamese overran the platoon. Sears had taken a round in the hip before the artillery barrage, and along the way his helmet had fallen off. After a modest advance, he paused to look where he was going. Moments later a North Vietnamese soldier in a soiled, green-khaki uniform marched out of a stand of trees twenty meters away. Startled, the two men stopped and stared at one another. Then, without warning, the NVA raised his AK-47 and fired. Miraculously, Sears managed to duck a fraction of a second before the NVA pulled the trigger, and instead of getting hit in the forehead, the bullet lodged in his back near his spine.

Sears, jolted by the impact of the round, collapsed listlessly onto the M-16 he and Sgt. Bob Sanzone had shared. Helpless though still tethered to his senses, he watched silently as the North Vietnamese soldier approached him. Sears closed his eyes and played dead. The enemy soldier stopped beside him, crouched down, and placed a hand on his back, as if to examine the gunshot wound. Flipping Sears onto his back, the NVA unhooked his web gear—Sears felt the belt slide off his waist and tried not to breathe—and picked up his M-16 before turning him over onto his stomach. Oddly, the man stood up, squatted back down, and began running his hands through Sears's flaxen blonde hair. Sears, barely breathing, wondered if the man was curious because he had never seen hair that color before. Whatever the reason, the enemy soldier stayed there for a moment longer, then walked away.

Lying near the dry creek bed, Spc4 Ken Barker went through seven to ten magazines of M-16 ammo, pausing only to reload and to tend to the shrapnel in his arm and shoulder from an RPG, before Sergeant Grandstaff called artillery down on top of the Fourth Platoon. Barker had blacked out during the barrage, and he awoke sometime after the final shells had landed. The jungle was startlingly still at that point, and the vegetation that had obscured his field of view prior to the barrage was now largely charred or blown down. Barker, as he took in the devastation all around him, was instantly struck by the number of American bodies within his line of sight. Everywhere he looked the bodies of dead Americans lay strewn across the jungle floor. Barker eventually peered out into the jungle beyond the perimeter. There, on the opposite side of the creek bed, a swarm of North Vietnamese were working their way east toward the platoon perimeter.

Descending into the creek bed, the NVA disappeared momentarily before reemerging on the Fourth Platoon side of the dry waterway. Barker, following the NVA with his eyes, suddenly remembered his wallet. Inside it he had kept a photo of his wife and some phone numbers and addresses, personal items the twenty-year-old from Illinois did not want falling into the hands of the enemy. Dead or alive, his comrades were being stripped of their wristwatches, rings, wallets, and other personal effects. One NVA even sat on the head of a wounded American and combed through the man's pockets.[8] Web gear, ammunition, and canteens were also removed from the bodies, as were rifles and other weapons. Barker reached into his back pocket and retrieved his wallet. Rolling over onto his back, he shoved the wallet down the front of his pants and then flipped back over onto his stomach. *That's better,* he thought to himself. *Even the bad guys don't want to stick their hands down your pants.*

Ahead of him, the NVA were standing over the bodies of his comrades. Some of them, guys he admittedly did not know very well having been a replacement, but fellow Americans all the same, were shot prior to being searched. *Were those men still alive*? he wondered. At least two wounded Americans, according to subsequent reports, were shot by the NVA that afternoon. Barker, now expecting the worst, shut his eyes. *If I can just go to sleep*, he told himself, *it won't hurt. If I can just close my eyes, it won't hurt. Please, God, don't let it hurt.*

Voices, muted but unmistakably Vietnamese, could be heard on the east side of the creek bed. Soon the chatter grew louder. The NVA were near, *very near*. Barker held his breath. He had, it turns out, little time to do anything else, for he was rolled abruptly onto his back. His heart raced, and a dread the likes of which he had never experienced before swept over him. *They're going to know that I'm alive and they're going to shoot me*! he screamed silently. As the words echoed inside his head, he felt his watch slide off of his wrist and a set of hands slip into his pockets. Tucked neatly away in the crotch of his pants, the wallet with the photo Barker so cherished was left untouched. Relieved of his M-16 and some of his personal effects, he was then flipped back over onto his stomach. Barker, now lying face down, felt the hands of a North Vietnamese soldier folding his arms behind his back. Seconds later his hands were bound with rope. The ordeal finally came to an end when one of the North Vietnamese, apparently administering one last indignity before departing, kicked him in the ribs several times.

Nearby, Pfc. Gilbert Nash came to just as the NVA were lifting his torso off of the ground. "I think one lifted me up," he recalled, "while the others started to take things off me." Those things included his wedding ring, his watch, and the dog tags dangling from his neck. Stripping Nash of his personal effects, the NVA lashed his hands together with rope, much the same as they had done with Ken Barker, and then rolled him over onto his left side. Traumatized, Nash soon lost consciousness.

The same scene played out over and over again. Slightly to the north of Nash, Pfc. Cliff Rountree was approached from behind by three North Vietnamese soldiers. Shortly before, the NVA had buzzed his position with a quick burst of automatic weapons fire, hitting the canteen on his belt. Rountree escaped unharmed, but the short burst ruptured the canteen and splashed lukewarm water all over his fatigues. Wet, wounded, and now hearing Vietnamese voices, the feisty Californian wriggled out of what he thought was the line of fire and then ceased moving altogether. "I just went limp and played dead," said Rountree. "I could hear them talking to each other in that singsong gibberish. They were talking back and forth, and they were definitely shooting people."

When the NVA finally reached Rountree, one of the three bent down and snatched his M-16. His watch and wallet went next. Rountree, keeping his eyes closed and his breaths shallow, expected to get picked clean of his personal belongings. One of the enemy soldiers, however, lifted up his shirt and gently squeezed an area of skin between his belt and his ribcage. "Whoever he was, he knew that I was alive," said Rountree. "I thought to myself: Well, that's that. I just kind of embraced the end there." Amazingly, the North Vietnamese soldier withdrew his hand and departed along with his two comrades, leaving Rountree face down on the jungle floor.

Why the NVA elected to leave Rountree alive, or Pfc. Gilbert Nash and Spc4 Ken Barker for that matter, remains a mystery. Some have argued, although rather unpersuasively, that the North Vietnamese left the men behind to recount the grisly details of their defeat and, presumably, to warn their comrades about the futility of opposing "the heroic People's Army" of Vietnam. None of it ever made much sense to Rountree, then or now, but he has certainly heard his share of theories. "I remember talking about it to a photographer in Washington, D.C., years later," he recalled. "We were talking about the war back at the hotel, and I guess he had spent some time in Vietnam and knew the culture. Well, he told me that that North Vietnamese soldier was probably a Catholic, because if he had been a Buddhist I'd probably be dead."

Sadly, not all of the soldiers in B Company served courageously on the afternoon of May 18. Blinded by fear, panic, or rank self-interest—or conceivably some combination thereof—one staff sergeant abrogated his responsibilities and refused to fight. That soldier, whom Sgt. John McKeever described as a "chubby little NCO," was apparently in his early thirties and had spent a number of years in the Army before arriving in Vietnam. Nevertheless, when the fighting flared up around the company perimeter, the man, rather than lead his troops as one would expect from a longtime soldier and NCO, stubbornly refused to move. Twice, according to Spc4 Larry Gerken, a Silver Star recipient from an earlier action and a highly respected original, SSgt. Rock Smothers implored the sergeant to move his squad up and into position. Defiant, the man refused to budge. Exasperated, Smothers eventually resorted to threats, howling, "If you don't get off of your fat ass, I'm going to put a boot in it." Cooler heads ultimately prevailed, but no amount of prodding or cajoling could get the man to move.

Fellow soldiers, ironically enough, are often the most understanding when it comes to men who, for whatever reason, are unable or unwilling to fight. Few in B Company, however, expressed any sympathy for the sergeant. "Look, none of us were out there charging machine guns," said Specialist 4th Class Gerken, "but most of us did our job. And maybe one day, for whatever reason, you didn't do as much and maybe the next day you did. It's difficult to explain what goes through a guy's mind to a civilian or someone who hasn't been there. But this guy was a screw-up. What he did was rare for us."

Sgt. John McKeever agreed with Gerken and added that the wayward sergeant, by behaving unapologetically after the fact, did much to cast himself in a wholly unsympathetic light. "Everybody knew that he hadn't done anything during the battle—that he just sat on the ground," remarked McKeever. "Nobody challenged him on it, however, until he challenged us. He started saying things like how his mother hadn't raised no fool and how he would do the same thing if it happened again. Well, that's all it took. I walked away. I didn't want any part of that guy." Specialist 4th Class Gerken later learned that the sergeant, following a court-martial, was busted down to a private and eventually removed from the field. Gerken actually testified at the court-martial, and the last he had heard the sergeant was "burning shit back at the division base camp."

Work on a B Company LZ, meanwhile, began in earnest around 2 P.M. Lieutenant Allen, mindful of the growing number of wounded requiring a medical evacuation, sought to hasten the process of loading the men aboard incoming slicks by establishing a makeshift medical collection point close to the LZ. Unfortunately the slicks still had no place to land while the wounded, lying on the ground near the partially cleared landing zone, suffered grievously in the heat and humidity.

Getting the wounded to the collection point was often no mean feat. The remaining able-bodied grunts frequently had to brave machine-gun, AK-47, or RPG fire just to reach a fallen comrade and then, with the snap of bullets cracking past, had to drag or carry anywhere from 125 to 200 pounds of deadweight, depending on the size of the soldier, back through the same gauntlet of enemy fire. Uneven terrain and thick, tropical vegetation added to the difficulties the grunts faced in trying to recover the wounded.

Hardest hit, the Second and Third Platoons had wounded men in the ravine west of the company CP area. Sgt. Arthur Parker III, an African American original from Michigan and a former gridiron standout, served as a squad leader in the Second and had, to that point, escaped serious injury despite being in the thick of the fight. Petulant at times and occasionally abrasive, Parker had few close friends and rarely if ever indulged in idle chitchat with other soldiers. "A lot of times, even in the field, if you tried to talk to him he would just ignore you," said Spc4 Bill May. "He was really aloof and standoffish." Pfc. Rudy Dalton, a well-liked black trooper who knew Parker, described the broad-shouldered sergeant as "definitely something to deal with, but he was good." Parker was indeed a good soldier, and he had fought tenaciously during the battle.

Late that afternoon Parker decided to rescue some of the wounded soldiers in the ravine. "Cover me," he announced boldly as he stood up and prepared to leave the relative safety of his position along the Second Platoon line. Soon after, as 1st Lt. Larry Rodabaugh and several other soldiers nearby laid down a hail of covering fire, he dashed forward and was swallowed up by the surrounding vegetation. When Parker did not return after a minute or two, some began to fear the worst. Suddenly the jungle gave way and a figure burst through the foliage. Parker, the body of a wounded American draped casually over his shoulder, swept the remaining branches and leaves aside and marched into view. Striding effortlessly toward the rear of the company, past Lieutenant Rodabaugh and the surprised expressions of the other dirt-smeared soldiers providing covering fire, Parker reached the medical collection point and lowered the man over his shoulder to the ground. Finished, he turned around and quietly retraced his steps.

Parker returned to the ravine again and again, carrying one wounded man after another to safety, until finally, his mouth and face now a bloody pulp, he could do no more."That's it," he announced as he stumbled over to the collection point with one last body. "I'm done." Flesh dangled from his blood-splattered face. "He [Parker] had caught a round in the face, and it looked like it tore the side of his face off," Rodabaugh recalled grimly. "You could see his teeth. But he kept on going back out to get guys." Parker survived his wounds and the war, and word has it that he even killed the North Vietnamese soldier who had shot him. Inexcusably, however, his heroism has never been officially acknowledged. "Parker should have gotten the Silver Star," observed Bill May," but he just got lost in the shuffle."

Wounded earlier in the fight, a squad leader in the First Platoon, to the right of Lieutenant Rodabaugh and the Second Platoon, wailed pitifully over the sound of the gunfire. "Don't let me die!" he moaned again and again. "Oh please, don't let me die!" Tall, lanky, and a trifle awkward, Pfc. Gary Wayne Cripps, nineteen, of DeKalb County, Tennessee, heard the pleas from the stricken man and started through the underbrush to rescue him. Cripps was a replacement and had been trained as a transportation specialist yet, after a brief period of in-country training with the 4th Replacement Detachment in Pleiku, had found himself humping across the Highlands with B Company, 1-8 Infantry. None of that mattered now, though. What mattered, at least to Cripps, was that a fellow soldier—his squad leader—needed help. "Back at boot camp, no one would have thought it would be Cripps," said Pfc. John Barclay. "He wasn't even supposed to be infantry. But he did what he had to do."

Cripps had nearly made it to his injured squad leader when an NVA round slammed into his right knee, slowing him considerably. Undaunted, he continued crawling and began dragging the man to safety. Soon a second round tore into his body. Forced to stop, Cripps quickly contemplated his next move. Since neither man could drag the other, Cripps decided to lie across the body of his wounded squad leader and act as a human shield. Heroically he then remained in that position, blasting away at the NVA, until he lost consciousness.

There Cripps lay, in a contorted, blood-slicked heap, until Pfc. Ken Brosseau and a black sergeant named Squalls reached him later that afternoon. Brosseau, passing his M-16 to Squalls, bent over and tried to pick Cripps up, but the lanky replacement slid from his hands and slumped to the ground. "He had been hit a whole bunch of times, and when I tried to pick him up, I just couldn't because he was so bloody that he slipped right through," said Brosseau. "My hands were sticky after that with all of the blood, so the sergeant said, 'Let's get a poncho.' And when I did, we had to roll him over and carry him like that to the holding area, where they were trying to cut an LZ. He was blue, just blue, when we picked him up and he was a big boy, too. I never thought we were going to be able to pick him up with all of that blood."

Brosseau dumped Cripps off at the medical collection point and headed back out for the wounded Italian kid from New York. Cripps eventually recovered from the gunshot wounds he sustained to his right knee, right ankle, and left shoulder and was later awarded the Silver Star for his heroism on the afternoon of the eighteenth. Proud of his hard-earned commendation, Cripps derived greater satisfaction from the knowledge that he had willingly offered his own life to save the life of a wounded comrade.

Plodding along in dense jungle to the east of Cripps and Brosseau, Capt. Walter Williamson and his A Company, 1-8 Infantry troopers were marching steadily westward, toward B Company, when the voice of Lt. Col. Tim Gannon crackled over the radio shortly after 3 P.M. "Shortly after learning that contact had been lost with Fourth Platoon, I again contacted A Company—they popped smoke—and were still a kilometer away from B Company (-)," Gannon observed. "At 1512 I ordered A Company to move south to a cleared area—small, but after some preparation would take one helicopter."[9] Gannon, concerned with the time it was taking A Company to reach Lt. Cary Allen's beleaguered company by foot, had ordered Captain Williamson to head toward a small grove. Upon reaching the grove, Williamson was to cut an LZ and get his company ready to be airlifted to B Company.[10]

A Company, under the direction of Williamson, a twenty-nine-year-old former battalion S4 in his first combat command, had been beating the bushes, fraying both threadbare fatigues and jittery nerves, for nearly two hours before Gannon intervened to expedite the move with new orders.[11] Whether traveling by air or on foot, the grunts—originals and replacements alike—were acutely aware that a head-to-head with the NVA likely awaited them. Indeed, in the minds of some of the originals, the battle had all the makings of March 22, only in reverse.

Pfc. Tom Carty, an RTO in the Fourth Platoon and a veteran of the March battle in the Plei Doc, had learned of the trouble brewing with B Company while listening in on the battalion frequency. "We were stopped and I vividly remember listening to the radio—and it must have been tuned into the battalion net—and hearing that B Company had made contact with some NVA who had dropped their rucksacks and that the company had sent a platoon after them," Carty said. "I immediately thought, 'What a stupid thing to do!' Either the entire company goes, or no one goes. It was and is my personal opinion that sending one platoon was an error."

Gunfire, not garbled transmissions broadcast over the battalion net, alerted Pfc. Bill Dobbie, a nineteen-year-old replacement in Second Platoon, to the developing crisis in the B Company AO. "We could hear the firing, a lot of firing, and then it got real intense," said the Detroit, Michigan, native. "I guess that's when Bravo [Company] walked into that ambush. You could tell the difference between the M-16 and the AK-47 fire, and after awhile we didn't hear the M-16s that much anymore. That didn't bode too well."

Dobbie had been trained to operate crew-served weapons while back in the States, but when he landed in Pleiku aboard a C-130 in March of 1967, a salty old NCO informed him that his Military Occupational Specialty (MOS) was no longer 11H10 (crew-served weapons) but rather 11B10 (infantry). "All I could think," he later joked, "was that I had not been there two minutes yet and I had already got a promotion."[12] Scarcely a promotion, Dobbie had been arbitrarily re-designated, without a word of explanation, and was now little more than an ordinary rifleman, the least desirable and most hazardous occupational specialty in all of Vietnam.

Nor were the firefights and skirmishes in the weeks preceding May 18 on the scale or of the scope required to remove any doubt the A Company veterans may have had about Private First Class Dobbie and the other recent replacements. "After the March 22nd deal, we got a lot of replacements and we didn't really know how they would react under concentrated NVA fire," admitted Sgt. Ross Rembert, a Third Platoon original and a veteran of the costly battle in the Plei Doc. "A lot of us had been together for awhile, had been together under fire, and knew what to expect from one another. We didn't have that same trust in those [new] guys—yet." Sgt. Doc Bockover, the medic who performed an improvised tracheotomy during the battle on March 22 only to watch the man die soon afterward, lamented that A Company, as the originals had known her, was already gone, never to return. Too many good men had died that fateful day in March, and too many had been wounded and evacuated out of the field. Scarred by the subsequent turnover in the company, Bockover vowed to keep all of the replacements at arm's length.

Sgt. Jim Peirce felt the same way, but as a squad leader he was obliged to incorporate the new guys into his squad as best he could. Stern but patient, the bronze-colored twenty-one-year-old with Algonquin Indian in his blood sympathized with the replacements. New, green, and abruptly exposed to the horrors of war in an alien environment, the replacements had a hard row to hoe in the Highlands. Peirce, consequently, saw it as his duty to help the newcomers adjust.

Marching solemnly forward, each man in step with his respective platoon, Peirce, Bockover, and Rembert knew that if A Company ran into anything big along the way, their lives—as well as those of the B Company survivors—might well depend on the performance of the replacements.

6 FOURTH PLATOON—WHERE ARE YOU?

Twenty minutes past four or so on the afternoon of May 18, the battle-weary troopers of the Second Platoon, perhaps the most combat capable of the two B Company platoons facing the ravine on the western side of the company perimeter, gamely mounted one final, desperate attempt to break through the North Vietnamese and rescue the Fourth Platoon. Stiff enemy resistance greeted the attackers once again, however, and the assault quickly ran out of steam. Lieutenant Allen, with the welfare of his exhausted men in mind, halted the attack and instructed his platoons to remain within the company perimeter and continue work on the landing zone.[1] In time the NVA fire tapered off, and by 4:45 P.M. that afternoon the company reported only sporadic sniper and small-arms fire.[2] Meanwhile, to the west, the North Vietnamese had slipped back into the jungle, leaving the shaken survivors of the overrun Fourth Platoon alone in the shell-ravaged ruins of their former perimeter. The platoon they had once belonged to, that had marched north with the rest of B Company that very morning, had been utterly destroyed.

Holding his breath for what seemed like an eternity, Pfc. Cliff Rountree was at last able to exhale and open his eyes. The NVA, after systematically shooting and searching the soldiers of the Fourth Platoon for thirty to forty minutes, were finally gone and the jungle was quiet once again. Overjoyed, Rountree realized that somehow he had survived the firefight, the artillery barrage, *and*—while he was still very much alive, no less—the roving hands of the North Vietnamese soldier who had found him. And then it swept over the gutsy Californian like a wave, a sensation so strong that his mind was suddenly unable to conceive of anything else. "I felt like I was the only person left on the entire planet [at that point]," Rountree recalled. "It was surreal. It was like an outer-body [*sic*] experience."

Rountree then glanced down and saw his leg draped over the body of Spc4 Melvin Schultz. Not knowing what else to do, he stared anxiously at Schultz, hoping the rough-and-tumble medic would stir beneath his leg. Schultz, however, remained perfectly still. There the two men lay, the leg of one flopped over the body of the other, for some time until finally, with dusk creeping across the charred tangle of jungle that had once been their perimeter, Rountree took a chance and wiggled his leg. Schultz wiggled back. Although relieved to learn that someone else had made it, too, Rountree decided to remain quiet. "We had kind of figured out that we had gotten through it by playing dead," he noted. "I'm not sure if we fooled as many people as we think, but we were still alive." Schultz evidently agreed, and the pair continued to play dead.

A short while later Rountree heard rustling noises behind him. The noises, he soon discovered, were coming from Spc4 Tom Sears. Forced to play dead while a North Vietnamese soldier fussed with his blonde locks, Sears was squirming across the jungle floor without a helmet or a weapon. Rountree was glad to see that Sears was still alive, but he suspected that the former RTO had been wounded in the intense fighting. "I knew pretty much that Tom was hurt, because he was over there with Sanzone and there was an automatic weapon just shooting the shit out of him and really fucking them up," Rountree recalled. "That's the automatic weapon I took out with the rocket launcher." Worried, he crawled over to Sears and immediately noticed a gunshot wound in his back. Pulling Sears's shirt over his wound—Sears had lost his lone field bandage when the NVA unhooked his web gear—Rountree managed to staunch most of the bleeding before crawling off to find some water.

Soon afterward Rountree returned with two half-filled canteens he had scavenged off the bodies of dead Fourth Platoon soldiers. Everyone did it, and no one ever really thought twice about it. "That's just the way it was. Guys figured, well, he doesn't need it anymore so they started calling out or divvying up who got what," said Victor Renza. "It's crazy when you think about it now, all of these years later, but back then we were just so focused on surviving that no one really thought—hey, that's a buddy of mine we're talking about!" Sears and Rountree drank from the canteens in silence. Both were thankful to be alive. Sears would later credit Rountree with helping him survive the aftermath of the battle. "Cliff Rountree," he told another veteran of the battle, "was my hero [that day]."

Not far away, Pfc. Gilbert Nash awoke to find his hands still bound with rope. Slowly regaining his senses, Nash glanced over and saw another soldier, Spc4 Ken Barker, rubbing his wrists back and forth. The NVA had tied Barker's hands as well, and he was attempting to wriggle free. Following Barker's lead, Nash carefully untied his own hands but, unlike Barker, who continued to fidget even after he had loosened the rope, he decided to stop moving as soon as his hands were free. *What is that guy doing?* Nash wondered, terrified that the NVA would notice Barker moving and come back.

Gently extending his leg, Nash tapped Barker's boot with his own. Barker felt the tap and instantly froze. *An NVA soldier just tapped my boot*, thought Barker, *and he's probably standing over me. He's going to shoot me any second now.* Barker had heard the NVA shooting the dead and wounded as they moved out of the dry creek bed, and he was sure he was about to suffer the same fate. Curiously, though, seconds soon became minutes and he began to wonder if the NVA were still there.

As the shadows lengthened around him, Barker stared idly into the jungle across the dry creek bed. After a while he started to think that maybe it wasn't the NVA that had tapped his foot. Turning his head slowly around, he discovered Pfc. Gilbert Nash lying there behind him. Barker, cussing under his breath, briefly entertained the idea of shooting Nash for frightening him half to death. Then he realized—for the first time since the NVA had overrun the Fourth Platoon—that he was not alone; there were *other* survivors. Comforted, Barker breathed a deep sigh of relief. What had seemed so inconceivable only a short while before suddenly seemed possible. Maybe, just maybe, he would live through this nightmare after all.

Hobbling around back at the battalion firebase, Captain Sholly monitored events in the field from inside the TOC and quietly brooded. Sholly had returned to the firebase with Lieutenant Colonel Gannon when the C&C chopper they had been flying in landed at the firebase helipad to refuel. Rather than remain onboard while the bird refueled, however, Sholly had hopped out in the hopes of catching the first slick bound for B Company. Desperate to get back to his men, Sholly did not want to spend the rest of the day following the action from the air, as most would have expected from a company commander with a badly sprained ankle. Slicks would be shuttling supplies in and taking the wounded out just as soon as B Company finished clearing an LZ, and he was determined to be on the first bird in.

With dusk fast approaching, a Huey suddenly touched down on the helipad amid a cloud of dust and debris. A serviceable, one-chopper LZ—Sholly learned—had finally been cleared. Rounding up three or four medics, Sholly lumbered over to the slick and climbed in. The *whoop-whoop* of rapidly accelerating rotor blades grew steadily louder, and in an instant the small party was airborne and on its way to B Company. Following a short, tense flight, the slick descended slowly into the B Company LZ at 5:25 P.M. to a smattering of small-arms fire.[3] Unable to land completely, the Huey hovered atop a platform of cut timber as Sholly and the medics leaped out. Sholly, holding an M-79 grenade launcher in his hand, jumped awkwardly from one log to the next until he hit the jungle floor. It was not until later that night, when he attempted to contact B Company from his C&C ship, that Lieutenant Colonel Gannon first realized that Sholly had hitched a ride back to B Company. "He [Gannon] thought that I had stayed at the firebase when we got off the helicopter," said Sholly. "And the next thing he knew, he was up flying over the battle area and talking on the radio and he was surprised to be talking to me on the ground. He hadn't realized that I had gone back to the company."

Nor had 1st Lt. Larry Rodabaugh. Sprawled out on the ground with some of the other wounded, Rodabaugh spotted Sholly limping toward him and yelled fulsomely, "I didn't miss this one!" Often dispatched to participate in in-country training programs, Rodabaugh had been absent during a number of previous B Company contacts. Sholly smiled approvingly. "You sure didn't." The two officers spoke briefly before Sholly, noting the condition of Rodabaugh's wounded left arm and his general appearance, urged the leader of the battle-battered Second Platoon to find a seat on the helicopter behind them. "Go on," Sholly repeated, "get out of here." Rodabaugh offered to stay but Sholly politely declined.

Nodding, Rodabaugh walked over to the hovering slick and took a seat. "I would have stayed out there that night if Sholly hadn't told me to get on the chopper, and I think the reason he told me that was because I looked so goddamn bad," Rodabaugh recalled. "My arm was peeled like a banana, it had bled a lot, and when I cut that radio off of Claire Johnson, he had bled all over me. So I was covered with blood and all the rest of that crap. I looked worse than I was." Filled with wounded grunts, the slick carrying Rodabaugh jerked abruptly skyward, cleared the surrounding canopy, then droned noisily off into the late afternoon sky.[4] Five months later, in October 1967, Rodabaugh was awarded the Silver Star for his courageous exploits on the eighteenth.

Sholly next met with Lt. Cary Allen. Allen spoke calmly and coherently and appeared, despite the travails of the day and the calamity that had befallen the Fourth Platoon, to have matters well in hand. The three remaining platoons had settled into a defensible perimeter, many of the wounded had been evacuated to a centralized collection point, and a one-chopper LZ had finally been cut. Artillery fire, meanwhile, had been used to ring the company perimeter, and every so often aircraft from the U.S. Seventh Air Force would swoop in and make the surrounding jungle shudder and shake.[5] Two airstrikes, one at 3:25 P.M., the other at 4:23 P.M., were actually delivered in support of the company; after the second, the enemy fire around the perimeter began to slacken. Helicopter gunships were also on station, providing canopy-level air support to the company. At least one AC-47 fixed-wing gunship had also arrived on station. All in all, the enemy—Allen could report with some satisfaction—had been hit hard by supporting arms.

The conversation then turned to Sergeant Grandstaff. Grandstaff, Allen explained, had been advised to return to the company shortly before the NVA surrounded the Fourth Platoon. "One of the first things that Allen did was to tell me exactly how he had tried to get Grandstaff to not go down the trail as far as he did and to return," said Sholly. "He was a little apprehensive, I think, of what *I* was going to think about what he had done in my place. But he was holding it all together and doing fine." Sholly listened attentively while Allen summarized the situation, and when the young lieutenant was finally finished, he kindly offered a few words of encouragement and then suggested that the two of them take a tour of the company perimeter. Allen agreed, and the pair headed off for a trip around the perimeter.

Walking slowly, Sholly concluded that the perimeter was serviceable but lacking in one fundamental respect—the troops were not properly spaced. Surprised by the sudden NVA fire earlier that afternoon, the Second and Third Platoons had hit the dirt in search of anything—trees, logs, thick vegetation—that afforded the grunts some measure of protection. Maintaining proper spacing within fire teams and between squads was, understandably, very much of secondary importance in the chaotic opening moments of the struggle to reach the Fourth Platoon. As a result, however, the grunts were bunched too close together, making the perimeter too small to defend effectively in the event of a massed enemy ground assault.

Sholly, in response, pushed his remaining platoons farther out into the jungle. The expanded perimeter, he hoped, would "cover a little more territory and keep the NVA from getting in too close." Meanwhile, he deployed the battalion Reconnaissance Platoon, which had begun to arrive by helicopter around 5:30 P.M., on the eastern side of the perimeter. Dispatched by Lieutenant Colonel Gannon and placed under the operational control of B Company, the Recon Platoon continued to land in the one-slick LZ until 5:45 P.M., when the last of its elements closed on the perimeter.

Pushed farther out, the three B Company platoons fleshed out the new perimeter and started digging. The grunts soon realized, however, that their entrenching tools were no match for the rocky Highland soil. "You could not dig there to save your soul," lamented Sgt. Dick Surface. Sholly, looking around, advised the grunts to find the nearest tree to hide behind if they could not scratch out a shallow hole. While not ideal, a good sturdy tree, Sholly reasoned, at least offered some protection from enemy mortar rounds.

In the waning afternoon light, B Company prepared for the night ahead. The grunts dug shallow holes, cleared fields of fire, and evacuated the dead and wounded. "All WIA of Company B (-) were evacuated on the evening of the eighteenth," Sholly later wrote. "We had some KIAs from the action on the eighteenth that were not evacuated as well, because it was getting too dark and we generally didn't evacuate KIAs if it would create dangers for helicopters. In this case, we were still actively receiving fire and the small one-ship rickety platform was not Dulles [Airport]." Any additional WIAs and KIAs the company suffered that night—along with any discarded equipment—would have to wait until morning.

Getting the wounded out had not been easy. The grunts were already exhausted when they were ordered to load the wounded aboard idling choppers, and there were enemy stragglers and snipers lingering in the jungle beyond the perimeter. Shortly before 6 P.M., a medevac ship received enemy fire from a location southwest of the company.[6] The Americans responded with artillery and gunships. B Company also reported sporadic NVA automatic weapons fire from the north, albeit in steadily decreasing intensity.

Occasionally, an NVA soldier would emerge from behind a tree to shoot at the tired troopers or fire a random burst into the perimeter. Furious, the grunts would attempt to return fire, but the enemy always seemed to slide back behind a tree before the grunts could kill them. Sholly was visiting with the Third Platoon when an NVA soldier popped out from behind a tree and opened fire. Sholly, barely flinching, raised his M-79 grenade launcher, took aim at the tree *behind* the now hidden NVA, and remarked, "Here's the way you take care of that." Seconds later a 40-mm round smashed into the trunk of the second tree, spraying the North Vietnamese with shrapnel. Sholly, satisfied that he had demonstrated how to handle an enemy sniper hiding behind a tree, instructed the grunts to adopt the same basic approach. The order spread quickly, and soon the company's M-79 gunners, squinting in the murky twilight, began pumping rounds into tree trunks around the perimeter.

Sholly, meanwhile, returned to the company CP area to scribble in his journal. Evocative, if mildly disjointed, the entry read:

> Rounds incoming, small arms rattling. . . . People pushing faces into trunks of trees. . . . Looks of wrinkled anguish and expectation on face. . . . Body tense waiting for smash or bullet. . . . Sgt. Hunter on the radio, look of surprise and a question mark on his face while radioing for help.

Settling in, Sholly also understood that he would not be commanding the mission to rescue his Fourth Platoon that evening. Lieutenant Colonel Gannon, wisely, had already arranged to have A Company fly in and locate the missing platoon. Captain Williamson's people were to land, form up, and then sweep the jungle to the west. B Company was to stand down and consolidate in its night defensive position (NDP). Bitterly disappointed, Sholly opposed the decision to send A Company on an emotional level, but as a clear-eyed commander with a firm handle on the condition of his men, he recognized that Gannon had made the right call. "I was about to move, but he [Gannon] said that he was bringing A Company in. That was probably not a bad decision because a lot of my guys were—I won't say demoralized, because we definitely *weren't* demoralized—still a little uncertain as to where things were given how things had gone to hell in such a short period of time," Sholly acknowledged. "We got organized, had a good perimeter going, and were defending ourselves extremely well. It just took a little time [to recompose the company], because everybody knew that the Fourth Platoon was pretty well gone. Gannon reasoned that it would be better letting them [A Company] land and move through a defended position, rather than having them land and have to secure an entire perimeter and then move out. I agreed."

The first batch of A Company, 1-8 Infantry troopers landed in the small, one-chopper LZ at 5:55 P.M. Incoming mortar rounds and moderate small-arms fire greeted the anxious troopers as they hit the ground. It had been an arduous, all-day affair for the men of A Company. Patrolling along the high ground to the east that afternoon, the company had been ordered at 1:30 P.M. to move at once to help B Company, then embroiled in a major battle with a large NVA force. Dense jungle and intermittent sniper fire delayed Captain Williamson, however, and his troops were still thrashing through thick brush a kilometer away when Sergeant Grandstaff requested artillery fire on top of the Fourth Platoon. Foot-weary after more than an hour and a half of intense bushwhacking, Williamson and his flustered troopers were then ordered to head south toward a small grove, where they were to cut an LZ and prepare for an airlift. A Company reached the grove around 5 P.M. and less than an hour later began boarding slicks bound for B Company.[7]

Capt. Walter Williamson hopped off a slick and gazed around the B Company LZ. Born in Baltimore, Maryland, Williamson was an Army brat and the son of a soldier who had been stationed in Hawaii at the time of the Pearl Harbor attack. "I never knew anything *but* the Army," said Williamson. "The Army has always been my life." Following in his father's footsteps, Williamson enlisted in 1956, a little more than a month after he graduated from high school. For the next seven years, he served as an enlisted man, eventually earning a commission through OCS. Williamson arrived in Vietnam with the 4th Infantry Division in September of 1966 and spent his first six months in-country as the battalion S4 before assuming command of A Company in March of 1967, following the death of Captain Sands.

Williamson, as he waited for the rest of his company to land, mulled over the mission Lieutenant Colonel Gannon had given him. No company commander, he imagined, would relish the idea of stumbling around in the dark looking for a missing platoon. "We weren't exactly sure where they were and we weren't exactly sure where Charlie [NVA] was," said Williamson, "but we knew he was out there and we were out there. If you make noise, and he doesn't—guess who's going to find who first?" Next Williamson met with Captain Sholly. Listening attentively while Sholly described the B Company NDP and the situation overall, he resolved to do his best that night because "when somebody's in trouble, you go."

Around 7:15 P.M., a slick carrying the last group of A Company troopers landed in the B Company LZ.[8] A handful of men were on board, including Pfc. Tom Carty. Carty, then a twenty-two-year-old RTO from the Sacramento area, was in the process of jumping out when the door gunner, presumably to hasten his exit, shoved him out the door. Carty tumbled forward as his feet thudded forcefully on the ground below; regaining his balance, he quickly realized he had no idea where his platoon was.

Suddenly the voice of his platoon sergeant pierced the darkness. "Carty, Carty—where are you?" Carty, following the sound of the sergeant's voice, scampered anxiously over to the location of A Company's Fourth Platoon.

A Company by then had spread out around the B Company LZ, the grunts finding cover behind trees or in the thick vegetation. When the entire company was finally on the ground and accounted for, the four platoons—pushed and prodded by antsy officers and NCOs—hurried into position and prepared to move out. Captain Williamson organized the company into two columns. On the left, the First Platoon, under the command of 2nd Lt. Allen T. Rogers Jr., walked point followed by the Third Platoon. On the right, the Second Platoon, commanded by Sgt. Ron Snyder, took point while the Fourth Platoon pulled up the rear. At 7:23 P.M., a mere eight minutes after Tom Carty had stumbled off the last slick in, the two columns saddled up and marched off after B Company's "lost platoon."

Marching westward, A Company pushed past B Company and into the jungle beyond. Shortly thereafter the sun set on the western horizon, shrouding the two columns in darkness. Williamson, mindful of the pitfalls of wandering around the jungle at night with a large enemy force in the area, placed his two columns on a west-southwest axis. Williamson hoped that by avoiding the most obvious axis of advance—due west—his men could circle around any ambush the NVA had planned for them. He would do his best to find the missing B Company platoon that night, but he had no intention of leading his company into a North Vietnamese trap.

Sgt. Ross Rembert, walking along toward the rear of the column on the left, was a squad leader in the Third Platoon. Rembert had enlisted in the Army in September of 1965 at the age of seventeen—before his senior year of high school and against the wishes of his mother—with dreams of one day joining the 101st Airborne Division. Gung-ho, the Mobile, Alabama, native looked very much like a future Screaming Eagle until he tore cartilage in his left knee during a training jump at Fort Benning, Georgia. Placed on a medical hold, he was prohibited from jumping for three months. Rembert, fearing that he would spend the next three months on kitchen police (KP), requested a transfer to an infantry division bound for Vietnam. The Army obliged, and in February of 1966 he joined A Company, 1-8 Infantry.

Rembert watched his jittery squad maneuvering through the undergrowth in the inky black Highland night. "We'd been in country for awhile so we were relatively accustomed to working at night, whether it was night ambushes or LPs [listening posts]," said Rembert, "but on the night of the eighteenth we knew a large force was in the area. And it was scary as hell not knowing if we were going to stumble into a horseshoe ambush." Rembert tried to steady his nerves. Sooner or later his squad would look to him, and for their sake he knew he had to appear as poised and in command as possible.

Stumbling along, arms outstretched to keep squads of jumpy troopers organized and within reach of one another, the four A Company platoons eventually merged into a single column. The move improved command and control and allowed the company to move through the thick jungle more efficiently. Spc4 Raul Munoz, an affable twenty-year-old Mexican American original from the Phoenix area, grabbed ahold of the grunt in front of him so that he wouldn't become separated from his squad as the column moved westward. Munoz was not alone. "I could hear the flares sizzle and they'd float down, but when the illumination went out, you had to grab the guy in front of you," said Pfc. Tom Carty. "Moving that way was in contrast to our training, which called for staying at least fifteen feet apart." Few if any of the grunts, however, strayed more than *five* feet from the man in front of them.

Overhead a U.S. Air Force AC-47 "Spooky" flare ship dropped parachute flares at regular intervals to illuminate the tenebrous jungle below.[9] Animated by the artificial light, an army of shadows danced ominously about, eliciting a whole host of imaginary horrors. "You want to talk about eerie—those flares would drop down on these little parachutes and you'd start seeing all kinds of shit," recalled Pfc. Landis Bargatze, a replacement in the Fourth Platoon. "I swear I saw alligators, monsters, and a lot of other stuff that was none too pretty. I'm sure everybody did." Pfc. Charlie Bann, stumbling along with the Second Platoon, felt as though the blind were leading the blind. "Even though there was illumination going off, none of us had any idea what we were walking into," said Bann, then a nineteen-year-old replacement. "There were shadows to the right and left of me, and I didn't know whether those shadows were one of our guys, the enemy or what."

Despite the danger, A Company pressed on in search of the missing B Company platoon. "Fourth Platoon, Bravo Company—where are you?" the A Company grunts shouted desperately. Every so often, the column would stop and someone would fire a single shot into the air. Captain Williamson hoped that if there were any survivors from the ambushed platoon, they would recognize the familiar sound of an M-16 and start shouting. At one point the troops crossed a dry creek bed, prompting speculation that the missing platoon might be near, but as before their shouts and shots went unanswered. The Fourth Platoon was nowhere to be found.

Mercifully, at a quarter to eleven, Lieutenant Colonel Gannon contacted Williamson and suspended the search for the night. The entire enterprise, Gannon would later recall, had been long on effort but short on results. "Pulling A Company out of the jungle and placing it in B Company's position was a tedious task—[it] took until sunset," said the 1-8 Infantry CO. "When the entire company had arrived, it moved west to find B Company's Fourth Platoon. The AF [Air Force] provided flare ships. Couldn't locate the platoon that night."[10] Williamson was ordered to establish an NDP and resume the search for the missing B Company platoon the following morning.

Halting west of the dry creek bed, A Company curled into a perimeter for the night. Too tired to dig in, some of the grunts tossed their rucksacks on the ground and lay down behind them. Others dug shallow holes. Almost to a man, however, the grunts understood that the company had courted disaster that night. "If the NVA had had a machine gun," said Pfc. Tom Carty, "they would have wiped us out." Sgt. Ron Snyder bedded down behind the frontline squads of the Second Platoon. Promoted to platoon leader the day before, Snyder believed that his men and the men of the other three platoons had survived the ordeal largely because the North Vietnamese, for whatever reason, had decided not to attack. Long admired for their martial prowess at night, the NVA—in his opinion—had squandered a golden opportunity to strike the company when it was at its most vulnerable. Sitting back, the self-described "lieutenant for a day" felt certain that the company would never be asked to do anything like *that* again. "I thought to myself—if we don't all get killed tonight, we're invincible," said Snyder. "It was absolutely pitch dark, and we were walking in a single column. It's the scariest thing I've ever done over there."

Buried beneath the branches of a fallen tree east of the dry creek bed, Spc4 Victor Renza had heard voices somewhere off in the distance. It had been dark for a while, and since he could not tell if the voices were American or Vietnamese, he decided to remain quiet. At one point, however, he had heard someone yell, "This is A Company! If anyone is alive, then fire a shot in the air!" Renza momentarily considered reaching for his rifle nearby. "But then I thought—what if the NVA are still out there? I just couldn't take the shot," said Renza. "I couldn't risk it. If the NVA were still out there, A Company would have walked right into them. The NVA would have ambushed them, *at night*. It would have been a massacre." Risking an entire company for one wounded grunt—Renza had long since assumed that he was alone, an impression reinforced by the fact that no one else had responded to A Company—struck him as incredibly selfish, and before long the voices faded away.

Pfc. Cliff Rountree and Spc4 Tom Sears had also heard A Company shouting in the distance. Rountree and Sears had stayed together after the battle, and as the two grunts gazed through the trees, out beyond what had been the Fourth Platoon perimeter, they observed North Vietnamese soldiers smoking and talking casually. Visible whenever a flare floated overhead, the NVA were close enough that Sears could see that some of them had rolled up their shirtsleeves. Sears and Rountree weighed their options. They could yell out, and run the risk of drawing A Company into the NVA they saw mingling in the flare light, or they could remain quiet and maybe forfeit their last chance of being rescued. Neither one of them knew the extent of their injuries, or if they could make it through the night without medical attention. Whispering softly, the two grunts huddled for a moment longer and then decided that they, too, would remain quiet.

After a while the calls of the A Company troopers grew more distant. A Company would later learn that there *were* survivors from the missing B Company platoon and that those survivors had selflessly and heroically chosen to remain silent to spare their weary sister company from blundering into an enemy ambush. That night, back at the headquarters of the 4th Infantry Division, an Army spokesman issued a statement on the status of the missing platoon. "The platoon apparently was overrun," the spokesman said. "The last radio contact carried a request by the platoon leader for artillery fire on his position." The request was subsequently granted, the spokesman added, and a number of rounds were fired on top of the platoon. Three men were listed as dead at that time.[11]

The statement was released around 9 P.M. Meanwhile, in the B Company CP, Sgt. Dick Surface was busy contacting the four platoons manning the company perimeter. Surface typically performed a SITREP check every hour and then relayed the information to Captain Sholly and the S3 back at the battalion firebase. None of the platoons, however, had anything of note to report. Other than the sound of friendly artillery fire, in fact, all was relatively quiet around the perimeter. Surface relayed the news to Sholly and returned to his handset. "Three-Three, this is Eight-Two Charlie," he chirped into the radio, making sure he identified himself and his unit to the S3 sitting in the battalion TOC. "SITREP negative."[12]

Surface eased a poncho over his head and then carefully lit the cigarette dangling from his mouth. Smokes normally soothed his nerves after a long day in the bush, but nothing—not even smoking three cigarettes at once—seemed to calm the veteran RTO on the night of the eighteenth. "My mind was running a hundred miles an hour, [thinking] about Foreman [Sgt. James Foreman] and all of those guys down there [in the Fourth Platoon]," Surface admitted. "I just couldn't believe it. It was like a dream."

Nearby, in the First Platoon, Spc4 Larry Gerken mulled the passing of his platoon leader, Plt. Sgt. Clifford Johnson. Lieutenant Allen had ordered Johnson to move an element of his First Platoon out to the right to protect the flank of the company. Johnson led the charge and was fatally wounded while firing on NVA soldiers hiding in the trees and in the thick underbrush. Later that afternoon, after the firing had died down, Gerken and several other soldiers dashed out and retrieved Johnson's body. "The NVA had taken his watch, and they had taken things out of his pockets," said Gerken. "If anyone should have gotten the Medal of Honor, it should have been Cliff Johnson. He went out there by himself to see if he could relieve some of the pressure they [NVA] were putting on us. Cliff was probably one hundred yards or so in front of the perimeter when we found him." The week before the battle, Johnson had told Gerken that he didn't want to die in Vietnam, but if it happened he wanted his body returned to the United States.

That night Gerken was sitting, somberly recalling the events of the day, when Lieutenant Allen, now back in command of the First Platoon, approached him. Allen, sizing up the mood of the sullen sergeant, spoke first. "You lost your platoon sergeant today."

Gerken looked up and nodded. "Yes, sir—I guess we did."

"How do you think I feel?" Allen replied unsympathetically. "I lost a whole *platoon* today."

7 PICKING UP THE PIECES

Artillery fire ringed the B Company perimeter throughout the night, bolstering the morale of the battle-fatigued troopers. "That right there [artillery fire] was like a wall of steel around us," said Sgt. Dick Surface, who spent the night pulling radio shifts. "We knew the NVA would have to come through that barrier." Similarly, the illumination provided by dozens of air-dropped flares increased visibility and contributed to the sense of security Surface and many others felt. Whether the artillery fire had any material effect on the North Vietnamese that night remains unclear. B Company reported that it did not receive any small-arms fire on the evening of May 18–19. The company did, however, report enemy mortar fire around 2:19 A.M. Fired from the north at an estimated distance of about five hundred to six hundred meters, the thirty or so enemy rounds landed outside the American perimeter.[1]

Waiting anxiously in the damp underbrush, the bleary-eyed grunts on LP duty marked the first few rays of light on the eastern horizon and scampered back through the jungle. Dispatched to the jungle around the B Company NDP, the wary grunts slipped silently through the dewy brush and returned to the company perimeter at daybreak on the morning of the nineteenth. It had been a relatively uneventful evening for the LP teams and the company in general after an extraordinarily trying day on the eighteenth. Gradually, the grunts on the line began to stir. Sleep-starved privates yawned groggily, while veteran NCOs nearby downed cups of coffee. Many wondered what the new day would bring.

In the Second Platoon, a small group of grunts climbed out of their fighting hole, sat down, and began snacking on C-rats. Spc4 Joe Mancuso was one of them. Mancuso, looking for a decent place to sit, found a spot among the broad, aerial roots of a large Highland tree. Branching out from the base of the tree in all directions, the gnarled mass of aboveground roots was such that a man could fit comfortably in its folds and grooves. Mancuso leaned back against the trunk of the tree and hungrily plunged his plastic spoon into a can of C-rats.

While Mancuso and the others ate, two North Vietnamese soldiers crept into position near the company perimeter. Calmly leveling the business end of an RPG, one of the men fired at the small gathering. An ear-ringing explosion shook the Second Platoon seconds later, shattering the early morning calm. Tripping and stumbling about, the startled grunts scrambled for cover. As they peered out into the murky jungle, some of the grunts listened intently for the "thump" of an enemy mortar tube. Instead, the platoon heard something few will ever forget. "The next sound [we] heard was an unearthly moan coming from one of the men," said Bill May, a Spc4 in the Second. "Still stunned and searching for the enemy, everyone turned to locate that horrible sound. It was coming from one of the guys. He was staring at the tree. There sat what had been Joe Mancuso. A white plastic spoon was in his right hand and a C-ration can in his left, but his upper shoulders and head were gone. To use the word surreal doesn't do it justice. The simple act of acting human in an inhuman environment had led to disaster." Although shrapnel from the blast wounded one other soldier in the foot, the tree absorbed most of its concussive effects, sparing the rest of the soldiers sitting nearby.[2]

B Company received between two and five RPG rounds, including the round that decapitated Spc4 Joe Mancuso, at 6:27 A.M. on the morning of the nineteenth. All of the rounds, the company reported, were fired from positions north of the perimeter.[3] Artillery fire was subsequently requested, and later that morning a patrol found three dead North Vietnamese soldiers outside the perimeter. The patrol, however, could not say for certain if any of the three had participated in the attack that killed Mancuso.

Falling quietly into formation, the four A Company platoons marched out of their makeshift perimeter at 7:05 A.M. and headed north, through the early morning mist, in two columns. The nineteenth had dawned warm and muggy, much like the previous day, and the men soon worked up a sweat traversing the rolling, thickly jungled terrain. Farther back, behind his lead platoons, Capt. Walter Williamson monitored the progress of his advance elements and consulted his compass. Williamson, as he had done the night before, planned to take the company on something of a circuitous route—north and then east—to B Company's Fourth Platoon to avoid any possible ambushes the North Vietnamese might have established along one of the more direct avenues of approach.[4] Better to arrive a little later and in one piece, Williamson reasoned, than to hurry forth along the shortest and most predictable route and stumble into an ambush.

A Company had spent a long, restless night camped to the west of B Company. "Nobody could sleep. How could you?" said Pfc. Charlie Bann, a Second Platoon replacement from Pennsylvania. "You just couldn't get it out of your head. We knew that they [NVA] were out there, and we really felt like we were going to get hit and really hard." That morning Bann's Second Platoon fell in behind the Fourth Platoon on the left, while the First Platoon followed the Third Platoon in the column to the right.

Led by the Third and Fourth Platoons, respectively, the two columns marched steadily northward before shifting to the east. Sgt. Frank Patton was with the Second Platoon in the left rear of the two up, two back company formation. Originally from Picayune, Mississippi, the nineteen-year-old had enlisted in the Army without much forethought. "I was so stupid," he joked, "[that] I was on my way to Fort Polk before I even knew I was in." Patton, though, developed a penchant for detecting the enemy with his nose as well as his eyes and ears. If the North Vietnamese were around in any kind of number, he would often smell them before he ever laid eyes on them. Sniffing the humid Highland air that morning, Patton was certain he smelled *something* in the jungle around A Company.

The eastward march continued for a while thereafter, but before the men could advance much farther Captain Williamson ordered the company to halt. While the two columns paused in the thick underbrush, Williamson, perhaps sensing that the missing B Company platoon was somewhere close by, directed the First and Second Platoons to push on ahead of the rest of the company. The Third and Fourth Platoons, alternatively, were to remain in place and await further instructions.

Saddling up, the First and Second Platoons followed the sloping terrain east and soon crested a small hill. Spent casings and discarded machine-gun ammunition links were scattered atop the hill, and the area had all the outward appearances of a North Vietnamese ambush site. A mortar-firing position and five 82-mm mortar rounds were also found.[5] The platoons, moreover, discovered a high-speed trail running west to east-southeast through the jungle. Troops from at least one of the two platoons proceeded to search the surrounding area, but there were no reported incidents of enemy contact. Continuing on, the two platoons then descended the opposite slope in a single column, with the First Platoon, under the command of Lieutenant Rogers, on point.

Sgt. Joe Bauer, a tough twenty-year-old original from New Jersey, hit the bottom of the hill and glanced backward. Bauer had been promoted to platoon sergeant in the Second Platoon when Ron Snyder assumed command on the seventeenth and was walking near the back of the platoon column along with Spc4 Dave Miller. Bauer, slowing down long enough to survey the crest of the hill to his rear, suddenly saw a North Vietnamese soldier sprinting across it, no more than thirty meters away.

Bauer shouldered his M-16 and dropped the NVA with a short burst of fire. Cautiously approaching the body, Bauer and Specialist 4th Class Miller noticed that the enemy soldier was clean-cut and seemingly well nourished. The man also wore a fresh-looking khaki-colored uniform and a belt buckle adorned with a star. Bauer and Miller both eyed the belt buckle, but only Miller had a knife at his disposal. Slicing through the dead man's belt, Miller removed the buckle and held it in his hand. Pleased, he then stashed the prized souvenir away and joined Bauer in searching the man's body. "That guy *had* a weapon, but when we got to that guy—yes, he was NVA in a full uniform—he had no weapon, no ammo, no nothing," said Bauer. "So there had to be another guy in that area. We checked him for papers, but he had nothing of interest on him. In that short time [the time it took to reach the body], that guy was stripped. There had to have been another guy with him that we didn't see, because he had no weapon."

Miller, incidentally, did not actually see Bauer shoot the NVA nor did Sgt. Ron Snyder, the Second Platoon leader that morning. Snyder could not even recall whether there had been any gunfire. Nor is it entirely clear what occurred after the incident, but at some point the First and Second Platoons resumed heading east. In command of the First, Lieutenant Rogers placed a squad on the right and left flanks of the platoon for security and to expand the overall area covered by the search. Pfc. Robert "Ned" Bishop, a replacement from Pennsylvania, walked point for the squad on the left flank. Bishop, moving slowly through the leafy green undergrowth, suddenly saw an American soldier some distance up ahead. The soldier, from what Bishop could tell, had either spotted him moving through the jungle or had heard him approaching and was now attempting to attract his attention. Bishop informed his squad leader, and the sergeant relayed the information up the chain of command until it reached Captain Williamson back at the company CP.

Pushing on toward the signaling soldier, the First Platoon parted the thinning brush and entered what had been the perimeter of the missing B Company platoon at 8:20 A.M. on the morning of the nineteenth.[6] Nothing, however, not even the bloody battle on March 22 in the Plei Doc, had prepared the veterans of the First Platoon, to say nothing of the green replacements in their midst, for what they would find when they finally located the "lost platoon." Scores of downed trees—some yanked from the soil, roots and all—lay scattered about the shell-scarred landscape. Patches of jungle in and around the perimeter were flattened, shredded, or devoid of all vegetation. Brass casings and other debris littered the ground. Swarms of flies hovered over the corpses of the fallen. The air reeked of gunpowder and rapidly decaying flesh.

Spc4 Gary McMichael, twenty, of Springfield, Oregon, wandered through the perimeter and surveyed the devastation.[7] Though hardly a wide-eyed rookie, McMichael was taken aback by the carnage. "The first thing I remember was all the bodies with arms and legs missing," said the soft-spoken original. "The guys were all our guys in the area I was in. The NVA must have taken away all of their dead, or at least in my area. There was one guy who was dead, and he had had both of his legs blown off. Another guy had his left arm missing from the elbow down. There were just body parts *everywhere.* It was just a thing to have to see." McMichael's eyes then fell on Spc4 Ken Barker. Barker was lying on the ground near the dry creek bed, dirty, disheveled, and relieved of his rifle and personal effects. But he was alive, and that gave McMichael hope that others had survived as well.

Fanning out quickly, McMichael and the rest of the First Platoon formed a protective perimeter around B Company's shattered Fourth Platoon. Second Platoon, trailing behind the First, reached the perimeter shortly thereafter. Lieutenant Rogers, Sergeant Snyder, or both radioed Captain Williamson back at the A Company CP and informed him that they had found the "lost" platoon. It was later determined that A Company had passed no more than one hundred meters south of the ill-fated platoon on the night of the eighteenth.

Following the death of Spc4 Joe Mancuso, Captain Sholly directed the four platoons in the B Company perimeter east of A Company to fire simultaneously, and with all available weapons, for a period of one minute. "I ordered it to ensure that any enemy outside the perimeter would think again about making a ground attack, [but] I felt it would also give the troops a little morale boost that we were still a formidable fighting force capable of taking care of business," Sholly wrote candidly. "[That] even after the indignities of the day before, we were back on our feet and ready to take on whatever was out there." Sholly notified Captain Williamson of his intentions so that Williamson "wouldn't think the world was coming apart again," and then ordered the "Mad Minute" to commence.

On Sholly's signal, the B Company troopers opened up on the jungle around the perimeter. With a deafening roar, the outgoing rocket, machine-gun, and small-arms fire tore into the surrounding vegetation for roughly a minute, before Sholly, satisfied that the still-potent capabilities of his wounded company had been amply demonstrated, stepped in and stopped the firing. In retrospect the "Mad Minute" had virtually no effect on the existing tactical situation; B Company did not report any confirmed kills as a result of the firing, nor is there any evidence to suggest that it preempted a North Vietnamese assault on the company perimeter. Nonetheless the firing did seem to have something of a salutary effect on the morale of the troops. "Yes, I think it did help [with unit morale]," noted Sholly. "It got the troops in a proactive stance instead of merely reacting to what was going on outside the perimeter. It helped promote the thought that, 'Hey, we're still here and we're ready for anything.'"

Under no circumstances, Sholly had decided, were his men to sit in their holes and wallow in self-pity. For the time being each and every one of them belonged to

B Company, 1-8 Infantry, and as long as he had anything to say about it they were to carry on with the business of soldiering, regardless of what had happened the day before. If he had had his way, B Company would have mounted up and marched west after the missing Fourth Platoon. Lieutenant Colonel Gannon nixed the idea, however, in part, Sholly suspected, to spare B Company the anguish of having to evacuate the platoon's dead and wounded.

With A Company in charge of recovering what remained of the Fourth Platoon, Sholly tasked the four platoons under his command with policing up the battlefield and strengthening the company perimeter. By keeping his men busy and mentally engaged, Sholly believed that he could keep them sharp. Since most of the dead and all of the seriously wounded had been evacuated the night before, the troops spent a considerable amount of time on the nineteenth retrieving rucksacks to ensure, as Sholly put it, that "the admin was correct as to what had happened [and] to whom." B Company, excluding the separated Fourth Platoon, had suffered ten KIA and twenty-four WIA during the fighting.[8]

Rolling up their sleeves, the troops improved their fighting holes and other defensive positions around the company perimeter. Sholly, meanwhile, dispatched squad-sized and occasionally platoon-sized patrols to sweep the surrounding jungle. Attached to B Company the night before, the battalion Reconnaissance Platoon, an outfit expertly trained in tactical intelligence collection, conducted patrols throughout the day.

Pfc. Kent Coombs, a twenty-year-old replacement RTO in the Recon Platoon, went out on patrol that afternoon and marched right by the site of the ambushed Fourth Platoon. Coombs witnessed the extraordinary devastation firsthand but he still preferred patrolling, even if it meant encountering dead Americans, to the guard duty the Recon Platoon had been pulling at the battalion firebase. In-country for about six weeks, Coombs did his best not to stare as he moved nervously past the Fourth Platoon dead.

Other fill-ins drawn from the ranks of the battalion firebase and the division base camp, officially designated Camp Enari that May, had flown out on the nineteenth to reinforce B Company's understrength platoons.[9] "On the night of the eighteenth, because I did not know when I would receive replacements for my casualties, I called for everyone—no matter what their status, except those whom it would not be medically sound to have with us," wrote Captain Sholly. "I insisted that those guys who could hold a rifle and were not medically disqualified come out to reinforce us in the field. I even had the Company XO, Lieutenant Tupa, come out since the only officers I had left in the company were he [*sic*] and Lieutenant Allen [1st Plat]."

Of the men pressed into frontline service, however, few were as experienced or as fit for combat as the troopers of the Recon Platoon. "From time to time, the Recon Platoon would be attached to one of the line companies to beef them up with an extra platoon if it looked like things would be getting a little heavy," Sholly explained . "So they had worked with all of the line companies at one time or another and in my case, they fit right in to take the place of my Fourth Platoon." The platoon, furthermore, fielded more M-60 machine guns and radios than a standard infantry platoon. Private First Class Coombs and his comrades, Sholly well knew, had the firepower and the communications capabilities to get the job done.

Pfc. Gilbert Nash spent the night of May 18–19 lying perfectly still on the eastern bank of the dry creek bed. Nash, following the example of Spc4 Ken Barker nearby, had wriggled free of the rope the NVA had used to bind his hands. Content to play dead, the nineteen-year-old African American replacement then remained virtually motionless, in the same position the NVA had left him in, for hours on end. Nash, incredibly, moved only once the entire night, when he reached down and unzipped his fly to urinate. Slumbering on and off, he awoke early on the morning of the nineteenth on his side, in precisely the same position he had been in for the better part of sixteen hours. The gunfire had finally stopped, and for an instant it seemed as if the war had forgotten him.

Arching higher and higher in the Highland sky, the bright tropical sun burned through the morning mist and warmed the jungle floor. Still too afraid to move, Nash listened to the sounds of the jungle around him and quietly pondered the fate of the Fourth Platoon. Were there any other survivors? Was B Company coming to get them? Did anyone even know where they were? Barker was also awake, but neither dared to move, much less speak. Suddenly the jungle off to their west began to stir. "I heard some voices, and I definitely heard the voices of some GIs," said Nash. "Then I saw this sergeant—I know he was a sergeant because I could see the stripes on his sleeve—and I just thought to myself, 'Oh my God!'"

Nash sat up and studied the man. "Are you OK?" asked the A Company sergeant as he approached the embankment. "How do you feel?" Nash assured the sergeant, a man most likely from either the First or Second Platoon of A Company, that he was okay. Rising unsteadily, he then stood up and walked down the embankment toward the dry creek bed. There, in the shallow bed below, he saw the "bodies of American soldiers piled up and riddled with bullets." Nash stared into the bloodstained bed for a moment longer and then staggered back up the embankment. Overcome with emotion, the Harlem native sat down and started to sob.

Embarrassed, Nash immediately tried to wipe the tears from his face before anyone noticed. He was a soldier, after all, and soldiers were not supposed to cry. The A Company sergeant, however, would have none of it. "That's alright, soldier," he began soothingly. "If you want to cry, you go right ahead and cry. It's ok." Afterward,

Nash was escorted to a medical collection point A Company set up for the wounded survivors of the Fourth Platoon. A separate collection point, nearby but out of view, was established for the dead.

Nash sat down near some of the other survivors. Sadly, it would be years before he felt comfortable enough to recount the events of May 18, 1967. "I was afraid what might happen to me if I told them [the Army] I had to shoot a white soldier to get that North Vietnamese," said Nash. "Back then, in 1967, I didn't know how people would react to a black soldier having to shoot through a white soldier, even a dead white soldier, to get at a North Vietnamese. I was scared, and so I didn't tell anybody."

One by one, the survivors of B Company's shattered Fourth Platoon were located and escorted to the collection point established for the wounded. Seven survivors were found relatively quickly—Pfc. Gilbert Nash, Pfc. Cliff Rountree, Spc4 Tom Sears, and Spc4 Ken Barker among them—and for a while it appeared as if A Company would not find any more until a soldier searching along the eastern edge of the former Fourth Platoon perimeter suddenly exclaimed, "Here's one over here!"

Hidden in the branches of a downed tree, Spc4 Victor Renza heard the A Company soldier shouting. "When I heard him [A Company soldier] say that," said Renza, who had heard other voices that morning though none as distinctly, "I started to yell. He wasn't that far away, but I had to keep yelling so that he could find me." Sgt. Doc Bockover, an A Company medic with the Second Platoon, eventually spotted Renza and, with the help of another A Company soldier, pulled him out of the tree and sat him up. "I kept hearing someone yelling," wrote Bockover, "but I couldn't find him. I told him to keep yelling, and I found him in a bunch of blown trees."[10] Calmly explaining that they were from A Company, Bockover opened Renza's shirt and examined his chest and back. Renza had two puncture wounds in his back—one an entry wound, the other an exit wound—and leeches all over his chest and shoulders.

"You've got two holes in your back," Bockover remarked bluntly, looking over the bullet wounds.

"I *know*," answered Renza.

Bockover, working swiftly, bandaged the gunshot wounds first and then turned his attention to the leeches. Common to the rainforests of the Central Highlands, leeches were a persistent nuisance and a potentially serious medical matter the grunts often remedied with the smoldering end of a cigarette. Lighting a pair of Marlboro cigarettes, Bockover and the other A Company soldier took turns carefully burning the slimy, bloodsucking worms off of Renza's chest, shoulders, and lower legs. The process was hair-raising and painful, but before long the last leech had been burned from his body.

Helped to his feet, Renza walked with the two A Company soldiers around the downed tree and over to the collection point established for the Fourth Platoon survivors. "They brought me over to the other seven survivors," recounted Renza, "and some of the guys looked up at me and said: 'Renza, holy shit! You're still alive!' I just remember asking them what had happened. I couldn't believe it." Renza mumbled a response and gave the assembled survivors a quick once-over. Disheveled and visibly exhausted, the men were lying side by side in a neat row on the jungle floor. Six of the seven had already been bandaged up by the A Company medics. The seventh appeared uninjured. Sitting down beside one of the other survivors, Renza learned that Sgt. Robert Sanzone, the best friend he would ever have, had been killed on the eighteenth.

That afternoon the eight survivors of the Fourth Platoon boarded choppers and flew to the rear. Renza and Cliff Rountree landed at the 18th Surgical Hospital in Pleiku, the first stop on the long road to recovery. For Renza, Rountree, Pfc. Gilbert Nash, Spc4 Tom Sears, and Spc4 Ken Barker, the war was finally over. Heartbreakingly, however, the horrors of May 18, 1967, would revisit them often in the years to come.

On the morning of the nineteenth, Colonel Jackson placed A Company, 1st of the 22nd Infantry, under the operational control of Lieutenant Colonel Gannon's 1-8 Infantry. A Company, 1-22 Infantry arrived at the 1-8 Infantry firebase west of Duc Co at 9:40 A.M. and immediately assumed responsibility for the security of the base, relieving C Company, 1-8 Infantry. Earlier that morning, before the arrival of A Company, 1-22 Infantry, C Company received word that it had been relieved of firebase security duty.[11] Gannon, with C Company now available for commitment elsewhere, directed Capt. Curt Peterson, the company CO, to reinforce B Company, 1-8 Infantry and the battalion Recon Platoon in the field. The first contingent of C Company soldiers was subsequently airlifted from the 1-8 Infantry firebase to the B Company LZ at 9:41 A.M.

Bob Carlson, a young private first class in C Company, jumped out of a slick that morning with another soldier and plopped boots first into a pocket of surprisingly deep, brown-black mud. Carlson had moved from New York to Iowa when he was about fourteen, and when his draft notice arrived in the fall of 1965, he promptly quit his job and "partied for about a month" before he reported for duty. Sinking slowly into the mud, the fun-loving original suddenly seemed far removed from his carefree civilian days. Carlson, now ankle deep in the slop, yanked his boots from the sucking mud and lurched forward onto dry land. *Did I jump out of the wrong side of the helicopter or something?* he wondered, looking down at his mud-splattered boots. Carlson, quickly forgetting the muddy boots clinging to his feet, hurried along and fell in with his platoon.

Wisconsin born and bred, Pfc. Leslie Bellrichard was assigned to C Company in April 1967. Idealistic Bellrichard had envisioned serving in the 1st Cavalry Division and had playfully boasted that he and some of his buddies were "going to write a portion of military history in Vietnam."[12] After about a month in the bush, however, the twenty-five-year old draftee was more interested in surviving than making history. Survival had long been a way of life for Bellrichard. The second youngest in a family of five boys, Leslie had lost his father, Earl Bellrichard, in a truck-train accident when he was scarcely eleven months old. Already fatherless, Leslie would lose his eldest brother, Wayne, the following year when his mother, Lizetta Bellrichard, was struck by a train while driving in their hometown of Janesville, Wisconsin. Tragically the violent collision killed five-year-old Wayne Bellrichard. Andrew Bellrichard, then only four, suffered critical injuries in the crash.

Inconsolable, Lizetta Bellrichard tumbled into a deep depression and her life began to unravel. "My mother couldn't handle it," said Mark Bellrichard, the youngest of the Bellrichard boys. "She started drinking and didn't take very good care of us. Rock County stepped in and took us away from her."[13] Rock County separated the boys, though Mark and Leslie remained together. The pair then bounced around the system, spending time in numerous foster homes before finally landing with Victor and Beryl Bloedel. The Bloedels lived on a farm near Evansville and always treated the boys like family. When Leslie was eleven or twelve, however, he suffered a "nervous breakdown," according to Mark, and was sent off to the Martin Luther Home in Stoughton, Wisconsin.[14] Restless, Leslie eventually dropped out of high school and moved to California to be closer to their birth mother.

Leslie Bellrichard, after earning his GED, went to work as a lathe operator for Lockheed Missile Systems in San Jose, California. Soon after, he began dating a bubbly brunette named Shirley Jean, and in 1962 the happy couple tied the knot. Deeply patriotic, Bellrichard also rediscovered his faith; drafted in 1966, he promptly volunteered for Vietnam. "I'll have to take it one step at a time," he wrote of his decision, "and trust Jesus Christ, my personal Lord and savior, to see me through."[15] No conscientious objector, Bellrichard landed in the B Company LZ on the morning of the nineteenth fully prepared to fight and die for his country and his buddies.

C Company was finally on the ground and in the field by 11:30 A.M. B Company—busy reorganizing, running patrols, and evacuating injured personnel when Capt. Curt Peterson's three platoons were airlifted in—enlarged its existing perimeter to accommodate the new arrivals. Peterson chatted with Captain Sholly, and the two officers quickly organized a single perimeter. Peterson's Third Platoon, meanwhile, spent part of the day operating with a CIDG unit and did not arrive until 2:40 P.M. that afternoon.[16]

Shortly after his lead platoons reported that they had found B Company's Fourth Platoon, Captain Williamson pushed forward with the rest of A Company. Securing the area around the B Company platoon first, Williamson established separate collection points for the dead and wounded. In the meantime, A Company was to search the denuded jungle for B Company soldiers.

Sgt. Jim Peirce, a hardnosed twenty-one-year old original, led his Fourth Platoon, A Company squad through the shallow ravine where the missing B Company platoon had met its fate. Peirce had originally enlisted in the Marines and had planned to leave for boot camp after high school when he injured one of his legs in a car wreck; deemed unfit for duty, he was released from his military obligation and granted an honorable discharge. Nine months later, Peirce, now fully healed, attempted to reenlist but before he could depart for Paris Island his father intervened and had a physician insist that he (Jim) had asthma. The Marine Corps relented and Peirce was again released with an honorable discharge. The Army, curiously enough, drafted Peirce in the fall of 1965 and sent him to the 4th Infantry Division, where he trained for months in A Company's Fourth Platoon—the so-called "weapons platoon"—alongside B Company's Fourth Platoon.[17] "I personally knew a lot of the guys in the Fourth Platoon of Bravo Company," said Peirce. "We used to train with them as mortar platoons, so I knew Sergeant Grandstaff and a lot of those guys." Knowing that some of the mangled bodies strewn about in that shell-shattered ravine were men he trained with made the carnage all the more difficult for Peirce to swallow.

Circling back around, Pierce eventually found the remains of an unusually muscular soldier. Pierce, catching his breath, realized almost immediately that the powerfully built torso lying on the jungle floor belonged to Sergeant Grandstaff. Upset, he walked a ways and saw what looked like a slab of skin stuck to a tree. Moving closer he noticed that the skin had the words "Born to Lose" tattooed across it. The tattoo, which had been torn from a human body and hurled violently against the tree, belonged to Pfc. Michael Sessa, Sergeant Grandstaff's erstwhile RTO. "I was stunned when I saw it," Peirce admitted. "My initial reaction was that a B-40 rocket or a machine gun had torn it off and had thrown it onto that tree. B-40 rockets can just obliterate a body. I will always remember it, though, that skin from the guy's arm stuck on a tree."

Troops from A Company's Second Platoon, meanwhile, began sweeping the jungle around the perimeter. Sgt. Ron Snyder, the acting platoon leader that morning, believes that rank played a role in the decision to send the Second Platoon, and not one of the other three platoons, to search the surrounding jungle. "I guess I have the feeling that I was picked because I was only an E5, basically a nobody," said Snyder. "That's just my personal feeling—that if I hadn't been an E5, they wouldn't have sent my platoon out there. I could be 100 percent dead wrong on that, but it was just my personal feeling at the time." Irritated, Snyder eased his squads through the first few sweeps around the perimeter. Farther out, the jungle grew noticeably thicker, increasing—in Snyder's mind—the likelihood of enemy contact. The tension, as the platoon broadened the search into the dense foliage beyond, was almost palpable. "Having to be out there, and then thinking that the reason we had been picked was because of me, made it a little tougher," Snyder continued. "If any of my guys had been killed while we were out there searching for bodies, I wouldn't have been able to help feeling responsible."

A squad leader in the Second Platoon, Sgt. Frank Patton paused and inhaled the sticky Highland air. Patton was born in Mississippi and lived in the state for a time before moving with his family to Arkansas. Eager for something more out of life, he signed up in November 1965 with the expectation of entering the Army on a delayed enlistment. Patton returned to the recruiter's office in Little Rock the following day to complete the process, only to learn that his enlistment had not been delayed. "I don't think so, buddy boy," a crusty sergeant told him gruffly. "You're going to be on that two o'clock plane this afternoon." Ushered aboard a commercial aircraft that afternoon, he was flown to Fort Polk, Louisiana, and later to Fort Lewis, Washington, for basic training.

Patton exhaled and immediately recalled a familiar scent. The NVA had been in the area. "In an area like that, you could *smell* them," explained Patton. "Anytime you went in an area and came across a strange odor—we knew we stunk but you got used to it—you just *knew.*" *Wherever they were now,* thought Patton as he crept anxiously along, *they must have been around here for quite a while.*

Second Platoon, moving cautiously through the undergrowth, swept the jungle in wider and wider arcs around the missing B Company platoon and along the way stumbled upon a number of well-worn, high-speed trails. The North Vietnamese had been in the area and in large numbers but, much to the relief of Sergeant Snyder, who resented the fact that his guys were risking their backsides on a mission he believed had everything to do with rank, the only NVA his tightly wound platoon encountered that morning were already dead. The platoon also found dead Americans, including one man who had seemingly been killed some distance from the rest. "The very last guy we found was way up the [dry] creek [bed] kind of in a hole, on our side of the creek—on the same side that the 'lost platoon' was at," said Snyder. "I have no idea who that was. I'm not sure if we ever checked, or whatever. But he must have been on flank or on point or something, because he was a *ways* from the rest [of the Fourth Platoon, B Company bodies]. Of course, you didn't have to go far to get lost because that was about the thickest jungle I'd ever seen."

With one man still unaccounted for, Snyder and the Second Platoon scoured the bush some more, venturing farther and farther out with each succeeding loop around the "lost platoon." The missing soldier, the grunts would eventually learn, was Pfc. Joe DeLong, the young replacement to whom Spc4 Victor Renza had handed his trusty M-60 machine gun back in April. DeLong, however, was nowhere in sight. It was time to come in. The Second Platoon, Snyder decided, had been out there long enough.

"Sir, we've gone farther and farther out," he informed Captain Williamson over the radio, "and there are no more bodies out here."

Williamson finally relented. "If you're sure there's nobody left, come on in."

Suspending the search, Snyder gathered up his squads and returned to the A Company security perimeter. Tragically the body of Pfc. Joe DeLong was never recovered. Postwar investigations into the incident suggest that DeLong was captured by the North Vietnamese after the battle on May 18, 1967, and was later killed while trying to escape from captivity. Former North Vietnamese official Cao Tien Phiem, for example, told American investigators in 1996 that he interrogated DeLong, whom he described as a short, brown-skinned man with a small build. Phiem, then an interpreter in the Central Highlands Front Enemy Proselytizing Office (EPO), claimed he received word in early 1968 that DeLong had stolen an AK-47 and had escaped from a POW camp in Cambodia. Soldiers from a Front military-political school, according to Phiem, hunted DeLong down and killed him.[18] Unfortunately Phiem did not know where the soldiers had buried his remains.

Eight survivors, including Pfcs. Robert Young and Grover Harrison, the latter a young African American soldier who had been shot in the head, were found in the former Fourth Platoon perimeter. The men were examined, treated, and then escorted to the collection point organized by Captain Williamson. With the B Company wounded present and accounted for, the A Company mission shifted from rescuing the survivors of the ill-fated platoon to recovering the dead.

Pfc. Landis Bargatze, twenty-five, of Nashville, Tennessee, stared at the severed limbs scattered across the jungle floor on the morning of the nineteenth and gasped in disbelief. Known affectionately as "the Old Man" within his Fourth Platoon, A Company squad, Bargatze had worked in a Chevy dealership and for a printing press company, boxing now and then at a local Boys Club, before he received his draft notice in October 1966. Bargatze had also attended Middle Tennessee State University but became, by his own admission, too immersed in "the social life aspect of things" and flunked out after his freshman year. Humbled, he left school, returned home, and went to work. Maturing immeasurably in the succeeding years, he entered the Army in 1966 a man, physically and mentally. Bargatze breezed through basic training and AIT, the latter down at Fort Polk's famed "Tigerland" training grounds in Louisiana, and, like many replacements, completed his in-country processing at the 90th Replacement Depot near Bien Hoa prior to joining A Company in April of 1967. A quick study, Bargatze developed into a reliable soldier under the watchful eye of his squad leader, Sgt. Jim Peirce.

Hardened by months of training in the States and four long weeks in the Highlands, Bargatze grabbed a poncho that morning and, surveying the embankment above the dry creek bed, looked for a body to bag. As gingerly as circumstances would permit, he helped lift the body of a dead B Company trooper onto the poncho and assisted in carrying the man over to the collection point established for the dead. Bargatze and the other A Company grunts stacked the body and then headed back out for another KIA. The cloying tropical air carried with it the unmistakable scent of death, adding to the sense of despair hanging over them. Some of the bodies, Bargatze noted gratefully, were still in one piece. Others had to be put back together again to ensure that every KIA departed the field with the correct number of arms and legs.

Bargatze and a fellow grunt collected up the remains of another deceased soldier a short while later and slung what was left of the man, poncho and all, beside the other dead bodies."You could smell the gunpowder—that sulfur-like smell—and you could smell that stench of death, even though it was the next day [and] it was just a terrible thing to see, having to stack our dead on top of each other like that," recalled Bargatze. "It may have been the lowest point of my life. Death was just *everywhere.* We had ponchos to put the dead in, and there were half-bodies and body parts everywhere. One skull just came apart like a pumpkin. Some guys had taken rounds in the midsection, so you had to be careful that their intestines didn't fall out when you moved them. Or else you were putting different body parts in a poncho without ever being sure [if] they belonged to the same body. It was just tough, that's all."

Nearby Spc4 Jay "Joby" McAulay retrieved the arms and legs of a fallen soldier and carefully arranged them in a body bag. Piecing together a complete body, without inadvertently mismatching any of the parts, was in some instances exceedingly difficult. "We tried to gather enough parts to make a complete body—two arms, two legs, a head and torso—and then we put them together, whether they actually went together or not," McAulay remembered ruefully. "I hope the families understand that we were doing the best we could, considering we didn't have a lot of time and didn't know if the gooks were still out there." Earlier in the month, McAulay was back in Pleiku, running patrols and re-acclimating himself to life in the Highlands after a brief bout with malaria. McAulay welcomed the brief respite, but he yearned to return to A Company and his buddies in the Fourth Platoon. The gung-ho twenty-year-old original had rejoined the company expecting to fight, not rummage through the underbrush "collecting body parts and putting them in bags."

A Company eventually bagged and stacked all of the dead from B Company's Fourth Platoon. Numbed by the experience, many of the A Company troopers shut down emotionally and withdrew behind the unfeeling, uncaring, "don't mean nothing" attitude the grunts often adopted to avoid internalizing the horrors of war. For some, however, the experience was life-altering. "My life has never been the same since then," Landis Bargatze conceded. "It changed the way I viewed life and death. I began to feel that, if you died the way these guys did, there wasn't anything that came after. You were just dead—period—and there wasn't anything that was going to come afterward that was going to make it any better. You were just dead. When you're growing up and attending church and listening about all of the good things to come in the afterlife, well, none of that means shit out there in the jungle when you're putting pieces of people in goddamn ponchos."

A Company, after the return of Sergeant Snyder's Second Platoon, finished up the recovery phase of the relief effort and began the process of evacuating the dead and wounded. First Platoon, under the command of Lieutenant Rogers, maintained perimeter security during the evacuation phase while the Second hacked an LZ out of the jungle. Greeting the incoming dustoffs, troopers from the Second and Third Platoons loaded the surviving members of B Company's Fourth Platoon, and by early afternoon all eight had been medevaced out. The bodies of the deceased, most wrapped or covered in ponchos, went out next. Pfc. Bill Dobbie groaned as he and Spc4 Bob Feigan, a powerfully built twenty-two-year-old Second Platoon original, lugged the body of a large African American soldier toward an awaiting slick. Tall and of considerable weight, the soldier hung over the stretcher Dobbie and Feigan had fashioned out of a poncho and some cut tree limbs.

"Damn, he's heavy!" moaned Dobbie, straining under the weight of the dead man.

"Well," Feigan began matter-of-factly, "I always figure that if I can help someone who can't help themselves then maybe the Good Lord will take care of me."

Poor, black, and fatherless from the age of six on, Feigan struggled mightily growing up in rural Alabama. Feigan picked cotton as a boy to help make ends meet, and he occasionally skipped school to work in the fields so that he and his four siblings could purchase clothes and books. There never seemed to be enough time in the day to do all that was required of him but he stuck it out, balancing work and school when many of his peers would have quit, and he eventually graduated from high school in 1963. Profoundly spiritual, the hardworking draftee drew strength from his faith, regardless of whether he was in the fields of Alabama or the jungles of Vietnam. "I talked to the Lord every day [in Vietnam]," said Feigan proudly, "and I prayed for the Lord to carry me through."

Feigan and Dobbie loaded the black soldier onto a whirring chopper and scurried out of the way. Both men then went back to find another body to load. The process was utterly dehumanizing. Dobbie, at one point, had to scoop brain matter off the ground to ensure that it flew home with the right body. Later, while assisting in loading the body onto an awaiting slick, he glanced down and noticed that some of the man's brains had fallen out of the poncho and onto the jungle floor. "I was thinking to myself 'Son-of-a-bitch! I've got to pick this guy's brains up *again?*'" said Dobbie. "I couldn't just leave it there, though." Bending down, Dobbie collected what he could and stuffed the slimy mess back inside the poncho. "I told the guys on the chopper, 'Hey, this goes with him,'" Dobbie added. "I just felt it should go home with him, with the body.".

Just kids themselves, the young A Company troopers, Private First Class Dobbie included, treated and evacuated the B Company dead with extraordinary dignity. "Company A will never know how much a recovered body means to a family," said Betty Workman Sturgeon, sister of Fourth Platoon KIA James Workman. "It is the beginning of closure and grief. It is a symbol of saying to the world, 'This is my boy. He did exist. He has died too young. See what war is capable of?'"[19] That afternoon, as the last of the Fourth Platoon, B Company dead were evacuated from the field, all that remained of their desperate last stand were bits and pieces of discarded equipment, scores of spent shell casings, and splotches of dried blood.

On July 10, 1969, a little over two years after the battle on May 18, 1967, Bruce Alan Grandstaff was posthumously awarded the Medal of Honor. Sgt. Phillip Venekamp, a fire team leader in the Fourth Platoon, received the Silver Star, posthumously, for aiding wounded comrades and eliminating an NVA position with a hand grenade during the fighting. A Silver Star was also awarded (posthumously) to Sgt. Leland Thompson, the intrepid forward observer attached to the Fourth Platoon that fateful afternoon.[20] Thompson received the commendation for capably directing artillery fire, some of it after he had been wounded, around the doomed platoon. Sgts. Robert Sanzone and James Foreman, meanwhile, were awarded (posthumously) the Distinguished Service Cross, the nation's second-highest award for bravery. Pfc. Michael Sessa and a number of other Fourth Platoon soldiers, moreover, received Bronze Stars (posthumously) for their actions during the battle. And it could certainly be argued that Spc4 Victor Renza, Spc4 Tom Sears, and Pfc. Cliff Rountree deserved similar recognition for selflessly placing the welfare of their comrades in A Company above their own on the evening of the eighteenth.

Few platoons have ever been so decorated. Encircled, outnumbered, and under intense assault, the Fourth Platoon beat back two NVA attempts to overrun the platoon perimeter and, despite increasingly overwhelming odds, fought courageously until the bitter end. Medals and citations, however, should never obscure the awful truth that the Fourth Platoon had been utterly destroyed. Of the twenty-eight men in or attached to the platoon on the morning of the eighteenth, only eight would survive the daylong ordeal. Nineteen of their comrades would perish in the vicious, close-quarters fighting and one, Pfc. Joe DeLong, would disappear altogether, never to return.[21] No medal, no matter how prestigious, could ever fill the void left by the dead—the lost sons and brothers, fathers and uncles who perished that day.

Numbingly final, that loss—that sobering realization of what might have been, what *should* have been for the men who were taken much too soon—was felt first by the survivors of the Fourth Platoon. "I knew that Bob [Sanzone] was dead," said Spc4 Victor Renza, "but I just couldn't bring myself to see him. It wasn't just that we were

Army buddies, but the families started to get to know one another through us. My sisters wrote Bob. Bob wrote my sisters. Charlie Ranello's younger sister wrote to me. I wrote to her. We were like relatives, and by the time we left for Vietnam, that was the level we were on." Renza's parents, in fact, would attend the funeral of Sergeant Sanzone back home on Long Island.

For the rest of B Company, news of who had made it did not reach the grunts until A Company radioed over the roster numbers of the Fourth Platoon survivors. "I was listening for Jim's [James Foreman's] number," said Sgt. Dick Surface, an RTO in B Company, "but I didn't hear it." Surface wept inconsolably. "James Foreman, from my hometown, was my best friend," he continued bitterly. "We were drafted the same day in 1965. We did everything together. Why couldn't I have been with him? I felt I let him down. Maybe we could have done something different to survive had I been there with him."[22] Surface left the field on the twenty-third and flew home to Indiana on a thirty-day compassion leave to attend the closed-casket funeral of his best friend.

Betty Workman Sturgeon glanced out the window one Saturday afternoon in May of 1967 and stared, spellbound, as a man in an Army dress uniform exited a vehicle parked outside the Indiana apartment she and her mother were living in at the time. "My heart began to pound," recalled Workman Sturgeon. "I clung to the thought that perhaps he was just injured badly. Military families all know what it means when a full-dress-uniformed person arrives at your home."[23] Spc4 James Workman, her beloved twenty-one-year-old brother, the good-natured teenage boy who had taken her out in his prized '57 Chevy for milkshakes and cheeseburgers on the weekends, had been killed in Vietnam.

So, too, had Sgt. James Burch, a handsome twenty-year-old farm boy from the same small county in Indiana. Burch had grown up a few miles from Workman, toiling away on the farm and honing his skills on the basketball court. A school-boy standout, he had played for Freedom High School and was a junior on the team that knocked off mighty Spencer High, the top team back then in that part of the state. Duty bound, yet more concerned about his buddies than any crusade to stop Communist expansion in Southeast Asia, Sergeant Burch died with them and *for* them in that fateful patch of jungle near the Cambodian border. "It wasn't about apple pie, or Mom and Pop, or fighting against Communism," said Mary Wheeler, Burch's younger sister. "Jim was fighting for his buddies out there that day. World War II had heroes before they were named, thanks to John Wayne and the movies. It was a way of taking the country to war with the troops. Factories retooled and people sacrificed to help the boys. No one remembered to do that when we sent our boys to Vietnam. We sent them off alone, with only each other and their families back home to support them. They still take care of each other, and the memories of those they lost. Together, with the families, we will make sure no one forgets."

Heart-wrenchingly, some of the families of the fallen and many of the B Company veterans will always wonder if the Fourth Platoon could have been spared if it had not chased the North Vietnamese that fateful morning. "They [NVA] were like choreographers," said Spc4 Victor Renza. "If you took one step to the left, they moved in between you and the guy next to you. They led us right where they wanted us, and we walked right in. We never should have followed them." Cliff Rountree agreed with Renza. A fellow survivor, Rountree admired the NVA's ability to manipulate the battlefield, particularly at the small-unit level, and believes that the platoon should not have pursued them so aggressively.

Colonel Jackson, meanwhile, concluded that the Fourth Platoon had been lured into an all-too-familiar trap. "The pattern the enemy followed was simple," noted the 1st Brigade commander. "We would move with patrols in all directions over rugged terrain. It's slow and tedious and hard on our troopers. Perhaps one platoon would sight two or three NVA. There would be a quick and brief exchange of fire. The enemy would beat it down the trail. Then there would be a second sighting. Perhaps eight or ten or even fifteen enemy. To new officers and men this might appear that we had them outnumbered. Actually, it was the old sucker treatment for it invariably happened that 15 or 20 minutes [later] the lead patrol or platoon would find itself under fire from three sides. The other platoons would begin to move toward the action and they too might be jumped." Nor was it uncommon, Jackson observed, for the NVA to have a 3:1 advantage on the ground.[24]

Nevertheless, it is not altogether clear that the battle would have turned out any differently if the Fourth Platoon had remained behind with the Second and Third Platoons. "First of all, there's nothing to say that if the Fourth hadn't chased the NVA that the whole company wouldn't have run into an ambush that day," said 1st Lt. Larry Rodabaugh. "In retrospect, when this whole thing started with three NVA coming down that trail, the thought should have crossed my mind that they just might have been the point element for a larger unit. But it was a tough situation and a really tough decision for Allen, because you want prisoners and you want information."

Haunted by the loss of so many men that day, Rodabaugh wonders if B Company would have been better served putting a couple of platoons on-line, astride the high-speed trail the Fourth Platoon eventually followed. The platoons could have then waited, machine guns positioned at either end of the two-platoon line, for the NVA to come to them. "Neither I, nor Aronhalt, nor Allen stopped to think—maybe with my Second Platoon on-line, we should put Chuck's [Lieutenant Aronhalt] platoon on-line and then just sit there quietly and wait," said Rodabaugh. "There would have been a bunch of them coming down that trail. If we had done that, we could have taken out a *ton* of them." Interestingly, Captain Sholly acknowledged that if he had been on the ground with B Company that morning he would have considered moving two platoons on-line, as Rodabaugh suggested, in order to put "the preponderance of [the company's] firepower a little more forward." Sholly, however, stands by the decisions the company made in his absence.

Significantly, none of the B Company survivors dispute the extraordinary courage displayed by Plt. Sgt. Bruce Grandstaff after the Fourth Platoon was encircled. Fearless in battle, Grandstaff fought tenaciously and even began *taunting* the North Vietnamese. "When I spoke to him near the end of that thing, he sounded angry not afraid," Sholly recalled. "He sounded like a man who was pissed off that he was about to die, and he seemed determined to take as many of them with him as he could." Sholly added that he and Lieutenant Colonel Gannon agreed that Grandstaff's actions merited the Medal of Honor.[25] On that point, the opinion of the survivors is virtually unanimous.[26]

Sweeping the battlefield on the morning and afternoon of the nineteenth, the three companies of Lieutenant Colonel Gannon's 1-8 Infantry reportedly counted a total of 119 NVA dead. B Company, by comparison, had suffered twenty-nine KIAs (and one MIA) in the fighting, good for a fairly robust 4:1 kill ratio. As always, however, that figure presumes that the enemy body count had not been inflated, either arbitrarily or through counting errors, but instead represents an accurate measure of the damage inflicted on the North Vietnamese.[27] In this instance, it is entirely possible that the body count approached or even exceeded 119, given the North Vietnamese practice of removing friendly KIAs from the battlefield to conceal the extent of their losses. The North Vietnamese, moreover, had ample time on the eighteenth to evacuate their dead. B Company, incidentally, recovered two AK-47s, an SKS rifle, an RPG with four or five unexpended rounds, lots of small-arms ammo, and a number of Chicom grenades as well. A shoulder board with a yellow stripe down the middle, two stars and a set of crossed cannons, presumably from the uniform of an NVA artillery soldier, was also found among the battle debris.[28]

Whatever the final body count, most of the NVA dead found on the nineteenth resembled the rank and file of a formation that had only recently returned to South Vietnam from Communist base areas in Cambodia. Clothed in clean, khaki-colored uniforms, the North Vietnamese appeared well fed, well groomed, and in reasonably good physical condition. Morale had also been quite high, as was sometimes the case with NVA units fresh out of Cambodia. Similarly, the highly disciplined, well-coordinated manner in which the North Vietnamese operated in battle on the eighteenth betrayed a level of fieldcraft that could not have been attained without professional training, training incidentally that would have been more difficult to conduct on the South Vietnamese side of the border.[29]

Materials recovered after the battle revealed that the North Vietnamese belonged to a battalion from the 32nd NVA Regiment. Formally established in North Vietnam on March 20, 1964, the 32nd consisted of three battalions and was composed initially of officers and men selected from three regular army units that had service records dating back to the war against the French. After training in the North for more than four months the regiment then started south, down the Ho Chi Minh trail, in August to reinforce Communist units in South Vietnam. Previously Hanoi had only sent down "independent battalions" or "cadre framework units" of ethnic Southerners who had regrouped to North Vietnam following the Geneva Accords in 1954. Thus the 32nd enjoyed the unique distinction of being the first "full-strength main force regiment" the North dispatched to fight on the battlefields of South Vietnam.[30]

A veteran of the war in the Highlands, the 32nd collided, famously, with the U.S. 1st Cavalry Division in the Ia Drang Valley in 1965, and elements of the regiment later opposed the 4th Infantry Division during Operations Paul Revere IV and Sam Houston. Battle-hardened, the 32nd's three subordinate battalions were well trained, well armed, and tactically proficient. Indeed, according to the authors of a 1-8 Infantry report, the battalion B Company engaged on the eighteenth had "made maximum use of terrain, cover, and concealment" and employed its mortars and machine guns "to maximum advantage."[31]

Ominously, at least for the hard-pressed 1-8 Infantry troopers chasing the enemy on the Cambodian border, the sudden appearance of the 32nd in the Ia Tchar Valley, coupled with the May 1 clash northwest of Duc Co involving elements of the 66th NVA Regiment, confirmed that the 1st NVA Division had reentered South Vietnam in strength. General Man and Colonel An had "lit the fuse" in western Pleiku Province, and now it was up to the 4th Infantry Division to respond.

8 NIGHT MOVES

Suspended momentarily in the sultry midmorning air, the C&C Huey slipped below the jungle canopy and glided gracefully down into the B Company, 1-8 Infantry landing zone. Lieutenant Colonel Gannon and Colonel Jackson, the 1st Brigade CO, exited the craft in a hurry and immediately looked for Captain Sholly, the senior officer on the ground. The joint B-C Company perimeter bustled with activity, but word eventually got around to the troops that both the battalion and brigade brass had come out for a visit.

Ostensibly Colonel Jackson had decided to visit the 1-8 Infantry on the morning of the nineteenth to confer with his battalions in the field, but the trip was as much a morale-building exercise as it was an effort to assess the situation on the ground. "Jackson was a soldier's soldier. He was a good guy, and he came out to see what his battalion and his companies had undergone," said Captain Sholly. "Part of his visit was to obtain that information firsthand, but [it] was also to 'show the flag' and show that people cared about us still, even at the brigade level. That's what commanders do. The meeting, as far as intelligence and everything else was concerned—that had all been exchanged on the radio and in the reports. At that level, the brigade commander wants to see what's going on, but really he has very little input [down] at that level of tactics."

Gannon and Sholly did most of the talking during the meeting, with the former assuring the latter that he would continue to have all the firepower he needed to get the job done. B Company had performed well in difficult circumstances, Gannon remarked encouragingly, but the battle had only just begun. "The meeting that we had was really just to say—you guys did a really great job, sorry about your losses, however we're going to continue the march and continue to chase the bastards," recalled Sholly. "Once you're in contact, you don't want to really break contact with the enemy. You want to follow him up and continue to do bad things to him." Gannon and Jackson agreed that the 1-8 Infantry would find, fix, and destroy the enemy in the days ahead.

If the North Vietnamese wanted to fight along the border, General Peers now seemed happy to oblige. The threat of a major enemy offensive had pulled Peers to the border, despite his initial plan to counter the North Vietnamese after they had pushed deeper into South Vietnam, and he was determined to find them before the 1-8 Infantry returned to Jackson Hole. "We were to seek out the enemy and destroy him, driving him back into Cambodia," said Brig. Gen. Glenn D. Walker, then the assistant division commander (ADC) of the 4th Infantry Division. "Once we found him, we were to seize the initiative and aggressively attack him. Because he was so difficult to find, we would fight him anywhere to include the border area. We wanted to please [General] Larsen and at that stage of the war had no qualms of engaging him close to the border."[1] Peers believed that General Larsen preferred fighting "as close to the border as possible."[2]

Larsen was certainly aware of the dangers associated with operating along the border. There, in double and triple canopy jungle within walking distance of their Cambodian sanctuaries, the North Vietnamese had been able to attack isolated American companies again and again. Yet, like most of the Army's commanders in South Vietnam, Larsen understood that the United States could not simply cede the Central Highlands to the North Vietnamese and withdraw into defensive enclaves on the coast. "I can see almost no psychological or military advantage to a strategy that would intentionally invite the war east towards the coast," Gen. William Westmoreland wrote in 1967. "It would be retrogressive, costly in casualties and refugees, and [would] almost certainly prolong the war."[3] Allied pacification efforts in the densely populated lowlands, where Westmoreland believed the war would ultimately be won, depended in part on an aggressive forward defense in the remote border regions of the country.[4] How far forward depended on the commander. Larsen favored hitting the enemy as soon as he crossed the border. Others preferred more of a defense-in-depth.[5]

Col. James Adamson, commander of the 4th Infantry Division's 2nd Brigade, claimed that General Larsen was also influenced by an incident that occurred in 1966. Speaking at a press conference in Washington, Larsen told reporters that a number of North Vietnamese regiments were operating in Cambodia, an assertion the Department of Defense quickly denied. When he was asked about it later, Larsen replied that he "was not going to question [his] superiors about what they say" and insisted that he had been mistaken.[6] "Instead, he returned to South Vietnam and seemed to have a fixation on the border—'don't let a single NVA into South Vietnam,'" Adamson recalled. "He would prove that the NVA came from Cambodia. General Peers got the message."[7]

Boarding his C&C chopper again later that afternoon, Lieutenant Colonel Gannon flew out for a visit with A Company in the shallow glen to the west of the emerging B-C Company perimeter. On the return flight, the NVA opened fire with an automatic weapon and reportedly wounded three Americans on board, one seriously. Gannon was unharmed. When the incident occurred, sometime around 5:38 P.M., the command ship was apparently in the process of completing a northwest turn from the A Company landing zone.

At approximately 5:30 P.M., shortly before the NVA fired on Lieutenant Colonel Gannon's command and control bird, B Company to the east was hit with a barrage of 82-mm mortar rounds. Captain Sholly responded with air and artillery strikes and the enemy mortar fire, estimated at some twenty-five rounds, suddenly ceased. Silencing the rash of enemy antiaircraft fire that afternoon was another matter altogether, however. Frustratingly Sholly, no matter how adroitly he handled the enormous firepower available to him, could not silence the enemy fire harassing the helicopters shuttling in and out of his one-bird LZ. Nor could the gunships escorting the incoming dustoffs and slicks. Buttonholed by enemy small-arms fire, some of the ships were fortunate to escape the area in one piece.

Spent emotionally and physically, A Company set up for the night along a ridgeline near the former Fourth Platoon, B Company perimeter. A Company's Second Platoon received a new platoon leader—Sgt. Ron Snyder, making good on his upcoming R&R, had hopped aboard an outbound slick earlier in the day—and carried on as usual, too tired to care at that point about the sharp-looking black lieutenant barking out orders. The other three platoons did much the same, and the entire company was dug in before dark.

Preplotted artillery rounds exploded around the A Company perimeter throughout the evening, providing a nominal layer of protection for the huddled-up troopers. Noises other than the familiar whistle of incoming artillery were also heard around the perimeter that night. "We could hear stuff—whether it was pulling away their dead or burying their dead or whatever," said Pfc. Landis Bargatze of the Fourth Platoon. "We weren't entirely sure [what it was], but there was a lot of movement around the area. It was spooky as hell that night." Although unnerving, the sounds did not presage an enemy ground assault. The night, in fact, passed relatively peacefully.

East of the dry creek bed, the combined B-C Company perimeter was shelled by the NVA. Captain Sholly and Captain Peterson, the C Company CO, had established the joint NDP on a ridgeline, and while not indefensible, the position was certainly not immune to attack by indirect fire. Scrambling for cover during the opening volley, Sholly hunkered down and began counting the incoming mortar rounds.

"The brigade log says only twenty-five [mortar rounds] were reported, but I stopped counting after forty," Sholly remarked. "And since we were busy trying to guess which was the right side of a tree to hide behind, we probably didn't report the others." Crouched behind trees or in shallow foxholes, B Company waited anxiously for the barrage to stop.

One by one the enemy rounds landed outside the perimeter, producing—in the end—more sound than fury. Sholly acknowledged, however, that, right up until the time the shelling finally ceased, he and his men experienced a "continuing feeling of fear, anxiety and just plain fright," because none of them ever knew "where the next one was going to land." Sholly and Peterson settled their people down after the mortar barrage and prepared the perimeter for the possibility of an enemy ground assault. Supported by artillery fire, the two companies hunkered down, ready to repulse an enemy ground assault, but the NVA chose not to attack on the evening of the nineteenth.

Patrolling the skies to the west of B and C Companies, a U.S. Air Force pilot observed flashes of light in the jungle below. Concerned, the pilot contacted the 1-8 Infantry to discuss the situation. The exchange could be heard over the radio inside the headquarters of A Company, 1-8 Infantry back at Camp Enari, the official name of the 4th Infantry Division base camp. Pfc. Tom Carty, an A Company RTO in the room at the time, downed a can of beer and listened in. Carty had been in the field, helping to police up the Fourth Platoon, B Company ambush site, when he happened upon the headless body of Pfc. Michael Sessa and "just kind of doubled over." Traumatized, Carty admittedly "couldn't function after that" and was eventually sent back to Camp Enari later that afternoon, where he then overheard the conversation between the pilot and the 1-8 Infantry. "I heard a pilot talking to battalion—I can only assume it was to the colonel [Lieutenant Colonel Gannon]—and he was saying that he could see flashes at such and such coordinates and that he could take them out," recalled Carty. "That pilot was not given permission to do so, though, because he was advised that the coordinates were in Cambodia. Our guys were taking rounds, but we couldn't bomb them back. And we were sacrificing people for *this?*"

Disturbingly, the incident reflected the farcical constraints imposed on American arms operating near the border. Visible from the air, the flashes of light on the night of the nineteenth indicated the presence of North Vietnamese forces in the jungle below, yet the pilot could not strike because American policy at the time restricted the use of *offensive* force on Cambodian territory. Washington, implausibly enough, continued to maintain the façade of Cambodian neutrality, and as a consequence of that public posture, American forces were compelled to extend undue deference to Cambodian territorial sovereignty. Hanoi, however, imposed no such restraints on the NVA. NVA transit routes, training camps, and base areas were all established on

Cambodian territory, often with the tacit approval of Cambodia's mercurial dictator, Prince Norodom Sihanouk. North Vietnamese troops, moreover, moved back and forth across the border at will.[8]

That one side was uncompromisingly committed to victory, irrespective of an arbitrary line in the jungle, was evident, even to a distraught private downing beers in the rear.

North Vietnamese mortars, fired from a location roughly five hundred meters to the northwest of the joint American perimeter, shelled B Company at 5:13 A.M. on the morning of the twentieth. None of the fifteen to twenty 82-mm rounds landed inside the perimeter. Two hours later, at approximately 7:25 A.M., a C Company LP observed three North Vietnamese soldiers moving north. Spotted in the jungle approximately one hundred meters to the east, the enemy soldiers were dressed in green uniforms and were observed carrying weapons of some sort. The Americans opened fire but could not confirm if they had killed or wounded any of the three.[9] Meanwhile, to the west, A Company radioed in and reported that there had been little enemy activity.

Following a second NVA mortar attack—ten rounds, none of which landed inside the American perimeter, were fired in the direction of B Company just after 10 A.M.—B and C Companies began preparing for the long day ahead. Determined to find, fix, and destroy the NVA in his area of operations, Lieutenant Colonel Gannon directed his three companies to sweep west to a nearby ridge after a short artillery preparation. The three companies were to then turn north and advance on to a predetermined location. Artillery prep would also precede the push north. A and C Companies, under the commands of Captain Williamson and Captain Peterson, respectively, were to spearhead the effort and advance abreast at the head of a two up, one back formation. B Company, meanwhile, would pull up the rear.

Badly battered on the afternoon of the eighteenth, B Company had regrouped largely on the strength of its platoon-level leadership and the addition of the battalion Reconnaissance Platoon. "On the seventeenth, I had one hundred and sixty [men] total strength on the books with one hundred and forty guys in the field," wrote Captain Sholly. "On the nineteenth, not counting the Recon Platoon, I had something like seventy-seven—a 45 percent casualty rate. Because of my insistence on the leaders exercising the chain of command and training their replacements, even though we had lost the Fourth Platoon, the company was just as experienced and strong as it had been on the seventeenth. My platoon leaders were 1st Lt. Cary Allen for the First Platoon, Sgt. 1st Class [Alhandro] Yuson for the Second Platoon, Sgt. 1st Class [Felipe] Morales for the Third Platoon. As far as experience, Yuson and Morales were outstanding NCOs and were both battle-hardened veterans who knew what they were doing and just as importantly, knew how I operated." Yuson, as if to illustrate the point, would later receive the Silver Star for his leadership in the Second Platoon on the eighteenth.

Allen, Morales, and Yuson commanded a handful of outstanding squad leaders between them, none more so than SSgt. Frankie Molnar. A freewheeling country boy from Logan County, West Virginia, Molnar had hitchhiked with a friend to Fresno, California, after high school and once there had moved in with his older brother, Paul. Partying as often as he could, Molnar soaked up the California social scene and looked for work. With steady jobs hard to come by, he enlisted in the Army in 1963 and served a three-year hitch, spending part of it overseas in Germany. Molnar left the Army after his enlistment ended and moved to New Brunswick, New Jersey, where his widowed mother had previously relocated. Discouraged by the employment market in New Brunswick, he eventually re-upped before his Army reenlistment bonus expired. Molnar was subsequently assigned to the 4th Infantry Division, and he arrived in Fort Lewis in time to deploy with the division to Vietnam.

Molnar, then an E5, served as the communications sergeant in B Company, 1-8 Infantry. The position, unfortunately, could not accommodate a rank above E5, meaning that Molnar had to decide whether to stay put, and postpone the prospect of a promotion indefinitely, or leave the company and seek an opening and the opportunity for advancement elsewhere. Molnar, not wishing to leave the company, requested a transfer out of the communications section prior to leaving for Vietnam. Reassigned to the Third Platoon, he was promoted to staff sergeant (E6) in early November 1966 and placed in charge of a squad. The following March, Molnar would earn a Bronze Star for his actions during the fight in the Plei Doc.[10]

Molnar spent time with his wife Sharon and their baby girl while on leave in early May and then flew back to Vietnam, rejoining B Company in the field on the fifteenth. In April, before flying up to Canada to see his wife, Molnar had visited his brother Paul in California. Things were *bad* over there, he told his brother solemnly. The fighting was fierce at times, and good men were being killed and maimed. Over there it was increasingly becoming a question of *when* and not *if* he would be killed or wounded, and he wanted some assurances from Paul to help put his mind at ease. "If I don't come back," he began delicately, broaching a subject his brother Paul had probably hoped to avoid, "will you take care of my family?"

Reverberating through the jungle, the preplanned artillery preparation commenced on schedule at 11:59 A.M. Soon after, the three line companies (A, B, C Companies) of the 1-8 Infantry saddled up and marched off toward the first objective of the day, an otherwise unremarkable ridgeline to the west. By 12:33 P.M. the three companies had swept the ridge and, following another short artillery preparation, had begun moving north.[11] On the lookout for North Vietnamese troops, camps, and weapons caches, the companies discovered additional evidence of enemy activity in the area. B Company, for example, found fifteen Chicom stick grenades, approximately forty pounds of rice, and sufficient clothing for several individuals around 1 P.M. Tallied up and reported, the enemy grenades and supplies were then swiftly destroyed.[12] C Company, meanwhile, found five unused 82-mm mortar round fuses, as well as two enemy mortar positions located along a northwest-southeast trail.

Finding no enemy troops to fight, the three companies swept onward through the dense jungle. Shortly before 3 P.M., however, C Company observed a lone North Vietnamese soldier in the jungle and opened fire.[13] The soldier, most likely a route watcher dispatched to track the American companies, fled to the west.[14] C Company swept the area where the incident occurred but reported no sign of the enemy soldier or his parent unit. Cautiously the three companies then advanced, more or less on-line, up the slope of a modestly steep ridge. B Company, advancing on the far left flank, fixed bayonets. "We were all pissed off," recalled Captain Sholly, "and we were looking for those guys [NVA]." C Company, under the command of Captain Peterson, anchored the center of the line to Sholly's right while A Company, led by Captain Williamson, clambered up the slope on the right flank of the formation.

Progress was slow but steady as the troops pushed up the side of the ridge. Reaching the top in relatively good order, the three companies then followed the ridgeline for some distance before ambling down into a shallow draw. Barely breaking stride, the Americans scaled the small knoll on the other side of the draw and stumbled, unexpectedly, on an abandoned NVA base area. The time was ten past three in the afternoon.

Large enough to accommodate a large enemy unit, the camp sat on the summit of the knoll and contained fifty well-dug fighting holes, some neatly constructed with overhead cover, arranged in a defensive perimeter. Three mortar positions, each facing east, were found in the perimeter, along with an area that apparently served as a fire direction center (FDC). Poking around the enemy camp, the Americans found the frame of a U.S.-issued rucksack and fifteen empty 82-mm fuse containers.[15]

The three companies eventually pushed on down the ridgeline but, with fatigue setting in and dusk descending swiftly on the western Highlands, the sweep soon ended and the search for a suitable NDP began. Captain Sholly suggested that the companies return to the NVA camp on the small knoll. The ridgeline offered no immediate alternative, and the rapidly diminishing daylight ensured that the companies would have little time to establish a better position anywhere else. The NVA position was also situated on high ground, Sholly reminded the other two company commanders, and it contained a number of serviceable fighting holes that would require very little if any additional digging. "The fact is that it was late in the day, and it was an excellent defensive position," said Sholly. "The overriding concern was that we didn't have the time to dig the holes as deep as we would have otherwise. And it was on top of a hill. It was the best defensible terrain we had found." Peterson and Williamson concurred with Sholly, and the three company commanders informed Lieutenant Colonel Gannon of their decision.

Gannon and the battalion S3 objected to the proposed location. Certain that the North Vietnamese would know the precise coordinates of the position, the exact configuration of the perimeter, and the most auspicious avenues of approach, Gannon expressed surprise that his company commanders would choose an abandoned enemy camp to spend the night. The NVA typically maintained a network of temporary camps, and they possessed intimate details about the layout of each. Consequently, if the companies were to establish a battalion NDP in one of these camps, the NVA would enjoy a significant tactical advantage in the event of an attack. It was as if the companies were asking to set up in the belly of the beast. The battalion S3 agreed. Together, the three company commanders continued to lobby on behalf of the enemy camp, and in the end Gannon reluctantly agreed to the arrangement. A, B, and C Companies, however, were to set up for the night in one large perimeter.

Two hundred meters long by two hundred and fifty meters wide, and approximately eight hundred to one thousand meters northwest of where the engagement on the eighteenth had taken place, the American perimeter sat atop a knoll above a narrow draw.[16] A Company occupied the western and northern sides of the perimeter, opposite a modestly thick tangle of trees and underbrush. B Company manned the south side, overlooking the draw and a small, wooded hill. To the left of B Company, on the eastern and northern sides of the battalion perimeter, Captain Peterson and his C Company troopers took up positions facing the long, tree-lined eastern slope of the main north-south ridge.

Settling in before sundown, the three companies quickly converted the abandoned NVA camp into a well-defended NDP. The troops shoveled out existing holes, dug new ones, and cleared fields of fire. Trip flares and Claymore mines were placed in front of friendly positions, and small teams of men from each of the companies were selected for LP duty. On the western side of the perimeter, Captain Williamson toured the positions held by A Company. "We had a couple of replacements, and one thing that I always told the troops when we stopped was that they needed to dig in and clean their weapons," said Williamson. "So I had gone out to check the perimeter and there were a couple of new guys who had dug their hole about eight or nine inches deep. I told those guys that that hole was not going to cut it, and that they were to dig that hole until I told them to quit." Chastened by Williamson's pointed remarks, the two replacements grabbed their entrenching tools and started digging.

Captain Sholly, from his CP hole near the edge of the draw, plotted a series of artillery fire plans to cover potential enemy staging areas and all likely avenues of approach. Concerned about the possibility of an enemy attack that night, Sholly registered artillery on the main ridgeline farther south but stopped the rounds short of the draw to avoid hitting friendly positions. Sholly also instructed the artillery to fire several defensive concentrations. Williamson and Captain Peterson, tied in to the right and left of B Company, respectively, worked out similar fire plans for A and C Companies.

Shortly after he and several other C Company troopers had finished digging a medium-sized bunker, Pfc. Leslie Bellrichard paused for a moment, as he would often do, to read from the Bible. The day had been long and hard, even for the old hands in the company, so he turned as always to the Good Book to see him through. Nearby, Pfc. Kent Coombs of the Reconnaissance Platoon noticed Bellrichard and walked over to his bunker. Dug in on the left flank of B Company, the Recon Platoon abutted the right flank of C Company. Coombs knew Bellrichard, and the two chatted briefly before parting company. Coombs, walking away, hoped the night would be a quiet one for both of them. The young RTO had no idea that the 1-8 Infantry had settled down in a camp that likely belonged to elements of the 32nd NVA Regiment.

Stealthily negotiating the dense jungle, two battalions of the 32nd NVA Regiment quietly converged on the small knoll. Foot trails in the area, some leading right to the camp, hastened their movement. Markers consisting of white tape were conspicuously placed along trails leading into the American position to help facilitate the movement of assault troops at night. The North Vietnamese then laid wire through the jungle and tied the ends to bushes beneath the lip of the shallow draw, presumably to guide the assault elements from their staging areas to their assault lanes in the B Company sector.[17] NVA mortar crews, moreover, returned to positions established during the battle on the eighteenth. For coordination in the upcoming attack, the crews relied on telephone wire laid between the mortar locations and the main assault elements.[18] The sun, meanwhile, sank below the western horizon.[19]

Shortly after dark, the 1-8 Infantry noticed lights in the jungle to the east, near the site of the LZ A Company had cleared on the nineteenth. Suspicious, the battalion called in artillery fire on the suspected location of the strange lights. Around 8:20 P.M., not long after the lights were detected to the east, the three American companies reported receiving mortar fire from the southwest. North Vietnamese troops, moreover, were attacking the perimeter from the south, southeast, and southwest.[20] Almost immediately, the Americans requested a forward air controller (FAC), a flare ship, and air support. The battle for the battalion NDP had begun.

Hidden in the brush in front of A Company, Spc4 Joe Anya, a diminutive but gritty Hispanic original, had heard noises around his four-man LP team, followed by the sound of mortar rounds falling on the small knoll. "After we got out there, it wasn't very long before we heard noises all around us," said Pfc. Landis Bargatze. "We could hear movement in the bushes and voices. There wasn't any firing yet, but the movement was maybe thirty to forty yards from us. We radioed in and told them what was going on, and that's when we heard the mortars dropping. We got the word to get back in, so we basically got our shit together and got out of there." Anya, Bargatze, Pfc. Ray Mankowski, and a fourth soldier turned around and low-crawled back toward the perimeter. Chased in by exploding mortar rounds, the four scratched and clawed their way through the underbrush and scrambled back into the A Company line, winded and gasping but elated to have outrun the enemy mortars.

The euphoria was short-lived, however; Anya, in his haste to get back in, had left the radio behind. One of them would have to go back out and recover the radio before the NVA got a hold of it. Anya and the fourth soldier knew one another and both outranked Bargatze and Mankowski, the two replacement E3s on the LP. And since Mankowski was nowhere in sight, having slid into a shallow fighting hole somewhere else along the line, responsibility for retrieving the radio invariably fell to Bargatze, the lowest ranking man present.

Scampering out of the bunker he had tumbled into moments before, Bargatze low-crawled back to the general area where he believed Anya had left the radio. Mortar rounds exploded in the jungle all around him, but he scuffled along on his hands and knees through the underbrush and eventually found the PRC-25 about thirty yards from the perimeter. Relieved, Bargatze hooked the radio around his left leg and started dragging it back to A Company. Bushes and shrubs along the way tugged stubbornly at the antenna, while the body of the radio clanked noisily over roots and rocks. On several occasions, the entire unit became entangled in the undergrowth and had to be yanked loose. "Don't ask me how I got to that radio but I did—but once I got it, getting it in was no easy task," Bargatze reflected. "That radio did not exactly *slide* over the ground. I had one leg pulling it, and the other leg crawling forward because I sure as hell wasn't going to stand up and announce I had a damn radio. I was just trying to get in any way I could without getting killed."

Bargatze, arms burning, the radio skidding unevenly behind him, neared the A Company line when, out of the corner of his eye, he noticed shadows to his left. Bargatze froze. Simultaneously the jungle crackled with the sound of small-arms fire. "I didn't know what to do at that point," said Bargatze. "I didn't know if I should go after them [the shadows], ignore them and keep moving, or continue lying there and get shot. The last alternative didn't really appeal to me." Rolling onto his side, Bargatze raised his M-16 and ripped off a burst on full auto. The shadows disappeared. Bargatze, hooking the radio around his left leg once again, crawled back to his squad in the battalion perimeter and found cover in a small fighting hole.

By then enemy mortar rounds were exploding inside the American perimeter. Paul Hardeman, a platoon sergeant in A Company's First Platoon, heard the distinctive *thump* of a round leaving the tube and hollered out as loud as he could, hoping that the troops up-front in the company line would hear him and find the bottom of a hole. The grunts within earshot of Hardeman, for the most part, did exactly that. "We were on the perimeter and jumped into our foxhole, which was about 10 meters in front of Lt. Rogers [PTL of the First Platoon]," wrote Pfc. Ned Bishop. "It seemed the mortars started hitting just outside the perimeter and then 'walked' into our position. When the mortars stopped I looked around and saw that three of the four air mattresses in our hooch were flat." Behind Bishop, Lieutenant Rogers, twenty-four, of Johnson City, Tennessee, lay dead, struck down by shrapnel. Hardeman was wounded in the head in the same shell burst that killed Rogers, but his steel pot absorbed most of the shrapnel discharged in the blast.

NVA mortar and small-arms fire wounded several more troopers. SSgt. James Gaskins Jr., an African American replacement who had joined the First Platoon in March, left his hole to treat the wounded and soon found Sergeant Hardeman. Gaskins promptly bandaged Hardeman's head wound and then relocated the platoon sergeant to a safer spot inside the perimeter before assuming command of the platoon. Moving thereafter from one position to the next, actions that would ultimately contribute to a Bronze Star commendation for his role in the battle, Gaskins distributed ammunition and flares and later assisted in the evacuation of A Company's wounded.[21]

Glued to a radio behind the A Company line, Sgt. Joe Bauer, then a squad leader in the Second Platoon, learned that a mortar round had scored a direct hit on the four-man LP he had sent out into the jungle in front of the platoon. All four men, Bauer discovered, had been hurt in the blast. Alarmed, he immediately left his fighting hole and began crawling toward the wounded men. Bauer had walked out with the four men earlier that night and had personally selected the site for the LP. Remembering the location, he retraced his steps and quickly found the injured soldiers. Wounded by shrapnel, none of the men could walk or crawl without some assistance. Bauer would have to drag the men, one at a time, back to the battalion perimeter.

Hurriedly grabbing hold of one of the wounded troopers, Bauer began dragging the man in when he suddenly stumbled on four North Vietnamese soldiers. Somehow the four had slipped between him and the perimeter and only then did Bauer realize that he had left his M-16 back at the LP. Startled, the New Jersey native then remembered that he had two hand grenades and, pulling both pins before the NVA could fire a shot, heaved the two grenades, one right after the other, at the enemy soldiers. Two ear-ringing explosions quickly followed, killing all four North Vietnamese. "It seemed like when the first grenade went off," Bauer recalled, "it was raining shrapnel all over the area."[22] Bauer, waiting for the dust to finally settle, hauled the wounded man past the dead NVA to the battalion perimeter. Fearlessly ignoring the mortar rounds and the increasing small-arms fire, Bauer returned to the LP three more times and rescued, one by one, the remaining members of the team.

Safely inside the perimeter, the four wounded men received basic medical care. Bauer dutifully lent a hand. "Not mentioning any names, [but] one man had a leg wound," he remembered. "After cutting his pant leg, I felt what I thought was ground up flesh. Wrong. The man was wounded, but he had also shit himself and I ended up with shit all over my hands. I received the Bronze Star with 'V' device for my actions, but I prefer to say I received it for being shit on."[23]

South of Sergeant Bauer, beyond the forwardmost positions of B Company, 1-8 Infantry, North Vietnamese troops had tripped a flare in front of a four-man LP led by Sgt. James Bloom. Bloom opened fire unhesitatingly—silhouetted in the bright white light of the flare, the NVA were clearly visible in the jungle beyond the LP—as did Spc4 John Richey, Spc4 Larry Gerken, and Pfc. Eugene Poeling. Gerken, firing as fast he could, squeezed off a magazine. "They [NVA] were lit up by the trip flares, and I saw NVA—fully silhouetted," said Gerken. "I fired at them and I saw some of them go down, but I'm not sure if they were taking cover or if I had hit them." Certain that the tripped flare and ensuing gunfire had betrayed the location of their LP, Gerken scampered, along with Bloom and Richey, back through the undergrowth toward the B Company line. Poeling stayed behind to cover the withdrawal.

NVA small-arms fire crackled behind them but the three grunts, covered by Private First Class Poeling, managed to reach the B Company line. Specialist 4th Class Gerken found a sturdy log some twenty meters inside the perimeter and leaped behind it. Poeling, dashing back through the jungle moments later, huddled up behind the same log. Soon after, a mortar shell exploded near the two grunts, filling the air with jagged chunks of metal. Poeling, twenty-one, of Worden, Illinois, was killed instantly. Cheerful and easy going, he had only been in-country for about a month. "He [Poeling] wasn't six feet from me, and he got killed and I didn't get a scratch," Gerken noted. "And it wasn't because I was any braver or a better soldier than Gene. Gene was a damn good soldier, but that's just the way things were." Private First Class Poeling, whom Gerken described as a "good kid" and a "no-trouble guy," was posthumously awarded the Bronze Star for singlehandedly covering the withdrawal of his LP team.[24]

Exploding in the canopy above the 1-8 Infantry, the incoming mortar rounds showered the troopers below with bark and, occasionally, chunks of red-hot shrapnel. Others crashed through the trees and exploded near foxholes and bunkers along the battalion perimeter. Frighteningly accurate—Captain Sholly identified one NVA tube near the old A Company LZ and another on the ridgeline south of B Company—the rounds were soon landing inside the perimeter with alarming regularity. "When those mortar rounds started coming in," said Sgt. Frank Patton of A Company, "they were right on target. There's no way that was by accident. The NVA *had* to have had some forward observers." Spc4 Joby McAulay had been sitting down before the battle, scribbling a letter to his family with his legs dangling in a foxhole, a poncho pulled over his head and shoulders to conceal the soft beams of light radiating from his flashlight, when a mortar round exploded to his right, sending a hunk of hot metal whistling by his face. So close, in fact, that McAulay could feel the wind on his skin as the shrapnel flew past.

B Company suffered a handful of casualties in the first few volleys. Aware of the injuries, and the increasing likelihood that his company would suffer many more if he could not silence the enemy tubes, Captain Sholly called in artillery fire on the strange lights he had observed that night. For a while, the mortar fire would cease. "Then it would start up again," Sholly recalled, "and I would see the lights. I would keep shooting artillery at it—it was obviously too far for us at several hundred meters away—and they kept firing into the trees in our area." Adjusting the incoming arty from his command post some forty to fifty feet behind the lip of the shallow ravine, Sholly blasted the ridgeline to the south and the old A Company LZ to the east. No matter how much shellfire he placed on those two locations, however, the enemy tubes continued to fire on the perimeter.

Pfc. Ken Brosseau, a replacement in B Company's First Platoon, wriggled out of the lean-to he had fashioned out of a poncho and scurried off into a large fighting hole to escape the incoming mortar rounds. Spc4 Ronald James Moore sought cover in the same hole. Moore, though, never made it. "He was right next to me, and all of a sudden I didn't hear anything," Brosseau recalled. "He was lying there, and I reached over [to touch him]. His body was still warm. I put my hand all up and down his back, and I didn't feel anything. I lifted him up to feel underneath, and I didn't feel anything. The poor kid was just dead. He died right next to me." Specialist 4th Class Moore, twenty-one, of Columbus, Ohio, had been killed by shrapnel fragments, just a few feet from the hole that might have saved his life.

On the eastern side of the 1-8 Infantry perimeter, to the left of B Company, Sgt. Chuck Runde, a twenty-one-year old squad leader in C Company, hurried back to his platoon. Runde had been out on an LP with a Starlite scope when the enemy mortar fire began. Advised that he had been entrusted with a piece of equipment reportedly worth around $25,000, the straight-laced original turned the scope in as soon as he returned to the perimeter. Born in Elmhurst, Illinois, Runde grew up in southwest Wisconsin and was offered an academic scholarship to the University of Wisconsin in 1963. Runde, however, followed in the footsteps of his father and older brother and attended Lawrence College in Dubuque, Iowa.

Bored, Runde dropped out of college after his freshman year and went to work in a shoe store in Cedar Rapids. No longer in school, a politically unconnected working-class kid like Runde, no matter how gainfully employed (by then he had been promoted to a managerial position within the store), could almost count on a draft notice from Uncle Sam. Runde's arrived in the latter half of 1965. "It wasn't the highlight of my day—let's put it that way—but it didn't depress me in any way whatsoever and I wasn't upset about it," he later recalled. "I guess I have always had a strong feeling about the debt that I owed my country. It was paid by hundreds of thousands before me, and I felt it was my personal obligation to do that." In Vietnam he felt obliged to lead and to enforce basic standards of professionalism in the field, even if it rankled some of the guys in his squad.

Runde had nearly reached his hole when a mortar shell exploded nearby, spraying his chest with shrapnel. Blinded by dirt and debris, he hit the ground with a thud. Blood oozed from the wound in his chest. Shaken up, he paused momentarily and then opened his eyes, fully expecting to see a battle raging all around him. Instead, the former shoe store manager could not see anything at all. The blast had robbed him of his sight. Runde pawed frantically at the dirt and debris burrowed in his eyes. Little, or at least not enough to restore his vision, came out and he closed his eyes to alleviate the burning pain. He briefly considered hollering for help but, doubtful that anyone would hear him over the gunfire and explosions, decided against it. Friendly artillery fire was exploding around the battalion perimeter; one shell went off in a nearby tree, knocking the upper half of it down on top of him. Half shattered, the tree smacked painfully against his right hip.

Runde sat calmly under the broken tree and waited for the NVA to appear, screaming and shouting and looking for Americans to kill. *Fuck it,* he figured, *no sense worrying about it now.* They would be there soon enough. "Sitting there, under that tree, I flipped my M-16 on automatic and reached down and pulled out two grenades," Runde recounted. "I pulled the pins on them and I said to myself that I'd just wait for the sons of bitches. I thought I was dead."

9 CAN YOU HOLD?

Long bursts of rifle and automatic weapons fire lashed the American perimeter. Grenades were hurled uphill, over the lip of the shallow draw in front of B Company. Smoke trails lingered momentarily as RPGs flashed across the jungle and exploded against tree trunks inside the perimeter. Rolling the mortar barrage farther north, the North Vietnamese swept in behind the shifting shellfire and assaulted the battalion NDP from the south. The all-out push to destroy the 1-8 Infantry was now under way.

Shirtless, Sgt. John McKeever jumped into his foxhole with another First Platoon soldier named "Smitty." McKeever, who had been with Plt. Sgt. Clifford Johnson on the eighteenth, covering the right flank of B Company with rifle and machine-gun fire, grabbed his M-60 and started spraying the jungle. Some of the branches draped across the top of his hole clawed at his bare back—Sergeant Lopez had shouted for him to "get some overhead cover on that damn foxhole"—but he refused to let up on the trigger.

"McKeever!" Spc4 Bill May shouted suddenly. "What the hell are you shooting at?" May had attended high school with McKeever in New York State, and the two men were friends. Dug in that night to the left and slightly below McKeever, May had been holding his fire on the right flank of B Company's Second Platoon until he could actually see something worth shooting at, and even then he intended to use grenades for as long as possible to avoid disclosing his position to the enemy.

"I don't know," McKeever hollered back, "but they aren't getting up this hill."

Shortly thereafter a North Vietnamese soldier charged up the shallow draw and tripped a flare, illuminating the jungle near the tie-in point between the First and Second Platoons. "We had put out trip flares and our usual night defenses, not realizing that they [NVA] didn't care that the trip flares were there," said Specialist

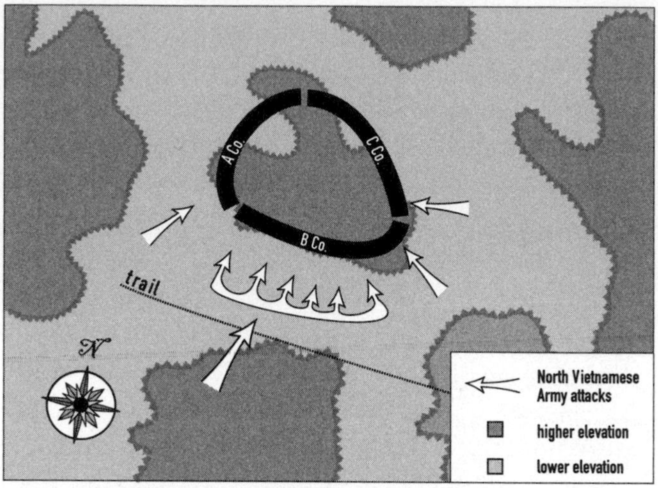

A, B, and C Companies, 1-8 Infantry, May 20, 1967. Situation at 8:30 P.M. *Map by Charles Grear, adapted from original drawn by S. L. Dowdy in Robert Sholly,* Young Soldiers, Amazing Warriors.

4th Class May. "By the time the trip flares went off, they had already run through them and the trip flares were *behind* them." Sprinting toward the gap between May and McKeever, the North Vietnamese soldier was nearly past May when he turned his head at the last second and noticed May and Spc4 Terry Levendowski, M-16s raised, in a hole to his right. "He looked right at us and the whole look on his face was like—*Oh fuck!*" said May. "He was absolutely stunned, and I think he realized it was over for him."

Specialist 4th Class Levendowski fired first, hitting the man in full stride, and within seconds the grunts to the left and right of Levendowski had also opened fire. Staggering forward, the NVA soldier fell face down, a few feet from the foxhole Levendowski shared with Specialist 4th Class May. "Levendowski hit him first, and then the whole line sort of emptied on him," said May. "In a few more steps, he would have been past us." Curious, May looked the man over. Dressed in a tan uniform, the soldier was wearing a helmet and appeared to be armed with an AK-47 assault rifle. Moments later a wave of North Vietnamese charged out of the jungle and up the draw, shrieking wildly and tripping flares along the way.

Angry orange-red muzzle flashes erupted up and down the American line as B Company, recovering from the initial sound and fury of the NVA assault, unleashed a torrent of fire on the sprawling, screaming mass of enemy troops surging up the draw toward the perimeter. "It was mass pandemonium," said May. "They [NVA] got into their position, and they just ran straight forward." Firing until the barrel on his M-60 turned "cherry red," Sergeant McKeever poured machine-gun fire into the draw and up the opposite slope. Specialists 4th Class May and Levendowski pitched in with steady M-16 fire, while off to their left, in the Third Platoon sector, SSgt. Frankie Molnar, returning presently to his foxhole after gunning down five NVA during the mortar barrage, rallied his squad and calmly assisted in stemming the enemy tide.

Struck down in the ongoing maelstrom, the wounded on both sides howled in agony, rattling the nerves of the grunts on the line . "I'm not sure whether they were ours or theirs," recalled Sgt. John McKeever, "but I could hear men screaming in pain and agony. *That* was horrendous." Medics rushed over to attend to the American wounded, while the assaulting NVA crawled forward to drag some of their injured comrades back from the front line. A number of NVA went to ground in the shallow draw just short of the B Company line, beyond the range of rifle butts and bayonets, but well within the outermost band of American artillery fire.

Captain Sholly was tempted to call in artillery on the NVA in the shallow draw. Mindful of the risks associated with calling in rounds that close to friendly positions, however, Sholly decided instead to concentrate his artillery fire farther back—*behind* the draw—to interdict enemy reinforcements and to isolate the battlefield. "What I was trying to do was break up their support areas and their assembly areas over on the hill and [get at] their mortar positions, rather than trying to get it down into the gully," said the B Company commander. "I did try that a couple of times, but I don't know how it ended up."

Eyeball to eyeball, toe to toe, the two sides slugged it out in the shadows on the southern side of the 1-8 Infantry perimeter. The fighting, as one might expect given the close proximity of the combatants, was particularly chaotic and confusing. Reduced at times to firing at flashes in the night, some of the grunts in B Company relied on hand grenades to kill the enemy. The NVA responded in kind, and soon both sides were hurling hand grenades back and forth. Occasionally a grenade would fail to explode, frustrating the thrower and sparing the intended target.

Pfc. Carlos Renteria, a young Mexican American replacement from Arizona, poked frantically at his jammed M-16 as he glanced around his First Platoon foxhole. Green NVA tracer rounds buzzed overhead. Finding the can of oil he was looking for, Renteria sliced the metal container in two with a knife and poured the lubricant into the receiver of his rifle. Oil splashed onto his fatigues as he emptied the can, but it served the purpose and got his rifle working again. While Renteria poured oil into his M-16, North Vietnamese troops moved toward the hole he occupied with Pfc. John

Barclay, the self-described "Mc" from the south side of Chicago who had unloaded a LAW on the Y-shaped tree during the battle on the eighteenth, and a third soldier.

Renteria, perhaps sensing the approaching NVA, swung his M-16 over the top of the hole and blazed away. The following day, the grunts discovered three dead bodies within six feet of their foxhole. "Without doing any forensics on the bodies of those three, I would say it's a good possibility that it was Carlos that killed them when he popped up and fired out in front of our hole," said Private First Class Barclay. "I had met Carlos back at LAX Airport on the way to Oakland, and we were on the same plane together coming over. And to think just a few weeks later he might have saved my life."

Barclay, though, never laid eyes on a single North Vietnamese soldier. Trained to hold his fire until he had a discernible target, he lowered his M-16 at one point and removed the hand grenades he carried on his web gear. *If they get in close,* he thought to himself as he lined the grenades up, side by side, *I'll take them out with these!*

Machine gunners along the B Company line, meanwhile, were hammering the North Vietnamese with continuous fire. "Come on—you sons of bitches!" taunted one intrepid gunner. Small groups of NVA pressed the company in spots, yet they were never able to overrun a section of the line and force a breakthrough. "We probably hadn't put the machine guns out properly," Spc4 Bill May averred, "but it probably turned into a good thing." May, from his foxhole near the junction of the First and Second Platoons, judged that the weight of the NVA assault was falling most heavily on the B Company line to his left, often on sectors of the line thoroughly covered by friendly machine guns.

Down in the draw, not far from the foxhole occupied by Specialists 4th Class May and Levendowski, a North Vietnamese light machine gun, more than likely a Soviet 7.62-mm RPD (Degtyaryov light machine gun) or its Chicom equivalent, chattered away, sending steady bursts of fire up toward the B Company line. Set up below the Americans, the NVA gunner was firing high, over the heads of May and Levendowksi, because he could not simultaneously overcome the angle created by the slope of the draw and aim the gun low enough to hit May's foxhole. It is highly probable, in fact, that the NVA gunner could not even *see* the two Americans in the hole. Similarly, neither May nor Levendowski could see the enemy gun, much less put accurate M-16 fire on it.

May pulled the pin on a grenade and tossed it down into the draw where he thought the enemy machine gun, chattering away at a distance of no more than twenty meters, was most likely located. "If I was in a closet, I doubt I could throw it and hit the back wall—I had no athletic ability whatsoever," May later joked. "But that was an easy throw." The machine gun, however, continued firing. Annoyed, May lobbed two more grenades into the draw, and one of the two finally knocked the gun out.

The North Vietnamese ground assault engulfed much of the 1-8 Infantry perimeter, with the heaviest blows falling on B Company and the southern sector of C Company. Captain Peterson, the C Company CO, coordinated the company's defenses and assisted in directing artillery fire on the attacking NVA. Peterson, having done just about all that he could as a company commander, realized that the outcome of the battle would now depend largely on the young troopers manning foxholes and bunkers along the company line.

Pushing ahead, through the exploding shellfire, the NVA closed with the C Company line and attacked with machine guns and AK-47s. C Company returned fire. Spc4 Leon Wangerin, gawking out from the relative safety of a bunker, was blasting away at the advancing North Vietnamese when he saw three C Company troopers suddenly go down, clipped by incoming bullets or flying shrapnel. Wangerin had been out on a four-man LP, but when an enemy mortar round exploded and wounded his team leader, he immediately took charge of the team and guided it back to the perimeter. Convinced that the three wounded troopers needed assistance, Wangerin left his bunker and braved the intense NVA fire to lead the three, one trooper at a time, back to his bunker.

Just as Wangerin managed to escort the last wounded trooper to safety, however, shrapnel from an enemy mortar round whistled through the jungle, gravely injuring the twenty-year-old. Near death, the wounds on his body more severe than he had initially imagined, Wangerin, who would earn a Bronze Star for his gallantry, fought on and prevented the NVA from overrunning his bunker. Sadly the Milwaukee, Wisconsin, native died not long after the NVA attack in his sector had been repulsed.[1]

Shrieking North Vietnamese soldiers, some blazing away with AK-47s, charged the perimeter at other points along the C Company line. Heavy mortar fire preceded the ground assault, as had been the case with B Company to the south, and it likely contributed to the speed with which the NVA were able to close with the company line. One group of enemy soldiers charged a foxhole occupied by Pfc. Leslie Bellrichard and four other grunts. Crouching down in the hole, Bellrichard promptly rose to his feet and heaved hand grenades at the oncoming enemy. Several NVA were killed in the ensuing explosions, and the rest were forced to pull back.

Increasingly the NVA wave assault on the south, southeast, and eastern sides of the American perimeter began to falter. B and C Companies, while certainly hard-pressed, had held the line. On the western side of the perimeter, the sudden enemy mortar barrage and ground assault caught some of A Company's grunts by surprise. "Where's my helmet? Where's my boots?" one A Company soldier asked frantically. "Where's my rifle?" Roused by the sound of incoming mortar fire, the man had leaped into his foxhole without his gear. Pfc. Bill Dobbie had jumped into the same hole moments before. Dobbie, who had a habit of sleeping with his boots on and his helmet and rifle nearby, gazed at the man disapprovingly. "Hey, you're going to have to go *get* them!"

Over in A Company's Third Platoon, several panicky FNGs hopped into the foxhole of their squad leader, Spc4 Raul Munoz. Munoz had been sleeping in his poncho liner when he heard "popping noises," followed by an explosion close by. In charge of a squad for the first time that night, Munoz grabbed his rifle, jammed his steel pot onto his head, and jumped into his foxhole. The FNGs tumbled in behind him, unarmed and helmetless. Visibly frightened, the men seemed incapable of any kind of action. Munoz, leaving the huddling greenhorns behind, crawled out of the hole and returned with their rifles and helmets. Fuming, he then cussed the men out until they finally appeared capable of functioning on their own.

A Company was soon under assault, hit as B and C Companies had been, by a determined force of well-armed NVA infantry. Rifle fire from a small hill opposite the Fourth Platoon attracted the attention of Sgt. Jim Peirce, an experienced squad leader and a savvy veteran of numerous firefights. The hill was more or less directly in front of Peirce, and as he scanned it for the source of the fire, he suddenly saw sparks followed by a rocket. Ducking down ahead of the rocket, he slid into his foxhole seconds before it exploded against the tree next to his hole. Two soldiers to the right of him, neither of whom had bothered to dig much of a hole that night, were killed instantly.

Peirce immediately examined his own body, certain that he would find a gash or a gouge somewhere. Surprisingly, however, he had escaped the shrapnel and the concussive effects of the blast unscathed. Peirce then checked on the soldiers in the hole to his left; none of them had been injured in the blast. Still, the rocket had come much too close to have been an accident or a lucky shot. Peirce was convinced that the NVA had seen him, and the other A Company soldiers nearby, digging in earlier that night.

Maneuvering through the tangled forest beyond the perimeter, the NVA followed up the RPG strike with a ground assault on segments of the Fourth Platoon. "I could hear their gear—canteens or whatever it was they were carrying—clinking," Peirce remembered, "so I knew they were coming up on us on foot." The troopers in the hole to the left of Peirce apparently heard the clinking as well and opened up in the direction of the noise. Muzzle flashes lit up the jungle, and in the glimpses of illumination provided by the sudden gunfire, Peirce spied a number of North Vietnamese soldiers, most no more than fifteen meters away. Startled, Peirce moved to detonate the Claymore mine he had planted in front of his position but the device, surprisingly, failed to explode. Only later would he discover that the Claymore had been disarmed by an NVA soldier or sapper who, after sneaking up on the perimeter undetected, had carefully removed its blasting cap.

Peirce aimed his M-16 and started firing. Bursts of AK-47 fire snapped past foxholes and bunkers along the line, but the volume of outgoing M-16 and M-60 fire the Fourth

Platoon put out prevented the NVA from advancing any farther. "I opened up on them [NVA], and that's when I saw them coming at us," Peirce said. "They started hollering, and they were firing back, but I think we were out-firing them because we were holding them off and they started falling back." Halted without achieving a breakthrough, the North Vietnamese pulled back and regrouped.

Pfc. Landis Bargatze, a squad mate of Sergeant Peirce, used the lull in the fighting to abandon the shallow, one-soldier hole in which he had weathered the first enemy attack in favor of a large, sturdily constructed bunker manned by three other A Company soldiers. Bargatze had burned through several magazines of M-16 ammo fighting off the first assault, and he felt reasonably certain that the enemy would eventually mount another. If they did, he figured he would have a better chance of surviving in a bunker with overhead cover and a narrow firing aperture than in a partially shoveled hole.

Pick your shots carefully, Sgt. Ross Rembert warned his A Company, Third Platoon squad, and conserve your ammunition whenever possible. Rembert did not want his people firing indiscriminately. That kind of sloppy fire discipline would betray their positions prematurely and expend valuable ammo, mistakes that could leave the squad vulnerable in the event of a massed enemy ground attack. But, he added, if the NVA tripped a flare or set off a Claymore mine, all bets were off. For a while the only noises Rembert heard that night were the sound of exploding enemy mortar rounds. And then, suddenly, a Claymore went off out in front of the squad, followed immediately by a number of trip flares. "In between the flares, I could see a number of NVA moving—five to eight of them, maybe ten—out in front," said Rembert. "There'd be a small group of them, and maybe thirty to forty yards away there'd be another group of them moving abreast. When the flares were lighting the area up, they'd duck back down."

Responding to the blown Claymores and trip flares, Rembert's squad unleashed a tremendous volley of fire on the attacking North Vietnamese. "They're inside the Claymores," some of the young troopers shouted breathlessly as they cut loose with their M-16s, "Fire for effect!" The NVA employed fire and maneuver to close the gap between the two forces, but against a dug-in and equally determined opponent, the assault uphill quickly stalled. "They were firing and moving, so I taught my guys to put rounds all around the muzzle flashes they saw," recalled Rembert. "We were ready for them. Whenever a Claymore went off or a flare went up and we could identify their outline, we went to work on them." More men, more firepower, or both would have to be committed—he imagined—if the NVA hoped to penetrate his sector of the line.

In another Third Platoon squad not too far from Rembert, Pfc. Bob Warden pumped M-16 fire into faceless silhouettes. Small trees were falling nearby, most knocked over by the intense back-and-forth fire. Nineteen and still new to the war—the Illinois native had only been with A Company since early April 1967—Warden had learned to carry a lot of hand grenades, six to be exact, and he knew how to make every one of them count. Warden, in fact, liked to use grenades, especially when the enemy drew close. Over the next hour or two, Warden would throw all six of his grenades.

Blown Claymores in the Second Platoon sector prompted Pfc. Charlie Bann, a relatively green replacement in the same squad as Pfc. Bill Dobbie, to shoulder his M-16. Bann detonated one Claymore himself and began firing in the general vicinity of where the mines had exploded; nothing, however, seemed to halt the groups of NVA assaulting the platoon. "I could see them running toward my position and running to the right and left, past other guys' holes," Bann remembered. "You could hear them [NVA] screaming, and some of our guys yelling: 'They're inside the perimeter!' You're looking three hundred and sixty degrees around at that point, trying the best you could to protect yourself." Pfc. Hector Vega-Tirado who, like Private First Class Bann, had joined the platoon as a replacement earlier that spring, was manning a hole slightly to the rear of Bann along with another soldier. Set up on a machine gun that night, Private First Class Vega pumped rounds of M-60 fire into the attacking North Vietnamese and eventually blocked, along with other troopers in the platoon, the furious enemy advance.

Vega was in position to engage the NVA when he did and prevent a breakthrough in part because his squad leader that night, Sgt. Joe Bauer, had pulled some of the squad back to avoid casualties from the incoming mortar rounds that preceded the enemy assault. Not coincidentally then, when the NVA raced past Bann, thinking perhaps that they had broken through the American line, some of them ran headlong into what Bauer termed "the secondary line" of Second Platoon. Vega and a few of the other replacements occupied fighting holes in that secondary line. "In that area [near Private First Class Vega] you could see them [NVA] coming through and around, trying to run a line up on us," explained Bauer. "But it was just the volume of fire we were returning on them. We had lost a lot of our old guys in March, and you really didn't know how the new guys were going to handle it. But they really just got the concept that once you put down a field of fire to gain fire superiority, you didn't want to just back off and put out a couple of rounds because you've just made yourself a target. I think that Vega fell in with that [because] he was just pumping it out there, putting it out there."

Hardest hit by the NVA assault on the western side of the perimeter, the left flank of A Company had held, much like the right flank of C Company and the four embattled platoons with B Company to the south and east. Groups of NVA were now falling back everywhere, repulsed by the three dug-in American companies, and an uneasy lull soon settled over the battalion perimeter. Flying with his artillery liaison officer, Capt. Ray Harton, Lt. Col. Tim Gannon was monitoring the battle from his C&C ship overhead. Gannon wanted to be on the ground with his men that night and would have been if not for the objections of Colonel Jackson, the brigade CO. Jackson was adamant that Gannon remain at the battalion firebase, where he would be more accessible to higher commands. "I felt that [with my battalion] was where I belonged but the brigade commander, Colonel Jackson, insisted that his battalion commanders remain at FSBs [fire support bases]," Gannon lamented. "He wanted them available to answer questions concerning their units. On the nineteenth and twentieth I wanted to remain with the battalion, [but] he said 'no.' When the NVA hit the battalion perimeter on the twentieth, the senior captain [Capt. Robert Sholly] had to act as the battalion commander."[2]

Had he been consulted on the matter, Captain Sholly would have sided with Colonel Jackson. "We fought a different kind of war in the Highlands than in the Delta or anywhere else," said Sholly, "and so for a battalion commander to go out in the field with his companies just wasn't practical." Good battalion commanders, Sholly had long since learned, facilitated fire support for their companies in contact and then stepped back while their company commanders managed the battle on the ground.

Although confined to his C&C bird, Gannon conferred with Sholly via radio throughout the battle, addressing among other concerns how to effectively harness all of the fire support available to the battalion. Shortly after the start of the NVA assault, for example, helicopter gunships appeared in the skies overhead to provide aerial support to B and C Companies. According to Sholly, however, the fire from the gunships was *too* close in some instances to his frontline troopers. To avoid repeating some of those earlier near-misses and to avert an even worse mishap when the fast-movers—fighters and fighter-bombers from the U.S. 7th Air Force—arrived on station, Gannon and Sholly designated specific target areas for each firepower asset. "We gave the artillery assets those targets that were on the east, southeast, south, and southwest of the perimeter, and the air assets the targets to the northeast, north, and northwest of the perimeter," said Sholly. "That way, the aircraft would not be flying into or under the artillery rounds being fired in our support. It eliminated a conflict of fires as well."

Moreover, by redirecting much of the incoming artillery fire onto targets south of the battalion perimeter, the fire scheme decreased the number of rounds flying directly *over* the perimeter, thereby reducing the possibility of an errant round falling *inside* the perimeter. Captain Harton, incidentally, coordinated much of that artillery support, sometimes adjusting the fires of more than one battery at a time from high over the battlefield. Awarded an Air Medal for his time in the air during the fighting, the seemingly indefatigable artillery officer kept the guns firing wherever and whenever the 1-8 Infantry needed support. "The only time we were not in the air," Harton wrote, "was when we ran from one chopper to another."[3] Indeed, on one occasion when a lieutenant reported that his guns had fired so much that the tubes had gotten hot, Harton asked the man if he could still touch the tubes with his hands. Barely, the lieutenant responded tersely. Harton replied that the tubes were not hot enough, and the guns continued firing.[4]

Supported by helicopter gunships and heavy artillery fire, the troops of the 1-8 Infantry had defeated the first NVA assault on the battalion perimeter. Each of the three companies had suffered casualties repelling the violent assault, and some of the men used the lull in the fighting to administer to wounded comrades. Harassing mortar and small-arms fire, meanwhile, kept the grunts on edge while the North Vietnamese regrouped in the jungle around the American perimeter.

Crawling out of his foxhole in the A Company CP area, Captain Williamson moved around and checked in with his platoons. Encouragingly, the troops on the line were in relatively good shape and none of his platoons, not even the First Platoon, now under the command of Sergeant Gaskins, appeared out of sorts or incapable of functioning effectively. Over on the B Company side of the perimeter, Captain Sholly sat with his artillery forward observer (FO) and Sgt. Don Hunter in a large hole right behind his platoons, no more than forty to fifty feet from the lip of the draw. The rest of the CP group, composed of Sgt. Dick Surface and 1st Sgt. Victor Lopez, were in a large foxhole twenty feet away. A thick wall of vegetation separated the CP group from the center of the battalion perimeter. Sholly, when deciding where to set up for the night, worried that if he located his CP on the *other* side of that wall, the dense undergrowth would prevent him from observing the action as it unfolded along the perimeter. Accordingly he selected a position on the side closest to his troops.

Straying temporarily from his three-man hole, Sholly snuck out to the edge of the draw and peered over. On the slope below, he observed a swarm of North Vietnamese troops scrambling uphill, toward the B Company line. Some of them had already made it a ways up the slope. "I had one white phosphorus grenade that I had been lugging around for a long time and it was heavy," Sholly wrote. "I decided that this was a good time to get rid of it. So I tossed it down into the crowd and removed myself backwards quickly while warning everyone that they were on the way." Exploding either on the slope or in the draw below, the grenade produced a rash of anguished yelps from the attacking North Vietnamese. Sholly was shielded from the effects of the blast by the lip of the draw. Back in his hole, he waited for the attack to hit the company line.

Bugle blasts suddenly rang out over the rattle of small-arms fire. Regrouping after the first assault, the North Vietnamese rushed forward again and attacked the southern half of the battalion perimeter. Communist machine guns barked loudly in support of the attack, with one gun zeroing in on a sector of the B Company line held by the

Recon Platoon. Tied in with C Company on the left flank of the line, the platoon's three squads were quickly engulfed in enemy fire. "[They] were taking all kinds of shit—grenades, small-arms fire," recalled Pfc. Kent Coombs. "There was absolutely no doubt that they were under heavy assault."

Prior to the assault Coombs had been leaning against a tree, talking on the radio, when an RPG exploded above him, blowing a six-inch hole in the tree. Hot shrapnel and bits of bark flew through the platoon CP. Sgt. Charles Tiede, the acting platoon leader on the evening of the twentieth, was wounded in the explosion, as was Sgt. Raymond Borowski, a battalion medic serving with the platoon. Tiede, who would earn a Bronze Star for his courage and leadership during the battle, remained in charge of the platoon, despite the painful wound in his back.

Armed with an M-60, Pfc. Dennis Carney relocated to another position to silence the NVA machine gun buzzing part of the Recon Platoon. Carney, now somewhat more exposed, attracted heavy enemy fire, and the furious exchange continued uninterrupted until Carney, on his way to a Bronze Star commendation, eliminated multiple enemy positions with bursts from his M-60. Soon after an RPG denoted nearby, slicing his back with shrapnel. Carney, however, refused to retreat. Farther back, Sergeant Tiede repeatedly lobbed hand grenades at the NVA. "As far as I knew, we were holding the line," said Private First Class Coombs. "I didn't hear anything over the radio about anyone getting overrun or anything to that effect. It was pretty hot and heavy, though."

Guided in some instances by communications wire, the assaulting NVA scurried up the slope of the draw, closing at times to within five to ten meters of the B Company line. Enemy soldiers armed with AK-47s and RPGs also climbed trees and fired down on B Company from above, while some on the ground held their fire until they had closed to within ten meters of the perimeter.[5] Others tossed hand grenades at the nearest American bunker or foxhole. One grenade bounced in the direction of Sgt. Paul Domke, a machine gunner in the Second Platoon. The twenty-one-year old from Detroit was on the way back to his hole from the company CP following an ammo run when the enemy grenade appeared out of nowhere.

Reacting instinctively Domke snatched the grenade up and hurled it back at the North Vietnamese. Domke, realizing after a few seconds that the enemy grenade had failed to detonate, threw one of his own grenades but it, too, refused to explode. "We were plagued by a lot of duds," recalled Spc4 Bill May. "Some of theirs didn't go off, and some of ours didn't go off." Domke then threw a second grenade and covered up. Moments later an explosion rang out. Domke, certain that the blast had wiped the NVA out, darted past the general area where the first enemy grenade had landed and returned to his foxhole.

Arguably more furious than the first, the second NVA assault adhered to the same basic tactical script and generally targeted the same sectors of the B Company line, namely the three platoons to the left of the First Platoon. "What I always found amazing was that they came back in the exact same way that they had the first time," recalled May, who was dug in on the right flank of the Second Platoon. "They were running right into these machine guns. They kept coming back the same way. I truly believe that had they shifted, more towards us and [Sgt. John] McKeever, they could have overrun us." Instead, the enemy's principal attacks struck the squads dug in to his left, including those of the Third Platoon and the attached Recon Platoon.

Nearby in the Third Platoon, deployed at the time between May's Second Platoon and the hard-pressed Recon Platoon, SSgt. Frankie Molnar was crawling about, distributing grenades and ammo to the men in his squad, moments before the second assault hit. Fierce fighting engulfed the squad as enemy troops equipped with AK-47s, RPGs, and, in some cases nothing but hand grenades, pressed the attack. Molnar and his men, however, threw the North Vietnamese back.

Sgt. Chuck Runde sat quietly under a half-broken tree and waited for the North Vietnamese on the east side of the 1-8 Infantry perimeter. Two grenades, their respective pins carefully removed, waited with him. In his hands he held an M-16. Blinded by dirt and debris, Runde wondered when the NVA would finally burst through the perimeter. Bolstered by ample artillery support, C Company, particularly those elements tied in with B Company farther south, had certainly buckled, but it did not break under the weight of the first NVA assault.

Waiting for the firing to subside somewhat, Runde hollered out for assistance. Pfc. Van Waugh and two other soldiers heard him and crawled out of their foxhole near a small tree. Waugh had never dug in at night before, preferring instead to sleep on the ground behind a tree or in the underbrush, but sleeping as nature had intended sounded a whole lot more dangerous once word got around that there might be some contact that night, something they had not seen much of in the preceding weeks.

Private First Class Waugh and the two soldiers found Runde and escorted him back to their foxhole. Five foot seven and barely "one hundred twenty pounds wringing wet," according to Runde, Waugh squeezed in alongside the other three men. Waugh had grown up in Michigan and had volunteered for the draft in 1966 after a couple of years of college, hoping that his education and typing skills would land him a clerical position in the Army. Grunts—not clerks—were in demand that fall, and the twenty-two-year-old former college frat boy was soon sent to Advanced Infantry Training (AIT) at Fort Jackson. Disappointed but not surprised, Waugh graduated AIT in late February of 1967 and by March of that year was serving in Vietnam with C Company's Second Platoon. "Don't ever salute me in the field," his platoon leader had told him brusquely on his first day in the field, "and take your underwear off."

Waugh was still in the four-man hole near the small tree, searching the jungle for muzzle flashes and silhouettes, when a sudden burst of brilliant red appeared before his very eyes. "The next thing I know," Waugh recalled, "the other three guys were asking me if I was ok." Confused, Waugh mumbled that he was but moments later felt something burning through his fatigues. Whatever had emitted the bright red flash of light had also cast scalding hot shrapnel onto his clothing. Brushing the shrapnel from his fatigues, Waugh noticed that his rucksack had vanished, along with the small tree that it had been leaning against. "Whatever hit that tree and the rucksack totally just . . . the tree was gone and my rucksack was gone," he recalled. "There was just a small stump at the level of the ground. I don't have a *clue* what it was [that hit the tree]." Remarkably, neither Waugh nor any of the three other soldiers in the hole with him were injured.

Two, however, were left with damaged M-16s while the third—the man farthest from Waugh—stood helplessly by as the force of the blast blew the rifle right out of his hands. Sergeant Runde would eventually regain his sight after boarding a dustoff bound for Jackson Hole the next day, but even while temporarily blinded, he never let go of his M-16. "Just tell me where and when to shoot," he told Waugh, "if the North Vietnamese attack again."

A short while later, the second NVA assault—preceded again by mortar and RPG fire—slammed into B Company and the southern sections of A and C Companies. Flares lit up the jungle near Private First Class Waugh yet, other than the shifting shadows created by the artificial light, he did not see much of anything in front of his Second Platoon hole. Elsewhere twenty-one-year-old Spc4 Peter Hayges, an earnest RA (Regular Army) with three years in, aimed and fired his M-16 repeatedly. Hayges had trained as a combat engineer but later switched specialties when he was assigned to the 4th Infantry Division in September 1965, following a stint with a mechanized infantry division in Germany. Handy with a rifle, Hayges zeroed in that night on muzzle flashes and the periodic glimpses he caught of the enemy whenever they tripped a ground flare or wandered under the light of an aerial flare provided by a USAF "Spooky" flareship circling overhead.

C Company continued to engage in small firefights as the NVA probed the wary grunts. Pfc. Bob Carlson served in the Fourth Platoon with Hayges, but unlike the former combat engineer he could neither see nor hear the NVA, other than the ubiquitous crack of their AK-47s. *Where are those rounds coming from?* Carlson wondered, gazing up into the trees. While Carlson searched in vain for any sign of the enemy, a group of North Vietnamese soldiers stormed out of the jungle and advanced on a large foxhole occupied by Pfc. Leslie Bellrichard, Pfc. Robert Braun, Spc4 Michael Gustafson, and two other C Company troopers. Bellrichard bravely stood up and threw hand grenades at the onrushing enemy. Just as he was about to throw another grenade, however, a mortar round exploded a short distance away.

Hurled backward by the concussive force of the explosion, Bellrichard tumbled to the ground and inadvertently dropped the grenade. The pin had already been pulled. Horrified, Bellrichard dove on the live grenade and smothered the ensuing explosion with his body before his comrades realized what had happened.

The blast blew off Bellrichard's left leg and severely mangled the left side of his body. Astoundingly, the Wisconsin native managed to pull himself up long enough to retrieve his M-16 and empty a magazine at the enemy. Dying, Bellrichard mouthed the words "good bye" to his shaken comrades.[6] The soft-spoken replacement who carried a small Bible in his pack would die a hero. "The medic came to help," said Specialist 4th Class Gustafson, "but there was nothing he could do for him. Private First Class Bellrichard's complete disregard for his own life will never be forgotten by those of us in his foxhole. There is no doubt that his courageous and willing sacrifice saved my life as well as the other men in the foxhole."[7] An equally grateful Private First Class Braun echoed Gustafson's sentiments. "The ultimate sacrifice which he made in order to save the lives of his buddies is indicative of his courage and complete unselfishness," he said. "His heroic actions will never be forgotten by me or any of the other men in the foxhole with him that night."[8] Braun, Gustafson, and 2nd Lt. James Flaiz issued formal statements testifying to the extraordinary courage of Private First Class Bellrichard on the evening of May 20, 1967. Laid to rest in Oak Hill Cemetery in his hometown of Janesville, Wisconsin, Bellrichard was posthumously awarded the Medal of Honor.

Wide-eyed and seemingly half-crazed, a horde of North Vietnamese, armed mostly with grenades and AK-47s, pushed uphill toward Spc4 Raul Munoz. "They looked like those damn hyenas—all you could see was their eyes," recalled Munoz, "and the sons of bitches were all over the place. The NVA were like ants coming up that hill!" A Company was suddenly under attack again, although the second enemy assault on the western side of the American perimeter seemed smaller in number and arguably less violent than the ongoing attacks against B Company and the southern flank of C Company. Munoz and the other troopers in his squad tossed hand grenades downhill at the North Vietnamese and sprayed the slope with rifle fire. Neither side knew enough to quit. "You just kept firing with your M-16 until you couldn't fire anymore," said Munoz, "and if you had to you grabbed an M-16 from a dead or wounded buddy and kept on firing!" In the same general area, Sgt. Ross Rembert's squad dutifully matched the output of Munoz and his men. Rembert would later assert that "there just wasn't [*sic*] enough of them to get through us that night."

Numbers alone, however, could not account for the success of the Third Platoon. Leadership, particularly at the squad level, was exceptional throughout the platoon.

Specialist 4th Class Munoz, Sergeant Rembert, and Sgt. Ralph Ely III—the latter a well-respected A Company original and one of the first in the company to earn a Combat Infantryman's Badge—coaxed, cajoled, and cussed at their squads, especially the FNGs, to save lives. "Ely was next to me and he was cussing out his new guys," Munoz remembered. "I don't know exactly what I said to mine, but I was definitely cussing them out like everyone else. Eventually they got it together." Sergeant Ely, much like Munoz and Rembert, led by example. During the battle, the nineteen-year-old from Haddam, Connecticut, would earn his second Bronze Star for killing an enemy sniper and rescuing a wounded trooper some thirty-five meters from his hole.[9]

While Munoz, Rembert, and Ely fended off NVA attacks in the Third Platoon sector, Pfc. Landis Bargatze in the Fourth Platoon shoved the barrel of his M-16 through the firing port of a four-man bunker and blazed away at a swarm of screaming North Vietnamese. Bargatze had moved into the bunker shortly before the second assault and was now firing frantically at the enemy, along with another soldier, while the two grunts at the back of the bunker busily loaded magazines. Periodically the four men would switch positions. NVA machine-gun and AK-47 fire crackled around the bunker, and every so often an RPG would *whoosh* out of the jungle and explode close by.

Doggedly advancing through the small-arms fire, some of the North Vietnamese closed to within grenade range of the Fourth Platoon bunker. "At that point, we started to see people," said Bargatze. "We could see the sandals they were wearing, and some of the North Vietnamese were bent over and some of them were crawling. They were almost at point-blank range. They were ready to die, and they were certainly ready to kill." Bargatze attempted to blast the NVA back with 40-mm grenade rounds from an M-79, but when he failed to hear any explosions in the bush beyond the bunker, he quickly abandoned the weapon and resumed firing his M-16.

Scrambled to support the 1-8 Infantry, fighter-bombers and AC-47 gunships began pounding tracts of jungle to the north, northeast, and northwest around the time of the second NVA assault. The ordnance employed in these strikes, as had been the case since the eighteenth, consisted mainly of general purpose bombs and cluster bombs (CBU).[10] These strikes, however, were largely designed to interdict and isolate the battlefield, sparing the NVA that were already engaged from the worst effects of American airpower. "I do know that we didn't let the Air Force do much close air support, certainly not in the B Company area," said Captain Sholly. "Just not reliable enough and certainly not at night. We did have the perimeter marked with strobe lights, and I think the gunships were able to use those to good advantage on the northern side. The Air Force assets were too fast to be truly accurate, so we used them in a general support role away from the company positions."

North Vietnamese snipers, meanwhile, remained a problem for all three American companies, even as the second assault ground to a halt. Perched high up in the trees, several snipers targeted Sgt. Frank Patton in A Company's Second Platoon. Patton was lying in a slip trench behind his squad, but when the shooting started he gradually worked his way through the undergrowth until he was within twenty meters of the enemy snipers. Quietly moving into position, the sure-handed squad leader shot the first sniper then pressed on, toward the location of the second. The NVA quickly returned fire, and for a while he was forced to stop and play dead. Patton waited calmly for the firing to cease, and when he was certain that the NVA had moved on to another target, he leaped to his feet and shot several more snipers, actions for which he would later earn a Bronze Star.[11]

The second North Vietnamese assault on the 1-8 Infantry perimeter ended, much like the first, in failure. For the tired grunts on the B Company line, however, the margin of victory had been uncomfortably close. "I had guys fix bayonets on the lip [of the draw]," recounted Captain Sholly, "in case they got through." Sobered by the realization that the last wave had carried the North Vietnamese to within two or three feet of the company line, Sholly accepted, resignedly, that the outcome of the battle was bound to come down to rifle butts and bayonets.

That the NVA knew where the company was probably assisted the assault troops attempting to overrun the American perimeter but, according to Sholly, the impact of that advantage has been somewhat overstated. Second-guessed for suggesting that the battalion set up for the night in a vacant NVA base camp, Sholly contends that the carefully considered manner in which the troops were positioned inside the camp, a consideration he believes his critics have often overlooked, contributed to the defeat of the first two NVA assaults. "One thing that often comes out as criticism for our selecting the NVA position is that the late quarterbacks, who weren't there, complain that the NVA knew where our holes were located and therefore had good mortar information on them," said the former B Company commander. "We, of course, knew that as well, so at least in B Company's sector, wherever possible, we dug new holes *closer* to the lip of the gully to confront the NVA as soon as they got close." Setting aside the larger question of whether it was advisable to set up in an enemy camp in the first place, the results of the first two NVA ground assaults on the B Company line certainly appear to support Sholly's contention. Plagued by American hand grenades, rifle fire, and the inevitable difficulties of attacking uphill, the NVA—despite their numbers and determination—were never able to secure a foothold on the crest of the small knoll or above the well-defended lip of the draw.

Following the second enemy assault, B Company redistributed ammo among the squads and fire teams on the line and quietly licked its wounds. The fierce, close-quarters combat had left the company with a number of casualties, including Pfc.

William Lumsden. Assigned to B Company with the rest of the 33rd Infantry Platoon (Scout Dog), Lumsden served as a tracker with Combat Tracker Team #3. Tracker teams like Lumsden's used military dogs to perform a variety of duties, from tracking VC guerillas to detecting mines and booby traps. Eager to help out that night, the nineteen-year-old Maryland native dashed to the perimeter to take up arms alongside the frontline troopers of the company. Lumsden would fight, shoulder-to-shoulder, with soldiers whom he did not know, until an NVA mortar round landed close by, mortally wounding him. Private First Class Lumsden was posthumously awarded the Bronze Star for his bravery and exemplary dedication to duty.[12]

Others suffered serious if not fatal wounds that required medical evacuation. In the Third Platoon, some of the wounded were treated by SSgt. Frankie Molnar and then relocated to a relatively safe area inside the perimeter. Molnar, at one point, was preparing to move a seriously wounded comrade with several other troopers when an NVA grenade landed unexpectedly in their midst. Noticing the enemy grenade first, Molnar immediately flung himself on top of it and absorbed the subsequent explosion with his body.

Fond of playing back-alley softball with his siblings, Molnar, the former vending machine technician who loved the Army and a good time, died in the blast, selflessly and with the welfare of his comrades foremost in his mind. "He could have gone to Canada while on leave and stayed there until the war was over, like some did, but his family obviously had standards and had raised him to be true to himself," observed Captain Sholly. "I have always been impressed with the Molnar family in that they raised their children to serve ably and well. I thought so much of him that I was going to recommend him for OCS after Vietnam. He would have made a fine officer." Molnar was posthumously awarded the Medal of Honor, marking the third extraordinary example of heroism in three days—and second that night—for which a trooper from the 1-8 Infantry would be so decorated. "It's pretty much what I would have expected from him," said 1st Lt. Larry Rodabaugh. "He was an *outstanding* squad leader, and he was a really good soldier."

Sometime after 9 P.M. the North Vietnamese attacked the 1-8 Infantry perimeter for the third time. The assault, which fell primarily on the B Company line, surged up the slope of the draw and, in some places, spilled *over* the lip. Lieutenant Colonel Gannon, circling over the battle in his C&C chopper, radioed Captain Sholly in the midst of the attack and asked, bluntly, "Can you hold?"

"This is the 82 element [B Company]," Sholly responded confidently, "and nobody is coming through us!!"

Low on ammunition and nearing exhaustion, the battle-dazed troopers of B Company, 1-8 Infantry held on and fought off the third and final NVA assault. "Another wave and we would have been down to spit, teeth, and blades," Sholly confessed years later. "Fortunately the NVA were more or less convinced [that] their tactics were not 'optimal' for a fourth try." By 9:45 P.M. the enemy assault had all but collapsed.[13] North Vietnamese troops probed the perimeter from the south and east around 10:15 P.M., around the same time that all three American companies reported experiencing some enemy jamming on the radio net, yet neither the probe nor the attempt to disrupt radio communications amounted to more than a minor inconvenience.[14] Soon after, the battalion reported that all NVA small-arms fire had ceased.[15]

Sporadic enemy mortar and RPG fire continued throughout the evening. At approximately 10:37 P.M., for example, a U.S. Air Force FAC observed flashes in the jungle some four hundred meters south of the battalion perimeter. The FAC, believing that the flashes were the result of mortar fire, relayed enough information for the artillery to be able to fire on the suspected location of the enemy tube. By 11:09 P.M. that night the North Vietnamese mortar fire had finally stopped. Intermittent RPG fire persisted, though, and for a while, around midnight, the battalion reported that the perimeter was receiving rocket rounds every ten to fifteen minutes.[16] The battalion later estimated that the NVA had hit the three-company perimeter with 175 mortar rounds and approximately forty-five RPG rounds between the start of the battle and the stroke of midnight.[17]

Three wave attacks, dozens of mortar rounds, and the destructive power of nearly fifty RPGs, some fired at close range, failed to dislodge the dug-in defenders of the 1-8 Infantry. Around midnight, the North Vietnamese finally withdrew to the west and reportedly crossed the Se San River on rafts.[18] The American victory owed much to the courage and skill of the grunts on the line, the availability of external fire support, and the performance of the three company commanders. Tasked with managing the defense of a three-company perimeter, at night and in dense jungle near the Cambodian border, Captain Sholly deserves considerable credit for juggling the demands of his own company—fighting for much of the battle at the very center of the enemy assault—with those of the battalion overall. "When the NVA hit the battalion perimeter on the twentieth, the senior captain [Sholly] had to act as the battalion commander," noted Lieutenant Colonel Gannon. "He did an outstanding job since the NVA's main attack hit his B Company [and] also C Company." Sholly, who would go on to earn a Bronze Star for his role in the battle, reflected instead on the demeanor and determination of his entire company. "We were a roused citizenry," he would write proudly, "and [we] were not going to permit a breakthrough in our sector no matter what they threw at us!"

While the three companies regrouped in the early morning hours of May 21, Captain Williamson supervised the grunts he had detailed to clear a landing zone. Williamson, expecting to evacuate some of the more serious casualties that night, had detached part of A Company to begin work on an LZ following the second NVA assault. Spc4 Lou Macellari was standing guard over a group of wounded soldiers near the LZ, not far from where Sgt. Doc Bockover was treating Sgt. Raymond Borowski. Borowski, then a senior medic serving in the Recon Platoon, had been seriously wounded during the fighting. Removing the St. Christopher's medal from around his neck, Borowski handed the keepsake to Macellari and assured the young A Company trooper that it would bring him luck. It was a simple yet profound gesture, one that possessed the power to unite two strangers in a moment of mutual humanity. Macellari accepted the medal graciously and resumed standing watch over the wounded.[19]

Nearby, Captain Williamson, well on his way to earning a Silver Star, stood in a clearing that morning, exposed to enemy small-arms fire, waving a strobe light to guide the helicopters in.[20] Around dawn a dustoff arrived to evacuate some of the wounded. Hovering overhead to avoid landing in what was still a relatively hot LZ, the dustoff lowered a basket down for Sergeant Borowski. Sergeant Bockover eased Borowski into the basket and waited for the chopper to lift the wounded medic out. Differing accounts exist as to what occurred next, but there is general agreement among the grunts on the ground that the basket was in the air and in the process of being hoisted up when the cable supporting it suddenly snapped. The actual cause of the break (enemy fire, faulty cable) has never been definitively determined. As soon as the cable snapped, however, the basket crashed to the ground, killing Sergeant Borowski instantly. "[Ray] was one hell of a man," Bockover wrote after the war. "I wish I could have spent more time around him. The men who did respected him, and he was like a father figure."[21]

Inconsolable, the distraught dustoff pilot apologized to Williamson over the radio for the mishap. Williamson, recognizing that no one was to blame, attempted to comfort the shaken aviator. "Hey, you guys are just standing up there hovering with all of this shooting coming at you," he told the pilot firmly. "It wasn't your fault." Williamson greatly admired the courage and dedication of chopper pilots in general. There were no braver men in the whole of the Army, he would later contend, than the medevac pilots in Vietnam.

The tragic circumstances surrounding the death of Sergeant Borowski proved difficult for the grunts to reconcile. "To be so close to going home and then for that to happen," said Pfc. Landis Bargatze, speaking for many on the ground that night, "was very emotional for all of us. We were all used to death, seeing bodies all blown up or in horribly grotesque, inhuman positions—positions no human body should be in. But that [Borowski] was different because every one of us could relate to being wounded and having a chance to get on a chopper and get out of the field. Those choppers, to us, meant no more humping, no more *living* death, no more *smelling* death, no more misery. Those choppers were our lifeline, so to see that lifeline lose one of us—or one of our guys not be able to get on it and have a chance to survive and go home—was incredibly difficult for all of us." Decades later, Lou Macellari returned the St. Christopher's medal to the Borowski family.

On the morning of the twenty-first, troops from the 1-8 Infantry swept the battlefield and found four dead NVA.[22] Subsequent sweeps produced a final tally of thirty-eight confirmed NVA KIA and eight enemy weapons. No estimate was provided for the number of dead the NVA almost certainly dragged off during and after the battle. American losses were listed as sixteen KIA and sixty-five WIA. A low cloud ceiling had hampered efforts to evacuate the dead and wounded the night before, but by 11:30 A.M. all of the battalion's casualties had been flown out.[23]

That morning, while searching the jungle near the battalion perimeter, B Company captured a pair of wounded NVA soldiers. One of the men would die before the company could send him in, but the other was flown back to the 1st Brigade Headquarters at 9:45 A.M.[24] Identified as a platoon sergeant in the 32nd NVA Regiment, the prisoner claimed that three battalions of the 32nd and elements of the 88th NVA Regiment had participated in the night battle. Organic 82-mm mortars, and possibly much larger 120-mm mortars recently transported into Pleiku Province from Cambodia, supported the enemy assault.

Additionally, according to the prisoner, twenty soldiers either from his platoon or company—the 1st Brigade could not confirm which—were killed on the twentieth before he got wounded. The man also indicated that the 32nd had been hard hit by air and artillery strikes over the previous few days.[25] Incredibly, nearly 18,000 artillery rounds, the blood, sweat, and tears of four batteries (A Battery, 6-29 Artillery; B Battery, 5-16 Artillery; C Battery, 5-16 Artillery; B Battery, 6-14 Artillery), were fired in support of the 1-8 Infantry from May 18 to May 24.[26] Arm-weary American artillerymen, toiling away in the heat and humidity, day after day, could find solace in the knowledge that at least *some* of those rounds inflicted damage on the enemy. Joining the 1-8 Infantry on the ground on the twenty-first, Lieutenant Colonel Gannon established the battalion TOC within the existing perimeter and settled in. "If this battalion goes down," he declared defiantly amid the sandbags surrounding his new CP, "then I'm going down with it!" Gannon arranged to have all nonessential personnel from the battalion trains and the division base camp sent forward to reinforce the battalion forward area.[27]

For the remainder of the twenty-first and the following two days, the 1-8 Infantry encountered light enemy contact and occasional mortar fire. On the twenty-fourth, the battalion, replaced in the forward area by B and C Companies, 3-8 Infantry, withdrew to Jackson Hole to rest and refit. Bloodied but unbowed, the Bullets would remain at Jackson Hole until the end of June.[28]

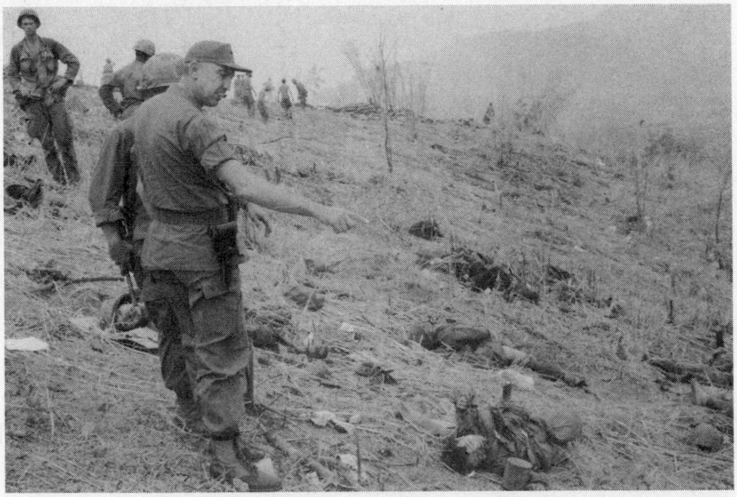

(top)
Gen. William R. Peers,
November 1967.
Courtesy Jim Stapleton.

(middle)
Pfc. Landis Bargatze,
A Company, 1-8 Infantry.
Courtesy Landis Bargatze.

(bottom)
Spc4 Bob Feigan,
A Company, 1-8 Infantry.
Courtesy Bob Feigan.

B Company, 1-8 Infantry on the move in the Central Highlands. *Courtesy Larry Rodabaugh.*

(above)
Plt. Sgt. Bruce Grandstaff, B Company, 1-8 Infantry. Grandstaff was awarded (posthumously) the Medal of Honor for his actions on May 18, 1967.
Courtesy Victor Renza.

(left)
Capt. Robert Sholly, B Company, 1-8 Infantry.
Courtesy Robert Sholly.

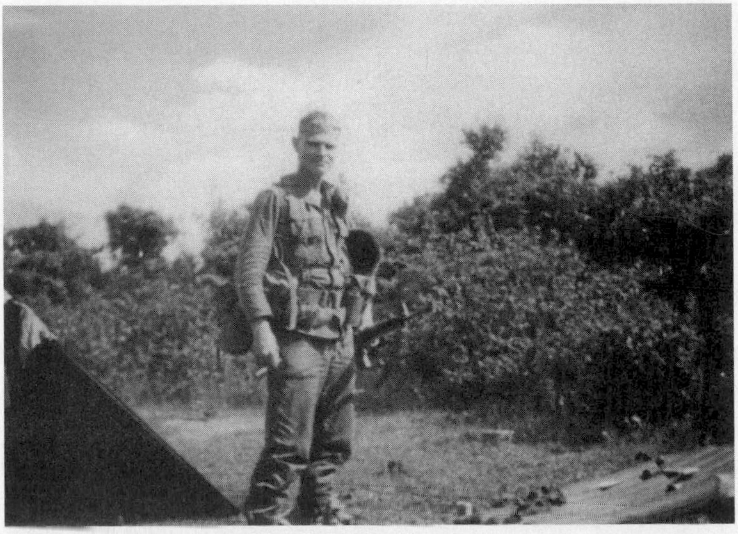

1st Lt. Larry Rodabaugh, B Company, 1-8 Infantry. *Courtesy Larry Rodabaugh.*

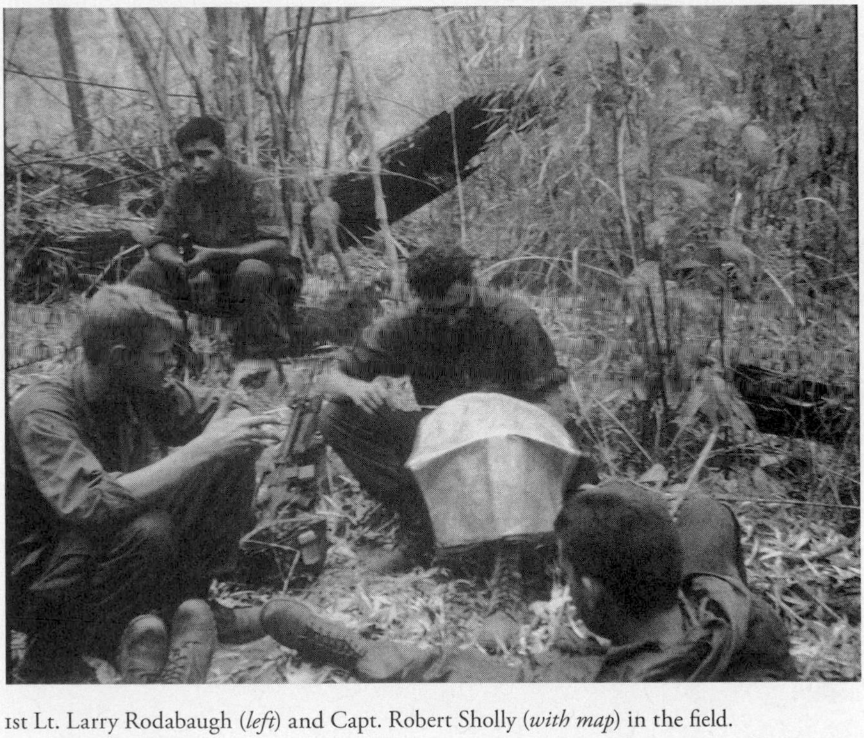

1st Lt. Larry Rodabaugh (*left*) and Capt. Robert Sholly (*with map*) in the field. *Courtesy Robert Sholly.*

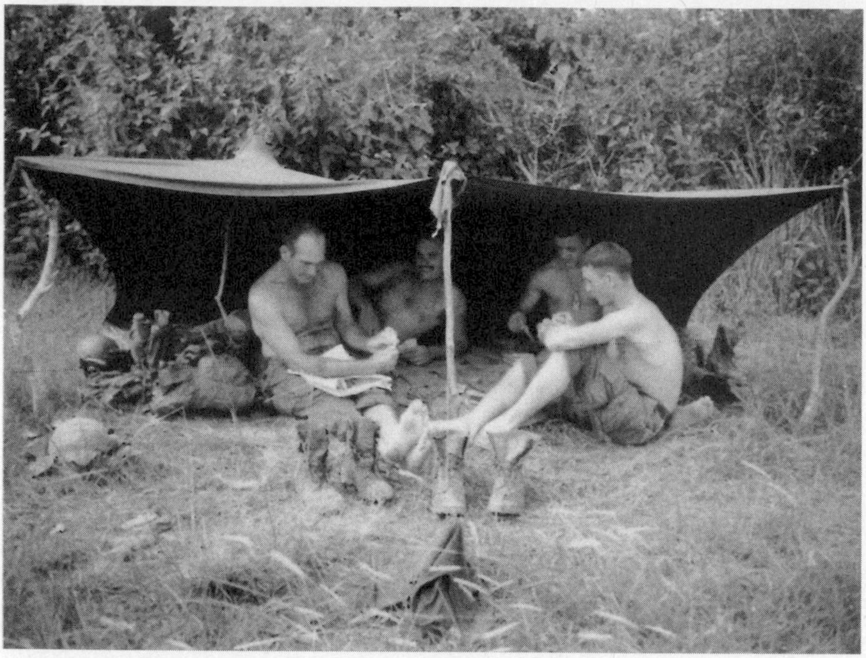

SSgt. Frankie Molnar (*right*), B Company, 1-8 Infantry. Molnar was awarded (posthumously) the Medal of Honor for his actions on May 20, 1967. *Courtesy Larry Rodabaugh.*

Pfc. Cliff Rountree, B Company, 1-8 Infantry. *Courtesy Cliff Rountree.*

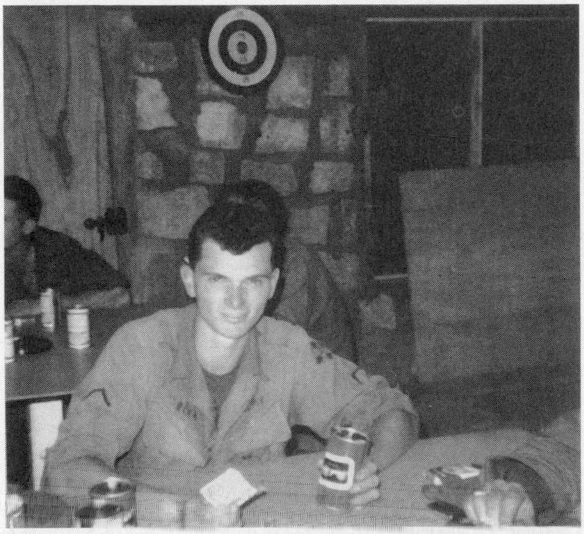

Spc4 Victor Renza,
B Company, 1-8 Infantry.
Courtesy Victor Renza.

Pfc. Gilbert Nash, B Company, 1-8 Infantry.
Courtesy Gilbert Nash.

Smoke billows up through the jungle canopy as artillery rounds crash down on the Fourth Platoon, B Company, 1-8 Infantry.
Courtesy Robert Sholly.

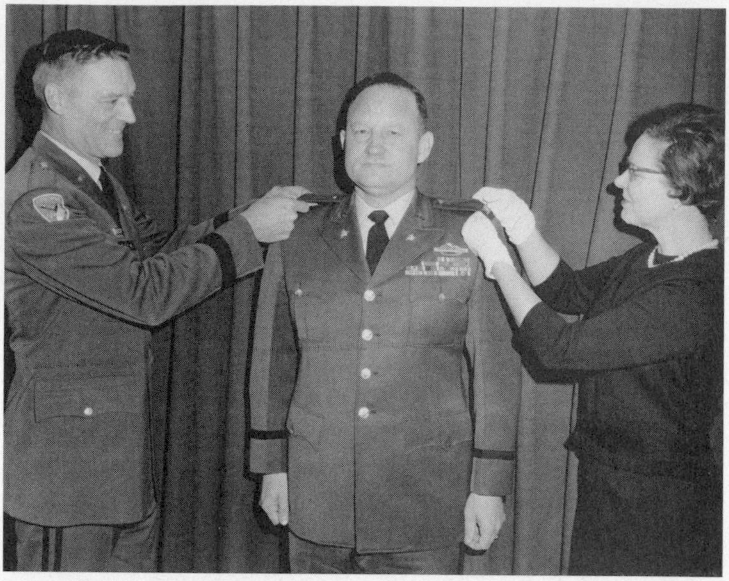

Lt. Col. John Vollmer, CO 3-12 Infantry, receiving a promotion to colonel, January 1970. *Courtesy John Vollmer.*

(above)
Pfc. Leslie Bellrichard, C Company, 1-8 Infantry. Bellrichard was awarded (posthumously) the Medal of Honor for his actions on May 20, 1967.
Courtesy Mark Bellrichard.

(right)
Capt. Mike Hamer, B Company, 3-12 Infantry, shortly after the battle on May 24, 1967.
Courtesy Mike Hamer.

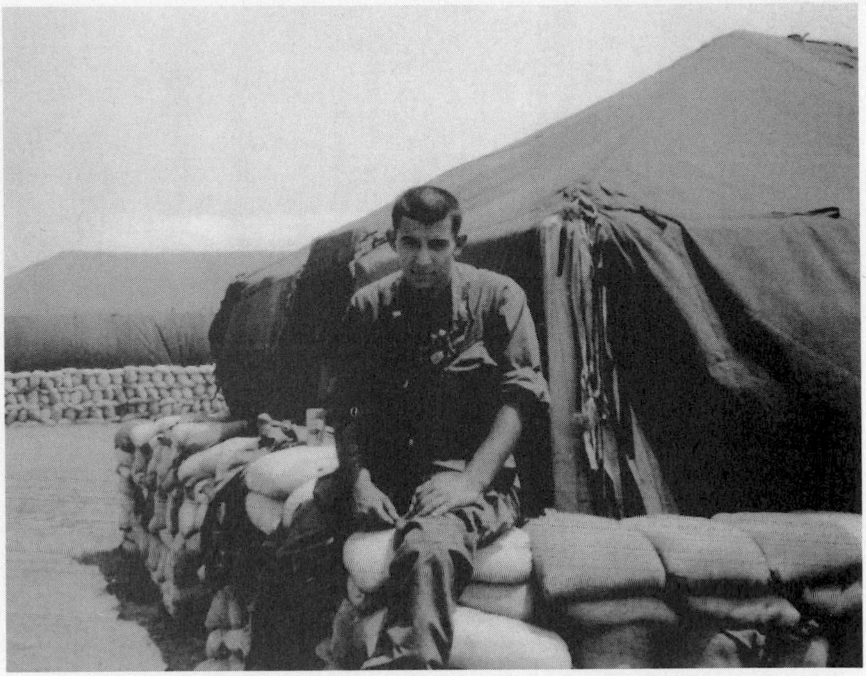

1st Lt. Steve Pestikas, B Company, 3-12 Infantry. *Courtesy Steve Pestikas.*

Spc4 Scott Reitenauer, B Company, 3-12 Infantry. *Courtesy Scott Reitenauer.*

Spc4 Mike Horan, B Company, 3-12 Infantry, with an M-16/XM-148. *Courtesy Mike Horan.*

Spc4 Mike Horan relaxes inside a makeshift bunker. Horan was in a similar bunker on May 22, 1967. *Courtesy Mike Horan.*

North Vietnamese weapons and equipment left behind after the battle on May 22, 1967. *Courtesy Mike Hamer.*

Capt. Tom Pearson, C Company, 3-12 Infantry. Pictured here as a lieutenant colonel, ca. 1971. *Courtesy Tom Pearson.*

C Company, 3-12 Infantry, crossing a river in the Central Highlands. *Courtesy Tom Radke.*

1st Lt. Doyle Volkmer, C Company, 3-12 Infantry. *Courtesy Doyle Volkmer.*

Spc4 Roger Strand, C Company, 3-12 Infantry, holding an M-79 in one hand and an M-16 in the other. *Courtesy Roger Strand.*

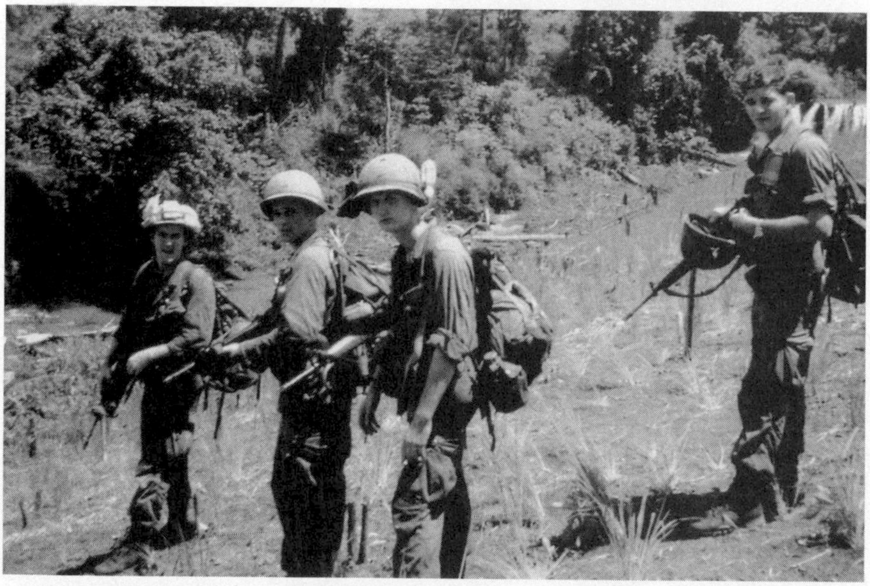

Sgt. Tom Radke (*far right, helmet off*) and Spc4 Larry Schindeldecker (*second from right*), C Company, 3-12 Infantry. *Courtesy Tom Radke.*

Lt. Col. Tom Lynch (*right*), CO 3-8 Infantry, with Capt. James Powers (*middle*) and MSgt. Richard Childers (*left*) of C Company. *Courtesy Bill Bodine.*

B Company, 3-8 Infantry, on patrol in the Central Highlands.
Courtesy Branko Marinovich.

1st Lt. Branko Marinovich,
B Company, 3-8 Infantry.
Courtesy Branko Marinovich.

1st Lt. Branko Marinovich (*far right, wearing watch*) discusses the day's events, May 25, 1967.
Courtesy Branko Marinovich.

(above)
MSgt. Richard Childers (*right*), C Company, 3-8 Infantry.
Courtesy Robert Childers.

(left)
Spc4 Bob Gamboa, B Company, 3-8 Infantry.
Courtesy Bob Gamboa.

(right)

Sgt. Erin Stroh, C Company, 3-8 Infantry. *Courtesy Erin Stroh.*

(below)

Spc5 Richard Jackson, C Company, 3-8 Infantry. *Courtesy Richard Jackson.*

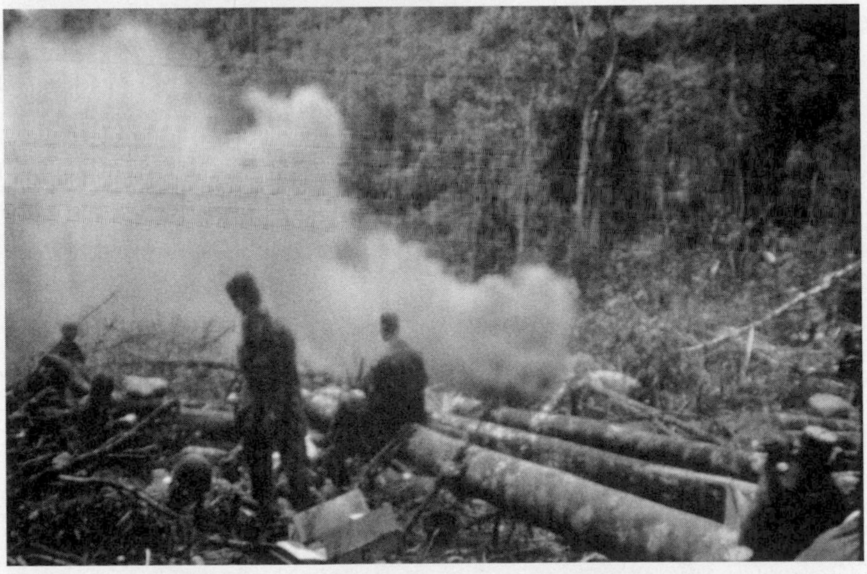

The LZ on Hill 521, May 26, 1967. By "popping" smoke, the grunts were able to mark the LZ for incoming helicopters. *Courtesy Ed Goehring.*

(left)

Sgt. Michael Scott, 6-29 Artillery, poses with an AK-47 captured on May 26, 1967. The photo was taken at Jackson Hole after the battle. *Courtesy Michael Scott.*

(below)

A 105-mm howitzer from C Battery, 6-29 Artillery. The battalion motto "Can Do" is written on the howitzer. *Courtesy Michael Scott.*

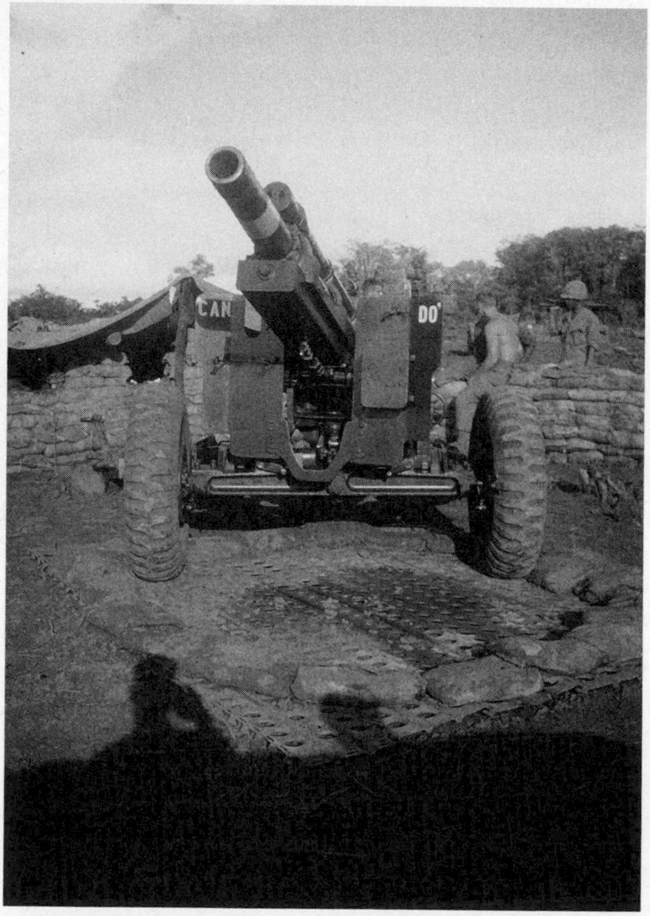

PART II

3-12 Infantry

THE BRAVES

10 INTO THE FRAY

Cruising high above the canopy, unheard and unseen, U.S. Air Force B-52s arrived over an area three kilometers to the west of the 1-8 Infantry perimeter around midnight on May 22 and promptly laid waste to the jungle below. Two more B-52 bombing runs targeted the same general area later that morning, while a fourth and final strike that night devastated a swath of jungle to the southwest.[1] Apart from reducing the affected areas to a cratered wasteland, however, the strikes produced no immediately verifiable result. Nevertheless General Peers hoped that the avalanche of bombs dropped by the B-52s would smash some of Col. Nguyen Huu An's 1st NVA Division and its estimated troop strength of 5,743, if it was still within striking distance of American supporting arms after the battles on the eighteenth and twentieth.[2]

Hours earlier, before the big bombers arrived to deliver their deadly payload, General Peers decided to return the 3-8 Infantry to the 1st Brigade. Colonel Jackson's reserve battalion was then sent to Duc Co and placed under the operational control of the 2nd Brigade. The boundary between the two brigades, meanwhile, was moved north of Highway 19 to the Chu Goungot Mountains. Peers ordered Col. James Adamson, CO of the 2nd Brigade, to dispatch two battalions to the north of Highway 19. Adamson was to use his remaining battalion to defend Plei Me.[3] To assist Peers, General Larsen asked General Westmoreland at MACV to hasten the deployment of the 173rd Airborne Brigade (Sep.), presently based in III Corps, to the Central Highlands. Westmoreland had promised Larsen the 173rd to help offset the loss of two brigades that had recently been removed from IFFV and combined with another brigade to form Task Force Oregon.[4]

Peers also directed the 3-12 Infantry, operating at the time in the upper Ia Tchar Valley, to move south and link up with the 1-8 Infantry. Nicknamed "the Braves," the 3-12 Infantry arrived with the 1st Brigade in the fall of 1966 and spent the next five months working the rice paddies and fertile valleys of Phu Yen Province on the coast of II Corps during Operation Adams. The operation was designed to destroy enemy forces in the area and protect the local rice harvests.[5] More often than not, however, the battalion—as with the 1-8 Infantry, the 3-12 Infantry consisted of originals and replacements—encountered small bands of guerillas armed with an assortment of rifles, carbines, and the occasional AK-47. Contacts were usually of the hit-and-run/ambush variety, typical of guerilla warfare, and seldom did the encounters last for any length of time. "We had VC and usually the local variety," said Capt. Mike Hamer, S2 of the 3-12 Infantry from the fall of 1966 to the spring of 1967. "We operated in an area of villages and little hamlets, and the VC would follow us by day and then operate against us at night. Booby traps abounded."[6] Rarely if ever did the battalion run into a major enemy unit.

On March 9, 1967, however, a force of 100–150 well-armed Viet Cong attacked and overran a platoon from A Company, 3-12 Infantry on Hill 86, approximately thirteen kilometers west of Tuy Hoa. Elements of A Troop, 1st Squadron, 10th Cavalry Regiment hurried to the scene and secured the American position. Ten Americans died and twenty-five more were wounded in the carefully orchestrated enemy assault.[7] Returning to the hill, A Company discovered that some of the dead had been dismembered. "That was the day—March 9, 1967—that a lot of us became heartless," said Sgt. Billy Lomnicki, an A Company original in the Fourth Platoon. "They [VC] didn't just kill those guys up there—they butchered them. They cut off their arms, their legs and one guy was found with his hands together, like when you're praying, with a bullet in his head. That was the day that the worm turned for A Company, 3-12 Infantry. We realized right then that we weren't playing cowboys and Indians out there." A little over a week later, the 3-12 Infantry, then a part of Task Force Ivy, conducted a combat assault east of Dong Tre Special Forces Camp and once on the ground swept northwest for several days. Outraged over the massacre on March 9, the battalion hunted the enemy with a vengeance and reportedly killed twenty-five in operations west of Tuy Hoa.[8]

Operation Adams concluded on April 2, 1967, effectively ending the 3-12 Infantry's tour in Phu Yen Province. On April 3 operational control of the 3-12 Infantry reverted back to the 1st Brigade, 4th Infantry Division—from February 19 to April 3, 1967, the Braves had operated as a separate task force under the control of IFFV—and by April 6 the battalion had joined the 1st Brigade in Pleiku Province for the opening of Operation Francis Marion. As the 3-12 Infantry would soon learn, however, combat operations in the Central Highlands were dramatically different than those on the coast. "The battles that we fought around Tuy Hoa as compared to those in the Highlands were as different as night and day," confessed 1st Lt. Steve Pestikas, then a platoon leader in B Company, 3-12 Infantry. "In Tuy Hoa, there were many times when you could get on top of a mountain and could see the ocean for klicks all around. We did not experience the same in the Highlands. Once we got out to Pleiku and began operations, we dug foxholes every night and everyone was in a three-man foxhole. That *never* happened at Tuy Hoa. We also stopped sooner in the Highlands so we could dig in."

Initially the 3-12 Infantry conducted search-and-destroy operations southwest of New Plei Djereng. For the better part of four weeks, from April 6 to May 1, the battalion pushed southwest, toward the Cambodian border, in search of the North Vietnamese. Days of seemingly endless searching and patrolling helped acclimate the troops to the unique rigors of Highland warfare, yet even modest improvements in fieldcraft were not matched by any corresponding increase in the battalion's ability to find the NVA.[9] Significant contacts with the enemy, in fact, were few and far between. Then, on the morning of May 1, the battalion CP received an intelligence report indicating that two North Vietnamese companies were possibly located in the vicinity of A and B Companies. A Company, which had been preparing to depart from its NDP, was informed of the report at 7:10 A.M.[10]

Five minutes later, an A Company patrol on its way back to the perimeter found telephone wire running alongside a trail some three hundred meters south of the company position. The trail led right back to the company. Soon after, in the jungle southeast of the company, an alert LP radioed in that a force of about thirty to forty North Vietnamese were advancing on the perimeter. Concerned, the A Company CO that morning, a sharp African American captain named Jones, ordered all of his platoons, then in the process of packing up, to cease at once and return immediately to their former positions in the perimeter.[11]

Moments later a company-sized force of NVA assaulted the A Company perimeter from the southeast. Rockets, mortar rounds, and heavy machine-gun fire pounded the First Platoon. Spc4 Kenny Dempich, age twenty-one, from Lincoln Park, Michigan, slid down behind an M-60 and glared out through the firing port of his bunker. "Demp" to his buddies, Specialist 4th Class Dempich disliked the high-powered machine gun at first, complaining that it was too heavy and "kicked his butt." Dempich was drafted in 1965 and tested well enough to attend flight school. Stuck instead in an infantry battalion ticketed for Vietnam, Dempich eventually adjusted and, though slightly built, learned to handle the firepower of "the pig."

Out in front of Dempich, an A Company trooper staggered awkwardly forward, tugging at his trousers. The trooper had been outside the perimeter, attempting to relieve himself before the company saddled up and moved out, when the North Vietnamese assault began. Hit in the back with a piece of shrapnel, the man could hardly pull his pants up, much less outrun the NVA. Two other troopers, seeing the man in trouble, dashed out of the perimeter and grabbed him before the NVA could finish him off. On the way back to their positions, the troopers dropped the injured man in Dempich's bunker and kept moving. To make room for the man, Dempich snatched his M-60, climbed out, and took up a position nearby.

Small-arms fire crackled through the A Company perimeter from multiple directions. Captain Jones placed artillery fire around the perimeter and called in air strikes. Jones, who would suffer a head injury later on in the fight, worked the enemy with artillery and after several more minutes of intense firing, the company reported that the volume of enemy small-arms fire around the perimeter had begun to subside. Stopped short of the American line, the NVA assult from the southeast gradually petered out.

As the assault slowed around him, Specialist 4th Class Dempich suddenly felt uncomfortably warm. *Son of a bitch, it's hot,* he thought to himself, as he grabbed the left side of his neck above the collar. Smeared with streaks of red, the palm and fingers of his left hand were nearly covered with blood. Dempich glanced down and noticed that the upper left side of his shirt was soaked with blood as well. Somehow he had been wounded in the assault on the company perimeter. "There were multiple guys throwing grenades at us," said Dempich, "and there were mortar rounds, too. I had gotten hit in the neck with shrapnel, but from what—a grenade, the mortars, or whatever—I can't say."

Dempich then felt an intense burning sensation, akin he imagined to being on fire, radiating from his neck. A medic rushed to over to assist him and immediately poured water on the wound. Nothing, though, seemed to alleviate the burning sensation on his neck. "Basically what it felt like was if you took a butane lighter, lighted it, and then held it to your neck while it heated you up," said Dempich. "That's *exactly* what I felt like, like I was heating up." Short on time and with other soldiers to treat, the medic suggested morphine but Dempich, fearing that if he took the shot he would not be alert and lucid when the shooting started up again, declined. Only later, after the battle had ended, did he finally consent to any kind of medical treatment. Dempich was then herded onto a slick bound for the rear, where he would receive a Purple Heart for his wound and a promotion to E5.

After the first NVA assault, a patrol attempting to return to the A Company perimeter reported that a large contingent of enemy soldiers was approaching the company from the southwest. Captain Jones quickly shifted the artillery to cover this new threat, but the weight of incoming shells was not enough to prevent the NVA force from assaulting the perimeter with machine guns, mortars, and RPGs at 7:37 A.M.[12] Within ten minutes of the assault a FAC arrived on station to coordinate the first batch of air strikes—Jones, redirecting the company's artillery support to the eastern side of the perimeter, carved out a corridor for the fighters to operate in—and by 9 A.M. the battle was over. A Company, although victorious, sustained losses of three KIA and sixteen WIA in the fighting.

Late that afternoon, A Company linked up with B Company, 3-12 Infantry. Captain Jones, still suffering from the head wound he suffered during the battle, was evacuated from the field. The following day, the Americans swept the area and counted twenty-four North Vietnamese KIA. Nearly two dozen enemy weapons along with a modest cache of mortar and RPG rounds were recovered as well, suggesting that at least some of the NVA dead had been carried off.[13] The Americans also captured a prisoner, who revealed that his unit—the 66th NVA Regiment—intended to strike the Special Forces camp at Duc Co in early June before advancing on Plei Me. Considered credible, the POW contributed to the intelligence picture that ultimately convinced General Peers and Colonel Jackson to dispatch the 1-8 Infantry and the 3-12 Infantry to the Ia Tchar Valley.

A Company, in the span of two months, had been involved in two significant engagements, including the first major battle the 3-12 Infantry would fight in the Central Highlands. Fear of the Highlands, the jungle, even the NVA gradually subsided, and many of the originals began to suspect that the company was little more than an expendable cog in a mismanaged machine. "We weren't afraid of combat. I think we were seasoned and [had been] there long enough that we had our shit together and were able to help the new guys around that had just gotten there," said Sgt. Ken Ethier, a twenty-year-old Fourth Platoon original. "But we were angry with the way we were treated and angry with the lousy situations they had put us in. We'd be the ones on the ground, doing all of the fighting and getting all of the shit, and this battalion commander would fly overhead and get a Bronze Star. We never got any hot meals or any kind of good treatment. The intelligence in Vietnam was terrible. I think *we* knew more than the intelligence we were given. I always thought that when we went out, we were going to run into a superior force and get our asses kicked."

Lt. Col. John P. Vollmer, age thirty-nine, recipient of a Purple Heart for his service in Korea, had assumed command of the 3-12 Infantry shortly before the battle on May 1. Previously Vollmer had served as an operations staff officer with the Review and Analysis Division, Revolutionary Development Support Directorate (Headquarters, U.S. MACV). Industrious yet personable, Vollmer worked tirelessly in that capacity and was judged an "independent, original thinker" with a "keen mind that is sharply analytical, pragmatic, and tough" by one of his superiors in the Review and Analysis Division.[14] Vollmer was also extraordinarily thorough and after assuming command of the 3-12 Infantry had insisted on relocating and rebuilding all of the bunkers at the battalion base.

Raised in Washington State, Vollmer, the studious son of an Army cavalry officer, attended high school in Washington, D.C., and, following graduation, received an appointment to the United States Military Academy. Graduating from West Point in 1949, Vollmer later served as a platoon leader in Korea. There the young lieutenant learned a valuable lesson. An American platoon had been traveling down a road on foot, making better time than if the troops had been hiking across the Korean countryside, when the enemy suddenly sprung an ambush, catching the platoon in a deadly trap. Arriving too late to be of any assistance, Vollmer and his men were subsequently tasked with recovering the bodies of the ambushed platoon.

Vollmer, while policing up the dead that day, gained a newfound appreciation for the importance of terrain and the potential perils of selecting the easiest route of advance. "Either find yourself some high ground," Vollmer would later advise his company commanders in the 3-12 Infantry, "or locate the nose of a ridge and get on it." In Colonel Jackson he would find something of a kindred spirit. "Don't pay any attention to those folks pontificating about high ground and terrain," Jackson told Vollmer. "Even in the jungle, high ground and terrain are important."

Strong, inspired leadership, or someone, in short, who would command the battalion with conviction and compassion, was precisely what the 3-12 Infantry needed. Most of all, though, the troops wanted an advocate, not an out-of-touch ticket puncher motivated solely by the prospect of professional advancement. Vollmer certainly had aspirations of someday earning a promotion to full bird, but the stout, raw-boned West Pointer—he adopted the name "Husky" for his radio call sign—also cared about his people, a trait he shared with some but not all of his peers.

Vollmer also deflected interference from higher up the chain of command and for the most part resisted the urge, not uncommon among some battalion commanders, to micromanage his companies in the field. "Normally the battalion commander flies overhead in his little helicopter and talks to the company commanders," said Capt. Mike Hamer, CO of B Company, 3-12 Infantry beginning in March 1967. "Lieutenant Colonel Vollmer will probably tell you that he liked the idea of his company commanders telling him what they needed, and then he'd go and get it for them. The company commanders were down there under the trees, shooting at those guys [NVA], and he [Vollmer] didn't feel like he should tell them how to maneuver or what to do. For that, Lieutenant Colonel Vollmer was a godsend. But the real importance of Lieutenant Colonel Vollmer as an individual was that he would keep the *other* commanders away. In other words, the brigade commander would come over in his own helicopter. And, of course, in a pitched battle with parts of two battalions involved, the division commander would send someone out or he might come out himself. They'd all want situation reports about what was going on." Vollmer, according to Hamer, would step in and deal with the brass while his company commanders went about the business of fighting the war.

Despite a wealth of personal combat experience and years of professional development, however, Vollmer was not especially well versed in some of the tactical innovations the Army had perfected in Vietnam. Helicopters, for example, were still something of a novelty to him on the eve of the May 1 battle. "I had an instinct for fighting. However, I had not been trained in helicopter combat," Vollmer admitted. "The helicopter was somewhat new to me. And the damn thing made a lot of noise. As a battalion commander, I of course also had headphones on, so as far as outside ambient noise was concerned, you really couldn't even hear gunfire. It was all noise and vibrations in those damn things."

On the morning of May 21, Colonel Jackson summoned Vollmer to Jackson Hole for a conference. Vollmer, boarding his C&C bird, departed the 3-12 Infantry firebase at 9:23 A.M. The 3-12 Infantry, Jackson explained, was to move south from the upper Ia Tchar Valley and link up with Lieutenant Colonel Gannon's 1-8 Infantry. Flying back to the battalion firebase after the meeting, Vollmer ordered A and B Companies to move south with "deliberate speed and security." Vollmer, to better support the two companies moving south, decided to relocate the battalion firebase and arranged to have reinforced Apache teams from the battalion Reconnaissance Platoon scout and secure an area for the new base.[15] The old base, meanwhile, was to be dismantled while troops and equipment were airlifted out. C Company, 3-12 Infantry provided security at the existing base and conducted patrols during the move while awaiting orders to fly south with the rest of the battalion.[16]

Firm, outspoken, and something of a taskmaster, Capt. Thomas Pearson, United States Military Academy (USMA) Class of 1962, commanded C Company. Pearson had served as a platoon leader in a mechanized infantry regiment in Germany and as a battalion S1 before volunteering for service in Vietnam. Two months later, in December 1965, Pearson arrived in South Vietnam, and for much of the following year would serve as an advisor with two different ARVN Ranger battalions in two different theaters of the war. The assignments, though mentally and physically exhausting, provided an opportunity to oversee operations in the Central Highlands, an experience he would later draw on while in command of C Company. Relations with his South Vietnamese counterparts, strained as they were by cultural differences and the relentless stress of combat, deteriorated over time, however, and by the end of his tour as an advisor, Pearson was no longer on speaking terms with the commander of the ARVN battalion to whom he had been assigned. Disillusioned, he wrapped up his tour, happy he would never have to see or speak to the ARVN officer again, and briefly considered quitting the Army altogether.

In late 1966, while serving in the Headquarters of the 4th Infantry Division in Pleiku, Pearson unexpectedly ran into a lieutenant colonel who, as luck would have it, had been one of his English professors at West Point. Shortly, the lieutenant colonel informed Pearson, the 4th would have a number of openings available for new company commanders, if he was interested. Encouraged, Pearson left Vietnam in December 1966 for a thirty-day leave; returning in early January, the trim twenty-seven-year-old—Pearson would turn twenty-eight on April 5, 1967—received command of C Company, 3-12 Infantry.

Whatever doubts the men of C Company had about their new skipper, and some privately wondered if they were about to be led by some gung-ho, medal-chasing, spit-and-polish West Pointer, were quickly laid to rest during an ambush in the Tuy Hoa area a few weeks after Pearson took over command of the company. Pearson calmly pulled the company into a perimeter at the first sign of trouble and called in massive fire support. By employing a "firepower first" approach, he salvaged a potentially disastrous situation and, critically, signaled to his skeptical troops that he intended to expend shells—and not lives—to achieve operational objectives.

Crucially, Pearson believed that tactical maneuver, the traditional response to enemy contact but one that entailed significantly greater risk in a non-lineal combat environment, was of limited value in Vietnam and would only be used sparingly. "I didn't maneuver," recalled the West Pointer bluntly. "We'd bring in fire first. We'd make sure we had control of the artillery before we did anything, because if you maneuvered without knowing what was going on, it habitually led to absolute disaster. In other words, if you didn't bring the company up into that little circle, you were likely to lose a platoon. If you separated a platoon out and sent them off onto a flank, the chances were very good that you'd lose it. And that happened frequently. I wasn't about to let that happen. So the first thing we'd do is kind of circle the wagons, bring in artillery, and based on the situation as could be determined, then maneuver."

Pearson also believed in "piling on." Whenever the NVA appeared in large numbers and engaged friendly units, division and brigade commanders had an obligation, in his opinion, to commit the resources (troops, artillery, airpower) required to smash the enemy. Something big had manhandled the 1-8 Infantry, that much he and most of the other officers in the 3-12 Infantry knew for certain, and yet the brass had decided to commit only *two* companies to the rapidly developing meat grinder in the lower Ia Tchar Valley. The entire exercise struck him as absurdly inadequate. "If we were going to clean up that area down there [1-8 Infantry AO], and we knew there was a large enemy force down there, [then] you hit it with everything," he noted angrily. "Well, they [4th Infantry Division leadership] didn't do that." Pearson, however, never raised the issue with Lieutenant Colonel Vollmer. It is unlikely in any event that his objections would have had any impact on the decision to reinforce the 1-8 Infantry with A and B Companies.

Large enemy forces were indeed operating in and around the Ia Tchar but not all of them belonged to the 32nd NVA Regiment, the unit that had attacked the 1-8 Infantry.

Rumored to have established base camps northwest of Duc Co, the battle-hardened 66th NVA Regiment, veteran of several earlier Highland campaigns, had also moved elements into the area.[17] Celebrated for its courage and determination in battle, the 66th was a lineal descendant of one of the oldest regiments in the Vietnamese Communist armed forces. In late 1945, shortly after the conclusion of the Second World War, the Vietnamese Communists raised a number of main force regiments to oppose the restoration of French Colonial rule, including the 9th Regiment under the command of Le Trong Tan. Tan's regiment, according to a Vietnamese Communist history of the 66th NVA Regiment, would later become the "predecessor unit from which the 66th Regiment was born."[18] Initially based in Son Tay Province, the 9th was re-designated the 37th Regiment in December 1946. The following year the regiment was reorganized and formally renamed the "66th Regiment."

Incorporated into the newly formed 304th Division in 1950, the 66th campaigned extensively in the final years of the war against the French. The 66th fought primarily in Vietnam, but in 1953 the regiment was dispatched to central Laos where, in the space of just six short months, it achieved such spectacular results that General Vo Nguyen Giap, though addressing cadres on the Dien Bien Phu campaign, proclaimed: "In central Laos, the 66th Regiment alone is performing as if it was an entire division."[19] Triumphant, the 66th marched out of Laos in June 1954, scarcely a month after the fall of Dien Bien Phu, and returned to Vietnam. "When the resistance war against the French colonialists ended," a regimental history explained, "the 66th Regiment received the honor of being allowed to keep Chairman Ho Chi Minh's 'Determined to Fight, Determined to Win' flag."[20] Eleven years later the 66th hiked south into the Central Highlands of South Vietnam and again shed blood for the cause, this time in the Ia Drang Valley opposite the American 1st Cavalry Division.

Comparable to the 32nd NVA Regiment, the 66th was a professional, frontline formation very much akin to the straight-leg infantry units of the 4th Infantry Division. As a fighting force, the regiment had an excellent reputation for reliability in battle. Moreover, like those of the 32nd, the battalions of the 66th consisted of hard-nosed, well-equipped North Vietnamese regulars who, despite pronounced disadvantages in firepower and mobility, were not afraid of Americans.

Snaking through the jungle in a single column, B Company, under the command of Capt. Mike Hamer, had been on the move for nearly two hours on the morning of the twenty-first when the battalion TOC crackled over the radio at 10:43 A.M. Headed in a southerly direction at the time, the same general heading he had been on since breaking camp shortly before 9 A.M., Captain Hamer immediately recognized the voice of Maj. Richard Jones, the battalion S3. B Company, Jones explained, was to suspend its search-and-destroy operations and move at once to the 1-8 Infantry. Jones then relayed the coordinates of the 1-8 Infantry and instructed Hamer to move as quickly as possible.[21]

Hamer, hurriedly mapping out a route based on the coordinates furnished by Jones, briefed his platoon leaders on the new mission. Word of the move south to reinforce the 1-8 Infantry spread quickly, from the four platoon leaders to their respective squad leaders and on down the line, until most of the grunts had at least some understanding of the situation. "Did I know that we were hooking up [with the 1-8 Infantry]? I did. My sergeants did," recalled 1st Lt. Steve Pestikas, PTL of the Third Platoon. "Did that filter all the way down to the men? I'm sure it did. To what extent I do not know, but I thought the communications were very good in our particular unit—B, 3rd of the 12th. The company commander [Captain Hamer] was very attuned to communicating what he envisioned was happening and what our goals and objectives were."[22]

Spc4 Class Mike Horan, twenty-one, had hoped that with Buddha's birthday, and the twenty-four-hour truce the 4th Infantry Division intended to observe in honor of it, coming up on May 23, the company would enjoy a couple of quiet days in the bush. Horan never worried about firefights; Brooklyn born and bred, the young Irish-American kid from Park Slope felt almost indestructible at times, as if Vietnam had nothing on him. Nonetheless, the idea of marching headlong into an area with beaucoup NVA made him nervous. Horan, trying to shake it off, figured the sterling silver St. Christopher's medal his mother had given him and the green rosary beads he had picked up in Tuy Hoa would keep him safe if he ran into any trouble down there.

Hurried along, B Company double-timed it to the south-southeast, down a narrow jungle path, toward a north-south draw. Ordinarily Captain Hamer avoided moving along trails and footpaths, but with orders from battalion to expedite the march south, he could not afford to waste time tramping cross-country through the jungle. The company would have enough trouble getting to the 1-8 Infantry, Hamer well knew, without having to bushwhack the entire length of the proposed route.

Third Platoon, led by 1st Lt. Steve Pestikas, pulled up the rear of the company column. Having created a homemade patch with the words "Hell's Saints" inscribed above a halo-wearing, pitchfork-brandishing devil, the Third Platoon, perhaps more than any other platoon in the company, had a keen sense of unit identity. "The Third Platoon, B Company, 3-12 Infantry was known throughout the 1st Brigade, 4th Division as the 'Hell's Saints.' Every member of the platoon wore a patch labeled 'Hell's Saints,'" wrote Lieutenant Pestikas. "My platoon sergeant, Jim Morris, approached me with the suggestion that we establish a nickname for our platoon. Early in our tour we worked independent of the rest of the company on numerous occasions and felt great camaraderie among us. For numerous reasons, esprit de corps being a factor, I agreed with the concept." Pestikas, after receiving a number of design suggestions, had a drawing of the proposed "Hell's Saints" emblem made into patches, which were then sewn onto the helmet cover of every member of the platoon. The Third wore the "Hell's Saints" patch for months, until brigade brass intervened and forced the platoon to remove them shortly after the 3-12 Infantry arrived in the Central Highlands.

Accustomed to operating independently, the Hell's Saints, while certainly no better than the other platoons in the company, quickly developed a "don't tread on me" attitude in the field. "These guys weren't going to take anything from anyone," said Pfc. Eddie Meier, a replacement who joined the platoon in April 1967. "They would not back down." That mentality, Meier would soon discover, emanated from the top. Born in Hammond, Indiana, in August 1946, Steve Pestikas enlisted in the Army at eighteen, determined to serve in an airborne outfit. Gung-ho, he completed airborne and Special Forces training after AIT and was subsequently offered a duty assignment with the 10th Special Forces Group or a slot at Officer Candidate School. Pestikas opted for OCS. Commissioned in April 1966, at the age of nineteen, he was assigned to Fort Lewis, Washington and assumed command of the Third Platoon, B Company, 3-12 Infantry.

Traveling overseas with the 3-12 Infantry advance party, Pestikas arrived in South Vietnam ready to lead troops into battle. Olive-skinned, with shocks of charcoal-colored hair buzzed neatly above his forehead, the hard-charging Midwesterner was one of the youngest officers in the entire division, younger in some instances than the grunts in his platoon. Pestikas, however, preached professionalism and had little patience for sloppiness or insubordination. Everyone in the platoon had a job to do, and everyone was expected to do it right. "I was more afraid of Pestikas," said Private First Class Meier, "than I was of the NVA." Fond of LAWs and nighttime ambushes, the latter a rarity among junior officers, Pestikas believed that, if properly led and adequately equipped, his platoon, the Hell's Saints, would perform as well as any similar-sized North Vietnamese unit operating in the Central Highlands. The North Vietnamese were good, he reminded his youthful charges, but so were they.

A Company, 3-12 Infantry, humping south along the high ground to the west of B Company, halted briefly around 10 A.M. to get resupplied before continuing on through the dense, column-slowing jungle. Security elements flanked the company with little concern for the speed or pace of the column since the main body could scarcely move any faster in the thick undergrowth. Commanded now by a Captain Lee, an officer dispatched to the field after the battle on May 1, A Company had moved out at 8:17 A.M. that morning, expecting to push south for another day of routine operations. The slow but steady slog had progressed without incident, and with few interruptions, until 10:43 A.M., when Major Jones radioed with the location of the 1-8 Infantry in the lower Ia Tchar Valley. A Company was to join B Company in heading south to reinforce the regrouping battalion.

Half-briefed, and now in a hurry, platoon and squad leaders communicated the new mission to the troops. Another battalion in the valley had run into trouble, the grunts were told, and the higher-ups wanted A Company, 3-12 Infantry, to move quickly to reinforce it. "We didn't get all that much information," said Sgt. Arthur Klassen, a squad leader in the Second Platoon. "I don't know if they didn't want to scare us or whatever, but they said that the 1-8 Infantry had been involved in contact with an NVA unit and were getting continuous probes at night. They said that we were to move into that area to reinforce them. We knew that scenario, and we knew there was a large contingent [of NVA] in that area and that's why we were going to that area." Tall and intelligent, if somewhat ambivalent about the Army and the war, Klassen had survived the debacle on Hill 86 in March by hiding in the brush near the base of the hill. The twenty-year-old draftee from Detroit was handed a squad in April 1967, and he planned to get all of his people home safely.

Promoted to E5, Sgt. Kenny Dempich had recuperated from the wound he sustained on May 1 and had rejoined the company in the field, fully expecting that his M-60 machine gun would be waiting for him when he returned. Pfc. Shelby Bullard, however, had taken over on the M-60 and he, diminutive Demp, one of the least imposing soldiers in the First Platoon, had been placed in charge of the squad. On the morning of the twenty-first, Dempich was told that the 1-8 Infantry had stumbled into some "deep shit" and that *two* companies from the 3-12 Infantry had to move south without delay to reinforce the Bullets. Dempich, still very much a machine gunner at heart, planned to set up next to an M-60 that night "just in case something happened."

Hacking through thick jungle, A Company started down the heavily vegetated high ground to the west of B Company around 2:45 P.M. that afternoon after Lieutenant Colonel Vollmer ordered the company to move southeast, to more level terrain. Captain Lee was to then head south.[23] Much like A Company, 1-8 Infantry, which had moved to reinforce B Company, 1-8 Infantry, three days before, A Company, 3-12 Infantry marched downhill with a mixture of replacements and originals. Most of the replacements would become capable infantrymen; a small minority, conversely, would struggle with the most rudimentary of tasks and would never earn the trust of their more experienced peers. "Some of them," observed Spc4 Hank Fischer, an RTO in the Third Platoon, "were dumb as a box of rocks."

Fischer's less than charitable critique was not uninformed. One evening he had accompanied the Third Platoon PTL at the time around the perimeter to check if the new guys were digging in and setting up properly. The platoon leader, observing each defensive position in turn, asked the men if they had put out Claymore mines. Yes, the young troopers said confidently, they had put out their Claymores. The troopers then marched over to the mines. "With a Claymore mine, there's two ways you can tell if you've put it in right," said Fischer. "Right on the front of the mine it says: 'This side toward enemy.' So, you'd put it in the ground facing towards the enemy. The mine is shaped like a half-moon, so you'd put it up against your stomach. If it took the shape of your stomach, you would put it right down in the ground—just the way it was. So they made it so that if you couldn't read, that showed you the way it was supposed to go in." Incredibly, the troopers had put the mines in backward. Rather than facing out, toward the enemy, the business side of the mines were pointing inward, toward the American perimeter.

Around 11 A.M. B Company, marching at the time to the east of A Company, exited a tangle of thick, double-canopy jungle and began moving through a more open area covered with brush and elephant grass. The ground in the area was littered with small, unexploded, grenade-sized bombs from larger cluster bomb units (CBUs) dropped by the Air Force. A fallen tree trunk, not uncommon in the Highlands, lay across the narrow trail stretched out before the company. Four platoons strong, the company column bobbed noisily along as the grunts stepped over the tree trunk and continued on down the trail. Sgt. Thomas Modisette, nineteen, of Irving, Texas, approached the tree trunk in the trailing Third Platoon. Several soldiers, including Lieutenant Pestikas, had stepped over it moments before and were striding down the trail with their backs to him.

Normally one of the more bush-savvy grunts in the Third Platoon, Modisette appeared pensive and preoccupied that morning. For two weeks he had been in a funk, haunted, most guessed, by the tragic events of May 6, 1967. That night a green nineteen-year-old replacement assigned to his fire team was shot and killed when he was mistaken for the enemy while out on an LP with other grunts from the First Squad. Modisette blamed himself for the man's death and privately confided that he believed God would punish him for what had happened. Sgt. Robert Ramirez, the squad's even-keeled leader and an experienced original, noticed the change in Modisette almost immediately and told another soldier in the squad to look after him, trusting that in time the cocksure kid from the woods of Texas would come around.

Modisette lumbered up to the fallen tree trunk, started to step over it, and then disappeared in a cloud of smoke and debris. Wedged alongside or underneath the tree trunk, hidden in any event, an unexploded CBU had detonated suddenly and violently at his feet. The time was approximately 11:15 A.M.[24] SSgt. Loya Mallory, a twenty-four-year-old African American original, was next in line behind Modisette. Blown backward in the blast, the flesh on his chest and shoulder laced with shrapnel, Mallory tumbled to the ground.

Earlier, while the company was traversing a small rise, Mallory had handed Modisette a bunch of letters to mail when he and Sergeant Ramirez left the field for

R&R in a couple of days. As the company marched onward, Mallory grew increasingly unnerved by a premonition that something awful was about to happen. *If Modisette gets killed*, he found himself wondering forebodingly, *what will happen to all my mail?* Ten minutes later that nagging premonition had become a horrifying reality: Sergeant Modisette was on the ground, fighting for his life. "It blew him [Modisette] just about in half," Mallory recalled. "When he fell, I couldn't see the extent of his wounds. He had fallen on his stomach. Then I saw the medics who were working on him turn him over, and my heart just broke. When they turned him over, I could see that all of his stomach was gone." Mallory, scrambling to his feet, rushed over to assist Modisette but was pulled back by other soldiers.

Sergeant Ramirez, who was walking behind Mallory when the CBU exploded unexpectedly, was lifted off of his feet and spun around. "When I was hit, all of a sudden I felt like I had been hit in the face," recalled Ramirez, then a twenty-two-year-old Mexican American kid from Texas. "I was thrown up in the air, and I landed and was turned around. I was facing toward the *back* of the trail, and my face was burning. I didn't recognize it [the trail], because I was facing backwards. I didn't recognize where I was at. I was disoriented. I recall that I tried to reach for my rifle, but I couldn't because my arm was almost severed. It was numb, so I couldn't pick my rifle up. When I landed, my rucksack fell over and I was on my knees. I was staring around and couldn't get up because my rucksack was holding me down." Several soldiers hurried to his side and cut the straps on his rucksack.

Dirt-smeared and still a bit dazed, Ramirez slipped out of his rucksack and immediately began checking his body for injuries. Shrapnel, flying debris, or both had left wounds, in addition to the deep gash on his right arm, on his lower left leg, calves, upper left leg, right foot, and right ankle. An artery and a nerve on his right arm, moreover, were sheared above the elbow. "C'mon, take my picture," he joked with the soldiers hovering around him. "They're going to come pick me up. I'm fine." Ramirez, jungle-wise yet soft-spoken, the product of a migrant family that understood poverty and hard times, tried desperately to downplay the extent of his injuries, not for his own sake but for the troops in his squad. Long faces, aged in some cases beyond their youthful years, stared glumly down at him. "C'mon, take my picture," he demanded playfully. Ramirez then asked for Tommy.

Tommy, however, was dead. Sgt. Thomas Glen Modisette, the blonde-haired, fair-skinned free spirit who turned red in the sun and carried a snub-nosed .38, had died in the explosion. "The entire company had passed over that location without making the CBU explode," said Lieutenant Pestikas. "I was between the First and Second Squads, and it happened just after I had crossed that section of path where the explosion occurred. There was a tree trunk and branch across the trail, and probably close to a hundred guys had already passed over it when it exploded." Modisette's death had a particularly sobering effect on Pfc. Bill Avery, an RTO for an artillery forward observer attached to B Company. That kind of thing happened to other people, not guys like Modisette. "He had a pistol, and I remember he was one that didn't take any prisoners," noted Avery. "To me, he was the John Wayne guy, and he was there to fight. He was a real soldier. He stood out for me. When that happened, it was hard to believe. That probably had more of an effect on me than to [*sic*] the other guys."

Staff Sergeant Mallory, Sergeant Ramirez, and a third injured soldier, meanwhile, were alive but in desperate need of a dustoff.[25] Mallory, clenching his teeth, looked up at the grim-faced soldiers standing around and exclaimed, "Fuck it, I'm going to make it!" Few at the time believed him. "If you took a large sheet of rice paper and placed it tautly over a door frame, stood back ten feet and threw several handfuls of BBs at it, this man's body appeared to have resembled what the rice paper would have appeared—like a colander," observed Lieutenant Pestikas. "No way should he have survived what he did. From my perspective, his survival was the result of a positive mental attitude. It made an impact on me that day and every day since as the embodiment of the power of a positive mental attitude." B Company secured an LZ in a patch of elephant grass and at 11:17 A.M. radioed for a dustoff.

Around noontime a dustoff arrived to pick up the wounded. Loaded aboard the chopper, Ramirez felt guilty for leaving his squad behind. "Well," he intoned solemnly, "I guess I'm going home." Remarkably both he and Staff Sergeant Mallory would survive the explosion. For Ramirez, though, the death of Sgt. Thomas Modisette remains a painful reminder of the war in Vietnam. "Tommy was one of my fire team leaders," he stated proudly years later, "but most of all he was my friend. He will always be remembered and not forgotten."

Following the evacuation of Sergeant Modisette's body, B Company resumed marching south-southeast and eventually entered a north-south draw sometime after noon. Temperatures by then had climbed well into the eighties and perhaps even the nineties, and many of the grunts were relieved when the company approached a fast-moving stream. Captain Hamer, concerned about the welfare of his troops, instructed the platoons to replenish their water supplies before they splashed across the stream. Habitually thirsty, the grateful troopers dunked empty and half-empty canteens into the drink and filled them to the brim.

Hill masses and forested ridges flanked the company as it moved south. The advance took on the appearance of a training march back at Fort Lewis until the point element of the company column, moving along a trail running through the bush, spotted communications wire running parallel to the trail. Nervous, the point element tapped the wire, determined that it was "hot," and notified their platoon leader who, in turn, informed Captain Hamer. Dark green in color, the wire eventually merged with other wires to form noticeable bundles on the jungle floor. "I started noticing more and more, and then I would see the bundles as more and more lines ran into the main dark green commo wire," said Spc4 Mike Horan of the First Platoon. "You'd see them [wires] coming out from different areas and running into the main branch, so to speak, and then they'd run together in a bundle. And the bundles started getting bigger to me. To me that meant only one thing—that we were getting close to a command post or control, or a large group of [enemy] troops." Carefully tracing the route of the main enemy line, a B Company soldier followed the wire into the bush to the left of the trail and up the slope of an adjacent hill.

Along the way the trooper spied a North Vietnamese trail watcher and immediately opened fire. The NVA fled, apparently unharmed, and the trooper returned to the company. Captain Hamer noted the incident, and the column began moving again shortly thereafter. *If the NVA didn't know we were here before*, Hamer thought to himself as the column gained speed, *then they certainly know now*. Bundles of communications wire, moreover, told him that wherever they were, there had to be a lot of them to warrant that kind of command and control equipment.

Hamer had been in command of B Company, 3-12 Infantry since April, having replaced Capt. Jim Hegglund after a six-month stint as the battalion S2. Right away, Hamer realized he had inherited a dependable outfit: tough, resilient, and devoted to one another, if not necessarily to the war, the troops—kids, mostly—would soldier if ably led. Hegglund had earned their respect, yet after just a few short weeks, even some of the old hands had to admit that their new skipper could do the job. "Mike Hamer may have been my best company commander," recalled Lieutenant Colonel Vollmer, CO of the 3-12 Infantry. "He was one hell of a good company commander." Unflappable, Hamer rarely resorted to "rah-rah" speeches or gung-ho rhetoric to motivate the troops, most of whom he concluded would fight regardless of who was leading them. The troops, he believed, would respond more effectively to honesty, capable leadership, and a calm command presence.

Blue-eyed and broad shouldered, every bit the all-American boy, Martin Ernest Hamer—"Mike" for short—grew up in a middle-class family in football-mad Columbus, Ohio. Hamer played high school ball, and while he chased glory on the gridiron his mother volunteered as a fundraiser for legendary Ohio State football coach Woody Hayes. Hanging up his cleats after high school, he put off college and went to work in a Goodyear warehouse before enlisting in the Marine Corps in 1956. Hamer enjoyed the experience and even found time to play on the Regimental Football team at Camp Pendleton in 1957. Fulfilling his enlistment obligation, he left the Marines in 1958 and enrolled at Henderson State in Arkansas on a football scholarship. By his junior year, however, he had fallen behind and was in danger of not graduating on time. Should he require a fifth year to graduate, school officials warned, the tuition bill for the extra year and other out-of-pocket expenses would not be covered by his athletic scholarship. Hamer, on the advice of an academic counselor, signed up for Army ROTC to make up the credits he needed to earn a bachelor's degree in four years. In 1962 the accidental cadet graduated from Henderson State on schedule and received a commission in the Army.

Hamer began his Army career at Fort Benning, Georgia, in the basic infantry course for officers, before moving on to Fort Ord, California. Stationed at Fort Ord from 1962 to 1965, the onetime collegiate end practiced the art of war making, gradually advancing from platoon leader to a battalion S3. Hamer then applied to flight school and, after passing the physical and all relevant exams, patiently waited for an opening with fixed-wing aircraft; the Army, however, cut orders for helicopter flight school. Disappointed, he declined the offer and ended up in Germany prior to being reassigned to the 4th Infantry Division in July 1966. Assigned to the 3-12 Infantry, Hamer served as the battalion S2 in Vietnam until Lt. Col. David Peters, then CO of the battalion, approached him in late March 1967 and asked, "Do you want Bravo Company?"

Hamer replied unhesitatingly, "Absolutely!"

A and B Companies, the former rumbling down from the high ground to the west, the latter pushing through a north-south valley to the east, marched south on the afternoon of the twenty-first on roughly parallel axes of advance. Lieutenant Colonel Vollmer, planning for the night ahead, ordered B Company at 3 P.M. to move to an LZ approximately two hundred meters to the south-southeast.[26] B Company was to establish an NDP in the area and then wait for the resupply ships—slicks generally delivered supplies to line companies every three or four days—to arrive first thing the following morning. Once resupplied, B Company was to resume marching south to the 1-8 Infantry.

Captain Hamer estimated that B Company had enough ammo for the night, but the slicks would certainly have to deliver additional food and water, along with fresh fatigues to replace the tattered rags rotting off the bodies of some of the men, before the march south could resume the next morning. More than the supply situation, however, Hamer was troubled by the prospect of setting up that night within a few hundred yards of where his point element had fired on a North Vietnamese trailwatcher. "As soon as we received resupply [on the morning of the twenty-second], we were going to get orders on where to go and what to do," remembered the B Company commander. "We knew the 1-8 Infantry had been in a lot of contact, but we didn't know where or how much it was. We did know that they had been in contact for two days, so we knew there was something going on. Then we saw that trailwatcher, [and] we knew that the NVA were around somewhere." Wherever that somewhere happened to be, the NVA—thanks to that trailwatcher— would soon hear all about the arrival of an American company in the area, if they hadn't already. Hamer quickened the pace of the company column. *Before it gets dark out here*, he reminded himself, *we had better be dug in.*

Meanwhile, to the north, the arduous process of relocating the 3-12 Infantry firebase by helicopter proceeded slowly. Apache scout teams were lifted out first, beginning at 1:01 P.M., and the teams secured the site selected for the new base. Colonel Jackson visited briefly with Lieutenant Colonel Vollmer around 2 P.M. at the old base, in between the scheduled lifts, and at that time only fifty-five men and one officer were on the ground at the new location.[27] Nearly five more hours would pass before the move to the new firebase was finally completed. In the unsettled skies above the western Highlands, the 52nd Combat Aviation Battalion, the famed "Flying Dragons," supported the 1st Brigade throughout Operation Francis Marion. The 119th Assault Helicopter Company, for example, committed an average of seven UH-1Hs and two armed UH-1Bs daily during the operation. The 179th Assault Support Helicopter Company, meanwhile, contributed an average of two CH-47s (Chinooks) a day.[28]

Late that afternoon, Lieutenant Colonel Vollmer, influenced perhaps by the events in the 1-8 Infantry AO, ordered A and B Companies to link up and then consolidate in a single perimeter. Vollmer placed Captain Hamer in charge of the joint perimeter. Hamer was also entrusted with choosing the exact location, within the area already designated by the battalion, for the two-company NDP. Briefed on his new orders, the twenty-nine-year-old former Marine led B Company along a dry stream bed and up another trail to a modest clearing surrounded by a wood line of single- and double-canopy jungle. A ridgeline of some height rose out of the jungle to the west.

Hamer, surveying the area, halted the company column. The wood line seemed like a perfect place to anchor the perimeter while the two company CPs and the B Company mortar crew set up in the more open center. The middle of the modest clearing, moreover, was something of a natural LZ, sparing his worn-out troopers the hassle of having to clear one in the morning. "When we stopped, we consolidated a position where we could bring in a helicopter the next day because we needed resupply," said Hamer. "There was an open spot in the middle. It was there, so we could bring in helicopters. I wanted a place where I could bring in some stuff." There was also sufficient space to accommodate a second company.

Captain Hamer, satisfied that he had found what he needed, selected the site for the two-company NDP. Trudging out into the wood line, his exhausted platoons began digging in along one-half of the anticipated two-company perimeter. Sandbags were filled with dirt and stacked on the sides of fighting holes. Logs and chopped-down tree limbs were laid carefully across the stacked sandbags and then padded with additional sandbags to create overhead cover. In the jungle adjacent to their fighting positions, the troopers hacked modest fields of fire and made note of prominent terrain features and possible avenues of approach.

Pfc. Rey Ramirez, twenty-one, a product of the parochial school system in Dallas, Texas, studied the terrain around the perimeter and immediately grew uneasy. Busted down to private for drinking at an off-limits bar back in Tuy Hoa, the Third Platoon original bucked authority from time to time, but he never forgot what his instructors had told him back in boot camp: "Don't ever get caught in a valley," they had warned, "because the enemy can then surround you." And yet, glancing around the perimeter that afternoon, Ramirez could not help but notice that the company was setting up in a shallow draw.

"Remember when they told us we should never be in valleys?" he asked a buddy nervously as the two of them dug in for the night. "Well, this is a valley, and I don't feel too comfortable around here. Something's not right. We shouldn't be camping down here."

"Yeah," agreed the soldier, "it probably isn't a good area to be camping in."

As dusk descended on the Ia Tchar Valley, A Company closed the distance between the two companies and ambled into the B Company perimeter around 6:33 P.M.[29] Together the two companies had marched over six thousand meters on the twenty-first, a not-insignificant feat considering the steamy tropical conditions and the often difficult terrain the companies had to traverse along their respective routes.[30] A Company, exhausted after pushing along the high ground for much of the afternoon, was to spread out and take up positions on the side of the perimeter Captain Hamer had deliberately left undefended.

Vegetation, terrain, and the timing of its arrival dictated to some extent the defensive positions A Company was able to establish around the modest clearing, but in the end the two companies merged into one large—one hundred yards by fifty to sixty yards—oval-shaped perimeter approximately five thousand meters north of the hilltop NDP the 1-8 Infantry had defended on the evening of the twentieth.[31] Each company assumed responsibility for roughly half of the perimeter. Critically, both companies had elements facing in a westerly-southwesterly direction.

The four A Company platoons spread out and began digging in before nightfall. In the First Platoon, Sgt. Kenny Dempich, as he had vowed to do earlier that afternoon, sought out an M-60 machine-gun position and, finding one, set up immediately to the left of it. *If anything happens to that gun crew*, he murmured to himself, *I'm going over there and getting that gun firing again*. Dempich, gazing around the perimeter, suddenly realized that he had never seen so many American soldiers setting up, together, in one position.

A small Highland stream flowed past elements of A Company's Second Platoon, commanded by Lt. Thomas E. Blake. Sgt. Arthur Klassen, a squad leader in the Second, faced the stream but could not see the water through the dense undergrowth covering the sloped ground in front of his partially completed bunker. Six foot three without boots on, Klassen preferred a bunker with enough depth and elbow room to accommodate a soldier of his proportions. Accordingly Klassen had the grunts shovel out a six- or seven-foot-long, deeper than usual three-man bunker. Afterward, the grunts used sandbags and foraged tree limbs to build a bunker with overhead cover.

Behind Klassen, in the center of the rapidly consolidating two-company perimeter, the CP elements of both companies, along with an 81-mm mortar team, dug in for the night. Largely treeless, the clearing offered little natural protection. "Normally we wouldn't do that—we wouldn't set up in a spot where there was a big open area, because that just invites mortar fire to come in," Captain Hamer admitted. "But the only people in the center, there, were my people and the other company commander [Captain Lee] and his people. All of the troops were in the wood line." Those troops, of course, did not include the men of the 81-mm mortar crew or the corresponding fire control component of 1st Lt. Thomas Burke's Fourth Platoon, B Company, 3-12 Infantry.

Officially organized as a "heavy weapons platoon," the Fourth Platoon had found the mortar too weighty and too unwieldy to lug around in rugged, triple-canopy jungle and had decided shortly after arriving in the Central Highlands to dispense with two of its three authorized 81-mm mortars. A Company's Fourth Platoon, meanwhile, had ceased carrying mortars altogether and had been functioning for some time as a standard maneuver platoon. That night B Company's mortar crew and its lone 81-mm mortar were under the command of Sgt. Bob Mervosh, a twenty-one-year-old original who had tried to enlist in the Air Force. With three brothers, each having served in a different branch of the military, the Pittsburgh, Pennsylvania, native received his draft notice in 1965 and briefly considered joining the Air Force so that his mother "could have four pictures, with one from every branch of the service." Mervosh, though, like many working-class kids at that time, wound up in the Army, sporting olive green instead of Air Force blues.

Situated behind Captain Hamer and the B Company CP hole, the mortar pit, when finally completed, would measure about eight feet wide and three to four feet deep, ample room for a fully assembled weapon and supporting crew. The pit would not, however, have overhead cover in an area Mervosh likened to a basin. "If we don't get hit tonight or tomorrow," said Mervosh, talking then to his gunner, Spc4 Clarence Morris, "we ain't never going to get hit!"

Nearby, behind the frontline squads of the Fourth Platoon, the foxhole Lieutenant Burke would share with his radioman that evening was nearly complete. Burke, age twenty-five, regarded by most as an approachable sort with the brains to go along with his bars, wondered as well if the NVA would hit the company that night. The Gloucester, Massachusetts native, with a little bit of guile and a whole lot of luck, had already survived several brushes with death while in command of the Fourth. On one occasion, while covering the right side of a rice paddy near Tuy Hoa with his platoon, he unwittingly crossed paths with a fleeing Viet Cong soldier. Flushed from the paddy, the VC spied Burke, aimed his .30-caliber carbine at the lieutenant, and was about to pull the trigger when the platoon point man that day opened fire first, dropping the guerilla in his tracks. Burke, walking over to the body, picked up the carbine and ejected the cartridge. "I guess this bullet had my name on it," he joked nonchalantly, "but my point man erased it."[32]

A and B Companies registered their supporting artillery before nightfall and quietly posted a number of LPs around the joint perimeter. C Company, in the meantime, continued to provide security for the new battalion firebase. Around 9 P.M. Colonel Jackson contacted Lieutenant Colonel Vollmer to check in and to inquire if the two companies had established defensive positions with overhead cover. Vollmer assured Jackson that almost all of his people had done so. Jackson then informed Vollmer that he planned to visit the 3-12 Infantry firebase sometime the following morning.[33]

By that time A and B Companies would presumably be up and marching south to reinforce the 1-8 Infantry.

11 THE JOINT PERIMETER

The first few mortar rounds to fall from the murky, overcast sky at 7:10 A.M. on the morning of the twenty-second crashed unexpectedly around the American perimeter, sending startled A and B Company troopers scurrying for cover. The surrounding jungle had been relatively quiet that morning and many of the troopers were out of their bunkers, drinking coffee and dining on C-rats, when the shelling began. Worse, since the two companies were expecting to move out shortly, some of the grunts had removed the overhead cover from their bunkers, inadvertently creating positions that were suddenly vulnerable to incoming mortar fire.

Sgt. Art Klassen, coffee in one hand, an M-16 within reach of the other, was out of his Second Platoon bunker, chatting and catching up with buddies nearby, when an ominous *thump thump thump* reverberated across the jungle. Instinctively Klassen sprang to his feet and sprinted back to his bunker. "I got up and I covered thirty feet in what seemed like six steps, going head first and sliding into my hole head first," he later recalled. "I *literally* went down into my hole head first." Explosions shuddered across the perimeter, and as he waited anxiously in his bunker amid the thudding crash of incoming mortar rounds, B Company troopers in a hole behind him agonized over a fallen comrade."I heard them talking and one of the fellas had died, and they weren't sure what to do with him," said Klassen. "Their platoon leader, or whomever, said to push him out of the hole behind them. He said that [since] the man was dead now, and it wouldn't make any difference." A short while later another mortar round crashed through the canopy and exploded on the jungle floor. *Man, is this really happening*?" he wondered in awe.

Hidden in a tangle of vines and bushes well beyond the A Company line, SSgt. Rudy Dunn, leader of a small ambush patrol from Lt. Thomas West's Third Platoon, could only gnash his teeth in frustration. The point man for the patrol had spotted

North Vietnamese troops setting up a mortar in the jungle, but when Dunn attempted to warn A Company, the radio malfunctioned and refused to transmit the message. Maddeningly, Dunn could listen to other messages being transmitted over the radio, but he could not transmit any outgoing messages over the company net. Afraid of being seen and unable to communicate with A Company, Dunn hid quietly in the bush and waited for an opportunity to dash back to the perimeter. "One of the VC popped his head up and I was afraid they would see us," Dunn recalled. "We were really right up on top of them. If I had the radio, I could've put artillery right on top of them."[1]

Meanwhile, in the jungle all around the A Company patrol, troops from the 66th NVA Regiment raced eastward, toward the two-company perimeter. Cut off and now heavily outnumbered, Sergeant Dunn went to ground with his men beneath a large log.[2] Around the same time Spc4 Gary Terrell, "TZ" to his Third Platoon, B Company buddies, watched breathlessly as several North Vietnamese soldiers appeared in the jungle before him. Terrell, Pfc. Richard Munson, and Sgt. Jerry Sewell had set up an LP in a slight depression formed by running water and were leaning against a small, earthen bank. Fearful of staying put, the three grunts raced out of the depression and jumped into an old shell crater.

"Get in the bunker, Meier!"

Too green to tell whether the *thump thump* he had heard were incoming or outgoing mortar rounds, Pfc. Eddie Meier, a nineteen-year-old replacement in B Company's Third Platoon, deferred to his squad leader, Sgt. Terry Hawkins, and ran immediately to their three-man bunker. Meier, not bothering to slow down once he got going, lunged through the opening of the bunker and onto Hawkins, momentarily entangling the two men. A third soldier, an FNG whom Meier recognized, was also in the bunker with an M-60. Outside of the bunker soldiers from both companies were still shouting and running for cover. Trembling between Hawkins and the new kid, Meier found himself thinking, fearfully, *Holy shit! This is it. They're trying to kill us*. None of it made any sense to Meier at that moment, and then he realized that his leg had stopped shaking; Hawkins, without saying a word, had reached over to steady it.

While Hawkins and Meier jostled at the bottom of their bunker, Spc4 Wallace Dworaczyk, twenty, of Yorktown, Texas, lay helpless atop the bunker of Spc4 Scott Reitenauer, the fire control coordinator for the 81-mm mortar crew. Fatally wounded, presumably by an exploding enemy mortar round as he attempted to leap over the bunker, Dworaczyk landed with a thud on the sandbags above Reitenauer. What was left of his leg dangled lifelessly inside the bunker. "His leg was split right down the middle," said Reitenauer, a Fourth Platoon original. "I saw every bone in his leg.

It was like someone took a knife and slit his leg in half, right down the length of his leg. I got splattered with some of his blood, and part of his foot landed in my lap!" Shocked, Reitenauer picked up the man's bloody foot and threw it out of the bunker.

Scattering as soon as the first few rounds exploded in the jungle, A and B Companies reoccupied the bunkers and foxholes composing the joint perimeter and were soon functioning as a cohesive entity. Captain Hamer, meanwhile, requested immediate air and artillery support.[3] "Get all you can get," Hamer urged his artillery FO, "and start bringing it in." Named overall commander of the two-company perimeter the night before, Hamer feared the intense mortar fire was designed to keep their heads down while the NVA moved into position for a major ground assault. And when it came, he intended to hit the enemy with all the firepower he could muster.

Scrambling down a ridgeline to the west past some of the A and B Company patrols and LPs, a company-sized force from the 66th NVA Regiment scampered through the morning mist and attacked elements of both companies at 7:23 A.M., eight minutes after Hamer's urgent request for air support.[4] Small-arms fire swept the perimeter from the west and southwest, while mortar rounds crashed down among the bunkers and fighting holes in the wood line. "I can't tell you what landed outside of the perimeter but, buddy, they had us zeroed in," remarked 1st Lt. Steve Pestikas, dug in at the time behind the front line of B Company's Third Platoon. "A lot of those rounds came within our perimeter, and there were some *big* rounds coming in."

Not too far away, on the A Company side of the perimeter, the sound of an exploding Claymore rattled the First Platoon. Disastrously the mine had exploded *inward*, toward the bunkers and foxholes of the platoon, rather than *outward* toward the assaulting North Vietnamese. Showered with shrapnel, the grunts quickly realized that some of their Claymores had been turned around by the NVA, either the previous night or sometime earlier that morning. "We quit detonating the Claymores," noted Sgt. Kenny Dempich. "[No point] blowing ourselves up with those things." Dempich, nestled in the middle of a three-man hole, escaped injury, but the two soldiers on either side of him had received minor wounds from either an errant Claymore or an enemy mortar round.

An A Company machine gun to the right of Dempich barked to life and unleashed a branch-snapping burst of fire on the North Vietnamese attacking through the underbrush. The familiar sound of an M-60 in action comforted Dempich—the pint-sized A Company NCO had deliberately set up near the gun—but the other First Platoon gun, the one off to his left, was disconcertingly silent. "Who's got that other sixty?" Dempich demanded brusquely, worried that the heavy volume of enemy fire would prevent him from fetching additional ammo if either of the guns ran out during the firefight. "It's OK," a loud voice suddenly shouted over the sharp report of rifle fire, "everything has been taken care of." Satisfied, Dempich hollered back, "OK,

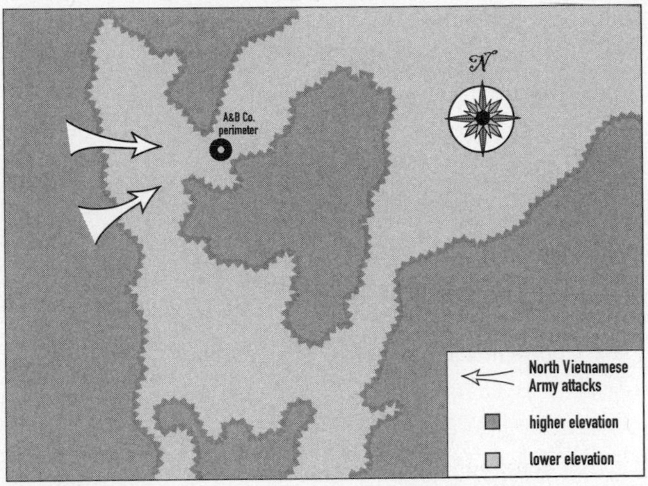

A and B Companies, 3-12 Infantry, May 22, 1967. Situation at 7:23 A.M.
Map by Charles Grear, adapted from original drawn for John P. Vollmer.

you take care of it. It's all yours!" Steady NVA small-arms fire, meanwhile, buzzed the two-company perimeter from the west-southwest.

Nineteen-year-old Spc4 Randal Aylworth, a replacement RTO from Jenison, Michigan, was among the first to be wounded in the First Platoon. Locating his radio, which was lying next to a bunker in plain sight, Aylworth began crawling toward it so that he could call in artillery fire on the North Vietnamese. When the radio was finally within reach—Aylworth might have gotten to it sooner if he had not been firing back at the NVA—an enemy grenade exploded nearby. Severely wounded in the blast, the intrepid RTO died unexpectedly in the arms of a fellow First Platoon grunt. Specialist 4th Class Aylworth was posthumously awarded the Bronze Star.[5]

Farther inside the American perimeter, a stream of grazing fire crackled over the B Company mortar pit. Primarily AK-47s and SKSs, the increasingly intense fire included bursts from an enemy light machine gun. Sgt. Bob Mervosh, crouching down in the pit with the other three members of his 81-mm mortar crew, felt vulnerable as the enemy rounds snapped overhead. Without overhead cover, the mortar pit practically invited a direct hit from a mortar round. A number of rounds had hit the perimeter thus far, but none of them had landed close enough to do any real damage.

Mervosh had all but predicted an enemy attack on the perimeter while digging in with his gunner, Spc4 Clarence Morris, the night before. Then it had sounded like just another grunt second-guessing the site selected for the two-company NDP. Trapped, the four mortarmen—Mervosh, Morris, Spc4 Terry Straub, and a soldier named

Pedro—huddled together in the mortar pit, terrified that a round would land on top of them. Mervosh, at one point, thought he heard the sound of trumpets blaring.

No one, though, heard the bullet that caught Morris in the right lung. Genuinely pious, Morris studied scripture enthusiastically—the twenty-one-year-old from Spencer, North Carolina, never gave much thought to foxhole conversions—and treated cleanliness like a virtue. "GIs are GIs—they got their *Playboy* magazines or whatever but Morris, well, when we took a break, he'd break out the bible," said Mervosh. "He was very religious. He would wash himself with his canteens of water. He'd drink it, too, but he'd also wash himself, whereas we could've [*sic*] cared less. We didn't shave and, well, you know what I mean. That's just the way he was." Hit in a major organ, Morris cringed in pain inside the mortar pit, the shooter all but invisible in the dense vegetation.

Suddenly the ground around the pit began to tremble. Somewhere in the surrounding jungle, an NVA mortar crew, assisted in all likelihood by a forward observer close to the American perimeter, was dropping rounds on the clearing and churning up the earth around the pit. Sergeant Mervosh, edging out toward the center of the pit, knocked the 81-mm mortar tube over, hoping that if the tube looked as if it had been put out of action the enemy mortar crew would move on to another target. The tube had been silent to that point anyway, and with artillery presently thundering down all around them and gunships most likely on the way, the two companies would be just fine without it. If not, he could always stand it up and crank some rounds out. Certain that he had acted in the best interest of all concerned, Mervosh then told Specialist 4th Class Morris that he was going to fetch his web gear, which he had left on a tree stump on the other side of the pit earlier that morning. There were bandages in his web gear, and he would use them to patch up the gunshot wound.

Mervosh started across the mortar pit, but as he soon as he reached the tree stump, a series of explosions rocked the center of the joint perimeter. Masterful with mortars, the NVA, after practically bracketing the four Americans moments before, had dropped a round directly into the mortar pit. Dazed and deaf in one ear, Mervosh turned around and nearly gasped in horror. Spc4 Terry Straub, twenty, of Lykens, Pennsylvania, and the assistant gunner on the four-man crew, had been blown out of the pit and was nowhere in sight. Neither was Pedro, the ammo bearer for the 81-mm mortar. Only Spc4 Clarence Morris remained behind in the shell-blasted pit. Morris, however, had lost an arm in the explosion and was wailing, "God make them stop! God make them stop!"

Without thinking, Mervosh immediately tried to account for his own arms and legs, praying all the while that he would not come up a limb or two short. All of his limbs, he quickly discovered, were still attached. Ripped in the explosion, his left ear drum hurt and he could not hear much out of that ear—the hearing in his other ear had been affected as well, though only slightly—but for the most part he had no serious wounds to speak of. Morris, on the other hand, was not nearly as fortunate. Shot in the lung and missing an arm, his badly broken body folded in a heap, Morris pleaded with Mervosh to put him out of his misery. "Shoot me," he implored Mervosh, "please just shoot me." Mervosh briefly contemplated honoring Morris's request but in the end could not bring himself to pull the trigger.

The company-sized enemy assault was falling heavily on elements of B Company. Clothed in khaki-colored uniforms and in some instances sun helmets camouflaged with leaves and branches, the NVA maneuvered forward, supported by RPD light machine guns and the occasional RPG, through the undergrowth to within hand-grenade range of the company. Reaching the tall grass and scrub brush in front of elements of the First Platoon, some of the NVA tossed hand grenades at the American bunkers blocking their advance. "I looked up and all I could see were Chicom grenades flying and heading in my direction," said Spc4 Mike Horan. "I remember thinking—Jesus, their quality control must stink because a lot of the grenades weren't going off. They were just lying there, and they weren't going off. Years later I talked to some of our guys—reliable sources, to be sure—who told me that the NVA were using these catapults made of bamboo, which I thought was pretty crafty, to hurl grenades into our perimeter." Horan, Pvt. Antonio Garza Jr., and a third soldier responded by detonating a couple of the Claymore mines they had put out the previous night.

Helmetless—the sandbagged roof covering their bunker left little room for headgear—Specialist 4th Class Horan steadied his M-16/XM-148 and scanned the brush in front of the First Platoon. Developed to combine the firepower of a grenade launcher with an ordinary assault rifle, the XM-148 was originally mounted under the barrel of an M-16 and fired 40-mm grenades. Horan liked the weapon, even though many of his peers preferred the simplicity, durability, and general functionality of the standard M-79 thump gun.

Still largely hidden in the underbrush, the NVA followed up the grenade assault on the First Platoon with a flurry of RPGs. Some of the shoulder-fired rockets, however, sailed right over the American bunkers on the line and exploded noisily further inside the perimeter. "They were flying in and kind of wobbling—you know, up and down like they were front heavy and tail light," said Horan. "They were coming in like that, [and] I could see that they were firing them from the brush line." Sun helmets suddenly popped up out of the brush and began moving toward the platoon. Sneaking forward in groups of five or six, the North Vietnamese were attempting to infiltrate the forward positions of the platoon and push on into the interior of the joint perimeter.

Relaxed, the butt of the M-16/XM-148 wedged firmly against his right shoulder, Specialist 4th Class Horan picked out a sun helmet and opened fire as if he were on a weekend hunt back in upstate New York. The firefight quickly escalated, and before long high-velocity rifle rounds were hitting soft flesh within earshot of his bunker. "A couple of guys that I shot, I could actually hear the *ta-wock.* That's how close they were," recalled Horan. "I'd fire the rifle and I'd hear it hit. It's like going to a target range, and I had done a lot of target shooting so I was familiar with that sound of shooting and hearing it hit. People would ask—how do you hear a bullet hit? You *do* hear it hit. It's like you're hitting a wet coat. It's like a slap noise." Attacked initially with grenades and rockets, the First Platoon had suddenly become embroiled in an intimate, close-quarters shootout with small groups of NVA.

Horan, bullets flying, peered out into the brush and noticed a North Vietnamese soldier in a sun helmet. Troublingly the enemy soldier was working his way forward, through the brush, carrying an RPD light machine gun. Conscious of the need to conserve ammo, Horan flipped the selector switch on his M-16/XM-148 to "semi-automatic" and snapped off a few shots as the NVA machine gunner disappeared into a slight depression off to the left. Moments later Horan's M-16 jammed. Irritated, he switched over to the XM-148 grenade launcher and quickly fired a 40-mm shell into the depression. Wherever the shell landed, it failed to kill either the NVA gunner or his assistant, and as the two enemy soldiers maneuvered out of the depression, the assistant grabbed the gunner by the shoulder and pointed directly at Spc4 Chuck Ahearn, presently to the left of Horan. Ahearn had crawled out of his own bunker moments before to treat a wounded soldier who was lying on the ground between the two bunkers, screaming hysterically. Panic-stricken, the wounded man had convinced himself that the perimeter was about to be overrun. "Don't let them take me alive," he shouted frantically. "Just shoot me!"

Calmly approaching the wounded grunt, Specialist 4th Class Ahearn found the man's field dressing and wrapped it around his bleeding neck. "Don't worry," he reassured the solider, "we aren't going to get overrun. We'll get you a medic and you'll be fine." Before Ahearn could finish bandaging the soldier up, an enemy grenade exploded nearby, showering the area with shrapnel. Closest to the blast, the wounded grunt absorbed most of the shrapnel and debris; Ahearn caught a couple of chunks in his right arm. Neither man, though, was seriously wounded.

Glancing up after the explosion, Ahearn saw the NVA assistant gunner grab the gunner by the shoulder and point in his direction. Scared, the twenty-year-old original began low-crawling back to his bunker. Within seconds, however, the enemy machine gun opened up and shredded the foliage above him. Bits and pieces of shredded leaves and broken branches rained down on him as he crawled frantically across the jungle floor. *Oh man,* Ahearn thought, *they're going to kill me.* Suddenly he heard a funny hovering noise above him, and at first he thought it was a helicopter flying in to drop off ammo. But then, for some strange reason, he imagined that it was the sound of wings, like those of a large bird. The next thing he knew he was back at his bunker, clearing and reloading the M-60 he had sitting atop some sandbags, while the FNG beside him looked for the North Vietnamese machine-gun team. "To this day I swear to God that it [the hovering noise] was my guardian angel," said Ahearn. "That sounds kind of crazy, I know. They [NVA] should have hit me. They must have been the worst machine gunners in the world." Ably assisted by the alert FNG, Ahearn found the two NVA gunners, swiveled the barrel of the M-60 in their direction, and started working through the entire belt of ammo. The flurry of fire sliced through the jungle and killed the enemy machine-gun team.

"Hold your fire! Hold your fire unless you've got a target!" a trooper somewhere up the line shouted brusquely.

Ahearn punched off the last few rounds of ammo left on the belt then eased up on the trigger. "Yeah," he declared angrily, responding to the voice up the line, "I've got a fucking target." In the bunker next to Ahearn, Specialist 4th Class Horan had a target as well. Horan, while scouring the wood line for North Vietnamese, spotted an enemy soldier creeping forward with an RPG and immediately pumped the area with 40-mm grenades. Apparently discouraged, the NVA fell back without firing the rocket.

Shortly thereafter, two American soldiers burst through the brush adjacent to Horan's position. "Cease fire! Cease fire!" the soldiers screamed. Crouched at the waist and moving toward the B Company line at a trot, the troopers, men whom Horan recognized as members of the First Platoon, had been out on an LP when the battle began and were now desperately trying to get back to the perimeter without being mistaken for the enemy. Bobbing up and down, their steel pots visible above the brush, the two Americans were quickly identified by other grunts in the platoon, prompting shouts of "Cease fire, cease fire!" from bunkers and foxholes up and down the line. Horan was shouting as well, and it was not long before the crackle of outgoing machine-gun and rifle fire had ceased.

The two troopers soon had company. Hunched over, as if deliberately mimicking the movements of the two Americans, a group of khaki-clad enemy soldiers appeared out of nowhere, behind and to the right of the two men. Stunningly, the NVA were trotting, step for step, through the tall grass and shrub brush in front of the First Platoon. Horan realized that the NVA were attempting to sneak inside the perimeter with the returning troopers and, borrowing an M-16 from another soldier, fired a series of single shots at the sun helmets mixed in with the two steel pots. Bunkers up and down the line started firing as well. "Cease fire! Cease fire!" yelled one of the North Vietnamese, trying to trick the grunts into thinking that they, too, were American soldiers attempting to return to the perimeter. The grunts kept firing. Halted in the adjoining scrub brush, the enemy soldiers went to ground some thirty yards from the platoon line.

Pfc. Rey Ramirez, chest heaving, his lungs aching for air, sprinted back through the jungle toward the B Company line. Up ahead he could see the small rise that led back to the American perimeter. Behind him, he could hear the crack of AK-47s and the snap of rounds whistling past. Too scared to turn around, Ramirez realized that if he and the other two Third Platoon troopers running along with him did not hurry, none of them would make it back alive. The Hell's Saints were already missing one LP—Spc4 Gary Terrell, Pfc. Richard Munson, and Sgt. Jerry Sewell were still huddling in an old shell crater somewhere in the jungle—and could not afford to lose any more men with a major enemy ground attack sweeping toward the platoon.

Ramirez sprinted to the top of the small rise and headed straight for the Third Platoon. "Don't shoot," he screamed frantically, "Don't shoot!" Caught between the incoming fire of the North Vietnamese and the outgoing fire of the platoon, Ramirez expected to get hit either in the chest or in the back at any moment, but he kept on running and eventually skidded to a halt inside the perimeter. Matching Ramirez stride for stride, the other two members of the LP sprinted in together and crammed into a foxhole manned by another grunt. The hole was only large enough to accommodate three soldiers. Ramirez, wriggling across the jungle floor, assumed a prone position not far from the three-man hole.

Audible over the steady chatter of small-arms fire, the shrill shriek of a whistle warned the grunts of an impending ground assault. "The first thing I remember was the whistles," said 1st Lt. Steve Pestikas, PTL of the Hell's Saints. "After the whistles, and I don't know how many people [NVA] were on the other sides [of the perimeter], but on our side we had literally human wave attacks. Now I can't tell you whether it was a second before the whistles or a second after the whistles, but you could hear the *thump thump thump* of the mortars. Had the NVA waited—and I don't know how many minutes it would have had to have been—they would have found us without canopies on our foxholes."

Rockets, machine guns, and a recoilless rifle supported the NVA assault on the Third Platoon. Lieutenant Pestikas, observing the action from behind the platoon line, noted soberly that the attackers appeared to possess a greater number of AK-47 assault rifles than the platoon had experienced before. Previously the Hell's Saints had encountered enemy forces equipped with a more even mix of AK-47s and semi-automatic SKSs (Simonovs).[6]

Deployed in depth, the Third Platoon withstood the initial blow and returned fire with M-16s and M-60s, slowing the enemy assault. The heavy defensive fire, in fact, forced some of the NVA to regroup. "Some of them at first were—I could tell—just coming forward," said Private First Class Ramirez. "They were coming forward, and then we started shooting at them and some of them started going to the side and then coming back." Ramirez fired on anything that moved, confident that with ten magazines of ammo he could keep it up until the NVA pulled back for good. Within shouting distance of Ramirez, Pfc. Eddie Meier, his leg no longer shaking uncontrollably, stayed busy loading magazines for Sgt. Terry Hawkins, who was presently blazing away with a CAR-15 through the opening of their three-man bunker. On the other side of Meier, an FNG was working the underbrush with an M-60.

Meier, when he had the time, slid over and fed the machine gun for the new guy. The son of a hardworking Army Air Corps veteran, Meier grew up in Wisconsin in a loving if fairly strict middle-class home. As a boy he sported a military-style "flattop" hair cut, like his father, and every day—summer, winter, spring, and fall—he would have to polish the shoes his father wore to work. Chores and discipline were simply a way of life in the Meier household. Interested in marketing, Meier graduated from high school and enrolled in a two-year college in the fall of 1965. After just one year of college, however, he dropped out and went to work with his father at a trucking company. Meier was subsequently drafted in the fall of 1966, and by the end of April 1967 he was in South Vietnam, serving with B Company, 3-12 Infantry, in the Central Highlands. Few arrived in the bush any greener. "I was so new, I couldn't tell my butt from a piece of cold meat," recalled Meier, then a scared nineteen-year-old FNG. "I couldn't really go out on ambush patrol, because I would have stood out like a shiny penny."

Crouched down in a bunker on the morning of the twenty-second, Meier alternated between feeding the machine gun and stuffing magazines for Sergeant Hawkins. Curious, Meier stood up a little at one point and peeked through the firing port. Dirt was piled up in front of the bunker, and there was a smattering of trees and some scrub brush off to the left. Meier was still gazing out on the flat terrain to his left when Sergeant Hawkins reached over and abruptly shoved his head back down below the firing port, moments before a swirling cloud of shrapnel engulfed the bunker. Meier caught a small sliver of shrapnel in his nose, the machine gunner a quarter-sized piece in his arm, but other than a couple of flesh wounds the three stunned troopers emerged from the sudden explosion in front of their bunker miraculously unharmed.

Meier removed the shrapnel from his nose and helped Hawkins bandage up the machine gunner. It had all happened so fast. Meier then glanced at Hawkins and, without uttering a word, conveyed what both men were undoubtedly thinking. "If he hadn't have done what he did—pushing my head down like that—when he did," said Meier, "I would have caught a face full of shrapnel. I remember we were just looking at each other like—'Holy shit, that could have been so much worse!' We looked at the top of that bunker after the battle, and it was just shredded like Swiss cheese. It was just full of holes."

Hawkins, brushing the dust from his fatigues, peered out of the bunker and watched, utterly astounded, as a North Vietnamese soldier just beyond the Third

Platoon line hurled 60-mm mortar rounds at the platoon with his *bare hands*. One of the shells had caused the explosion that shredded the top of their bunker. "I never knew that the round had been thrown," Meier confessed. "All I remember was Sergeant Hawkins shoving my head down." Dumbfounded, Hawkins eventually recovered and gunned down the North Vietnamese soldier before he could throw another shell at their bunker.[7]

"Medic! Medic! Medic!" The frenzied shouts, Hawkins and Meier would later learn, were not for them but for a Third Platoon soldier who had been shot in the head. More shouts would follow, some for the medic, others with instructions, as the battle raged on along the stretch of the B Company line held by the hard-fighting Hell's Saints.

Elements of A Company were also under assault. Spc4 Hank Fischer, a bespectacled twenty-one-year-old from Long Island, New York, was ensconced in a four-man hole with Lt. Tom West, who was in charge of the Third Platoon at the time, a soldier the grunts called "Peaches," and the recently arrived PTL of the Fourth Platoon, 2nd Lt. Harold Ford. Fischer had served as an RTO in the Third Platoon since the fall of 1966, when he first arrived in Vietnam, and had remained on the radio voluntarily despite the dangers typically associated with the job. Squeezed in beside his pack, Fischer stayed on the radio and his M-16 as the fighting intensified around the platoon. Lieutenant Ford was right beside him. "When the shit hits the fan, everybody's shooting," said Fischer. "We [RTOs] had M-16s, and we always did that. And shit was flying all over the place [on the twenty-second]." Later on Lieutenant West would leave the hole to check on the troops manning the platoon line.

West could do little to help the small ambush patrol led by SSgt. Rudy Dunn. Stranded in a tangle of vines and bushes, Dunn and the five troopers under his command sat helplessly by while American artillery rounds intended for the North Vietnamese blasted the jungle all around them. One of Dunn's troopers would eventually catch a chunk of shrapnel in the shoulder.[8] The wound, while certainly not life-threatening, only served to heighten the troopers' concern that sooner or later a round would find the entire patrol. Friendly-fire incidents had certainly claimed the lives of other American servicemen in the conflict, and without the ability to communicate with A Company, Dunn had no way of relaying his location to any of the supporting gun batteries.

Firing furiously in support of A and B Companies, the gunners of B Battery, 6-29 Artillery hammered the jungle west of the joint perimeter with heavy shellfire. 1st Lt. Ernest Putoff coordinated much of the support the battery furnished on behalf of A Company. An artillery FO assigned to the company, Putoff had developed an effective fire plan prior to the battle, and as soon as the shooting started that morning, he had B Battery firing for Captain Lee. Putoff would often stand in exposed areas or crawl around, sometimes beyond the frontline positions of the company, to observe the movements of the North Vietnamese. The plucky FO then used that information to adjust the incoming artillery fire accordingly.[9] Putoff was later awarded the Bronze Star for his bravery on the morning of the twenty-second.

Lieutenant Putoff's extraordinary courage and professionalism throughout the battle stand in stark contrast to the new artillery FO attached to B Company. The FO, upon hearing the gunfire that morning, apparently lost his nerve and instead of communicating with the artillery, sat idly by while the battle raged on all around him. "When the shooting started on the twenty-second, he just froze up," recalled Captain Hamer. "The FO I had been working with had gone out on R&R a day or two before, and this guy came out to replace him. Well, he wasn't responding over there, so this black kid—a Spc4 and the FO's RTO—grabbed the radio and started adjusting the artillery fire. The kid had gotten into some trouble before in the Army—it may have been in Germany, I'm not sure—but he was talking into the radio that morning and had taken over for the FO." Hamer was so impressed, in fact, that he allowed the young RTO to continue adjusting the company's artillery support.

Five minutes after the start of the NVA ground assault, Hamer, confronted with heavy enemy pressure from the west and southwest, asked the artillery to begin firing defensive concentrations (DEFCONs) immediately. Pre-plotted on expected enemy assembly areas and avenues of approach, the DEFCONs were designed to disrupt and ideally defeat an enemy assault on the two-company perimeter. The guns received the request and thundered away. As the storm of shells rumbled through the jungle to the west, Hamer noted after just a few minutes of firing that the defensive concentrations he had requested at 7:28 A.M. had succeeded in knocking some of the starch out of the enemy assault. Pleased, he informed the battalion TOC that the enemy attack had "let up some" on his company.[10] Cautiously optimistic, Hamer attributed some of the let-up to the devastating effects of concentrated artillery fire, but he also suspected that the North Vietnamese had not been defeated and instead were quietly massing for another assault. All the while, as if to confirm his suspicions, the NVA stubbornly fired RPGs into the B Company line.

North of the embattled perimeter, on a soggy strip of land inside the 3-12 Infantry firebase, the battalion mortar platoon thumped out rounds beside the guns of B Battery, 6-29 Artillery. Equipped with four 4.2-inch mortars and four 81-mm mortars, the platoon had started firing the 4.2s—larger than the 81s, the 4.2s also possessed greater range—in support of the two companies. "Fire mission! Fire mission!" an excited sergeant had hollered moments before as he raced out to the mortar crews. Twenty-one-year-old Jim Coughlan, a Philly native and a loader for one of the 4.2s, rushed into action. Four men to a tube, Coughlan's crew set up quickly and had shells in flight and on the way in no time at all.

Specialist 4th Class Coughlan slid a shell down the tube of the 4.2-incher and covered his ears. Belching noise and smoke, the heavy mortar flung the 35–40-pound shell skyward and then sank into the soil. "Each time we dropped a round down the tube and fired, the base plate would sink into the ground," said Coughlan. "We would then have to pull them out and set them up again. We had to pull two of the mortars out of service, while we kept the other two firing. We would dig the first two guns out, get them back up and sited in, and then start firing them. We would then take the other two guns out of service."

Meanwhile, in the center of the joint perimeter, an enemy mortar round had knocked B Company's 81-mm mortar crew out of action. With two members of his crew unaccounted for and a third, Spc4 Clarence Morris, shot in the lung and missing an arm, Sgt. Bob Mervosh clambered out of the mortar pit and crawled over to the bunker of Spc4 Scott Reitenauer, the acting fire control coordinator for the mortar team. The mortar crew had taken a direct hit, Mervosh told Reitenauer bluntly, and Straub was dead. Morris probably wasn't going to make it, either. *Holy shit*, Reitenauer thought to himself as Mervosh spoke. Clearly distressed, Mervosh then muttered something about an artillery round hitting the mortar pit, speculation that was subsequently disproven, before scurrying off in the direction of the company CP.

Responsible for plotting coordinates and relaying that information to the B Company mortar, Specialist 4th Class Reitenauer worried that the loss of the crew would reduce the company's organic firepower at a time when the grunts needed all the help they could get. *We're getting the shit kicked out of us*—that thought, and little else, kept running through his head—*and we've got to get that mortar going.* Thin, with a baby face and dirty-blonde hair, Reitenauer would never have been mistaken for a gridiron standout who had quarterbacked his varsity football team, much less a battle-hardened grunt with guts to spare. Yet the twenty-year-old millworker from eastern Pennsylvania was both a stellar athlete and a superb soldier.

Someone, though, had to do something about the mortar. Reitenauer, making up his mind before thinking it through, squirmed out of his bunker near the center of the perimeter and sprinted toward the mortar pit fifteen yards away. Steady bursts of enemy machine-gun fire made the short trip a harrowing experience, but he reached the pit without getting hit and leaped in. Sliding over to the slightly bent mortar tube, Reitenauer adjusted the elevation and deflection on the weapon, then immediately looked around for shells to fire. Another soldier joined him on the mortar at one point, though it is unclear whether that soldier was Spc4 Clarence Morris—missing an arm and wounded in the lung, Morris would seem an unlikely candidate—or someone who had followed the former high school signal caller into the pit to assist with the weapon.[11] "When you're in the middle of it, and bullets are flying around and people are getting killed, you don't always remember who was doing what," said

Reitenauer. "I'm not sure who was with me. I knew what elevation and deflection to set, and I just set it [the mortar] for distance." That soldier, whoever he was—Morris, a trooper from one of the CP groups—risked his life to help Reitenauer on the mortar.

Exposed to flying shrapnel and sheets of enemy machine-gun fire, Reitenauer stood in the pit and began dropping mortar rounds around the two-company perimeter. Within seconds, however, a frantic voice from somewhere on the line cried out, "Scott, it's too short! It's too short!" Some of the rounds, apparently, were falling too close to the frontline positions of A and B Company. Mortified, Reitenauer adjusted the mortar and was soon dropping rounds in the same circular pattern around the perimeter, only much farther out.

Shortly before 8 A.M. the gloomy overcast shrouding the shallow draw began to clear up. Capitalizing on the brightening skies, Lieutenant Colonel Vollmer, the West Point–educated CO of the 3-12 Infantry, was airborne by 8:05 A.M. and in contact with A and B Companies on the ground.[12] "You're running the show," he reminded Captain Hamer from the cramped confines of his C&C bird. "Just tell me what you need, and I'll get it for you."

Hamer wanted more artillery, air strikes as soon as the Air Force could scramble some fighter-bombers, and the freedom to conduct the battle on the ground without the inhibiting effects of "Vietnam Helicopter Syndrome" (VHS). Broadly defined as the tendency on the part of battalion, brigade, and divisional commanders to converge in the air over an ongoing battle, VHS reflected the worst bureaucratic impulses of the U.S. Army in Vietnam and complicated the job of company commanders. "A battle would start and pretty soon they'd all be stacking up in helicopters overhead wanting to know what was going on, but I never talked to anybody on the twenty-second except for Colonel Vollmer, the forward air controller, and some of the other support people," said Hamer. "I was never quizzed by any colonels or generals at any level about what was going on. That happens to a lot of company commanders. They'd get caught up in something and would be trying to sort it out and fight their way out, and then some colonel from somewhere else would come on [the radio] and say, 'What's your situation?' It doesn't work that well that way." One general referred disdainfully to these colonels and generals as "squad leaders in the sky."[13] Vollmer agreed, and from the moment the battle started on the morning of the twenty-second, he did his best to keep the radio clear for his company commanders.

Shielded from meddling generals and with air support presumably on the way, Hamer felt reasonably confident that the situation was more or less under control. The company-sized assault along the western and southwestern sides of the joint perimeter had been contained, and in the thirty or so minutes since the artillery began firing defensive concentrations, the enemy had made little attempt to breach the frontline positions of either A or B Company.[14] Further, the longer the enemy remained in the area, the more American firepower would tip the scales in favor of the defenders, now that the skies were beginning to clear.

The North Vietnamese, however, clung stubbornly to the perimeter and raked the Americans with small-arms fire. A Company requested gunships on the west side of the perimeter at 7:39 A.M. to suppress some of that fire. Dug in with the Second Platoon, Sgt. Art Klassen had received very little small-arms fire in his sector, but he did hear a number of explosions to his left. Operating under the cover of mortar fire, the NVA continued to probe the company, and the grunts reported seeing enemy troops around the perimeter at 8 A.M.[15] Enemy snipers supposedly climbed up some of the trees to Klassen's right, but a buddy of his saw one of them and blew the man out of the tree with an M-79.

Hidden beneath a log, far removed from the fighting around the Second Platoon, SSgt. Rudy Dunn and his cutoff A Company ambush patrol winced silently amid a swarm of angry insects. The patrol, while attempting to hide from the North Vietnamese, had unwittingly disturbed a wasps' nest. Buzzing furiously about, the insects emerged from the nest and descended on the stricken troopers. Amazingly, Staff Sergeant Dunn and his men would remain quiet throughout the painful ordeal for fear of alerting the North Vietnamese nearby.[16]

Meanwhile, in the jungle west-southwest of B Company, Sgt. Jerry Sewell, Spc4 Gary "TZ" Terrell, and Pfc. Richard Munson, the three stranded troopers from the cut-off Third Platoon LP, huddled in an old shell crater. Three North Vietnamese soldiers, evidently unaware that there were three Americans hiding in it, started crawling toward the crater. Inching forward, the NVA crawled to within fifteen meters of the crater before eyeballing the Americans. Startled, perhaps, by the sudden appearance of three Americans, the NVA did not open fire on the huddling Hell's Saints, but one of the enemy soldiers ducked down behind a log and tossed a hand grenade.

Tumbling down the shallow slope of the crater, the grenade was about to explode when Private First Class Munson, already wounded by shrapnel from an American artillery round, scooped it up and threw it back out. "If it hadn't been for Munson's quick thinking," said Sergeant Sewell, "we would have all been dead in that hole."[17] A gun battle then broke out between the two groups, and in the ensuing firefight Munson, Sewell, and Specialist 4th Class Terrell shot and killed the three North Vietnamese soldiers. Afterward Terrell reassured Munson that if he could just hold on, a helicopter would soon be on the way to take him out.

Stalled by punishing artillery strikes and two companies of entrenched infantry, the North Vietnamese committed additional troops to the battle, eventually marshaling the strength of an entire battalion to smash the stubborn American perimeter. The two American companies, in the meantime, reported that they were still receiving heavy fire more than an hour after the NVA first began mortaring the combined perimeter. There were also indications the NVA were using the cover of mortar and small-arms fire to sneak closer to the Americans.[18] Captain Lee, who was on the horn talking to the battalion TOC around 8:15 A.M., estimated that the perimeter had been hit by a "company-plus" force of North Vietnamese supported by three to five mortar tubes. Enemy snipers, moreover, had been spotted in the trees southwest of the company. A Company, Lee argued, had not received enough supporting artillery fire at times—pointed criticism Lieutenant Colonel Vollmer did not dispute—and he echoed the battalion call for gunships to work the jungle to the west and southwest.[19]

Lt. Tom West, back presently in his CP hole, which was no bigger than a midsized couch, watched the battle unfolding along the front line of the Third Platoon. West was joined by his RTO, Spc4 Hank Fischer, Lt. Harold Ford, the new PTL of the Fourth Platoon, and a soldier nicknamed "Peaches." Located behind but also between two frontline fighting positions, the CP hole allowed Lieutenant West to observe the perimeter and, when necessary, spray the adjoining jungle with rifle fire. Fischer had been alternating between his M-16 and the radio, double duty the salty Long Islander had grown accustomed to, for much of the morning.

Third Platoon, Lieutenant West could confidently report, had not been breached in the initial NVA assault, and the troops upfront—men whom he had risked his life to visit, albeit briefly—showed no signs of quitting, despite the persistent chatter of enemy machine guns and AK-47s. West, though, would soon notice an increase in the intensity of the incoming fire. Snipers lurking in the trees and bushes around the perimeter were taking pot shots at the company line, and heavy small-arms fire continued to lash his men from the west. No one, though, saw the NVA who fired an RPG directly at the platoon. Dancing atop a trail of white smoke, the enemy rocket hissed across the jungle and exploded in a fiery ball right in front of West's CP.

West, who was standing in the hole to the right of Lieutenant Ford, survived the explosion, as did "Peaches" and Specialist 4th Class Fischer to the left of Ford. Lieutenant Ford, twenty-three, of Pittsburgh, Pennsylvania, a squared-away soldier by all accounts but still relatively new in-country, was killed instantly.[20] "He [Ford] took the initial blast, and it took the whole left side of his head right off of him," said Fischer. "He was blown backwards and was killed instantly. How I didn't get killed is beyond me, because if we had twelve inches between our two heads, we had *a lot*."

Fischer, spitting out dirt and debris, brushed himself off after the blast and started pawing at the left side his face. Half a dozen shards of red-hot shrapnel were embedded in his skin, his eyeglasses had been shattered, and a mixture of dirt, debris, and shrapnel from the blast had closed his left eye shut. An uncle of his had lost an eye in Korea, and the thought immediately crossed his mind that another generation of the Fischer family was about to suffer the same fate in Vietnam. "The only thing I could see," recalled Fischer, "was two fingers at two feet." Behind him in the hole, "Peaches" was also shaking off the effects of the blast, although unlike Fischer, he had not been seriously injured.

Stuck, still, in an old shell crater with Sgt. Jerry Sewell and Pfc. Richard Munson, Spc4 Gary Terrell guessed that it was probably too late to make a run for it back to B Company. Raised in Hackett, Arkansas, Terrell was just a boy when his coal miner father passed away suddenly. His mother died shortly thereafter, yet almost incredibly he was still drafted in 1965 and sent to Fort Lewis, Washington. Fair-skinned and slightly freckled, Terrell graduated from basic training with the rest of the B Company originals, but even then he had a peculiar habit of appearing strangely preoccupied. "He had an expression like he was somewhere else," said Sgt. Robert Ramirez. "He would have this twinkle in his eye whenever you told him something or asked him something, so the sergeant at basic said he wasn't there but was in the twilight zone. We then joked that he was in the *Zone.*" Soon Ramirez and many of the other Third Platoon originals began calling Terrell "Twilight Zone" or "TZ" for short.

Terrell encouraged Private First Class Munson—the Peoria, Illinois, native had been wounded earlier in the fight by a friendly artillery round—to hold on until a helicopter arrived to evacuate him out. Small-arms fire had been crackling around the old shell crater when suddenly an enemy slug whistled through the jungle and slammed into Terrell's head. Almost certainly fired from above, presumably by an NVA sniper perched high up in the trees, the bullet damaged Terrell's ear and left him feeling nauseous. Queasy, he returned fire, vomited, and then passed out.

Terrell awoke to find that Private First Class Munson and Sgt. Jerry Sewell had vanished. The two troopers, thinking perhaps that Terrell was not merely unconscious but dead, had hurried back to the perimeter. Groggy, Terrell looked around—he was relieved to discover that there were no NVA in the crater with him—and quickly realized that he could *smell* the enemy in the jungle nearby. Slipping in and out of consciousness from time to time, he would come to, jerk to attention, and reflexively fire off a burst with his M-16. The NVA, though, never approached the crater. Light-headed, Terrell cried out for help, even as his thoughts began to wander. *I bet I could probably get an AK-47,* he mused. *I'll keep it as a souvenir.*

Terrell belonged to a squad commanded by Sgt. Dennis Palmer, arguably the finest NCO in B Company's Third Platoon. "Dennis Palmer was a squad leader [for me] and a damn good one," said 1st Lt. Steve Pestikas, PTL of the platoon. "He was intelligent, loyal, and dedicated. He always followed directions, yet he possessed the ability to think fast and accurately when he made split-second decisions—which ultimately made him a valuable member of the Hell's Saints. His men were dedicated to him as their squad leader, because they knew he 'took care of them.'" Palmer had heard Terrell crying out for help and knew that someone had to bring him back to the platoon.

Covered by one of his fire team leaders, Sergeant Palmer yelled over to Captain Hamer in the B Company CP. Terrell was still out there, Palmer told Hamer, and he intended to go out and get him. Racing out of the perimeter and down a dry creek bed as rifle rounds snapped through the brush, the Jarboro, North Carolina, native found Terrell, wounded and unable to walk, about a hundred meters from the two-company perimeter. Bravely, Terrell had called out to advise the Third Platoon against attempting to rescue him, telling the grunts that it was much too risky; barely conscious when Palmer finally reached him, he could no longer move under his own power. Steadying himself, Sergeant Palmer reached down, picked Terrell up, and started in with the wounded Spc4 in his arms. Incredibly Palmer then carried Terrell across one hundred meters of NVA-infested jungle, in the middle of an ongoing firefight, to reach the safety of the B Company line.[21]

Pfc. Charles A. Richardson Jr., twenty, of Jasper City, Tennessee, had overheard Palmer talking before he left the perimeter to retrieve Terrell. "Junior" to his buddies, Richardson had also observed North Vietnamese advancing toward the perimeter in the same general area as his squad, which was set in just to the right of the shallow ravine Palmer had climbed out of carrying Terrell. "Being young and dumb, me and Vinny Brock and Stan Coker were more or less shooting at where we thought they might be," Richardson recalled. "We could see them [NVA] moving, and we'd shoot at where we thought they had stopped. We were also trying to put as much suppressive fire out there as possible to help cover him [Palmer]. His team leader was out there covering him, and I saw him [team leader] shoot a North Vietnamese soldier while firing from the hip. Sergeant Palmer came right up through there with that man."

That man, Spc4 Gary "Twilight Zone" Terrell, survived the battle and returned to his home state of Arkansas. Nowadays Terrell has his ups and downs living with the memories of Vietnam, like most veterans, but he remains forever grateful to Sgt. Dennis Palmer.

North Vietnamese pressure, particularly along the western and southwestern sides of the combined A-B Company perimeter, gradually increased. The NVA hurled grenades at A Company and buzzed the grunts with AK-47s and SKSs. One bullet smacked into the company radio around 8:30 A.M., damaging the unit.[22] Across the perimeter, the grunts reported that a number of larger-than-usual enemy mortar rounds—120-mm, according to some of the grunts—were exploding in the bush. Measurably more destructive, the 120-mm rounds—if they were indeed 120s—augmented the deadly chorus of 82-mm rounds bursting inside the B Company bunker line.

Captain Hamer concluded that the mortar rounds were coming in from the west, possibly from a location near the Se San River. Hamer had been hugging the perimeter with artillery fire for over an hour, trying to break up the enemy's assault groups and disrupt his initial attack, but he was not about to push the artillery farther out to deal with the mortars when he could *feel* another major attack brewing in the jungle to the west. Hamer was still considering his options when a gunship pilot raised him over the radio.

"Where do you want us to go?" the pilot asked, circling overhead.

"We're taking mortar fire and it's coming from the west, toward the river," Hamer responded. "Can you go out there and take a look around, because they've got to have an open spot in the jungle to be able to fire those things."

Speeding off, the gunships headed west toward the Se San River. Approximately ten minutes later the ships got on the horn again and proudly announced that they had discovered three enemy mortar tubes and had "put them out of their misery."

B Company had suffered its share of casualties as well. Violent explosions in the trees above and around the company from enemy mortars and RPGs had sent shrapnel, bark, and branches hurtling across parts of the perimeter, injuring some of the grunts. Enemy snipers, grazing fire, and repeated ground probes accounted for much of the rest. "There'd be a lull in the fighting," said 1st Lt. Steve Pestikas, "and then all of a sudden you'd hear whistles and, buddy, they'd come at us again." Several of Pestikas's Hell's Saints had been wounded in the fighting and had abandoned their bunker to seek medical treatment behind the platoon line.

The abandoned bunker, however, had created a potentially dangerous gap in the frontline defenses of the Third Platoon. To close that gap and restore the defensive integrity of the entire line, the squad leader in charge of the wounded troopers moved forward and occupied the empty bunker. The shift occurred in the center of the line, directly in front of Lieutenant Pestikas. Tactically innovative, Pestikas had previously reduced the number of squads in his platoon from four to three by disbanding the "weapons squad" and dispersing its armaments and personnel throughout the three remaining squads. Two of the squads were equipped with an M-60 machine gun, while the third was converted into a "LAW" squad and armed with an extra M-79 grenade launcher. This simplified structure, Pestikas believed, improved the platoon's communications and enhanced tactical flexibility. The troops, moreover, were able to concentrate their firepower more effectively in battle.

With the NCO in charge of the middle squad now manning a bunker on the front line, Lieutenant Pestikas, flanked by radio operator Spc4 Juan Trevino and Spc4 Jim Matyas, scrambled out of his CP hole and hopped into the foxhole formerly occupied by the quick-thinking squad leader. Trevino and Matyas, the latter a forward observer with the platoon, joined Pestikas in the hole. Trevino, incidentally, formed one-half of the Hell's Saints "wind talkers" radio team. "Whenever we communicated within our platoon, the two radio operators—Trevino and Valdez—spoke 'b-bob-Spanish,'" said Pestikas. "The Marines had used American Indians for radio traffic [during World War II] in order to prevent the Japanese from being able to understand them. We in essence did the same thing, except our two guys from Texas only spoke in 'street Spanish' on the radio and the NVA were never able to understand anything they said. I got the idea from our World War II brothers." All requests for fire support, however, were communicated in English.

Around the same time that Pestikas, Trevino, and Matyas were settling into their new foxhole, 1st Lt. Thomas Burke left his position, apparently unannounced, and occupied the hole the three of them had just abandoned. Lieutenant Burke, then in command of B Company's Fourth Platoon, had lived something of a charmed life in Vietnam, having survived several brushes with death, and seemed to relish being in the thick of the action. Burke, though, would not remain in the hole for long before disaster struck. "I could hear mortar rounds hitting behind me, and then one of them went into the hole that I had just been in. All I could think was, 'Thank God I am not in that hole,'" said Pestikas. "I don't know what caliber round they hit it with, but structurally there was nothing left of the hole. I did not know then that Burke had gone in there. Burke never communicated to me that he was going to move into my hole after I had moved up. To this day I don't know why he did." Lieutenant Burke, age twenty-five, the pride of Gloucester, Massachusetts, died instantly.

Busy working the 81-mm mortar in the B Company pit nearby, Spc4 Scott Reitenauer felt the shuddering impact of the round that killed Lieutenant Burke but at first had no idea what had happened. *What's going on here*? he wondered, half dreading the answer. Burke, Reitenauer then discovered, was dead. The blast, whatever it was, had killed him. No one was irreplaceable but the loss of Lieutenant Burke, the officer in charge of *his* platoon, a man whom he had come to regard as a friend, hurt more than he cared to admit. "He was like an older brother to me," Reitenauer remembered. "He even wrote a letter home to my wife [stating] that I did really well during one fire mission." Reitenauer, who would earn a Bronze Star for manning B Company's 81-mm mortar that morning in the face of intense enemy fire, acknowledged that Burke was "gung-ho" and "used to take the night patrols out." Tragically that uncompromising urge to lead from the *front,* to embrace the responsibilities of command, cost Lieutenant Burke his life on the morning of the twenty-second.

Fitful bursts of North Vietnamese fire, meanwhile, raked the joint perimeter. The moment of decision was now at hand.

12 WINNERS AND LOSERS

About an hour after the initial assault on the two-company perimeter, North Vietnamese pressure, which had been limited for a time to probing attacks and attacks by fire, suddenly matured into a full-blown, battalion-sized push to annihilate the dug-in Americans.[1] Rockets smashed into trees around the clearing, choking the startled grunts with dust and debris, and machine guns swept the front lines as the assault gathered momentum. As before, however, the North Vietnamese assault bubbled up out of the jungle to the west and southwest. A Company, deployed in part along the enemy's axis of advance, absorbed some of the onslaught. Advancing in twos and threes, sometimes in groups of ten, the NVA fought through a blizzard of M-16, M-60, and M-79 fire to close to within twenty-five meters of the First Platoon. There the advance slowed before a wall of fire so intense that it reminded Sgt. Kenny Dempich of a "Mad Minute," only considerably longer.

Fields of fire had been cleared in front of the bunker Dempich shared with two other First Platoon troopers, and he could see groups of North Vietnamese maneuvering in the adjacent jungle. Deliberate, purposeful, and seemingly well coordinated, their movements had all the hallmarks of a professionally trained adversary. "You just had that feeling that these guys weren't your local VC," said Dempich. "These guys were much more organized and skilled. That's kind of how we determined that they were not your local VC. They were maneuvering around and trying to maneuver in, [and they were] just much more organized. For example, three of them would run from twelve o'clock over towards eleven o'clock, or from twelve o'clock over towards ten o'clock. Four or five of them might move towards one o'clock or two o'clock. It was definitely more skilled, and they knew what they were doing. No doubt about that." There were certainly enough of them, Dempich noted uneasily, to penetrate the platoon line if one of the squads buckled.

Sergeant Dempich had been firing on single-shot to conserve ammo, but with the North Vietnamese now clinging stubbornly to the First Platoon, some no more than twenty-five meters from his bunker, he needed more firepower to push them back. *Fuck this*, Dempich thought. He flipped the selector switch on his M-16 to automatic and ripped through two magazines. Shoulder to shoulder, Dempich and the two troopers with him—both men bloodied by shrapnel but still blasting away—raked the brush beyond their firing position. The fighting quickly escalated. "The enemy was all over the damn place," said Dempich. "We could see them running and charging and lobbing grenades." A machine gun to the right of their position was also hammering away at the jungle in front of the platoon.

Some distance away, in A Company's Third Platoon, bright red tracer rounds were smacking off tree trunks beyond the platoon line. Spc4 Hank Fischer tracked the friendly tracers with his uninjured right eye and poured M-16 fire into the same general area. Thick jungle surrounded parts of the platoon, making it difficult to see the North Vietnamese assaulting the bunker line forward of the CP bunker he shared with Lt. Tom West, a trooper he and the others called "Peaches," and Lt. Harold Ford. Lieutenant Ford had been killed, the left side of his skull hideously disfigured, and was lying at the back of the bunker. The same RPG that had killed Ford had closed Fischer's left eye shut, forcing him to rely on his right eye. Partially blind, he was scanning the underbrush when suddenly the platoon began to buckle. "They're getting closer! We're starting to get overrun!" the grunts on the line screamed in panicked desperation.

Alarmed, Lieutenant West ordered Fischer to call in artillery and then walk the rounds in, toward the platoon line. Fischer grabbed the radio and looked out at the bunkers in front of him. Only fifty feet or so of jungle separated the two positions. "Keep your heads down," Fischer yelled out to the line squads, "we've got artillery coming in and we're going to walk it all over." Tricky in the best of circumstances, the delicate process of walking artillery in over the radio was made even more difficult by the dense foliage surrounding the perimeter, as an artillery FO attached to A Company discovered when he attempted to walk rounds in toward the company line. The frustrated FO reported that he could scarcely hear, much less see, the rounds exploding in the thick vegetation.[2]

Artillery fire alone, however, could not stem the enemy tide building along the western edges of the A Company line. Faced with a potential penetration, the company dispatched troops from the eastern side of the perimeter, where the situation appeared well in hand, to the western side to bolster the hard-pressed First and Third Platoons.[3] Lt. Thomas Blake, PTL of the Second Platoon, rounded up some of the troops that were shifted to the west. "He [Blake] had grabbed guys, and he came to my position and he took one of the guys from my position and went off to my right," said Sgt.

Art Klassen, a squad leader in the Second Platoon. "He said that we were moving people over to the right, because if the enemy was going to make another attack, it was going to come from that side. It was a real quick explanation—more or less I need someone from your position and we're going to move them over to the right hand side." Blake positioned his people behind the First and Third Platoons. If the NVA broke through, his Second Platoon would have to hold the line.[4]

Trotting toward the B Company line, a column of North Vietnamese soldiers reached the end of a narrow jungle path and spilled out into a slight clearing in front of the Third Platoon. Well trained, the NVA fanned out into assault groups of ten to twelve and charged, AK-47s blazing, toward the dug-in platoon. Shoulder-fired RPGs, backed by chattering machine guns, streaked across the jungle in support of the attackers.

The assault crashed headfirst into the Hell's Saints. "The second assault was extremely intense. Not only did they use more personnel, it was spread over a greater area in front of our positions," said 1st Lt. Steve Pestikas, who observed the attack from a hole just behind the front line. "They'd come in a straight line on a path, and once they broke into the clearing, they'd fan out. We had [NVA] really close to our perimeter, *really* close. The guys that carried the M-79s also carried a .45, and I know that some of them took out that .45 and used it." Two of his squads relied mainly on M-16s and M-60s to repel the attackers, while the remaining squad—the aptly named "LAW Squad"—added rockets to the deluge of outgoing fire. Partial to the destructive effects of the weapon, Pestikas had requisitioned a supply of LAWs for his men prior to the battle; most if not all were expended that morning, and of the fifteen or so that were fired the majority were directed at enemy snipers, machine guns, and recoilless rifles.

Slowed by the intense defensive fire, the North Vietnamese hugged the platoon line and responded with AK-47s. Pfc. Junior Richardson, dirt dribbling down around him from a bullet-punctured sandbag sitting atop his bunker, saw North Vietnamese soldiers no more than fifty yards from his bunker. Sired by a Tennessee coal miner, Richardson needed only one day in the mines to realize that he had no desire to follow in his father's footsteps. A safe, secure municipal job *above* ground sounded a lot more appealing to him than working in a coal mine, so he went to work for a water company in Jasper City, Tennessee, after high school. Richardson was still working for the city when he was drafted in October 1966. Handed what he considered a "one-way ticket to Vietnam," Richardson left for basic training that fall and turned twenty the following April aboard an airplane bound for South Vietnam.

Firing at the NVA to his front, Richardson suddenly noticed an NVA light machine gun off to his right. Pointed uphill the gun—most likely a Soviet RPD or its Chicom cousin, the Type 56—was set in at an angle behind a fallen log and had been chewing up the front of the Third Platoon. Pfc. Stan Coker and a soldier named Brock were to his left, and while both could probably make out the gun, neither was in position to take out the gunner. Left-handed, Richardson lined up the gunner with his M-16 and continued squeezing the trigger until the enemy gun finally fell silent. No one can say for certain who killed the enemy gunner—the gun had drawn fire from other grunts on the line—but some have since concluded that it was probably Richardson.

Heavy North Vietnamese pressure, meanwhile, extended across the B Company front to include elements of the First Platoon. Aided by the disorienting effects of exploding mortar shells and rocket-propelled grenades, groups of determined NVA, most armed with AK-47s and SKSs, assaulted the platoon with hand grenades and small-arms fire. Spc4 Mike Horan dropped some of them with his XM-148 grenade launcher before a soldier nursing a badly injured foot, the same panicky grunt Spc4 Chuck Ahearn had attempted to bandage up earlier in the fight, crawled up behind the bunker Horan shared with Pvt. Antonio Garza and another trooper.

"I'm hit! Let me in the hole!" the wounded soldier demanded.

Horan reluctantly refused. "I can't. If we let you in the hole, we're going to be standing on top of you! Stay behind the hole."

Moments later the wounded soldier moaned that he had been hit again. Curiously, he then asked Horan if he should throw grenades at the North Vietnamese. Afraid that the grunt might short-arm the throw and accidentally put a grenade right on top of their bunker, Horan cautioned the soldier against throwing anything at the NVA while he was still behind them. Just sit tight, he told the soldier sternly, and stay behind the hole. The injured grunt crawled off in search of cover.

Ten to twenty yards behind the front line of the First Platoon, Spc4 Gary Specht, a recently promoted fire team leader from Hershey, Pennsylvania, gathered bandoliers of spare ammunition and flung the belts up to the hard-pressed troopers manning the line. Specht, well protected in a four-man bunker with sandbags for overhead cover, tossed the last of the ammo forward, then turned back to the slanted patch of jungle sloping upward before him. Periodically Specht or one of the other troopers in the bunker, two of whom he knew had already sustained minor head wounds from mortar shrapnel, would spray the slope with rifle fire, mainly as a precaution. Some of the brush in front of the platoon was on fire, but he had yet to see any NVA on the slope. Still, Specht preferred to remain vigilant. *If they ever get on the high ground*, he thought to himself, *they'll be able to charge right down that slope and right into our line.*

About two hours into the battle, A Company revised its original estimate of the size of the North Vietnamese force attacking the perimeter from a "company-plus" sized element to a full battalion. Larger than the earlier push that morning, the ongoing NVA assault, while still heaviest to the west and southwest, had now engulfed much if not all of the joint perimeter. North Vietnamese troops, B Company reported within minutes of the revised A Company estimate, were now "all around," with the largest number opposite the western and southwestern sectors of the perimeter.[5] "They were in position around the perimeter, and they began to attack. It was pretty much about three-quarters of the way around [the perimeter]," said Capt. Mike Hamer, B Company commander. "From what I could tell from my people—Pestikas and a couple of others who were on that side—they were being attacked by small arms, and they could see them [NVA]. And on the A Company side, it was pretty much the same." Both companies, moreover, were low on ammunition.

Expecting air support, Lieutenant Colonel Vollmer shifted his supporting artillery east of the perimeter shortly after 9 A.M. to clear the way for a napalm strike along a line running southwest to northeast.[6] Captain Hamer, in charge at the time of coordinating fire support for the entire perimeter, had been reluctant to lift the artillery fire pounding the jungle to the west and southwest long enough to accommodate an air strike, telling the FAC on station—a pilot he knew who went by the nickname "The Mad Mexican"—to stand by and hold off until he had "a really good target for it." Hamer's judgment was tactically sound. A subsequent examination of the most effective use of supporting fires, in fact, confirmed that "air support should not be used at the expense of reducing direct support and reinforcing artillery."[7] Accurate artillery fire, moreover, had assisted in breaking up the first North Vietnamese assault. With the better part of an NVA battalion now to the west and southwest, however, the need to bring in close air support more than justified the risks involved in temporarily lifting the artillery firing in support of the two companies. Hamer, satisfied that he now had "a really good target," reversed course and requested a napalm strike on the southwest side of the perimeter several minutes before Vollmer issued his orders to shift the artillery eastward.[8]

Artillery fire, in the meantime, continued to devastate the jungle around the two-company perimeter. Overhead 1st Lt. Joseph T. Makalusky, an air observer dispatched by divisional artillery, skillfully managed the fires of all five batteries supporting the embattled companies. Makalusky, flying aboard an OH-23 piloted by Maj. Gerald Cross, adjusted some of the shellfire to within fifty meters of the perimeter. Later, before he left for a refueling run, Makalusky coordinated with observers on the ground to ensure that accurate, effective fires continued in his absence.

Poor visibility and low cloud cover that morning might have impaired Lieutenant Makalusky's ability to call in adjustments if it had not been for the exceptional courage and skill of Major Cross, who routinely maneuvered the OH-23 into position to observe the battle despite intense enemy ground fire. Cross stayed aloft for nine hours, landing only to refuel, in the hazardous skies over the battlefield, and because of that unwavering dedication Makalusky was able to effectively coordinate the fires of all five gun batteries. For their meritorious service on the morning and afternoon of the twenty-second, both men were awarded the Air Medal.[9]

Spread out on the jungle floor, NVA troops no more than twenty to twenty-five meters away, Pfc. Rey Ramirez ripped off a burst on full auto, hoping that he would hit one or two of them and maybe push the rest of the sons of bitches back. Ramirez had been lying flat on his belly, next to a foxhole in B Company's Third Platoon, ever since he had raced in from an LP, NVA nipping at his heels, earlier that morning. Gunshots rang out behind him on the way in, and he could hear some of the rounds whistling past. Bellying up beside a three-man foxhole inside the perimeter, Ramirez had turned around in time to witness the first assault on the platoon line. North Vietnamese soldiers in sun helmets and light-colored uniforms, not shabbily equipped guerillas dressed in black pajamas, were moving swiftly through the jungle, firing AK-47s. *Jesus*, Ramirez thought at the time, *these guys aren't VC. We're in trouble now*!

In the earlier assaults that morning, when the numbers of NVA attacking his section of the Third Platoon seemed more manageable, Ramirez fired mostly on semi-automatic. Now, however, with the jungle crawling with North Vietnamese, the twenty-one-year-old Mexican American relied almost exclusively on full auto, scared that there were just too many of them to deal with on any other mode of fire. Bursts from his M-16, as well as those from the other grunts nearby, sent some of the NVA scurrying for cover; moving parallel to the platoon line, the enemy soldiers would dart into the brush and then return to pressure the platoon again.

Ramirez listened for the sound of AK-47 rounds crackling past. For awhile the shooting would stop, but it never seemed to last for very long. The bursts he had been putting out with his M-16 were not enough to suppress the small-arms fire clipping through the bush. Nor were the North Vietnamese falling back, as he had hoped. "They [NVA] just kept coming at us and firing at us," said Ramirez. "That North Vietnamese Army just kept coming and coming. They would not stop. We kept shooting them, and for a little bit the shooting would stop. I'd think that maybe they were backing off. But then they came again. They kept coming." Haunted by the prospect of being overrun, Ramirez slapped in a fresh magazine and, blocking out the screams of the wounded nearby, fought on with grim determination.

LAWs and M-79s quieted some of the enemy machine-gun fire raking the platoon, but neither weapon had any effect on the incoming mortar fire. After a while, a round landed near Ramirez, peppering his right hip and leg with shards of scalding-hot shrapnel. "When that mortar round hit me," he recalled, "all that I felt was heat. What I noticed was the heat. It wasn't that painful, but it was really hot." The round had exploded somewhere off to his right. Ramirez, remembering how he had heard other grunts say that "whenever you lost a limb—leg or arm—the only thing you felt was the heat," panicked and began cursing and screaming. "Fuck!" he shouted in frustration, certain that he would be returning home with only one leg.

Several minutes of dreadful uncertainty passed before he finally mustered up the courage to glance down at his wounded right leg. His pant leg had been ripped open in the blast, and there was blood on his fatigues. Fortunately, it was all still there, every muscle and joint from the tip of his right boot to the top of his hip. Painful to touch, the wounds were serious but hardly life-threatening. The shrapnel from the mortar shell had not severed any major arteries, and the pieces that were still inside of him were not burrowed into the bone.

Unable to walk, shards of shrapnel visible through the holes in his pants, Ramirez crawled away from the foxhole relieved that he had survived the blast with his limbs intact. "If I had been standing up," he later noted, "I would have easily been killed." Flopping forward onto his belly, the gritty Texan found a new position and settled in behind his M-16. The firing angles there, he soon discovered, were much more to his liking.

A faithful workhorse, along with the ubiquitous Huey, of Army aviation in Vietnam, the CH-47 "Chinook" transport helicopter, a sling load of mortar ammunition swaying gently beneath its fuselage, descended on the 3-12 Infantry firebase north of the joint perimeter. Releasing the sling with the push of a button as soon as it touched the ground, the Chinook then gained altitude and lumbered out of sight. Sling loads of shells were also delivered to the 105-mm battery that day.

Nearly out of high explosive (HE) rounds, the battalion mortar platoon dashed over to the drop zone immediately after the Chinook departed and began hauling in boxes of HE ammunition. Spc4 Jim Coughlan, tired already after loading and re-loading a 4.2-inch mortar for much of the morning, was among the troopers grabbing boxes of ammo. Each box contained two mortar shells; Coughlan, carrying a box on each shoulder, shuffled across the firebase—a distance of some forty to fifty yards—to the mortar section. While he and the other mortarmen had to carry heavy boxes of ammo on foot, the artillery crews drove back and forth in a jeep. "The artillery was right next to us, and they had a jeep. They were lucky," said Coughlan. "They were able to drive to the LZ. The [artillery] rounds were pushed on the jeep, and they'd drive them back so all they'd need was a couple of guys. We had to go out and carry our rounds." A and B Companies, entangled at the time with a large North Vietnamese force to the south, needed the mortar platoon to hammer the jungle around the joint perimeter.

North Vietnamese probing attacks and ground assaults on A Company, which had fallen primarily on the First and Third Platoons earlier in the battle, had now spread to include sections of the Fourth Platoon. Separated by a stretch of brush and bamboo, the grunts and the assaulting NVA, many of whom could be seen crouch-walking—not running—toward the platoon line, exchanged heavy bursts of small-arms fire. Two-deep, the NVA aimed and fired deliberately, each shot or burst targeting a specific bunker or foxhole, as they maneuvered downhill through the bamboo.

Some of them ambled down a small hill near the two-man hole occupied by Spc4 Ralph Lent and another Fourth Platoon trooper. Lent lost track of the attackers in the bamboo and was soon forced to shoot mainly at muzzle flashes. The twenty-one-year-old original from Newburgh, New York, flipped his M-16 to automatic and banged away at the flashes, figuring that if he put enough lead into a particular area he was bound to hit the little bastards even if he couldn't see them. As soon as enemy soldiers began to emerge from the bamboo, however, he switched back to semi-automatic and tried to make every shot count. Lent and the other troopers defending that section of the Fourth Platoon delayed but did not destroy the North Vietnamese assault group.

A wave of tan- and khaki-clad soldiers, undeterred by the roar of M-16s, advanced on the dug-in defenders with single-minded determination. "They were coming right at us. We'd shoot them down, and they'd drag the bodies away and more would come after us," said Lent. "They were like two-deep, and as soon as we hit someone in the front, that person in the back would start dragging him away. One of the other ones that was out there would then come forward and start shooting and take his place." Fewer now in number, the North Vietnamese forged ahead and eventually closed to within thirty-five to forty yards of Lent's hole. *Make your shots count*, Lent told himself, *make every shot count.*

"That one hit the bunker!" exclaimed Pvt. Antonio Garza Jr. North Vietnamese had been throwing hand grenades at the cramped B Company bunker Garza occupied alongside Spc4 Mike Horan and another soldier for much of the morning, but most had failed to explode. So many, in fact, that Horan began to wonder—only half-jokingly—about the quality control standards of the manufacturer. Not one of those grenades, though, had landed on *top* of the bunker.

Garza, determined to find out what had landed on their bunker, scrambled halfway out of the firing aperture and inspected the roof the three of them had constructed out of logs and sandbags. Moments later a bone-rattling explosion reverberated through the entire structure. "I felt like a *whoosh-boing* and then the pressure changed, and I knew something had exploded above my head," said Spc4 Mike Horan. "It was like someone put a bell over my head, and all I heard was a loud *boing.* The whole bunker and everything collapsed down on top of me. Somebody was lying on top of me—it could have been Garza—but I was lucky to be conscious. To this day, I don't know what landed on the bunker. We had had RPGs flying overhead, grenades thrown in our direction, and mortar rounds landing behind us." Exploding suddenly and violently, the unidentified grenade/mortar/RPG killed Garza, then a twenty-year-old replacement from Jourdanton, Texas, and reduced the bunker to a pile of smoking rubble.

Disoriented, blood oozing from both ears, an ugly gash stretched across the width of his upper back, Specialist 4th Class Horan was alive amid the blast-shattered jumble of broken logs and shredded sandbags that had once been their bunker. Wood splinters and shell fragments were embedded in his head and back, and something had punctured his right lung. Conscious, if still reeling from the initial shock of the explosion, Horan realized that he had to wriggle out of the ruins of what had once been their bunker as quickly as possible if he wanted to survive the enemy assault. "I felt that if I didn't get up somebody was going to come by and stick a bayonet in me, because I could see them [NVA] running around," said Horan. "I could see the NVA coming through in certain areas, and I said to myself—they're going to stick me if I don't get up out of this hole."

Horan, crawling painfully out of the smoking debris, worked his way around behind the collapsed bunker he had shared with Garza and another grunt, neither of whom he could presently locate. There was a hand grenade in the left front pocket of his pants. Tales of how the NVA treated American POWs frightened him, so he decided then and there to pull the pin if they ever got too close. They would never take him alive.

Strangely calm, Horan slumped to the ground and rolled over onto his back. Shell bursts, small-arms fire, even shouts from other troopers on the line—noises that normally would not have occasioned any great pain or discomfort—now hurt so much he had to cover his ears with his hands. By then his right lung cavity had collapsed, making the simple act of breathing increasingly more difficult, so he did his best to inhale slowly and deliberately. Horan eventually gazed up into the sky and spotted a prop plane dropping napalm near the edge of the perimeter. "Oh shit," he muttered softly. "Don't drop that on me!"

Scrambled to provide air support for the two embattled companies, Air Force fighters arrived on station at 9:41 A.M., prompting Lieutenant Colonel Vollmer and Captain Hamer to shift the artillery to the east side of the perimeter. This adjustment allowed the fighters to work the jungle to the west, southwest, and northwest without having to fly through incoming artillery fire.[10] Slow movers like the A-1 Skyraiders, one of which Specialist 4th Class Horan had observed, participated in subsequent strikes and produced surprisingly effective results. "Many of the parallel flight patterns of the A-1 Skyraiders were in that portion of the terrain in which they [NVA] would have been grouping," said 1st Lt. Steve Pestikas, PTL of B Company's Third Platoon. "We could notice the difference in the timing of the frontal assault. There were greater differences in time, so you know that those guys in the Skyraiders had an effect on their staging areas. And, actually, right where the vegetation became less, you could see where there was a tremendous amount of damage done. I will tell you unequivocally that if we wanted ordnance in a certain location, those sons of guns put it right on it. They were, on a scale of one to ten, a twenty." Napalm was used in the strike. Earlier the fighters targeted the suspected location of an enemy mortar tube to the northwest.[11]

Gunships rolled in immediately after the first air strike to strafe and rocket enemy troops around the two-company perimeter. Prowling the jungle to the southeast and southwest, the gunships swooped in, blew North Vietnamese snipers out of the trees, and blasted the jungle near friendly positions.[12] Squeezed into a three-man bunker with two other troopers, both of whom he noticed were still fighting despite bleeding from shrapnel wounds to the face, neck, and shoulders, Sgt. Kenny Dempich listened to the gunships rocketing and machine-gunning the NVA beyond the A Company line. The gunships created enough of a commotion, particularly since the artillery had been temporarily redirected to the eastern side of the perimeter, that it attracted the attention of the First Platoon. "You could definitely hear those bad boys firing," said Dempich. "We'd hear explosions out in front of us, and since the artillery wasn't firing at the time, we knew it was either a bomb or rockets from the rocket pods on the gunships. I didn't see them [gunships], but we knew they were there."

In need of fuel, ammo, or both, the gunships completed their final passes and departed, replaced by the fire of multiple artillery batteries. Captain Hamer had insisted that the artillery be shifted back around to cover the western side of the perimeter as soon as the gunships had finished. Five batteries in all (B Battery, 6-29 Artillery; A Battery, 6-14 Artillery; B Battery, 6-14 Artillery; B Battery, 5-16 Artillery; C Battery, 5-16 Artillery) would continue firing in support of the two companies on the twenty-second. Together, the gunship runs and the close tactical air strikes had some effect on enemy pressure around the joint perimeter. Pounded for much of the morning by artillery fire, the North Vietnamese had clung stubbornly to the front lines of both companies, obscured to some extent by the low cloud cover. Alternatively, when the skies over the battlefield began to clear, the NVA's staging areas and forward positions became more susceptible to American airpower. Indeed, Hamer would later note that, while enemy mortar, machine-gun, and rifle fire did not cease entirely, the intensity of the fighting subsided somewhat after the air strikes.

While gunships were working the jungle to the southeast and southwest shortly after the first air strike, Spc4 Hank Fischer, an RTO in A Company's hard-pressed Third Platoon, was communicating over the radio with an incoming slick from the 170th Assault Helicopter Company (52nd Combat Aviation Battalion). "We need ammunition bad," Fischer told the pilots bluntly, "and we need it now." Injured earlier in the battle by an RPG, Fischer knew that the line squads of the Third, and probably those of the other platoons as well, were desperately short on ammo. Fischer's appeal, however, fell on deaf ears. "We're not landing," the aviator responded flatly. "It's too hot. There's shit all over the place."[13]

"If you don't deliver ammo," Fischer replied angrily, "then take that shit back and bring in body bags."

"Tell you what we'll do."

"What's that?"

"Just shoot the shit out of everything you've got, and we're going to come in and kick the shit out. Then we're outta there!"

"Alright."

Third Platoon, guided throughout the battle by the courageous personal leadership of Lieutenant West, dutifully obliged and began laying down heavy suppressive fires. Meanwhile, overhead, the copilot of the slick, Warrant Officer (WO1) Gregory Waltz, aided the pilot in maneuvering the bird down through a storm of antiaircraft fire. In back, 1st Lt. George "Skip" Rice, nineteen, of East Stroudsburg, Pennsylvania, stood by, ready to kick crates of ammo out of the hovering craft.

The executive officer (XO) of B Company, Lieutenant Rice had earned a commission through OCS and was one of the youngest officers in the division. "He was a cheerful, high-energy, well-liked individual who could be stubborn and tough when the situation called for it," recalled Capt. Jim Hegglund, the battalion S2 and onetime commander of B Company. Rice always seemed to be in the right place at the right time, too. That morning the pint-sized lieutenant was in the rear, badgering and cajoling anyone who would listen, until he finally got a chopper loaded up with small-arms ammo for the companies in contact. Rice was equally adamant that he would accompany the crew out to the beleaguered perimeter to ensure that *his* people received the ammo they needed to continue the fight.

Angling into position, the slick carrying Lieutenant Rice and the crates of desperately needed ammo descended down toward a drop point near the center of the two-company perimeter. Small-arms fire followed the Huey down, but Warrant Officer Waltz and the pilot remained composed and fearlessly lowered the bird to within twenty to thirty feet of the jungle floor.[14] There the Huey hovered, visible and vulnerable, while Rice kicked crates of ammo out of the craft and into the clearing below. North Vietnamese fire chased the Huey off before Rice could finish unloading all of the crates, however, and it would be another twelve minutes before the two pilots returned to unload the remaining ammunition at 10:29 A.M.[15]

Few on the ground would have criticized Waltz or the pilot if they had decided against returning to deliver the rest of the load, "hot" as the perimeter was that morning, and many marveled at the courage the two Army aviators displayed in bringing a bird in under those conditions. Remarkably, such displays were not uncommon. "Some of the bravest guys over there were our helicopter pilots," noted Lieutenant Colonel Vollmer.

"They would hover over our positions and drop ammo down to the troops, which was quite dangerous. The actions of the pilots were extremely valorous." Dangerously exposed to enemy fire while hovering above the clearing that morning, the Huey was reportedly hit on the first attempt to resupply the two engaged companies and could just as easily have been hit, with potentially fatal consequences, on the second run.[16]

Although most of the airdropped ammo had landed safely inside the joint perimeter, some of it—too much, apparently, for the outnumbered grunts to do without—crashed to the ground in the surrounding jungle. A number of crates ended up near B Company's Third Platoon, and without being told, Sgt. Dennis Palmer rushed out and grabbed as many as he could handle. "Dennis was the type of soldier who, if he saw something that needed to be done, he did it," said 1st Lt. Steve Pestikas. "We were in dire straits, and he did not need to get my permission to go out and get them. He was a hell of a soldier." Twice more, amid the snap and crack of enemy small-arms fire, Palmer left the safety of the perimeter to recover the errant crates. Palmer, whose exploits on the twenty-second would later result in a Silver Star commendation, then hustled from position to position, distributing ammunition and encouraging the troops in his squad.[17]

Next to Sergeant Palmer's squad, and to the right of a well-worn jungle track leading up to the platoon line, Pfc. Junior Richardson jumped up and ran into the clearing to gather ammunition that had fallen *inside* the joint perimeter. "Follow me!" he shouted to Pfc. Eddie Meier, Pfc. Stan Coker, and a soldier named Brock. Richardson had been in his bunker, scared he would run out of ammunition before the North Vietnamese ran out of men, when Warrant Officer Waltz's resupply slick appeared with crates of ammo. The fighting that morning had been fierce in his sector, and some of the old hands in the platoon had advised him to stuff a sandbag, rucksack, or anything else he could put his hands on—including a dead American—behind his bunker to keep the enemy from shooting him in the back. "The dead don't feel nothing anyway," the veterans told him matter-of-factly, "so use them for cover." Richardson stuffed sandbags and a rucksack behind his bunker.

While Richardson, Coker, and Brock gathered up crates near the B Company CP, often with their backs to the enemy, Meier stood guard, silently watching the jungle in front of the Third Platoon. Temporarily exposed to enemy fire, the three men were knowingly risking their lives to fetch the airdropped ammo, but staying put and hoping the NVA ran out of men seemed even riskier. "We were running out of ammo, and we were dead without it," said Richardson. "They were shooting at us. We could have been killed going after it, but we *had* to have it. That was the whole thing in a nutshell." On their third and final run, the men collected what they could and, quickly traversing the twenty-five to thirty yards between the scattered ammo and the platoon line, cracked open the crates and began distributing the boxes and bandoliers inside.

Desperate soldiers from both companies hauled in the crated ammo and handed it out to the grunts on the line. Greedily reloading, some of the grunts realized that they had never fought for so long, or had expended so much ammunition, in a single battle. The battle, however, would soon be over. Melting back into the jungle, the North Vietnamese, battered and bruised by American supporting arms and having failed, after more than three hours of fierce close-quarters fighting, to penetrate the joint perimeter, quietly withdrew from the battlefield. B Company apparently noticed the enemy withdrawing first. "Look! They're leaving!" the grunts shouted back to Captain Hamer. "We can see them, and they're just moving away in the jungle!" B Company continued to receive mortar, rifle, and automatic weapons fire until approximately 10:45 A.M., but by 10:50 A.M. all enemy fire around the perimeter had ceased.[18]

Curiously, for the second time in three days, elements of Colonel An's 1st NVA Division had decided to attack a static defensive position rather than a company or platoon on the move in the jungle. The 66th NVA Regiment, moreover, attacked in broad daylight, when the full effects of American firepower could be brought to bear on its assault force, rather than at night like the 32nd NVA Regiment. Firepower clearly played a role in the successful defense of the joint A-B Company perimeter. Assaulted repeatedly by large numbers of North Vietnamese, some of the B Company survivors believe that more lives and quite possibly the battle would have been lost without air support. "I would not be here today if it were not for those guys [the Air Force]," said 1st Lt. Steve Pestikas. "They were absolutely outstanding. Between the air support and the artillery support, you could not have asked for better support. The people that were making it happen were instrumental in us being successful and maintaining that line." Pfc. Rey Ramirez also witnessed some of the air strikes and insists that "if it wasn't for the air cover, we would have gotten run over." Air power, according to Ramirez, allowed B Company to overcome the numerical superiority the NVA enjoyed throughout the battle.

The timing of the North Vietnamese withdrawal certainly suggests that American airpower had an effect on the enemy assault. Nonetheless, it is not entirely clear that the two companies would have been overrun even without air support given that the NVA had failed, despite considerable effort, to penetrate the perimeter in the critical hours *preceding* that support. It is also worth noting that the sentiments expressed by Ramirez and Pestikas are not shared by all of the B Company survivors. Captain Hamer, though somewhat removed from the fighting along the company line, followed the ebb and flow of the battle closely and never believed the company was in any imminent danger of being overrun. Hamer also understands why some of the grunts feel differently. "If they could see them [NVA], and there was a lot of firing, they would immediately think that we were about to be overrun," said the B Company commander. "That was a *natural* thing for any of the guys."

Shortly before 11 A.M., Lieutenant Colonel Vollmer advised Captain Hamer to consider pushing troops to the west, southwest, and northwest.[19] Vollmer suspected that the North Vietnamese were withdrawing westward, toward the Se San River and the safety of the Cambodian border, and would likely escape unless his forces could catch them before they crossed the river. Offensive operations beyond that point were expressly forbidden. "I wanted like hell to chase 'em but we couldn't," said Vollmer. "When they're coming over the border trying to kill you, your blood gets going and you want to go get 'em. I knew it tore the guts out of our people when they could come across the border looking to kill us, and we couldn't fire a round across the Se San River." Vollmer, moreover, had already been warned about the consequences of violating the Johnson administration's policy regarding the border. "Husky, you've got to stop your people from firing across the river," Colonel Jackson had told him, "[or] we'll all get fired." Jackson had a right to be concerned. During Operation Sam Houston, General Peers, upset after learning that a LRRP team had been inadvertently airlifted into Cambodia, called the transgression an "almost unbelievable mistake" and then very nearly sacked the commander responsible.[20]

Philosophically Vollmer espoused the virtues of pursuing a defeated enemy. Pursuit, he argued, presented the victorious commander with a rare opportunity to transform a successful attack or defense into a decisive military victory. "If you can pursue the enemy and he does not have established or prepared defenses behind him," Vollmer explained, "the situation can become a rout rather than an orderly withdrawal or what some might call a retreat." Whether he intended to actually pursue the North Vietnamese on the twenty-second, or merely probe the jungle beyond the joint perimeter, is a matter for debate. Several critical factors would have influenced his decision, perhaps none more so than the condition of his forces on the ground. A and B Companies had earned, with the assistance of supporting arms, a hard-fought victory over elements of the 66th NVA Regiment. The struggle had been a costly one, however. Between the two companies, the defenders had suffered ten KIA—eight from B Company—and seventy-seven WIA. Added up, the total number of dead and wounded amounted to about a third of the entire two-company force.[21] Many more were emotionally and physically exhausted and likely in no shape to pursue the NVA through the jungle, something Vollmer himself had once considered "a pretty damn difficult thing to do" in the best of circumstances.

Captain Hamer also suspected that the North Vietnamese were withdrawing toward the Se San River and the Cambodian border. Hamer contends that he too wanted to round up some troops and chase after them. Vollmer, according to the B Company commander, took the matter under advisement but ultimately decided against pursuing the NVA, citing the reduced troop strength of the two companies and the lack of adequate intelligence as to what they might encounter along the way. In all likelihood, the decision to stand down and evacuate the wounded was probably reached by mutual consent. The two companies may not have had enough troops to pursue the NVA and secure an LZ in any event, and no one in the brigade or battalion could say for certain what was lurking between the perimeter and the border.

Vollmer claimed that he *would have* pursued the NVA with mortar fire were it not for the rules regarding the Cambodian border. "The sanctuary business with the Se San River really upset a lot of us. We broke the enemy at one point, and he was withdrawing and he was within mortar range," he recalled. "But once he got across that Se San River, we weren't allowed to fire over there. The II Corps area is heavily wooded with forests and so on, but when you get to the banks of the river it was a little bit open. They would have to come in the open, so our air could get at them. They were withdrawing, [and] you can hurt an enemy a hell of a lot more when he's withdrawing than any other time. That's why pursuit is so important. But we had orders not to fire across the river." In the end, Vollmer abided by the existing policy.

It is also conceivable that Colonel Jackson had to remind Vollmer to exercise restraint near the border. "If Vollmer told Jackson that he wanted to pursue and Jackson said 'no,' Vollmer would not have told me that," said Hamer. "That would have sounded like he was passing the buck, and he wouldn't have done that." The decision not to pursue the North Vietnamese with elements of A and B Companies was almost certainly the correct one. Hamer would have been obliged to leave some of his troops behind to protect and evacuate the wounded, weakening an already compromised pursuit force. More significantly, Hamer admitted that even if Vollmer *had* ordered him to give chase, by the time the troops were assembled, organized, and moving west, the NVA "could have been halfway to the river."

Reluctant to pursue the retreating North Vietnamese with ground troops, Lieutenant Colonel Vollmer relied on air strikes and artillery fire to block the enemy's withdrawal routes. Sometimes the air strikes were delivered against a specific target, such as the strike that targeted an NVA recoilless rifle that had been firing off to the east-southeast, but for the most part the strikes were placed around the perimeter to prevent the enemy from withdrawing from the battlefield.[22] At one point, the FAC orbiting overhead radioed Captain Hamer to report that he had aircraft on station. The planes, said the FAC, were available but would soon be out of fuel. Hamer immediately requested an air strike between the perimeter and the Se San River to catch the NVA before they could scurry across the border into Cambodia. Gunships worked the jungle west of the perimeter, engaging targets of opportunity out to a distance of six hundred to seven hundred meters.[23]

B-52s were available to strike North Vietnamese escape routes as well and later on that day, after the shooting had finally tapered off, a familiar voice crackled over the radio. The voice belonged to the "Mad Mexican," a FAC captain Hamer knew well. "He came on the net not long after the fighting had stopped and said to me that, if I wanted them, he had a flight of three B-52s out of Thailand that were going to a target somewhere," said the B Company commander. "He said that he could divert them if I had a really lucrative target." Hamer had a target, the fleeing troops of the 66th NVA Regiment, but it appeared as if they were on the verge of escaping. The big birds would have to hurry. "There's five kilometers between us and the Se San River," Hamer shouted into the radio, "and that's where they're all going!"

Before long a B-52 pilot came on the horn. "This is the big birds in the sky," said the pilot, introducing himself to the commander on the ground, "where do you want us to put it?" Hamer, consulting his map, quickly found a series of targets. "The FACs had FM radios—the fighter pilots did not—and the B-52s had FMs. So I gave him [the B-52 pilot] a block of eight grid coordinates, four long and two wide, right there between us and the [Se San] river," he recounted. "It was about three klicks away from us, and the B-52s dropped it on them. They stitched that place. They were highly accurate, and I wasn't afraid of them dropping stray bombs on us. If they've got a set of four or five grid squares, all of their ordnance is going to fall into those grid squares. They don't miss." In the meantime, Hamer organized a medical collection point for the wounded near the B Company CP and arranged to have an LZ prepared for the incoming dustoffs, the first of which, he learned, would depart around 11:16 A.M. along the same route the resupply slicks had travelled.[24] Gunships were instructed to provide support, while a resupply bird guided the dustoffs in to the perimeter. Additional arrangements were made to shift all supporting artillery fire east and southeast to accommodate the incoming choppers.[25]

With the first dustoff finally en route, B Company reported at 11:35 A.M. that it had prepared an LZ capable of accommodating one ship. The most seriously wounded were to be evacuated first. Many would never return to the field again, their part in an American tragedy now mercifully at an end, and yet rarely did the men who were left behind have any idea what became of them. "When we put those kids on a chopper, whether they were dead or whether they were wounded, we couldn't figure out necessarily what hospital they went in," said Pfc. Eddie Meier. "We didn't necessarily know whether they went home. We'd think—did they go home? There was never a final closure. We lost all of these people, especially the dead, and they were going back home and their families were going to be devastated by their passing. We never got that final closure."

1st Lt. Steve Pestikas, Meier's no-nonsense platoon leader, visited with the surviving members of the Third Platoon. For Pestikas, it was a privilege just to stand among them. "My chest that day was sticking out because of how proud I was of the men that I had been with for all of those months, over how well they had performed as a unit," he recalled. "We held up our sector, and to this day I've never been prouder of a group of men than I was that day. Anytime that you survive, and you can look upon those people to whom you gave training for all of those months, you're at a loss for words [explaining] how proud you are of them. What needed to be done—they did it and they did it without hesitation." Quietly, indeed often wordlessly, Pestikas attempted to convey to his men what they meant to him that day.

Scared, dirty, and surrounded by death and destruction, the weary grunts of A and B Companies, 3-12 Infantry, many just a few years removed from homecoming games and high school dances, did—with little fanfare and even less glory—what needed to be done.

13 ALL HANDS ON DECK

Awake early that morning in his C Company bunker back at the battalion firebase, Spc4 Oliver Butler reached for his helmet and M-16 as soon as he heard gunfire and the distinctive boom of outgoing artillery. A and B Companies were under assault in the hazy, mist-shrouded draw to the south, and the 105s behind him were firing frantically in support of the two companies. Butler stuffed a .45—he had found the weapon, along with dozens of spent shell casings, in a hooch on top of Hill 86—in his belt as he listened to the distant rumble of battle. C Company had been providing security for the firebase, duty most of the grunts preferred to humping the boonies, while A and B Companies conducted search-and-destroy operations, but he had a feeling that whatever was happening in the draw would eventually drag them all in.

Easy-going with a colorful country drawl, Butler grew up on a farm in Polk County, Illinois, the third of four children. After high school he made plans to marry his sweetheart and build a life together in a house the two of them had spent hours cleaning, painting, and decorating. In the fall of 1965, however, while visiting with his future in-laws, he learned that his mother had phoned with an urgent message to return home immediately. Butler respectfully complied, and when he arrived at his parents' house, he found a draft notice waiting for him. Married on November 27, 1965, Butler spent less than two weeks with his new wife before he left for basic training at Fort Lewis, Washington.

Originally an assistant machine gunner, Butler had heard the chatter of automatic weapons many times before but the din emanating from the draw that morning, coupled with the feverish activity around the firebase in response, convinced him that the battle raging to his south was no ordinary affair. "There was heavy machine-gun fire, rifle fire, and grenades going off and it just kept going," said the then–twenty-year-old original. "It was just *bang! Bang! Bang!* And *boom! Boom! Boom!* When that firefight broke out down there, that firebase just came *alive.* The artillery guys just about jerked their boots on, grabbed a helmet, and ran over to the guns in their skivvies—some had pants on, but some were in their skivvies with a helmet and no shirt—and started hammering away. You couldn't hear yourself think [because] they were just hammering away, one round after another." Next to a radio, Butler was listening in to the transmissions of a forward observer attached to either A or B Company and could hear screaming, shouting, and the chopping drone of heavy AK-47 fire in the background. *Oh my God,* he thought to himself, *do something to help those poor sons of bitches down there.* Later that morning, his prayers were answered when a fighter zoomed overhead after completing a bombing run in the draw.

More help was on the way. At 11:47 A.M., while three flights of fighters were stacking up in the skies above the battlefield, ready to pound NVA targets and routes of withdrawal, Colonel Jackson instructed C Company to prepare to move. Jackson planned to dispatch a company from Lt. Col. Tom Lynch's 3-8 Infantry to the 3-12 Infantry firebase to relieve C Company, so that the latter would be available to reinforce A and B Companies in the draw.[1] Talk of the move soon spread around the firebase. "You heard all kinds of stuff, [and] then we learned that C Company was going," said Spc4 Jim Coughlan, a loader with the 3-12 Infantry mortar platoon. "It was like—*oh man.*" Spc4 Oliver Butler checked his M-16 and cleaned his .45. His intuition had been right; C Company—and a number of unfortunate souls scraped up from the battalion rear areas—were about to join "them boys down there."

The first helicopter to land in the joint perimeter on the twenty-second arrived with two female reporters and several cameramen on board. Cameras in tow, the men hopped out and headed, along with the two women, toward Captain Hamer. News of the battle had apparently reached the press, and the reporters wanted a quick recap of the fighting and some photographs to document its aftermath. Hamer, surprised to see members of the press in the Highlands, met the group and established the ground rules. "Do whatever you want to do," he told them politely, "but just stay out of the way." Interested mainly in the particulars of the battle, the two reporters, one of whom he would later run into back in the rear, peppered Hamer with questions. "How big was the North Vietnamese force?" they wondered "What was the fighting like? Was there ever any concern that the enemy might overrun the perimeter?" Cordial if understandably distracted, Hamer responded tersely then returned to the business of commanding what was left of his company.

Disheveled, raggedy holes torn in his faded jungle fatigues, Spc4 Gary Specht had been walking around B Company's First Platoon, checking in on buddies and seeing who needed what, when he noticed the reporters wandering through the perimeter.

The NVA never raced down from the high ground in front of his position during the battle, something he had feared would happen when the enemy assaulted the platoon, but seeing the number of dead and wounded lying around and the condition of the surviving grunts was upsetting enough without having to put up with reporters crawling all over the place. The thought of them out there, asking questions and snapping pictures, did not sit well with the twenty-year-old fire team leader. "They're bringing [them] out, and I believe there were males and females, and we're sitting there with our crotch ripped out of our pants and stuff like that," said Specht. "Then they're out there and they're coming around taking pictures." To have their dignity taken, too, after what they had already lost that morning, struck Specht as especially cruel. Not too far away, on the A Company side of the perimeter, Sgt. Art Klassen stopped momentarily to watch a camera crew dismount from an idling slick. "Don't you people realize that this is a hot area?" he muttered to himself in disbelief. "We just went through a four-hour battle here. Has anybody thought about that?"

Klassen believes that the cameramen he saw worked for a major television news station, possibly even NBC. There are others who also remember news crews, cameras rolling, walking around the perimeter. Some, however, only recall seeing photographers. Print or broadcast, male or female, the press that showed up that afternoon to cover the battle had opponents and supporters among the surviving grunts. Nearly killed when an NVA soldier threw a 60-mm mortar shell at his bunker, Pfc. Eddie Meier was "appalled and amazed at the time that those people were out there taking pictures." Many agreed with Meier. Pfc. Stan Coker, on the other hand, did not object to the press filming or photographing the aftermath of what had been a hard-fought battle. Folks back home in the States deserved to know the truth, he reasoned, and it was not as if the public had never seen a dead American soldier before. "It didn't bother me because it was a war that was on TV every day even before I got drafted, because I had seen it," said the then–twenty-year-old replacement. "It was a nightly thing—somewhere they were showing combat every night on the national news. I wasn't shocked. I didn't care. People back home, I thought, needed to know what was going on." Coker, incidentally, was never approached for an interview.

Ignoring the press for the most part, the able-bodied survivors of A and B Companies, many resigned to the grisly business of policing up the perimeter, went about their work with an almost grim resolve. Coker, helping out at the time in B Company's Third Platoon, noticed that the jungle around the perimeter was littered with dead North Vietnamese. The condition of some of the corpses was disturbing, particularly for an FNG barely a month into his tour. "I remember seeing a lot of dead NVA—burned up, heads gone, feet blown off," said Coker. "That was the first time I had seen anything like that. They [Air Force] had dropped napalm real close to the perimeter—you could feel the heat from it—and the [NVA] bodies were like in rigor mortis, with their hands and arms all curled up. They were just burnt. With some of them, you could not recognize the features. You just knew it was a body." Admittedly Coker felt an enormous sense of relief that the blackened corpses in the bush were North Vietnamese and not some of his B Company comrades.

A Company encountered similar scenes of death and destruction. Uninjured during the battle—miraculously, in fact, considering that the two soldiers beside him in his cramped three-man bunker had both been hit by shrapnel—Sgt. Kenny Dempich was among the grunts searching the surrounding jungle for dead NVA and weapons. Dempich had not ventured far from the perimeter, twenty-five to thirty meters at most, when he discovered numerous dead bodies, parts of bodies, discarded weapons, and spent shell casings scattered across the jungle floor. The enemy had also suffered grievously, more so it seemed than either A or B Company.

Conditioned to produce a body count for higher commands to digest and report, the two companies made a preliminary tally of North Vietnamese dead. An extension of Washington's attempts to measure progress in the war through statistical metrics, the oft-derided "body count" had long been an immutable feature of operations in the Highlands, and everywhere else in South Vietnam. The American war machine, far from being a stumbling colossus, succeeded in killing tens of thousands of enemy combatants during the conflict. Counting burned and dismembered bodies, however, did not appeal to most of the grunts, even if it affirmed their own performance in battle. "I always thought that the whole body count thing was political," said Sergeant Dempich. "The war was not very popular and I think they just used it to show the public—for propaganda or whatever."

Political considerations notwithstanding, and one could argue that a majority of Americans still supported the war in May of 1967, the grunts generally objected to the practice on more pedestrian grounds.[2] "It was just *gross*," said Sgt. Billy Lomnicki, who was at Jackson Hole awaiting a flight out to A Company on the afternoon of the twenty-second. "It *stunk*—you can never really forget that smell—it was messy, and it was just not a fun thing to do. We had better things to do."

Formerly a gunner with B Battery, 6-29 Artillery, Pfc. Bill Avery never imagined that *he* would be counting bodies when his tour started in the fall of 1966. Avery, age twenty, the son of a carpenter, grew up in Nevada and volunteered for the draft in 1965. Assigned to an artillery battery in basic training, he served with a 105-mm gun crew until March of 1967, when he approached his section chief and asked to be reassigned. Avery, convinced that their CO would never promote him, wanted to carry a radio for an FO attached to a line company. Skeptical, his section chief warned him that FOs and RTOs didn't last long in the bush and then suggested that he reconsider. Avery assured the sergeant that he understood the risks and had no intention of remaining with the battery, unless he received a promotion. When his CO adamantly refused to sign off on a promotion, Avery joined the HQ section of B Company, 3-12 Infantry as an RTO for the attached artillery FO.

Crouched inside a bunker on the morning of the twenty-second, Avery wandered out to the front line after the battle and followed some B Company troopers into the jungle for a quick body count. Avery, combing through an area not far from the perimeter, counted eight to ten NVA bodies in the brush. Most of the enemy dead appeared unharmed other than a trickle of blood around the ears and nose, leading Avery to conclude that the men had probably been killed by the concussive effects of American artillery fire. The rest had been killed by small-arms fire. Blood and enemy equipment were also found in the area.

Avery returned to the perimeter and walked over to a pile of gear that had belonged to Lt. Thomas Burke, formerly of the Fourth Platoon. Burke and two other troopers from the Fourth, Spc4 Clarence Morris and Spc4 Terry Straub, both members of the ill-fated 81-mm mortar crew, were dead.[3] Pawing through Burke's belongings, Avery found a poncho, sleeping gear, and some ammunition to replace the items he had lost when the NVA shot up his rucksack during the battle.[4]

Avery gathered up the items he intended to take and walked away. If it had been his stuff lying around out there unattended, just waiting to be tossed aboard a slick and sent to the rear along with his dead body, someone would have done the same thing to him. Everyone did it.

Around noontime, the first dustoff arrived to evacuate the wounded.[5] Carried over to the LZ, the most seriously wounded, their limbs dangling limply over the sides of dull green ponchos, were quickly loaded aboard the awaiting bird. Half a dozen dustoffs would shuttle in and out of the perimeter, some carrying medical supplies for the harried medics on the ground, before 1 P.M.[6]

Tossed onto an idling Huey that afternoon, Spc4 Mike Horan—skull dented, the breadth of his back lacerated by shrapnel—slid across the floor of the cabin behind the door gunner. Jarringly, several bloody bodies were then thrown on top of him. Buried beneath a pile of dead bodies, Horan, anxious to avoid being mistaken for a KIA, began squirming about as the bird slowly powered up and gained altitude. The door gunner, glancing down at the jumble of bodies near his feet, saw Horan and alerted the crew. "This guy's moving here!" the gunner exclaimed. "You're going to be alright, pal, just hang in there. Don't go to sleep. Stay awake! Stay awake!" Lucid, Horan heard the man shouting and tried to remain conscious.

For a while after the battle, Horan doubted that he would live long enough to ever see the inside of a chopper again. Sgt. Eddie Connor, Horan's squad leader in the First Platoon, had found him lying flat on his back, not far from the bunker he had shared with Pvt. Antonio Garza Jr. Horan was laboring with a collapsed right lung, and the wound on the right side of his head resembled a "sticky mess." Calmly peeling the cellophane paper off of a pack of cigarettes, Connor leaned down and placed the paper over the gaping shrapnel wound in his back. "He put it over the hole because I had been hit with fragments all the way from shoulder to shoulder down my back," said Horan. "One of them penetrated my back, and he put the cellophane on it and it allowed my lungs to fill again. As soon as he did that it stabilized the pressure, and I could catch my breath and breathe normally."

Feeling better, Horan asked Connor for a cigarette—that's what the wounded always do in the movies, Horan thought—and had a few puffs before realizing that "it tasted like shit." Disappointed, he put the cigarette out and sat still while Sergeant Connor positioned sandbags on either side of his head to protect it from further injury. Connor, needed elsewhere in the perimeter, left Horan moments later but a medic stopped by soon after to examine his head and back. Horan asked for something to help with the pain but the medic, citing his head injury, refused to give him a morphine shot. "Fuck," Horan muttered to himself, "there goes my one big chance to get high." Instead of morphine, the medic gave Horan a tag that read "expectant"—medical shorthand for "expected to die"—and then hurried off to treat the rest of the wounded. Horan refused to die, however, and he was eventually helped back to the main medical collection point near the center of the perimeter, where he would remain until he was evacuated later that afternoon.

Hobbled by shrapnel wounds in his right hip and leg, Pfc. Rey Ramirez never made it to the collection point. Unable to stand or walk, he stayed on the line, stubbornly defending his small piece of the perimeter. *Don't worry,* he told himself, *everything is going to be OK.* Approached by two medics after the battle, Ramirez insisted that he was fine and urged the men to treat the more seriously wounded first. Ramirez, told at one point to keep an eye out for the NVA, waited patiently for nearly an hour and a half before finding a spot on the floor of a departing dustoff. One of the last of the B Company wounded to fly out on the twenty-second, he peered down on the battle-scarred perimeter as the bird rose slowly above the jungle canopy. "The one thing I will remember as long as I live is when I was being lifted out, I could see along the perimeter and I saw a lot of our guys lying there," recalled the Third Platoon original. "One particular guy had half his body blown away. I could only see from his torso up." Ramirez's eyes welled up with tears as he stared at the bodies of the fallen, youthful souls gone much too soon, and yet at the same time he was overcome with a profound sense of relief at having survived the battle. *I'm so lucky,* he thought to himself. *I'm so damn lucky.*

Ramirez, Specialist 4th Class Horan, and Sgt. Bob Mervosh, head of the 81-mm mortar crew, were among the B Company wounded evacuated on the afternoon of the twenty-second. Ramirez and Horan would spend considerable time in Japan, recuperating physically and mentally from the wounds of war. Neither man, as a result, would experience the psychologically disorienting effects of being returned to the United States from the battlefields of Vietnam with little more than a handshake in between. "The time I spent in Japan was really nice. I enjoyed it, and I think it helped me a lot as far as my recovery, especially mentally," said Ramirez. "In Japan I was by myself, didn't have any family around me, and I started getting back to being a regular guy. I think a lot of guys who were over there [Vietnam] and then came right back [to the United States] had trouble with their recovery."

Firing furiously in support of A and B Companies, a 105 from B Battery, 6-29 Artillery, paint peeling from its smoking barrel, unloaded another round on the draw to the south with a thunderous boom. The loud report resonated across the 3-12 Infantry firebase, prompting Spc4 Richard Blair to begin collecting his gear. *Whenever the guns let loose like this*, thought the twenty-one-year-old Second Platoon original, *C Company ends up back in the bush.* Blair's intuition proved prescient. At 12:15 P.M. the decision was made to send C Company in to reinforce A and B Companies. Captain Pearson's company was to move by helicopter in groups of three.[7]

Although news of the airlift did not reach the C Company troopers right away, many—including Specialist 4th Class Blair and Spc4 Oliver Butler—already had an inkling that something was afoot. Butler, as he listened to the battle over the radio that morning, figured somebody with bars was bound to tell his platoon to saddle up because the company was heading down there to that godforsaken draw. Putting on a clean pair of socks, Butler refilled his canteens and loaded his pack with rations. Later on he watched while some of the wounded from A and B Companies were choppered in to the battalion firebase for medical treatment.

C Company had been on alert since the previous morning, when the enemy in the area mortared the battalion firebase between 1 A.M. and 2 A.M.[8] Tracking the incoming rounds with radar, the Americans responded with mortar and artillery fire and dispatched patrols later that morning to search for the enemy's mortar sites. One patrol, conducted by C Company's First Platoon, discovered three fighting holes arranged in a "T" formation. Dug a couple of weeks before but not recently occupied, the holes were facing toward the east. The First Platoon found other indications that the enemy had been in the area. "There were all kinds of trails around, and some of them were fourteen or so inches wide," said Sgt. Tom Radke, then a twenty-year-old squad leader in the platoon. "And you could smell them. As bad as we must have stunk, you could still smell them. That gave me the willies, because you knew there had to be a whole lot of them around." Radke, though, refused to dwell on it, and while he had heard the scuttlebutt about A and B Companies, he decided to approach the twenty-second like any other day. Until somebody said otherwise, it was business as usual for his First Platoon squad.

Practical, patriotic, and purposefully plainspoken, in many respects the perfect embodiment of traditional Midwestern values, Sergeant Radke grew up in Hastings, Minnesota, in a large family of seven girls and three boys. Radke considered college after high school, but like many students of modest means he could not afford the cost of tuition. Without a deferment, the prospect of some form of military service seemed inevitable, and he was eventually drafted in 1965, along with four other young men from Hastings High School. Radke received the news with a shrug and a smile. Two years in the Army, after all, did not seem like too much to ask. "I wanted to do what the guys did in World War II," said Radke. "They wanted to do what their country wanted from them. I know a lot of people went the other route. They went to 'Hippyville,' or they went to Canada or some other direction. But I figured that two years of my life wasn't a lot to give my country." And if that meant boarding a slick and flying out to a fight on the afternoon of the twenty-second, then so be it. Radke had done it before and would do it again.

C Company as a whole, however, preferred running patrols and protecting the 105s at the battalion firebase. Rotating through the firebase at regular intervals, the line companies of the battalion took turns providing security for the base so that the troops off all three would have an opportunity to regroup after search-and-destroy operations in the bush. Base security required, among other things, a good deal of patrolling, but the troops could generally retire to a semi-secure defensive perimeter every night without having to dig a fresh bunker or foxhole. When it became clear that C Company was flying back out to the bush, leaving the relative comfort and safety of the base behind, many of the grunts grumbled aloud, and some blamed A and B Companies for dragging them into a fight.

Capt. Tom Pearson, the C Company CO, faulted the judgment of those farther up the chain of command. "They sent two companies down there and allowed them to set up a perimeter in an indefensible position," noted Pearson. "They were down there in a valley, and it was late afternoon. You just don't do that. I know *why* they [A and B Companies] did it, but it seemed to me to be reinforcing failure. My issue was not with [Lieutenant Colonel] Vollmer, understand." Vollmer, incidentally, summoned Pearson to the battalion TOC on the twenty-second to discuss the situation with A and B Companies and the planned C Company airlift. Pearson learned that his company was to chopper out to the battle zone, deliver some replacements to B Company, and then—as he interpreted the mission—"clean up that mess" in the draw.

Captain Pearson left the TOC and prepared for the airlift that afternoon. Pearson, twenty-eight, on his second tour in the Highlands after a stint with the ARVN back in '66, expected a fight as soon as his people hit the ground.

Stumbling out of an incoming Huey, cameras snapping, a group of photographers crowded around Spc4 Hank Fischer as he waited patiently for a chopper ride out of the two-company perimeter. Bandaged over one eye, the normally bespectacled RTO was standing next to Lt. Tom West, his platoon leader, when the photographers pounced. "What happened to him?" the cameramen asked Lieutenant West pryingly. "Get the fuck out of here," West snarled, "and let me take care of my men!" West then helped Fischer onto the chopper. Flown back to Jackson Hole, Fischer was herded into a large tent and advised to take a seat. Sitting down, he noticed that the tent was crowded with wounded and had probably been set up as casualty collection point. Shortly thereafter a soldier carrying a clipboard approached him.

"I need your name, your serial number, and the company you were in," the soldier began, barely glancing up from his clipboard.

Incredulous, Fischer cocked to his head to one side and asked, "You're telling me you don't know who *I* am?"

Confused, Sgt. Billy Lomnicki looked up and immediately recognized Fischer. "Jesus Christ—it's you! Are you OK?"

"Well," Fischer replied facetiously, "I've got a little hole in my head!"

Lomnicki, elated to learn that his childhood buddy was still alive, leaned over and wrapped his arms around Fischer. "You don't know how worried I was about you!" As the two embraced, Lomnicki thought about how lucky Fischer had been. Handed a clipboard earlier that afternoon, Lomnicki, then a twenty-one-year-old A Company original, was told to record the name, serial number, type of wound, and the company—A or B—of the casualties arriving at Jackson Hole. Later on, as he recorded the names of the A Company wounded, he realized that Fischer's name was not among them. "We were watching the guys come in, and I kept looking for him [Fischer]," said Lomnicki. "I had seen moderately wounded guys, severely wounded guys, and a few guys that had suffered mental breakdowns. I didn't see him, and it started to get down toward the end of the company. I was thinking—Jesus Christ, if he doesn't come in with the next couple of choppers, he's probably dead." Lomnicki put a fresh bandage on Fischer's eye and quietly arranged for another soldier to look after him. Loaded onto another chopper later that day, Fischer flew back to a hospital on the coast before moving on to a facility in Japan, where doctors carefully extracted the remaining material from his injured left eye.

Satisfied that he had done all that he could for his best friend, Sergeant Lomnicki walked out of the tent and into the searing afternoon heat. Nearby, on the base helipad, another medevac was arriving with casualties from the morning battle. Standing up on the skids of the bird, waving around a .45, was Lt. Tom West, Fischer's platoon leader. West spotted Lomnicki and immediately launched into a half-crazed rant. "C'mon, Lummy," he shouted deliriously, "get back on this chopper! We gotta go back out there! We gotta help those guys." Lomnicki would have liked nothing better; killing time at Jackson Hole after attending an NCO leadership school in Pleiku, he had planned to catch a slick out to A Company that morning but was instead handed a clipboard and told, along with another grunt, to jot down the name, rank, and so on of the incoming casualties. A and B Company were in contact, the executive officer of A Company explained gruffly, and no one was going anywhere.

West, Lomnicki was relieved to note, did not appear to be a danger to himself or anyone else. Nevertheless, a loaded firearm in the hands of a highly agitated soldier suffering from severe battle fatigue increased the chances of a deadly misunderstanding. Lomnicki believed that what West needed most was a fucking break, from the field, the Army, the war in Vietnam—but first he had to hand over that .45. Steadying his voice, Lomnicki approached the chopper and delicately declared, "Sir, you've got to give me that weapon."

"I'm not giving anybody any weapon!"

Distraught, West stumbled out of the chopper holding the .45 over his head. The standoff ended moments later, however, when Lomnicki finally coaxed the pistol from his hand. Where the Army sent West after that, he could only guess, but he never saw the lieutenant again. Lomnicki had never been particularly fond of West—the two had butted heads back in Tuy Hoa—but after seeing West wounded, wild-eyed, and waving around a .45 that afternoon, his attitude softened. Speaking to other A Company veterans years later, Lomnicki discovered that Lieutenant West, unlike some of the officers he had encountered in Vietnam, had performed valiantly under fire and was indeed worthy of the Bronze Star the Army had awarded him for his actions on the twenty-second.

Lieutenant West and Spc4 Hank Fischer were among the thirty-three A Company wounded evacuated from the joint perimeter. Thirty-six B Company troopers were also evacuated, along with eight men from the HQ Company, 3-12 Infantry. Hit with shrapnel from an enemy grenade, Spc4 Chuck Ahearn was milling about the triage area, waiting for a bird out, when he suddenly found himself staring at a line of ponchos flapping in the wind. "I just remember looking down as the prop wash from a chopper rustled the ponchos covering the dead and seeing the scuffed jungle boots sticking out from the ponchos," Ahearn recounted. "They were all scuffed and muddy, and it just seemed like such a waste." Those boots belonged to some of the soldiers (eight B Company KIA, two A Company KIA) that had died defending the perimeter that morning.

A Company, reinforced with a platoon from B Company, pushed out of the perimeter at 1 P.M. and began sweeping the jungle to the west, northwest, and southwest. Colonel Jackson radioed the battalion TOC shortly before the start of the sweep. The element policing the battlefield, Jackson made clear, was to have good security on all sides and on the way out. Jackson also requested the latest casualty figures from the morning battle, and he urged Vollmer to have the policing element capture a prisoner if at all possible. B Company, meanwhile, was to remain in the perimeter and guard the LZ while the wounded were evacuated.[9]

Sidestepping shell craters and half-smashed trees, A Company and the platoon from B Company swept through the jungle in search of enemy bodies and weapons. Pfc. Bill Avery, the erstwhile 105 gunner turned RTO from the 6-29 Artillery, noted the number of trees in the area with roots sticking up above the ground and worried that they would make excellent hiding spots for enemy soldiers. Avery had moved cautiously around one tree and was about to move on to the next when he noticed a North Vietnamese soldier squatting down behind it. Startled, Avery stopped and stared at the crouching figure. "Here's this NVA soldier, all in one piece, with blood coming out of his ear and nose, [just] squatting there," he said. "He was dead, but it was scary when you came around [trees], because you didn't know." Exhaling, Avery hurried past the dead NVA behind the tree.

A Company troopers, meanwhile, found a wounded North Vietnamese soldier in the jungle outside the perimeter. Captured less than ten minutes into the sweep, the soldier, a private first class in the 66th NVA Regiment, revealed that his battalion was in the process of withdrawing with many of its dead and wounded. The POW, however, did not know the route of withdrawal.[10] Around 1:30 P.M., after Colonel Jackson had contacted the 3-12 Infantry for an updated body count and to urge Lieutenant Colonel Vollmer to continue sweeping the battlefield, A Company reported a total of eight enemy KIAs and two POWs.[11] Sgt. Art Klassen greeted one of the prisoners on the outskirts of the perimeter. Left behind to stand guard while most of the company swept the jungle to the west, Klassen grabbed the POW by the scruff of his neck—skinny and scared, the man looked no more than sixteen or seventeen years old—and dragged him back to the LZ.

Hands bound, the young North Vietnamese prisoner stumbled along beside Klassen, apparently unwounded, in a pair of black pajamas. Few of the B Company troopers walking around seemed to notice the man, much less interact with him, but the striking juxtaposition of a scrawny Vietnamese soldier standing next to a six-foot-three American sergeant caught the eye of a photographer. Klassen guarded the prisoner for about fifteen or twenty minutes and then stood aside while the man was hustled onto a helicopter and flown back to a base in the rear.

A handful of North Vietnamese prisoners were captured on the twenty-second and evacuated from the field. From these sources, the 1st Brigade gleaned valuable intelligence on the enemy forces involved in the morning attack.[12] One of the POWs, for example, stated that a reinforced battalion had attacked A and B Companies and was now withdrawing with many of its dead and wounded, reiterating much of what A Company had reported earlier that afternoon. Colonel Jackson passed this intelligence on to Lieutenant Colonel Vollmer and then directed the 3-12 Infantry CO to close off all potential avenues of escape with artillery fire.[13] Forty or so minutes later, at 3:14 P.M., Vollmer received word from Jackson that the enemy unit involved in the attack had been hit by air strikes, according to one of the POWs. Disorganized, apparently, and carrying many of its dead and wounded, the enemy unit was said to be withdrawing toward a rallying point on the Se San River. Fighters arrived on station within the hour—Vollmer requested strikes on enemy escape routes to the northwest—and at least two additional groups of fighters worked the jungle west of the joint perimeter before nightfall.[14]

Mentally and physically spent after the morning battle, A Company and the attached platoon from B Company, despite the sweltering heat and humidity, continued to search the jungle around the perimeter. SSgt. Rudy Dunn, head of the six-man A Company ambush patrol that had been hiding under a log for hours, heard over the patrol radio that a company was sweeping the area. Cut off and virtually surrounded, he and his men had survived the North Vietnamese, scores of friendly shell bursts, and a swarm of angry wasps. The company conducting the sweep would find them sooner or later, Dunn imagined, but he was deathly afraid that his troopers would not survive the curtain of incoming artillery fire the gunners were walking out in front of the company.

Shells crashed and exploded in the jungle nearby, but when the artillery fire finally rolled past, sparing the huddling patrolmen, Sergeant Dunn heard the sound of voices. Overjoyed, the cut-off patrolmen began shouting, and before long they could see American infantry approaching. The time was approximately 2:14 P.M.[15] "It sure was a pretty sight to see our own men," said Dunn, adding that he "should've been dead six times already."[16] Three of his troopers were wounded during the ordeal.

Cut off from the perimeter, the patrol observed elements of the enemy battalion withdrawing after the battle. The North Vietnamese, the patrolmen reported, used porters to haul away more than forty enemy casualties.[17] Colonel Jackson had hoped that a speedy search of the battlefield would result in a more accurate—and preferably higher—enemy body count.[18] Dunn's patrol, however, revealed that the post-battle sweep had not been conducted swiftly enough to prevent the North Vietnamese from hauling away some of their dead and wounded. "If we took too long in getting on the battlefield following a sharp action, he'd [North Vietnamese] clean it up despite our denial fires," Jackson later admitted. "The body counts are cold statistics but when our troopers could see for themselves the damage they had done to the enemy, then it's a big morale factor. Our troopers want to be winners."[19] Feeling more like survivors than winners, the able-bodied men of A and B Companies, their buddies dead, others badly wounded, would spend years in some cases searching for validation.

Airlifted in from Jackson Hole, A Company, 3-8 Infantry arrived at the 3-12 Infantry firebase around 1 P.M. and assumed responsibility for the defense of the base.[20] A Company became available when General Peers returned operational control of the 3-8 Infantry, which had been operating in Darlac Province to the south, to Colonel Jackson on the twenty-first. With another infantry company on hand to protect the battalion firebase, C Company, 3-12 Infantry was free to reinforce its sister companies to the south. Shortly before 2 P.M., news of the planned airlift reached the troops.[21] C Company, they were told, was to land near the joint perimeter and link up with friendly forces on the ground. Gunships would escort the incoming slicks, and rumor had it that the First Platoon was to fly out first.

By 2:07 P.M. slicks were in the air and en route to the battalion firebase to pick up C Company.[22] 1st Lt. Doyle Volkmer, twenty-six, of Bay City, Texas, summoned his squad leaders in the Third Platoon. "Get your men ready," he barked, "we're going out to reinforce A and B Companies." In command of the platoon since January 1967, Volkmer made a habit of sleeping with his boots on, carried a CAR-15 like many officers, and, for a while, after his men had found a couple of skeletons with AK-47s, had decorated his foxhole with a human skull. Smart and unshakeable, edgier, in many respects, than his bespectacled, mild-mannered appearance would suggest, Volkmer enlisted in the Army in 1959 and spent the next four years in Germany, meeting and marrying a German girl along the way. Returning to the United States in November 1963, he remained in the Army and eventually graduated from OCS in October 1966.

Ticketed for a combat tour overseas, Volkmer, then a newly commissioned second lieutenant, flew to South Vietnam later that month and was subsequently assigned to the 4th Infantry Division. Volkmer also spent time in a reconnaissance unit and attended the MACV "Recondo School" in Nha Trang. "Believe it or not that [Recondo training] came in somewhat handy," he recalled. "The type of recon I was trained in was for us to observe. We had more ways to break contact than to fight. Now, normally, we were operating in a much smaller unit then a platoon, but you could apply some of those Recondo School techniques to a platoon. In other words, you stayed hidden." Remaining hidden on the afternoon of the twenty-second, while slicks droned noisily overhead, hauling in all four platoons of C Company, would not be so easy, however.

Around the same time, Captain Pearson, annoyed that he had to escort a member of the press to the LZ, called for Spc4 Oliver Butler.

"Butler!"

"Yes, sir?" Butler answered tentatively.

"Take this person with you."

"*What?*"

"Take this person with you!"

Confused as to whom he was supposed to "take," Butler turned around and saw a woman standing there in jungle fatigues, jungle boots, and a baseball cap. Reasonably attractive, the woman wore her hair in a long ponytail, which spilled out of her cap and down her back. *Uh huh*, Butler thought as he glanced disapprovingly at the camera dangling from the woman's neck, *she's a reporter. We're going down there to help them boys out, and I ain't playing chaperone to no female reporter.*

Annoyed, Butler turned to Captain Pearson, who was already walking away after issuing what he considered a direct order, and sneered, "Hell, I ain't taking her!"

"What did you just say?" growled Pearson, whirling around to face the young specialist 4th class.

Cowed by Pearson's sharp tone and angry glare, Butler explained, somewhat sheepishly, that he just didn't have the time—not with everything else going on—to be messing around "with that woman." Pearson, not of a mind to quibble with subordinates, would hear none of it. "You *will* take her with you."

"I don't have time to fool around with her!"

"I'm not *asking* you. That's an order, and I don't want to hear any more."

Spc4 Bob Masching, twenty, 1st Squad, First Platoon, the same squad as Spc4 Oliver Butler, was standing nearby and overheard the exchange. "I'm sure as hell glad he picked you instead of me," Masching chirped good-naturedly, "because if she was with me, I am not sure she would make it." Butler sighed and turned once again to the reporter. "Do you even have a weapon?"

"No," the woman responded.

Butler, pointing toward the battalion perimeter, told the reporter to get a rifle. While he waited for the woman to return, a helicopter arrived with a sling load of shells for the ammo-starved artillery battery.

The airlift began at 2:34 P.M. Stepping anxiously into awaiting Hueys, jaws clenched, rifles in hand, the first group of C Company troopers choppered out of the battalion firebase and disappeared over the horizon. Seated next to a door gunner on one of the slicks, Sgt. Tom Radke gazed down on the lush, green foliage blanketing the countryside. Puffs of white-grey mist soon caught his eye as the chopper sped south. "You could see the bullets coming out of the trees, because it would blow up mist from the vegetation," said Radke. "The bullets coming through the vegetation were leaving a puff of mist."

Alarmed, Radke swung his M-16 into action and returned fire. When more puffs appeared in the trees, suggesting that the NVA had their Huey dialed in, Radke hollered at the door gunner to "turn it up" with his M-60. The machine gun, however, remained silent. Out of the corner of his eye, Radke then noticed that the gun was hanging idly down, as if it had been left unattended. *Why the hell isn't this guy shooting?* he wondered. Puzzled by the position of the gun, Radke glanced back and saw the gunner slumped forward with a bullet hole in his forehead.

Soon after, the slick carrying Radke and the 3rd Squad, First Platoon approached the LZ near A and B Companies. Told that the pilot did not intend to land, Radke and his men leaped out of the hovering chopper and onto the jungle floor; a few landed gracefully while some of their comrades, weighted down as they were by heavy rucksacks and forced to jump in bamboo, tumbled to the ground in a heap. A squad leader in the Second Platoon, Spc4 Rich Blair hopped out of another hovering slick and, landing somewhat awkwardly, slipped and fell on his back. Comically, several of the grunts in line behind Blair did not bother to look before they jumped and wound up in a pile on top of him. Some mishaps were more serious than others. Not long after Radke hit the ground, a helicopter dropped off another batch of C Company troopers and then took off again with a hapless grunt dangling from the door. "His web gear had gotten caught on the straps of the seat, and he was swinging around above the skid plate," said Radke. "The chopper flew away with him hanging out of the side of the chopper."

Arriving in small groups, the First Platoon pushed out from the LZ and waited for the rest of the company to land. Spc4 Oliver Butler leaped out of a slick as soon as its landing skids touched something solid, flattened bamboo or some kind of large log he later guessed, and quickly fell in with the 1st Squad. Butler surveyed the surrounding jungle and counted his blessings. No one was shooting at them, and the female reporter he had been asked to escort had disappeared. Delighted to be relieved of the woman, Butler could not help thinking about the coveted CAR-15 someone back at the battalion firebase had given her, a weapon he would have given "his right nut" to use.

Thirty sorties were required to complete the airlift, but by 3:40 P.M. that afternoon, C Company was on the ground and ready to move out.[23] Lieutenant Colonel Vollmer, anxious to get his people out of the draw, ordered Captain Pearson to move into the high ground west-northwest of A and B Companies and prepare an NDP for all three companies.[24] C Company would almost certainly cross paths with A Company along the way, so it was important for Pearson to coordinate his movements with Captain Lee. All units, moreover, were to be notified when friendly troops were in the area.[25]

Fifteen minutes later, at 3:55 P.M., Lieutenant Colonel Vollmer joined C Company on the ground. "For somebody to sit back in a comfortable area all of the time and not be on the ground, well, you've got to show up with your troops," he explained, noting that at West Point cadets are taught that commanders have an obligation to share some of the hardships of their men. "Then they figure—hell, if that colonel can do it, we can do it. And it was pretty miserable. There were bugs and snakes, and we even had people run into wild bees. It wasn't pleasant. But it was just a good idea to get down there." USMA, Class of '49, Vollmer had thought it best to "show the flag" after a tough day of battle, and he decided to spend the night with his companies.

14 HAPPY VALLEY

C Company, after a short walk from the LZ, approached the scene of the morning battle. Bent and twisted trees, some splintered like kindling, blackened shell craters, and broken bits of bamboo littered the battle-torn landscape. The stale jungle air reeked of gunpowder and charred flesh. Struck by the extent of the devastation, the anxious troopers, hearts racing, moved cautiously through the jungle.

Third Platoon, under the command of Lt. Doyle Volkmer, initially passed several dead NVA. Fleshed out with a number of replacements—including Pfc. Ronnie Tenney, a journal-scribbling twenty-one-year-old from Mound City, Missouri—the platoon continued on, however, and eventually encountered the kind of wanton destruction few could ever have imagined, much less thought possible. "At first we saw a few dead gooks that must have been killed in the firefight only that morning, but as we made our way farther we saw something different—something most horrible," Tenney wrote years later. "Evidence of the mighty destruction of an air strike was everywhere. Death overwhelmed the scene. Dead gooks lay in twisted and contorted form. The smell of burnt flesh was sickening. Bodies, like bloated animals, were stiffened and body parts splattered the area. It was like my mind was acting separate from my body as we moved through the destruction. The moment ran before me as if in slow motion—time was not a factor. Each of us was going through a sort of shock as we walked by the death scene."[1]

Dead North Vietnamese, skulls smashed, their bodies pressed up against tree trunks, were scattered throughout the area. Others were sprawled out across the jungle floor. Lieutenant Volkmer stepped over one body and noticed that the man was lying on the ground with his mouth wide open. Nearby, several recent replacements were staring at the corpse, visibly shaken. None of them, apparently, had ever seen a dead body before. Volkmer, hoping to break the tension with a little gallows humor, pointed at the NVA's mouth and joked, ham-handedly, "Look Ma, no cavities!" Unamused, the replacements just stood there looking at him.

Fascinated by the carnage, a couple of grunts in the Third Platoon decided to take pictures of the NVA. Specialist 4th Class Tenney, sickened by the sight of so many bodies and body parts, wondered why anyone would want to photograph the dead, whether they had a camera or not. When word came down asking if anyone was taking pictures, the two grunts, afraid that they would have to turn over their film if they stepped forward, remained quiet. Sticking together, the platoon covered for the men and reported that no one in the Third had taken any photographs. Afterward one of the men involved insisted that he would have the film developed and stored in a lockbox. "If my son ever thinks that war would be fun," the sergeant announced, "I'm going to show him these pictures. Then perhaps he will change his mind."[2] Tenney and the others agreed.

C Company's First Platoon, meanwhile, swept through the shallow draw under the watchful eye of Plt. Sgt. Calvin Rohrbough, a strict but well-respected Korean War veteran. The battle, the platoon quickly discovered, had been a bitterly contested, close-quarters affair. "It looked like, when we got off the helicopter, that they [A and B Companies] had walked the artillery right up to the edge of the perimeter," recalled Spc4 Oliver Butler. "There were hardly any trees or anything standing. It was just blown all to pieces." Pushing on, the platoon found dead NVA lying around the perimeter. Spc4 John Sobaski, twenty-one, of St. Paul, Minnesota, was startled to see an enemy KIA lying no more than ten feet from an American foxhole. *What the fuck?* thought Sobaski. *Why did they do this? Why did A and B Company set up in a valley when they had hills all around them? Man, it's like they were asking for it.*

Sobaski, however, was hardly the only First Platoon grunt to question the battalion's decision to set up a two-company perimeter in a draw. "I'm not trying to put a thorn in anybody's side but it was like a football stadium, where the seats all around were like the hills surrounding parts of that perimeter and the field down below was the perimeter," said Sgt. Tom Radke, Sobaski's squad leader at the time. "From most any vantage point where they [A and B Companies] had set up there, you could see down onto where they were. If the NVA had set up a mortar tube somewhere, they could actually see down where they were to move the mortar around. They would have been able to visibly see where the rounds were hitting. We could never understand why they [A and B Company] would have ever set up in a spot like that." Radke assumed that someone had selected the flat, relatively open location with helicopters in mind.

Searching near the joint perimeter with his 3rd Squad, Radke stumbled on a wire running across the jungle floor. "Look at this," he exclaimed, drawing attention to the wire. Similar in appearance to the lines used for land phones, the wire was located approximately fifty to sixty yards from the perimeter. A second wire, this one some ten to fifteen feet farther away, ran parallel to the first. Radke had heard that the NVA used commo wire, but it was the first time he had actually seen any in the bush.

Troopers from another squad found sections of wire near a tree, and when elements of the Third Platoon reported similar findings, Lieutenant Volkmer posited that the NVA had used the wires to guide their forces into position for the attack on the joint perimeter. "I do not recall that wire, but it's possible," wrote Captain Hamer. "They [NVA] would have had very little time to lay in a perimeter wire before dark. At dark our listening posts were in place, so it would have been difficult to avoid detection. On the other hand, I've seen where they had crawled through concertina wire carrying satchel charges successfully, so who knows." Hamer also suspected, perhaps correctly, that the wires B Company found on the afternoon of the twenty-first belonged to a North Vietnamese headquarters element, and it is certainly conceivable that the wires C Company discovered on the twenty-second were a part of the same communications network.

Capt. Tom Pearson, the confident, almost cocksure CO of C Company, had thought it foolhardy to dispatch two infantry companies, scarcely two-thirds of the line strength of a *single* battalion, to reinforce the 1-8 Infantry if the situation in the southern Ia Tchar concerned General Peers and Colonel Jackson. Setting up in a draw made even less sense to him. Why, then, were A and B Companies allowed to set up there, not far from a bundle of North Vietnamese commo wire, especially when Jackson and Lieutenant Colonel Vollmer had previously expressed the importance of terrain and the advisability of establishing NDPs on high ground? Vollmer, in selecting the general area for the joint perimeter, gambled that the two companies could pause for the night in a draw, where it would be easier for helicopters to land the following morning without courting disaster. Expected to reach the 1-8 Infantry quickly, Vollmer wanted to get Captain Hamer resupplied and both companies on the move as soon as possible on the twenty-second. The draw, with its even topography and modest clearings, satisfied both operational imperatives.

More concerned with food and water than the next leg of the journey south, Hamer believed B Company would make do regardless of where it set up for the night, as long as there was an LZ available to resupply the troops in the morning. "Vollmer had emphasized that it was critical that we moved quickly to reinforce the 1-8 Infantry," said Hamer, "[but] we had to stop for supplies. We had to get them before we moved forward." While certainly more defensible, much of the high ground in the area—as A Company could attest—was heavily forested with fewer openings in the canopy. Noting as much, Hamer observed that if B Company had camped in the hills, it would have taken until mid-morning on the twenty-second to cut an LZ comparable to the one he had found in the draw.

Lieutenant Colonel Vollmer, moreover, seems to have understood the need to balance operational demands with basic force protection when he ordered A and B Companies to establish a large, two-company perimeter on the evening of the twenty-first. Hamer surmised at the time that Vollmer had ordered the two companies to unite in a single, mutually supporting position to compensate for the questionable choice of terrain. Later he wondered whether the NVA had misjudged the strength of the American position:

> I think that may have been why Vollmer decided to have both companies set up together. I still say they [NVA] did not know our strength. They thought they were attacking a normal infantry company, because that was the way we always travelled around. But we had two full companies in there, and so instead of ninety guys, they were looking at [maybe] two hundred and thirty or two hundred and forty. Now, they [NVA] had to plan this thing on the spur of the moment and they only had a few hours to figure out what they were going to do, because we hadn't gotten there until late in the day on the twenty-first. So they had to scout us, see where we were, and look at the perimeter with only a couple of hours of daylight left. I didn't think we'd be attacked, because I thought that all of the NVA were committed to [attacking] the 1-8 Infantry. The other part was that I had two-thirds of a battalion [with me] in the field.

Contrary perhaps to Hamer's expectations, the NVA assaulted the joint perimeter but were beaten back by the combined strength of two infantry companies, amply supported by air and artillery strikes. Whether either company would have been able to hold off a reinforced enemy battalion without the assistance of the other is not altogether clear. It is also worth mentioning that the decision to camp in the draw, if only to expedite the move south, had its defenders in C Company. "While we would not ordinarily have set up in a position like that, we did not know what the circumstances were with those two companies," said Sgt. Wayne Watson, a squad leader in the Second Platoon. "There are a million different reasons why they might have been there. They could have been waiting for an aerial resupply that was running late, for example. We didn't know." Others put it more succinctly. "You set up wherever you stopped," noted 1st Lt. Doyle Volkmer of the Third Platoon. "That's just the way things worked, and that position was defensible."

♣ Somewhat limited in scope, Lieutenant Colonel Vollmer's attempts to police up the battlefield produced a final body count of seventy-nine enemy KIA. A handful of North Vietnamese POWs were recovered as well, along with ten AK-47s, eight SKSs, a pair of RPD light machine guns, and over two dozen 60-mm mortar rounds.[3] Significantly, the troops also found documents indicating that the "7th Battalion" of the 66th NVA Regiment had attacked the joint perimeter.[4]

Around 4:20 P.M. the battalion TOC received word that all three companies were consolidating at C Company's location.[5] Lieutenant Colonel Vollmer, addressing plans for the night ahead, ordered Captain Pearson to move up onto the ridgeline to the west. "Find a spot large enough for all of us," he advised Pearson, "and start digging in." A and B Companies would join C Company later on that evening. Vollmer added that the troops had to be dug in before dark because an NVA regiment was believed to be lurking in the area, reportedly within striking distance of the three companies. News of the move west trickled down to the troops, though few additional details were forthcoming. Some of the grunts, moreover, were unaware that Vollmer had choppered in to command the battalion on the ground.

Curiously, the three companies had very little contact with one another that day, despite their close proximity. Shortly after landing, C Company had interacted briefly with elements of A and B Companies, but the state of some of the survivors made conversation difficult if not impossible. Noticeably unnerved, several hollow-eyed, unshaven grunts stared blankly at 1st Lt. Doyle Volkmer—an empty gaze Volkmer imagined "must have been the thousand-yard stare mentioned so often in World War II"—and simply mumbled.[6] North Vietnamese lay scattered all around the two companies, and as he paused for a moment to reflect on the number of enemy dead, Volkmer realized just how tenaciously those mumbling, quasi-catatonic grunts had fought to defend the perimeter.

Spc4 Oliver Butler approached an A Company sergeant he recognized from Fort Lewis, Washington, and had a similar encounter. Relieved to discover that the man had made it, Butler was soon struck by the trembling, shell-shocked figure he saw standing beside a bunker, absently clutching an M-16. "It was that old saying—the lights were on but nobody was home," said Butler. "He was just standing around looking, but there wasn't anybody there." Another C Company trooper offered the sergeant a cigarette, and then had to step in and light it for him. "He [the sergeant] had the shakes so bad, he just couldn't do it," recalled Butler. "I remember what he looked like and I thought—he'll never get over this. There was a human there but it just wasn't—it's hard for me to explain. Mentally and physically, he was just in bad shape." Butler would later learn that the sergeant had shoved the body of a dead American soldier in front of his bunker like a sandbag to block some of the incoming fire.

Butler remained with the 1st Squad, First Platoon while the companies consolidated, but before long C Company was marching west toward the ridgeline Lieutenant Colonel Vollmer had selected for the battalion NDP. Brightly colored bands of sunlight poked through the canopy as the troopers hiked quietly across the draw. Shotgun in hand, Spc4 Roger Strand walked, stride for stride, with Butler and Spc4 Bob Masching. Strand was familiar with the Cambodian border from his days in the battalion reconnaissance unit, and had taken his bush-busting Stevens (Savage)

Model 77E pump-action shotgun with him when he left. Rough around the edges, the twenty-year-old North Dakotan was initially assigned to C Company at Fort Lewis, Washington, in 1965–66 but had left the company for the recon unit shortly after AIT.

Strand was a superb soldier in the bush, good as anyone in the company, in fact, but he never thought much of rules and regulations and usually got into trouble whenever he spent any time in the rear. Harmless in the grand scheme of things, his playful carousing nevertheless left his shirtsleeves short a stripe or two. "I probably set the record for the most times getting busted down from an E5," Strand joked. "I wasn't much good in camp, and sometimes I'd come in there and raise some hell. They'd get me in trouble and I'd say, 'What are you going to do? Put me in the bush with the recon?' I didn't care." Sgt. Tom Radke remembered Strand from basic training and was thrilled to have him around on the twenty-second. "Strand made his own decisions, but he was not insubordinate," said Radke. "He was a hell of a good soldier. I am glad he was on our side." Most of the C Company originals who had trained with Strand readily agreed.

Well to the west of Strand, the roar of Air Force fighters heralded another round of air strikes. By hammering suspected enemy escape routes with air strikes and artillery fire, Colonel Jackson and Lieutenant Colonel Vollmer hoped to inflict as much damage as possible on the North Vietnamese before they could scurry back across the border. In March, following a pitched battle involving the 2-35 Infantry, Huey gunships located and killed dozens of enemy soldiers wading across the Se San River toward Cambodia. Vollmer had helicopter gunships prowling the jungle as well, and he figured that between the gunships, fighters, and artillery fire, an opportunity existed to deliver a significant parting blow to the retreating elements of the 66th NVA Regiment.

Crackling across the jungle, the sudden burst of gunfire shattered the late afternoon calm and interrupted C Company's march into the high ground to the west. A lone North Vietnamese soldier with an automatic weapon opened up on the company from a distance of 150 meters or more and then abruptly fled. The Americans returned fire but made no effort to pursue the man.[7] Captain Pearson got his people organized and moving again and it was not long before the company was pushing uphill, toward the upper reaches of the ridgeline Lieutenant Colonel Vollmer had selected for the battalion NDP. Pearson, eager to reach the top quickly so that his troops could dig in, wanted to find a defensible knoll with decent fields of fire that was large enough to accommodate a three-company perimeter.

C Company, legs burning, shoulders aching under the weight of overstuffed packs, crested the ridge and found a suitable location for the battalion NDP on top of a knoll. The time was approximately 6 P.M. Spc4 Oliver Butler, still chuckling nervously, arrived with the First Platoon and started digging in. While marching up the slope of the ridge, Butler had come across a dead NVA soldier kneeling behind a broken tree with half of his head blown off. Butler then noticed a huge hole in the ground in front of the tree, no more than six to eight feet from the man. Several other First Platoon soldiers were with him at the time, and one of them remarked, morbidly, "I bet that son of a bitch wished he hadn't peeked." Butler laughed at the remark and continued chuckling, although he could not for the life of him say why, all the way up the slope. That night, as he was setting up with an M-60 crew on the south side of the knoll, Butler recalled his fit of laughter on the slope and attributed it to nerves.

Tightly wound, C Company cleared fields of fire and prepared mutually supporting positions, backbreaking labor that taxed the troops physically and mentally, under the direction of Captain Pearson. Tempers flared from time to time as the troops, tired and increasingly irritable, struggled to dig foxholes and bunkers in the waning daylight. Pfc. Ronnie Tenney snapped at Sgt. James Cartwright then stormed off in a huff. Cartwright, twenty-two, of Eugene, Oregon, was, in the words of 1st Lt. Doyle Volkmer, an "almost fearless man," yet he remained calm and addressed the young Third Platoon replacement respectfully when the two spoke a short while later. "I can't remember his exact words, but he told me that he hadn't meant to make me mad," wrote Tenney. "He was sorry, he said, but he had just wanted to help me do my best so someday, perhaps, I might make it out of there. He told me he would soon be going home, in about three months, and when they left I would be a prime candidate for squad leader. But I had a lot to learn, he said, and he had a short time to teach me what he knew. Then just like that my anger was gone. He was right. He always was."[8] Tenney apologized for his part in the dustup, and Cartwright quickly accepted. Amicably resolved, the flap was soon forgotten and the two got ready to go out on LP.

Thirty minutes after C Company reached the ridgeline west of the draw and began digging in, B Company, accompanied by Lieutenant Colonel Vollmer and additional troops rounded up from the battalion rear, closed on the knoll.[9] Curious, Spc4 Oliver Butler glanced over at the troops filing in to the perimeter, noticed what appeared to be an entourage accompanying one of the officers, and immediately wondered, *Now who in the hell is that*? Butler thought about it for a moment and then realized that it was Vollmer, the battalion commander. *Oh shit! Why in the hell is he coming out here? Maybe that's why Captain Pearson told us to set up an especially tight perimeter.*

Organized with three companies in mind, the perimeter had a number of positions prepared for B Company by the time Vollmer arrived. B Company, reduced to four under-strength platoons, limped in and began taking up positions on the line. Vollmer had arranged for choppers to deliver water and ammunition to the company before it marched up the ridge, supplies the troops desperately needed, and he warned Captain Hamer that night about a second NVA regiment in the area. Similar reports had crackled across the radio earlier that afternoon. "Hamer was, from my perspective, very concerned with the information he got from the S2, namely that we were not 'out of the woods' yet," wrote 1st Lt. Steve Pestikas of the Third Platoon. "The intel he received was that there was a high probability the twenty-second was not going to be an isolated occurrence. Therefore I, for one, made it very clear to my men that we had to be prepared for further contact with the NVA." Pestikas, in turn, relied on Plt. Sgt. Jerry Tharp to reinforce the message. Accordingly, the Hell's Saints prepared for the worst; Pfc. Junior Richardson, expecting that his area would remain on high alert all night, heard someone calling for fixed bayonets.

B and C Companies posted LPs in the jungle and waited for A Company to arrive. Colonel Jackson, meanwhile, directed Lieutenant Colonel Vollmer to "dig in extremely well" and to make certain the battalion had developed an effective artillery program for the night ahead. Jackson wanted Vollmer to use artillery to "box" the battalion position and "deny the battle area" to the North Vietnamese. Vollmer, moreover, was to request "any and all support" he needed that night without hesitation.

Night fell swiftly on the ridgeline, and soon the troops were cloaked in darkness. Private First Class Richardson swore he heard voices in the jungle beyond the B Company line. Set up in front of C Company, Sgt. James Cartwright and Pfc. Ronnie Tenney, eyes straining in the inky black, watched and waited. The two grunts chatted in hushed whispers, neither man hearing or seeing anything important enough to radio in. Talking helped pass the time, and the two became friends. "I remember thinking there was no one I'd rather be on LP with on such a night, and I was glad that we were no longer angry at one another," Tenney wrote. "I decided then and there to learn all I could from Jim Cartwright."[10]

Shortly after 9 P.M., the 1st Brigade ordered the artillery LNO assigned to the 3-12 Infantry to cease all fires other than illumination promptly at midnight. The artillery restrictions were scheduled to coincide with the start of the twenty-four-hour truce the 4th Infantry Division had agreed to observe in honor of Buddha's birthday. Earlier, Lieutenant Colonel Vollmer had asked the artillery to cease firing illumination rounds except on suspected enemy escape routes to the west.[11] Targeting grid coordinates between the battalion and the border, the FAC on station then put in a series of air strikes before midnight.

A Company, moving west out of the draw, stumbled up the ridgeline in the dark and entered the battalion position at 10:49 P.M.[12] A number of defensive positions had been prepared for the company in advance, and it did not take long for the tired troopers to fill in along the perimeter. In reasonably good shape after the fighting that morning,

Lieutenant Blake's Second Platoon improved some of its existing positions—the grunts heard that an NVA regiment was nearby and ready to strike—and started settling in. Sgt. Art Klassen, an experienced original who had survived the fiasco on Hill 86 in March, dug his foxhole a little deeper that night and even took the time to shovel out a smaller, secondary hole the grunts called a "grenade thump." Designed to absorb shrapnel, "grenade thumps" were located inside a foxhole or bunker and provided a place for grunts to safely detonate a grenade that had been thrown into their hole.

Klassen finished the "grenade thump" and picked up his M-16. Nervously recalling the smell of fish and rice as he hiked up the ridge, the veteran squad leader chambered a round and hunkered down for the night. "Normally, unless we were point squad or on guard duty, I would tell my squad—don't keep a chambered round unless you're expecting contact. But everybody was locked and loaded [that night]," said Klassen. "We were expecting something. We were really on pins and needles until the night of Buddha's birthday was over." Sgt. Kenny Dempich guessed that his First Platoon would spend the entire night on "100 percent alert" and would be lucky to get any sleep.

In no mood for another fight, A Company settled in and waited for morning. As a group, the young troopers had fought courageously that day. "To the best of my knowledge, we did not have one guy that laid down at the bottom of a foxhole and was scared shitless and scared so bad that he could not even fire a weapon," said Kenny Dempich. "We did not have *one* guy that did that. Everybody did their job. [And] our medics were phenomenal. *They* did their job." But the job was not over, Captain Lee reminded them, and everyone—medics, grunts, officers and NCOs—had to remain alert and prepared for another enemy attack.

Lee, Pearson, and Hamer set up behind their respective companies, much like a platoon leader would do in a single-company perimeter. Exhausted, Captain Hamer stretched out on a couple of C-rat boxes and retired for the night, relieved that Lieutenant Colonel Vollmer was in charge of the three-company perimeter. Normally Hamer would have stayed awake, monitoring the radio and communicating with his platoon leaders, until about 1 A.M. Attacks at night, when the North Vietnamese could operate under the cover of darkness, worried him the most. In the daytime the NVA were more visible and thus more vulnerable to American firepower. Hamer trusted that his troops would buy him enough time, regardless of the numbers involved, to batter the enemy with air strikes and artillery fire, if the attack occurred during the day. Nighttime assaults, however, were another matter altogether.

Farther back, in the center of the battalion perimeter, Lieutenant Colonel Vollmer fretted over reports of an uncommitted enemy regiment in the area and the approaching truce. The 1st Brigade had been ordered to suspend offensive operations on the twenty-third, and while the Communists had also pledged to honor the twenty-four-hour ceasefire to mark Buddha's birthday, the NVA were known to violate such agreements whenever it was militarily expedient. Vollmer expressed concern that the North Vietnamese would exploit the opportunity afforded by the truce to attack the battalion NDP, possibly with an entire regiment. Conferring with his company commanders, Vollmer also made it clear that if the NVA did attack that night, he intended to direct the battalion's defense.

Tuesday, May 23, dawned warm and humid. The previous night, much to the relief of the tired troopers manning the battalion perimeter, had ended uneventfully, and at 6:45 A.M. Lt. George "Skip" Rice, B Company's diminutive XO, requested three radios, two machine guns, and some poncho liners. As fears of an NVA attack gradually subsided, Lieutenant Colonel Vollmer contacted the battalion TOC at 7:25 A.M. for further instructions on the operation. Vollmer then ordered the companies to return to the draw to patrol the jungle around the abandoned A-B Company perimeter. Bemused by the decision to halt all artillery fire at midnight, particularly when the battalion had been using those fires to deny the NVA access to the battlefield, Vollmer suspected that the final enemy body count that day would be lower than if the guns had been allowed to fire throughout the night.[13]

Jumpy after the events of the twenty-second, the three companies moved down the ridge that morning and began running patrols in the draw.[14] Scared, Spc4 Gary Specht eased through the shattered jungle and passed a number of dead NVA who were crouching down behind trees. Specht, gazing uncomfortably at the bodies of the dead enemy soldiers, concluded that the men had likely been killed by supporting arms. Four years old when his father died, the twenty-year-old original was sent to the Milton Hershey School, then a private boarding school for orphaned or otherwise disadvantaged boys, in his hometown of Hershey, Pennsylvania.[15] Milton had made a man out of him, but nothing could have prepared him for the horrors of war.

Unsettlingly quiet, the jungle around the abandoned perimeter reeked of decomposing flesh. "I have never smelled anything so bad in my entire life," recalled Spc4 Larry Schindeldecker. "They [NVA bodies] were all bloated. They may have been wet and dried out in the sun, but they were all swelled up and you'd see them up against a tree somewhere. The bodies that I saw were mostly intact, but they were bloated and stunk *so* bad. One of the things that lives [on] in my memory is those bodies." Schindeldecker, twenty, of St. Paul, Minnesota, served with Sgt. Tom Radke in C Company's First Platoon, and neither man would ever forget the hideously bloated bodies, half-mangled corpses dangling from the trees, and the unbearable smell in that shallow draw on the morning of the twenty-third. "To come back to that spot, with all of those bodies lying around in one hundred degree heat, you can imagine what that was [like]," said Radke. "They were all blown up, full of maggots, and there were pieces falling off. And the stink—it was unbelievable."

C Company, however, continued patrolling near the abandoned perimeter. Tiptoeing along the bank of a stream, Sgt. James Cartwright, point man for the right front element of 1st Lt. Doyle Volkmer's Third Platoon, maneuvered past a fallen tree and pushed on through the undergrowth. Pfc. Ronnie Tenney, following close behind, crept forward to the tree next and noticed movement up ahead. Tenney thought it looked a human arm reaching down to pick something up. Confused, he turned to Sgt. Ray Flores, who had joined him behind the tree.

"I see someone up ahead," Tenney told Flores. "I'm not sure how many, or if they see me."

Flores sensed trouble. "Get Cartwright!"[16]

Moments later Sergeant Cartwright came ambling back, holding up at least two fingers. Flores and Tenney knew immediately what the show of fingers meant; there were two, possibly three, North Vietnamese soldiers in front of them. Suddenly the crack of small-arms fire echoed across the jungle. Cartwright, shot once in the chest near his left shoulder and once through the wrist, collapsed to the ground. The time was 9:20 A.M.[17]

Seventy-five yards to the rear, Lieutenant Volkmer heard the gunfire and soon after learned that one of his men had been hit. "I had sent two squads out in a modified 'cloverleaf' maneuver—one to the right front and one to the left front," Volkmer recalled. "Word came back that one of my men was hit, [and] we immediately went to the location to help."[18] Volkmer, rushing forward with the rest of the Third Platoon, reached the area where the shooting had occurred and was squatting down behind a large log when one of the grunts informed him that the wounded soldier was Sergeant Cartwright. Cartwright's wounds were apparently severe, and someone would have to go out and get him. Sgt. Jessie Garcia, third or fourth in line when the shooting started, volunteered and began crawling toward Cartwright while the platoon laid down heavy covering fire. Garcia, bullets rippling overhead, covered the ten to fifteen meters to Cartwright on his hands and knees and dragged the bleeding sergeant to safety.

Cartwright, badly hurt but still conscious, pleaded for his best friend, Sergeant Flores. "Ray, Ray, Ray," he moaned inconsolably. The platoon medic, a specialist 4th class named Rapa, hurried forward with another medic and the two began to treat the wounded sergeant. "We found out later that the shoulder wound had entered the chest cavity. Rapa was giving mouth to mouth and as another medic was performing CPR," Lieutenant Volkmer recounted, "he evidently forced some of the gore from the wound into Rapa's mouth, causing him to stop and vomit. As soon as he stopped vomiting, he immediately resumed mouth to mouth rescue breaths."[19] Dedicated, selfless, and never far from the very worst of the war, the combat medics assigned to the line companies often embodied the very best of the 4th Infantry Division.

Pfc. Ronnie Tenney and several other soldiers, meanwhile, crossed the stream to search the area where the North Vietnamese—three members of a trailwatching party, according to subsequent reports—had set up.[20] The shooting had stopped by then, and as the grunts neared a flat area near the stream, they discovered a small campsite where the North Vietnamese had probably spent the night, along with some of their belongings. The trailwatchers, however, had vanished. Hurrying back across the stream, Tenney and the others returned to find Specialist 4th Class Rapa working feverishly to revive Sergeant Cartwright. Nearby Lieutenant Volkmer was on the radio with Captain Pearson. "Cartwright's been hit bad," Volkmer told the C Company CO, "and we need to get him to a hospital." Pearson called back shortly thereafter to say that he had located an LZ on top of a hill; grabbing Cartwright, Tenney and three other grunts scurried down the bank, across the stream, and up the slope of the hill. Specialist 4th Class Rapa followed along beside them.

Numb, Tenney prayed silently as the small group staggered up the slope. "Oh please God," he mumbled to himself, "please save Jim Cartwright." Then, without warning, Rapa told the group to hold up. Tenney and the other men lowered Cartwright to the ground and waited, breathlessly, while the platoon medic huddled over his unconscious body. Time slowed to a crawl as they waited there, hoping, praying, dreading the worst, until Rapa, hunched down beside Cartwright, muttered, "He's gone." Hauntingly final, the words dulled the senses and deadened the soul. "And just like that, a life that was here just moments before was now gone," Tenney reflected after the war. "Fuck it—I thought. Fuck it all. And at that moment something in me died. It was not just a bad moment; it was a place in time that changed me forever. [It] changed the way that I looked at things, and life for me would never be the same."[21] Devastated, Tenney helped carry Cartwright up the hill, mindlessly planting one battered boot in front of the other, to the LZ.

Officially, Sgt. James Cartwright, Third Platoon, C Company, 3-12 Infantry, was pronounced "dead on arrival" at 11:24 A.M.[22] His comrades, however, the men for whom he had fought and died, remember the horrible truth of that muggy morning near the Cambodian border. "I have relived the moment time and time again," Tenney wrote poignantly. "Many times I've seen Cartwright go down. Many times I've heard him cry out. And each time I die in panic not knowing what to do. In every person's life there is that moment that we wish we could go back to and do over—to correct something about the moment. If I could I would go back to that dreadful moment when Jim Cartwright got killed, then perhaps there would be something I could do to save him."[23]

Following the brief firefight that killed Sergeant Cartwright, Lieutenant Colonel Vollmer received permission to use artillery fire if his companies made contact with the enemy, notwithstanding the terms of the truce, with the understanding that such fires were to be employed in a "discriminate" manner. A short while later, at approximately 10:15 A.M., Colonel Jackson reminded Vollmer that he had been authorized to employ artillery only in the area of contact and only for the duration of the engagement. When in contact, however, Vollmer's units were to request artillery fire immediately.[24]

For most of the morning, the three companies patrolled the steamy jungle and searched for bodies. A Company, operating for a time near the old two-company perimeter, policed the battlefield, cleaned individual and crew-served weapons, and chatted about the battle the day before. "We were talking—those of us that were still out there and were not wounded or KIA—about how lucky we were and how we had survived *something*," said Sgt. Kenny Dempich. "Again, at that time, we did not know the severity of what we had survived. We found that stuff out later. But, yeah, we just talked about how we had survived and how lucky we were. And again that's when some of the guys got to talking about how they were down to their last magazine of ammo." Dempich, as he talked to some of the other grunts, watched for snipers—the trees in the area were reportedly infested with them—and kept close tabs on his First Platoon squad.[25]

Southwest of A Company, B Company's understrength platoons limped along, beating the bush for bodies, blood trails, and enemy equipment. Captain Hamer reiterated reports that the NVA had an uncommitted regiment in the area and urged the platoons to stay alert. Lives depended on it. A replacement thought he heard gunfire while the Third Platoon was on a sweep and later recalled hearing a rumor that members of the platoon had shot and killed some wounded NVA. The incident and others like it, if true, exposed the ugly underbelly of the war waged in the Central Highlands. Atrocities, while perhaps less prevalent in the Highlands than in other areas of South Vietnam, where the civilian population mingled more freely with the combatants, were certainly not unheard of in the hills and valleys abutting the Cambodian border. Indeed, less than a week before the alleged incident on the twenty-third, North Vietnamese troops had shot survivors from the 1-8 Infantry's "Lost Platoon."[26]

Early that afternoon, a North Vietnamese sniper opened fire on a squad from C Company's Third Platoon. Spc4 Alfred McCalla crumpled to the ground in a heap, dropped by a round to the lower leg, but the squad—which had been walking point at the time—returned fire and forced the man to withdraw, possibly with one or two other snipers. McCalla, though, suffered a compound fracture and could not walk.

Dashing forward to reinforce his point squad, Lieutenant Volkmer and the remainder of the platoon arrived to find McCalla, bones protruding from his lower leg, lying on the ground. Specialist 4th Class Rapa, the platoon medic who had coughed up blood and gore while performing CPR on Sergeant Cartwright, hurried over to treat the wounded soldier. "As the medic was working on him, McCalla motioned me down and told me he had two extra canteens of water in the side pockets of his pack," Volkmer recounted. "Water was an important part of our existence, and it was a real gift when someone offered you a drink from his canteen. It didn't matter if he had green scum on his teeth. You took the drink and thanked him."[27] Touched, Volkmer accepted the canteens and arranged for a medevac to pick McCalla up. A search of the immediate area, meanwhile, produced a 60-mm mortar base plate and a North Vietnamese pack.[28]

Jostled painfully about, Specialist 4th Class McCalla grimaced as the troopers carrying him to the LZ staggered along through the jungle. Morphine shots did little to dull the pain shooting through his shattered leg, and for a while the stricken RTO seemed to cry out with every step the troopers took. Helpless, McCalla endured every trip, slip, and stumble until around 3 P.M. that afternoon, when he was loaded aboard a dustoff and evacuated to a medical facility in the rear.

Slicks also flew in to the old two-company perimeter to unload supplies and collect packs, rifles, and other discarded equipment before the three companies hiked up into the high ground northwest of the draw. Marching off with a fresh supply of food, water, and ammo, A Company left the perimeter around 4 P.M. and headed for the hills. Lieutenant Colonel Vollmer, departing aboard an outgoing bird, returned to the battalion firebase shortly before 5 P.M. and placed Captain Pearson in charge of the new NDP. By 7 P.M. all three companies had relocated to the high ground and were digging in for the night.

Spooked by the hit-and-run attacks on the Third Platoon, C Company tied in nervously with A and B Companies and waited for what Lieutenant Colonel Vollmer feared would be a major enemy attack. "Everybody was so uptight," said Spc4 Oliver Butler of the First Platoon, "that if anybody had farted they would probably have gotten shot." Farther north, in the battalion TOC, the results of the day's operations—eight NVA KIAs, one AK-47 assault rifle—were recorded for Vollmer to review. C Company accounted for the AK-47 and one of the KIAs.[29] Captain Pearson, however, questioned some of the metrics used to measure success in the field. "I know Westmoreland got caught up in that body count crap, but that was the worst thing we ever got into," said the C Company skipper. "The only realistic indicator of how well you're doing is the increase or decrease in the amount of time you see enemy activity."

That night, while the three line companies of the 3-12 Infantry were settling in on the high ground northwest of the draw, Colonel Jackson decided to recall the

1-8 Infantry to Jackson Hole and exchange it with the 3-8 Infantry, commanded by Lt. Col. Tom Lynch. Jackson planned to have slicks pick up both battalions on the twenty-fourth to complete the swap. Then at Jackson Hole, the 3-8 Infantry was to establish a new firebase and commit two companies to the Ia Tchar Valley. Elements of Colonel An's 1st NVA Division were still operating in the area, and Jackson wanted Lynch and Lieutenant Colonel Vollmer to push east and sweep the lower ridges of the Chu Goungot Mountains.[30]

With A Company, 3-8 Infantry slated to provide security for Lynch's new firebase, Vollmer made arrangements that evening to fly A Company, 3-12 Infantry back to the battalion firebase the following day. Vollmer expected Captain Lee to be in the draw and ready to board choppers by 11 A.M. on the twenty-fourth, after Colonel Jackson had replaced the 1-8 Infantry with the 3-8 Infantry. In the meantime, Vollmer warned his company commanders of a "strong body of enemy elements" in the area and advised all three to prepare for an enemy attack late that night. Intelligence passed down from brigade placed two North Vietnamese battalions to the east of the battalion perimeter and one to the southwest, near enough that there were Indications the enemy would attempt to overrun friendly elements if they appeared "lax."[31]

As a final precaution, Vollmer insisted that the companies dispatch LPs around the perimeter and check the overhead cover on bunkers and foxholes. The companies, moreover, were to distribute ammo and set their radios accordingly. Shortly after the call from Vollmer, Captain Pearson contacted the TOC and explained that if anything happened to the battalion net that night, they would switch to the Admin Log. Pearson then turned his attention back to the perimeter. The time was 11:05 P.M.[32]

Quiet for the most part on the twenty-third, American artillery unleashed a thunderous "time on target" (TOT) barrage around 12:35 A.M. on the morning of May 24, heralding the end of the twenty-four-hour-truce. The target of the TOT, identified by the brigade S2 as the headquarters of the 66th NVA Regiment, was reportedly only 1,300 yards from the location of the 3-12 Infantry CP.[33] Without boots on the ground to assess the results, however, neither the brigade nor the battalion could be certain if the artillery fire destroyed or even damaged the enemy command and control element.

Shrouded in darkness, many unable to sleep, the weary troopers manning the perimeter around Captain Pearson squinted at shadows, unaware that an enemy headquarters had been targeted for destruction. Glimpses of soft, grayish-colored light greeted the grunts eventually and many, after hours of waiting and wondering if the sun would ever come up, sighed with relief. A new day was dawning. The long, tedious, and at times terrifying night had come to a merciful end. Firefights during the day were bad enough but at night, when it seemed as if the battalion was fumbling about half-blind in the dark, that "pit-in-the-stomach" feeling they had all learned to live was always much more acute. Finally able to exhale, the grunts straightened up, looked around, and started the morning routine.

At 8:15 A.M. Major Jones, the battalion S3, notified Captain Pearson that he was to relinquish operational control of B Company to Captain Hamer, ending a temporary command arrangement Lieutenant Colonel Vollmer had ordered the previous day just before he flew back to the battalion firebase. Hamer, Jones added, was to move B Company onto a north-south ridge located to the east of the two-company perimeter he had shared with A Company on the twenty-second. Pearson, meanwhile, would march east-southeast and secure an LZ for A Company. Selected to replace A Company, 3-8 Infantry, Captain Lee's company was to follow C Company down to the LZ, where it would board slicks bound for the battalion firebase. Vollmer needed Lee to return to protect the firebase, and he needed Pearson to provide security during the lift. Once A Company had been airlifted out, Vollmer wanted C Company to head east and join B Company in a two-company perimeter.[34] The two companies were to then search the lower slopes of the Chu Goungot Mountains for elements of the 32nd and 66th NVA Regiments.[35] That same day, elements of the 173rd Airborne Brigade (Sep.) began arriving in Pleiku. Establishing a base at Catecka about twelve kilometers south of Pleiku City, the 173rd was to operate under the control of the 4th Infantry Division.

Hiking down from the high ground, C Company returned to the draw and secured an LZ by 10:26 A.M., six minutes after B Company had headed east out of the hills toward the north-south ridge identified by Major Jones. Earlier that morning, after Captain Hamer had received his marching orders from Jones, Lieutenant Colonel Vollmer had promised the B Company commander that he would try to get him some more troops before the end of the day.[36] For the fifty or so B Company survivors marching east, however, the prospect of additional troops meant nothing if the NVA hit the company again in the interim. Pfc. Eddie Meier, a Third Platoon replacement who had nearly been killed when an NVA soldier threw a mortar round at his bunker on the twenty-second, worried that the North Vietnamese were lurking somewhere in the jungle, just waiting to strike. Lieutenant Pestikas had cautioned the Third to stay alert, that the company was not out of the woods yet, but Meier knew that even an alert platoon was no match for a carefully laid ambush. *At any moment*, Meier cringed, *the NVA could come out of that damn jungle and hit us again!*

Mindful of the possibility of enemy contact, Captain Hamer maintained security elements on both flanks of the company column as it pushed steadily eastward, past the old two-company perimeter, toward the ridge. Making good time, the column advanced without interruption—the jungle covering the approaches to the ridge was not quite as thick—until about 1 P.M., when the point element spotted two

North Vietnamese soldiers and opened fire. Clad in khaki-colored uniforms and black sandals, the enemy soldiers fled, one to the north, the other to the south, but the Americans managed to kill one of the men before he could escape. Hamer had the area searched, and along with the dead trailwatcher the troops found an AK-47 assault rifle and three grenades.[37]

B Company called the incident in, destroyed the three grenades, and continued moving toward the crest of the ridge. Around quarter to two that afternoon, Captain Hamer contacted the battalion TOC and requested ten PRC-25 radio batteries. Running short after a couple of chaotic days in the field, Hamer hoped to have the batteries by nightfall, when the company would need them the most.

The first load of A Company troopers boarded slicks bound for the battalion firebase at 2:26 P.M., nearly three and a half hours behind schedule. Thrilled to finally be leaving "Happy Valley," the tired troopers lined up and climbed—one grunt at a time—inside the awaiting Hueys.[38] "We just wanted to get the hell out of there," said Sgt. Kenny Dempich of the First Platoon. "We needed to get out of there. Most of us were wearing clothes that were half rags. They were ripped and torn, and while I can't say for sure, I can almost guarantee that most of us had bloodstains on our clothes from all the wounded. Whether it was trying to help the medic trying to take care of somebody, or loading the wounded onto the choppers, the dead onto the choppers, there was blood all over the damn place. After the ordeal we had just been through, we were all just thinking—get me the hell out of here, let me back to a base camp, let me get a shower." When it was finally his turn, Dempich climbed inside a Huey and sat quietly on the cabin floor, comforted by the familiar *whoomp whoomp* of the rotors overhead.

Some of the slicks arrived in the LZ with reinforcements Lieutenant Colonel Vollmer had promised B Company. Dispatched to the field from Camp Enari, Paul Modafferi, John Ferrante, and Bill Moen, three Spc4s from the battalion communications platoon, hit the ground and reported to C Company. It had been a hectic afternoon, one that included a meeting with their platoon sergeant in the platoon tent. The sergeant and the soldiers standing beside him in the tent were all from the South; Moen, Modaferri, and Ferrante were from New York. "He [the sergeant] said that we had to send three guys out to the field and that we were going to draw straws," said Moen. "He said the Southern guys had drawn already and here are your three straws."

Moen, sensing that the fix was in, glanced suspiciously at Modafferi and Ferrante and then looked down at his straw. It was short. So, too, were the straws held by Modafferi and Ferrante. "Go on and grab yourselves some ammo, grenades, and food," the sergeant snorted, "and get on over to the helipad." Stomping out of the tent, Moen, Modafferi, and Ferrante packed up their gear and waited for a chopper. "The three New Yorkers had to go out in the field," Moen later mused, "and the three Southerners stayed."

The last of the A Company troopers landed at the battalion firebase a little after 3 P.M.[39] Meanwhile, back at the LZ, C Company got ready to join B Company on the ridge to the east. Not expecting any trouble, Captain Pearson decided to move in a column formation without any flank security. Eight hundred meters of Highland jungle separated the two companies, plenty of ground for his people to cover, he reckoned, before the sun went down.[40]

15 BRAVES ALWAYS FIRST

Critics of American military strategy in Vietnam have often argued that General Westmoreland was hopelessly wedded to conventional war and failed to grasp the socio-political, post-colonial context of Communist-inspired "national wars of liberation." Westmoreland, however, understood that a strategy based entirely on killing the enemy would not produce a stable, politically viable South Vietnam. Adopting a holistic approach to the war, the MACV commander stressed the importance of pacification. Critically, Westmoreland viewed civic action programs and other nation-building initiatives as key components of the pacification process. Westmoreland, moreover, encouraged his subordinates to consider the political aspects of the conflict. "The war in Vietnam is a political as well as a military war," he explained. "It is political because the ultimate goal is to regain the loyalty and cooperation of the people, and to create conditions which permit the people to go about their normal lives in peace and security."[1] One dead guerilla, Westmoreland averred, was worth two dead main force soldiers.[2]

The 4th Infantry Division, under General Collins and General Peers, engaged in civic action primarily to promote pacification. Keenly aware of the political-social dimensions of the war, Peers embraced and expanded the division's modestly successful "Good Neighbor Program." The program, like similar initiatives, was based on the belief that "killing the Viet Cong alone can't achieve the goal of defeating the enemy."[3]

Military commanders, however, are obliged to fashion a strategy that accurately reflects the enemy threat. In Vietnam, General Westmoreland correctly deduced the *dual* nature—Communist big-unit war and a well-entrenched Communist insurgency—of that threat and endeavored to blunt the former so that Allied pacification efforts could defeat the latter. President Johnson dispatched American combat troops to Vietnam in 1965 precisely because the enemy's big-unit war, waged by professionally trained and heavily armed North Vietnamese and Viet Cong regiments, was on the verge of destroying the South Vietnamese Army. Hanoi realized that it had to crush South Vietnam's conventional forces in high-intensity, big-unit battle if it wished to collapse the regime in Saigon. Westmoreland, unlike many of his critics, appreciated the immediacy of the main force threat facing South Vietnam and responded accordingly. Indeed, even the U.S. Army's 1966 PROVN report, which some have used to indict Westmoreland as a narrow-minded conventionalist fixated on firepower and attrition, placed the "*defeat of Peoples' Army of Vietnam [NVA] and Main Force Viet Cong units* [emphasis added] and the reduction of Viet Cong guerrillas and political infrastructure among the population" at the very top of its list of vital strategic objectives.[4]

Westmoreland preferred to fight in the largely unpopulated border regions of South Vietnam, where American commanders could bring enormous firepower to bear on the enemy without adversely affecting the civilian population. In the remote western Highlands, as in other border regions of the country, the American military used that firepower to interdict and attrite North Vietnamese forces. "It was a body count war," observed Lieutenant Colonel Vollmer, "and to a point our guys wanted to know if we were hurting the enemy. And we were. We beat the hell out of those guys on the ground. You can't believe how many people we were able to kill over there. The press, though, was not always interested in reporting it in those terms." Vollmer knew that he had hit the NVA hard on the morning of the twenty-second, but he also believed that a large enemy force was still in the area.

Ambling into the high ground east of the draw on the afternoon of the twenty-fourth, B Company stopped for the night on the crest of a steep-sided knoll. Sloped on three sides and large enough to accommodate two companies, the knoll seemed ideally suited for a joint perimeter. Captain Hamer, moving his people into position on the crest, set up a defensive line along an arc facing north. Hamer also marked off positions for C Company and deliberately left the back side of the knoll undefended so that Captain Pearson's troops could enter the perimeter from the southwest without having to pass through B Company. Hamer then surveyed the surrounding terrain—the former Marine was concerned mainly with potential enemy staging areas and avenues of approach—and began plotting firing points for his supporting artillery.

Giant boulders dotted the military crest of the knoll and some of the B Company troopers, tired after another long day of marching and climbing, removed their packs and slumped down between them. Spc4 Gary Specht dropped his pack near a termite mound and trudged off to find some wood for overhead cover. While some of the grunts found tree limbs and branches for their bunkers, others were reduced to using machetes to chop down what they needed. The rest of the company remained in the perimeter, reluctantly digging holes and clearing fields of fire.

Specht returned to the perimeter with wood and started digging in. Jabbing into the rocky soil, the First Platoon original was standing in a hole about a foot deep when he heard the unmistakable *thump* of a mortar round leaving the tube. Instinctively, he dove behind the termite mound near his hole. Pfc. Eddie Meier, ankle-deep in another hole along the B Company line, listened to the *thump thump* and stood, oddly transfixed, while his startled Third Platoon squad hit the dirt all around him. "Get my gun!" exclaimed one of the troopers. "Get my helmet!" hollered another. Several explosions then rocked the jungle around the knoll. The time was approximately 4:00 P.M.[5]

Down slope, no more than fifty meters from the Third Platoon, Pfc. Stan Coker and two other troopers abandoned their three-man LP and dashed back to the platoon as soon as the enemy mortar fire began. Coker was not alone. 1st Lt. Steve Pestikas and his RTO, Spc4 Juan Trevino, heard the mortars and sprinted up the south side of the knoll. Coker, Pestikas, and Trevino reached the crest unscathed; a young black trooper who had been cutting wood did not. Sliced open by shrapnel that had ricocheted off a rock, the trooper ran uphill, through the enemy shell bursts, and staggered into the perimeter.

Frantically tossing helmets and packs to the grunts near his hole, Pfc. Eddie Meier noticed the wounded trooper coming up the slope and rushed over to help. "It looked like the guy had been opened up by a lion or a tiger," he recalled. Meier, surprised that the wounded trooper could walk much less run, led the man to a group of large rocks nearby and promised that he would keep an eye out for a medic. Behind him, Lieutenant Pestikas and Specialist 4th Class Trevino sprinted across the crest and met up with Spc4 Jim Matyas, the platoon FO, and together they found a spot among the rocks for the platoon CP.

Mortar rounds continued to rain down on the knoll. Reaching for his handset, Captain Hamer got on the horn and called in artillery on the enemy tubes.[6] *We're in big trouble now,* Hamer thought to himself as he gazed down on the surrounding jungle from his half-dug hole behind the B Company line. *There's* [*sic*] *maybe fifty of us covering a third of what was supposed to be a two-company perimeter. If they hit us now, we aren't going to be able to hold 'em.* Barrels booming, the artillery opened up and within minutes the enemy mortar fire ceased.[7] Hamer exhaled and prayed that the mortars would not soon be followed by a wave of NVA.

Armed with rockets, rifles, and hand grenades, a force of approximately one hundred North Vietnamese soldiers from the 32nd NVA Regiment converged on the knoll and scrambled up its heavily forested slopes to assault B Company from the north, northeast, and northwest at 4:13 P.M. Steady SKS and AK-47 fire swept uphill

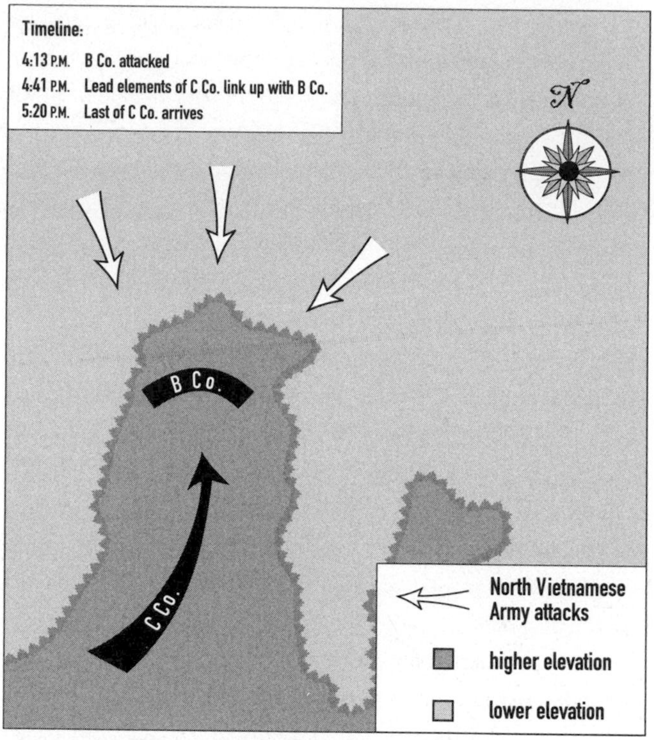
Timeline:
4:13 P.M. B Co. attacked
4:41 P.M. Lead elements of C Co. link up with B Co.
5:20 P.M. Last of C Co. arrives
N
B Co.
C Co.
North Vietnamese Army attacks
higher elevation
lower elevation

B and C Companies, 3-12 Infantry, May 24, 1967. *Map by Charles Grear, adapted from original drawn for John P. Vollmer.*

from three directions as the attackers closed on the crest and hurled hand grenades at the Americans. Sniper fire snapped across the knoll from the southeast and east, and by 4:19 P.M. enemy mortars were shelling the perimeter again.[8]

Cut down on the crest of the knoll, several B Company grunts were lying on the ground near Spc4 Gary Murray. Murray, a medic attached to the company that day, spotted the wounded troopers and immediately ran to their aid. The twenty-year-old original ignored the intense automatic weapons fire sweeping the company line and was attempting to treat the men, an act for which he was later awarded a Bronze Star, when he was struck and killed by shrapnel.[9]

Chunks of scalding-hot steel bounced off the boulders scattered atop the knoll. Crammed into a shallow hole, Pfc. Gary Mills of Wichita, Kansas, hugged the ground and waited for a lull in the fighting. Mills had leaped into the foot-deep hole—along with five other soldiers—after a mortar round had landed in front of him. Incredibly, the round did not go off, saving the six startled grunts. The hole, though, was dangerously vulnerable to 82-mm mortar and small-arms fire, but every time Mills or one of the other grunts attempted to wiggle away, a North Vietnamese sniper would snap off a round and force them back down.[10]

Directed downhill at the attacking NVA, the M-16s and M-60s chattering away along the B Company line eventually grew louder and more coordinated. Kneeling near his partially dug foxhole, Pfc. Eddie Meier, mindful of the grunts lying—rifles blazing—on the ground in front of him, zeroed in on the muzzle flashes twinkling across the northern slope of the knoll. Meier glanced around and saw other troopers in the platoon sprawled out behind trees, rocks, and whatever else they could find, and almost all of them were firing at the enemy. The Hell's Saints were clearly holding their own, thanks in part to the steadying influence of Plt. Sgt. Jerry Tharp. "Tharp was a platoon leader's 'made from heaven sergeant,'" said 1st Lt. Steve Pestikas. "He was a damn good soldier. Calm, collected, and intelligent. He had a different leadership style in that, for his age and experience, he was remarkably steady in his demeanor." Tharp got the platoon organized during the mortar barrage then rallied the troopers when the NVA attacked up the slopes of the knoll.

Listening to the outgoing fire, his ears acutely attuned to the sound of his M-60s hammering away on the line, Captain Hamer realized instantly that the North Vietnamese were attacking from the north. Hamer depended on the four machine guns to anchor his defensive front, but he did not want the gunners firing needlessly into the bush. "I hope you've got a target!" he yelled to the gunners, convinced that if they didn't they would run out of ammo when the company needed them most. Assured that the guns had targets, Hamer contacted his platoon leaders, then called out to the grunts on the line. "We're shooting them," the grunts shouted back breathlessly, "and we can see them going down!"

The North Vietnamese, however, had climbed to within twenty-five meters of the company line.[11] Precariously positioned on the extreme northern end of the crest, Captain Hamer was worried that the North Vietnamese would eventually commit enough troops—the initial assault on the morning of the twenty-second was also conducted by a company sized-force—to sweep around his line and attack up the undefended *backside* of the knoll. "The first one they'd [NVA] see if they came up that side of the hill would be me," recalled the B Company commander. "There was nothing there. That whole area had been left for C Company to fill in." With few troops to spare, Hamer ordered his two RTOs and a medic, troopers who would have ordinarily remained at his side, to set up about ten feet behind him and face south so that they could cover the backside of the knoll. Someone, probably Platoon Sergeant Tharp, then yelled for Pfc. Junior Richardson. "Take your men," the NCO barked at Richardson, "and hold Charlie Company's side of the perimeter. Hold until relieved." Richardson grabbed Pfc. Stan Coker and a kid named Brock and hurried across the crest.

Artillery rounds, meanwhile, crashed down on the northern slope of the knoll. Scurrying up through the shellfire, the North Vietnamese neared the crest and heaved hand grenades up at the Americans. Spc4 Gary Specht, peering out from behind a termite mound, gazed down the narrow jungle path leading away from the First Platoon and observed an NVA soldier in a brown uniform. Twenty to thirty yards down slope, the man was hurling grenades uphill at the platoon, some of them in his direction. A few of the grunts nearby were heaving grenades back at the man, so Specht decided to toss one or two more for good measure. Lying on his belly, he retrieved a grenade, pulled the pin, and tossed it over the termite mound. "My thought process at the time was that if I let it cook off for a second or two and then throw it, and it hits a branch or something and flings back at us, then we'd be in a world of hurt," said Specht, then a fire team leader in the First Platoon. "So I was just pulling the pin and throwing it. And you can't get too good of a throw when you're laying down."

Specht's grenade exploded somewhere in the brush just below the crest of the knoll—it was difficult to distinguish one explosion from another in the chaos—but it soon became apparent to him that the NVA had survived the blast. The enemy soldier, more lucky than good, continued hurling grenades at the First Platoon. Every one of them, however, fell short, good fortune Specht attributed to the steepness of the slope and the thick vegetation. Spooked, or perhaps finally out of grenades, the NVA attempted to flee at one point but was quickly gunned down by another grunt on the line.

Fierce fighting erupted to the right of Specht. The heavy gunfire—M-16s, M-60s, everything seemed to be going off over there—concerned him and he wondered if a swarm of NVA would come scrambling up the slope, guns blazing. Directly behind Specht, a frightened trooper was still trying to dig a foxhole while the battle for the knoll raged all around him. Fully exposed, the man was soon shot dead, possibly by a sniper in a tree. Specht, not wanting to be next, shrunk down behind the termite mound.

Reports of the battle reached Lieutenant Colonel Vollmer almost immediately, and within moments of receiving the news he ordered C Company to move at once to reinforce B Company. Vollmer also requested artillery fire around the entire perimeter except to the southwest, the direction from which Captain Pearson's people (then eight hundred meters to the west) were expected to move up the ridgeline.[12] Pearson, in turn, directed his First Platoon to lead the company column east-northeast to B Company.

C Company saddled up and headed east at 4:13 P.M. Spc4 Oliver Butler, hotter than "blue blazes" and sweating like a "Missouri mule," the straps of the PRC-25 radio he had been ordered to carry eating into his shoulders, tramped through the dense vegetation behind his squad leader, Sgt. Fred Roper. Butler, marching near the front of the First Platoon, hated humping the radio and had even less use for the M-16/XM-148 "over-under gun," yet somehow he ended up with both that day. Spc4 John Sobaski could certainly relate. A machine gunner in the platoon, the sturdy Minnesotan was hauling around an M-60 along with a rucksack crammed with Claymore mines, extra ammo, and three C-rats short of a box. "That was hell going over there [to B Company], being loaded down with all of that extra stuff and trying to get to them," said Sobaski. "I don't know what the distance was, but it was a ways. We weren't running, but we were going about as fast as we could go to get to those guys. You didn't want to take your time going over there when the enemy is trying to kill GIs."

Splashing across an ankle-deep creek, C Company plowed on, through a dense tangle of vines and bamboo on the opposite bank, and approached the high ground to the east. Led by the First Platoon, the company reached the western-southwestern slope of the knoll—thickly vegetated in spots, the slope was barely visible at first—sometime before 4:30 P.M. that afternoon.[13] Up above them, on the crest of the knoll, the troopers could hear explosions and the roar of gunfire.

Captain Pearson, under orders to reinforce B Company as quickly as possible, directed the First Platoon to move up the slope at once. Sgt. Fred Roper's 1st Squad was instructed to take point. Roper, twenty-one, of Barrier Mills, Illinois, objected and contacted Plt. Sgt. Calvin Rohrbough. "We need a break first," he told Rohrbough over the radio, hoping to buy a little time for his tired troopers. "We've been carrying around heavy packs since we got resupplied. We need a break." Rohrbough refused. "Start moving your people up the damn hill," he replied impatiently, "B Company's under attack." Disappointed, Sergeant Roper handed the radio handset back to Spc4 Oliver Butler.

Summoning Spc4 Bob Masching, a bush-smart original with considerable experience walking point, to lead the squad up the slope, Roper dispatched security to both flanks and instructed Masching to move out. Masching, smartly, climbed up the slope at an angle. The squad had not advanced very far when Masching heard a commotion in the trees and hit the dirt. Frightened by the sight of the approaching Americans, a herd of Highland monkeys were screeching and thrashing about in the trees, trying to make their escape. Relieved, Masching glanced back at the young black private lying on the ground behind him. "C'mon. We gotta go."Overcome with fear, the rattled trooper clung to the slope. "No—I ain't going."

Masching, growing increasingly frustrated, tried again. "C'mon! We gotta go!" The man, however, refused to budge. Fed up, finally, after the third or fourth try, Masching shouldered his M-16 and pointed it at the obstinate trooper. "If you don't get up, I'm going to shoot you right here." Reluctantly, the terrified private scrambled to his feet and started up the slope.

Shortly thereafter, Captain Pearson halted the company column. Still on point, Specialist 4th Class Masching moved quietly off the track he had been following—the 1st Squad had advanced about fifty to sixty meters up the slope— and slipped into some bushes. Others took a knee or crouched down. No one muttered a word. Shrapnel had been whistling through the trees, and the grunts could hear explosions and gunfire on the slope above them. Pearson, concerned about the possibility of running into friendly artillery fire on the backside of the knoll, wanted to sort it all out before he continued up the slope.

Strung out at the front of the column, the First Platoon paused silently in place. Noise discipline throughout the company was generally good, an attribute that served the troopers well in the bush, and had been for some time under Captain Pearson. While the troopers waited, however, the noises reverberating through the jungle grew louder and more ominous. "It was noisier than hell," said Spc4 John Sobaski. "I don't know if it was their bombs going off, or their mortars, or whatever, but it was unbelievable that noise. It was something else." Sagging under the weight of his pack, his M-60 growing heavier with every step, Specialist 4th Class Sobaski gazed exhaustedly at the steep slope stretched out before him and wondered if he would ever make it to the summit.

After a short pause, Captain Pearson was back on the horn getting elements of the First Platoon moving again.[14] Knifing up through the jungle, Sergeant Roper's 1st Squad advanced a ways up the slope and then halted once more. Pearson had discerned the sound of mortar rounds exploding along the left flank of the company and had heard Captain Hamer telling Lieutenant Colonel Vollmer over the battalion net that enemy mortar rounds were flying over his head. Launched from tubes located somewhere to the east-northeast, the rounds exploding to the left of C Company were landing close enough to spray the surrounding brush with shrapnel.[15]

Farther up the slope, Spc4 Roger Strand had flanked out to the right of the 1st Squad. Strand was peering into the dense brush, some thirty to forty meters from the company column, when a pair of North Vietnamese soldiers suddenly appeared in the jungle to his right. The enemy soldiers were walking along the slope, apparently unaware that there were Americans nearby. As soon as the men spotted Strand, however, they scurried off and hid behind some rocks.

Strand, thinking that the NVA were attempting to outflank the company, dropped his rucksack and ran after them. Sergeant Roper yelled for Strand to stop but the former high school fullback, who had volunteered for the draft because he "couldn't see any reason to stay in North Dakota during the wintertime," kept on running. Roper's radioman, Spc4 Oliver Butler, knew there was nothing the sergeant or anyone else could do to stop Strand once he had put his mind to something. Strand had always marched to the beat of a different drummer, and as long as there were no good guys in the way, things usually turned out alright. "We used to call him 'Shotgun' Strand, and when Roger pulled the trigger he didn't care who was in front of him," said Butler. "So you damn sure wanted to know where Strand was when the firefight started. I was as scared of him as I was of the enemy, because anything that was in front of him was bait. Roger was fearless and a little crazy." Butler and Sgt. Tom Radke joked about it often, amusingly insisting that they were only afraid of two things in Vietnam—booby traps and being in front of Roger Strand in a firefight.

Strand, nearing the area where the North Vietnamese had fled, lowered the barrel of his trademark Stevens (Savage) Model 77E pump-action shotgun—he had picked up the weapon in the Recon Platoon after adamantly refusing to walk point with an M-16—and reached for a grenade. Bigger than a backyard shed, the rocks on that part of the slope offered plenty of places to hide. Strand lobbed the grenade over one of the rocks, hoping that the concussive blast, razor-sharp shrapnel, or both would kill the two enemy soldiers. Tossing a second grenade, he then hustled back to the 1st Squad. Sergeant Roper, convinced that chewing Strand out in front of the squad wouldn't have done much good anyway, held his tongue. "Roger was a go-getter—a 'put me where the action is at' type," Roper recalled. "He wasn't a timid type of guy who was going to lay back. Besides, I had more important things to worry about at that time and it seemed to turn out alright."

A flurry of enemy mortar rounds, meanwhile, exploded near the company column. The time was approximately 4:33 P.M.[16] Realizing that the company had to "get the hell out of there," Captain Pearson informed his platoon leaders in no uncertain terms that there was nowhere for them to go but up. The artillery had left a narrow corridor open for C Company, Pearson continued, and it ran all the way up to the top of the knoll; they were to follow it right into the B Company perimeter. "So let's get going!" Pearson growled. "Get your ass into that perimeter!"

Spc4 William "Rusty" Pritchett, twenty, of Selene County, Illinois, carried a radio for Captain Pearson. Previously an RTO for Platoon Sergeant Rohrbough in the First Platoon, Pritchett well understood the duties of a dependable radioman. Pritchett remained by Pearson's side, handset at the ready, all afternoon, and whenever Pearson was too busy or otherwise occupied to relay an order himself, Pritchett was asked to repeat the order, word for word, over the radio. This Pritchett did, albeit reluctantly, but on occasion the salty language would rub a lieutenant the wrong way. Later, that same lieutenant complained to Pearson—the *old man*, according to Pritchett, had cussed and "goddamned" enough for the two of them that day—about the way Pritchett had spoken to him over the radio. The lieutenant wanted Pritchett punished. Pearson politely declined. Pritchett, Pearson patiently explained, had only been following orders and therefore he had no intention of subjecting the reliable RTO to any disciplinary action.

Halfway up the slope, Platoon Sergeant Rohrbough barked out orders to the First Platoon. Rohrbough had received Pearson's message to "get going" loud and clear, and now it was up to him to get his people to B Company as fast as possible. Up front, Sergeant Roper's 1st Squad, led by Spc4 Bob Masching, scampered up the slope. Roper and Spc4 Oliver Butler hurried along behind Masching as chunks of shrapnel buzzed through the trees above them. *Sounds like angry bees*, Butler thought nervously. *Please God, don't let one of those one-seven-five or eight-inch rounds misfire.*

On the northern slopes of the knoll, the North Vietnamese pressed doggedly onward, attacking the only side of the summit that was adequately defended by American troops. "As the luck of the war gods would have it, the attack on us was a company-sized unit—there were probably one hundred [NVA]—and it came right up the side of the ridge where I had all of my troops stationed," noted Captain Hamer. "If they had come up the other side, or the backside, the first people they would have seen would have been me and my radio operator. I was very, very fortunate that they came right into the teeth of what we had." Fifty troopers and four M-60s strong, B Company had put out enough fire to prevent the North Vietnamese, struggling as they were on the steep slopes below, from reaching the summit of the knoll.

Hamer also had more than half a dozen batteries firing in support of his outnumbered company, and by 4:30 P.M. a FAC and two fighters were on the way with instructions to run air strikes on a ridgeline to the west. Before the fighters arrived, however, Hamer had gunships sweep the high ground west of the knoll.[17] Reasonably confident that his troops could hold on, if not indefinitely than at least until C Company arrived, Hamer stayed on the radio and tried to dig in behind the B Company line.

North Vietnamese mortar rounds, meanwhile, were battering the knoll from the east and southeast in support of the enemy ground assault. Firing uphill with AK-47s and SKSs, NVA troops on the slope below B Company's Third Platoon raked the company line—the grunts responded aggressively with M-16s—and hurled grenades up through the bamboo. "There were a series of hand grenades that were thrown at our positions, but for whatever reason they did not explode," recounted 1st. Lt. Steve Pestikas. "One particular section, or one group of three guys, had more than what we considered normal. They [grenades] were the ones with the wooden handles." Pestikas, positioned directly behind the front line of the platoon, felt something—mortar round, grenade, RPG—explode against a rock near his CP. Rock fragments from the blast tore at the right side of his torso and left painful wounds that, while not life-threatening, required medical attention. A medic hurried over, treated the wounds, and got Pestikas back in the fight.

Spread out in shallow fighting holes, behind large rocks, and across the jungle floor, the Hell's Saints banged away at muzzle flashes on the northern slope of the knoll. Sgt. Terry Hawkins, a squad leader in the platoon, wanted Pfc. Eddie Meier to hurry up and get their M-60 firing again but Meier, realizing that the gun was probably jammed, opened the top of the weapon, removed the rounds inside and cleared the bolt. Meier then reloaded the rounds and buttoned the gun up; aiming downhill, he quickly ripped off five or six rounds before the gun jammed again. Furious, Sergeant Hawkins would later allege that the "dumb sons of bitches" in his squad "never cleaned the gun."[18] Meier was still fiddling with the gun when something exploded to his right, wounding Spc4 James Lee Kachline. Twenty years old, from Tatamy, Pennsylvania, Kachline died, tragically, despite the best efforts of the brave medic who rushed over to treat him.

Meier slid out from behind the jammed machine gun and grabbed his M-16. Heavy firing had erupted to his left—Hawkins and a few others were shooting at a group of NVA moving up a trail toward the platoon—while off to his right, past Specialist 4th Class Kachline, a black sergeant was throwing hand grenades at the enemy. Bare-chested, the sergeant was standing straight up, boldly heaving one grenade after another into the brush. Meier noticed that a few of the grunts were tossing the man grenades to throw at the North Vietnamese. Reaching for his web belt, Meier removed a grenade and underhanded it to the sergeant. The sergeant, still stripped to the waist, chucked the grenade at the NVA. As the two sides traded grenades and gunfire, a dark-haired machine gunner raced past Meier. The machine gunner, Meier would later learn, had been running up and down the line, firing at the NVA coming up the slopes of the knoll.

The North Vietnamese, though fewer in number and less organized than on the morning of the twenty-second, applied enough pressure to keep the issue in doubt. "It was a pretty good little battle there for awhile," said Captain Hamer, "but they didn't come around any other way except right up where the troops were." Several soldiers, led by Pfc. Junior Richardson, had the backside of the knoll covered, but they were soon joined by Pfc. Bill Avery. A radioman for the artillery FO attached to B Company, Avery had heard that the side of the perimeter facing south needed troops, so he volunteered to fill in alongside the soldiers who were already there.

Fourth Platoon, shorthanded after the loss of Lieutenant Burke and the platoon mortar team on the twenty-second, had held the line, but there didn't seem to be any end to the fighting in sight. Stretched out between two rocks, Spc4 Scott Reitenauer, rifle rounds crackling above his head, a wounded black trooper named Anderson wailing "Help me, help me" nearby, suddenly felt something warm on his neck. *Oh man*, Reitenauer thought, *I'm hit in the neck*. Reitenauer, fearing the worst, reached behind his head and felt a piece of shrapnel sticking out of his neck. *Oh God, just let me die right now*! Warm to the touch, the piece of shrapnel had penetrated the skin but he was able to yank it free.

Tossing the shrapnel aside, Reitenauer looked up—he was still lying flat on his belly—and observed a handful of muzzle flashes in the trees directly across from the Fourth Platoon. Level with the crest of the knoll, the height of the flashes seemed to suggest that the shooter had climbed up one of the trees on the slope and was hiding in its branches. Reitenauer fired six shots into the trees. "Nothing fell out of the trees but I really couldn't see that much because of the dense foliage," recalled the B Company original. "I didn't see any more flashes after that, though." A little while later, a North Vietnamese soldier appeared at the bottom of the knoll. Firing at the man with his M-16, Reitenauer pulled out a hand grenade and pitched it down the slope. The grenade had no sooner left his hand, however, when the distinctive crack of a single rifle shot forced him to duck back down behind a small rock.

Captain Hamer, from his makeshift CP near the center of the wooded crest, briefed Lieutenant Colonel Vollmer, then in his C&C bird, on the battle. "The line's intact," Hamer shouted into his handset, "and we're holding our own." Hamer also indicated that B Company was not in any imminent danger of being overrun. Vollmer, having been reassured that the battle was at least somewhat in hand, advised Hamer of C Company's location and its estimated time of arrival.

Clambering up the backside of the knoll, Sergeant Rohrbough's fast-moving First Platoon in the lead, C Company was within one hundred meters of B Company by 4:33 P.M.[19] Pfc. Junior Richardson was on the southern end of the crest, peering down through the jungle, when he thought he saw North Vietnamese soldiers maneuvering on the flanks of the C Company column. Richardson, however, held his fire. Whatever they were—soldiers, shadows, figments of his imagination—the "mortars and the artillery were keeping them driven back."[20] The narrow corridor the artillery had left for C Company ran up the slope, from what Richardson could tell, and right into the perimeter. C Company would be safe, as long as it stayed in the corridor.

Downhill, a round exploded in the canopy above C Company's First Platoon. Thrown to the ground with a brain-scrambling thud, Sgt. Tom Radke, then in charge of the 3rd Squad, felt as if he had been hit by a heavyweight. Woozy, Radke glanced around glassy-eyed and noticed that the blast had also knocked Spc4 Larry Schindeldecker and another member of the 3rd, a trooper named Wenberg, to the ground. Wenberg was on his knees, too shaken to stand up but still very much alive; flattened by the shell burst, Schindeldecker, twenty, of St. Paul, Minnesota, a self-described "skinny little twit" and a good friend of Radke's, was lying motionless on the slope. Radke, recovering from the initial shock, crawled over to Schindeldecker and began shaking him, scared that whatever had exploded in the trees above them—Radke would later insist that it was an American artillery round—had killed the easygoing original. Cussing as he came to, Schindeldecker awoke to find that he had been knocked momentarily unconscious.

"Where the hell did everybody go?" he asked Radke bewilderedly.

"Larry, just keep going up the hill."

While Radke was helping Wenberg up, Schindeldecker pulled himself together and scrambled to his feet. The three men then scurried up the slope. Radke, keeping an eye on their rear as they moved uphill, glanced over his shoulder at one point and spotted a soldier lying face down with a box of machine-gun ammo about twenty yards back. "Wait up!" Radke shouted, figuring the man had gotten hit and needed assistance. More importantly, he knew they could not afford to leave the machine-gun ammo behind—a medic would eventually treat the trooper—when no one, not even Sergeant Rohrbough, could say for certain what awaited them at the top.

Maintaining his balance on the steep pitch, Radke crawled back down the slope to the prostrate trooper. "Are you hit?"

Lucid, the soldier lifted up his head, looked at Radke, and replied, "No, no. I'm not hit." Radke then remembered the machine-gun ammo. "You've got to get up and get moving."

"No, I'm not going," the trooper responded defiantly. "I can't go! I can't go!"

"No, you're going!" Radke snarled, nudging the man. "They need that ammo up there. If you stay down here, it ain't going to be pretty what they do to you!"

Nudged to his knees, the man glared at Radke resentfully. He had felt safe, lying there on the slope, and in that moment he hated Radke for making him move. Try as he might, though, he could not bring himself to stand. Radke, realizing that the terrified trooper required additional motivation, stood up, stepped back, and lowered the barrel of his M-16. "Either you're going to go up that hill, or I'm going to shoot you myself!" Shocked, the trooper grabbed the ammo box, leaped to his feet, and dashed up the trail the First Platoon had been following.

Near the end of the company column, 1st Lt. Doyle Volkmer's Third Platoon was double-timing up the slope, packs jouncing, exhausted troopers stumbling, when the whine of incoming rounds forced some of the grunts to hit the dirt. Pfc. Ronnie Tenney, still struggling with the death of his squad leader, Sgt. Jim Cartwright, felt the earth shudder beneath his body. "Those mothers were close!" howled one trooper. Tenney paused for a moment then hopped up and started moving again.

Ahead of Tenney, on the slope above the Third Platoon, some of the replacements Lieutenant Colonel Vollmer had scraped together to reinforce B Company—drawn mainly from the rear, the men were to march over with C Company that afternoon—were lying on the ground, apparently too frightened to advance any farther. Thick jungle surrounded the men on either side, and it was immediately obvious to Lieutenant Volkmer that his platoon would not be able to maneuver around them. "We're not going to sit around here and get shelled," Volkmer hollered up to the rattled replacements. "Now get up and get going. C'mon!" A thudding blast then shook the jungle, knocking him to the ground. "I was trying to explain to these guys that they had to get up and get moving," Volkmer later recalled, "and about every third or fourth word an artillery or mortar round would land, and of course I would fall down. I'd then have to get up and have to start this talk about how we had to get out of that area, otherwise the artillery or mortars were going to continue to fall." Yet no matter what he said, or how many times he said it, the men refused to budge.

Out of ideas, Volkmer turned to his troops and directed them to run right over the replacements lying in their way. Some of the men lying on the ground, however, were more tired than scared. Sandbagged by his platoon sergeant back at Camp Enari, Spc4 John Ferrante, twenty-one, one of three New Yorkers from the battalion communications platoon to fly out to C Company, had fallen out of the company column to rest. Ferrante, like most of the emergency replacements from Camp Enari, was not accustomed to humping the rugged hills of the Central Highlands. Volkmer's men could have trampled him, for all he cared. But when Ferrante heard Spc4 Paul Modaferri, his buddy from the commo platoon, pushing, cajoling, begging him to move, he immediately sat up and tried to explain himself.

"Paul, I can't go on anymore," he groaned despairingly. "I'm beat. Just go on without me."

"John, c'mon!" pleaded Modaferri. "I'm not going to leave without you! You gotta go!"

Before Ferrante could respond, however, a shell blew up in the jungle near the company column, wounding one of the replacements in the left elbow. The sudden explosion sent Ferrante and Modaferri ambling up the slope. Herd-like, the rest of the replacements, spooked in all likelihood by the very same shell burst, got up and moved with them. Lieutenant Volkmer's Third Platoon, spared the hassle of having to trample over fellow soldiers, followed close behind.

With elements of his company nearing the top of the knoll, Captain Pearson switched one of his radios to B Company's frequency. "If Vollmer had any faults at all it was that he wanted to command so bad that he occupied the [battalion radio] net to such a degree that I couldn't get a word in edgewise," said Pearson. "He was just constantly talking on the damn thing, so I took that battalion net and put it on B Company's frequency so that I could talk to Mike [Hamer]. Now that's a violation of protocol, and you're not supposed to do that. I don't think he [Vollmer] even knew that I did that. I'm sure the brigade commander was on his back and the division commander and so on. But the natural control of that battle—I'm talking about the ground battle, not the air force and artillery—was on Mike's company frequency. I didn't mean any disrespect to Vollmer, because I truly liked the guy, but he started giving instructions on this May thing. It was a company commander's war. I don't think that *any* of the battalion or brigade commanders had a full appreciation of exactly what was happening out there."

Pearson raised Captain Hamer over the company frequency. "Where do you want us to go?" he asked, trying to coordinate the movement of his people with the B Company commander. Hamer thought about it for a moment then directed Pearson to take up positions along the eastern and western sides of the crest until his troops had linked up with B Company. C Company would then be in a position to cover B Company's flanks and complete the perimeter. Staring down through the trees, Pfc. Junior Richardson and the small detachment of B Company troopers covering the backside of the knoll, meanwhile, waited for C Company to arrive.

First in line, Spc4 Bob Masching climbed—stomach churning—up the last stretch of jungled slope leading to the top of the knoll. *Those B Company guys are going to shoot me as soon as they see me,* Masching thought to himself. *It's always the point man that gets it. If that was me and I saw something coming up the hill, I know I'd shoot first and ask questions later.* Bob Rider, a twenty-one-year-old Spc4 from Shawnee Town, Illinois, Spc4 Roger Strand, and the black trooper Masching had threatened to shoot if he didn't get up and get moving, were right behind him. Strand, shotgun in hand, was already looking for something to shoot. Muscles tight, the back of his throat drier than dust, Specialist 4th Class Rider crept quietly forward, afraid for the first time since he had been in Vietnam that he was about to die.

Thrashing up through the brush, Specialist 4th Class Masching stepped out into a partial opening in the jungle, unaware at first that he had reached the top of the knoll, and immediately noticed the business end of an M-16 pointing directly at him, thirty feet to his left. Speechless, Masching stood perfectly still. Eyes, big as saucers, stared back at him from behind the barrel of the gun. For a moment, the two men simply stared at one another, neither daring to move. Masching, barely breathing, eventually moved first. Slowly raising his right hand, he waved innocuously then waited for a response. It came, finally, when the B Company trooper motioned for him to come forward. "When I got to where he was and came out into that opening, it was like what war looked like on TV," said Masching. "There were mortars going off, dirt and debris flying all over, and a couple of soldiers running. I remember other ones lying on the ground."

NVA mortar fire had stripped away some of the vegetation where the two men were standing—enemy rounds were presently landing on the eastern side of the crest, to Masching's right—but much of the summit was still heavily jungled. Masching crouched down next to the B Company trooper. Moments later, Roger Strand, Bob Rider, and a third soldier burst into the partial opening on the southern side of the knoll, where they were soon joined by Sgt. Fred Roper, Spc4 Oliver Butler, and the rest of the 1st Squad, First Platoon. Butler, desperate to dump the PRC-25 on his back, wriggled out of his shoulder straps and left the rucksack, radio and all, lying on the ground. The time was approximately 4:41 P.M.[21]

Shortly before the two companies linked up, Lieutenant Colonel Vollmer called down and placed Captain Hamer in command of all units on the ground. Hamer, in turn, ordered Plt. Sgt. Jerry Tharp to coordinate the movements of the C Company troopers entering the perimeter.[22] Masching and Butler heard someone shouting at them to move across the knoll and take up positions on the other side of the perimeter. That person was probably Sergeant Tharp. "A guy said to cover that side over there [northern side of the perimeter], because there was hardly anybody over there," Butler recalled. "It was a sergeant or a lieutenant. . . . I came into the perimeter, and he told me to go that way and that they needed me over there." Tharp would later earn a Bronze Star for his actions during the battle.

Wandering to the right of Butler, Spc4 Roger Strand saw Sergeant Tharp in a foxhole with another man. Strand recognized Tharp from their time together in the battalion recon platoon. Tharp hollered for him to get down. An NVA soldier, Strand soon discovered, was up in a tree and had that part of the perimeter fairly well covered. Hunching down, Strand noted a small platform hidden in the branches of the tree. A knapsack was hanging next to it. *Thanks for warning me,* Strand told himself as he zeroed in on the platform, *but why the hell didn't one of you guys take this son of a bitch out?* Determined to do it himself, Strand blasted the tree with buckshot, and before long "a big old bunch of crap" tumbled out and crashed to the ground. "You got the sniper!" cheered a nearby grunt. "I see him down there!" Strand, lowering the barrel of his shotgun, hurried off through the underbrush.

Sergeant Roper was heading in the same direction, and he directed the rest of the 1st Squad to move north with him. Roper, without direction from Sergeant Tharp or anyone else, led his troops across the crest of the knoll and filled in along the B Company line. Some of the grunts, lying down behind their packs for cover, set up near a large rock next to a tree. Thick with smoke, the jungle in front of them sloped down toward a shallow saddle just below the crest. The North Vietnamese had not gotten as far as the saddle, but they were well within striking distance of the Americans above it. "The NVA were coming up the hill, close enough that we were looking at them eyeball to eyeball," Roper recalled. "They were close enough that you could see their faces. Getting up that hill and then being able to match up, face to face with the enemy—you shooting at them and they're shooting at you—it's a little bit scary." Taking aim at the stocky figures he observed moving up the slope, Roper wondered whether he would live long enough to see his mother's birthday on the twenty-eighth.

As if on cue, Roper's squad tore into the approaching NVA with M-16s and M-79s. Spc4 Oliver Butler, huddled down between a tree and a waist-high rock, the closest cover he could find, was peeking downhill when a North Vietnamese soldier with an AK-47 leaped out from behind a big tree. Butler, ducking instinctively, dropped down behind the rock in front of him. "He [NVA soldier] had an AK-47 and he was beating the hell out of that rock," Butler noted. "You could hear the bullets ringing off that damn thing." Spc4 Bob Masching and a grunt with an M-79 returned fire, but the NVA slipped back behind the tree before either man could hit him. "Hit the tree!" Masching hollered to the thump gunner. Fifty yards down slope, the NVA reemerged and, opening up again with his AK-47, sprayed the squad with a long burst of fire. Head down, rounds ricocheting off the rocks around him, Butler shuddered to think what the rock he was hiding behind looked like.

Masching tried to shoot the NVA down but repeatedly missed. Three times the man whirled around the tree and fired up at the squad. Masching, staring down at the big tree, waiting to pull the trigger as soon as he caught *another* glimpse of the man's khaki-colored uniform, suddenly recalled an incident back at Fort Lewis, Washington. "I was in AIT training, and the first day they gave us live ammunition training, we were out there on this big prairie hillside," said the C Company original. "And what was there to shoot at [there]? Well, there was a patch of thistles out front, and two or three of us kind of got into a competition of shooting the thistle stem to shoot the head off of that thistle. For whatever reason, that came back to me and I knew I had about that big of a target beside that tree." Masching, recalling the concentration required to hit a small target, blocked out everything but the big tree. Motionless, he waited until he saw a flash of khaki slip back into view. Gently squeezing off two or three rounds with his M-16, Masching dropped the NVA near the tree he had been hiding behind.

Soon after, a North Vietnamese soldier snuck into the saddle below the 1st Squad and stood up behind a large rock. Wide-eyed, the soldier spotted Masching, realized that Masching was looking back at him, and immediately ducked back down behind the rock. *Shit*, Masching thought as he reached for a grenade on his belt, certain that the enemy soldier had the same thing in mind and would probably get to his first. The grenade, however, had gotten caught or stuck on something and refused to come off. "It seemed like it took for [*sic*] an eternity to get it off," said Masching. "It didn't want to come off my belt." Finally yanking the grenade loose, Masching held it up so the grunt beside him could see it. "Get ready!" Masching then lobbed the grenade behind the rock where he had seen the enemy soldier. Seconds later it exploded in the saddle, sending the NVA stumbling out into the open. The grunt next to Masching then dropped the man with a quick burst of rifle fire. Masching, glancing over at the grunt approvingly, flashed the "thumbs up" sign, grateful that the two of them had been able to eliminate the threat.

Embroiled in the ongoing battle on the northern side of the perimeter, the 1st Squad was soon joined by the rest of the First Platoon. Captain Pearson, hotfooting into the perimeter with his RTO, Spc4 William Pritchett, ordered Sergeant Rohrbough to move across the crest and reinforce the B Company line. Pearson then instructed Second Platoon, next in line behind the First, to take up positions along the undefended western side of the perimeter. Still on the slope behind the C Company CO, Lieutenant Volkmer's Third Platoon was to turn around and cover the exposed southern side of the perimeter as soon as it reached the top of the knoll.

Steady under fire, Sergeant Rohrbough led his remaining squads through the underbrush to the B Company line. There the troopers waged a spirited defense of the hard-pressed perimeter. "They [First Platoon] did a marvelous job of getting behind rocks—there were a lot of rocks up there—and putting down a rain of fire on them [NVA]," said Captain Pearson. Spc4 Larry Schindeldecker, 3rd Squad, First Platoon, credited Sergeant Rohrbough with improving the professionalism of the platoon. "Why we are here today is probably because of him," Schindeldecker observed. "He knew what he was doing over there, but he also knew that he wanted to make us into something that he wanted to take over there. I know a couple of platoons that got their butts run over, but it was never going to happen to us with him around." Rohrbough's exceptional leadership that afternoon, both on the slope and inside the perimeter, resulted in a Bronze Star commendation.

Sgt. Tom Radke, three members of his 3rd Squad somewhere to the right, three more to the left, tossed his rucksack to the ground not far from Sergeant Rohrbough and flopped down behind it. Shouldering his M-16, Radke studied the jungle below. There were North Vietnamese on the slope, and some of them were sticking their AK-47s around trees and firing at the American line. Others were *in* the trees firing down on the line. The grunts, in response, fired back and threw hand grenades down the hill. Occasionally, the grenade blasts would force the NVA to scurry from one position to another, exposing them to concentrated M-79 and M-16 fire from the summit of the knoll. Radke, working his way through a magazine, tried to catch the enemy soldiers dashing between the trees.

Blocked by elements of the 3rd Squad, the NVA fell back, regrouped, and attacked another sector of the line. The lull did not last very long, however, before the crack of AK-47s and M-16s rang out across the slope. Surprised to suddenly see Spc4 Roger Strand, half crouched, brazenly pumping out buckshot from his trademark Stevens (Savage) 77E, Sgt. Tom Radke stopped shooting and shouted, "Strand, what the hell are you doing over here? Get back with your men!" Strand continued firing. "Tom, the shooting slowed down over there." Pumping off a few more shells, Strand then pulled out a canteen of water and poured it over the barrel of his shotgun.

Off to Strand's left, along the western side of the summit, soldiers from C Company's Second Platoon were hurrying through the brush. Spc4 Rich Blair, a squad leader in the Second, found a spot overlooking a steep incline and started firing at the khaki-green uniforms he saw maneuvering in the jungle below. Visible in ones and twos, at least in his immediate area, the NVA blazed away at his position from a distance of about fifty yards, but did not attempt to move up the slope. "So much fire was coming in, we couldn't really keep our heads up all the time," said Blair. "We'd come up, put down some suppressive fire, and then put our heads back down." Blair, using nothing but his helmet and bare hands, dug up enough dirt to fashion a small earthen berm in front of his position.

Fourth Platoon followed the Second into the perimeter and then fanned out to the right. Under the command of Sfc. Felipe Sierra, who moved from position to position, tirelessly directing his harried troopers, the Fourth filled in along the undefended eastern side of the perimeter. As the platoon was approaching the top of the knoll, however, one of the grunts fell and accidentally discharged his M-16, killing the man ahead of him. There were apparently several soldiers who witnessed the incident at the time, but most of the company would not learn of the man's tragic death until after the battle.

One plucky C Company soldier, meanwhile, shot and killed the NVA sniper who had kept six B Company troopers pinned down and bunched together in a shallow hole. "That gave us the chance to get out of our half-hole," said Pfc. Gary Mills. "As soon as the firing died down, we dug like crazy."[23] Mills had jumped in the hole after a close call with what turned out to be a dud mortar round early in the battle and had not been able to get out.

By 5:03 P.M. three of C Company's four platoons had reached the top of the knoll. The linkup, though disjointed at times, had gone about as well as could be expected, given the circumstances. Another wave of air strikes was on the way—to be delivered from south to north, along a gridline west of the two companies—and the wall of incoming artillery fire had been adjusted to within fifty meters of the joint perimeter.[24] North Vietnamese troops continued to attack from the north and west, but the knoll remained firmly in American hands.[25]

Stretched thin, mentally and physically exhausted, the fifty or so "effectives" manning the B Company line had held the northern third of the crest long enough for C Company to arrive. Excellent leadership, the courage, skill, and personal initiative of the individual B Company soldier, and steep slopes had prevented the NVA from overrunning the company line before C Company could get there. "Some of those B Company guys were sounding like they were having a pretty good time," said Captain Hamer. "There was laughing going on, and I was thinking—what the hell's going on?" Guarding the backside of the knoll, Pfc. Junior Richardson, Pfc. Stan Coker, and a third soldier dashed back across the partially denuded summit and rejoined B Company's Third Platoon as soon as C Company arrived. The platoon, along with much of the northern and western sides of the perimeter, was still receiving heavy small-arms fire. Richardson, pointing his M-16 down slope, suddenly realized that the North Vietnamese were already "within hand grenade distance of us." There were more NVA nearby, and one of them picked up a grenade Sgt. Terry Hawkins had thrown at him and calmly threw it back. Hawkins grabbed another grenade, pulled the pin, and after counting to three, hurled it at the NVA. Stunningly, the man scooped up the grenade and was about to throw it back when it went off in his hand.

Smaller than the average American soldier, the North Vietnamese often had difficulty throwing grenades far enough up the slope to reach the B Company line, and some of their older wooden handle models failed to explode altogether.[26] Rocket-propelled grenades, however, could reach the line in the blink of an eye, and a number of them were fired at both companies during the battle. Troopers from C Company's First Platoon, at one point, eyed an enemy soldier with an RPG no more than twenty-five yards from Sgt. Fred Roper's 1st Squad. Swiftly shouldering the tube, the man aimed the rocket directly at the grunts. "I heard a whoosh, and then I saw something that looked like a big old red light bulb flying up at us," said Spc4 Oliver Butler. "That thing flew up out of that draw and over our heads and out of the back end of our perimeter." Butler and Spc4 Bob Masching shouted "incoming" and then ducked for cover. After the rocket flew harmlessly overhead, a couple of grunts to the left of Masching popped up and gunned the NVA down.

Still standing, despite the rocket, rifle, and mortar fire, Captain Pearson alternated between commanding the company as a whole and, when necessary, personally assisting the First Platoon in front of him. The North Vietnamese were hitting the First hard, searching the perimeter for weak points, and two enemy soldiers in mismatched uniforms were seen maneuvering through the underbrush to the left of Sgt. Fred Roper's 1st Squad. "You could see them coming around towards my side," said Spc4 Bob Rider, "so I started firing. They were definitely moving. They were definitely going to flank us." Rider did not see either man again after he opened fire on them with his M-16. Concerned about the fighting in the First Platoon area, Captain Pearson would later note, with considerable satisfaction, that the North Vietnamese failed to punch through the platoon line or outflank the northern third of the perimeter.

Three-quarters of the way up the hill, the North Vietnamese assault, hard hit by M-16, M-60, and M-79 fire, finally began to run out of steam. "We were really putting down some withering fire," said Oliver Butler. "We were really putting some ammunition downhill. There was more going down the hill than coming up." Maintaining that level of fire, however, forced the grunts to reload often. "When you get in a firefight, one of the hardest things you have to do is change magazines," recalled 1st Lt. Doyle Volkmer. "You have to take that empty magazine out, put a fresh one in, jack a round into the chamber, and then start shooting again. And that seems to take forever." Up on one knee, his rifle down by his hip, Sgt. Tom Radke was desperately trying to reload when an NVA soldier armed with an AK-47 suddenly popped up in front of him. No more than twenty feet away, the man was wearing a dull, greenish-colored uniform and a floppy bush hat. Radke, slapping in a fresh magazine, ripped off a quick burst from his waist. Blown backward by the burst, the NVA tumbled to the ground without firing a shot.

Shaken, Radke dropped to the ground and slid behind his pack. Later on, after the firing had tapered off around the perimeter, he walked down the slope to examine the North Vietnamese soldier he had shot at point-blank range. Removing the magazine from the dead man's AK-47, Radke stared at the lifeless body in the dull green uniform and wondered why the man didn't shoot him when he had the chance. Recalled Radke:

> There was only one round in the magazine, and there was one in the chamber. He did pull the trigger on me. When I started looking at him, I saw that somebody had shot him from the side while he was standing there—before I shot him—and that had killed him. It had to be just a fraction of a second before I shot him in the chest, because he had three fingers shot off his hand and a bullet had gone through the receiver on his rifle. That must have been enough to just slow that pin down enough, so that it didn't set the bullet off. That bullet had my name on it, and somebody must not have wanted me to go, because he [NVA soldier] had that thing crammed right at my chest. He must have gotten hit just as he was pulling the trigger, because there was a little dent in the primer. I'm thinking that a bullet from the side went through the receiver and slowed the action down enough where it didn't fire off.

Radke climbed back up the slope and rejoined his squad, certain that his life had been spared by a bullet fired by someone else along the line.

Waved in by Sfc. Felipe Sierra of the Fourth Platoon, 1st Lt. Doyle Volkmer's Third Platoon, along with the replacements Lieutenant Colonel Vollmer had promised B Company, scrambled up the slope and into the perimeter around 5:20 P.M.[27] Sierra, who would later earn a Bronze Star for his actions on the twenty-fourth, then helped position the Third Platoon on the southern side of the crest. Turning around, the grunts dropped their packs and took up positions overlooking the undefended backside of the knoll. Lieutenant Volkmer ended up in front of the platoon with his RTO, a specialist 4th class named Lynch, and was still there when something hit him in the neck. Volkmer, thinking he had been shot, clutched his throat but did not feel any blood. "The lieutenant's hit!" one of his squad leaders suddenly shouted. Volkmer reassured the man that he was okay and resumed firing downhill.

Third Platoon, aided by Sergeant Sierra, had also linked up with the Second and Fourth Platoons, completing the two-company perimeter. While the last of the C Company troopers were filling in around the perimeter, Lieutenant Colonel Vollmer, haunted by the specter of another Dien Bien Phu, was on the radio, talking to the battalion fire support coordinator (FSC) about the next wave of incoming aircraft. "If they've got napalm," he told the FSC brusquely, "then hit some of it behind 'em!" Worried that the two companies were still within range of the NVA's heavy mortars and modest Highland artillery, Vollmer decided to disengage and figured that the sheer spectacle of a fiery napalm strike, if visible from the slopes of the knoll, might encourage the enemy to withdraw. It was late in the afternoon, and while the North Vietnamese would not introduce long-barreled 85-mm guns and 105-mm howitzers to the Highlands until 1968–69, his people had already suffered about as many dead and wounded as he was willing to accept for a nameless knoll in the middle of nowhere.[28]

Streaking across the sky shortly after Vollmer's call to the FSC, Air Force fighters and fighter-bombers sealed off the western, southwestern, and northwestern sides of the perimeter as soon as C Company had taken up positions along the southern end of the crest.[29] The napalm strike Vollmer requested on a nearby ridge left a roiling ball of smoke and flame billowing up through the jungle canopy. "Napalm goes off like a nuclear bomb, for God's sake," Vollmer noted. "Even in the jungle, you can see that exploding ball. Enemy firing stopped almost immediately. I didn't realize it would be that effective. I was kind of hoping it would get behind them [NVA] and screen them and maybe even catch a few of them. But I didn't want to drop it on them, because we had artillery fire going on in there, and that would be duplicating it all. Napalm might splash over on your own people, so I wanted it to be [farther] back." North Vietnamese pressure along the perimeter decreased considerably following the run, and by 5:38 P.M. B Company was reporting only light enemy mortar and small-arms fire. Approximately fifteen minutes later, the firing ceased altogether and the NVA began to withdraw.[30]

Hampered by steep slopes, stiff resistance, and the disruptive effects of American firepower, the North Vietnamese abandoned the assault and melted into the jungle. "Moving on to a knoll on the end of a ridgeline might require an additional hour of effort, so you have to give Hamer credit for recognizing that it was worth it," said

Lieutenant Colonel Vollmer, acknowledging the effects of terrain on the conduct and outcome of the battle. "Hamer had the good sense to work for that high ground." Awarded a Bronze Star for his part in the battle, Captain Hamer instead credited the young B Company troopers holding the line. "The troops had that one in hand, all the way," he said selflessly. "They didn't need anything from me, and they didn't need any kind of support." Captain Pearson would also earn a Bronze Star for his actions on the twenty-fourth. Pearson guided C Company up the slope of the knoll, and when his First Platoon finally reached the top, he shrewdly ordered Sergeant Rohrbough to reinforce B Company—rather than take up positions on the eastern and western sides of the perimeter—on the northern end of the crest.

Relative to the outcome of the contest, the material effect of the napalm strike Lieutenant Colonel Vollmer ordered on the ridge was almost certainly negligible, yet it is not unreasonable to conclude—given the timing of the withdrawal—that the strike had a *psychological* effect on the North Vietnamese.[31] "I didn't think it would be *that* visible through the forest, but it was," said Vollmer. "It was a big ball of fire. I don't know if it was a coincidence or not, but the firing let up pretty damn quickly and the enemy began to bug out."

With the sun setting fast on the western horizon, Vollmer thought about B Company, which had been reduced at that point to about thirty effectives, considered how much ammo the two companies had left—both were running short—and decided to keep his people in place and pursue the retreating North Vietnamese with supporting fires. The grunts received some relief when a bird dropped much needed supplies into the perimeter at 5:56 P.M. Gunships escorting a second supply run twenty-three minutes later spotted twenty to thirty NVA in an open area to the southeast. Soon after, the battalion dispatched gunships to a draw west of the knoll. While gunships strafed the draw to the west, artillery fire continued to work the jungle in support of the two companies. Stormy weather forced Cider 10, the Air Force FAC on station that night, to arrange one final air strike at 7:25 P.M. on a location south of the knoll.[32]

B and C Companies, meanwhile, conducted a limited sweep of the area and prepared for the night. Captain Hamer wanted to evacuate the dead and wounded before it got too dark, but without chain saws and C4 to cut an LZ, he knew he would have to wait until morning. Bone-weary, a handful of B Company troopers, too tired to finish their foxholes and bunkers, settled in among the rocks and nodded off standing up. "I will never forget that for as long as I live," said Pfc. Eddie Meier who, along with Sgt. Terry Hawkins and a few other Third Platoon soldiers, fell asleep on his feet that night. "There's a little dance you do when you fall asleep standing up. Your knees buckle, and your whole body gets almost a huge shake. It's almost as if someone has struck you and made your whole body waver like a tuning fork. It wakes you right up." Meier awoke often during the night, sleeping for the most part in restless fits and starts.

Heartbreakingly, the anguished cries and pitiful moans of the wounded kept some of the grunts awake. "The saddest part of that battle was that we couldn't get our dead and wounded off of that hill," recalled Spc4 John Sobaski, a machine gunner in C Company's First Platoon. "They had to stay there overnight." Sobaski noted that several men eagerly donated blood in a desperate attempt to save the life of one wounded trooper. Sharing the perimeter with dead comrades proved equally unnerving. Covered with a poncho, the body of the C Company soldier accidently shot and killed while advancing up the knoll had been laid to rest near the foxhole of Spc4 Rusty Pritchett. Pritchett was sitting in his hole, not far from the company CP, when he suddenly heard an odd gassy sound and gurgling noises emanating from the body. The noisy processes at work inside the man's body continued throughout the night. "It [the body] was shutting down—like gasses in his stomach and the gurgling," recounted Pritchett. "He was right there beside me all night. When you hear it [the noises], you can't forget it."

Three chain saws and two cases of C4 were flown in to the perimeter early on the morning of the twenty-fifth, and by 9:15 A.M. an LZ had been cleared to evacuate the dead and wounded. The two companies had suffered four dead, three from B Company, and seventeen wounded in the fighting on the twenty-fourth.[33] Of the seventeen, fourteen belonged to B Company, including Spc4 Scott Reitenauer. Winged during the battle—he had no idea he had been shot in the shoulder until a fellow trooper pointed out the hole in his shirt—Reitenauer left the knoll on a dustoff and never returned to B Company.[34] Spc4 Roger Strand, injured after the battle when another grunt blasted an NVA sniper out of a tree with an M-79, was medevaced out with the C Company wounded. Packs, rifles, and other equipment left behind by the dead and wounded were also evacuated.

Combing the jungle around the perimeter, the grunts found thirty-seven enemy dead, three AK-47s, three SKS rifles, two rocket launchers, and a machine gun.[35] That afternoon Lieutenant Colonel Vollmer ordered C Company to send out patrols to search the area for more enemy dead and wounded. Gunshots rang out as the patrols pushed north, however, and when Captain Pearson radioed to call a halt to the shooting, the troopers replied that they were firing back at wounded NVA who were leaning against trees, pretending to be dead. "They're faking it," stammered the grunts, "and they're shooting at us!" Pearson, impatiently, reminded the patrols that they were there to count bodies and capture prisoners.

Sweeping out of a shallow ravine around 2 P.M., elements of Sergeant Rohrbough's First Platoon found a North Vietnamese soldier in black pajamas lying on a makeshift stretcher. Alive, the man was missing his right arm—the stump had been cauterized and wrapped in clean sandbags—and appeared to be unconscious. Spc4 Oliver Butler, upon seeing the wounded NVA, turned and hollered, "There's a guy laying here!" Shortly thereafter, Butler and another soldier hauled the man back through the jungle and up the knoll. The prisoner was later loaded aboard a resupply chopper and evacuated out at 3:47 P.M.[36]

C Company's Second Platoon, flanked at the time to the right of the First Platoon, discovered an enemy base camp a short distance from where Butler had spotted the one-armed man. Heavily damaged by artillery fire, the camp was approximately fifty by one hundred and fifty meters and had been built within the last day or two. Twenty bunkers, some large enough to accommodate as many as ten men, and two underground facilities were located within the complex. Poking around inside, the two platoons found rice, mortar rounds, and medical supplies.[37] There were also rumors that a warm kettle had turned up in one of the bunkers. "We were so close to where their camp was, and I think that's why they attacked us [on May 24]," said Captain Hamer. "We were almost on top of them when we were on that ridge. I don't think we were more than three hundred to five hundred meters away."

Whether the North Vietnamese attacked B Company to protect a base camp north of the knoll, as Hamer has suggested, or merely to annihilate a small American force before it could dig in for the night is open to debate. The 3-12 Infantry eventually confirmed, however, that the attackers belonged to a battalion from the 32nd NVA Regiment that had assaulted the 1-8 Infantry on the evening of the twentieth.[38] For the third time in a week, elements of the 32nd had attacked American troops in and around the Ia Tchar Valley.

General Peers and Colonel Jackson visited the 3-12 Infantry firebase on the morning of the twenty-fifth. That night Lieutenant Colonel Vollmer learned that B-52 bombers were scheduled to strike targets well to the west of B and C Companies at 6 A.M. on the twenty-sixth.[39] The two companies moved south after the bombing runs and searched for the North Vietnamese until the twenty-eighth, when Vollmer decided to replace B Company with A Company. A and C Companies then swung back to the north before running into a dug-in enemy force on the afternoon of May 30. Seven NVA, some wearing camouflage uniforms and straw helmets, were killed in the ensuing clash. Two Americans were wounded and medevaced out.[40]

On June 23, 1967, the headquarters of the 3-12 Infantry returned to Jackson Hole. For the next eight weeks, the battalion conducted blocking operations west of the brigade base, light duty after the May battles in the Ia Tchar Valley. Nevertheless the "Nine Days in May" had taken a toll on the Braves, so much so in fact that the line companies of the battalion were pulled out of the field during this period and rotated back through the divisional base camp at Camp Enari to train and refit.[41]

An April replacement, Pfc. Eddie Meier, B Company, 3-12 Infantry, had heard about the NVA long before the "Nine Days in May." The North Vietnamese were well armed and well trained, the cadre back at Fort Polk had warned him, and they were tough, dedicated, and courageous in battle. Meier found out firsthand what he was up against on May 22 and 24, when B Company battled elements of the veteran 32nd and 66th NVA Regiments. Recalling those long-forgotten battles, the Wisconsin native believes he learned something about the troops of the 3-12 Infantry as well. Young kids, fighting in a war half a world away, the grunts—and the officers and NCOs who led them—had tried their very best to embody the battalion motto Braves Always First. "You can say what you want about the Airborne and the Marines and all this other crap, but I guarantee you our guys would stand toe-to-toe with those cats," said Meier. "I don't know what the NVA thought of us—I know that American soldiers aren't supposed to have a hair across their asses or whatever—but we didn't give any quarter, and we gave it right back."

PART III

3-8 Infantry

THE DRAGOONS

16 HILL 521

Airlifted in on the morning of the twenty-fourth, Lt. Col. Tom Lynch's 3-8 Infantry replaced the 1-8 Infantry in the lower Ia Tchar Valley and began pushing east-northeast in search of the 32nd and 66th NVA Regiments, the two enemy formations reportedly in the area.[1] The push east in to the foothills of the Chu Goungot Mountains marked the return of the 3-8 Infantry to Operation Francis Marion. Rushed to the Central Highlands in February 1967, the battalion participated in Operation Sam Houston before joining the 1st Brigade headquarters at Jackson Hole for the start of Francis Marion in early April. Initially the battalion patrolled around Jackson Hole and conducted modest search-and-destroy operations north of Highway 19.[2] On April 24, however, General Peers sent Lynch south to deal with a developing threat in Darlac Province.

Partnered with an ARVN battalion, Lieutenant Colonel Lynch launched Operation Hancock I on April 26.[3] Less than a week later, B Company, 3-8 Infantry, while maneuvering through thick brush near the banks of a river, bumped into a force of about thirty to forty North Vietnamese. Hidden in the tree line on the other side of a small clearing, the NVA unleashed a furious volley of small-arms fire and pinned the Americans down. C Company, sweeping to the north at the time, was engaged by a small group of VC.[4]

Regrouping under fire, B Company's Fourth Platoon found cover in the dense undergrowth near the river and began firing into the tree line. Red and green tracers zipped back and forth across the clearing as the two sides exchanged shouts and cusses. Spc4 Bob Gamboa, hurrying forward with the platoon radio, realized that one of the squads was not firing at all. "C'mon, guys! Open up! Let's go! Open up!" Gamboa shouted impatiently.

Part Portuguese, part Mexican, Robert "Panch" Gamboa grew up in San Fernando, California, with his mother and maternal grandparents. Fluent in English and Spanish,

Gamboa graduated from high school in 1963 and eventually saved up enough money to buy a Buick Wildcat. Romeo, or so he thought, behind the wheel of his brand new Buick, Gamboa spent his days chasing girls and drinking beer with his buddies. The party ended abruptly in November 1965, however, when he was drafted and sent to Fort Lewis, Washington, with dozens of other 3-8 Infantry originals. Well liked, Gamboa had a colorful way of saying and doing things in Vietnam, including wearing belts of M-60 ammo slung across his chest like Pancho Villa. A medic jokingly called him "Panch" and the name stuck. Gamboa didn't mind. "Mexican American, Portuguese—whatever man," he joked. "I'm a fucking beaner."

Gamboa hurried over to the shaken squad and got the grunts firing at the North Vietnamese. Throwing himself down behind his pack, Gamboa pulled the grunts in tighter and yelled for someone to cover the flanks of the squad. Reorganized, the troops began to fight back more effectively. Gamboa, meanwhile, laid his M-16 on top of his pack and began firing into the tree line. Suddenly a stream of green sliced through the undergrowth. "They're up in the trees!" Gamboa screamed, noting the downward angle of the enemy's green tracer rounds. "They're up in the trees!"

M-79s thumping, the grenadiers blasted the trees with 40-mm shellfire, sending bark, branches, and hidden enemy soldiers tumbling to the ground. Gamboa sprayed the upper half of another tree—nothing fell out—then felt something hit his lower back and buttocks. Shrapnel from whatever had hit him had also smashed up his radio. Sore from what felt like a baseball bat slamming into his backside, Gamboa cussed at the North Vietnamese in Spanish, loud enough he hoped for them to hear, and bravely insisted that he was okay.

High above the battle, an Air Force FAC came on station with a flight of F-100s. "Charger, this is Cider One-One," the FAC announced. "I've got four canisters of CBU. I'd like to run 'em down the river bank. Over."

"This is Charger," Lynch replied. "Run 'em. Over."[5]

Fast and accurate, the F-100s roared in and pounded the North Vietnamese near the river. A second air strike followed and the enemy eventually withdrew, leaving two dead behind. Farther north, C Company chased the Viet Cong off and captured a prisoner.[6] Wounded in the fight, Specialist 4th Class Gamboa was evacuated from the field later that day. "I went out after my radio," he recalled. "When they were pulling out the wounded, they took my radio on the chopper [first] and left my ass there." Gamboa was awarded the Bronze Star for his actions during the battle.

General Peers, responding to the heavy contact in the Ia Tchar Valley, terminated Hancock I on May 22 and returned the 3-8 Infantry to the 1st Brigade.[7] The next day, Colonel Jackson decided to replace the 1-8 Infantry with the 3-8 Infantry. As soon as his people were on the ground and in position, Lynch was to sweep east and search the lower ridges of the Chu Goungot Mountains with two companies. Lynch, leaving

A Company behind to provide security for the battalion firebase, dispatched B and C Companies on the morning of the twenty-fourth.

That night the two companies set up in separate perimeters and dug in. Mindful of the earlier battles in the Ia Tchar Valley, Lynch wanted the two companies to control the high ground as much as possible and discussed the matter at length with his company commanders. "It's probably not like a typical by-the-book strategy, but I'd sit with my company commanders and say, 'Here's what I think,'" said Lynch. "Then I'd get their input, and all of us would make a decision as a group. Everybody knows what the other companies are doing." To that end, it was decided that one company would move onto a hill or ridge while the other company remained in place. The first company would then remain in place while the second company moved forward onto another key terrain feature.[8] Lynch hoped that by moving by bounds, from one key terrain feature to the next, his people would be able to stay out of the densely forested draws in the area.

Six foot one, one hundred and eighty five pounds, a soldier for more than twenty years, Lt. Col. Tom Lynch looked and acted like a battalion commander. Drafted in 1945, Lynch served initially with the 508th Regimental Combat Team. "I was an enlisted man for six years," he recalled proudly. "For five of those years I made a stripe a year."[9] Lynch then earned a commission and went on to serve in the Korean War. After the war, he spent time in an armored unit and eventually completed the rigorous Command and General Staff course. Volunteering for service in Vietnam, Lynch was assigned to the rapidly rebuilding 4th Infantry Division, where he assisted in evaluating the division's three brigades before serving as the executive officer of the 1st Brigade. Lynch was promoted to lieutenant colonel shortly after he arrived in Vietnam and in December 1966 assumed command of the 3-8 Infantry.

Driven, demanding, by all accounts the very embodiment of his radio call sign, "Charger," Lynch pushed himself and his troopers hard, a point facetiously reflected in the "Dragoons—We Try Harder" sign someone had put up when the battalion was still in Phu Yen Province.[10] Not surprisingly, some of the grunts disapproved of Lynch's hard-charging, "go get 'em" style. "He *sucked*," said Spc5 Richard Jackson of C Company. "We were always in the bush and for days at a time. We never got to go in it seemed." Aggressive, Lynch wanted his Dragoons in the bush, patrolling, searching, taking the fight to the enemy, but he was anything but hard-hearted. "Now I knew that he was a man who could brood in the night about his lost troops," said author Charles Flood, "and get up the next morning and work hard all day trying to find the enemy, doing a job he had sworn to do when he raised his right hand one day in 1945."[11] Flood considered Lynch "a soldier's soldier" and believed that because "he'd been all of those different ranks he *understood* what [his] soldiers were thinking about."

Energetic, Lynch also knew how to motivate the men in charge of the line companies that were beating the bush, day after day, rain or shine, in search of an elusive enemy who, more often than not, did not wish to be found. "He was more flamboyant [than the previous battalion commander] and had more of a leadership style that was in-your-face," said 1st Lt. Branko Marinovich, B Company's CO. "He was the kind of guy that would come in, get you all riled up, pat you on the back, and tell you to go get 'em. I think everybody liked him."

Moving out on the morning of the twenty-fifth, B Company pushed east into the foothills of the Chu Goungot Mountains. C Company, led by Capt. James Powers, a tall, strapping West Pointer, broke camp soon after and eventually found twelve to fifteen foxholes roughly three hundred meters northeast of its NDP. "This guy [NVA]," Lynch had warned the company, "will only try to take you when he thinks he has you outnumbered."[12] Ten minutes later, at 11:10 A.M., C Company discovered the body of a North Vietnamese soldier dressed in gray fatigues. Dead for about a week, the man had been killed by American artillery fire.[13]

B Company, advancing to the north of C Company, reached Hill 521 later that afternoon. Steep and slippery, the hill was approximately 1,500 meters east of the battle the 1-8 Infantry had fought on May 20.[14] The company was to set up for the night near the summit. Strung out in a column, the exhausted Dragoons, slipping and sliding on the soggy slope, started up the hill. After a while, some of the grunts, often after falling down and sliding backwards, began climbing on their hands and knees, using branches, vines, and anything else they could get their hands on to pull themselves up.

Spc4 Ed Goehring, then a twenty-year-old RTO in 2nd Lt. Bill Berg's Third Platoon, grabbed a tangle of vines with his left hand and immediately grimaced in pain. Laced with long, sharp thorns, the vines punctured the palm of his hand and left a deep, painful wound. Goehring, glaring down at the reddish-looking hole in his hand, grumbled under his breath. Born in Allentown, Pennsylvania, he had considered enlisting in the Coast Guard after high school but decided to take his chances in the draft. Two years in the Army, if it came to that, sounded better than four years in the Coast Guard. As his wounded left hand began to swell, however, he was once again reminded that two years in the Army *was* worse than the Coast Guard, much worse. The steep, slippery slope slowed the advance to a crawl as the grunts, sagging under the weight of heavy packs, inched up the side of Hill 521. "It took you a full minute to make a step, because you couldn't really get anything firm [to step on]," noted Pfc. Gary Retana, then a twenty-year-old replacement from California. "You'd have to put your foot on the side of a tree or a root just to hold you firm so that you could gradually go up. We were carrying all that weight that we had behind us in our rucksacks to begin with, and it was almost as if we were going straight up. And it just kept going and going and going."

Thorny plants and steep, muddy hills were immutable features of the hostile environment the Dragoons discovered in the Central Highlands. Far from the sandy beaches of the South China Sea, the young Americans were soon stumbling around in dense tropical rain forests teeming with unusual wildlife. "Everything imaginable up there was scary," Retana recalled. "Every kind of insect was larger than anything I had ever seen in my life, and then you'd have these birds that looked like ravens. They'd fly around and get up on the trees, and the way that they would sound was almost as if they were saying 'fuck you.' We'd always have a low-lying fog in the morning, [and] it was maybe about two feet from the ground up. So we'd have this little fog, and I'd be looking out and for whatever reason it always reminded me of a horror movie."

B Company also encountered an altogether different adversary in the Central Highlands—the North Vietnamese Army. Landing with the 1st Brigade at Nha Trang in October 1966, the 3-8 Infantry trucked up to Tuy Hoa on the South China Sea and, like the rest of the 1st Brigade, spent months prowling the sloping hills and lush lowlands of Phu Yen Province. B Company participated in Operation Adams, but for the most part the troops were opposed by marginally effective local force VC and part-time guerillas. "We chased VC around the countryside," said Spc4 Bob Gamboa. "After fucking around with 'Charlie,' we thought we were invincible. We bumped into 'Mr. Charles' [NVA] in the Highlands, instead of 'Charlie.' We had respect for that motherfucker." Well armed, well trained, and willing to stand and fight, the NVA were arguably the first professional soldiers the company had faced in Vietnam.

1st Lt. Branko Marinovich, having personally led small unit patrols in the Highlands, knew well what his B Company troopers were up against. Marinovich, in fact, expected a tough fight if the troopers ran into any North Vietnamese on the way up Hill 521. A part of him, however, hoped that they would. "The NVA were like the big prize, and that's who we were out there looking for," he recalled. "We had heard that they were operating in the area, and we knew that they were good. But if you could latch on to one of those big units, and they were certainly elusive and difficult to find, you could use everything we had on them and then you had a chance to really do some damage to the other side." Chasing Viet Cong guerillas, part-timers he had likened to "farmers with a cause," never made much sense to him, not when there were North Vietnamese regulars roaming the country. More than that, though, he wanted to know if he was any good against other *professional* soldiers, an itch only the NVA could scratch.

Marinovich, twenty-seven, had emigrated to the United States as a boy from a small town in present-day Montenegro. His father, a merchant seaman who had jumped ship to enlist in the U.S. Army during World War II, moved the family to Fresno, California, shortly after the war to pursue the American dream. "My dad saw the light and got me to the Promised Land," Marinovich joked. "He used to always say, 'God bless America.'" Proud of his adopted country, Marinovich enlisted in the National Guard following his junior year at Fresno State and, finding the military to his liking, attended OCS in 1964. Idealistic, he applied for active duty in 1965 and was assigned to the 3-8 Infantry in November of that year. Ten months later Marinovich sailed with the battalion to South Vietnam.

Older than many of the other lieutenants, Marinovich had commanded the battalion mortar platoon before he took over B Company in April 1967. Gung-ho, he would often take half the platoon out on patrol, leaving the other half back at the battalion firebase to support the line companies in the field. Relying on stealth, the patrols produced excellent results. Constant patrolling, moreover, helped season the eager lieutenant, and the success of his small-unit operations against enemy irregulars eventually led to his promotion to company commander.

One day, however, while on patrol with the mortar platoon, he ran into a small group of Viet Cong. After a short firefight, the enemy melted back into the jungle. Marinovich was still searching the brush with one of his sergeants when he stumbled on a badly wounded VC lying against a tree. Conscious, the man spotted the two Americans approaching and, boldly pointing his Thompson submachine gun at Marinovich, pulled the trigger. *Click.* Incredibly the Thompson had jammed, but before the VC could fix whatever had caused the malfunction, the sergeant standing next to Marinovich stepped in and finished the man off with a burst from his M-16. Marinovich breathed a long sigh of relief. Had the man's submachine gun not misfired, the deadly game of "hide and seek" he had been playing with half of a platoon in the Highlands might have ended prematurely.

C Company, exhausted after a long day in the bush, stopped for the night to the southwest of Hill 521 around twenty minutes to five.[15] Noise discipline had been strictly enforced throughout the day—one officer had told his men to bury any item that they couldn't keep quiet—as the company, warned about the possibility of enemy contact, moved through the jungle. Pfc. Dan Shayotovich, a recent replacement who had been working in the avionics industry in California before he got drafted in October 1966, stuffed his dog tags in his boot to keep them from jingling. Shayotovich had been with the Second Platoon for over a month, shorter than most of the grunts in the platoon but long enough to recognize this was no routine sweep. *Something big must be going down*, thought the twenty-year-old RTO, *if we have to be this quiet*!

Transferred to the 4th Infantry Division in May, Sgt. Richard Crooks, twenty-one, then a fire team leader in the Second Platoon, had never been in jungle that thick before. Crooks, the nephew of a Marine Corps veteran who had fought on Guadalcanal, thought about joining the Marines after high school but decided instead to volunteer for the draft. Called up in late 1965, he was assigned to the 9th Infantry Division, which was reactivated in early 1966 at Fort Riley, Kansas, and arrived in Vietnam in 1967. His unit, the 4th of the 39th Infantry, operated in III Corps near Saigon, poor preparation in retrospect for combat in the rugged Central Highlands. "You talk about being a virgin—well, I was," said the Michigan native. "Those guys [in C Company], they knew their shit out there in the jungle. They weren't beginners like me. Down in the south, some of the black guys were taking their boom boxes out on patrol. If anybody did that in the 4th Infantry Division, somebody would nail their ass to a tree. Nobody played [around] up north like they did in the south."

C Company's professionalism was in large part a result of its superb leadership, beginning at the top. Capt. James Powers, USMA, Class of '64, had taken over command of the company in early 1967 after a six-month stint as a general's aide.[16] "He was a good officer," said Lt. Col. Tom Lynch. "I knew him from way back in Fort Lewis, Washington. He asked to come to our battalion, and I agreed to take him. They put him in C Company, and he did a fantastic job." Comfortable with a map and compass, Powers stayed off trails as much as possible and insisted on marching in a diamond formation so that his people would be able to form a perimeter quickly if they were ever attacked. Powers, twenty-seven, knew what a good company looked like and made sure that his people did, too. "Every time he *moved*," noted Pfc. Dan Shayotovich, "something got done." Shayotovich grew to admire Powers, believing—almost reverentially—that the tall, blonde captain "knew everything there was to know" about how to command a company.

James Conrad Powers grew up on a farm outside of Dubuque, Iowa. Powers, along with his seven brothers and sisters, worked in the fields and cared for the cattle, chickens, hogs, goats, and sheep his father raised on their 150-acre farm. There was always more to do, never enough time, and for nearly five months when he was in the seventh grade, he had helped run the family farm with two of his brothers while their father recovered in the hospital. Powers joined the junior ROTC cadet program at Loras Academy High School and made plans to attend the United States Military Academy. Graduating from Loras Academy in 1958, he left Dubuque and enrolled in a prep school in Minneapolis. The former altar boy then spent a year at the U.S. Merchant Marine Academy in King's Point, New York, before receiving an appointment to West Point in 1960.

Handsome, clean-cut, and a natural in uniform, Captain Powers resembled an officer straight out of central casting, whether walking the parade grounds at West Point or the jungles of western Pleiku Province. "Lieutenant Johnson [1st Lt. Clayton Johnson] and Captain Powers—my God, those guys were like they came out of Hollywood," said Don Tienhaara, then a twenty-year-old private first class in C

Company's Fourth Platoon. "Those guys were movie stars. I'm not kidding. They were good looking, fit, and damn good leaders."

Powers was also very much at ease around his men, a trait he shared with Lt. Branko Marinovich. Pfc. Bill Perkins was walking behind Powers in the jungle one day when the normally long-striding captain suddenly whirled around and exclaimed, "Hey lookout! Be careful!" Startled, Perkins stopped and immediately scanned the jungle floor. The originals had taught him to watch for mines and booby traps, but he didn't see anything near his feet.

"What?" he finally asked Powers bewilderedly. "What am I looking for?"

Powers grinned wryly, "There's a grid line right there. Be careful you don't step on it." Scheduled to rotate home that June, Powers had asked Richard Childers, his thirty-five-year-old first sergeant, to stay on a little longer so that the two of them could return to the United States together. Powers wanted to introduce Childers to his wife Ann, whom he had married after a whirlwind courtship in 1965, and the rest of his family back home. Loyal to a fault, Childers agreed to remain with the company until Powers had completed his tour in Vietnam.

After twenty years and two wars, Master Sergeant Childers was quietly considering retiring from the Army. His enlistment was up in June, and he had a wife and five children waiting for him at home in Ohio. No one would have blamed him if he had decided to skip the operation in the Chu Goungot Mountains. Childers, in fact, had only "five days and a wake up" left on his tour when the company broke camp on the morning of the twenty-fifth. The Army was more than just a paycheck, however. It had been a career and a calling. Childers also had a deep, abiding respect for Captain Powers. "This guy's going to go somewhere," he had told his brother Robert. "He is really good. I really like him."

If Captain Powers had been carefully groomed—junior ROTC, West Point, six months as a general's aide in Vietnam—to command men in battle, the same could not be said of Childers. One of seven children, Childers grew up in Norton, a small town near Akron in northeastern Ohio. Fiercely independent, even as a kid, he ran away from home at the age of twelve and was found three months later in Kentucky. In 1947, after completing his freshman year at Akron Kenmore High School, he accompanied a friend to the local draft board. Childers, though only fifteen at the time, ended up joining the Army. Serving alongside men more than twice his age, he went on to fight with an airborne unit in the Korean War and at one point was offered a field commission. Devoted to his men, Childers declined the offer, telling his wife Sonya that NCOs had a more important job because they were closer to the troops.

Childers eventually bought a house in Norton and was serving as an ROTC instructor when the Army transferred him to the 4th Infantry Division. Tough but fair, the former airborne trooper adapted quickly to the challenges of serving in an untested, straight-leg infantry company. "The first guy we had was a dickhead and a drunk, but Childers was a soldier's first sergeant," said Sgt. Erin Stroh, a squad leader in C Company's Second Platoon. "He was this little short guy, and he was an *old school* first sergeant, but once you got to know him he was really a good guy. As long as you told him the truth, he could deal with it and he'd get you out of it if you were in trouble. But don't you dare lie to him—Holy Jesus! I can tell you that he didn't put up with any bullshit. He'd just as soon fight. But you could approach him, and you could talk to him." Most of the grunts in C Company agreed.

Something of a throwback, Childers, beneath his gruff, Army-to-the-bone exterior, worried more about the young C Company soldiers digging in on the afternoon of May 25 than he probably cared to admit. To him, they were all just kids, too young and too immature to appreciate the harsh realities of war. It was almost as if, deep down, they could not quite wrap their heads around the fact that they might actually have to *use* the training they had been given. C Company had already been in the Highlands for three months, but other than a few minor skirmishes, it had yet to fight a major battle. Childers knew that sooner or later their luck would run out.

C Company set up for the night in the rugged terrain southwest of Hill 521. *Man, this place feels eerie*, thought Spc5 Richard Jackson as he slipped out of his pack. *There's no messing around up here*. An African American medic attached to the Third Platoon, Jackson had heard that the 1-8 Infantry had gotten hit, and like many of the grunts had felt uneasy about operating in the same general area. In the Second Platoon, Pfc. Dan Shayotovich turned the "squelch" up on his PRC-25 to reduce the *chhhhhhh* sound the radio made when he released the button. His platoon leader, 1st Lt. Jack Cannello, spoke mainly in hushed whispers.

As they had done countless times before, the C Company troopers dug holes, gathered branches for overhead cover, and cleared fields of fire. 1st Lt. Clayton "Buddy" Johnson, twenty-one, of Evanston, Illinois, supervised the troops in the First Platoon. Johnson had been a leader for as long as the folks back home in Evanston could remember. "People looked up to him," said childhood friend Dan Mangas. "But he was a very personable person. He didn't lead by intimidation or anything else. He had a sister who was deaf, and he was very protective of her. Buddy was always for the underdog. He was [just] a leader. He said things to people, and they wanted to do what he wanted to do. He had a gift."

Growing up, Johnson cherished an old photograph he had kept of his father, a combat veteran who had served with Sergeant Childers in Korea, and spoke frequently about joining the Army. "That was his whole thing—he wanted to get old enough to go into the service," said Mangas. "That was his dream. Back in the late '50s and early

'60s, the big thing was the Green Berets—the Army Special Forces—because they had just started to become popular. We didn't know much about them, but Buddy and I decided we were going to go be Green Berets." Mangas eventually earned a spot in the Special Forces; Johnson, after attending college out west, graduated from OCS and was eventually assigned to the 4th Infantry Division at Fort Lewis, Washington. Both men ended up in Vietnam.

Full of "piss and vinegar," according to one grunt, Johnson decided that if C Company had a war to fight, he was going to fight it. "Yeah—I'd say he probably liked looking for contact, but he was one of those guys that would lead from the front," said Spc4 Roger Tenbrink, a twenty-year-old First Platoon original from Cottage Grove, Oregon. "Obviously, as an officer, he couldn't always do that but if the situation was such that he could, he'd be right there with us. Johnson was the kind of guy that if we were getting shot at, *he* was getting shot at. I'm surprised sometimes that we didn't get ourselves killed with his leadership, because he was the kind of guy that was a leader and we'd follow him. He never did anything really stupid, but he was definitely gung-ho."[17]

Fond of racing his Jaguar XKE back at Fort Lewis, Lieutenant Johnson had pushed his platoons in Vietnam, but by the spring of 1967 he had grown tired of serving in a line company. Johnson, more than anything else, needed a change.[18] Intrigued about an opening he had heard about in the LRRPs, Johnson met with 1st Lt. Robert Walden in Walden's dusty command tent at Jackson Hole, shortly before the operation in the Ia Tchar Valley. Walden, in charge of the 1st Brigade LRRP platoon, was scheduled to rotate out in August and had been asked by the brigade S2 to interview some possible replacements. "I've got good people," Johnson assured Walden, "but I want to do something else." Walden had interviewed several other candidates for the position but had found Johnson to be the most intellectually engaging. Field savvy, the charismatic young lieutenant had asked all the right questions and seemed to understand the unique challenges associated with leading a LRRP platoon. Impressed, Walden decided that, when the time came, he would recommend Johnson for the job.

Johnson, unaware that Walden intended to select him as his replacement, watched as the First Platoon finished digging in. Soon the perimeter would be finished, and the company would begin sending out ambush teams. *Same shit, different day.* Meanwhile, to the north, B Company had set up a perimeter near the summit of Hill 521.[19] The climb that afternoon had been long and difficult, and some of the grunts were too tired to dig anything more than a prone shelter. Hungry, Spc4 Richard Elam, then a twenty-one-year-old Second Platoon original, set his entrenching tool down and opened a can of peaches. The shallow hole he had been digging could wait. Homeless as a boy, Elam had lived at a Catholic mission in San Diego for nearly six years with his brother and sister before the nuns there sent him and his brother to

Boys Town in Nebraska. "Don't mean nothing," as the grunts would say, had been a way of life for him long before he ever got to Vietnam.

Finishing the can of peaches, Elam stood up, grabbed his entrenching tool, and started digging. Normally, he would have shoveled out something a little deeper than a shallow hole, especially with all the talk going around about what had happened to the 1-8 Infantry. But the long climb had taken it out of him, and he didn't have the time or the strength to dig a fighting hole with overhead cover. Exhausted, Elam stared for a moment at the reddish-brown dirt beneath his boots. "Don't mean nothin'."

At 5:50 P.M. B Company radioed in the coordinates of its night location on Hill 521.[20] Both companies were then issued instructions for the following day. C Company was to march northeast and close with B Company on Hill 521. Marinovich, meanwhile, was to sit tight, patrol the hill with platoon-sized elements, and wait for C Company to arrive.[21] Marinovich and Powers, moreover, were advised to prepare for the possibility of enemy contact.

In the murky twilight, the two companies, exhausted after a long day of marching, hunkered down for the night. Ambush teams from both companies were sent out—Powers and Marinovich reported that all teams were in place by 7:15 P.M.—and an uneasy silence settled over the jungle. "There wasn't a sound [around B Company]," said Pfc. Gary Retana. "There were no rumblings in the air or anything else." The jungle was also quiet around C Company to the south. Shortly after 8 P.M., the grunts heard the distinctive *thump* of mortar rounds leaving the tube. The grunts counted seventeen rounds in all, fired most likely from a location to the southwest, but could not hear where the rounds were landing.[22] Lieutenant Colonel Lynch had the report of the mortar attack kicked up to brigade before he notified C Company at 8:25 P.M. that he planned to engage the "target area" with artillery fire. Booming away in the distance, the guns fired nearly three dozen rounds on the suspected location of the enemy mortar tube.

Around 11 P.M., the TOC keyed the battalion net and waited for a response from B and C Companies. Neither company responded, however. Twenty minutes later, the TOC indicated that it had stopped keying the net but was still awaiting a response from the two companies. Concerned, the TOC eventually asked the 3-12 Infantry to contact B and C Companies over the 3-8 Infantry command frequency. At 12:30 A.M. the 3-12 Infantry reported that it had made contact with both.[23] Moments later, the 3-8 Infantry reestablished communications with the two companies.

For a while, the jungle around the two companies remained quiet. Then, around 2:30 A.M., C Company heard ten mortar rounds being fired from a location approximately five thousand meters to the north. This time the grunts could hear the rounds exploding in the jungle some three thousand to four thousand meters south of the company perimeter. C Company reported the attack, and the battalion notified the 1st Brigade.[24]

Gray, overcast skies typical of the southwest monsoon greeted the grunts on the morning of the twenty-sixth. Asleep in a small puddle, Sgt. Richard Crooks woke up clutching his M-16. Crooks, a recent replacement from the 9th Infantry Division, had been put in charge of a fire team in C Company's Second Platoon. He hadn't been with the platoon long, but he could already tell that his team didn't think much of him or the 9th Infantry Division. As far as they were concerned, he was just another swinging dick from some half-stepping outfit in the Delta. Crooks, scared that they might be right, sat up and checked his wet rifle.

Awake in their holes, a number of grunts were already eating, chatting, and pawing at their M-16s. Pfc. Bill Perkins, a replacement in C Company's Fourth Platoon, opened his eyes and peered out into the damp jungle. *It's not a dream*, he thought to himself. *I'm really here. Oh God—I'm still here.* Attached to the Third Platoon, Spc5 Richard Jackson, twenty-one, was sitting beside his rucksack, quietly munching on C-rats. Jackson had shined shoes as kid growing up in Boston and sometimes, after he was done, he would listen to the radio while his mother cooked dinner in the kitchen. Fascinated by the news reports on the Korean War, he walked over to his mother one day, tugged on her apron, and asked, innocently, "Am I going to have to go to war when I get big?" Poor, black, and working in a mail room at the time, Jackson was drafted in 1965 and sent to Fort Lewis, Washington, to help flesh out the 4th Infantry Division.

Hustled off the bus at Fort Lewis, Jackson was originally assigned to A Company, 3-8 Infantry. After completing basic training with A Company, Jackson volunteered for duty as a combat medic. "I had no idea that the whole division might be going to Vietnam, so I was thinking—hmmm, medic? I can deal with that," he recalled. "Even as a kid, when one of my buddies or somebody had fallen outside, I'd tell them to come to my house and we'd put a Band-Aid on it. I was always good at that. If I had known—oh brother! It was ghastly the stuff we were trained for. But that's what happens. It's not going to be someone with a splinter, and you aren't going to be treating anyone for pneumonia." Trained as a combat medic, Jackson went to Vietnam with A Company but was then reassigned to C Company after only a few weeks in country. Standing atop a bunker one afternoon in Tuy Hoa, fists clenched, arms held high above his head, he playfully announced to his C Company comrades that he was the only male witch in all of Vietnam and when he left there would be no more witches in the 'Nam. A sergeant overheard Jackson and nicknamed him the "Witch Doctor," and before long the entire Third Platoon was calling him Witch for short.

Jackson, hungrily consuming his breakfast in a can, noticed that the ambush teams Captain Powers had sent out the night before had already returned to the perimeter, bleary-eyed but generally no worse for the wear. The company would be moving out shortly. Jackson packed up his gear and grabbed his rifle. His platoon leader, 1st Lt. Charles Barrett, had offered him a .45 when he joined the Third—medics could carry a sidearm instead of a rifle—but he insisted on carrying an M-16. "What if a bunch of them charge me at once?" he had asked Barrett. "What am I going to do with a *.45*?" Barrett, however, was not with the company on the twenty-sixth.

Forming up in the fog-shrouded foothills of the lower Chu Goungot Mountains, C Company broke camp and headed northeast, toward Hill 521, around 7:20 A.M.[25] Captain Powers, hiking alongside Sergeant Childers and the rest of the company CP group, deployed his four platoons in a diamond formation for the march to B Company. John Wheeler, an Associated Press (AP) correspondent, was accompanying C Company on the operation. Despite the overcast skies that morning, the twenty-sixth had dawned warm and humid, sticky weather that made it easy for the grunts to work up a good sweat humping the hills and draws in the area. Thick, double-canopy jungle covered the surrounding slopes and draws, while higher up, on the rugged peaks and narrow ridgelines lining the valley, tall trees, scattered underbrush, and single-canopy jungle marked the landscape.

The early morning fog limited the troops' visibility, but as the company pushed across the uneven terrain without incident, Pfc. Dan Shayotovich realized that the knot in his belly had finally subsided. Exhaling, Shayotovich suspected that the strict noise discipline the platoon had been observing for the last two days had been nothing more than typical Army bullshit. Spc5 Richard Jackson was walking alongside the Third Platoon, asking the grunts about their feet, when he heard someone yelling, "Witch, Witch!" Jackson turned around and saw his friend, Spc4 Donald Mesarosh. Easy going, Jackson smiled at the eager RTO and said, "Hey Mezzy—what's up?"

"Doc, only one hundred and eleven more days to go!"

Jackson grinned uncomfortably. "That's great, Mezzy." Mesarosh, twenty, from Louisville, Kentucky, was the kind of grunt other grunts enjoyed being around. Mezzy handled the PRC-25 like a pro, never complained, and was always upbeat. Jackson liked Mezzy a lot, but the thought of spending another three and a half months in Vietnam sent a cold chill up his spine. *One hundred and eleven days*, Jackson thought to himself. *One hundred and eleven days before we get out of this place*. Sighing, Jackson walked toward the head of the Third Platoon column. "Later, Mezzy."

C Company stumbled on a high-speed trail shortly after 8 A.M. The trail was approximately two feet wide, but it did not appear as if it had been used recently. The trees along the trail were marked, however, possibly to guide the movement of an enemy unit operating in the area.[26] Captain Powers passed the information on to battalion and the advance continued. Taught to keep up without bunching up, the soldiers of the Fourth Platoon, their Camel-puffing platoon sergeant pushing the pace, crashed noisily through the damp jungle. "Watch where you're going and keep an interval between you and the man in front of you," warned Plt. Sgt. Paul Ingram, "or one round will get you all!" Pfc. Bill Perkins glanced up at the soldier in front of him. *Hold your interval*, he reminded himself sternly, *and don't get too close.*

Perkins, nineteen, had spent a semester at Texas Western College, now the University of Texas–El Paso, before enlisting in the Army in September 1966. Shipped to Vietnam after AIT, Perkins met up with his older brother Ray, then a specialist 4th class, while awaiting orders at the reception center in Long Binh. The two went shopping together and then parted company, confident that they would see each other again. In April 1967, Bill Perkins was assigned to the 4th Infantry Division as a replacement.

Marching in a diamond formation with the Second Platoon on point, the Fourth Platoon to the right, the Third Platoon to the left, and the First Platoon in the rear, C Company reached Hill 521 before 9 A.M. Snatches of gray overcast peeked through the canopy, but the early morning fog had started to recede. Second Platoon, led by Lt. Jack Cannello, started up the slope and found a well-worn trail. Farther back, Private First Class Perkins, mouth open, sweat dripping down his brow, wondered if he had the strength to make it to the top of the hill.

Soft, reddish-colored mud stuck to the bottom of the grunts' boots as they advanced up the hill. Spread out across the slope, the four platoons then stuttered to a stop. "Well, hell—that's about it for this sweep," remarked one grunt, jamming a half-crushed cigarette into his mouth. "Yeah," agreed another man, "I guess ole Charlie isn't goin' to show this time."[27] It had been a long morning, and many of the grunts sank to the ground to rest their aching backs and feet. Others drank greedily from lukewarm canteens.

C Company had just crested a small knoll when the ridgeline the troops had been following suddenly fell off sharply. The steep, downward slope in front of the company leveled off near the base of the knoll and then, after another short descent, began arching upward again. Captain Powers, confused as to why the company was suddenly heading downhill when it should have been heading uphill, toward the summit of Hill 521, halted the four platoons and called for a short break. "We took the wrong arm on that ridge," said Sgt. Michael Scott, an artillery forward observer attached to C Company. "We took the right-hand arm instead of the left-hand arm, and that's why he [Powers] called for the company to stop. Everybody realized after about a hundred yards that we were supposed to meet B Company on top of the mountain. We were heading downhill. We all knew we had made a mistake. We just didn't know quite where we were."

Scott, 1st Lt. Ronald Beckham, and the radioman assigned to Beckham formed the small artillery observer team assigned to C Company. While Beckham and his RTO remained almost exclusively with the company CP group, Scott was usually attached to either the First or Third Platoons. Assigned to the First Platoon that morning, Scott was at the back of the platoon, in front of a black grunt with an M-60, when Captain Powers brought the company to halt. Up ahead, on the sloped terrain leading down from the small knoll, Scott could see the company CP group and some troops from the Second Platoon. Both groups were downhill from where he was standing, as were elements of the Fourth Platoon to his right. Third Platoon had stopped in the jungle to his left.

Turning around to cover the knoll, the black machine gunner dropped down behind his M-60 and pointed the barrel slightly upward, toward the high ground. Scott, lying down beside the grunt, agreed to feed the gun. *We better keep an eye on that knoll*, Scott thought to himself as he studied the small rise in front of them, *because they could hit us from up there*. Twenty years old, Scott had grown up on a cattle ranch in Washington before he was drafted in 1965 and sent to Fort Ord, California, for basic training. Scott was then assigned to the artillery and trained as a forward observer. "Scotty was good man, *real* good," said Spc5 Richard Jackson. "He knew what he was doing out there." Set up beside the M-60, Lt. Clay Johnson and his platoon CP group not far behind, Scott figured that he could get to the radio in a hurry if he needed to call in a fire mission.

Meanwhile, in the Second Platoon, Lt. Jack Cannello wanted to know why his veteran point man, twenty-year-old Yakima, Washington, native Erin Stroh, had wandered off the route Cannello had expected him to take up the hill. "You're getting off your azimuth—what's wrong?" Cannello barked.

"It's too quiet," Stroh replied anxiously. "You can't hear anything. There's something wrong."

Stroh had worked at Elmendorf Air Force Base in Alaska after high school and had tried to enlist in the Air Force. Healthy, clean-cut, and already a civilian employee, Stroh seemed like a perfect fit; the Air Force, however, had already filled its enlistment quota and turned him down. Drafted in 1965, he ended up in Fort Lewis, Washington, with the rapidly rebuilding 4th Infantry Division.

Stroh had walked point a number of times before—most of the originals had taken a turn on point at one time or another—but something just didn't feel right to him. The jungle was just too quiet, and the trail he had been following ran up the slope into a modest clearing. "I'm not walking through that," he mumbled under his breath. "Jesus Christ. There's hardly any cover up there." A call then came in from the company CP. The Second Platoon was to send out a small reconnaissance party to determine where the company was and whether it should continue on or turn around and hike back up the knoll. Cannello dispatched a team led by Sgt. Terence Fitzgerald, a hard-charging Irishman who had immigrated to the United States from London, England.[28] Stroh remained behind with the main body of the platoon.

To the left of the company CP, the foot-weary squads of the Third Platoon waited quietly in the damp brush. Pfc. Russell Belden, twenty-one, from Hartford, Illinois, leaned back against a tree and opened a can of peaches. Hungry, he greedily swallowed a spoonful of fruit and looked around. Belden dreamed of making it big in country music one day, but when the Army called in December 1965, he put away his guitar and boarded a plane for Fort Lewis, Washington. Miserable, he went home after basic training and returned with his guitar, determined to play and practice whenever he could. "I did a lot of entertaining in the Army," said Belden. "I'd plug in my amp and sing and play music, and the guys would come and listen."

Shedding his pack, Spc5 Richard Jackson got up, informed one of the squad leaders in the Third Platoon that he needed a minute to do his business, and then walked a short ways up the hill. Jackson, turning back around so that he was facing the platoon, dropped his pants and relieved himself in the bushes. "I was doing *everything*," he recalled. "Those C-rations were running [right] through me." He had pulled up his pants and was about to head back when, out of the corner of his eye, he thought he saw someone ducking down in the jungle behind him. Startled, he whirled around, heart pounding, and peered into the brush. *Damn, man—don't tell me I'm seeing stuff now*, he thought to himself as he scanned the jungle. *Maybe I'm just tired. We've been humping all morning, and it is hotter than a motherfucker out here.* Unnerved, Jackson hurried back down the hill and told Sgt. Cleveland Lewis, a tough, no-nonsense NCO, that he thought he saw something in the bushes.

Before Sergeant Lewis could respond, however, a series of loud "pops" rang out toward the rear of the company. Pfc. Russell Belden heard a gunshot and then a sharp *crack*. The shot made the hair on the back of his neck stand up. "If you can *hear* an incoming bullet, you can tell someone's shooting at you," said Belden. "If you can hear a *pop* and then a *crack*, you can tell that you're being shot at." On the other side of the company, Pfc. Bill Perkins heard several loud "pops" and looked around. Moments later an older soldier in the Fourth Platoon yelled at him to get down because the platoon was taking fire. The time was 8:55 A.M.[29]

Near the center of the company formation, Captain Powers and Sergeant Childers were sitting down, mulling over their next move, when the popping began. "What's that?" Powers asked uneasily. Childers, grabbing his rifle, replied, "I'll go check."

"Wait a minute," Powers interrupted. "I'll go with you."

17 THEY'RE IN THE TREES!

Struck below the left eye, the tall Iowan collapsed to the jungle floor, mouth open, eyes gazing up vacantly at the gray Highland sky. Captain Powers, USMA Class of '64, CO of C Company, 3-8 Infantry, was dead, moments after he had scrambled to his feet to investigate the loud popping sounds he had heard with MSgt. Richard Childers. Stunned, Childers hurried over to help but there was nothing he could do. Powers had died instantly, robbing the old warhorse of the chance to comfort him in the final moments of his life. *You're gonna be alright*, Childers would have told him. *Just hang in there.*

Perched in the trees, the North Vietnamese had waited for the Americans to lumber into position before opening fire at 8:55 A.M.[1] Powers fell in the initial volley. Some of the grunts, startled by the sudden gunfire, hit the dirt and clambered for cover. Others screamed in pain as the enemy snipers fired down on the company with deadly accuracy. On the left flank of the company, not far from Pfc. Russell Belden, a young Third Platoon trooper was shot in the hip. "I've been hit!" the man moaned in agony. Belden leaned his pack against a small tree and lay down behind it.

Steadying himself, Sergeant Childers, now just four days and a wake-up from returning to the United States, alive and in one piece, turned to the troopers around him and shouted, "They're in the trees! Start shooting up in the trees!" Spc4 Don Tienhaara, a burly original from Bremerton, Washington, shouldered his M-16 and sprayed the canopy above the Fourth Platoon. While the riflemen were spraying the trees with M-16s, some of the machine gunners in the company joined in, the heavier *chug, chug, chug* of their M-60s adding to the roar of rifle fire echoing across the slope.[2] Childers thought the company was burning through too much ammo and immediately called for a ceasefire. 1st Lt. Clay Johnson, meanwhile, left Plt. Sgt. Karl Hoopes in charge of the First Platoon and rushed forward to assume command of the company.[3]

Almost immediately, C Company radioed the battalion TOC and reported that it was receiving sporadic sniper fire and had responded with rifle, machine-gun, and artillery fire. The enemy force was approximately the size of a company. Shortly thereafter, at 9:05 A.M., the jungle around the First and Third Platoons reverberated with the crack of heavy sniper fire.[4] "At first it was just like . . . *pow, pow, pow, pow*—like sporadic fire you know," recalled Spc5 Richard Jackson, "but then it just reached a *crescendo.* It was like rain drops hitting the ground and going through the air. If you were lying on the ground, you couldn't stick your hand up in the air or it would have gotten shot off. All hell just broke loose. I didn't know whether to shit or go blind."

Shoulder-fired RPGs shrieked angrily across the slope, sending chunks of hot shrapnel flying through the jungle. Bursts of machine-gun fire shredded the undergrowth around the stunned Americans as mortar rounds exploded in the canopy above them. Riddled with bullets, some of the grunts died instantly. Others wailed in agony on the rain-slicked slope. "I'm can't see! I can't see!" moaned a soldier who had been hit in the face. "God help me. Where's some cover?"[5] Lying against the legs of a wounded comrade, one grunt was struck over and over again by the withering fire engulfing the company. Another man, choking on the blood filling up in his lungs, sang and sobbed out loud. Forgotten in the confusion, the man eventually fell silent.

Crouching in the jungle to the west-southwest, a wave of North Vietnamese, supported by RPGs, mortars, and light machine guns, dashed across Hill 521 and slammed into elements of the First and Third Platoons.[6] The NVA closed on the two platoons so quickly that the artillery firing in support of the company could not break up the assault before it reached the grunts. In the confusion, Spc4 Don Tienhaara ended up near Lt. Clay Johnson, the acting company commander, and at one point an enemy soldier popped up in front of them. No more than twenty-five feet away, the man spotted Johnson and squeezed off a burst with his AK-47, narrowly missing the young lieutenant. Johnson returned fire and dropped the man.

Hard hit, C Company pulled into a defensive perimeter and returned fire.[7] Savage, close-quarters fighting, meanwhile, broke out along the line as the First and Third Platoons, recovering from the initial shock of battle, blazed away at the North Vietnamese with M-16s, M-60s, and M-79s. Facing the small knoll behind the First Platoon, a young black machine gunner opened up on a group of about twenty-five enemy soldiers moving through the jungle toward the Third Platoon. Sgt. Michael Scott fed the gun and figured that they were probably doing some damage, even if it was not enough to halt the enemy assault.

"Watch that area!" yelled one Third Platoon trooper.

"Medic! Medic!" screamed another.

Doggedly clinging to its defensive positions, the Third absorbed the enemy attack and held firm. Pfc. Russell Belden was lying behind his rucksack, facing downhill, when he heard someone shout, "Belden—get your men over there and fill in that gap!" Belden told the two grunts in his fire team to move out, then began low-crawling toward a small depression about ten to fifteen yards away. Armed with an M-16 and a handful of grenades, he reached the depression first and wriggled in. The two grunts slid in beside him to the right. Suddenly the volume of enemy fire sweeping across the sparsely covered depression increased. Scared, Belden crawled behind a small tree and yelled for the two grunts to get as low as they possibly could. "I could see the bullets hitting the bark above my head, and some of them were [hitting] right beside my head," he recalled. "Bullets were hitting everywhere."

Pfc. Paul Wooldridge Jr., the grunt lying closest to him, was already dead, however, along with the soldier lying to the right of Wooldridge. Both had apparently been shot, although it was not entirely clear where the two men had been hit. "I don't know where he [Wooldridge] got shot at on his body because I didn't see any blood," said Belden. "It was just that his eyes were black." Shot and killed while attempting to smother an enemy grenade, Wooldridge, twenty-one, from Metropolis, Illinois, was posthumously awarded the Silver Star.[8]

Shocked that his fire team had been killed right beside him, Belden squirmed out of the depression and crawled up next to a black sergeant named Allman. Allman had run out of hand grenades and wanted to know if Belden had any left. Belden replied that he did and was about to hand one to Allman when the sergeant shouted, "Throw a grenade behind that tree!" Wide enough to conceal a man, the tree was about twenty yards from the two Americans. "Sergeant—I can't," Belden stuttered. "I'm lying on my belly. I can't throw on my belly. You know what? I'll throw my grenades to you."

Belden then pulled out a grenade and tossed it to Allman. Yanking the pin, Allman leaned back and, in seemingly one fluid motion, lunged forward and heaved the grenade at the big tree. The grenade exploded near the tree, but the blast did not kill the North Vietnamese soldier hiding behind it. "It was a big tree—it was a *real* big tree—and we could see this arm coming around the side of that tree," said Belden. "He [NVA soldier] must have had a basket full of grenades, because he must have thrown a half dozen of them or better at us. Some of them looked like they were homemade devices made of bamboo and some sort of explosive."Fortunately, a lot of the grenades, regardless of the type, were duds that bounced harmlessly across the jungle floor.

Belden at one point threw two of his own grenades past the tree, hoping to catch the North Vietnamese soldier hiding behind it in the blast, but neither he nor Allman had been able to put one close enough to the tree to kill the man. Frustrated, Belden pulled the pin on another grenade and, sitting up slightly to get a little more leverage on the throw, lobbed it just beyond the trunk of the tree. The grenade went off moments later, the blast marked by a swirl of smoke and debris. "It must have got the NVA," said Belden, "because he didn't throw any more grenades at us after that."

The intensity of the North Vietnamese assault, coupled with the intimate nature of the fighting, produced a number of casualties in the Third Platoon. Spc5 Richard "Witch Doctor" Jackson, AK-47 rounds snapping through the underbrush above his head, grabbed ahold of his pack and wriggled off in search of wounded grunts. "Medic! . . . Doc! . . . Witch!" The screams of the wounded seemed as if they were coming from everywhere all at once. Nearby Spc4 Joe Perez, a good-natured grunt from Guam, had taken cover behind a fallen log along with several other grunts. Pinned down, Perez was banging away with his M-16, trying desperately to suppress some of the small-arms fire chopping up the jungle all around them.

Head down, eyes fixed on the dirt in front of his face, Jackson was low-crawling on his belly, past the log where Specialist 4th Class Perez had taken cover, when he suddenly heard the sound of two hand grenades landing in the brush behind him. A third grenade landed near Perez. The startled grunt picked it up but before he could throw it back, the grenade exploded in his hand. Jackson, lifted up by the blast, crashed to the ground with a thud, forcing the air from his lungs. Turning around, Jackson saw Perez lying in a prone position with his upper body resting on his forearms. His eyes were closed and one of his hands was missing, replaced by a bloody stump.

Jackson, crawling as fast as he could over the uneven terrain, scrambled over to Perez. "Can you see?" Jackson asked worriedly. Perez, however, did not respond. The blast had thrown shrapnel in his face, closing his eyes shut, and it seemed as if he had either been knocked unconscious or was simply too dazed to talk. The explosion, moreover, had blown his hand off at the wrist. Working quickly, Jackson put a tourniquet on Perez's arm and bandaged the raw, blast-blackened stump where his hand had once been. Jackson also placed bandages over the wounded man's eyes. "Stay down and don't move!" Needed elsewhere, Jackson left Perez by the log and crawled off through the underbrush. Remarkably, Perez survived the battle and was later awarded the Distinguished Service Cross for saving his fire team from an enemy grenade.

Meanwhile, on the other side of the emerging C Company perimeter, the elements of the small reconnaissance party led by Sgt. Terence Fitzgerald scampered back to the Second Platoon.[9] The Second was already in contact with the NVA, and there was at least one enemy machine gun firing nearby. Sgt. Richard Crooks, new to the division and the Highlands, heard the gun opening up—Crooks thought the gun was probably somewhere in front of the platoon—and tried to remain calm. Scanning the jungle, he was struck by how *loud* the rifle shots sounded. "To me, that determined how close they were or how far away they were," said Crooks. "Those shots were *very loud*, so I figured they were awfully close."

Sgt. Erin Stroh, Crooks's squad leader and the point man for the Second Platoon that morning, had slipped behind a small shrub farther up the hill. Alone on the slope, half a hill it seemed between him and the next GI, Stroh began searching the bush around him for the rest of his squad. "We got completely disoriented," he recalled. "We got screwed up. I couldn't even find my squad. We were just scattered all over the place." Stroh, discouraged by the heavy enemy fire clipping through the underbrush, decided to stay put until the firing slowed down some.

Slightly more organized, the Fourth Platoon had taken up positions to the right of the Second Platoon and to the left of Sgt. Michael Scott in the First Platoon. Parts of the Fourth Platoon were receiving heavy automatic weapons fire, and two rocket blasts had rocked the troops on that side of the perimeter. "I probably saw twenty people wounded from the two B-40 rocket shells," said Spc4 Don Tienhaara. "I think about twenty people got knocked out from those two shells." The platoon had also been hit by mortar fire, likely from the southeast. Trained as a mortarman, Tienhaara worried that the enemy crews would eventually start walking rounds across the slope, toward his position.

Most of the rounds, however, were exploding prematurely in the same thick canopy that had concealed the enemy's snipers at the start of the battle, sparing the grunts fighting on the slope below.[10] Later, there was even some question as to the number of mortar rounds the North Vietnamese actually fired during the battle. "A lot of times our people would say that it was mortars, but it wasn't mortars—it was those damn RPGs," said Lt. Col. Tom Lynch, CO of the 3-8 Infantry. "The NVA would fire them, and they would get in the canopy in the jungle and they'd break into fragments. For our guys on the ground an RPG [round] would be fired three or four feet ahead of them, but the fragments would hit them."

Lynch's theory is not without merit. The battalion after-action report, for example, observed that "snipers in trees were employing the B-40 rocket launcher as an anti-personnel weapon with good results."[11] It is certainly possible then, given the angle of fire, that the grunts on the ground mistook RPGs fired from high up in the trees for enemy mortar rounds.

News of the battle raging on the side of Hill 521 reached the battalion TOC to the north shortly after 9 A.M. C Company had been hit on the hill, Lieutenant Colonel Lynch learned, but it is unclear if the company knew at that point that it had bumped into a *battalion* of North Vietnamese. The enemy, in any event, was apparently well armed, well led, and highly motivated.

Someone in C Company—Lynch cannot recall who—asked for gunships. Lynch, however, refused. "They gave coordinates to the attack helicopters, and they wanted artillery on the same spot. Unfortunately, that was B Company," said Lynch. "They were giving me the coordinates for right on top of B Company! The B Company commander [1st Lt. Branko Marinovich] recognized it, and I wouldn't fire. I didn't want the attack helicopters, because when you get single and double canopy, the rockets going in there can't always penetrate the canopy. And I wouldn't put them on top of B Company." Nine artillery batteries, including the big guns of the 6-14 Artillery (175-mm, 8-inch) and the 5-16 Artillery (155-mm, 8-inch), would eventually fire in support of the hard-pressed Dragoons on Hill 521, with seven of the nine providing heavy blocking fires around the contact area.[12]

Taught to "pile on," Lynch immediately ordered B Company to dispatch three platoons to assist C Company.[13] Lieutenant Marinovich, following the battle over the radio, selected his First, Third, and Fourth Platoons. The First was to move southwest, alongside the main ridge running down from the company NDP, while the Third pushed west on the other side of the ridge. Fourth Platoon, under the command of 1st Lt. Rick Nelson, was to advance southwest down the spine of the main ridge. Nelson also received instructions to improve the existing trail on the ridge. While the other three platoons rushed off to help C Company, the Second Platoon, commanded by 1st Lt. Richard Schell, was to remain behind and clear an LZ near the company NDP.[14] Marinovich briefed the leaders of all four platoons, stressing as sternly as he could the seriousness of the C Company situation, then threw together a small relief force composed of troopers from the company CP and whoever else he could find.

Earlier that morning, B Company had sent out patrols to search the surrounding jungle, and at least one of those patrols was still down slope, some distance from the company CP, when Lynch ordered Marinovich to reinforce C Company. Rather than return to the top of the hill, however, the patrols were instructed to move toward the sound of the guns. "It's been a long time, and I'm a bit foggy on the details, but I know there wasn't enough time to recall the patrols and get organized," said Marinovich. "So I probably gave them the coordinates and told them to get down to the point of conflict. It was a matter of getting as fast as we could to what was left of C Company to reinforce them."

A Fourth Platoon patrol led by Spc4 Bob "Panch" Gamboa was already down slope, half a klick from the summit of Hill 521, when it heard heavy gunfire around 9 A.M. "It was *loud*, man," said Gamboa. "We could hear the NVA opening up on C Company. There were AKs, M-16s—both sides just going at it." Shortly thereafter, the patrol received a call from the company CP. Gamboa spoke directly to Lieutenant Marinovich and was told to "go help C Company." *Help C Company*? thought Gamboa. *What the fuck*?

Smaller than a squad, Gamboa's hopelessly outnumbered patrol marched off moments later in a tight, diamond formation. Shards of white hot shrapnel whistled through the air as the patrol approached C Company, forcing the grunts to hit the dirt. "Big chunks of fucking metal were landing all over the place," said Gamboa. "They were hitting the trees." Bursting above and around the crouching grunts, shells from enemy mortars and American artillery were blowing holes in the canopy above the small patrol, showering the slope with twigs and bark. Gamboa, afraid that his people would never make it to C Company alive, radioed Lieutenant Marinovich and asked for permission to return to the top of the hill. Permission granted, the nervous grunts turned around and raced back up the slope.

The frenzied rush to get troopers *down* the hill was nearly as chaotic. Hurriedly directing his First, Third, and Fourth Platoons to "marry up with me as soon as you can," Lieutenant Marinovich gathered his small relief force and headed down the slope toward C Company around 9:05 A.M.[15] "We didn't even think about security," recalled the former B Company commander. "We just headed as fast as we could to reinforce Charlie Company. I had my command group and some other men—I cannot honestly recall who they were or from what platoon—and we basically double-timed it through all kinds of jungle and vines." Lt. Rick Nelson thinks that some of the men in the relief force belonged to 2nd Lt. Richard Schell's Second Platoon, the platoon tasked with clearing an LZ near the company NDP.

Forming up in a hurry, Nelson's Fourth Platoon marched out of the B Company NDP and down the main ridge.[16] Nelson, walking in the center of the formation, had a squad in front of him, one on each flank, and an element in trace. Powerfully built, the Salem, Oregon, native played college football at Oregon State and was a teammate of Heisman Trophy–winning quarterback Terry Baker, seeing action in the 1962 Liberty Bowl. Nelson joined the ROTC program in college, and after graduating in 1965 earned a commission in the Army. The squared-away second lieutenant was eventually sent to Fort Lewis, Washington, where he was assigned to B Company, 3-8 Infantry. Nelson assumed command of the Fourth Platoon and knew as well as anyone in the company "who was good and who was bad and who we could trust, because we had taken them through their training at Fort Lewis."

To the right of the Fourth Platoon, the First Platoon, led by 1st Lt. Fletcher Bass, was moving down the hill in a column. C Company had gotten hit bad, Bass's squad leaders had told the grunts, and they had to get down there as fast as they could. Near the front of the column, Pfc. Gary Retana, M-16 in one hand, a LAW slung over his back, negotiated the slippery slope without losing his footing. It was not always easy. "We were trying to go as quickly as we could without falling down and causing more injuries to people," said Retana. "Everybody was moving fast but not running. We didn't want to build up speed and then start stumbling." Retana, like most of the soldiers in his squad, had left his pack behind when the platoon marched off to help C Company.

Slowed by downed trees and thick, thorny vines, 1st Lt. Bill Berg, a former bush pilot from Seattle who had survived two plane crashes near the Arctic Circle, struggled to keep his Third Platoon moving to the left of the Fourth Platoon. Pfc. Larry Orr, twenty, cleared a tangle of vines and heard gunfire on the slope below the Third Platoon. Thick jungle, though, obscured the ongoing fighting. "We couldn't see anything," said Orr, "but we knew we were getting close because you could tell the difference between the weapons [M-16s and AK-47s] pretty easily." Orr had worked on his family's cattle ranch in Wyoming after high school; drafted in 1965, he sustained shrapnel wounds during an enemy mortar attack near Tuy Hoa and received a Purple Heart. Picking his way through the dense underbrush, Orr questioned whether the platoon would make it down to C Company.

They had lined up behind Captain Powers and Sergeant Childers on that February afternoon in New Plei Djereng, all one hundred and forty of them, men of every size, shape, and complexion. Sweating, their boots already covered in red dust, the troops listened quietly while Lt. Col. Tom Lynch spoke of the challenges they would now face in the Central Highlands. Lynch explained that they would have to build more bunkers, dig more shelters, and fill more sandbags if they wanted to survive in their new area of operations. The Highlands were going to be tougher than Tuy Hoa, he warned, but if they worked hard, stayed sharp, and used their heads, they would be okay.

When he had finished addressing the company, Lynch looked to Captain Powers and remarked approvingly, "Carry on." Sergeant Childers, turning to face the troops, lifted his hand like a conductor and then dropped it abruptly. On cue the men of C Company, 3-8 Infantry roared, "Fight fiercely, sir!"[17] By then it had become something of an inside joke within the battalion, a pseudo battle cry the grunts had humorously applied to virtually every occasion. "Eat fiercely . . . wash fiercely . . . dig fiercely!" Visibly amused, Lynch saluted the grinning troops and walked away.

Relying initially on instinct and then, as the fighting progressed, on its leadership and professionalism, C Company turned back the enemy's initial ground assault on Hill 521. Ironically, Captain Powers had played a pivotal role in defeating the enemy assault, despite losing his life in the opening moments of the battle. If Powers had moved the company up the slope that morning in a column, rather than in a diamond formation, his strung-out troopers might have been overrun.[18] Instead the company was ideally positioned to form a rudimentary perimeter and hold the enemy off. Laid to rest in Seattle, Washington, the tall Iowan was posthumously awarded the Silver Star for his lifesaving foresight on the twenty-sixth.

Following the assault, C Company began blowing enemy snipers out of the trees with shotguns, machine guns, and M-79s.[19] While the grunts were clearing the trees around the company, Lt. Clay Johnson ordered the Second and Fourth Platoons to move onto higher ground and close the perimeter on the north and northeast sides.[20] Facing the small knoll, Sgt. Paul Ingram, platoon sergeant of the Fourth Platoon, repositioned his people on the backside of the perimeter. Older, at age forty, than Master Sergeant Childers, Sergeant Ingram had served with the Marines in World War II and Korea before enlisting in the Army. Years of military service had molded the hard-bitten Ohio native to the point where he walked, talked, and even *looked* like a lifer. "I thought he was a tough old bastard," said Pfc. Bill Perkins. "He could out-walk any guy in the company. Nineteen-year-old guys would be falling out, but he'd walk by smoking a Camel. He was the kind of guy that would get up in the middle of the night and inspect your foxhole." Perkins trusted Ingram implicitly, as did most of the grunts in the Fourth Platoon.

Meanwhile, behind Sergeant Ingram on the other side of the perimeter, elements of Lt. Jack Cannello's Second Platoon had moved back toward the small knoll. Filling in along the line, some of the troopers took up positions on the high ground near the Third Platoon. Spc4 Richard Wilkins, a shy, bespectacled twenty-year-old original from Mountlake Terrace, Washington, followed his squad leader. "They treat us like crap here," Wilkins had told his younger brother Dan, then a high school student in suburban Seattle. "We don't know what we're doing, we don't know where we're going, and we don't even know why we're here." Tired of the war, Wilkins wanted nothing more than to go home with his best friend, Spc4 Lynn Wanzak, and forget all about Vietnam. Friends since basic, the two had become virtually inseparable, so much so that the other grunts had teasingly referred to them as "Mr. and Mrs. Wanzak."

Nineteen-year-old Pfc. Dave Fessler hurried back up the slope, past the company CP, and hit the dirt near a thorny bush that looked like a large fern. Fessler, a former Forest Service firefighter from California who had joined the company in late February, settled in with his Second Platoon squad and immediately scanned the trees for snipers. Many were carefully concealed in the canopy, but whenever a gunshot rang out, the grunts would determine where the shot came from and then concentrate their fire on that tree.

Knocked unconscious when two bullets slammed into his helmet, leaving a large bump above his left brow, Pfc. Dan Shayotovich awoke to find Plt. Sgt. Paul Cox hovering over him. Cox had been slapping Shayotovich, hoping to wake him up.

"I'm dead," Shayotovich whimpered. "Now leave me alone."

"You're not dead until I tell you you're dead!"

Dizzy, Shayotovich gazed glassy-eyed at Sergeant Cox. The entire right side of his body felt funny, and he could barely move his right arm or leg. Second Platoon troopers were scurrying past—Cox was apparently directing some of them—but, lacking the strength to stand up, Shayotovich could only watch while the platoon shifted positions. Someone then grabbed him by the leg and pulled him back.

Troops from both the Second and Fourth Platoons were still moving into position when the NVA launched a second ground assault. Heavier than the first assault, the

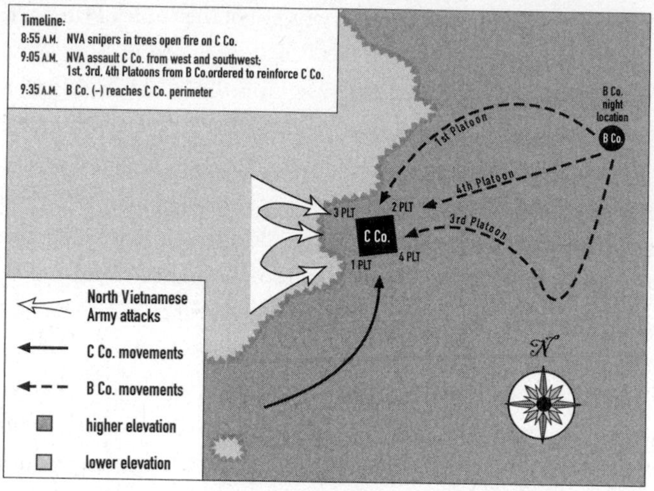

B and C Companies, 3-8 Infantry on Hill 521, May 26, 1967.
Situation at 9:35 A.M. *Map by Charles Grear, adapted from 3-8 Infantry AAR.*

attack hit the First and Third Platoons holding the south and southeastern sides of the perimeter. "They had tremendous, *tremendous* firepower," recalled Spc4 Don Tienhaara of the Fourth Platoon. "The bullets, the mortars, the B-40 rockets—they had so much firepower that it was amazing. You can't run and you can't stand up. It's not like the movies." Somewhat exposed, Tienhaara crawled down the slope, chipping a bone in his elbow, to retrieve ammo from his pack. Dirt and debris closed one of his eyes shut, but he hurried back into position along the platoon line.

A fierce firefight, meanwhile, broke out between elements of the Second Platoon that had moved back toward the knoll and a group of North Vietnamese. "They were on that side of the bushes and we were on this side of the bushes, and the bushes would shoot at us and we would shoot at the bushes," said Pfc. Dave Fessler. "The fire kind of came on in waves. They'd attack, then we'd attack and there was just so much fire going between us that it just *roared.* Everybody's shooting, so you have to stay down. It's very surreal. You shoot for a while and then everybody stops and reloads. Then everybody starts shooting again and it just *roars.*" Three months before, Sgt. Terence Fitzgerald had told him that he was in the best platoon, in the best company, in the best division in Vietnam. Fessler, putting a burst of fire into the line of bushes in front of him, prayed that Fitzgerald was right.

Lying on the slope near the front of the Second Platoon, sheets of small-arms fire sweeping through the underbrush, Sgt. Richard Crooks had a man to his right, another to his left, and a third covering the jungle behind him. The three grunts were members of his fire team, but he had no idea where the rest of the platoon had set up. "I'm hit, I'm hit!" . . . "Over there, goddammit!" . . . "Motherfuckers!" All around him men were screaming, cussing, and moaning, sounds he "never really got used to hearing." Crooks had been in firefights before, but he had never experienced anything like the battle on Hill 521. His entire tour to that point, in fact, suddenly seemed like one long training exercise in comparison. "What we had down in the 9th was like a scrimmage," said Crooks. "Somebody would be walking down a trail, and he'd spot us and we'd spot them and we'd start shooting. But they'd never stay and fight. They got out of the area. I didn't see *anything* in the 9th like I did in the 4th."

Crooks was afraid that if he yelled he would give away his position, so he used hand signals to communicate with the rest of his team. One man was already firing, where or at what Crooks could only guess, but the other two were apparently waiting for something to shoot at. Suddenly Crooks saw something moving in the jungle. "I figured it had to be the enemy because it was probably only one man," he recalled. "GIs like to get together in a firefight." Crooks leveled his M-16 and pumped a few rounds into the bush. His stomach in knots, the smell of gunpowder thick in the air, he waited for a moment then realized that the movement had stopped.

The weight of the enemy assault had fallen primarily on the troops of the First and Third Platoons. Scrambling up the small knoll, six North Vietnamese soldiers darted across the slope in front of Sgt. Michael Scott on the left flank of the First Platoon. Thirty to forty yards away, the enemy soldiers were moving from tree to tree, headed toward the Third Platoon to Scott's right. Scott could see that some of the men were dressed in khaki-colored uniforms, while others were wearing khaki pants and a black shirt. All of them were armed with AK-47s and SKSs.

In position near the base of the knoll, Scott and the black gunner, the latter armed with an M-60, the former an M-16, cut loose on the North Vietnamese, killing two of them. Undeterred, the four survivors ignored the two Americans and continued on across the knoll. "I couldn't figure out why they didn't come right toward us," said Scott. "Maybe it was because of the heavy machine-gun fire. It was like they were trying to get to a certain area over there [to the right], and everyone was congregating on it." Afterward Plt. Sgt Paul Ingram advised Scott to check the area in front of them. Tied in to the left of Scott, Ingram probably wanted to make sure that his Fourth Platoon, stretched as it was across the hill, was in no danger of being outflanked by an assault on the First Platoon.

North of the knoll, in the broken country to the right of Sergeant Scott, the North Vietnamese were embroiled in an increasingly ferocious fight with the Third Platoon. Locked in mortal combat, the two sides savaged each other with rockets, rifles, and machine guns, blasting the surrounding jungle. Spc4 Donald Mesarosh, the happy-go-lucky RTO who had cheerfully announced how many days he had left in-country earlier that morning, remained in regular contact with the company CP, and every now and then he would leave the radio and distribute ammo to the grunts on the line. His buddy, Spc5 Richard Jackson, was low-crawling nearby when he stumbled on a soldier with a shotgun.

"Doc, I'm hit!" the man cried out suddenly. "I'm hit!"

"Where?" Jackson asked, looking the man over.

"In the back! I think I got hit twice in the back!"

Sitting up, Jackson slid behind the man and lifted up his shirt. Unable to find any wounds, and with desperate troopers screaming for help up and down the platoon line, Jackson ducked down—heavy small-arms fire was cutting across the jungle inches above his head—and shouted, "You're not hit! You're *not* hit!"

"I know I'm hit! I felt it! I got hit! I got hit!"

Jackson looked again and this time noticed two small wounds on the man's back. Strangely, neither wound appeared to be bleeding out. "I guess they fused—I don't know," said Jackson. "The only thing I can possibly think of is that we had snipers in the trees, and he [the wounded trooper] may have been hit at close range. That's the only thing I can think of. The bullets from the AK—that's usually what the gunshots were from—didn't have time to travel that far." Covering the wounds with a couple of gauze bandages, Jackson tossed the rest in his pack, grabbed his M-16, and told the trooper that he had to go. As he was low-crawling up the platoon line, it suddenly occurred to him that he "could have gone straight up in the air and *still* found someone to patch up."

Those that could fight did fight, however, and by 9:15 A.M. the First and Third Platoons, with help from the adjoining Second and Fourth Platoons, had defeated the second enemy assault. Forced to regroup, the NVA pulled back and pounded the perimeter with heavy rocket and sniper fire. "It seemed like they [RPGs] were everywhere," noted Pfc. Bill Perkins of the Fourth Platoon. "You could *hear* them. You could hear them hissing and burning as they came through the bush, and when they hit something they exploded. They would make a pretty big bang." Afraid, Perkins buzzed the bush from time to time with his M-16 to "at least act like I was trying to kill somebody and to keep their heads down if there was anybody around." Perkins also noticed a lot of smoke and movement in the jungle, and as the four platoons tightened up around the company CP after the second assault, the grunts killed a number of NVA who had fought their way inside the perimeter.[21]

While the grunts worked to clear the perimeter, Lt. Clay Johnson crawled over to Sgt. Michael Scott in the First Platoon. "Scotty, I need you to go down to the CP and get a radio," Johnson explained. "One of my radios got shot up and we need artillery.

It doesn't make any sense having them calling it in from down there. They can't see where we are up here. I can't let you use mine, because I've only got one left. Captain Powers is dead, but he's got three. Go down there and get one." Scott was to use that radio to call in artillery fire when he returned to the First Platoon.

There had been plenty of artillery support on that side of the perimeter during the first two assaults, but with Lieutenant Beckham—the senior FO attached to C Company—calling it in from the company CP, where it would have been difficult if not impossible to see the front lines of the First and Third Platoons, many of the rounds were falling *behind* the North Vietnamese. Johnson wanted to bring the artillery fire in closer, but he needed Scott to do it while he used his remaining radio to communicate with Sergeant Childers. Scott agreed that Johnson could not call in artillery fire and run the company on one radio. Scott also knew that Lieutenant Beckham would have trouble walking the artillery in from the company CP. Someone, though, had to help the black gunner on the M-60.

"I'll get somebody to feed the gun," Johnson assured him. "Don't worry."

Nodding, Scott slipped past Johnson and low-crawled down the slope to the company CP. After assisting with a wounded grunt, he reported to Sergeant Childers, who was talking on the radio at the time, and explained the situation. Scott then asked the first sergeant for a radio. "We'll find you one in a minute," Childers replied. "And watch that knob up there." Scott got his radio a few minutes later and started up the slope.

"Where are you going?" Childers asked.

"I'm going back to where Lieutenant Johnson is!" Scott shouted back.

As Scott pushed up the slope, the four C Company platoons tightened up the perimeter around the company CP and prepared for another assault. Pfc. Dan Shayotovich, conscious but still dizzy, his head throbbing from the two bullets that had slammed off his helmet, was on the radio. A Second Platoon replacement, Shayotovich remembered Sergeant Cox telling him to call in an air strike, but he had no idea what to say when the voice on the other end asked for the company's coordinates. Near the base of the knoll, Pfc. Dave Fessler, Shayotovich's friend and a fellow replacement, continued to watch the line of bushes in front of his position. Fessler was wearing his web gear and had grabbed a few belts of M-60 ammo that were lying on top of his pack, but he had left a bag full of magazines behind when he moved back up the slope with his squad. "Next time," he mumbled under his breath, "I'm going through my damn pack first."

Crawling behind the Third Platoon line, Spc5 Richard Jackson found another medic, Pfc. Richard Mason, huddled behind a tree. Good friends, the two men stopped for a moment to talk. "We were both black guys but I think all of the color had drained out of our faces," said Jackson. "We were scared *shitless*, man. Both of us were shaking like leaves, [and] we talked about how fucked up the situation was and how many guys were getting hurt." The two medics were still talking—Jackson nose deep in the dirt, Mason behind the tree—when Jackson suddenly heard and felt a loud *crack*. Terrified, he immediately began pawing at the left side of his face. "I'm hit!" he hollered. "I'm hit in the face!" Mason pulled Jackson's hand from his face and looked for a gunshot wound. "You're not—you're not hit!"

Jackson glanced down at his dirty left hand and was shocked to discover that it was not covered in blood. Mason was right. The round had missed him. "The rifle shot must have come so close between me and that tree that I felt the velocity of it," Jackson recalled. "That's the only thing I can imagine, because I heard it and felt it. But I wasn't hit." Frightened by the near miss, Jackson snatched his pack and crawled away from the tree as fast as he could.

Winded, the small patrol led by Spc4 Bob "Panch" Gamboa scampered up Hill 521 and dashed into the B Company NDP. Nearby troops from Lt. Richard Schell's Second Platoon were clearing an LZ on the side of the hill. Digging in, Gamboa learned that the rest of the Fourth Platoon had been sent down to help C Company. Lieutenant Marinovich, however, had ordered his patrol to stay put, presumably to protect the LZ in the event of an enemy attack

Flanked by the First and Third Platoons, Gamboa's Fourth Platoon had moved down the main ridge in an arrow formation. Lt. Rick Nelson, listening to the "crack and thump" of bullets snapping through the brush, concluded that "there was one hell of a battle going on" below them. Mortar rounds were exploding in the canopy above the platoon, and at one point he stumbled and twisted the same surgically repaired knee that he had injured in college. Following the ridge down the hill, past the bodies of dead enemy soldiers, the Fourth began taking fire from enemy snipers in the trees. Nelson, however, did not know if the North Vietnamese had deliberately dispatched snipers to block his platoon, or if they were simply part of a larger effort to encircle C Company.

Half running, half crawling, Sgt. Larry Jumper, twenty-one, one of the fastest men in the Fourth Platoon, crashed through the jungle in a final, frantic push to reach the C Company perimeter, now only thirty yards away. Jumper, dodging tracer rounds slicing down through the canopy, laced the treetops with his M-16. Tightly knit, his squad of mostly black and white draftees did their best to keep pace. The platoon medic, Spc4 Ronyal Jacobs, had been out on a patrol that morning but had made it back in time to accompany the troops down the hill. Raised in Columbia, South Carolina, Jacobs, twenty-one, figured that someone was bound to get hit before they got to C Company.

B Company's First Platoon, meanwhile, was moving quickly but cautiously alongside the main ridge when the jungle suddenly erupted in small-arms fire. Attacked by a small enemy force, the platoon took up defensive positions and returned fire. Pfc. Gary Retana, taking cover in the brush, fired at puffs of smoke and at any sign of movement in the jungle around the platoon. The North Vietnamese punched back with AK-47s and SKSs, and one round smashed into the tree next to him. Stung by small bits of shattered bark that flew into his eye, Retana got up and moved behind a large tree stump.

Farther along than the First Platoon, Lieutenant Marinovich and his hastily assembled relief force had also run into heavy small-arms fire near the C Company perimeter. Marinovich, not sure where the fire was coming from, stayed on the horn with Sergeant Childers, who did his best to relay where the NVA were located in relation to the two companies. Several men were wounded coming down the hill but the group, reduced at that point to crawling on all fours, pressed doggedly on. "We're coming," Marinovich shouted into the radio, hoping to reassure Childers that help was on the way. "We're coming and we'll be there as fast as we can!"

Doggedly defending their positions on the side of Hill 521, the four C Company platoons had turned back a second enemy ground assault by 9:15 A.M. Twenty minutes after the second assault, however, the North Vietnamese charged out of the jungle from the west-southwest and, heavily supported by RPGs, attacked the perimeter again.[22] Hissing angrily across the slope, the enemy rockets exploded among the huddling Dragoons, hurling shrapnel and debris in every direction. "They were using big stuff then," said Sgt. Michael Scott. "They had to be using rockets, either that or they were using mortars. There was shit blowing up everywhere."

Much louder, Scott recalled, than the previous attack, the third assault on the C Company perimeter, its initial momentum broken by heavy defensive fires, quickly devolved into another hellish exchange of rocket, rifle, and machine-gun fire."I remember thinking [at one point] that it couldn't get any worse than *this*, but it could and it did," said Pfc. Dan Shayotovich. "I used to watch war movies when I was a little boy, and I would envision myself there and it's *nothing* like the movies. Everything is real and it's final." Queasy, the bump above his left brow throbbing, Shayotovich manned the radio and watched while a blizzard of leaves and twigs rained down on the Second Platoon.

Forced to attack uphill in some areas, the NVA tried to put more troops in the trees, presumably to bring more effective direct fire down on the C Company perimeter. Many were killed while climbing into position. The assault, however, continued. Low-crawling along the Third Platoon line, Pfc. Russell Belden had bullet holes in his shirt and one pant leg, and a round had knocked his helmet off his head. *Jesus Christ*, he thought to himself as he searched for cover, *there's gotta be a machine gun out there for this much shit to be coming in.*

Some of it was from enemy snipers, and the steady crack of rifle fire followed Belden and Spc5 Richard Jackson as they moved through the brush. Jackson was wriggling across the jungle floor on his belly, trying to get out of the line of fire, when he suddenly felt a sharp pain in his right leg, as if someone had just slammed a nail through the back of his thigh. "I'm hit!" he yelped in agony.

Jackson, remembering that *he* was the platoon medic, whirled around and checked the back of his leg for blood. *Good*, he thought, *at least I'm not bleeding out*. The gunshot had pierced the flesh just below his right buttock, but the wound did not appear especially serious. For a moment, he considered crawling back to Spc4 Richard Mason, but he was too far away at that point to turn around. If he kept moving forward, though, he was certain he would find someone who could put a dressing on his wound.

Fierce firefights continued around the C Company perimeter. In the Second Platoon, the rippling crack of an AK-47 sent Sgt. Erin Stroh, a squad leader in the platoon, scurrying behind a small shrub. Stroh, peeking through the branches of the shrub, was amazed to see Lt. Jack Cannello racing up the hill toward the modest clearing above the platoon. Cannello charged in to the clearing then sank to his knees, dropped, some believe, by a burst of machine-gun fire. "I'm hit! Help me!"

Stroh thought about rushing over to help but quickly reconsidered. Rifle fire had already stripped the leaves off the shrub he was hiding behind, and there was just too much hill and not enough cover between him and the wounded lieutenant. "I'll get you in a minute," Stroh yelled out from behind the shrub. "Lay down and play dead, and I'll come and get you in a minute!" Stroh then clambered up the damp slope, beyond the sparsely covered area to the right of the clearing, and slipped into some bushes.

Stroh waited there for a while then crept back down the slope. Crouching down in the brush, he gazed out onto the clearing and suddenly felt his heart skip a beat. *Where the hell did he go*? Stroh wondered as he scanned the empty clearing. *He was right there!* Lieutenant Cannello, he finally concluded, had either crawled off on his own or had been pulled to safety by another grunt. Stroh, worried that he would be next if he waited there any longer, checked the clearing one last time—there was no sign of Cannello anywhere in the tall grass—then scuttled back up the slope.[23]

Scuffling along on their hands and knees, the harried B Company troopers closed on the C Company perimeter at 9:35 A.M., just as the North Vietnamese were attacking across the hill.[24] 1st Lt. Branko Marinovich, in command of the small, hastily assembled relief force, had been talking to C Company over the radio and whoever was on the other end at the time—Marinovich could not recall if it was Sergeant Childers or his RTO—was trying to tell him where the NVA were located. "And that's when I started to use my forward observer to bring in artillery," said Marinovich. "What I felt was that Charlie Company was all hunkered down with no command and control left, other than [individual] units just defending themselves. So when I came in, I started bringing in indirect fire." Marinovich also requested gunships and fixed-wing air support.

Thrown together at the last minute, Marinovich's small relief force had beaten the First, Third, and Fourth Platoons down the hill. Marinovich had kept in contact with his three platoon leaders on the way down, but with C Company under assault and only twenty to thirty grunts from his group there to assist, the situation was becoming increasingly dire. "Where are you?" Marinovich thundered over the radio. "Why aren't you here yet?"

His First and Fourth Platoons had made contact with the NVA but were pushing on toward the C Company perimeter. Slowed by a slew of downed trees and thick, thorny vines, Lieutenant Berg's Third Platoon had apparently fallen behind. "We're doing the best we can to get to you and C Company," Bill Berg told Marinovich, "but we've run into some thick stuff and some wait-a-minute vines with thorns. Some of the guys have gotten scratched up pretty bad. We're having a hard time getting through it."

"Goddammit!" Marinovich barked angrily. "I don't care if the thorns rip your skin off! C Company's in trouble! Now get your ass down here and quit making excuses!"

Marinovich would later acknowledge that he "kind of lost control of the platoons and where everyone was at" when he approached the C Company perimeter. His own group, moreover, was having trouble linking up with the perimeter, so he switched radios and got back on the horn with the C Company CP. Marinovich wanted C Company to mark the perimeter with smoke grenades and then report where the North Vietnamese were located in relation to the smoke. C Company quickly agreed and began popping smoke on that side of the perimeter.

"We're getting fire north of the smoke!" yelled one C Company trooper.

"They're northeast of the smoke!" bellowed another.

Lost in the thick undergrowth, Marinovich and his men, some still on their hands and knees, followed the colored smoke billowing up through the jungle and inched closer to the perimeter. As the group moved warily forward, few if any knew where the North Vietnamese were located. "The truth is that it was massively confusing, and the real challenge was trying to figure out what was going on while we were trying to fix the enemy. The best that we could do was [listen] to C Company, and some of my own people, but we really were guessing as to where the enemy was," said Marinovich. "We kept getting incoming fire, but it was hard to tell where it was coming from. In fact, it got so damn frustrating that, in my command group, I was handling two or three radios and I was still getting shots fired my way. I was getting frustrated because I had a hard time figuring out where it was coming from." Marinovich also radioed his First, Third, and Fourth Platoons. C Company was starting to panic, he told his three platoon leaders. If they didn't hurry up, the North Vietnamese would probably overrun C Company *and* the small relief force he had led down the hill.

Hunched low, radios squawking in his ear, Marinovich eventually noticed that some of the rounds were kicking up dirt around him. "Spread out and keep going," he shouted to his small group. "Try to get to C Company." Not one to lead from the rear, Marinovich pressed on with his RTOs, the company FO, and a medic. *Follow the smoke*, he reminded himself as he moved through the underbrush toward the C Company perimeter, *and watch out for friendlies.*

Pinned down shortly thereafter by heavy enemy fire, Marinovich was weighing his options—he and his FO were already calling in artillery fire—when he spotted what he thought was a North Vietnamese soldier perched in a distant tree. Without thinking, Marinovich leaped to his feet and emptied his M-16 in to the tree. As he was slapping in a fresh magazine, however, a bullet slammed into his rifle right below the carrying handle, shattering the weapon.

Pieces of the shattered rifle sliced through Marinovich's left hand, all but severing his left thumb, and for a moment the shaken B Company commander stared numbly at the bloody digit dangling from his wrist. Tenuously attached to the rest of his hand by a small flap of skin, his thumb looked like a prop from a horror movie. There were also bits of metal lodged in his left shoulder. Marinovich then realized that he was still standing, completely exposed to enemy fire, and immediately crouched back down. The medic attached to the group hurried over and, placing Marinovich's left thumb inside the palm of his left hand, wrapped the entire area with bandages.

Severely wounded, his tiny command group pinned down somewhere near the C Company perimeter, Marinovich waited anxiously for help to arrive. The fate of the men under his command, he now feared, depended on the three B Company platoons rumbling down the slope.

18 TURNING THE TIDE

Fought to a standstill, the North Vietnamese—later identified as the 6th Battalion of the 32nd NVA Regiment, according to American intelligence—had charged sideways across the hill for the third time that morning, only to have the momentum of their assault broken once again by heavy defensive fires.[1] During the fighting, however, the NVA managed to set up on the small knoll behind C Company. From the crest of the knoll, the attackers were able to fire directly into the American perimeter. "Get the high ground," a worried MSgt. Richard Childers shouted from the company CP. "We've got to get the high ground."[2]

Lt. Clay Johnson, C Company's acting CO, decided to attack the knoll. "He came over and he was talking [about] how he was going to do this, and he was going to do that, and I'm thinking—gosh, this guy's pretty squared away," recalled Pfc. Dave Fessler. "He wasn't scared at all. I started to feel a little better, and I started thinking that I might survive [because] this guy's doing alright. He kind of gave everyone else the feeling that—hey, we can do this." Johnson then told Fessler and some of the other grunts in his squad to get on-line, because they were going to assault the NVA on the knoll. Once the assault started, every third man was to fire on automatic. *We're gonna get on-line and attack them?* Fessler thought to himself, the can-do optimism he had felt only moments before suddenly vanishing. *Man, that sounds pretty stupid.*

Warily moving into position, Fessler switched his M-16 to automatic and waited for the assault to begin. Lieutenant Johnson, gazing back over his shoulder at the grubby, sweat-soaked grunts standing behind him, raised his right hand and shouted, "Follow me, men!" Lurching forward, the line of First, Second, and Fourth Platoon troopers started up the slope of the knoll.[3] "We would shoot and then stop, shoot and then stop," said Fessler. "That's kind of how it was." Spc4 Edward Renck watched the grunt in front of him collapse in a hail of bullets. Renck, a Second Platoon original from Spokane,

Washington, eyeballed the enemy soldier who had shot the man and quickly returned fire. A bullet then smashed through Renck's rifle, tearing off one of his fingers.[4] To the left of Renck, an enemy mortar round knocked some of the grunts in the Fourth Platoon to the ground. Plt. Sgt. Paul Ingram stopped to assist the dazed troopers. Ingram had caught a round in the chest during the fighting but incredibly, the bullet, likely at the end of its trajectory, burrowed harmlessly into his skin, leaving his internals undamaged.

The hastily planned attack on the knoll was eventually halted by heavy enemy fire. Pfc. Dave Fessler, firing from a prone position to the right of Lieutenant Johnson, banged away at the NVA on automatic, unaware at first that most of the rounds were slamming into the dirt in front of him. Sheepishly adjusting his M-16, Private First Class Fessler, worried that he would run out of ammo if he wasn't careful, buzzed the bushes upslope, then flipped the selector switch on his rifle back to semi-automatic. A Fourth Platoon grunt to the left of him stood up at one point and spotted the enemy machine gun on the knoll, but before he could get off a shot, the crew opened fire, forcing him to drop back down. There were three NVA on the knoll, the grunt blurted breathlessly, but he could not get at them without standing up again. The two artillery batteries providing close support, moreover, were having a difficult time hitting the knoll with accurate shellfire.[5]

North Vietnamese mortar rounds, meanwhile, were exploding in the canopy above the C Company perimeter. Private First Class Fessler heard something coming in—what it was, he could not say for certain—and was abruptly lifted off the jungle floor by a loud explosion. Slamming back down, Fessler, half dazed, his ears ringing, turned to the grunt to his left. Shrapnel from the blast had hit the man in the eye, ears, and shoulder, and he looked as if he had been knocked unconscious. Pfc. Rodolfo Perez, lying to the right of Fessler, knew the wounded man and immediately wriggled over to help. "Medic!" Perez shouted frantically. "Medic!"

Perez then noticed the horribly burned remains of Lieutenant Johnson. Blown apart in the blast, Johnson had been hit—some say in the chest—by a B-40 rocket, not an 82-mm mortar round.[6] Shocked, Perez told Fessler that Johnson had been killed. Fessler, convinced that if he saw the lieutenant's charred remains he would never be able to forget it, refused to look. "Don't need to see that," he mumbled to himself. "Don't want to see that." Dead at twenty-one, Clayton Winslow Johnson was posthumously awarded the Silver Star.

Sent down to the company CP to retrieve a radio for Lieutenant Johnson, Sgt. Michael Scott returned to the First Platoon after the attack on the knoll. Scott, hunkered down behind a tree, noted that the black machine gunner had moved and had taken the M-60 with him. Several dead Americans were lying on the slope of the knoll. In front of the dead Americans, he noticed four or five dead NVA. Another ten or twelve were lying farther up the slope. Slowly piecing it all together, Scott deduced that the grunts had tried to take the knoll while he was down at the CP retrieving the radio. Some of the fighting, he heard, had been hand-to-hand.

Scott stared glumly at the burned body lying in the brush. He was still staring when a voice somewhere off to the right called out, "Yes—that's Lieutenant Johnson."

"You've got to be kidding me," he replied incredulously.

"No."

"Well, I'm the only one here. There's nobody here but me."

Out of nowhere, a second voice chimed in—Scott did not recognize either voice—and offered to send some troops. A few minutes later three men moved into position to his right. Sergeant Ingram then had a couple of grunts take up positions to his left. Scott, part of the artillery forward observer team attached to C Company, had come back with a radio to call in artillery fire for Lieutenant Johnson. Lt. Ronald Beckham, the senior FO attached to the company, was having a hard time locating the front lines of the First and Third Platoons from the company CP, and a lot of the direct support they were receiving was landing *behind* the North Vietnamese. Beckham, Johnson had told Scott, could not adjust the incoming fire as effectively as an observer attached to either of the two platoons. Johnson would have done it himself, but he needed his remaining radio to communicate with Sergeant Childers, the company's first sergeant. With a second radio, though, Scott could call in fire missions and make adjustments from the front line.

Scott could hear the crunching thud of artillery rounds landing on the other side of the knoll. Confused as to who was firing what and where, Scott contacted the artillery and requested a cease-fire. "They were firing three different batteries at once, and I couldn't tell which was which," he recalled. "So I told them to cease fire and [then] only shoot one artillery battery at a time so I could determine who was who. And I told them that I wanted to talk to someone direct." Shortly thereafter, an enemy mortar round or RPG exploded in the jungle behind him, spraying the backs of his legs with shrapnel and debris.

While Scott sorted out C Company's artillery support, news of Lieutenant Johnson's death eventually reached Sergeant Childers at the company CP. Childers had nearly been killed himself when an NVA machine gun buzzed the bushes above his head. "I could watch the leaves fall from the wind of the bullets," he recounted. "After a while I said the hell with it. If you're going to get it, you're going to get it. That's the way I always felt about it. If it's your turn, I don't care if you're driving or walking down the street or what it is. It's just your turn, and that's all there is to it."[7] Childers, now helmetless, both of his hands sliced and swollen from enemy shrapnel, was doing what he could to hold the company together when word came in that Johnson, the last able-bodied officer in the company, had been killed by a rocket. Next in line, the Ohio native got on the horn and calmly announced that he was assuming command of the company. Childers then notified the battalion TOC.[8]

Curiously, there is still some debate as to *when* Sergeant Childers assumed command of C Company. According to an article written by John T. Wheeler, the Associated Press reporter attached to C Company that morning, the NVA ambushed the company during a rest break and "within minutes all its officers were dead or too badly wounded to act." Wheeler, who had been humping the bush with the Dragoons for a possible feature story on the daily life of an American infantry company, wrote that after Powers had been killed, Childers "announced over the radio that he had taken command."[9] Subsequent accounts of the battle, perhaps piggybacking off Wheeler's gripping dispatch, tell a similar tale.[10]

These accounts, however, directly contradict the battalion after-action report (AAR) and the testimony of several key veterans. In describing the opening moments of the battle, the AAR noted that "the Company Commander, Captain Powers, was killed in the initial action and Lieutenant Johnson assumed command." Later, the report states that "Lieutenant Johnson, the acting C Company commander was killed during the third ground attack. Command of the company was assumed by 1SGT Childers."[11] Sgt. Michael Scott, meanwhile, remembers fetching a radio for Lieutenant Johnson *before* Sergeant Childers assumed command of the company, and Pfc. Dave Fessler vividly recalls the young lieutenant organizing the ill-fated counterattack on the knoll. "Childers was a hero and so was Johnson, but no one ever talks about him [Johnson]," said Spc4 Don Tienhaara, a Fourth Platoon original who heard Childers telling Johnson to take over the company. "He [Lieutenant Johnson] was like John Wayne out there. Johnson and Childers were like John Wayne '1' and John Wayne '2.'"

The moist, tropical air reeked of gunpowder and freshly overturned jungle. Mortar rounds were hitting the hill from the south and west, and the crack of gunfire rattled ominously across the slope.[12] Thirty yards from the C Company perimeter, Sgt. Larry Jumper, half running, half crawling, dropped down behind the body of a dead North Vietnamese soldier. Jumper, a twenty-one-year-old squad leader in B Company's Fourth Platoon, crept cautiously forward, often crawling from body to body, until he eventually reached the perimeter. A wounded grunt with a shotgun was lying nearby. "There was a world of them [shotgun shells] around him and I could still smell that shotgun smoke," said Jumper. "There were also about ten to fifteen dead NVA to his front. I think he may have helped hold them off [because] there were so many dead people in front of him. Where he had been shooting, there were a lot of bodies." Chillingly, most of the enemy dead had been killed at close range.

Jumper approached the wounded grunt. Bookish-looking with pale skin, strawberry blonde hair, and thick glasses, Spc4 Richard Wilkins—"Radar" to the grunts in C Company's Second Platoon—was helping his squad leader close a dangerous gap in the company line when the NVA shot him in the chest.[13] While Jumper looked on, a medic came by to give Wilkins a shot of morphine, but there was little else he could do for the well-liked original. Wilkins would later die on Hill 521. Honored with a full military funeral, he was posthumously awarded the Silver Star.

Spc4 Ronyal Jacobs joined Jumper inside the C Company perimeter. Jacobs, then a skinny African American medic attached to B Company's Fourth Platoon, wrinkled his nose as the acrid stench of gun smoke filled his nostrils. Green tracer rounds were snapping through the underbrush, and he was assailed from all sides with endless cries of "Medic! Medic!" Forgetting the piece of shrapnel lodged in his right arm—a mortar round or stray artillery shell had caught him on the way down the hill—Jacobs slipped off his rucksack and began treating the wounded. One injured trooper led to another, and after a while he grew numb to the noise and the nameless, faceless figures around him. "I was functioning but I think I was out of it," noted Jacobs. "All I know is that people were calling me, and I was going where they were. The rounds that were moving through the air? I didn't even pay any attention to them. I heard them cutting the air, and I heard the rockets buzzing." Nothing, not even the *whoosh-bang* of incoming B-40 rockets, seemed to distract the South Carolina native as he moved from grunt to grunt.[14]

Shot in the back of the leg, Spc5 Richard Jackson spotted Jacobs crawling toward him and yelled, "I'm hit!"

"Where?" Jacobs asked.

"In the ass!"

Jacobs, wriggling over to Jackson, ripped open his pants, looked at the wound, and gasped, "Oh shit!"

"How bad is it, Jake?" Jackson stammered.

"Not bad, Rich, not bad."

A lump began to form in Jackson's throat. *Why did he say, 'Oh shit!' if it wasn't that bad?* he wondered. *Did my leg fall off while I was crawling away? Is it still attached but only connected by a couple of tendons?*

"Everything's still intact," Jacobs responded reassuringly, "and we'll get you patched up right away." Sprawled out on the slope, scratches on both his hands and knees from crawling up and down the Third Platoon line, Jackson waited quietly while Jacobs finished bandaging the wound. The two medics then parted ways, Jackson dragging his rifle, rucksack, and right leg behind him.

Marching alongside the main ridge running down the hill, B Company's First Platoon, led by Lt. Fletcher Bass, had run into a small but determined enemy force near the C Company perimeter. "We met quite a bit of resistance and it wasn't resistance of just scattered people," said Pfc. Gary Retana. "It seemed like a nice, organized group that was trying to prevent us from hooking up with C Company. They put enough firepower against us that, once we took cover and started firing back, it took us a little while to start moving from one location to another." Scattered by the initial burst of enemy fire, the platoon had regrouped and was now advancing on-line, the grunts firing from behind trees and bushes as they moved forward.[15]

Private First Class Retana, before continuing on down the hill, examined the bodies of several North Vietnamese soldiers he found lying on the slope. *Not going to jump up and shoot me in the back*, he mused as he checked the bodies to make sure that the men were actually dead. *I know all about you sneaky little bastards.* Retana discovered that, in addition to being dead, all of the NVA were wearing mismatched clothing and either boots or sandals on their feet. One man, for example, was wearing a khaki-colored tunic with black pajama pants and a straw hat.

Pushing the North Vietnamese back, Lieutenant Bass's First Platoon closed on the C Company perimeter from the north-northeast. Smart, disciplined fighting had put the perimeter within reach, but it was not altogether clear what the grunts were supposed to do when they got there. Private First Class Retana reached the C Company line and slid behind a log. "Don't go there!" shouted a grunt to his right. "That's where I got shot!" Startled, Retana scrambled behind another log and immediately noticed two dead C Company soldiers lying nearby. Both men had been shot in the head near the top of the skull.

Convinced that an NVA sniper hiding in the trees had shot the two men, Retana scanned the canopy, eventually stopping on a tall tree about fifty feet from the dead GIs. Way up high, near the top of the tree, he spotted what looked like a man's boot, half-hidden in the leaves and branches. Sitting up, Retana swung the M-72 LAW he had carried down the hill onto his shoulder and squeezed the trigger. Moments later the top of the tree disappeared in a cloud of smoke and debris. "It was a semi–Fourth of July," recounted Retana. "Once it hit the tree, the tree exploded and all I saw basically was the smoke. Once the smoke cleared, then I could see that I had taken out about four feet off the top of the tree. When I saw that foot, there were no ifs, ands, or buts about it. That was one of the reasons why I took it [the LAW] with me. I hated that LAW rocket and wanted to get rid of it anyway." Satisfied, Retana tossed the tube aside and picked up his M-16.

Meanwhile, to the left of the First Platoon, on the opposite side of the main ridge, Lt. Bill Berg's Third Platoon had climbed out of a shallow gully and was continuing west-southwest, toward the C Company perimeter. Delayed earlier that morning by thick, thorny vines and fallen trees, the Third was moving down the slope in a column when the troops upfront started taking small-arms fire. Berg halted the column long enough to put his people on-line, then pushed forward into the enemy fire.

Side by side, the young Third Platoon troopers engaged the NVA in a rolling firefight. Pfc. Larry Orr, age twenty, half a world away from the ranch his family owned in Wyoming, crept through the jungle in a low crouch. Orr fired mostly at sounds—the terrain, tall trees, and thick brush concealed the NVA—and kept moving, hurried along by the steady crack of small-arms fire. Occasionally, an RPG would streak across the jungle and explode in a fiery ball. Close enough to hear the muffled blasts, Orr moved quickly from one tree and bush to the next, and as he approached the perimeter, some of the C Company grunts began laying down covering fire for the platoon.

Orr, aware that the Third Platoon had been in contact with C Company, broke into a dead sprint. Legs churning, he covered the final twenty to thirty yards of jungled slope as fast as he could and dove behind a mound of dirt inside the perimeter. "We just kind of fell in with them [C Company]," he recalled. "They knew where we were, and we knew where they were. We had been talking with them." Safe behind the mound of dirt, Orr asked a few of the C Company grunts where the NVA were located. "They're in the jungle," the grunts replied uneasily, "and there's an awful lot of them. They've got good weapons, but we'll be okay if we can keep them out of the perimeter."

Capably led, the three B Company platoons had finally reached the C Company perimeter. *When* they arrived, however, is not entirely clear.[16] "I honestly never knew when they [the three platoons] got there or even if they got there," said 1st Lt. Branko Marinovich, B Company's CO. "I was so involved in my own thing—calling in artillery, communicating with Sergeant Childers—that I don't know if their getting to C Company was ever communicated directly to me. I was really only communicating with my artillery and Sergeant Childers at that point." Squeezing in wherever they could, the B Company troopers merged with the existing C Company perimeter, often with very little direction.

As the B Company troopers moved in to the perimeter, C Company informed the battalion TOC that the two companies had linked up. Drizzly overcast skies and the close proximity of the two forces on the hill adversely affected American air support, but with nearly two companies now in or around the perimeter, North Vietnamese hopes for a swift decision were beginning to fade.[17]

MSgt. Richard Childers sat, radios crackling, in the center of the C Company perimeter and surveyed the action. C Company, on its own, had held off a much larger enemy force for nearly forty minutes without air strikes or the type of close-in artillery support companies in contact had come to expect in Vietnam. Outnumbered, the Dragoons—many of them reluctant draftees—had fought tenaciously, erasing any doubts he might have had about their ability to perform under fire.

Restless, Childers set up resupply points for ammo and water and helped pull wounded men to safety.[18] The troops seemed pretty well tied in, and most of B Company had made it down the hill. The small knoll was still in North Vietnamese hands, however, and an enemy machine gun was hammering the Third Platoon. Childers knew that he had to push the NVA off the knoll, so he sent a grunt up to the First Platoon to talk to Sgt. Michael Scott. Scurrying off with a PRC-25, the man found Scott lying behind a tree.

"The gooks got a machine gun up there and the Third Platoon can't do anything," the man blurted excitedly. "The gun ain't hitting 'em, but it's keeping 'em down. They can't fight!"

Scott, using the radio the man had carried up from the company CP, contacted Childers, who confirmed that an enemy machine gun on the knoll—Scott could hear it but couldn't see it—had pinned the Third Platoon down. Childers wanted Scott to take out the gun and capture the knoll.

Nearby, Pfc. Dave Fessler thought he heard someone yelling something about another attack on the knoll. "I got up and started moving up the [knoll]," said Fessler. "When I started looking around, I realized there wasn't anybody else moving with me. I don't know if maybe I had misheard something, but I was the only one who got up." Stunned to see a line of grunts lying on the slope behind him, Fessler raced up the shoulder of the knoll alone and hid in some bushes. Breathless, he paused there for a moment, then began picking his way through the vines and branches tugging at his dirty fatigues. Stopping behind a big tree, he noticed a well-worn trail, three feet wide and recently travelled, running across the jungle floor.[19]

Fessler decided to take cover behind another large tree on the other side of the trail, but as soon as he moved, the NVA raked the area with AK-47s. Chased across the trail, Fessler curled up in a ball behind the second tree and waited, bullets ripping off chunks of bark above his head, for the firing to die down. His hip began to cramp up, but after awhile the AK-47s and SKSs fell silent. Scrambling to his feet, he was about to dash back down the shoulder of the knoll when the firing started again.

Startled by the sudden gunfire, Fessler slid back down the tree, his ailing hip tightening into a knot. *I don't give a shit if my hip does hurt*, he told himself. *I'm running the next time they stop shooting.* When the firing stopped shortly thereafter, he dashed across the trail, past the first big tree, and into a thicket of bushes. Full of sharp, clingy thorns, the bushes ripped his helmet off and scratched his face as he stumbled forward, twisting and turning, through the undergrowth. Regaining his footing, he yanked his M-16 out of the thorny bushes and turned around. "I remember looking up and seeing them [the grunts at the bottom of the knoll], and I just kind of noticed that they all had their rifles pointed toward me," said Fessler. "I saw the spot where I had been, and the ground was kind of smooth there so I ran down the small hill and took a big dive. I landed on my belly and slid down the hill. I got caught on something, slid around, and then just stopped." Moments later a helmet rolled down the slope. Fessler, surprised to see his steel pot again, picked it up and put it on his head.

Pfc. Wilson Barnett stared at Fessler from behind the barrel of his M-60. "Damn—we almost shot you!" exclaimed the young machine gunner. "We thought you were dead!"

Above them, on the crest of the small knoll, the North Vietnamese machine gun Sergeant Childers desperately wanted to silence was still firing down on C Company's Third Platoon. The gun was not doing any real damage to the platoon, but the heavy fire was enough to keep the grunts pinned down. Meanwhile, in the First Platoon, Sgt. Michael Scott and the grunt Childers had sent up from the company CP managed to slither farther up the slope of the knoll without drawing any fire. Two C Company soldiers had heard Scott talking to Childers over the radio—Scott, the soldier from the CP, and the two C Company grunts were all within eight to ten feet of one another—and had moved up the slope with him.

Scott, gazing up at the wooded crest, heard the enemy gun firing but could not find it in the brush. A young rifleman from Sergeant Ingram's Fourth Platoon advised Scott that he had stood up earlier in the battle and had seen the gun and three North Vietnamese soldiers. "If you can put enough fire up there," the grunt said confidently, "and if I stand up, I can shoot one of them." Scott readily agreed, and while the four of them sprayed the crest with M-16s, the grunt from the Fourth Platoon darted behind another tree, stood up, and shot one of the North Vietnamese. Mortally wounded, the NVA rolled down the slope to the right. A second NVA soldier popped into view, but before he could drop back down or scurry off into the brush, Scott, the three troopers with him, and the grunt from the Fourth opened fire, sending the man tumbling down the slope.

Scott and the four grunts scanned the knoll for the third NVA, but after a while they began to suspect that the man had either been wounded or had already fled. Tired of waiting, the five Americans started up the slope, Scott carrying the radio he had borrowed from the C Company CP. Moving from tree to tree, the group passed the two dead NVA and reached the crest of the knoll. There they found a Soviet RPD light machine gun and drums of ammunition. Scott called Sergeant Childers on the radio and reported that they had knocked out the enemy gun and taken the knoll. The knoll was secure, he informed Childers, but there were only five of them holding it. "I'll try to send some men," Childers replied, "but they're still attacking us hard from the southwest and west."

Childers then explained that since the Third Platoon could now move around again, Scott and the four C Company grunts would have to hold the knoll until reinforcements arrived. At Scott's direction, the grunts set up four Claymore mines to cover the partial clearing below the crest of the knoll, then took up defensive positions in the brush.

Harried by the heavy enemy fire sweeping through C Company's Third Platoon, Pfc. Russell Belden crawled out into the open and immediately stopped. *Well, this was dumb,* he thought to himself as he glanced around the relatively bare, treeless stretch of slope. *I gotta get out of here.* Belden had run out of grenades, and no matter where he went he could not escape the snap and crack of rifle rounds. The twenty-one-year-old original had bullet holes in his loose-fitting fatigues, and one round had knocked his helmet off of his head.

As Belden began inching backward, out of the open area, he accidentally bumped into a small sapling. The swaying sapling attracted the attention of the NVA, who promptly swept the area with AK-47s and SKSs. Caught in the open, Belden was hit five times, all in the rear end. Three of the five rounds tore through his hip. The remaining two went through his abdomen. "The bullets hit me so hard and there were so many that hit me all at once," said Belden. "It flipped me backwards and I sort of rose up into the air and then fell forward. When I fell forward, I hit the ground real hard. Then they started shooting some more, and they shot me in the back." The last round, after skimming the surface of his skin, left a long flesh wound on his back.

Knocked crooked, Belden collapsed in front of the small sapling. There were some other Third Platoon troopers nearby, Sergeant Allman among them, but he could not bring himself to crawl over the sapling—his legs had become partly entangled in its branches—and into the underbrush where they were lying. "I wasn't scared at all during the battle, what I would call a firefight, but after I got shot that's when I experienced the *fear,*" he recalled. "I guess at that point I realized that I was in a battle." Crumpled up in a heap, Belden waited for the fear to pass then wriggled out of the open area, dragging his legs behind him.

Belden was still crawling into position when he accidentally brushed up against Sergeant Allman's pant leg. "Move over!" Allman barked angrily, upset that the wounded private had wriggled up beside him in the middle of a firefight. Thick-skinned, Belden slid over without saying a word.

Countless smaller battles, many involving only a handful of soldiers on each side, continued along the C Company line as the North Vietnamese, bloodied but unbeaten after nearly an hour of heavy fighting, pushed and probed the weary Dragoons. Often the battles pitted grunts on the ground against NVA snipers in the trees. In the Second Platoon, not far from Pfc. Dan Shayotovich, a young black trooper named Paul Toby had gotten up onto his knees and was blazing away with an M-16. Suddenly, Toby's arms went limp and his head slumped forward. Bleeding from the mouth, the young black trooper had been shot in the face.

Enraged, Shayotovich glared up into the canopy, convinced that an enemy sniper had shot Toby. "You fucker," he mumbled to himself. "I'll gut you for that!" His head ached, however, and the whole right side of his body felt weak and uncoordinated. He knew that the sniper was still up there somewhere, just waiting to shoot some other poor bastard in the face, and all he could do was turn the knobs on his PRC-25 radio. Dizzy from the two bullets that had smacked off his helmet earlier in the battle, Shayotovich, feeling helpless, slumped back down beside his pack.

While Shayotovich sat and seethed, a black grunt named John Logan rushed forward to rescue Paul Toby. "Stuff was flying through the air when Logan went up there and pulled Toby down and then dragged him away," said Shayotovich. "I'm here to tell you that *that* was above and beyond. He [Logan] looked at me as he was dragging him away, and I don't know what he thought, but I couldn't do it because I just didn't have any coordination. There really aren't enough awards to give that guy, though." Courageously, Logan had risked his own life to save Toby's.

Shayotovich, relieved that someone had pulled Toby to safety, returned to the chatter crackling over the radio. Dirt from a burst of enemy rifle fire flew up in his face, and for a split second he caught a glimpse of something moving in the trees. Holding his M-16 in his left hand, he leaned to one side and, using his pack for support, ripped off a magazine on automatic. With the same hand, he discarded the spent magazine, slid in a new one, and sprayed the trees again. "I never saw a man and I cannot confirm that I shot a guy in the tree," noted Shayotovich, "but I know that it [dirt flying up in his face] stopped." The sniper, he figured, had most likely been killed, wounded, or had found another tree to hide in.

Nearly an hour into the battle, C Company reported that it was still receiving significant sniper and mortar fire from the south, southwest, and west.[20] Plt. Sgt. Paul Cox, who had been appointed first sergeant when Sergeant Childers assumed command of the company, low-crawled across the slope and retrieved the packs of dead soldiers. Cox, always thinking ahead, wanted the packs so that he could distribute extra water and ammo to the able-bodied survivors on the line.[21] Spit-and-polish, the kind of old school NCO Childers could relate to, Cox had a well-deserved reputation for getting things done.[22] "He [Cox] was a great soldier who knew what to do," said Private First Class Shayotovich. "Cox never had a speck of dirt on him, and even his hair was combed. He always looked *fresh.* I don't know how he did it." That attention to detail, however, rubbed some of the grunts in the Second Platoon the wrong way. Cox, according to his detractors, insisted on enforcing minor regulations—nitpicking, chickenshit stuff the grunts resented—even in the bush.

Medics from both B and C Companies, meanwhile, were treating the wounded around the perimeter. Sgt. Erin Stroh, then a squad leader in the Second Platoon, scampered up the slope to assist the wounded and eventually stumbled on Paul Toby. "Jesus Christ," Stroh gasped silently. "His upper and lower jaw's been shot off! How the hell am I supposed to fix that?"[23] Afraid that Toby would choke on his own blood,

Stroh laid the wounded trooper down on his stomach, then carefully positioned his head so that it was lying at an angle facing uphill. The new position seemed to help, but it was obvious to Stroh that the horribly disfigured grunt needed more medical help than he could possibly provide.

Reluctantly, Stroh crawled farther up the slope and took cover behind a large tree. There was nothing else he could do for Toby, he told himself as he scanned the jungle for puffs of smoke, and he sure as hell didn't have the time to look around for a medic. While he was lying there, quietly peering out from beneath his steel pot, the selector switch on his M-16 flipped to automatic, something slammed into the other side of the tree. Four to five feet in diameter, the tree absorbed most of the blast, sparing the Second Platoon original. "The only thing I was thinking about," said Stroh, "was that I was never going to make it to my twenty-first birthday [on June 3]." Rattled, the echo of what was most likely an RPG still ringing in his ears, Stroh slid out from behind the tree and crawled uphill into some brush.

Stroh would later learn that Sgt. Terence Fitzgerald, one of the best squad leaders around, had been killed. Fitzgerald, twenty-seven, well known for his fiery Irish disposition, was posthumously awarded the Silver Star for his bravery on the morning of the twenty-sixth.[24]

Shortly after 10 A.M. the mortars fell silent and a wave of North Vietnamese, some wearing khaki-colored uniforms, most carrying AK-47s and SKSs, swept across Hill 521 and attacked the American perimeter from the west and southwest.[25] Hunkered down on the small knoll, Sgt. Michael Scott observed a force of about thirty to forty NVA leapfrogging forward, one squad at a time, through the jungle to his right. Scott, turning the RPD around, raked the NVA with the captured gun, while two of the C Company troopers on the knoll opened up with their M-16s. Together, the three Americans shot a number of NVA, but the survivors pressed on, moving from tree to tree as they closed on the company line.

Nose to nose, the two sides hammered away at one another on the blood-stained slope, the desperate cries of the wounded drowned out by the relentless roar of battle. Some of the heaviest fighting occurred near C Company's First and Third Platoons. Patched up by a B Company medic, Spc5 Richard Jackson crawled up a small rise and ducked down behind a log. The NVA were hitting the Third Platoon hard, but he could not tell where the fire was coming from. As he peered out through the smoky haze, mortar rounds exploding once again in the treetops, two other soldiers—men Jackson had never seen before—bellied into position nearby. Sgt. Cleveland Lewis, proud, black, and in charge of a squad in the Third, flopped down next to the two grunts.[26] "Don't let those motherfuckers up in here," he growled, glaring out over the lip of the rise. "Don't let them up in here!" Lewis, Jackson immediately realized, had spotted enemy soldiers moving in their general direction.

Sergeant Lewis was banging away on an M-16 alongside the two grunts, the three men putting out as much fire as they could, when his rifle suddenly jammed. Alarmed, Lewis turned to Jackson. "Doc—give me your weapon!"

Jackson handed his rifle to Lewis. "I hadn't used it up to that point, so I figured I probably didn't need it," he noted. "A lot of the medics in Vietnam carried .45s, but when I was with C Company, I told Lieutenant [Charles] Barrett that I would not go into the field without an M-16. I always carried an M-16. I even remember telling Barrett—what am I going to do with a .45 if we get overrun? But if there was ever somebody to give your rifle to, it was Sergeant Lewis. That man was a *soldier's soldier.*" Armed with Jackson's M-16, Lewis was working the jungle beyond the small rise, oblivious to the throaty *chck-chck-chck-chck* of an AK-47 firing nearby, when a bullet slammed into his right bicep.

"Doc, I'm hit!" he screamed, wriggling back down the rise. "Give me some morphine!"

Jackson, worried that a shot of morphine would numb the area, making it difficult to hold a rifle, looked at Lewis and asked, "Are you *sure*?"

"Just give me a shot of morphine!"

Wrapping the wound with bandages, Jackson grabbed a morphine syrette from his pack, pricked the seal, and jammed the attached needle into Lewis's right thigh. Lewis waited impatiently for Jackson to finish administering the shot, then low-crawled back up the small rise. M-16s blazing, the hard-charging sergeant and the two grunts Jackson had never seen before helped hold the line on that side of the platoon.

Like Sergeant Lewis, most of the C Company lifers would serve admirably on the morning of the twenty-sixth. There were, however, some exceptions. "Don't get me wrong—we had very good training sergeants and they certainly got us ready for Vietnam, but once we got over there some of them weren't any good in a firefight," recalled one C Company original. "Some of those guys just weren't any good in combat, and from what I understand, they didn't do much on the twenty-sixth, either." Others expressed similar sentiments. "They weren't worth a shit," complained another grunt. "They were scared shitless [on the twenty-sixth]. That's not to say that we weren't scared, because we were, but we definitely expected more from them. And it was the RAs [Regular Army] who always seemed to get the Bronze Stars, Silver Stars, and everything else. We didn't get shit."[27]

Medals never mattered much to Richard Jackson. What mattered were the young kids fighting and dying on that godforsaken hill. Unarmed, Jackson crawled down the small rise, leaving Sergeant Lewis and the two grunts behind. The ground was damp and rocky, but he pushed on guided by the cries of the wounded. Jackson eventually wandered over to the Second Platoon, where he found two soldiers—one black, one white—lying on the jungle floor.

"Are you a medic?" the white soldier asked tersely.

Jackson nodded, certain that the man was either an officer or a senior NCO. "Yes, sir."

"Get over here!"

Covered in mud, Jackson hurried across the slope, dragging his wounded right leg behind him. "The way he was talking and acting, I could tell that he had some *juice* [rank]," Jackson said of the white soldier. "He said that the other guy had been hit and needed medical attention. Then I looked at the wounded guy he was talking about. I didn't panic, but for a split-second, I thought—shit, what do I do?" The wounded grunt was Paul Toby. Jackson could see that a bullet had hit Toby in the face, between his nose and his upper lip, and had sliced through his chin, all but splitting the lower half of his face in two. Bandaging the mash of flesh and blood as quickly as he could, Jackson turned Toby's head to the side and laid it on the slope. Another grunt suggested moving Toby onto his side, but Jackson and some of the grunts nearby, concerned that the wounded trooper would bleed into his throat and suffocate, insisted that he be left on his stomach until a chopper could take him out.

Farther up the hill, Sgt. Erin Stroh was firing at puffs of smoke from behind a tree. Each short, sharp burst from his M-16 drew heavy fire in return, but he did not see any movement in the smoky jungle around him. Lying in the underbrush down slope, Sgt. Richard Crooks saw what he thought was a rocket shrieking toward his four-man fire team. Crooks, thinking that the NVA had fired an RPG, ducked and waited for the blast. The rocket, fired from an American M-72 LAW, smashed into a tree about ten feet from Crooks, peppering him with bits of bark and shrapnel. Another grunt, he later learned, had fired the LAW. "When you're spread out like that in the jungle and you get hit [by the enemy], you don't have time to really form a good line," said Crooks. "So you not only have to pay attention to what the enemy is doing, you damn sure have to pay attention to what *your* troops are doing." An NVA soldier in a light brown uniform, meanwhile, jumped up and dashed across the slope in front of Sergeant Stroh. "Shit," Stroh muttered to himself as the man disappeared from view. "Sons of bitches are everywhere."

That feeling, that the North Vietnamese were everywhere, stayed with the grunts, even as the enemy paused to regroup in the murky jungle around the perimeter. The enemy ground assault, the fourth to hit the Dragoons that morning, lasted less than ten minutes.[28] C Company, with the help of 1st Lt. Branko Marinovich's small B Company relief force and his First, Third, and Fourth Platoons, had repulsed the assault without gunships, fixed-wing aircraft, or the kind of close-in artillery support a company in contact could normally expect in Vietnam. The close-quarters fighting, in fact, had prevented the artillery from firing directly on the enemy. Constrained by the relative proximity of the two forces, the guns fired *around* the contact area to prevent the NVA from reinforcing its troops on the hill.[29]

Huddled around a radio in the battalion TOC, Charles Flood listened to the battle unfolding in the foothills of the Chu Goungot Mountains and held his breath. Flood, a civilian reporter and novelist who had spent time with the 3-8 Infantry and the 31st Tactical Wing, thought highly of Lieutenant Colonel Lynch and the companies he commanded. "I just kept thinking one thing," Lynch had told him one night. "I hope what I'm doing out here—I just hope we never have to run this thing through again."[30] Critical of American military strategy in Vietnam, Flood believed that the United States needed to do more to knock the North Vietnamese out of the war. Otherwise, he feared the war would continue to be a game of numbers decided by groups of armed men hunting each other in the jungle. "The least we could do was to put in more hunting parties than the other side had, which it was certainly clear that we could do on a population basis alone; but we were not doing it," Flood would later write. "When we were not trying to hit a mosquito with a hammer by sending supersonic jets against tiny, scattered targets, we were playing six-man touch against an eleven-man tackle team on the ground."[31]

On the steep, forested slopes of Hill 521, Lynch's hard pressed troopers were waging a desperate battle for survival against a numerically superior force, exactly the kind of fight the enemy preferred. The Dragoons had turned back four determined ground assaults, but at 10:20 A.M. the North Vietnamese attacked again, closing to within ten to fifteen meters of the American perimeter.[32] Fighting, not for God or country, but for the buddy lying next to them, the grunts opened up on the NVA with everything they had. "That's the only reason that I was able to crawl around," said Spc5 Richard Jackson. "Those guys were putting out so much shit on the perimeter."

Bits of metal lodged in his left shoulder, what remained of his nearly severed left thumb wrapped neatly inside the palm of his left hand, Lieutenant Marinovich ducked down and tried to determine the direction of the NVA attack. "All we could see was about a foot vertical, because we had trees and bushes and everything else in the way," recalled the B Company commander. "I was calling in artillery and asking C Company—is it effective? Should I adjust? Should I go right? Should I go left? Am I too close to your front lines, where your people are? I never really linked up with him [Sergeant Childers]. He was handling his own firefight, and I was on my end." Marinovich, injured when a bullet shattered his M-16 just below the handle, knew that if he could bring in accurate artillery fire, he could slow the enemy assault.

Firing furiously, the embattled Dragoons clung to the smoky slope. "I never really did see any of them [NVA]," said Pfc. Larry Orr, "[but] I was just firing out there to keep them off. We knew they were close. The weapons fire was awfully close, and sometimes you could hear them hollering just like they could hear us hollering back and forth." Mixed in with C Company, Orr had moved down the hill with B Company's Third Platoon. The line would hold, the C Company grunts assured him, as long they kept the NVA out of the perimeter.

As the fighting raged around elements of C Company's Fourth Platoon, Spc4 Don Tienhaara hugged the dirt behind a large tree—he had tried to dig in near the tree but could not get past the tangle of thick roots protruding through the soil—and blazed away at the NVA on the other side of a small saddle. There were wounded grunts lying on the slope nearby, and at one point he heard a man with a Vietnamese accent yelling, mockingly, "Here we are! We've come to save you!"[33] Laughing, the brazen NVA then taunted the grunts. Furious, Tienhaara hurled grenades at the man until the taunting finally stopped. Afterward, a soldier behind him struck up a conversation with one of the medics.

"Are you going to pick up a weapon and start firing if they come again?" the grunt asked.

Rumored to be a conscientious objector, the medic looked at the grunt and replied, "I won't know that until it happens."

As the number of dead and wounded increased around the perimeter, the calls for effective, close-in artillery support grew more acute. Lieutenant Marinovich, upset that the artillery could not bring fire directly down on the NVA, would later allege that the forward observer attached to B Company relied on 155-mm howitzers for support—rather than the 105s Marinovich claims he requested—and was relieved by Lieutenant Colonel Lynch after the battle. Larger and arguably less accurate, the 155-mm rounds Marinovich insists the FO called in could not be fired as close to the perimeter as 105-mm rounds without endangering friendly troops. C Battery, 6-29 Artillery (105-mm) and A Battery, 5-16 Artillery (155-mm), however, were the only two batteries that provided close-in support on the twenty-sixth.[34] Moreover, regardless of the size of the round, the proximity of the opposing forces prevented Lynch's supporting artillery from firing any closer to the perimeter for much of the battle.

The FAC on station attributed some of the problems the artillery experienced that morning to the rugged terrain. Radioing Sgt. Michael Scott from the cockpit of his spotter plane, Lt. Charles Munsch, a former FO who had served with Scott in the 6-29 Artillery, explained that there was a mountain between the artillery batteries and the small knoll. The gunners, Munsch continued, were having a hard time firing over the mountain and onto the coordinates Scott had called in. Munsch advised Scott to mark the front lines with smoke so that he could adjust the artillery fire on that side of the perimeter from the air. Scott, figuring that the "mountain" was either the main ridge they had been following or the summit of the hill, had the four C Company grunts on the knoll pop smoke grenades. Soon after, the radio crackled again.

"Are there any Americans to your south?" Munsch asked nervously.

"No," Scott responded "There's nobody down there."

"Then I've got some bad news for you guys. There's a bunch of people coming up the hill. This don't look real good."

Scott, worried that the enemy would overrun his small group, implored Munsch to find an artillery battery that could fire down on the knoll. "If I could've gotten artillery, I could have blown 'em off the face of the earth," said Scott. "But I couldn't get any artillery on them. I could only talk to one battery, and I couldn't even talk to my people at the 6-29 Artillery. I don't even know who I was talking to, but he [Munsch] could talk to everybody. I was hoping that maybe he could find another battery to fire for me and get in on them [NVA advancing up the knoll]." While Munsch searched for another battery, Scott told the four C Company grunts that a large enemy force was approaching them from the south. Together the five Americans then turned to the left, Scott behind the captured RPD, and waited for the North Vietnamese to march up the hill.

Meanwhile, in the drizzly, overcast skies above Hill 521, Lieutenant Munsch located the smoke wafting up through the canopy from his low-speed observation craft.[35] Munsch called it in and had a battery of 105s fire a spotting round on the southern slope of the knoll. A few minutes later, a shell from one of the 105s exploded on the slope about 100 to 150 yards below the crest of the knoll, exactly where Scott had been trying to get the artillery to fire. Feverishly calculating the distances in his head, Scott grabbed his handset and radioed Munsch. "You're onto something," he exclaimed, "now drop fifty and fire for effect!"

Peering down from the crest of the knoll, confident that he could now adjust some of his supporting artillery, Scott suddenly noticed thirty to forty NVA, many wearing red berets, walking casually up the slope.[36] The enemy soldiers were moving more or less on-line, rifles in some cases slung comfortably over their shoulders, in all manner of attire, from black pajamas to khaki-colored pants and camouflage shirts. There were a couple of men with RPGs, but many were armed with nothing but hand grenades.

The knoll sloped gently to the south, and through the partial clearing just below the crest, Scott and the four C Company grunts watched, wide-eyed, as the North Vietnamese ambled up the hill. "I think they thought that their guys were still up there [on the knoll]," said Scott. "Originally we thought there were three of them on that knoll. We shot two of them, but when we got up there, we only found two guys. We knew they didn't have radios, so then we thought that maybe they had sent down a runner to bring more of them up. I don't think that they knew that we had taken it over in the meantime." As the NVA were entering the clearing, a round from a 105 exploded in the jungle behind them. Spooked, the enemy soldiers spread out and hurried up the hill.

Scott's group waited for the NVA to get within thirty-five feet before they blew the four Claymore mines covering the clearing. Shrieks of pain rose up from the jungle below as hundreds of steel ball bearings tore into the first row of enemy soldiers.[37] Pouncing on the shattered enemy line, the five Americans on the knoll—two had been wounded but were still able to fight—threw hand grenades and raked the NVA with M-16s and the captured RPD. A grunt to their left opened up with an M-60. "He'd been my radio operator for about two months," said Sgt. Richard Childers. "I was trying to get this guy promoted. He was a machine gunner that day. He was the one that, when we'd seen those fifty [North Vietnamese] in the open, well, he probably killed about half of them."[38] Nicknamed "Gator," the young black machine gunner from Florida was killed later that morning.

What was left of the shattered North Vietnamese line regrouped and returned fire. Scott, sliding another drum into the receiver of the RPD, swept the slope below the crest. Trapped in the clearing, the surviving NVA were wiped out by the Americans on the knoll. "There really wasn't much left of them when we got through," said Scott. "All the NVA in front of us were lying on the ground. We probably did most of our damage with the Claymores." Scott was subsequently awarded the Silver Star for his actions on Hill 521.

A long, uneasy lull followed the North Vietnamese assault. For the fifth time in a little over an hour, the exhausted Dragoons had beaten back a major enemy attack. The NVA continued to mortar the hill, however, and at one point a mortar round landed near a group of grunts, killing or wounding all ten of them.[39] Medics from both companies, in the meantime, used the pause to treat the wounded. Spc4 Ronyal Jacobs, then a twenty-one-year-old medic in B Company's Fourth Platoon, stumbled on a soldier lying on the jungle floor with a "big ole chunk out of his head." Unresponsive, the man appeared as though he had been knocked unconscious. *Man*, Jacobs thought to himself as he bandaged the injured soldier's skull, *this guy's a goner*. Turning at one point to a B Company sergeant, Jacobs shook his head and muttered, "I don't think this guy's gonna make it."

"Oh yes I am!" the wounded soldier blurted out unexpectedly. "I'm gonna make it!"

Embarrassed, Jacobs looked down at the man and replied, sheepishly, "I'm not talking about you. I was talking about somebody else."

Jacobs finished patching the man up then slinked off into the brush. "That was the worst feeling in the world," he later recalled. "I didn't know he [the wounded man] was awake. I thought he was out of it."

Spc5 Richard Jackson felt numb when he happened upon the charred remains of an American soldier later that morning. Blown apart by an enemy rocket, the body was barely recognizable. "A guy turned around and saw me looking at the body," said Jackson. "I don't know if the guy saw the look on my face when I was trying to figure out who it was, but he just said, 'That's Lieutenant Johnson.'"

Upset, Jackson scurried off through the underbrush and eventually found Spc4 Donald Mesarosh lying on the slope. Always smiling, the twenty-year-old RTO from Louisville, Kentucky, had been shot in the back of the head. *He's gone*, thought Jackson somberly. *No sense checking for a pulse*. Jackson, fighting back tears as he remembered the young radioman cheerfully announcing how many days they had left on their tours earlier that morning, crouched over his friend and whispered, haltingly, "Sorry this happened to you, Mezzy." Overcome with emotion, Jackson paused beside the body for a moment longer, then scooped up his pack and crawled away. Mesarosh was posthumously awarded the Bronze Star.[40]

The long lull allowed the two sides to regroup and, while some of the Dragoons were busy helping the wounded, handing out ammo, and tightening up the line, a group of about ten NVA approached C Company's Third Platoon. "These guys were walking like there was nothing to it, like it was an exercise," said Pfc. Russell Belden. "They were carrying their rifles by their sides, with the bayonets facing toward us. They weren't afraid of *nothing*." Belden, hobbled by a handful of bullets that had ripped through his hip and abdomen earlier in the battle, warned the wounded troopers behind him and advised them all to play dead.

Slumping down in the bushes, Belden watched the small group of NVA moving through the jungle. The men were walking upright, not crouched at the waist like the grunts were accustomed to seeing, and some were wearing brown uniforms. "They got within ten yards of me and then one of them—I think he was maybe their leader or something—pointed to the left," said Belden. "They all turned to the left and walked that way. They didn't see me, and they didn't know I was sitting there." Shortly thereafter, heavy gunfire erupted in the jungle to his left. Belden, sitting up some, figured the NVA had gotten into a shooting match with the grunts over there.

Meanwhile, in a small draw below the B Company NDP, Terry Turner and Joe Gutierrez, "Little Joe" to his thirteen brothers and sisters, rigged a tree with C4 and, using the blasting cap and "clacker" from a Claymore mine, detonated the explosive. Spc4s in B Company's Second Platoon, Turner and Gutierrez had been working on the LZ, blowing down trees and clearing brush, for nearly two hours. Spc4 Richard Elam and Spc4 Jim Congrove were standing on the slope nearby. Elam and Congrove met at Boys Town and were later reunited at Fort Lewis, Washington. "I didn't even know he was there [at Fort Lewis]," said Congrove, "until that day when they read off his name."

Congrove scanned the jungle around the LZ. Sometime after the battalion had arrived in the Highlands, he was walking point with another grunt when he noticed four North Vietnamese soldiers talking on the other side of a clearing. The men were wearing uniforms, unlike the guerillas they had encountered on the coast, and were facing one another. Squatting down on one knee, Congrove shouldered his M-16 and shot all four; three went down in a heap but the fourth man scurried off into the bush. Armed with a shotgun, the grunt with Congrove chased after the wounded NVA and shot the man in the face. Some months before, while moving along a paddy dike in the Tuy Hoa area, a young machine gunner was shot in the face during an ambush. Congrove had helped carry the wounded trooper to a medevac. It was that kind of war.

"We gotta go!"

Grabbing his helmet, Lt. Col. Tom Lynch, CO of the 3-8 Infantry, raced out of his tent at the battalion firebase and sprinted toward his C&C helicopter on the base helipad. Spc4 Thomas Bruce Thompson, twenty, a member of the battalion reconnaissance platoon, followed Lynch out of the tent and into the idling chopper.[41] After a short flight, the helicopter exited a small valley and approached Hill 521. At 11:03 A.M., the NVA on the hill attacked again, drawing troops from both companies into another vicious, close-quarters fight. White smoke could be seen drifting up through the canopy, but every time the pilots tried to swoop down for a closer look, the NVA would respond with heavy small-arms fire. "The only yelling he [Lynch] did was at the pilots," said Thompson. "The pilots would fly low, and we'd start catching incoming rounds. So then they'd fly back up again, and Lynch would get mad at them. They couldn't go low enough for him."[42]

While the grunts hugged the slope, artillery shells crashed around the embattled perimeter. AP correspondent John T. Wheeler heard the shells exploding in the jungle and later noted that it was the first time the artillery had "closed up near the American lines."[43] At 11:12 A.M., however, Lieutenant Colonel Lynch shifted the artillery to the south and west.[44] "I took artillery fire and put it around the rear of the contact, so that the NVA could not withdraw and get out of there," said Lynch. "I wanted to isolate the contact area. If you didn't, the North Vietnamese would continue to maneuver or put additional units on top of you." Gunships arrived to attack targets closer to the perimeter, but by 11:15 A.M. the Dragoons had defeated the sixth and final enemy assault.[45]

Shortly before noon, the North Vietnamese began to withdraw, covered by rockets and mortar fire.[46] The battle was finally over.

EPILOGUE

Ambushed on a steep hill near the Cambodian border, the Dragoons, outnumbered and forced to fight without close artillery support for most of the battle, had beaten back—sometimes in vicious, hand-to-hand combat—an entire enemy battalion.[1] Filthy, wet, surrounded by the dead and the dying, the embattled C Company troopers had fought magnificently. "I've been in some tight spots with the Marines and some Army companies," AP reporter John Wheeler would tell a colleague in Saigon, "but I've never seen a rifle company as good as that."[2] The battle had been costly, however. Nine C Company soldiers, including Capt. James Powers, were killed on the hill and another sixty-one were wounded. B Company suffered one KIA and eight WIA in the fierce fighting.[3]

Content to hit the retreating NVA with supporting arms, Lieutenant Colonel Lynch ordered B and C Companies to move up the hill to B Company's NDP. Lynch hoped the move would prevent additional casualties. "All right, get all the dead and wounded in here," barked Sgt. Richard Childers, C Company's acting CO. "Every squad make a check and see if anyone's missing. Get the guns and the ammo and the packs. We ain't goin' to leave a damn thing for them." Childers then watched impatiently as the exhausted C Company survivors, working alongside some of the B Company troopers who had marched down the hill, retrieved the dead and wounded from around the perimeter.

Shortly after 1 P.M., the two companies shuffled out of the perimeter and, covered by a small rear guard, pushed up the steamy slope toward the B Company NDP.[4] Some of the wounded were able to walk on their own; others hobbled along on crutches made from tree limbs. The rest had to be carried up the hill on ponchos and makeshift litters. Lightheaded from the large bump above his left brow, Pfc. Dan Shayotovich, stumbling forward, the entire right side of his body straining under the weight of the heavy-set grunt he had been carrying up the slope with three other soldiers, suddenly dropped his end of the litter they had fashioned out of a poncho and two tree limbs. The grunt, shirtless and bleeding, slid off the poncho and tumbled to the ground.

"Pick that thing up," snapped one of the C Company soldiers, "and don't drop it again!" Shayotovich glared at the three soldiers, furious that they had put him on the left side of the litter even though he had told them that he could not carry anything with his right hand. "I can't! I'm injured!"

Fuming, Shayotovich eventually exchanged places with a soldier on the right side of the litter. Later that afternoon, a medic examined the bump on his head. "He asked me to recite my name and service number, do some basic arithmetic, and walk in a straight line," said Shayotovich. "If you could walk around, see straight, and pull a trigger, you had to stay." Shayotovich passed the test and was pronounced fit for duty.

As the two companies moved up the slope toward the B Company NDP, North Vietnamese were observed dragging their dead into a ravine to the north. The grunts shot and killed some of the NVA in the ravine, but as the slow march up the side of Hill 521 continued, the sniper fire that had been crackling through the jungle all morning suddenly increased. Concerned, Lieutenant Colonel Lynch ordered B Company to halt so that it could cover C Company's withdrawal. Lynch also instructed Lieutenant Marinovich to conduct a limited sweep of the battlefield.[5]

Around 1:45 P.M., a helicopter carrying Lieutenant Colonel Lynch and Spc4 Thomas Bruce Thompson landed in the LZ B Company had cleared in a small draw below the summit of Hill 521. Resting the skids of the chopper on a landing platform made of crisscrossed logs, the pilots waited for Lynch and Thompson to hop out, then pulled out of the draw.[6] Thompson, who had been shadowing the battalion CO as part of the 4th Infantry Division's "Soldier of the Month" program, jumped down off the platform and looked around.

"I'd like to stay, sir."

"Well," Lynch began gruffly, "you don't have your stuff."

"I'm sorry, sir, but I think there's a lot of stuff here."

Lynch reluctantly agreed. The lieutenant colonel and the young specialist 4th class, incidentally, would spend the night on the hill. "For me going in there and spending the night, they [division and brigade] raised hell but I didn't care," Lynch intoned. "It wasn't discussed. I wanted to get in there, because I knew they were hurting. If you come in and get exposed to a little bit of it, that's the time you have to demonstrate leadership on the ground and not on the other end of a radio. In Vietnam, if you didn't have contact with your units, you didn't command anything. I only had two units that were in contact, so I stayed with them." Assuming direct control of both companies, Lynch ordered B Company to continue sweeping the jungle around the

C Company perimeter. The two companies, meanwhile, were to withdraw to the B Company NDP. In addition, Lynch directed his artillery liaison officer to prepare heavy suppressive fires in the area where the contact had occurred.[7]

Higher up the hill, in the B Company NDP, Spc4 Bob Gamboa heard that Lieutenant Marinovich needed help evacuating the wounded. Gamboa, angling past a pair of grunts on their way up the hill, moved down the slope with his Fourth Platoon squad and walked into the C Company perimeter. Rifles and rucksacks were scattered across the slope, and the damp jungle air reeked of gunpowder and rotting flesh. "There were dead gooks all over the place and some Americans, too," said Gamboa. "The bodies were already beginning to stink. The cordite from the artillery, the gunpowder, and the decaying bodies combined into one smell and I'll never forget that smell."

Sweeping the slope, B Company found a number of dead enemy soldiers dangling from the trees. "I had never seen them tied in the trees before," said Spc4 Jim Congrove, a Second Platoon original who had moved down the hill to assist with the wounded. "As I recall, their arms or their feet were tied to the branch they were sitting on, and when they got shot they fell backwards or forwards and were hanging from the trees. The gun was dropped on the ground below them. We just left them there."

Congrove, twenty-one, was walking back down the hill later that afternoon when he ran into some B Company grunts carrying a wounded North Vietnamese soldier up the hill on a litter. Angry after a long, hard battle, the grunts had little sympathy for the hapless NVA. "The guys were really screwing with him," said Congrove. "They were hitting trees with him on the way up. I told them to knock it off and to get him up the hill, because he might have valuable information that could save lives. I think that they thought about what I had said, and then they started carrying him up the hill in a more orderly fashion." Congrove eventually returned to the LZ. By then, a resupply slick had brought in chain saws and more C4.

The two companies received sporadic sniper fire throughout the afternoon, and at one point a heavy burst reverberated across the hill. Down near the C Company perimeter, a B Company NCO told Sgt. Larry Jumper, who was overseeing the evacuation of some of the dead and wounded, that two C Company troopers were lying on the slope below a North Vietnamese machine gun. "Let's go get 'em!" shouted a C Company sergeant. Jumper immediately volunteered, and the two Americans took off up the hill.

As they raced up the slope, the two men shot a handful of NVA—Jumper accounted for two—out of the trees. The ground was covered with scattered brush, but Jumper could see the enemy machine gun in a bunker about thirty yards away. Hurling hand grenades uphill, Jumper and the C Company NCO charged the bunker, Jumper firing from the hip as a loud explosion rocked the slope above him. Suddenly smoke began pouring out of the bunker. "One of our grenades had to have landed in that bunker, because it blew two NVA *up*," said Jumper. "It blew the two of them right out of the bunker. Another one of them stumbled out and tried to run. He was trying to get away, limping and sort of dragging, when that boy from C Company shot and killed him." Hurrying on, Jumper and the C Company sergeant knocked out an enemy mortar pit farther up the slope, grabbed the two wounded troopers on the way back down, and returned to the perimeter. Jumper would receive the Silver Star for rescuing the two men.

Limping up the side of Hill 521, C Company closed on the B Company NDP at 2:08 P.M.[8] The wounded, many of them unable to walk without assistance, were moved to the LZ and loaded onto slicks bound for the 1st Brigade base at Jackson Hole. Spc5 Richard "Witch Doctor" Jackson, wounded when a rifle round slammed into the back of his right leg, was among the first to be evacuated that afternoon after an officer noticed him hopping around the LZ on one leg. "Get on the chopper," the man said sternly, "and get out of here." Surprised, Jackson hopped into the Huey and, kneeling down on the cabin floor, stared back at the wounded troopers lying on the slope. Overwhelmed with emotion, the young C Company medic began to sob. Jackson was eventually sent to the 36th Evacuation Hospital in Vung Tau.

Carried up the hill on a poncho fastened to a pair of freshly cut saplings, Pfc. Russell Belden waited for nearly an hour before he was finally loaded onto a Huey. "Get him to the hospital!" the grunts screamed as they pushed him inside the cabin. "He's losing a lot of blood!" Filled with wounded soldiers, the chopper cleared the canopy above the LZ and headed east. Belden, bleeding badly but thrilled to be alive, landed at Jackson Hole and was taken to a large tent with other wounded soldiers. Treated for multiple gunshot wounds, the twenty-one-year-old C Company original was then transported by helicopter to the 67th Evacuation Hospital in Qui Nhon, where he would undergo emergency surgery to remove two bullets from his intestine.

B Company's wounded were also evacuated that afternoon.[9] Nursing a sprained knee, Lt. Rick Nelson, then in charge of B Company's Fourth Platoon, helped 1st Lt. Branko Marinovich onto a chopper. Barely lucid, his left thumb heavily wrapped, Marinovich stumbled in and sat down. "I think I was in a fog because I don't even remember being evacuated off the hill," he recalled. "My parents back home in Fresno picked up the newspaper a few days later and saw me on the front page. It was a hell of shock to them, so they called the Army but couldn't get much information because I was in a combat zone. They contacted a congressman after that and eventually found out that I had been sent to Japan. Later I was transferred to Letterman Hospital in San Francisco for almost four months for reconstruction of what was left of my thumb." Marinovich was later awarded the Distinguished Service Cross.

Nelson, holding his helmet as he hobbled away from the chopper, assumed command of B Company. Soldiers from both companies, meanwhile, continued carrying the dead and wounded up the steep, slippery slope. "As we were moving up, we were slipping and sliding and two of us lost our footing," remarked Pfc. Gary Retana, a replacement in B Company's First Platoon. "When we leaned [to one side], the dead body we were carrying rolled off the litter and started rolling down the hill a ways until it was stopped by a tree trunk. The body just rolled out of the poncho. It was the most difficult job I ever did, carrying those bodies up that hill. It almost seemed like you were going inch by inch, not only to keep your footing, but again to keep that body solid and not leaning so that it wouldn't roll off again." Trudging back down the hill, Retana and the three B Company soldiers with him put the burned, lifeless body back onto the poncho and started up the slope. As the four grunts neared the LZ, blood from the dead man's body ran down Retana's forearm and dripped off his elbow. That night, while the rest of the company was digging in, Retana rinsed the blood off his arm with water from a canteen.

Forced to land in a narrow draw on the side of the hill, often under enemy fire, the pilots and crew of the helicopters involved in the evacuation flew with extraordinary courage and dedication. One chopper crew, however, objected to picking up the dead, insisting instead that they had been sent to evacuate the wounded. "The medevacs *were* supposed to evacuate the wounded as a priority," recalled Lieutenant Colonel Lynch, "[but] I had a dead captain and a dead lieutenant and I said, 'No way!' They started again, and I told them to knock it off. Well, they took the dead officers out and the dead NCOs. That's important because you have to get the dead out of there. And plus there were a few that we didn't know if they were dead or not. There was blood all over them and body parts, and you didn't know if they were still alive so you wanted to get them out of there."

Lynch offered to send all of the wounded in that afternoon, but many of the C Company soldiers refused to leave the hill. "No—we don't want to go back," the grunts insisted. "We're staying in case those bastards attack again." Mindful of another attack, Lynch flew the battalion reconnaissance platoon in from the battalion firebase; on the ground by 5:30 P.M., the platoon was eventually placed under the operational control of C Company.

By 5:45 P.M., B Company had finished sweeping the battlefield and had moved the rest of the dead and wounded up the hill to the LZ.[10] Sgt. Michael Scott, the young forward observer who helped capture the small knoll with a handful of C Company soldiers, boarded one of the last birds out. Still in command of C Company, Sgt. Richard Childers left later that night.[11] Childers received the Distinguished Service Cross for his heroism on Hill 521. "You can't make everybody heroes," he observed poignantly, "but they'd done an outstanding job. I just made a few decisions and I'm thankful they came out right for the company. My men did an outstanding job."[12]

Joining C Company near the summit of Hill 521, B Company reported an initial body count of ninety-two enemy KIAs. All of the enemy soldiers, the troopers noted, had been killed by small-arms fire.[13] The two companies then prepared for what many feared would be a long, sleepless night. Around 6 P.M., as the grunts were digging in for the night, Lieutenant Colonel Lynch requested an air strike on a target to the southwest. Lynch also directed his supporting artillery to fire throughout the night to prevent the North Vietnamese from policing up the battlefield. B-52 strikes would hit the enemy to the west-northwest, between the battalion and the Cambodian border.[14]

Lynch was monitoring the radio that night when he heard a North Vietnamese soldier talking over the battalion net. "He knew who I was and he addressed me by my call word, Charger," said Lynch. "They monitored our radio frequency, and after you've been in contact, all of your security doesn't mean shit. He said that it was too bad about 8-3-6, my C Company commander, and then he named him. He told me that they were sorry that they had killed poor Captain Powers, and he said that my men were valiant soldiers so eager to die for the great United States." Furious, Lynch called the man a son of a bitch and vowed that he would "get him yet."

The following morning, B Company and the battalion reconnaissance platoon searched the entire area and found four dead NVA, raising the body count to ninety-six. Artillery fire accounted for three of the four enemy KIAs.[15] That same morning, the last of the 173rd Airborne Brigade (Sep.) arrived in Pleiku. Placed under the operational control of the 4th Infantry Division, the 173rd was to serve as the "Strategic Reserve Force" for the Central Highlands during the upcoming rainy season.[16] Lynch, meanwhile, replaced C Company and the reconnaissance platoon with A Company, 3-8 Infantry. A and B Companies were resupplied the next day, May 28, and another search of the entire area was ordered.[17]

General Peers observed that the move west into the Ia Tchar Valley–Chu Goungot Mountains resulted in "nine days of vicious contact during the period of May 18–26, in which the 1st Brigade's three battalions—1st Battalion, 8th Infantry, 3d Battalion, 12th Infantry, and 3d Battalion, 8th Infantry—had almost continuous contact with never less than a battalion of the two well-armed and well-trained NVA Regiments contacted."[18] For its role in the aptly named "Nine Days in May border battles," the 1st Brigade was awarded the Presidential Unit Citation (Army); three of its soldiers, Plt. Sgt. Bruce Grandstaff, SSgt. Frankie Molnar, and Pfc. Leslie Bellrichard, meanwhile, were posthumously awarded the Medal of Honor.[19]

Over the course of those nine days, the 1st Brigade fought five major battles against elements of the 32nd and 66th NVA Regiments, often on the enemy's terms. Relying on tracking parties to locate the Americans, the North Vietnamese, backed by mortars and RPGs, had then attacked them while they were on the move or in temporary NDPs. These attacks, moreover, were apparently designed to overwhelm the hapless Americans before reinforcements arrived.[20]

Far from a drug-addled mob, however, the grunts fought back and defeated the NVA in savage, close-quarters combat. "We'd strike him with artillery first and then bring in the air and never halt our shelling of his positions," noted Colonel Jackson, " . . . but these engagements were won within a fifty-yard area of heavily jungled terrain where the fighting was man to man, our guys against the bad guys."[21] The combatants were so close, in fact, that the brigade used air strikes and artillery support primarily to isolate the battlefield and hammer the enemy's escape routes. Tellingly, the grunts would also report that small-arms fire had killed most of the 369 NVA dead.[22]

General Peers hoped that by striking first, before the heavy clouds and drenching rains of the southwest monsoon had gripped the Central Highlands, he could hit the enemy hard enough to preempt a possible attack on Duc Co. After the "Nine Days in May," Peers was convinced that he had defeated a major enemy offensive:

> In Operation SAM HOUSTON the enemy had been soundly defeated and forced back into his CAMBODIAN sanctuary. With the beginning of the summer monsoons he began deploying back across the border into South Vietnam. This challenge was met squarely and in nine days in May the enemy's monsoon offensive was halted hardly before it had begun.[23]

At the very least, Peers had disrupted the enemy's timetable in Pleiku Province. Captured on May 2, a North Vietnamese soldier informed the 3-12 Infantry that two battalions from his unit, the 66th NVA Regiment, were building base camps northwest of Duc Co. The 66th, according to the prisoner, was to attack the camp on June 6 before pushing on to Plei Me.[24] The following day, May 3, the 2-8 Infantry (Mech.) found a notebook in the shattered remains of an enemy base camp. In it the enemy listed Duc Co, Plei Me, New Plei Djereng, the 2nd Brigade base at Oasis, and the South Vietnamese district headquarters at Than An as potential targets for the upcoming rainy season offensive. As in previous offensives, the North Vietnamese were apparently planning to lure the Americans out of their bases by threatening key allied military and administrative installations.[25] Yet, after the heavy fighting in the Ia Tchar Valley–Chu Goungot Mountains, the threat of a major enemy offensive in Pleiku in early June gradually subsided.

Nevertheless, the "Nine Days in May" had kept the 4th Infantry Division busy in the rugged Central Highlands. Drawing the 1st Brigade into the remote valleys and foothills of western Pleiku Province, the North Vietnamese killed 69 Americans and wounded another 259 in the five major engagements along the border, losses General Peers could ill afford.[26] General Larsen considered reinforcing Peers with a brigade from the 1st Cavalry Division in Binh Dinh Province but eventually decided against sending troops from the coastal provinces of II Corps. Instead Larsen arranged to have the 173rd flown up from Bien Hoa. Pulled out of III Corps, the 173rd would remain in the Highlands, far from the battles brewing around Saigon, until mid-September.[27]

Peers, leaving his 2nd Brigade in place around Duc Co, sent the 173rd south to the Ia Drang Valley–Chu Pong Mountains. Farther north, his 1st Brigade, encouraged by the heavy contacts in May, continued to search the Ia Tchar Valley–Chu Goungot Mountains with the 3-8 Infantry and the 3-12 Infantry. By then, however, the North Vietnamese had melted back into Cambodia, and on June 23 the two battalions returned to Jackson Hole.[28] "This sanctuary [Cambodia] for a large NVA force is the biggest single challenge in all of II Corps," wrote General Larsen. "Such a military sanctuary, contiguous to the battlefield, in a supposedly neutral country, in effect ties up nearly one-half of key U.S. ground combat power in II CTZ, with no means in sight for us to destroy the enemy except when he decides on his terms when and where to fight on the Vietnam side of the border."[29] Pedaled as an appropriate use of American restraint, the decision to restrict the ground war to South Vietnam ceded the strategic initiative to the enemy and ensured that his sanctuaries in Cambodia—and with them the wherewithal to continue the war in the Central Highlands—would remain inviolate.

Meanwhile, in Kontum Province, a sharp increase in enemy activity forced General Peers to dispatch two battalions of the 173rd Airborne Brigade, commanded by Brig. Gen. John R. Deane, to Dak To. Commencing Operation Greeley on June 17, the 173rd pushed south into the hilly jungle around the Special Forces Camp. At first the airborne troopers searched for the North Vietnamese without success, but on the morning of the twenty-second a company from the 2nd of the 503rd Infantry (Airborne) bumped into an enemy battalion and was nearly annihilated before reinforcements arrived later that afternoon. Alarmed, General Larsen sent a brigade from the 1st Cavalry Division to Kontum.

To the south, in Pleiku Province, Peers continued Operation Francis Marion with his 1st and 2nd Brigades. After a relatively quiet June, the fighting resumed in July when two companies from Lt. Col. Corey Wright's 1st of the 12th Infantry, a 2nd Brigade unit operating near the Cambodian border north of the Ia Drang Valley, ran into elements of the 66th NVA Regiment. Scurrying back across the border, the North Vietnamese left behind 142 dead. The battle cost the Americans thirty-one killed, thirty-four wounded, and seven missing.[30] "As has often been stated, the choice of time and location for a sizable engagement in the Central Highlands basically rests with the NVA," Wright acknowledged. "Occasionally, our forces are postured and located in areas favorable to the enemy choosing to fight. . . . From his Cambodian sanctuary the enemy is capable of staging sizeable forces, alerted to be employed at a time and location of his choosing."[31] Eleven days later, on July 23, two companies from the 3-8 Infantry, aided by F-100 Super Sabres, Huey gunships, and eight batteries of artillery, held off an estimated 1,000–1,200 enemy soldiers from the 32nd NVA Regiment in a fierce, five-hour battle south of Duc Co. The Dragoons lost eighteen dead and thirty-seven wounded. Nearly two hundred North Vietnamese were killed in the fighting.[32]

Checking the enemy's rainy season offensive at the border, the 4th Infantry Division concluded Francis Marion on October 11, 1967. Largely successful, the operation killed hundreds of North Vietnamese, many of them during the "Nine Days in May," and frustrated a major enemy initiative in western Pleiku Province.[33] Still, the B3 Front had kept the Americans tied down in the remote border regions of II Corps and had forced General Larsen to dispatch reinforcements from the coast, as Hanoi had hoped. In the end, however, the fighting would do little to change the strategic trajectory of the war in the Central Highlands.

NOTES

ABBREVIATIONS USED IN NOTES

AAR After Action Report
CMH Center for Military History
DSC Distinguished Service Cross
DSJ Daily Staff Journal
NARA II National Archives and Records Administration II, College Park, Md.
PACAF Pacific Air Forces
RG Record Group

INTRODUCTION

1. For quoted words, see Westmoreland, *A Soldier Reports*, 142. See also Carland, *Stemming the Tide, May 1965 to October 1966*, 68–69.
2. For quoted words, see Sharp and Westmoreland, *Report on the War in Vietnam (As of 30 June 1968)*, 100.
3. For an excellent overview of the Plan, see Carland, *Stemming the Tide, May 1965 to October 1966*, 152.
4. Quote from Sharp and Westmoreland, *Report on the War in Vietnam (As of 30 June 1968)*, 113–14.
5. For Westmoreland quotes and the division of labor between South Vietnamese and American forces, see Sharp and Westmoreland, *Report on the War in Vietnam (As of 30 June 1968)*, 113–14, 116. The South Vietnamese divided South Vietnam into four tactical corps. Ranging from north to south, these corps consisted of: I Corps Tactical Zone, II Corps Tactical Zone, III Corps Tactical Zone, and IV Corps Tactical Zone. American military operations in the aforementioned corps came under the auspices of American commands. In I Corps, III Marine Amphibious Force handled American operations. In II Corps, I Field Force, Vietnam (U.S. Army) supervised American operations. In

III Corps, II Field Force, Vietnam (U.S. Army) handled American operations. American command arrangements evolved slightly as the war wore on, however. In 1968, for example, MACV (Military Assistance Command, Vietnam) established MACV Forward headquarters to handle American units in northern I Corps. Meanwhile, in something of a compromise arrangement, U.S. Army units involved in riverine operations in III and IV Corps came under the command of II Field Force. Later on, in 1969, Delta Military Assistance Command was established to control U.S. Army units operating in the delta. See Eckhardt, *Command Control, 1950–1969*.

6. General Westmoreland decided in July 1966 that the 4th Infantry Division would establish a base camp south of Pleiku City. For details on the deployment and activities of the 4th Infantry Division advance planning groups in South Vietnam in July of 1966, see Activity Reports from the Advance Planning Group, 4th Infantry Division, 14 July 1966–31 August 1966: Activity Report Number 1 (14 July 1966), 1–2; Activity Report Number 2 (18 July 1966), 1. For a brief history on the origins of the 4th Infantry Division, including its "Ivy" Division nickname, see St. John, *4th Infantry "Ivy" Division*, 70; Hymoff, *Fourth Infantry Division in Vietnam*, 2.
7. Lieutenant Enari was the division's "first posthumously awarded Silver Star winner." See Whitis, "General Peers Pays Tribute to First Lieutenant Enari," 1–2.
8. See Activity Reports from the Advance Planning Group, 4th Infantry Division, 14 July 1966–31 August 1966: Activity Report Number 6 (8 August 1966), 1.
9. See "2 Divisions Beefed Up by Army," 26.
10. For the reorganization of the 4th Infantry Division, including the dispatch of new recruits to the division, see Wilson, *Maneuver and Firepower*, 327. For an organizational listing of the 4th in Vietnam, see St. John, *4th Infantry "Ivy" Division*, 70.
11. See Wilson, *Maneuver and Firepower*, 327.
12. For IFFV strategy under General Larsen, see General Stanley Larsen, Senior Officer Debriefing Report, 21 August 1967, NARA II, RG 472, U.S. Forces in Southeast Asia, 1950–1975, Entry A1–887, Senior Officer Debriefing Reports; 1967–1972, Box 283, Annex B, 1–2, 5.
13. For quoted words and General Larsen's advice and suggested approach for General Collins, see MacGarrigle, *Taking the Offensive*, 67.
14. Quoted text from Minh et al., *Luc Luong Vu Trang Nhan Dan Tay Nguyen Trong Khang Chien Chong My Cuu Nuoc*, 18. This source will henceforth be referred to as *People's Armed Forces of the Central Highlands* in subsequent notes.
15. Erik Villard, a historian with the U.S. Army Center of Military History in Washington, D.C., has done much to articulate the symbiotic relationship between the Central Highlands and the lowlands, and the relationship between the rhythm of Communist operations in both theaters and the production and distribution of rice.
16. It has been said that the Central Highlands or B3 Front was the largest North Vietnamese command organ outside of North Vietnam. Such a description is open to interpretation, depending on the definition of a "North Vietnamese" command organ. Since COSVN [Central Office for South Vietnam] was organized by and answered to Hanoi, it could

conceivably be classified as a "North Vietnamese" command organ, in which case it would be the largest. See MacGarrigle, *Taking the Offensive.* , 67.

17. For biographical information on Man, see Do, *Tu Dien Bach Khoa Quan Su Viet Nam* [Military Encyclopedia of Vietnam], 189. Man held several positions between 1954 and 1965 in addition to those cited.
18. For establishment of the 1st NVA Division, see Military History Institute of Vietnam, *Victory in Vietnam*, 156.
19. See Minh, *People's Armed Forces of the Central Highlands*, 50–51.
20. Collins sent the 2nd Brigade, 4th Inf. Div. and the 3rd Brigade, 25th Infantry Division, into the Plei Trap. See AAR, Opn PAUL REVERE IV, 4th Inf Div, 28 Jan 67 (Historians Files, U.S. Army Center of Military History), 16–20. The Center of Military History will be referred to as CMH in subsequent notes.
21. Quoted words from Collins, Letter to Richardson, 26 November 1966 (Historians Files, CMH).
22. Quoted passage from AAR, Opn PAUL REVERE IV, 4th Inf Div, 28 Jan 67, 83.

CHAPTER 1

1. Quoted words found in: USMACV GENERAL 1967 Command History Part 1, 1967, Folder 01, Bud Harton Collection, The Vietnam Archive, Texas Tech University, 323. The phrase "inevitable general" comes from Ernest B. Ferguson's 1968 biography, *Westmoreland: The Inevitable General.*
2. General Westmoreland entitled a chapter on military operations in South Vietnam in 1967, "The Year of the Offensive—1967." See Sharp and Westmoreland, *Report on the War in Vietnam (As of 30 June 1968)*, 131.
3. For all quoted words pertaining to the Combined Plan, see JGS (Joint General Staff)/ MACV (Military Assistance Command, Vietnam) Combined Campaign Plan for Military Operations in the Republic of Vietnam, 1967 [7 Nov 66] (Historians Files, CMH), 4. Here again, though the Combined Campaign Plan did not specify that American forces should shoulder the lion's share of the fighting, American capabilities and sheer troop strength ensured it would be American forces, and not those of the Free World Military Assistance Forces (FWMAF), that did.
4. Free World Military Assistance Forces, or FWMAF, consisted of those forces from Australia, Thailand, South Korea, New Zealand, and the Philippines as well as advisors from Taiwan.
5. See Combined Campaign Plan for Military Operations in the Republic of Vietnam, 1967 [7 Nov 66], 7.
6. Quoted words found in Sharp and Westmoreland, *Report on the War in Vietnam (As of 30 June 1968)*, 133.
7. See "Maj. Gen. Peers Assumes Command of the Division," 1.
8. See David W. Hogan Jr., *U.S. Army Special Operations in World War II*, 99–100; Lieutenant General William R. Peers, March 1969, Folder 07, Box 13, Douglas Pike Collection:

Unit 08—Biography, The Vietnam Archive, Texas Tech University. The Peers bio mentions that he achieved the rank of captain in October 1941. Other sources indicate that he was a first lieutenant when he joined OSS.

9. See John Whiteclay Chambers II, *OSS in the National Parks and Service Abroad in World War II*, http://www.nps.gov/history/history/online_books/ossindex.htm. Peers was promoted to lieutenant colonel in January of 1944.

10. For an excellent source of biographical information on Gen. William R. Peers, see Lieutenant General William R. Peers, March 1969, Folder 07, Box 13, Douglas Pike Collection: Unit 08—Biography. Peers served as assistant division commander with the 4th from September 1963 to July 1964.

11. Quoted words and Peers analysis from Lieutenant General William R. Peers, Senior Officer Debriefing Report, 9 March 1969, NARA II, RG 472, U.S. Forces in Southeast Asia, 1950–1975, Entry A1–887, Senior Officer Debriefing Reports; 1967–1972, Box 283, 1–3.

12. Quoted words from Lt. Gen. William R. Peers, CG, 4th Inf Div, interview with George MacGarrigle, 21 Oct 75 (Historians Files, CMH).

13. See Operation SAM HOUSTON After Action Critique Notes, 4th Infantry Division, 24 May 67 (Historians Files, CMH), 2. The 4th's organic armored cavalry squadron was the 1st Squadron, 10th Cavalry, and the attached tank battalion was the 1st Battalion, 69th Armor.

14. The 2nd of the 35th Infantry, a 3rd Brigade unit, remained in the Highlands as a task force (TF 2-35 Inf.) and was later placed under the control of the 1st Brigade, 4th Infantry Division.

15. See AAR, Opn SAM HOUSTON, 4th Inf Div, 16 May 67 (Historians Files, CMH), 10; Operation SAM HOUSTON After Action Critique Notes, 2; Lt. Gen. William R. Peers, CG, 4th Inf Div, interview with George MacGarrigle, 21 Oct 75; CHECO Rpt, Opn PAUL REVERE/SAM HOUSTON, PACAF 27 July 67 (Historians Files, CMH), 72.

16. For a detailed analysis of Communist strategic thinking and decision-making, see Warren Wilkins, *Grab Their Belts to Fight Them: The Viet Cong's Big Unit War against the U.S., 1965–66* (Annapolis, Md.: Naval Institute Press, 2011), 127–134.

17. See Pribbenow, "General Vo Nguyen Giap and the Mysterious Evolution of the Plan for the 1968 Tet Offensive," 9–13.

18. Quoted words from *Lich Su Cuc Tac Chien, 1945–2000* [History of the Combat Operations Department, 1945–2000].

19. Quoted words from An and Duong, *Chien Truong Moi* [New Battlefield], 31. Man had also claimed that he and his troops had used the formula "work and study at the same time . . . fight and hone our skills at the same time." See Man with Trieu, *Thoi Soi Song* [Time of Upheaval], 420.

20. See Man with Trieu, *Thoi Soi Song* [Time of Upheaval], 423; An with Duong, *Chien Truong Moi* [New Battlefield], 39.

21. Quoted words from An with Duong, *Chien Truong Moi* [New Battlefield], 57; Hiep with Trieu and Binh, *Ky Uc Tay Nguyen*, [Highland Memories], Part 4, 62.

22. See Bieu, *A Number of Battles Fought by Units of the Central Highlands Corps*, 5:70. Interestingly enough, in the second phase of the Communist spring offensive, Man sent a "mobile force across to the east side of the Sa Thay River with the goal of either luring the enemy to push across to the western side of the river so that we could destroy his force or of forcing the enemy to withdraw and abandon his Dat Do-Pong Giong-Po Ko defense line."
23. See Summary of Operation SAM HOUSTON (Headquarters 4th Infantry Division) 20 June 1967. On February 18, the 1st Brigade was ordered to move the brigade CP as well as an infantry battalion and support elements to reinforce the 4th Infantry Division. See 1st Bde, 4th Inf Div, ORGANIZATIONAL HISTORY, NARA II, RG 472, U.S. Forces in Southeast Asia, 1950–1975, Box 1.
24. A slick is a troop-transporting UH-1 "Huey" helicopter. Slicks were used to transport troops and supplies, and to evacuate the wounded.
25. For the change in NVA tactics and its effect on American casualties during Operation Sam Houston, see AAR, Opn SAM HOUSTON, 4th Inf Div, 16 May 67, 10–12; 50 (Inclosure 1); MacGarrigle, *Taking the Offensive*, 175–76.
26. The 1st Brigade, 4th Inf. Div., and the 1st Brigade, 101st Airborne Div., were based at TUY HOA SOUTH in Oct. of 1966. See MacGarrigle, *Taking the Offensive*, 81. Interestingly enough, after the tragic drowning of an MP, swimming in the South China Sea was severely restricted.
27. Quoted words from Bockover, "The Untold Stories of the Men from Companies A & B, 1/8 Infantry" (unpublished source), 34.
28. During Operation Adams, NVA and Viet Cong main force units generally avoided contact with U.S. forces. See AAR, Opn ADAMS, 1st Bde, 4th Inf Div, 18 May 1967 (Historians Files, CMH), 4.
29. For Sholly's quotes and an account of the meeting, see Sholly, "Ivy Vines Tie Special Bonds," 3.
30. Quoted words from Bockover, "Untold Stories," 100.
31. Quoted words from Sholly, "Ivy Vines Tie Special Bonds," 3.
32. See Bockover, "Untold Stories," 17.
33. For quoted words and incident, see Bockover, "Untold Stories," 82. The Combat Infantryman Badge (CIB) was originally established during World War II to recognize Army infantrymen engaged in ground combat. CIB eligibility was expanded somewhat during the Vietnam War. For details see Summers *The Vietnam Almanac*, 128.
34. AAR, Opn SAM HOUSTON, 4th Inf Div, 16 May 67, 12 (Inclosure 10).
35. Quoted words from Bockover, "Untold Stories," 17.
36. Rawlinson, incidentally, received a Distinguished Flying Cross for returning to A Company over and over again to unload supplies and evacuate the wounded in the face of intense hostile fire.
37. See Sholly, "Ivy Vines Tie Special Bonds," 11.
38. Casualty figures for the battle were derived from Bockover, "Untold Stories," 17. A Company sustained twenty-two of the reported twenty-seven KIA.

39. Quoted words from Maj. Gen. James B. Adamson, Comdr, 2d Bde, 4th Inf Div, interview with George L. MacGarrigle, 4 April 79 (Historians Files, CMH).
40. See AAR, Opn SAM HOUSTON, 4th Inf Div, 16 May 67, 12 (Inclosure 10).

CHAPTER 2

1. For quoted words and the multiple missions assigned to the 4th Infantry Division, including pacification/population security, see AAR Opn FRANCIS MARION, 4th Inf Div, 25 Nov 67, 11, 30.
2. Quoted words from Peers, interview with MacGarrigle, 21 Oct 75.
3. For the dispositions of the 4th Infantry Division at the start of Operation Francis Marion, see AAR Opn FRANCIS MARION, 4th Inf Div, 25 Nov 67 (Historians Files, CMH), 11–12; MacGarrigle, *Taking the Offensive*, 290. The 3rd Brigade, 25th Infantry Division had been attached to the 4th since February 13, 1967, but it was under the operational control of the 1st Cavalry Division in Binh Dinh Province at this time. The brigade remained under the control of the 1st Cavalry until April 25, when it reverted to the control of Task Force Oregon. Additionally, the CIDG (Civilian Irregular Defense Group) were indigenous outfits advised by U.S Special Forces.
4. See AAR Opn FRANCIS MARION, 4th Inf Div, 25 Nov 67, 25.
5. Ibid., 20; the 52nd Artillery Group (IFFV) participated as well. The 1st Battalion, 69th Armor, which was attached to the 3rd Brigade, 25th Inf. Div., and the 1st Squadron, 10th Cavalry participated in Operation Francis Marion.
6. Quoted words from "Col. Jackson Succeeds Col. Austin," 1.
7. For biographical info on Jackson, see U.S. Army Heritage and Education Center (Carlisle Barracks, Pa.), *U.S. Army Heritage Collections Online*, http://www.carlisle.army.mil/ahec/index.cfm.
8. See Hymoff, *Fourth Infantry Division in Vietnam*, 96.
9. See MacGarrigle, *Taking the Offensive*, 290. The three independent regiments in the Highlands were the 95th (Pleiku Province), 33rd (northern Darlac Province), and the 24th Regiment (Kontum Province). There were also some independent NVA and VC battalions operating in the area. In May 1967 the 1st NVA Division was composed of the 32nd and 66th NVA Regiments, but it is not clear if the remaining unit was the 88th or the 174th NVA Regiment. Colonel An claimed that "not long after the end of the Sa Thay River Campaign" in the fall of 1966, the "88th Regiment received orders to move down to Cochin China. . . . In fact, only a few months after 88th Regiment left, 174th Regiment arrived from North Vietnam with orders to join 1st Division." See An with Duong, *Chien Truong Moi* [New Battlefield], 59. Another North Vietnamese source, the *People's Armed Forces of the Central Highlands*, also claims that the 174th arrived early in 1967. It remains unclear, however, exactly when the 88th left the Central Highlands and when the 174th arrived.
10. See 1st Bde, 4th Inf Div, AAR Opn FRANCIS MARION, 24 October 1967, NARA II, RG 472, U.S. Forces in Southeast Asia, 1950–1975, Box 1, 18; AAR Opn FRANCIS MARION, 4th Inf Div, 25 Nov 67, 1 (Inclosure 1).

11. For VC/NVA activity in Darlac Province, see AAR Opn HANCOCK, 3d Bn, 8th Inf, 7 June 67 (Historians Files, CMH), 6; MacGarrigle, *Taking the Offensive*, 290.
12. The 1st and 2nd Brigades of the 4th Inf. Div. would often OPCON (place under the "operational control") one of their battalions to the other brigade for a certain period of time. This occurred frequently during Operation Francis Marion. For example, on April 26, just two days after the decision to send the 3-8 Inf. to Darlac, the 1st Brigade consisted of the 1-22 Inf. and the 3-12 Inf., while the 2nd Brigade was composed of the 1-8 Inf., 2-8 Inf., and 1-12 Inf. Then, on May 13, the 1-8 Inf. was returned to the 1st Brigade.
13. See MacGarrigle, *Taking the Offensive*, 290.
14. See MacGarrigle "NINE DAYS IN MAY," (Historians Files, CMH), 7. The NVA POW was captured south of Highway 19. At that time, the 2-8 Infantry was in the process of converting from a regular infantry battalion to a mechanized infantry battalion.
15. For details of the action, see AAR Opn FRANCIS MARION, 4th Inf Div, 25 Nov 67, Inclosure 7; MacGarrigle, *Taking the Offensive*, 291.
16. For casualties, see AAR Opn FRANCIS MARION, 4th Inf Div, 25 Nov 67, 13. American sources often refer to the 95th NVA Regiment as the "95B" NVA Regiment.
17. Quoted passage from Captured NVA Document—"Outline of Campaign Plan of B3 for the 1967 Rainy Season" (Historians Files, CMH), 13.
18. See Captured NVA Document—"Outline of Campaign Plan of B3 for the 1967 Rainy Season," 27; AAR Opn FRANCIS MARION, 4th Inf Div, 25 Nov 67, 1–2; MacGarrigle, *Taking the Offensive*, 291.
19. See Operational Report Lessons Learned (ORLL), 1 May 67–31 July 67, 4th Inf Div, 20 August 1967 (Historians Files, CMH), 3; MacGarrigle, *Taking the Offensive*, 291.
20. For an excellent summation of the decision and events surrounding the dispatch of the 1-8 Inf., see MacGarrigle, *Taking the Offensive*, 291.
21. See Maj. Gen James B. Adamson, Comdr, 2d Bde, 4th Inf Div, interview with George L. MacGarrigle, 4 April 79. Adamson thought that "B-52 post-strike reconnaissance by ground troops was useless and dangerous."
22. Quoted words from Col. Timothy G. Gannon, Comdr, 1st Bn, 8th Inf, 4th Inf Div, interview with George L. MacGarrigle, 31 August 78 (Historians Files, CMH). A copy of the interview was provided by Capt. Robert Sholly.
23. AAR, Opn SAM HOUSTON, 4th Inf Div, 16 May 67, 35–36 (Inclosure 1); see MacGarrigle, *Taking the Offensive*, 292. Earlier, during Operation Sam Houston, companies were instructed to remain within one to three hours of one another.
24. For an excellent synopsis of 1-8 Inf. activities from April 6 to May 13, see 1st Bde, 4th Inf Div, AAR Opn FRANCIS MARION, 24 October 1967, 18–19; AAR Opn FRANCIS MARION, 4th Inf Div, 25 Nov 67, 12.
25. Quote from Gannon interview with MacGarrigle, 31 August 78.
26. See MacGarrigle, *Taking the Offensive*, 292–93.
27. Quoted words from AAR, Opn SAM HOUSTON, 4th Inf Div, 16 May 67, Intro (Inclosure 1).
28. Quoted words from DuPre, "Letters Show Many Sides of Young Soldier."

CHAPTER 3

1. "Lifer" was a derisive term used to describe career soldiers, while the term "John Wayne, gung-ho, motherfucker" was used to describe an overly aggressive soldier in Vietnam, particularly those in leadership positions like an officer or NCO. Both terms were used frequently in Vietnam, most typically by draftees.
2. Quoted exchange from Bockover, "Untold Stories," 115.
3. See AAR Opn FRANCIS MARION, 4th Inf Div, 25 Nov 67, Inclosure 7 (1st Battalion, 8th Infantry).
4. See AAR Opn FRANCIS MARION, 4th Inf Div, 25 Nov 67, Inclosure 7 (1st Battalion, 8th Infantry); 4th Infantry Division G-2 Daily Staff Journal (18–27, May 1967), NARA II, RG 472, U.S. Forces in Southeast Asia, 1950–1975, Box 6. The Journal date is May 18, 1967.
5. For quoted words and anecdote, see Moore and Galloway, *We Were Soldiers Once . . . and Young*, 63. PAVN, or the People's Army of Vietnam, was the official name for the North Vietnamese Army or NVA.
6. For the cited times and official narrative of events, see AAR Opn FRANCIS MARION, 4th Inf Div, 25 Nov 67, Inclosure 7 (1st Battalion, 8th Infantry); 4th Infantry Division G-2 Daily Staff Journal (18 May 1967); 4th Infantry Division G-3 Daily Staff Journal (18–27, May 1967), NARA II, RG 472, U.S. Forces in Southeast Asia, 1950–1975, Box 2; 4th Infantry Division G-2 Intelligence Summaries (11–20 May 1967). All entries are derived from May 18.
7. See AAR, Operation FRANCIS MARION, 4th Infantry Division, 25 Nov 67, Inclosure 7 (1st Battalion, 8th Infantry).
8. Quoted words from Bockover, "Untold Stories," 117.
9. Ibid., 118.
10. The platoon leader and his RTO would typically be located toward the front of the platoon, while the platoon sergeant and his RTO would normally be located toward the rear. Each man, of course, had access to a radio via his RTO.
11. Quoted words from Headquarters, 4th Infantry Division; Summary of Recommendation for Award of Medal of Honor (Posthumous); Name: Bruce A. Grandstaff; Status: Platoon Sergeant E-7, U.S. Army; Organization: Company B, 1st Battalion, 8th Infantry, 4th Infantry Division, USA; June, 1967, Inclosure 9.
12. See 4th Infantry Division G-2 Daily Staff Journal (18 May 1967).
13. "PTL" stands for platoon leader.
14. For the actions of 1st Lt. Chuck Aronhalt on May 18, 1967, seeHeadquarters, U.S. Army Vietnam, General Orders No. 3832 (July 27, 1967), NARA II, RG 472, U.S. Forces in Southeast Asia, 1950–1975, Box 4 (Charles E. Aronhalt Jr., Distinguished Service Cross Citation).
15. Quoted words found in Sholly, *Young Soldiers, Amazing Warriors*, 302.
16. The term company (-), or company "minus," refers to a company lacking one of its elements, in this case the Fourth Platoon.

17. See Headquarters, 4th Infantry Division, General Orders No. 3574, 26 October 1967, NARA II, RG 472, U.S. Forces in Southeast Asia, 1950–1975, Box 4 (John E. Richey, Silver Star Citation).
18. See Headquarters, 4th Infantry Division, General Orders No. 3492, 22 October 1967, NARA II, RG 472, U.S. Forces in Southeast Asia, 1950–1975, Box 4 (James W. Smothers, Bronze Star Citation).
19. See MacGarrigle, "NINE DAYS IN MAY," 15.
20. Quote from Gannon, interview with MacGarrigle, 31 August 78.
21. Quote derived from interview with author, 1 Feb 2011; Bockover, "Untold Stories," 109.

CHAPTER 4

1. See "Spokane School Honors Heroes," 1; Bruce A. Grandstaff Memorial Dedication Pamphlet, September 10, 2011, published by the Fairmount Memorial Association in cooperation with Tamara Grandstaff.
2. Quote from Bockover, "Untold Stories," 119.
3. See AAR Opn FRANCIS MARION, 4th Inf Div, 25 Nov 67, Inclosure 7 (1st Battalion, 8th Infantry).
4. That Nash observed a Confederate flag seems beyond dispute. Some veterans of the battalion, however, have called into question the size of the flag Nash described, saying that it was unlikely that a flag of that dimension would have been hanging in such a location. The ambush incident could not be independently corroborated either way, however.
5. Quote from Bockover, "Untold Stories,"119.
6. Ibid., 119.
7. See AAR Opn FRANCIS MARION, 4th Inf Div, 25 Nov 67, Inclosure 7 (1st Battalion, 8th Infantry). Although the AAR stated that only one man survived the carnage in the dry creek bed, interviews with the survivors indicate that *two* men actually escaped unharmed.
8. Ibid.
9. For the communication difficulties Grandstaff experienced and the use of artillery fire in support of the Fourth Platoon, see ibid.
10. See Headquarters, 4th Infantry Division, Summary of Recommendation for Award of Medal of Honor (Posthumous); Name: Bruce A. Grandstaff; Status: Platoon Sergeant E-7, U.S. Army; Organization: Company B, 1st Battalion, 8th Infantry, 4th Infantry Division, USA; June, 1967, Inclosure 2.
11. Quoted words from Bockover, "Untold Stories," 120.
12. Quoted words from Headquarters, 4th Infantry Division, Summary of Recommendation for Award of Medal of Honor (Posthumous); Name: Bruce A. Grandstaff; Status: Platoon Sergeant E-7, U.S. Army; Organization: Company B, 1st Battalion, 8th Infantry, 4th Infantry Division, USA; June 1967, Inclosure 9.

13. See AAR Opn FRANCIS MARION, 4th Inf Div, 25 Nov 67, Inclosure 7 (1st Battalion, 8th Infantry).
14. Ibid.
15. Quoted words from Hymoff, *Fourth Infantry Division in Vietnam*, 98.

CHAPTER 5

1. Quoted words from Bockover, "Untold Stories," 109. Gannon's decision reflected the institutional deference commanders on the ground enjoyed with respect to close-in artillery fire. "However, the control and adjustment of close-in, direct supporting fires," noted a divisional report published in August 1967, "out 200–400 meters from the perimeter, must be left to the company commander and his artillery FO." See Operational Report Lessons Learned (ORLL), 1 May 67–31 July 67, 4th Inf Div, 20 August 1967, 55.
2. The "G1" was the personnel officer or section at division or corps level.
3. Quoted passage from "Spokane School Honors Heroes," 5.
4. One unnamed Fourth Platoon member reportedly said that the surviving members of the platoon had "reached complete agreement that the artillery be brought in on us." See "Spokane School Honors Heroes," 5.
5. Quoted passage from Headquarters, 4th Infantry Division, Summary of Recommendation for Award of Medal of Honor (Posthumous); Name: Bruce A. Grandstaff; Status: Platoon Sergeant E-7, U.S. Army; Organization: Company B, 1st Battalion, 8th Infantry, 4th Infantry Division, USA; June 1967, Inclosure 9.
6. A "first sergeant" (1st Sgt.) was generally the senior enlisted man in a rifle company.
7. See AAR Opn FRANCIS MARION, 4th Inf Div, 25 Nov 67, Inclosure 7 (1st Battalion, 8th Infantry).
8. See "Reds Pick 'Dead' GIs' Pockets," 6.
9. Quoted words from Gannon, interview with MacGarrigle, 31 August 78.
10. See AAR Opn FRANCIS MARION, 4th Inf Div, 25 Nov 67, Inclosure 7 (1st Battalion, 8th Infantry); MacGarrigle "NINE DAYS IN MAY," 17.
11. The S4 is the logistics officer or section at the battalion or brigade level.
12. Quote from Bockover, "Untold Stories," 132.

CHAPTER 6

1. See AAR Opn FRANCIS MARION, 4th Inf Div, 25 Nov 67, Inclosure 7 (1st Battalion, 8th Infantry); MacGarrigle, "NINE DAYS IN MAY," 17–19. The attack, according to the AAR, was launched at 4:20 P.M. and was said to have been "stopped at the ravine to the front."
2. See AAR Opn FRANCIS MARION, 4th Inf Div, 25 Nov 67, Inclosure 7 (1st Battalion, 8th Infantry).
3. Ibid. The AAR states that elements of the Recon Platoon, which is part of the Headquarters Co. (1-8 Inf.), flew out with Captain Sholly. Sholly, however, disputes the claim and stated that only he and medics were on the flight.
4. The term "dustoff" generally refers to a medical evacuation Huey.

5. The 7th Air Force provided close air support to the 4th Inf. Div. during this period. See ORLL, 1 May 67–31 July 67, 4th Inf Div, 20 August 1967, 13. The 7th Air Force was based at Tan Son Nhut Air Base outside of Saigon, but it had units under its command throughout the country, including the 12th Tactical Fighter Wing at Cam Ranh Bay in II Corps.
6. See AAR Opn FRANCIS MARION, 4th Inf Div, 25 Nov 67, Inclosure 7 (1st Battalion, 8th Infantry).
7. For the movements of A Company during the afternoon of May 18 and its subsequent airlift to B Company, see AAR Opn FRANCIS MARION, 4th Inf Div, 25 Nov 67, Inclosure 7 (1st Battalion, 8th Infantry); MacGarrigle, "NINE DAYS IN MAY," 17; MacGarrigle, *Taking the Offensive*, 293.
8. See AAR Opn FRANCIS MARION, 4th Inf Div, 25 Nov 67, Inclosure 7 (1st Battalion, 8th Infantry).
9. AC-47 flareships were often called "Spookies" or "Spooky" by the troops. For an excellent examination of the role and uses of fixed-wing gunships, see USAF 1965–73 Fixed Wing Gunships (undated), Folder 01, Bud Harton Collection, The Vietnam Archive, Texas Tech University.
10. Quote from Gannon, interview with MacGarrigle, 31 August 78.
11. Quote from "Platoon Calls Shells Down on Own Position," 24.
12. "Eight-Two" (8-2) refers to Bravo Company, 1-8 Inf. Alpha Company, 1-8 Inf. was "Eight-One" (8-1), while Charlie Company was "Eight-Three" (8-3). "Charlie" in "Eight-Two Charlie," refers to Surface, the radio operator. Had Sholly been on the radio, he would have announced: "This is "Eight-Two Six," with the "Six" of course denoting the company commander.

CHAPTER 7

1. See AAR Opn FRANCIS MARION, 4th Inf Div, 25 Nov 67, Inclosure 7 (1st Battalion, 8th Infantry).
2. Spc4 Joseph A. Mancuso was awarded a Bronze Star for the events of May 19, 1967. Mancuso's commendation, though not officially stated as such, was awarded as much for his efforts on May 18.
3. See 4th Infantry Division G-2 Daily Staff Journal (18 May 1967); AAR Opn FRANCIS MARION, 4th Inf Div, 25 Nov 67, Inclosure 7 (1st Battalion, 8th Infantry). The AAR indicates that five B-40 rocket rounds were fired, while the G-2 Daily Staff Journal states that two rounds were fired.
4. See AAR Opn FRANCIS MARION, 4th Inf Div, 25 Nov 67, Inclosure 7 (1st Battalion, 8th Infantry). A Company was said to have moved north and then east before locating the missing platoon.
5. See "Troops Reach Lost Platoon; 22 of 50-Man Force Killed," 6.
6. See AAR Opn FRANCIS MARION, 4th Inf Div, 25 Nov 67, Inclosure 7 (1st Battalion, 8th Infantry).
7. McMichael was originally from Anthony, Kansas.

8. For casualty figures, seeMacGarrigle, *Taking the Offensive*, 293.
9. The base camp was named in honor of 1st Lt. Mark N. Enari, the first soldier in the division to be awarded (posthumously) a Silver Star.
10. Quote from Bockover, "Untold Stories," 24.
11. See AAR Opn FRANCIS MARION, 4th Inf Div, 25 Nov 67, Inclosure 7 (1st Battalion, 8th Infantry). C Co., 1-8 Inf. was relieved of responsibility for the security of the battalion base at 8 A.M., just about the time A Co., 1-22 Inf. was placed under the OPCON of 1-8 Inf.
12. Quoted words from DuPre, "Letters Show Many Sides of Young Soldier."
13. Quoted words from DuPre, "He Gave His Life for the People He Loved."
14. Ibid.
15. Ibid.
16. Third Platoon, like the rest of C Company, was airlifted in. For the movement and arrival of C Company, 1-8 Inf. AAR Opn FRANCIS MARION, 4th Inf Div, 25 Nov 67, Inclosure 7 (1st Battalion, 8th Infantry). There are some discrepancies between the AAR and the 1st Brigade Log as to the precise arrival times of C Company.
17. Back at Fort Lewis, the Fourth Platoon of rifle companies carried mortars to provide organic fire support to the three remaining "maneuver" platoons. In Vietnam, however, the mortars were dumped by many Fourth Platoons—included those in A and B Companies, 1-8 Inf.—because the burdensome weight of the weapons proved unsuitable for the tactical environment in which the platoons operated. Thereafter the Fourth Platoons reverted back to ordinary rifle platoons.
18. For a summary of the interview Phiem conducted with investigators, see Oral History Program Report: Senior Colonel Cao Tien Phiem, 01 May 1996, Folder 11, Box 13, George J. Veith Collection, The Vietnam Archive, Texas Tech University.
19. Quoted words from Bockover, "Untold Stories," 148. Spc4 James Workman was posthumously awarded a Bronze Star for his exploits on May 18, 1967.
20. See Headquarters, 4th Infantry Division. General Orders No. 1877, 11 July 1967, NARA II, RG 472, U.S. Forces in Southeast Asia, 1950–1975, Box 4 (Leland H. Thompson, Silver Star Citation); Headquarters, 4th Infantry Division, General Orders No. 1876, 11 July 1967, NARA II, RG 472, U.S. Forces in Southeast Asia, 1950–1975, Box 4 (Phillip R. Venekamp, Silver Star Citation).
21. The final casualty count for the Fourth Platoon, B Company (1-8 Inf.) lists nineteen KIA, one MIA, and eight (one uninjured) survivors. See MacGarrigle, *Taking the Offensive*, 293.
22. Quoted words from Bockover, "Untold Stories," 126.
23. Ibid., 148.
24. Quoted words from Hymoff, *Fourth Infantry Division in Vietnam*, 97–98.
25. Quoted words from Sholly, *Young Soldiers, Amazing Warriors*, 340.
26. Divisional reports would later warn against separating platoons from the main body of a company when operating near the Cambodian border. See Operational Report Lessons Learned (ORLL), 1 May 67–31 July 67, 4th Inf Div, 20 August 1967, 44.
27. For casualty figures, see MacGarrigle, *Taking the Offensive*, 293.

28. See 4th Infantry Division G-2 Daily Staff Journal (19 May 1967). The RPG was of the B-40 rocket variety.
29. For the status and condition of NVA KIAs found on the nineteenth, see AAR Opn FRANCIS MARION, 4th Inf Div, 25 Nov 67, Inclosure 7 (1st Battalion, 8th Infantry); MacGarrigle, *Taking the Offensive*, 293.
30. For quoted words, see Diem, ed., *Lich Su Su Doan 8 Bo Binh Quan Khu 9* (1974–2000) [History of the 8th Infantry Division, Military Region 9 (1974–2000)], 20. This source will henceforth be referred to as *History of the 8th Infantry Division* in subsequent notes.
31. Quoted words from AAR Opn FRANCIS MARION, 4th Inf Div, 25 Nov 67, Inclosure 7 (1st Battalion, 8th Infantry).

CHAPTER 8

1. Quoted words from Lt. Gen. Glenn D. Walker, Asst Div Comdr, 4th Inf Div, interview with George MacGarrigle, 3 Apr 79 (Historians Files, CMH).
2. Quoted words from Peers, interview with George MacGarrigle, 21 Oct 75.
3. Quoted words from Letter from General Westmoreland to General Wheeler—re: response to 'Why do we fight the enemy near the borders?,' 10 December 1967, Folder 06, Box 01, Veteran Members of the 109th Quartermaster Company (Air Delivery) Collection, The Vietnam Center and Archive, Texas Tech University. Westmoreland argued persuasively that a withdrawal policy would have had a profound psychological, political, military, and economic impact on the allied war effort in South Vietnam.
4. For a superb revisionist appraisal of General Westmoreland's strategy in Vietnam, see Daddis, *Westmoreland's War* 46, 81–84.
5. CMH historian Erik Villard notes that the United States had limited strategic options with regard to the border and enemy infiltration. The Army could not simply ignore the enemy's major incursions into South Vietnam, but it also could not strike at the Cambodian base areas supporting those incursions. As a result, the Army had little choice but to fight in the remote border regions of South Vietnam, including the Central Highlands.
6. For quoted words, see "General Says Red Force Massed in Cambodia; Pentagon Issues Denial."
7. Quoted words from Maj. Gen. James B. Adamson, Comdr, 2d Bde, 4th Inf Div, interview with George L. MacGarrigle, 4 April 79.
8. Sihanouk initially indicated he would pursue a policy of Cambodian neutrality. Later on, in the 1960s, Sihanouk allowed Hanoi to use Cambodian territory to transit men and material for the effort in the South. By the end of the decade, however, Sihanouk seemed much less opposed to attacks on NVA bases in Cambodia.
9. See 4th Infantry Division G-2 Daily Staff Journal (20 May 1967); AAR Opn FRANCIS MARION, 4th Inf Div, 25 Nov 67, Inclosure 7 (1st Battalion, 8th Infantry).
10. The Bronze Star with "V" Device was awarded in July of 1967.
11. See AAR Opn FRANCIS MARION, 4th Inf Div, 25 Nov 67, Inclosure 7 (1st Battalion, 8th Infantry).

12. See Operations Report from 1 May thru 1 August 1967, 1st Bde, 4th Infantry Division, 1 August 1967, NARA II, RG 472, U.S. Forces in Southeast Asia, 1950–1975 Box 6, np. The term "Chicom" means "Chinese Communist."
13. See Ibid, np. The time listed for the incident was 2:55 P.M.
14. See Operational Report Lessons Learned (ORLL), 1 May 67–31 July 67, 4th Inf Div, 20 August 1967, 5. Throughout Operation Francis Marion, the NVA made use of route and trail watchers to track the movement of American ground units.
15. See Operations Report from 1 May thru 1 August 1967, 1st Bde, 4th Infantry Division, 1 August 1967; 4th Infantry Division G-2 Daily Staff Journal (20 May 1967); AAR Opn FRANCIS MARION, 4th Inf Div, 25 Nov 67, Inclosure 7 (1st Battalion, 8th Infantry). There are some discrepancies between the various sources on the discovery of the abandoned NVA complex. For instance, the Operations Report from 1 May thru 1 August 1967, 1st Bde, 4th Infantry Division states that A and C Companies, 1-8 Inf., found the enemy foxholes, while the 4th Infantry Division G-2 Daily Staff Journal indicates that A and B Companies, 1-8 Inf., found the enemy foxholes. Similarly the Operations Report states that the NVA position was found at 3:10 P.M., whereas the 4th Infantry Division G-2 Daily Staff Journal cites a time of 3:30 P.M. The AAR report, however, confirms the 3:10 P.M. time but only mentions A Company.
16. For distance from the battle that occurred on the eighteenth, see AAR Opn FRANCIS MARION, 4th Inf Div, 25 Nov 67, 14.
17. Captain Sholly, the B Company CO, revealed in an interview with the author that the NVA had tied wire right in below the lip of the draw.
18. For NVA movements and preparations prior to the assault, see MacGarrigle "NINE DAYS IN MAY," 19.
19. American sources estimated that two battalions of the 32nd NVA Regiment, with an additional battalion in reserve, ultimately participated in the attack on the night of May 20. See AAR Opn FRANCIS MARION, 4th Inf Div, 25 Nov 67, Inclosure 7 (1st Battalion, 8th Infantry).
20. See AAR Opn FRANCIS MARION, 4th Inf Div, 25 Nov 67, Inclosure 7 (1st Battalion, 8th Infantry). While MacGarrigle's official account—*Taking the Offensive*—indicates that the Americans called in artillery fire on lights they observed, it does not indicate where the lights were seen. Captain Sholly, however, recounted in an interview with the author that the lights appeared to be near the LZ A Company cleared on the nineteenth.
21. See Headquarters, 4th Infantry Division, General Orders No. 3583, 26 October 1967, NARA II, RG 472, U.S. Forces in Southeast Asia, 1950–1975, Box 4 (James Gaskins Jr., Bronze Star Citation).
22. Quoted words from Bockover, "Untold Stories," 47.
23. Ibid., 48.
24. See Headquarters, 4th Infantry Division, General Orders No. 1758, 5 July 1967, NARA II, RG 472, U.S. Forces in Southeast Asia, 1950–1975, Box 4 (Eugene F. Poeling, Bronze Star Citation).

CHAPTER 9

1. See Headquarters, 4th Infantry Division, General Orders No. 1759, 5 July 1967 (Leon A. Wangerin, Bronze Star Citation).
2. Quote from Gannon, interview with MacGarrigle, 31 August 78.
3. Quoted words from Bockover, "Untold Stories," 110. Harton received the Air Medal with "V" Device for his service in "aerial flight," May 18–24.
4. Ibid., 110.
5. See 1st Bde, 4th Inf Div, AAR, Opn FRANCIS MARION, 24 October 1967, 6–7.
6. See James Flaiz, 2Lt, Infantry, Co. C, 1st Bn, 8th Inf., undated witness statement in support of Leslie Allen Bellrichard Medal of Honor Citation.
7. Quote from Michael Gustafson, SP/4 (E4), Co. C, 1st Bn, 8th Inf., undated witness statement in support of Leslie Allen Bellrichard Medal of Honor Citation.
8. Quote from Robert J. Braun, PFC (E3), Co. C, 1st Bn, 8th Inf., undated witness statement in support of Leslie Allen Bellrichard Medal of Honor Citation.
9. For Ely's exploits, see Headquarters, 4th Infantry Division, General Orders No. 3595, 26 October 1967 (Ralph W. Ely III, Bronze Star Citation). Ely would also receive a Bronze Star for an action that occurred on May 2, 1967.
10. Air strikes delivered May 18–23 featured all of the aforementioned ordnance as well as napalm. See 1st Bde, 4th Inf Div, AAR Opn FRANCIS MARION, 24 October 1967, 3.
11. For Patton's exploits, see Headquarters, 4th Infantry Division, General Orders No. 1884, 26 October 1967 (Frank E. Patton, Bronze Star Citation). Patton refused to discuss the events that earned him a Bronze Star out of deference to his comrades in A Co.
12. See Headquarters, 4th Infantry Division, General Orders No. 1884, 11 July 1967 (William M. Lumsden, Bronze Star Citation).
13. See AAR Opn FRANCIS MARION, 4th Inf Div, 25 Nov 67, Inclosure 7 (1st Battalion, 8th Infantry).
14. For NVA probing and jamming efforts See 4th Infantry Division G-2 Daily Staff Journal (20 May 1967).
15. Ibid. American radio transmissions indicate that the small-arms fire ceased at 10:37 P.M.
16. Ibid., for NVA mortar and RPG fire, as well as American responses.
17. AAR Opn FRANCIS MARION, 4th Inf Div, 25 Nov 67, Inclosure 7 (1st Battalion, 8th Infantry); Operational Report Lessons Learned (ORLL), 1 May 67–31 July 67, 4th Inf Div, 20 August 1967. The ORLL states that 214 82-mm mortar rounds hit the 1-8 Inf.; the AAR puts the number at approximately 175.
18. See MacGarrigle, "NINE DAYS IN MAY," 20.
19. Specialist 4th Class Macellari, incidentally, was awarded a Bronze Star for his heroic actions earlier in the evening.
20. Williamson was later wounded by a mortar round.
21. Quote from Bockover, "Untold Stories," 155.
22. See 4th Infantry Division G-2 Daily Staff Journal (20 May 1967).

23. For American and NVA casualties, see AAR Opn FRANCIS MARION, 4th Inf Div, 25 Nov 67, Inclosure 7 (1st Battalion, 8th Infantry). MacGarrigle places the number of KIA at ten (see MacGarrigle, *Taking the Offensive*, 294).
24. See AAR Opn FRANCIS MARION, 4th Inf Div, 25 Nov 67, Inclosure 7 (1st Battalion, 8th Infantry). B Company reported that the two wounded NVA had been armed.
25. For intelligence disclosures provided by the NVA prisoner, see 4th Infantry Division G-2 Daily Staff Journal (20 May 1967). The NVA POW also stated that the "3Bn" of the 32nd had a base camp one hour north of Duc Co.
26. See AAR Opn FRANCIS MARION, 4th Inf Div, 25 Nov 67, Inclosure 7 (1st Battalion, 8th Infantry).
27. Ibid.; MacGarrigle, "NINE DAYS IN MAY," 21.
28. On June 28, 1967, the 1-8 Infantry began operations around the 4th Infantry Division base camp at Camp Enari (Dragon Mountain). For the actions and movements of the 1-8 Infantry during this period, see 1st Bde, 4th Inf Div, AAR Opn FRANCIS MARION, 24 October 1967, 19.

CHAPTER 10

1. For B-52 strikes conducted in the area around the 1-8 Infantry on the twenty-second, see MacGarrigle, *Taking the Offensive*, 294.
2. For estimated troop strength of 1st NVA Division, see Operational Report Lessons Learned (ORLL), 1 May 67–31 July 67, 4th Inf Div, 20 August 1967, 4.
3. For Peers's response to the fighting in Ia Tchar on the twentieth, see MacGarrigle, *Taking the Offensive*, 294. The 3-8 Infantry had been operating in Darlac Province since late April in a battalion task force dubbed "TF 3-8 Inf."
4. See MacGarrigle, "NINE DAYS IN MAY," 22. The two brigades consisted of the 3rd Brigade, 25th Infantry Division, and the 1st Brigade, 101st Airborne Division.
5. From Jan. 1, 1967 to Feb. 19, 1967, the battalion was attached to the 1st Brigade, 4th Inf. Division. Thereafter the battalion was OPCON to IFFV, where it would remain until April 3, 1967. See AAR, Opn SAM HOUSTON, 4th Inf Div, 16 May 67 (Inclosure 3). Much like the other battalions of the 1st Brigade, the advance party and the rear detachment of the 3-12 Inf. arrived by airplane while other elements arrived by boat.
6. The "S2" was the intelligence officer or section at battalion or brigade level.
7. For American casualties in the Hill 86 debacle, see AAR, Opn ADAMS, 1st Bde, 4th Inf Div, 18 May 1967 (Historians Files, CMH), 11. Two American personnel carriers were destroyed as well.
8. See AAR, Opn ADAMS, 1st Bde, 4th Inf Div, 18 May 1967, 12; "Operation Adams—3/12th Strikes Back at Enemy," 1. According to the *Ivy Leaf* article, twenty-eight enemy soldiers were killed in the fighting.
9. See 1st Bde, 4th Inf Div, AAR Opn FRANCIS MARION, 24 October 1967 .
10. See AAR Opn FRANCIS MARION, 4th Inf Div, 25 Nov 67, Inclosure 7 (3rd Battalion, 12th Infantry, 1 May 67).
11. Ibid.

12. Ibid.
13. Ibid for casualties. Some forty-four 82-mm mortar rounds were recovered, along with eleven RPG rounds.
14. For quoted words, see Performance Review, LTC John P. Vollmer, Review and Analysis Division, Revolutionary Development Support Directorate, Headquarters, U.S. Military Assistance Command, Vietnam, 6 June 66–23 April 67 (Period Covered), Rater—Col. Erwin R. Brigham, May 1 1967.
15. Quoted words from 3-12 Inf. Daily Staff Journal (21–25, May 1967), NARA II, RG 472, U.S. Forces in Southeast Asia, 1950–1975, Box 240. Vollmer issued the request at 10:40 A.M. and arrived back at the firebase at 11:00 A.M.
16. Ibid.
17. An NVA prisoner captured by the 3-12 Inf. on May 2, 1967, claimed that two battalions of the 66th NVA Regiment had been constructing base camps in an area not far from the location of the May 1 battle. See MacGarrigle, "NINE DAYS IN MAY," 11.
18. Quoted words from *Lich su Trung Doan 66—Doan Plei Me—1947–2007* [History of the 66th Regiment—the Plei Me Group—1947–2007], 9.
19. Ibid., 29.
20. Ibid.
21. See 3-12 Inf. Daily Staff Journal (21 May 1967).
22. Pestikas was promoted to first lieutenant in April 1967.
23. See 3-12 Inf. Daily Staff Journal (21 May 1967). The Daily Staff Journal records that Lieutenant Colonel Vollmer ordered A Co. to "move Southeast, then when you get to the bottom move south." The entry was recorded at "1445 hrs."
24. Ibid. The Daily Staff Journal records that B Company requested a dustoff for "three people hit by CBU dud" at 11:17 A.M. The explosion, therefore, probably occurred shortly before the request.
25. Ibid. The Daily Staff Journal indicates that one soldier suffered "serious" injuries and two others had to "go out" on a dustoff. One man was reported as having died.
26. Ibid.
27. Ibid.
28. See 1st Bde, 4th Inf Div, AAR Opn FRANCIS MARION, 24 October 1967, 4.
29. See 3-12 Inf. Daily Staff Journal (21 May 1967).
30. See AAR Opn FRANCIS MARION, 4th Inf Div, 25 Nov 67, 14. While traveling on separate routes, the two companies each travelled a distance of over six thousand meters.
31. Ibid., 14.
32. Quoted words from "3/12th Officer in Third Narrow Escape from Death," 6.
33. See 3-12 Inf. Daily Staff Journal (21 May 1967).

CHAPTER 11

1. Quoted words from "The Five-Hour Ordeal of an Army Patrol," 6.
2. See Hymoff, *Fourth Infantry Division in Vietnam*, 100.
3. See AAR Opn FRANCIS MARION, 4th Inf Div, 25 Nov 67, Inclosure 7 (3rd Battalion,

12th Infantry, 22 May 67). The Daily Staff Journal for the 3-12 Inf. on May 22 indicates that Hamer issued his request for air support at 7:15 A.M.

4. See 3-12 Inf. Daily Staff Journal (22 May 1967); AAR Opn FRANCIS MARION, 4th Inf Div, 25 Nov 67, 14. The AAR indicates that the NVA attack came from "a high ridgeline to the west."
5. See Headquarters, 4th Infantry Division, General Orders No. 1862, 9 July 1967 (Randal R. Aylworth, Bronze Star Citation).
6. The SKS (Simonov) was a Soviet 7.62-mm semiautomatic rifle.
7. For an excellent summary of the incident, see "NVA Arsenal Includes Human Mortar Tube," 3.
8. See "The Five-Hour Ordeal of an Army Patrol," 6.
9. See Headquarters, 4th Infantry Division, General Orders No. 3493, 22 October 1967 (Ernest E. Putoff, Bronze Star Citation).
10. See 3-12 Inf. Daily Staff Journal (22 May 1967).
11. Reitenauer insists that another soldier assisted him on the mortar on the morning of the twenty-second, but he cannot recall the name of that soldier or whether he was Spc4 Clarence Morris. Morris's Bronze Star Citation for the twenty-second, however, states that he "and another man" put "the mortar into operation." That man was Specialist 4th Class Reitenauer, but there is some doubt whether someone in Morris's reported condition could have performed the actions attributed to him.
12. Vollmer was airborne and communicating with his engaged units by 8:05 A.M. See 3-12 Inf. Daily Staff Journal (22 May 1967).
13. Quoted words from Ricks, "The Collapse of Generalship," 39.
14. See AAR Opn FRANCIS MARION, 4th Inf Div, 25 Nov 67, Inclosure 7 (3rd Battalion, 12th Infantry, 22 May 67); 3-12 Inf. Daily Staff Journal (22 May 1967).
15. See 3-12 Inf. Daily Staff Journal (22 May 1967).
16. See Hymoff, *Fourth Infantry Division in Vietnam*, 101.
17. Quoted words from "Rifleman Saves Lives with Quick Reaction," 6.
18. See AAR Opn FRANCIS MARION, 4th Inf Div, 25 Nov 67, Inclosure 7 (3rd Battalion, 12th Infantry, 22 May 67). What percentage of the NVA force moved closer to the perimeter during this covering fire is not entirely clear.
19. For the SITREP radioed in by Captain Lee at 8:15 A.M., see 3-12 Inf. Daily Staff Journal (22 May 1967).
20. Ford was awarded a Bronze Star.
21. For Sergeant Palmer's exploits, see Mira, "Sergeant Braves Enemy Fire to Rescue Wounded Soldier," 3.
22. See 3-12 Inf. Daily Staff Journal (22 May 1967). A Company reported that a radio had suffered damage at 8:32 A.M.

CHAPTER 12

1. See MacGarrigle, "NINE DAYS IN MAY," 23.
2. See Hymoff, *Fourth Infantry Division in Vietnam*, 100.

3. See AAR Opn FRANCIS MARION, 4th Inf Div, 25 Nov 67, Inclosure 7 (3rd Battalion, 12th Infantry, 22 May 67); Hymoff, *Fourth Infantry Division in Vietnam*, 100.
4. For Lieutenant Blake's repositioning of Second Platoon troopers, see Hymoff, *Fourth Infantry Division in Vietnam*, 100.
5. For quoted words and the A and B Company estimates and reports, see 3-12 Inf. Daily Staff Journal (22 May 1967).
6. Ibid. Lieutenant Colonel Vollmer indicated his desire to shift the artillery at 9:12 A.M.
7. See AAR Opn FRANCIS MARION, 4th Inf Div, 25 Nov 67, 62.
8. Ibid.
9. See Headquarters, 4th Infantry Division, General Orders No. 2505, 11 August 1967 (Gerald K. Cross, Air Medal Citation); Headquarters, 4th Infantry Division, General Orders No. 2516, 11 August 1967 (Joseph T. Makalusky, Air Medal Citation).
10. See AAR Opn FRANCIS MARION, 4th Inf Div, 25 Nov 67, Inclosure 7 (3rd Battalion, 12th Infantry, 22 May 67).
11. See 3-12 Inf. Daily Staff Journal (22 May 1967). This air strike occurred shortly after 10 A.M., but the results of the attack were not recorded in the Journal.
12. Ibid. Gunships were operating to the southeast and southwest of the perimeter at 10:18 A.M., and three minutes later there were reports of the gunships knocking NVA snipers out of the trees.
13. The "aviator" was likely the co-pilot that day, WO-1 Gregory Waltz.
14. The distance the Huey hovered above the ground is in some dispute. Captain Hamer, set up near the center of the perimeter at the time, probably had the best vantage point of the incoming craft and estimated that the chopper hovered about "twenty to thirty" feet off the ground while the ammo crates were thrown out.
15. See 3-12 Inf. Daily Staff Journal (22 May 1967). The first incomplete delivery concluded at 10:17 A.M.
16. For the exploits of Warrant Officer Waltz, see Headquarters, 4th Infantry Division, General Orders No. 3247, 6 August 1967, (Gregory A. Waltz, Army Recommendation Medal Citation). Waltz's citation notes that the chopper he co-piloted was hit "several times by enemy fire," but it does not specify what type of fire.
17. See Mira, "Sergeant Braves Enemy Fire to Rescue Enemy Soldier," 3.
18. See 3-12 Inf. Daily Staff Journal (22 May 1967); AAR Opn FRANCIS MARION, 4th Inf Div, 25 Nov 67, Inclosure 7 (3rd Battalion, 12th Infantry, 22 May 67).
19. See 3-12 Inf. Daily Staff Journal (22 May 1967). The time indicated in the Journal was 10:56 A.M.
20. Quoted words from MacGarrigle, *Taking the Offensive*, 172.
21. See AAR Opn FRANCIS MARION, 4th Inf Div, 25 Nov 67, Inclosure 7 (3rd Battalion, 12th Infantry, 22 May 67). B Company suffered eight KIA, thirty-six WIA; A Company two KIA, thirty-three WIA; and HHC eight WIA.
22. See AAR Opn FRANCIS MARION, 4th Inf Div, 25 Nov 67, Inclosure 7 (3rd Battalion, 12th Infantry, 22 May 67); 3-12 Inf. Daily Staff Journal (22 May 1967). The strike began at 11:09 A.M. and was the second air strike of the day.

23. Ibid.
24. See AAR Opn FRANCIS MARION, 4th Inf Div, 25 Nov 67, Inclosure 7 (3rd Battalion, 12th Infantry, 22 May 67); 3-12 Inf. Daily Staff Journal (22 May 1967). The AAR indicates that medical evacuation began at 11:15 A.M.; the Daily Staff Journal records that the "dustoff" was started at 11:16 A.M.
25. See 3-12 Inf. Daily Staff Journal (22 May 1967). The Daily Staff Journal stated that the "ammo supply ship that made 1st supply run will lead in dustoff ships."

CHAPTER 13

1. See 3-12 Inf. Daily Staff Journal (22 May 1967); AAR Opn FRANCIS MARION, 4th Inf Div, 25 Nov 67, Inclosure 7 (3rd Battalion, 12th Infantry, 22 May 67). The Daily Staff Journal states that a company "minus 1 platoon" from the 3-8 Inf. would assume responsibility for security of the 3-12 Inf. firebase. The AAR simply notes that "A Company, 3rd Bn, 8th Inf." arrived to take over security at the base.
2. A majority of Americans, according to some sources, continued to support the war until roughly October of 1967. See Summers, *The Vietnam Almanac*, 290.
3. Straub and Morris received the Bronze Star posthumously.
4. Avery stated in an interview conducted on February 25, 2011 that he took the equipment off the dead lieutenant from the "mortar platoon." The "mortar platoon" would have been the Fourth Platoon, commanded by Lt. Thomas Burke.
5. See AAR Opn FRANCIS MARION, 4th Inf Div, 25 Nov 67, Inclosure 7 (3rd Battalion, 12th Infantry, 22 May 67). While the Daily Staff Journal seems to indicate that B Company prepared the LZ, the AAR notes that both companies "prepared to secure the LZ."
6. See 3-12 Inf. Daily Staff Journal (22 May 1967). The Daily Staff Journal states that by 12:55 P.M. "six sorties of dustoffs lifted off."
7. Ibid.
8. See 3-12 Inf. Daily Staff Journal (21 May 1967); 1st Brigade, 4th Infantry Division S-2 Daily Staff Journal (21–24, May 1967), NARA II, RG 472, U.S. Forces in Southeast Asia, 1950–1975, Box 4.
9. See 3-12 Inf. Daily Staff Journal (22 May 1967); AAR Opn FRANCIS MARION, 4th Inf Div, 25 Nov 67, Inclosure 7 (3rd Battalion, 12th Infantry, 22 May 67).
10. See 3-12 Inf. Daily Staff Journal (22 May 1967). The Daily Staff Journal states that A Company reported the capture of a wounded POW at 1: 08 P.M.
11. Ibid.
12. See 3-12 Inf. Daily Staff Journal (22 May 1967); AAR Opn FRANCIS MARION, 4th Inf Div, 25 Nov 67, Inclosure 7 (3rd Battalion, 12th Infantry, 22 May 67); AAR, Opn FRANCIS MARION, 1st Bde, 4th Inf Div, 18 May 1967, 23. Both AARs state that four enemy POWs were captured on the twenty-second, while entries #134 and #135 in the Daily Staff Journal mention five POWs and state that "POWs were put on chopper."
13. How many prisoners talked and who said what is unclear. For example, the Daily Staff Journal recorded entries in which Colonel Jackson provides the 3-12 Inf. TOC with

intelligence garnered from a "POW," but the entries never state whether the information originated from the same POW or multiple POWs.

14. For intelligence gleaned from the NVA POWs and the subsequent American response, see 3-12 Inf. Daily Staff Journal (22 May 1967). The Daily Staff Journal reports that a FAC had three fighters on station, but it is unclear whether they belonged to the two groups mentioned.
15. See 3-12 Inf. Daily Staff Journal (22 May 1967). The Journal indicates that "6 missing persons from A Co have been accounted for." The time given was 1414 hrs.
16. For Sergeant Dunn quotes, see "The Five-Hour Ordeal of an Army Patrol," 6.
17. See Hymoff, *Fourth Infantry Division in Vietnam*, 101.
18. Quoted words from 3-12 Inf. Daily Staff Journal (22 May 1967), entry #81.
19. Quoted words from Hymoff, *Fourth Infantry Division in Vietnam*, 99–100.
20. See AAR Opn FRANCIS MARION, 4th Inf Div, 25 Nov 67, Inclosure 7 (3rd Battalion, 12th Infantry, 22 May 67).
21. Neither the AAR nor the Daily Staff Journal indicates exactly when the official order to reinforce A and B Companies reached C Company. Some of the C Company troopers, moreover, recall hearing the news and boarding choppers within fifteen minutes. Others, however, have little recollection of when they learned of the airlift and how long after they choppered out. Wayne Watson, a C Company trooper with an excellent memory of the period before the C Company deployment, believes the troops received word of the airlift shortly before 2 P.M. The Daily Staff Journal indirectly corroborates Watson's account. Gunships were allotted to escort the C Company airlift, and a 1:52 P.M. entry in the journal states that gunships were "going to rearm and will escort CA of C 3/12." See 3-12 Inf. Daily Staff Journal (22 May 1967), entry #89.
22. See 3-12 Inf. Daily Staff Journal (22 May 1967).
23. See 1st Brigade, 4th Infantry Division S-3 Daily Staff Journal (21–24, May 1967), NARA II, RG 472, U.S. Forces in Southeast Asia, 1950–1975, Box 1. The Journal date is May 22, 1967.
24. See AAR Opn FRANCIS MARION, 4th Inf Div, 25 Nov 67, Inclosure 7 (3rd Battalion, 12th Infantry, 22 May 67).
25. See 3-12 Inf. Daily Staff Journal (22 May 1967).

CHAPTER 14

1. Quoted words from Tenney, "On a Strange and Distant Hill," 105.
2. Ibid.
3. See AAR Opn FRANCIS MARION, 4th Inf Div, 25 Nov 67, Inclosure 7 (3rd Battalion, 12th Infantry, 22 May 67). The battalion found thirty-six Chicom grenades and twenty-six 60-mm mortar rounds.
4. See 4th Infantry Division G2 Periodic Intelligence Summary for Period May 11–28, 1967, NARA II, RG 472, U.S. Forces in Southeast Asia, 1950–1975, Box 1. The summary cited is from May 22, 1967.
5. See 3-12 Inf. Daily Staff Journal (22 May 1967).
6. Quoted words from Volkmer, "The Splinter," 27.

7. See 3-12 Inf. Daily Staff Journal (22 May 1967).
8. Quoted words from Tenney, "On a Strange and Distant Hill," 107.
9. See 3-12 Inf. Daily Staff Journal (22 May 1967). The Journal indicates that B Company "closed with C Company" at "1830H." Lieutenant Colonel Vollmer was awarded the Bronze Star for his actions with B Company on May 22.
10. Quoted words from Tenney, "On a Strange and Distant Hill," 107.
11. For the order to cease all firing at midnight and the decision by Lieutenant Colonel Vollmer to cut off illumination, excluding that which was used to highlight NVA escape routes to the west, see 3-12 Inf. Daily Staff Journal (22 May 1967).
12. Ibid. A Company arrived at "2249 hrs."
13. For Vollmer's opinion on the matter, see AAR Opn FRANCIS MARION, 4th Inf Div, 25 Nov 67, Inclosure 7 (3rd Battalion, 12th Infantry, 22 May 67).
14. Ibid. The 3-12 Inf. Daily Staff Journal indicates that "units are patrolling from center mass 731347" by 8:10 A.M. The location of the joint perimeter was previously listed as "732346."
15. The Milton Hershey School was originally for poor orphan boys, but by the time Specht arrived the qualifications had apparently been eased to include boys who had lost one parent.
16. Quotes from Tenney, "On a Strange and Distant Hill,"109.
17. For time of the incident and elements involved, see 3-12 Inf. Daily Staff Journal (23 May 1967); AAR Opn FRANCIS MARION, 4th Inf Div, 25 Nov 67, 7 (Inclosure 6). Both sources, incidentally, are only partially correct. The DSJ correctly identifies the time of the incident (9:20 A.M.) but mistakenly attributes the action to A Company. The AAR, meanwhile, correctly identifies C Company but states the incident occurred at 8:20 A.M.
18. See Volkmer, "The Splinter," 27.
19. Ibid.
20. For speculation that there had been three NVA from a trail-watching party involved in the firefight, see 4th Infantry Division G-2 Daily Staff Journal (23 May 1967).
21. Quote from Tenney, "On a Strange and Distant Hill," 111.
22. See 3-12 Inf. Daily Staff Journal (23 May 1967).
23. Quoted words from Tenney, "On a Strange and Distant Hill," 111–12.
24. See 3-12 Inf. Daily Staff Journal (23 May 1967).
25. For intelligence regarding snipers, see 4th Infantry Division G-2 Daily Staff Journal (23 May 1967); 1st Brigade, 4th Infantry Division S-3 Daily Staff Journal (23 May 1967).
26. The alleged shootings on the twenty-third and the alleged incident Lieutenant Pestikas described have not, to this day, been thoroughly corroborated. While atrocities were committed by both sides in the Highlands, the generally straightforward, conventional nature of the war there—both sides knew who the enemy was and there were relatively few civilians to complicate matters—seemed to reduce the numbers involved.
27. Quote words from Volkmer, "The Splinter," 28.
28. See 3-12 Inf. Daily Staff Journal (23 May 1967).
29. Ibid.
30. See MacGarrigle, *Taking the Offensive*, 294.

31. See 3-12 Inf. Daily Staff Journal (23 May 1967).
32. Ibid. The "Admin Log" refers to the radio frequency that would normally be used to communicate with the battalion S4.
33. See 1st Brigade, 4th Infantry Division S-3 Daily Staff Journal (23 May 1967); Hymoff, *Fourth Infantry Division in Vietnam*, 101.
34. See 3-12 Inf. Daily Staff Journal (24 May 1967).
35. For the 3-12 Inf. mission for May 24, 1967 and beyond, see AAR Opn FRANCIS MARION, 4th Inf Div, 25 Nov 67, Inclosure 7 (3rd Battalion, 12th Infantry, 24 May 67).
36. Ibid.
37. For the incident involving the two NVA soldiers, see 3-12 Inf. Daily Staff Journal (24 May 1967); 4th Infantry Division G-2 Daily Staff Journal (24 May 1967); AAR Opn FRANCIS MARION, 4th Inf Div, 25 Nov 67, 7 (Inclosure 6); "Six men cram into tiny hole," 3. The AAR, G2, and "Six men" article all indicate that B Company ran into the two NVA. The DSJ, however, states that it was C Company. The G2 Journal notes the incident occurred at 12:57 P.M.
38. For the term "Happy Valley," see Hymoff, *Fourth Infantry Division in Vietnam*, 101.
39. See AAR Opn FRANCIS MARION, 4th Inf Div, 25 Nov 67, Inclosure 7 (3rd Battalion, 12th Infantry, 24 May 67). The airlift of A Company, 3-12 Inf. was completed at 3:05 P.M. on May 24, 1967.
40. For distance between the C Company LZ and where B Company set up on the afternoon of May 24, 1967, see "NVA Force Makes Too Many Mistakes," 8.

CHAPTER 15

1. Quoted words from Birtle, "PROVN, Westmoreland, and the Historians: A Reappraisal," 1219.
2. Ibid., 1222.
3. For quoted words, see Daddis *Westmoreland's War*, 112.
4. Quoted words from Birtle, "PROVN, Westmoreland, and the Historians: A Reappraisal, 1223." PROVN was an acronym for "A Program for the Pacification and Long-Term Development of South Vietnam."
5. See AAR Opn FRANCIS MARION, 4th Inf Div, 25 Nov 67, Inclosure 7 (3rd Battalion, 12th Infantry, 24 May 67).
6. See AAR Opn FRANCIS MARION, 4th Inf Div, 25 Nov 67, Inclosure 7 (3rd Battalion, 12th Infantry, 24 May 67); 3-12 Inf. Daily Staff Journal, (24 May 1967).
7. See 3-12 Inf. Daily Staff Journal (24 May 1967). The mortar fire stopped at 4:04 P.M.
8. For the opening moments of the NVA ground assault, see AAR Opn FRANCIS MARION, 4th Inf Div, 25 Nov 67, Inclosure 7 (3rd Battalion, 12th Infantry, 24 May 67).
9. Murray was awarded a Bronze Star for his heroism. See Headquarters, 4th Infantry Division, General Orders No. 1768, 5 July 1967, NARA II, RG 472, U.S. Forces in Southeast Asia, 1950–1975, Box 4 (Gary D. Murray, Bronze Star Citation). Murray was from Elizabethton, Tenn.
10. For an account of the six trapped troopers, see "Six Men Cram into Tiny Hole," 3.

11. See AAR Opn FRANCIS MARION, 4th Inf Div, 25 Nov 67, Inclosure 7 (3rd Battalion, 12th Infantry, 24 May 67).
12. Ibid.; see also MacGarrigle, "NINE DAYS IN MAY." Eight batteries (B and C Batteries, 6-29 Artillery; A, B, and C Batteries, 5-16 Artillery; A and B Batteries, 6-14 Artillery; and C Battery, 1st of the 92nd Artillery) supported the 3-12 Infantry.
13. See 3-12 Inf. Daily Staff Journal (24 May 1967). The Daily Staff Journal notes that at 4:23 P.M. C Company was "moving up to support B Company from the southwest." The DSJ indicates that C Company's point was within "100 meters of B Co." at 4:23 P.M.
14. It is not entirely clear if Pearson ordered the entire company to move at the time or merely the lead elements of the company. Oliver Butler, who was on the radio that afternoon, remembers hearing Pearson ordering his First Platoon squad to "move up a ways."
15. Captain Pearson believed the rounds were coming in from the east-northeast.
16. See 4th Infantry Division G-3 Daily Staff Journal (24 May 1967). The Journal entry states that at "1633 hrs" C Company was under 60-mm and 82-mm mortar attack while moving to the aid of B Company. Captain Pearson believed the company had advanced about one-half of the way up the "hill" when the barrage began in earnest. Spc4 Oliver Butler, while less certain of how far the company had advanced, nevertheless recalls "all hell breaking loose" at some point along the way to the top of the knoll.
17. For the fire support available to Captain Hamer, see 3-12 Inf. Daily Staff Journal (24 May 1967); AAR Opn FRANCIS MARION, 4th Inf Div, 25 Nov 67, Inclosure 7 (3rd Battalion, 12th Infantry, 24 May 67).
18. Pfc. Junior Richardson indicated that the M-60 Pfc. Meier was using had malfunctioned on previous occasions.
19. See 1st Brigade, 4th Infantry Division S-3 Daily Staff Journal (24 May 1967).
20. Some of the other veterans on the crest with Richardson did not recall seeing any NVA near C Company.
21. See 3-12 Inf. Daily Staff Journal (24 May 1967); AAR Opn FRANCIS MARION, 4th Inf Div, 25 Nov 67, Inclosure 7 (3rd Battalion, 12th Infantry, 24 May 67). Both sources cite 4:41 P.M. as the time in which the lead elements of C Company linked up with B Company.
22. Captain Hamer was put in command of all units on the ground at 4:38 P.M., a few minutes before the linkup. See 3-12 Inf. Daily Staff Journal (24 May 1967).
23. Quote from "Six Men Cram into Tiny Hole," 3.
24. See 3-12 Inf. Daily Staff Journal (24 May 1967); AAR Opn FRANCIS MARION, 4th Inf Div, 25 Nov 67, Inclosure 7 (3rd Battalion, 12th Infantry, 24 May 67). The 4th Infantry Division G-3 Daily Staff Journal (24 May 1967) states that three C Company platoons had "closed with" B Company by 5:12 P.M., while the 1st Brigade, 4th Infantry Division S-3 Daily Staff Journal (24 May 1967) states that the three C Company platoons had closed by 5:11 P.M.
25. See 1st Brigade, 4th Infantry Division S-3 Daily Staff Journal (24 May 1967).
26. See AAR Opn FRANCIS MARION, 4th Inf Div, 25 Nov 67, Inclosure 7 (3rd Battalion, 12th Infantry, 24 May 67).
27. See 3-12 Inf. Daily Staff Journal (24 May 1967). The Journal states that "all C Company elements have closed B Company area at 1720."

28. For the use of NVA artillery in the Central Highlands, see *People's Armed Forces of the Central Highlands*, 152–62. NVA forces in the Highlands had 75-mm pack howitzers much earlier in the conflict, but their use seems to have been sporadic at best.
29. See AAR Opn FRANCIS MARION, 4th Inf Div, 25 Nov 67, Inclosure 7 (3rd Battalion, 12th Infantry, 24 May 67).
30. See MacGarrigle, "NINE DAYS IN MAY," 25; AAR Opn FRANCIS MARION, 4th Inf Div, 25 Nov 67, Inclosure 7 (3rd Battalion, 12th Infantry, 24 May 67); 3-12 Inf. Daily Staff Journal (24 May 1967). Fire coming from the NVA stopped at 5:52 P.M.
31. See MacGarrigle, "NINE DAYS IN MAY," 25; AAR Opn FRANCIS MARION, 4th Inf Div, 25 Nov 67, Inclosure 7 (3rd Battalion, 12th Infantry, 24 May 67).
32. For American attacks by fire following the battle, see AAR Opn FRANCIS MARION, 4th Inf Div, 25 Nov 67, Inclosure 7 (3rd Battalion, 12th Infantry, 24 May 67).
33. Ibid., 34. Reitenauer recovered from his wound and joined mortar units at the battalion and divisional level for the remainder of his tour.
35. For enemy casualties and captured enemy equipment, see AAR Opn FRANCIS MARION, 4th Inf Div, 25 Nov 67, Inclosure 7 (3rd Battalion, 12th Infantry, 24 May 67); 3-12 Inf. Daily Staff Journal (25 May 1967). There are some discrepancies between the two sources. The AAR, for example, mentions three AK-47s, three SKSs, and two rocket launchers. The battalion Daily Staff Journal, conversely, includes the aforementioned items as well as an enemy machine gun and five "B4 rockets."
36. For the discovery of the NVA prisoner and the timing of the subsequent evacuation, see 3-12 Inf. Daily Staff Journal (25 May 1967). The Daily Staff Journal entry indicating that a POW had been found was recorded at 2:10 P.M.
37. 4th Infantry Division G-3 Daily Staff Journal (25 May 1967); 3-12 Inf. Daily Staff Journal (25 May 1967). Other items were found in the base as well, including hand grenades, entrenching tools, and a roll of commo wire.
38. See AAR Opn FRANCIS MARION, 4th Inf Div, 25 Nov 67, 3.
39. See 3-12 Inf. Daily Staff Journal (25 May 1967).
40. For casualty figures, see 1st Bde, 4th Inf Div, AAR Opn FRANCIS MARION, 24 Oct 67, 23.
41. Ibid. A, B, and C Companies were rotated back through the 4th Infantry Division base camp south of Pleiku City between June 23 and August 16. The companies spent five days training and refitting. In May of 1967, the 4th Infantry Division base camp, nicknamed "Dragon Mountain" by the troops, was named Camp Enari.

CHAPTER 16

1. See 3-8 Inf. Daily Staff Journal (24–26, May 1967), NARA II, RG 472, U.S. Forces in Southeast Asia, 1950–1975, Box 170; AAR Opn FRANCIS MARION, 4th Inf Div, 25 Nov 67, Inclosure 7 (3rd Battalion, 8th Infantry, 26 May 67).
2. See 1st Bde, 4th Inf Div, AAR Opn FRANCIS MARION, 24 October 1967, 20.
3. See AAR Opn HANCOCK, 3d Bn, 8th Inf, 7 June 67, 9–10. The 3-8 Inf. and an ARVN battalion were to cooperate and coordinate during the operation. Anywhere from "two to

four" CIDG companies and "one to four" Regional Force Companies also participated in Operation Hancock I.

4. Ibid., 10, Inclosure 5.
5. Quoted exchange from Flood, *The War of the Innocents*, 177.
6. For enemy casualties during the contact, see AAR Opn HANCOCK, 3d Bn, 8th Inf, 7 June 67, 10. Since the enemy KIAs were listed as "NVA," it can be safely assumed that they occurred during the fight with B Company. American casualties for the contact were not given, but Gamboa and another B Company trooper were wounded in the fight.
7. Ibid., Inclosure 5. The 3-8 Inf. completed the move to Jackson Hole by the evening of May 22, 1967.
8. See AAR Opn FRANCIS MARION, 4th Inf Div, 25 Nov 67, Inclosure 7 (3rd Battalion, 8th Infantry, 26 May 67).
9. See Flood, *The War of the Innocents*, 93.
10. Ibid., 81.
11. Ibid., 216.
12. Ibid., 131.
13. For the discovery of the foxholes and the path the two companies took on May 25, 1967, see 3-8 Inf. Daily Staff Journal (25 May 1967). Neither of the companies would move due east on the twenty-fifth.
14. AAR Opn FRANCIS MARION, 4th Inf Div, 25 Nov 67, 14.
15. See 3-8 Inf. Daily Staff Journal (25 May 1967).
16. It is not entirely clear if Powers assumed command of the company in December 1966 or January 1967. Powers, however, left for Vietnam in June 1966, spent six months as a general's aide, and was scheduled to be promoted to captain in early January. At that point he would have been more eligible to command a company.
17. Tenbrink was originally assigned to the Second Platoon.
18. Johnson commanded the Second Platoon at one point as well.
19. See 3-8 Inf. Daily Staff Journal (25 May 1967). The Journal indicates that B Company reported its night location on Hill 521 at "1750."
20. Ibid.
21. For B and C Companies instructions for May 26, 1967, see AAR Opn FRANCIS MARION, 4th Inf Div, 25 Nov 67, Inclosure 7 (3rd Battalion, 8th Infantry, 26 May 67). It is unclear whether Lynch or the battalion S3 briefed B and C Companies.
22. See 3-8 Inf. Daily Staff Journal (25 May 1967); AAR Opn FRANCIS MARION, 4th Inf Div, 25 Nov 67, Inclosure 7 (3rd Battalion, 8th Infantry, 26 May 67). C Company reported hearing the rounds at 8:05 P.M.
23. For the communications difficulties that night, see 3-8 Inf. Daily Staff Journal (25 May 1967).
24. Ibid.
25. Ibid.
26. The trees were marked with vertical cuts.
27. For exchange between the two grunts, see Wheeler, "Hell Is a Hill They Call 571," D1. Wheeler mistakenly refers to "Hill 571," instead of "Hill 521," in his article. See MacGarrigle, *Taking the Offensive*, 295.

28. There is some dispute whether Lieutenant Cannello, Sgt. Terence Fitzgerald, or both led the patrol.
29. C Company reported receiving sniper fire from the trees at 8:55 A.M. See AAR Opn FRANCIS MARION, 4th Inf Div, 25 Nov 67, Inclosure 7 (3rd Battalion, 8th Infantry, 26 May 67).

CHAPTER 17

1. For presence of NVA snipers in the trees, see Operational Report Lessons Learned (ORLL), 1 May 67–31 July 67, 4th Inf Div, 20 August 1967, 5; 1st Bde, 4th Inf Div, AAR Opn FRANCIS MARION, 24 October 1967, 7.
2. See 3-8 Inf. Daily Staff Journal (26 May 1967).
3. For Johnson's ascension to company command, see AAR Opn FRANCIS MARION, 4th Inf Div, 25 Nov 67, Inclosure 7 (3rd Battalion, 8th Infantry, 26 May 67); Headquarters, 4th Infantry Division. General Orders No. 1870, 9 July 1967, NARA II, RG 472, U.S. Forces in Southeast Asia, 1950–1975, Box 4 (Clayton W. Johnson, Silver Star Citation). How he was notified of Captain Powers's death is not clear, however.
4. See 3-8 Inf. Daily Staff Journal (26 May 1967); AAR Opn FRANCIS MARION, 4th Inf Div, 25 Nov 67, Inclosure 7 (3rd Battalion, 8th Infantry, 26 May 67). The AAR indicates that C Company reported heavier sniper fire at 9:05 A.M.
5. Quoted words from Kuhne, "Norton Sergeant Takes Over, Leads GIs in Bloody Battle."
6. See AAR Opn FRANCIS MARION, 4th Inf Div, 25 Nov 67, Inclosure 7 (3rd Battalion, 8th Infantry, 26 May 67); Wheeler, "Hell Is a Hill They Call 571," D1. The AAR report indicates that the first wave attack was reported at 9:05 A.M. Wheeler, who was with C Company that morning, notes that the wave attack came after the mortar rounds began falling on the company. The AAR states that C Company reported "heavy sniper fire in the area of its 1st and 3rd Platoons" and "simultaneously received a heavy ground attack from the west and southwest" against the First and Third Platoons. The Daily Staff Journal, meanwhile, states that the company contacted an estimated enemy company at 8:55 A.M.
7. See "4th Div. Unit Fights Way Out of 'Red Beret" Ambush, Kills 71," 6.
8. The grenade, incidentally, did not go off.
9. Some of the C Company soldiers thought that Fitzgerald and some of the recon party were caught in a crossfire on the way back to the company and killed. Fitzgerald's Silver Star Citation, however, strongly suggests that he returned and fought for some time after that. See Headquarters, 4th Infantry Division, General Orders No. 1692, 1 July 1967, NARA II, RG 472, U.S. Forces in Southeast Asia, 1950–1975, Box 4 (Terence P. Fitzgerald, Silver Star Citation).
10. See AAR Opn FRANCIS MARION, 4th Inf Div, 25 Nov 67, Inclosure 7 (3rd Battalion, 8th Infantry, 26 May 67); MacGarrigle, *Taking the Offensive*, 295. The AAR noted that "82-mm mortars was [*sic*] employed in its conventional role with minimal effectiveness because of the closeness of contact and geography of the contact area."

11. Quoted words from AAR Opn FRANCIS MARION, 4th Inf Div, 25 Nov 67, Inclosure 7 (3rd Battalion, 8th Infantry, 26 May 67).
12. Ibid. The seven batteries were B Battery, 6-29 Artillery; B, C, and D Batteries, 5-16 Artillery; A and B Batteries, 6-14 Artillery; and C Battery, 1-92 Artillery. The remaining two batteries—C Battery, 6-29 Arty and A Battery, 5-16 Arty—provided blocking fires.
13. See MacGarrigle, *Taking the Offensive*, 295; AAR Opn FRANCIS MARION, 4th Inf Div, 25 Nov 67, Inclosure 7 (3rd Battalion, 8th Infantry, 26 May 67); 3-8 Inf. Daily Staff Journal (26 May 1967). The Journal notes that B Company began moving downhill toward C Company at 9:05 A.M.
14. See AAR Opn FRANCIS MARION, 4th Inf Div, 25 Nov 67, Inclosure 7 (3rd Battalion, 8th Infantry, 26 May 67).
15. See "Fresnan Leads Viet Unit to Halt Ambush," 1; 3-8 Inf. Daily Staff Journal (26 May 1967). The Journal notes that B Company began moving downhill toward C Company at 9:05 A.M., the same time Lieutenant Marinovich was ordered to send three platoons down the hill. It seems highly unlikely, however, that Marinovich could have briefed his platoon leaders, organized a relief force, and headed out in less than a minute.
16. It is unclear whether Specialist 4th Class Gamboa's squad arrived in time to accompany the platoon back down the hill.
17. Incident and quoted words from Flood, *The War of the Innocents*, 131.
18. See Wheeler, "Hell Is a Hill They Call 571," D1.
19. See MacGarrigle, *Taking the Offensive*, 295; AAR Opn FRANCIS MARION, 4th Inf Div, 25 Nov 67, Inclosure 7 (3rd Battalion, 8th Infantry, 26 May 67).
20. See AAR Opn FRANCIS MARION, 4th Inf Div, 25 Nov 67, Inclosure 7 (3rd Battalion, 8th Infantry, 26 May 67).
21. Ibid.
22. Ibid.
23. Ibid., for confirmation that Lieutenant Cannello was wounded during the third NVA attack.
24. See "Fresnan Leads Viet Unit to Halt Ambush;" Wheeler, "Hell Is a Hill They Call 571," D1; 3-8 Inf. Daily Staff Journal (26 May 1967); AAR Opn FRANCIS MARION, 4th Inf Div, 25 Nov 67, Inclosure 7 (3rd Battalion, 8th Infantry, 26 May 67). The AAR states that "Company B (-) and the B Company Commander closed on the C Company perimeter" at 0935. Yet, in an interview with the author, Lieutenant Marinovich claims that his ad hoc group arrived *before* his other platoons. Marinovich's hometown newspaper indirectly corroborates his claim, reporting that Marinovich fought "into the ambushed company's area after a second reinforcing platoon was driven back by heavy fire." Similarly, Wheeler's account states that "Lt. Marinovich and one platoon of B Company fought their way through to reinforce Charlie Company's perimeter."

CHAPTER 18

1. For identification of the NVA battalion involved in the attack, see AAR Opn FRANCIS MARION, 4th Inf Div, 25 Nov 67, Inclosure 7 (3rd Battalion, 8th Infantry, 26 May 67).
2. Quoted words from Wheeler, "Hell Is a Hill They Call 571," D1. Wheeler's description

of when Childers uttered the order, and who participated in the subsequent assault, indicate that the first sergeant had said the words prior to the first assault on the knoll.

3. For the participation of the First and Fourth Platoons in the assault, see Hymoff, *Fourth Infantry Division in Vietnam*, 103.
4. See Wheeler, "Hell Is a Hill They Call 571," D1.
5. C Battery, 6-29 Artillery and A Battery, 5-16 Artillery provided close-in support during the operation.
6. See Headquarters, 4th Infantry Division, General Orders No. 1870, 9 July 1967, NARA II, RG 472, U.S. Forces in Southeast Asia, 1950–1975, Box 4 (Clayton W. Johnson, Silver Star Citation).
7. Quoted words from Levenson, "No Matter What He Says, He's Hero," A12.
8. See Headquarters, 4th Infantry Division, General Orders No. 4468, 1 September 1967 (Richard L. Childers, Distinguished Service Cross Citation); AAR Opn FRANCIS MARION, 4th Inf Div, 25 Nov 67, Inclosure 7 (3rd Battalion, 8th Infantry, 26 May 67); Wheeler, "Hell Is a Hill They Call 571," D1. Pfc. Dan Shayotovich and others recall hearing Childers announcing over the radio that he was taking over the company. It is safe to assume that Lt. Jack Cannello, PTL of the Second Platoon, had already been wounded by the time Johnson was killed, otherwise it seems likely that he—and not Childers—would have assumed command of C Company (see also Hymoff, *Fourth Infantry Division in Vietnam*, 103).
9. Quoted words from Wheeler, "Hell Is a Hill They Call 571," D1. Wheeler also notes that "senior sergeants swiftly assessed the situation and smoothly took charge."
10. See MacGarrigle, *Taking the Offensive*, 295; Richard L. Childers, Distinguished Service Cross Citation. Childers's citation reads that "he took charge of the company in the early moments of battle when both the company commander and a platoon leader were killed."
11. Quoted words from AAR Opn FRANCIS MARION, 4th Inf Div, 25 Nov 67, Inclosure 7 (3rd Battalion, 8th Infantry, 26 May 67). Hymoff's *Fourth Infantry Division in Vietnam*, it should also be noted, correctly states that Lieutenant Johnson assumed command of the company before Sergeant Childers.
12. See 3-8 Inf. Daily Staff Journal (26 May 1967). Sniper and mortar fire were reported from the "SW/S/W."
13. See Headquarters, 4th Infantry Division, General Orders No. 1721, 3 July 1967, NARA II, RG 472, U.S. Forces in Southeast Asia, 1950–1975, Box 4 (Richard E. Wilkins, Silver Star Citation). The citation does not indicate what platoon Wilkins moved to assist, but it may very well have been the embattled Third Platoon.
14. The B-40 rocket is a variant of the RPG-2.
15. When the First Platoon first made contact, the troops scattered to the right and left in search of cover. That process spread the platoon out into a line of sorts, and it continued moving forward in that basic formation.
16. The 3-8 Inf. Daily Staff Journal (26 May 1967) states that the two companies linked up at "0935." Since Lieutenant Marinovich almost certainly arrived at the perimeter first, it is safe to assume that the three platoons reached the perimeter sometime after 9:35 A.M. The AAR, interestingly enough, is a bit more ambiguous. In the Tab devoted to

the 3-8 Inf. operation on May 26, 1967, the AAR states that "Company B (-) and the B Company Commander closed on the C Company perimeter" at 9:35 A.M. This suggests that Marinovich and *all three* of the B Company platoons that had moved down the hill with him had reached C Company at 9:35 A.M. On page 15 of the overall AAR, however, it states that "two platoons of B Company moved through heavy fires to link up with C Company." The eyewitness testimony of B Company veterans, however, strongly suggests that all three platoons linked up with C Company at one point.

17. See 3-8 Inf. Daily Staff Journal (26 May 1967). While both air strikes and gunships were requested, neither are mentioned in the relevant source material until the end of battle. Gunships, for example, do not appear in either the AAR or the Daily Staff Journal until 11:15 A.M. Similarly, air strikes do not appear in the Daily Staff Journal until after 1 P.M. The AAR mentions that two A1E Skyraiders were flown against an enemy mortar position. No time, however, is given for either air strike.
18. See Richard L. Childers, Distinguished Service Cross Citation. Childers, in the DSC citation, is said to have contacted the battalion HQ, set up resupply points, and assisted wounded men *after* he assumed command of C Company. Since Childers did not assume command of C Company in the opening moments of the battle, as the DSC Citation states, the activities described above must have occurred after Lieutenant Johnson was killed during the third NVA assault.
19. Fessler believes the trail was the same one C Company had been following before the NVA struck that morning.
20. See 3-8 Inf. Daily Staff Journal (26 May 1967).
21. See Hymoff, *Fourth Infantry Division in Vietnam*, 103–4.
22. Ibid., 103.
23. It is not entirely clear when Stroh reached Toby, but given Stroh's account of the events that came before and after the incident, it seems logical that it occurred somewhere in this time frame.
24. See Fitzgerald's Silver Star Citation.
25. See 3-8 Inf. Daily Staff Journal (26 May 1967). The mortars ceased firing at 10:10 A.M.; AAR Opn FRANCIS MARION, 4th Inf Div, 25 Nov 67, Inclosure 7 (3rd Battalion, 8th Infantry, 26 May 67).
26. The mortar fire resumed at 10:13 A.M. See 3-8 Inf. Daily Staff Journal (26 May 1967).
27. "RA," or Regular Army, was the prefix before the serial number of an enlistee. "US" was the prefix before the serial number of a draftee.
28. See AAR Opn FRANCIS MARION, 4th Inf Div, 25 Nov 67, Inclosure 7 (3rd Battalion, 8th Infantry, 26 May 67).
29. Ibid. According to the AAR, artillery fire "was placed all around the contact area to preclude reinforcement and hamper withdrawal of the enemy." These blocking fires would have little effect on the NVA troops engaged with B and C Companies. For the lack of close artillery support, see Wheeler, "Hell Is a Hill They Call 571," D4. Wheeler also noted that "no helicopter gunships or jet planes were overhead to join the battle."

30. Quoted words from Flood, *The War of the Innocents*, 179.
31. Ibid., 212–13.
32. See AAR Opn FRANCIS MARION, 4th Inf Div, 25 Nov 67, Inclosure 7 (3rd Battalion, 8th Infantry, 26 May 67). Most contacts, incidentally, occurred between ten and fifteen meters of the perimeter.
33. Tienhaara thinks the NVA may have shouted, "Here we are, *B*," or "Here we are, *A*," possibly referring to B or A Companies.
34. See AAR Opn FRANCIS MARION, 4th Inf Div, 25 Nov 67, Inclosure 7 (3rd Battalion, 8th Infantry, 26 May 67). B Battery, 6-29 provided blocking fires.
35. It should also be noted that a light rain fell twice during the battle. It is not clear, however, when the rains fell.
36. The number of NVA varies, depending upon the source. Scott, for example, insists that there were "at least thirty or forty" enemy soldiers. Other sources place the number at fifty. See "4th Div. Unit Fights Way Out of 'Red Beret' Ambush, Kills 71," 6; Wheeler, "Hell Is a Hill They Call 571," D4.
37. See Wheeler, "Hell Is a Hill They Call 571," D4.
38. Quoted words from Levenson, "No Matter What He Says, He's Hero," A12. It is unclear, however, if the black gunner was the same one that had been with Sergeant Scott in the First Platoon at the start of the battle.
39. See "Viet Cong Ambush GIs—Trap Sprung on Company While Taking Rest Break."
40. See Headquarters, 4th Infantry Division, General Orders No. 1767, 5 July 1967, NARA II, RG 472, U.S. Forces in Southeast Asia, 1950–1975, Box 4 (Donald E. Mesarosh, Bronze Star Citation).
41. Thompson had been named "soldier of the month," and as a reward he was pulled from the field and allowed to accompany the battalion commander for a week.
42. See 3-8 Inf. Daily Staff Journal (26 May 1967); AAR Opn FRANCIS MARION, 4th Inf Div, 25 Nov 67, Inclosure 7 (3rd Battalion, 8th Infantry, 26 May 67). The Daily Journal indicates that Lieutenant Colonel Lynch was over the battle area when the sixth NVA assault occurred.
43. See Wheeler, "Hell Is a Hill They Call 571," D4. Sgt. Michael Scott, the FO attached to C Company's First Platoon, believed that Lieutenant Munsch—the FAC on station that morning—would have been the only observer capable of bringing the artillery in closer to the perimeter.
44. See 3-8 Inf. Daily Staff Journal (26 May 1967).
45. See AAR Opn FRANCIS MARION, 4th Inf Div, 25 Nov 67, Inclosure 7 (3rd Battalion, 8th Infantry, 26 May 67); 3-8 Inf. Daily Staff Journal (26 May 1967). The AAR noted that the gunships were brought in at 11:15 A.M. Ten sorties were flown in support of the ground action. Six sorties were used as an "aircap" in a security role. Four sorties provided direct, close-in support to ground forces. According to the map coordinates, the gunships were to operate *inside* the artillery fire. The gunships were to work the jungle two hundred to four hundred meters west of a point to the southwest of the perimeter.

46. See AAR Opn FRANCIS MARION, 4th Inf Div, 25 Nov 67, Inclosure 7 (3rd Battalion, 8th Infantry, 26 May 67); 3-8 Inf. Daily Staff Journal (26 May 1967). The NVA broke contact at 11:50 A.M. The mortar rounds were 82-mm.

EPILOGUE

1. See Opn FRANCIS MARION, 4th Inf Div, 25 Nov 67, Inclosure 7 (3rd Battalion, 8th Infantry, 26 May 67). The Americans repelled some of the six attacks with hand-to-hand combat. It is nearly impossible to determine when and during which NVA assault the incidents of hand-to-hand combat occurred, however.
2. Quoted words from Flood, *The War of the Innocents*, 205.
3. For casualty figures, see AAR Opn FRANCIS MARION, 4th Inf Div, 25 Nov 67, Inclosure 7 (3rd Battalion, 8th Infantry, 26 May 67).
4. The two companies began moving up the hill at 1:05 P.M. See 3-8 Inf. Daily Staff Journal (26 May 1967); AAR Opn FRANCIS MARION, 4th Inf Div, 25 Nov 67, Inclosure 7 (3rd Battalion, 8th Infantry, 26 May 67); MacGarrigle, *Taking the Offensive*, 296. Interestingly, the Daily Staff Journal states that "elements" of B and C Companies began moving toward B Company's NDP at 1:05 P.M. The AAR, however, notes that "Companies C and B (-) began moving to B Company's night location." In this context, it is mostly likely that "B (-)" refers to all elements of the company other than Lieutenant Schell's Second Platoon, which was already at the NDP.
5. See AAR Opn FRANCIS MARION, 4th Inf Div, 25 Nov 67, Inclosure 7 (3rd Battalion, 8th Infantry, 26 May 67).
6. Lt. Richard Schell's Second Platoon used logs from cut trees to construct the landing platform.
7. See AAR Opn FRANCIS MARION, 4th Inf Div, 25 Nov 67, Inclosure 7 (3rd Battalion, 8th Infantry, 26 May 67). It is not clear if B Company was expected to finish the sweep before it moved up the hill, or if some elements were expected to conduct the sweep while others joined C Company in the NDP.
8. See 3-8 Inf. Daily Staff Journal (26 May 1967).
9. See AAR Opn FRANCIS MARION, 4th Inf Div, 25 Nov 67, Inclosure 7 (3rd Battalion, 8th Infantry, 26 May 67). According to the AAR, at 2:30 P.M. B Company "continued withdrawal to its company night location." Since B Company had not yet completed the sweep ordered by Lieutenant Colonel Lynch, it is safe to assume that only elements of the company starting moving back up Hill 521. It also safe to assume that B Company's eight wounded would have been evacuated, along with C Company's wounded, as soon as possible.
10. Ibid. The Daily Staff Journal, however, notes that by 4:40 P.M., forty-five WIA and six KIA had been evacuated.
11. See Wheeler, "Hell Is a Hill They Call 571," D4. Wheeler writes that "all the dead and wounded had been evacuated, except Sgt. Childers. He stayed behind until much later, even though his hands were badly swollen from the fragment wounds." The AAR also indicates that all of the wounded were evacuated on May 26.

12. Quoted words from Levenson, "No Matter What He Says, He's Hero," A12.

13. For NVA casualty figures, see AAR Opn FRANCIS MARION, 4th Inf Div, 25 Nov 67, Inclosure 7 (3rd Battalion, 8th Infantry, 26 May 67). Interestingly, Lieutenant Colonel Lynch recalled that there were reports over the radio that morning about "bigger, Caucasian types" fighting with the NVA. Lynch noted, however, that there were no "Caucasian types" found among the NVA dead after the battle.

14. See 3-8 Inf. Daily Staff Journal (26 May 1967); AAR Opn FRANCIS MARION, 4th Inf Div, 25 Nov 67, Inclosure 7 (3rd Battalion, 8th Infantry, 26 May 67). Two A1E Skyraider sorties were flown against a suspected NVA mortar position that day. The B-52 strikes were conducted against target boxes to the west-southwest and west-northwest at 8:46 P.M. and 9:06 P.M.

15. For the NVA casualty figures, see AAR Opn FRANCIS MARION, 4th Inf Div, 25 Nov 67, Inclosure 7 (3rd Battalion, 8th Infantry, 26 May 67). The 3-8 Inf. also captured two NVA POWs (in total), eighteen AK-47s, six B-40 (RPG-2) rockets, four RPD light machine guns, sixty-five Chicom grenades, and assorted enemy equipment.

16. See Operational Report Lessons Learned (ORLL), 1 May 67–31 July 67, 4th Inf Div, 20 August 1967 (Gen. Peers Inclosure).

17. For the 3-8 Inf. operations on May 27 and 28, see AAR Opn FRANCIS MARION, 4th Inf Div, 25 Nov 67, Inclosure 7 (3rd Battalion, 8th Infantry, 26 May 67). C Company and the Recon Platoon were returned to the battalion firebase on the afternoon of May 27.

18. Quoted words from AAR Opn FRANCIS MARION, 4th Inf Div, 25 Nov 67, 1.

19. The Presidential Unit Citation (Army) was awarded to the 1st Brigade, 4th Infantry Division and assigned, attached, and supporting units, including, for example, the 6-29 Artillery.

20. For North Vietnamese tactics, see MacGarrigle, *Taking the Offensive*, 296; AAR, Opn SAM HOUSTON, 4th Inf Div, 16 May 67, 10–12 (Inclosure 1); Operational Report Lessons Learned (ORLL), 1 May 67–31 July 67, 4th Inf Div, 20 August 1967, 9. The 4th Infantry Division noticed similar tactics during Operation Sam Houston earlier that spring. The NVA had been "hugging" American infantry to reduce the effects of supporting arms since the battle in the Ia Drang Valley in 1965, but the 4th noted that the "enemy continued to emphasize 'hugging tactics' to reduce his casualties from friendly supporting fires."

21. Quoted words from Hymoff, *Fourth Infantry Division in Vietnam*, 99.

22. See MacGarrigle, *Taking the Offensive*, 296; AAR Opn FRANCIS MARION, 4th Inf Div, 25 Nov 67, 1. The 1st Brigade was supported by 219 tactical air strikes and 31,304 artillery rounds, and most were used to isolate the battlefield and hammer enemy escape routes. Fourteen B-52 strikes were also used against NVA base camps and troop concentrations. The NVA managed to carry away some of its dead and wounded after every one of the five major engagements, so the actual number of enemy dead exceeded the confirmed body count of 369.

23. Quoted text from AAR Opn FRANCIS MARION, 4th Inf Div, 25 Nov 67, 75. See

also Operational Report Lessons Learned (ORLL), 1 May 67–31 July 67, 4th Inf Div, 20 August 1967, 1.

24. See MacGarrigle, *Taking the Offensive*, 291.

25. In 1965, for example, the North Vietnamese used the "surround/besiege a point and annihilate the relief force" tactic to help "lure" the 1st Cavalry Division out of its bases. The NVA laid siege to the Plei Me Special Forces camp with the aim of drawing in and destroying a South Vietnamese relief force. The destruction of the South Vietnamese relief force, it was hoped, would then lure the Americans into the fray. In the fall of 1966, the 32nd NVA Regiment was to surround and provoke enemy forces at "Plei Djereng" to lure an American battalion out. The American battalion was to be channeled toward the "decisive battle location" and destroyed. See *People's Armed Forces of the Central Highlands*, 23–24; Man with Trieu, *Thoi Soi Song* [Time of Upheaval], 424; An with Duong, *Chien Truong Moi* [New Battlefield], 29–30, 42.

26. For American casualty figures, see AAR Opn FRANCIS MARION, 4th Inf Div, 25 Nov 67, Inclosure 7. There were, of course, a number of wounded who would return to the field. Nevertheless, while it is difficult to determine the exact "foxhole strength" of every company in the division, it is fair to say that many of them were under strength. Col. James Adamson, for example, said the average "foxhole strength" of a 2nd Brigade rifle company was "never more than 110 men" while he was in command. See Maj. Gen. James B. Adamson, Comdr, 2d Bde, 4th Inf Div, interview with George L. MacGarrigle, 4 April 79; MacGarrigle, *Taking the Offensive*, 304.

27. The 173rd began arriving on May 24 and completed the move to Catecka south of Pleiku City on May 26. Reinforcements for the Highlands were supposed to come from the 1st Cavalry Division and then the 173rd Airborne Brigade. Larsen, however, decided to commit the 173rd first. The bulk of the 173rd left in mid-September, but some elements of the brigade remained behind until October. See Murphy, *Dak To*, 119–25; MacGarrigle, "NINE DAYS IN MAY," 22.

28. See 1st Bde, 4th Inf Div, AAR Opn FRANCIS MARION, 24 October 1967, 21–23; Operational Report Lessons Learned (ORLL), 1 May 67–31 July 67, 4th Inf Div, 20 August 1967, 3; MacGarrigle, *Taking the Offensive*, 296. The 3-8 Inf. conducted operations near Combined Arms Hill northwest of Jackson Hole.

29. Quoted words from General Stanley Larsen, Senior Officer Debriefing Report, 21 August 1967, Annex B, 4.

30. For casualty figures, see MacGarrigle, *Taking the Offensive*, 306.

31. Quoted words from AAR Opn FRANCIS MARION, 4th Inf Div, 25 Nov 67, Inclosure 7 (1st Battalion, 12th Infantry).

32. See MacGarrigle, *Taking the Offensive*, 306–307. The North Vietnamese body count for July 23 was listed as 184.

33. The 4th Infantry Division claimed an enemy body count of 1,204 for the entire operation. Nearly one-third of that total (369) occurred during the "Nine Days." See AAR Opn FRANCIS MARION, 4th Inf Div, 25 Nov 67, 36.

BIBLIOGRAPHY

ARCHIVES

The Vietnam Archive, Texas Tech University

52nd Combat Aviation Battalion Unit History. Undated. Folder 18, Box 05, Vietnam Helicopter Pilots Association (VHPA) Collection: Unit Histories—1st Aviation Brigade.

Esprit: The Famous Fighting Fourth Division, Fall 1969. Folder 09, Box 01, Jennifer Young Collection.

"Faces of the Famous Fighting Fourth—Vietnam." Undated. Folder 08, Box 01, Jennifer Young Collection.

"Face to Face with U.S. Armed Forces (II): Plei—Jirang N Kha," 18 October 1966. Folder 09, Box 07, Douglas Pike Collection: Unit 02—Military Operations.

Letter from General Westmoreland to General Wheeler, re: response to "Why do we fight the enemy near the borders?," 10 December 1967. Folder 06, Box 01, Veteran Members of the 109th Quartermaster Company (Air Delivery) Collection.

Oral History Program Report: Senior Colonel Cao Tien Phiem. 01 May 1996. Folder 11, Box 13, George J. Veith Collection.

Peers, Lt. Gen. William R. Unit 08—Biography. March 1969, Folder 07, Box 13, Douglas Pike Collection.

USAF 1965–73 Fixed Wing Gunships. Undated. Folder 01, Bud Harton Collection.

USMACV GENERAL 1967 Command History Part 1, 1967. Folder 01, Bud Harton Collection.

U.S. Army Center of Military History, Washington, D.C.

AAR, Opn ADAMS, 1st Bde, 4th Inf Div, 18 May 1967.

AAR, Operation FRANCIS MARION, 4th Infantry Division, 25 Nov 67.

AAR Opn HANCOCK, 3d Bn, 8th Inf, 7 June 67.

AAR, Opn PAUL REVERE IV, 4th Inf Div, 28 Jan 67.

AAR, Opn SAM HOUSTON, 4th Inf Div, 16 May 67.

Adamson, Maj. Gen James B., Comdr, 2d Bde, 4th Inf Div. Interview with George L. MacGarrigle, 4 April 79.
Captured NVA Document. "Outline of Campaign Plan of B3 for the 1967 Rainy Season."
CHECO Rpt, Opn PAUL REVERE/SAM HOUSTON, PACAF 27 July 67.
Collins, Maj. Gen. A. S., Jr. Letter to Brig. Gen. Edward P. Smith, 15 November 1966.
Collins, Maj. Gen. A. S., Jr. Letter to General Richardson, 26 November 1966.
Collins, Brig. Gen. Arthur S., Jr. Biographical sketch. Undated. U.S.A. Headquarters, United States Strike Forward Command, MacDill Air Force Base, Florida.
Collins, Lt. Gen. Arthur S., Jr. CG, 4th Inf Div. Interview with George L. MacGarrigle, 28 Feb 75.
Gannon, Col. Timothy G., Comdr, 1st Bn, 8th Inf, 4th Inf Div. Interview with George L. MacGarrigle, 31 August 78.
JGS (Joint General Staff)/MACV (Military Assistance Command, Vietnam). Combined Campaign Plan for Military Operations in the Republic of Vietnam, 1967.
Larsen, General. MEMO to General Westmoreland. Subject: Paul Revere IV. Date: Nov. 1, 1966.
MacGarrigle, George. "SAM HOUSTON." Chapter 12 (unpublished draft chapter) in *The United States Army in Vietnam, Combat Operations: Taking the Offensive, October 1966 to October 1967.*
———. "NINE DAYS IN MAY." Chapter 24 (unpublished draft chapter) in *The United States Army in Vietnam, Combat Operations: Taking the Offensive, October 1966 to October 1967.*
Operation SAM HOUSTON After Action Critique Notes. 4th Infantry Division, 24 May 1967.
Operational Report Lessons Learned, 1 Nov 66–31 Jan 67. 4th Inf Div, 20 Mar 67.
Operational Report Lessons Learned (ORLL), 1 May 67–31 July 67. 4th Inf Div, 20 August 1967.
Operational Report Lessons Learned, Nov 66–31 Jan 67. IFFV, 6 March 1967.
Peers, Lt. Gen. William R., CG, 4th Inf Div. Interview with George L. MacGarrigle, 21 Oct 75.
"Statement of Service, 4th Infantry Division."
Summary of Operation SAM HOUSTON (Headquarters 4th Infantry Division), 20 June 1967.
Walker, Lt. Gen. Glenn D. Walker, Asst Div Comdr, 4th Inf Div. Interview with George MacGarrigle, 3 Apr 79.

National Archives and Records Administration, College Park, Md.

AARs, Daily Staff Journals, Reports, Summaries, etc.

1st Brigade, 4th Inf Div, AAR Opn FRANCIS MARION, 24 October 1967.
1st Brigade, 4th Infantry Division S-2 Daily Staff Journal (21–24 May 1967).
1st Brigade, 4th Infantry Division S-3 Daily Staff Journal (21–24 May 1967).
1st Brigade, 4th Inf Div, ORGANIZATIONAL HISTORY.
4th Infantry Division G-2 Daily Staff Journal (18–27 May 1967).
4th Infantry Division G-3 Daily Staff Journal (18–27 May 1967).
4th Infantry Division G-2 Intelligence Summaries (11–20 May 1967).
4th Infantry Division G2 Periodic Intelligence Summary for Period May 11–28.
Operational Report from 27 April thru 27 May 1967, 1st Bde, 4th Inf Div. 27 May 1967.
Operational Report from 1 May 1967 thru August 1 1967, 1st Bde 4th Inf Div. 1 August 1967.

Senior Officer Debriefing Reports; 1967–1972: General Stanley Larsen, Senior Officer Debriefing Report, 21 August 1967.

Senior Officer Debriefing Reports; 1967–1972: Lieutenant General William R. Peers, Senior Officer Debriefing Report, 9 March 1969.

3-8 Inf. Daily Staff Journal (24–26 May 1967).

3-12 Inf. Daily Staff Journal (21–25 May 1967).

Individual Award Citations

Headquarters, 4th Infantry Division. General Orders No. 2978. 17 September 1967. (Cary D. Allen, Silver Star Citation.)

Headquarters, U.S Army, Vietnam. General Orders No. 3832. July 27, 1967. (Charles E. Aronhalt Jr., Distinguished Service Cross Citation.)

Headquarters, 4th Infantry Division. General Orders No. 1862. 9 July 1967. (Randal R. Aylworth, Bronze Star Citation.)

Headquarters, 4th Infantry Division. General Orders No. 3413. 16 October 1967. (Paul F. Burk, Silver Star Citation.)

Headquarters, 4th Infantry Division. General Orders No. 3553. 25 October 1967. (Dennis Carney, Bronze Star Citation.)

Headquarters, 4th Infantry Division. General Orders No. 4468. 1 September 1967. (Richard L. Childers, Distinguished Service Cross Citation.)

Headquarters, 4th Infantry Division. General Orders No. 2505. 11 August 1967. (Gerald K. Cross, Air Medal Citation.)

Headquarters, 4th Infantry Division. General Orders No. 3595. 26 October 1967. (Ralph W. Ely III, Bronze Star Citation.)

Headquarters, 4th Infantry Division. General Orders No. 1692. 1 July 1967. (Terence P. Fitzgerald, Silver Star Citation.)

Headquarters, 4th Infantry Division. General Orders No. 3583. 26 October 1967. (James Gaskins Jr., Bronze Star Citation.)

Headquarters, 4th Infantry Division. General Orders No. 1505. June 22, 1967. (Bruce Alan Grandstaff, Silver Star Citation.)

Headquarters, 4th Infantry Division. General Orders No. 1870. 9 July 1967. (Clayton W. Johnson, Silver Star Citation.)

Headquarters, 4th Infantry Division. General Orders No. 1884. 11 July 1967. (William M. Lumsden, Bronze Star Citation.)

Headquarters, 4th Infantry Division. General Orders No. 2516. 11 August 1967. (Joseph T. Makalusky, Air Medal Citation).

Headquarters, 4th Infantry Division. General Orders No. 1767. 5 July 1967. (Donald E. Mesarosh, Bronze Star Citation.)

Headquarters, 4th Infantry Division. General Orders No. 1884. 26 October 1967. (Frank E. Patton, Bronze Star Citation.)

Headquarters, 4th Infantry Division. General Orders No. 1758. 5 July 1967. (Eugene F. Poeling, Bronze Star Citation.)

Headquarters, 4th Infantry Division. General Orders No. 3493. 22 October 1967. (Ernest E. Putoff, Bronze Star Citation.)

Headquarters, 4th Infantry Division. General Orders No. 1865. 9 July 1967. (Frankie Z. Molnar, Bronze Star Citation.)

Headquarters, 4th Infantry Division. General Orders No. 3574. 26 October 1967. (John E. Richey, Silver Star Citation.)

Headquarters, 4th Infantry Division. General Orders No. 3354. 12 October 1967. (Robert L. Rodabaugh, Silver Star Citation.)

Headquarters, 4th Infantry Division. General Orders No. 3492. 22 October 1967. (James W. Smothers, Bronze Star Citation.)

Headquarters, 4th Infantry Division. General Orders No. 1877. 11 July 1967. (Leland H. Thompson, Silver Star Citation.)

Headquarters, 4th Infantry Division. General Orders No. 1721. 3 July 1967. (Richard E. Wilkins, Silver Star Citation.)

Headquarters, 4th Infantry Division. General Orders No. 3411. 16 October 1967. (Alhandro Yuson, Silver Star Citation.)

Headquarters, 4th Infantry Division. General Orders No. 1876. 11 July 1967. (Phillip R. Venekamp, Silver Star Citation.)

Headquarters, 4th Infantry Division. General Orders No. 3247. 6 August 1967. (Gregory A. Waltz, Army Recommendation Medal Citation.)

Headquarters, 4th Infantry Division. General Orders No. 1759. 5 July 1967. (Leon A. Wangerin, Bronze Star Citation.)

U.S. Army Heritage and Education Center, Carlisle Barracks, Pa.

U.S. Army Heritage Collections Online. Available on the Internet at http://www.carlisle.army.mil/ahec/index.cfm

Private Collections

Activity Report from the Advance Planning Group, 4th Infantry Division, 14 July 1966–31 August 1966.

Braun, Robert J. PFC (E3), Co. C, 1st Bn, 8th Inf. N.d. Witness Statement in support of Leslie Allen Bellrichard Medal of Honor Citation.

Bruce A. Grandstaff Memorial Dedication Pamphlet, September 10, 2011. Published by the Fairmount Memorial Association in cooperation with Tamara Grandstaff.

Flaiz, James. 2Lt, Infantry, Co. C, 1st Bn, 8th Inf. N.d. Witness Statement in support of Leslie Allen Bellrichard Medal of Honor Citation.

Gustafson, Michael. SP/4 (E4), Co. C, 1st Bn, 8th Inf. N.d. Witness Statement in support of Leslie Allen Bellrichard Medal of Honor Citation.

Headquarters, 4th Infantry Division. Summary of Recommendation for Award of Medal of Honor (Posthumous). Name: Bruce A. Grandstaff. Status: Platoon Sergeant E-7, U.S. Army. Organization: Company B, 1st Battalion, 8th Infantry, 4th Infantry Division, USA. June, 1967.

Performance Review. Vollmer, LTC John P. Review and Analysis Division, Revolutionary Development Support Directorate, Headquarters, U.S. Military Assistance Command, Vietnam. 6 June 66–23 April 67 (Period Covered), Rater—Col. Erwin R. Brigham. 1 May 1967.

Books and Articles

"2 Divisions Beefed Up by Army," *Pacific Stars and Stripes* 21, no. 322 (November 19, 1965): 26.

"357 Enemy Killed, 65 Captured As Paul Revere IV Continues." *Ivy Leaf* 1, no. 3 (November 18, 1966): 1.

"3rd Brigade's Arrival Completes 'Ivy' Move to Vietnam." *Ivy Leaf* 1, no. 1 (November 4, 1966): 3.

"3/12th Officer in Third Narrow Escape from Death," *Ivy Leaf* 1, no. 15 (February 15, 1967): 6.

"4th Div. Unit Fights Way Out of 'Red Beret' Ambush, Kills 71," *Pacific Stars and Stripes* 23, no. 147 (May 28, 1967): 6.

"4000 New Troops Going to Pleiku." *Pacific Stars and Stripes* 22, no. 219 (August 8, 1966): 1.

An, Colonel General Nguyen Huu, with Nguyen Tu Duong. *Chien Truong Moi* [New battlefield]. Hanoi: People's Army Publishing House, 2002.

Bleu, Lieutenant Colonel Nguyen Van. *A Number of Battles Fought by Units of the Central Highlands Corps.* Volume 5. Hanoi: People's Army Publishing House, 1996.

"Birthday Just Another Day for 4th Inf. Div." *Pacific Stars and Stripes* 23, no. 342 (December 9, 1967): 24.

Birtle, Andrew J. "PROVN, Westmoreland, and the Historians: A Reappraisal." *Journal of Military History* 72 (October 2008): 1213–47.

Carland, John M. *The United States Army in Vietnam, Combat Operations: Stemming the Tide, May 1965 to October* 1966. Washington, D.C.: U.S. Army Center of Military History, 2000.

Chambers, John Whiteclay, II. *OSS in the National Parks and Service Abroad in World War II.* Washington, D.C.: U.S. National Park Service, 2008.

Clark, Conrad. "'Bullets' Hold 1st Brigade Record for Number of Moves." *Ivy Leaf* 1, no. 35 (July 9, 1967): 4–5.

"Col. Jackson Succeeds Col. Austin As Commander of 1st Brigade." *Ivy Leaf* 1, no. 18 (February 17, 1967): 1.

"Cripps Awarded Purple Heart." *Smithville Review* 76, no. 29 (October 19, 1967): 2.

Daddis, Gregory A. *Westmoreland's War: Reassessing American Strategy in Vietnam.* New York: Oxford University Press, 2014.

Dai, Colonel Ho Son, chief ed. *Lich Su Bo Chi Huy Mien (1961–1976)* [History of the COSVN Military Command (1961–1976)]. Hanoi: National Political Publishing House, 2004.

Diem, Senior Colonel Tran Ba, ed. *Lich Su Su Doan 8 Bo Binh Quan Khu 9 (1974–2000)* [History of the 8th Infantry Division, Military Region 9 (1974–2000)]. Hanoi: People's Army Publishing House, 2002.

Do, Senior Colonel Tran, chief ed. *Tu Dien Bach Khoa Quan Su Viet Nam* [Military encyclopedia of Vietnam]. Hanoi: People's Army Publishing House, 1996.

Duc, Pham Gia. *Su Doan 325, Tap II* [325th Division, Volume II]. Hanoi: People's Army Publishing House, 1986.

DuPre, Mike. "'He Gave His Life for the People He Loved." *Janesville Gazette*, May 29, 2004, 1, 7A.

———. "Letters Show Many Sides of Young Soldier." *Janesville Gazette*, May 29, 2004, 7A.

———. "Fellow Soldier Tells Story of Bellrichard's Final Moments." *Janesville Gazette*, May 29, 2004, 7A.

Eckhardt, Major General George S. *Command and Control, 1950–1969*. Vietnam Studies. Washington, D.C.: U.S Army Center of Military History, Department of the Army, 1975.

Fasoldt, Al. "10 Red Attacks Pound Allies Hours before 2-Day Truce." *Pacific Stars and Stripes* 23, no. 143 (May 24, 1967): 1, 10.

"The Five-Hour Ordeal of an Army Patrol," *Pacific Stars and Stripes* 23, no. 144 (May 25, 1967): 6.

Flood, Charles Bracelen. *The War of the Innocents*. New York: Bantam Books, 1971.

"Fresnan Leads Viet Unit to Halt Ambush." *Fresno Bee* 88, no. 16064 (May 26, 1967): 1.

"Gary Cripps Receives Silver Star." *Smithville Review* 76, no. 44 (February 1, 1968): 1–2.

"General Says Red Force Massed in Cambodia; Pentagon Issues Denial." *The Blade* (Toledo, Ohio), Saturday, May 28, 1966, 1.

Hardy, Captain Lee F., Jr. "Ivy Division Carries Fighting Tradition to Vietnam." *Ivy Leaf* 1, no. 1 (November 4, 1966): 1.

Hiep, Colonel General Dang Vu, with Senior Colonel Le Hai Trieu and Colonel Ngo Vinh Binh, *Ky Uc Tay Nguyen* [Highland Memories], Part 4. Hanoi: People's Army Publishing House, 2000.

Hogan, David W., Jr. *U.S. Army Special Operations in World War II*. Washington, D.C.: Department of the Army, 1992.

Hymoff, Edward. *Fourth Infantry Division in Vietnam*. New York: M. W. Lads Publishing Company, 1968.

Irelan, Ken. "4th Div. Hit Again Near Cambodia." *Pacific Stars and Stripes* 23, no. 142 (May 23, 1967): 6.

Keating, Susan Katz. "Nine Days in May." *VFW Magazine* 92, no. 3 (November/December 2004): 34–35.

Kuhne, Ron. "Norton Sergeant Takes Over, Leads GIs in Bloody Battle," *Akron Beacon Journal*, July 22, 1967, A1–2.

Levenson, Sanford. "No Matter What He Says, He's Hero." *Akron Beacon Journal*, July 22, 1967, 12.

Lich Su Cuc Tac Chien, 1945–2000 [History of the Combat Operations Department, 1945–2000]. Hanoi: People's Army Publishing House, 2005. Available at Quan Su Viet Nam [Vietnamese Military History], http://www.quansuvn.net/.

Lich su Trung Doan 66—Doan Plei Me—1947–2007 [History of the 66th Regiment—the Plei Me Group—1947–2007]. Hanoi: People's Army Publishing House, 2007.

"Light Action in Adams, Revere." *Ivy Leaf* 1, no. 5 (December 2, 1966): 1–2.

MacGarrigle, George L. *The United States Army in Vietnam, Combat Operations: Taking the Offensive, October 1966 to October 1967*. Washington, D.C.: U.S. Army Center of Military History, 1998.

"Maj. Gen. Peers Assumes Command of the Division." *Ivy Leaf* 1, no. 10 (January 6, 1967): 1.

Military History Institute of Vietnam. *Victory in Vietnam: The Official History of the People's Army of Vietnam, 1954–1974.* Lawrence: University of Kansas Press, 1994.

Man, Senior General Chu Huy, with Senior Colonel Le Hai Trieu. *Thoi Soi Song* [Time of Upheaval]. Hanoi: People's Army Publishing House, 2004.

Minh, Nguyen Van, et al. *Luc Luong Vu Trang Nhan Dan Tay Nguyen Trong Khang Chien Chong My Cuu Nuoc* [People's Armed Forces of the Central Highlands during the Resistance War against the Americans to Save the Nation]. Hanoi: People's Army Publishing House, 1980.

Mira, Specialist 4th Class Bob. "Sergeant Braves Enemy Fire to Rescue Wounded Soldier." *Ivy Leaf* 1, no. 36, (July 16, 1967): 3.

Moore, Lieutenant General Harold G. (Ret.), and Joseph Galloway. *We Were Soldiers Once . . . and Young: Ia Drang—The Battle That Changed the War in Vietnam.* New York: Random House, 1992.

Murphy, Edward F. *Dak To: America's Sky Soldiers in South Vietnam's Central Highlands.* Novato, Calif.: Presidio Press, 2007.

Neel, Maj. Gen. Spurgeon. *Medical Support of the U.S. Army in Vietnam, 1965–1970.* Vietnam Studies. Washington, D.C.: U.S Army Center of Military History, Department of the Army, 1973.

"NVA Arsenal Includes Human Mortar Tube." *Ivy Leaf* 1, no. 35 (July 9, 1967): 3.

"NVA Force Makes Too Many Mistakes." *Ivy Leaf* 1, no. 36 (July 16, 1967): 8.

"Operation Adams—3/12th Strikes Back at Enemy." *Ivy Leaf* 1, no. 20 (March 24, 1967): 1.

Paddock, Barry, and Jonathan Lemire. "Honoring Our Heroes." *New York Daily News,* October 12, 2011, 12.

"Platoon Calls Shells Down on Own Position." *Pacific Stars and Stripes* 23, no. 139 (May 20, 1967): 24.

Pribbenow, Merle. "General Vo Nguyen Giap and the Mysterious Evolution of the Plan for the 1968 Tet Offensive." *Journal of Vietnamese Studies* 3, no. 2 (Summer 2008): 1–33.

"Reds Pick 'Dead' GIs' Pockets." *Pacific Stars and Stripes* 23, no. 141 (May 22, 1967): 6.

Ricks, Thomas E. "The Collapse of Generalship." *Vietnam Magazine,* June 2013, 30–39.

"Rifleman Saves Lives with Quick Reaction." *Ivy Leaf* 1, no. 35 (July 9, 1967): 6.

"Rockets, Mortars Hit GIs." *Pacific Stars and Stripes* 23, no. 145 (May 26, 1967): 6.

Sharp, Admiral U. S. G., and General William C. Westmoreland. *Report on the War in Vietnam (As of 30 June 1968).* Washington, D.C.: Government Printing Office, 1968.

Sholly, Robert H. "Ivy Vines Tie Special Bonds: A Perspective from Company B, 1st Battalion, 8th Infantry, 4th Infantry Division, Republic of Vietnam." *Ivy Leaves* 89, no. 4 (Summer 2007): 3, 11.

———. *Young Soldiers, Amazing Warriors: Inside One of the Most Highly Decorated Battalions of Vietnam.* Pearland, Texas: Stonywood Publications, 2014.

"Six Men Cram into Tiny Hole." *Ivy Leaf* 1, no. 35 (July 9, 1967): 3.

"Spokane School Honors Heroes." *Ivy Leaves* 84, no. 4 (June 2002): 1, 5.

Stanton, Shelby L. *The Rise and Fall of an American Army: U.S. Ground Forces in Vietnam, 1965–1973.* New York: Ballantine Books, 2003.

Stewart, Richard W., ed. *American Military History*. Volume II, *The United States Army in a Global Era, 1917–2003*. Washington, D.C.: U.S. Army Center of Military History, 2005.

St. John, Philip A. *4th Infantry "Ivy" Division: Steadfast and Loyal*. Volume II. Paducah, Ky.: Turner Publishing Company, 1994.

Summers, Colonel Harry G. *The Vietnam Almanac*. New York: Ballantine Books, 1985.

Toan, Nguyen Huy, and Pham Quang Dinh. *Su Doan 304, Tap II* [304th Division, Volume II]. Hanoi: People's Army Publishing House, 1990.

"Troops Reach Lost Platoon; 22 of 50-Man Force Killed." *Pacific Stars and Stripes* 23, no. 140 (May 21, 1967): 6.

"Viet Cong Ambush GIs—Trap Sprung on Company While Taking Rest Break," *Yakima Morning Herald*, May 27, 1967, 1.

Westmoreland, General William C. *A Soldier Reports*. Garden City, N.Y.: Double Day, 1976.

Whitis, Staff Sergeant Bill. "General Peers Pays Tribute to First Lieutenant Enari." *Ivy Leaf* 1, no. 28 (May 19, 1967): 1–2.

Wheeler, John T. "Hell Is a Hill They Call 571."*Akron Beacon Journal*, July 2, 1967, D1, D4.

Wilkins, Warren. *Grab Their Belts to Fight Them: The Viet Cong's Big Unit War against the U.S., 1965–66*. Annapolis, Md.: Naval Institute Press, 2011.

Wilson, John B. *Maneuver and Firepower: The Evolution of Divisions and Separate Brigades*. Army Lineage Series. Washington, D.C.: U.S. Army Center of Military History, 1998.

UNPUBLISHED SOURCES

Bockover, John W. "The Untold Stories of the Men from Companies A & B, 1/8 Infantry."

Tenney, Ronnie. "On a Strange and Distant Hill."

Volkmer, Doyle. "The Splinter."

AUTHOR INTERVIEWS

Note: Ranks reflect rank held during the "Nine Days in May"

Central Intelligence Agency

Merle Pribbenow (ret.), June 28, 2011.

1st Brigade, 4th Infantry Division

1st Lt. Robert Walden (LRRP Platoon), Apr. 27, 2014.

1st of the 8th Infantry

Pfc. Charlie Bann, Dec. 16, 2010.

Pfc. John Barclay, Sept. 27, 2010; Oct. 6, 2010.

Pfc. Landis Bargatze, Nov. 2, 2010; Nov. 4, 2010; Nov. 8, 2010; Nov. 17, 2010; Nov. 19, 2010.

Spc4 Kenneth Barker, Mar. 3, 2011.

Sgt. Joe Bauer, July 18, 2012; Nov. 19, 2012.

Pfc. Robert "Ned" Bishop, Oct. 25, 2012.

1st Lt. Howard Brooks, Nov. 16, 2010.

Pfc. Ken Brosseau, Oct. 9, 2010; Jan. 9, 2011.

SSgt. Jim Buckmaster, Oct. 18, 2010.

Pfc. Tom Carty, Nov. 22, 2010.

Pfc. Bob Carlson, Feb. 4, 2011.

Pfc. Kent Coombs, Dec. 4, 2010.

Pfc. Rudy Dalton, Jan. 24, 2011.

Pfc. Bill Dobbie, Dec. 22, 2010.

Spc4 Bob Feigan, Dec. 27, 2010.

Spc4 Larry Gerken, Oct. 11, 2010; Oct. 16, 2010; Dec. 29, 2010; May 24, 2012.

Spc4 Peter Hayges, Dec. 5, 2010.

Spc4 Lou Macellari, Jan. 3, 2013.

Pfc. Ray Mankowski, Nov. 30, 2010.

Spc4 Bill May, Nov. 10, 2010; Nov. 2, 2012.

Spc4 Jay "Joby" McAulay, Dec. 13, 2010; Dec. 19, 2010.

Sgt. John McKeever, Jan. 3, 2011; Feb. 17, 2012.

Spc4 Dave Miller, July 18, 2012.

Spc4 Raul Munoz, Nov. 27, 2010; Nov. 29, 2010.

Pfc. Gilbert Nash, Sept. 22, 2010; Sept. 25, 2010, Sept. 28, 2010, Oct. 2, 2010.

Sgt. Frank Patton, Jan. 4, 2010.

Sgt. Jim Peirce, Nov. 14, 2010.

Capt. Bob Quinn, Jan. 27, 2011.

Sgt. Ross Rembert, Nov. 28, 2010; Dec. 5, 2010.

Spc4 Victor Renza, Sept. 18, 2010; Sept. 26, 2010; Sept. 28, 2010; Oct. 12, 2010; Oct. 15, 2010; Dec. 12, 2010; Jan. 12,2011; Nov. 14, 2011.

1st Lt. Larry Rodabaugh, Sept. 21, 2010; Sept. 25, 2010; Oct. 10, 2010; June 8, 2011; June 11, 2012; Jan. 5, 2013.

Pfc. Cliff Rountree, Oct. 2, 2010; Oct. 27, 2010; Jan. 13, 2011; June 14, 2011.

Sgt. Chuck Runde, Jan. 30, 2011.

Capt. Robert Sholly, Dec. 1, 2011; Dec. 19, 2011; Dec. 22, 2011; Mar. 8, 2012; Apr. 19, 2012; May 3, 2012; July 25, 2012; July 28, 2012; Aug. 12, 2012; Sept. 25, 2012; Oct. 25, 2012; Nov. 5, 2012.

Sgt. Ron Snyder, Nov. 13, 2010; Nov. 15, 2010; Nov. 28, 2011; Aug. 30, 2012.

Spc4 Tom Sears, Jan. 9, 2011.

Sgt. Dick Surface, Oct. 24, 2010; Nov. 3, 2010; Jan. 19,2011.

Pfc. Van Waugh, Feb. 1, 2011.

Pfc. Bob Warden, Dec. 13, 2010.

Capt. Walter Williamson, Jan. 13, 2011.

Relatives of 1-8 Inf. Veterans

Tami Grandstaff (daughter of Plt. Sgt. Bruce Grandstaff), Apr. 1, 2014.

Mary Wheeler (sister of Sgt. James Burch), Oct. 22, 2010.

Betty Workman Sturgeon (sister of Spc4 James Workman), Nov. 4, 2010.

Gaza Molnar (brother of SSgt. Frankie Molnar), May 1, 2012.

Sharon Mills (widow of SSgt. Frankie Molnar), May 3, 2012.

3rd of the 12th Infantry

Spc4 Chuck Ahearn, July 22, 2013.
Spc4 Richard Blair, July 27, 2013.
Spc4 Oliver Butler, Apr. 11, 2011; Apr. 20, 2011; April 21, 2011; Jul. 6, 2013.
Pfc. Stan Coker, July 12, 2013.
Spc4 Jim Coughlan, Feb. 25, 2011; Apr. 12, 2013; June 2, 2013.
Spc4 Kenny Dempich, May 18, 2011; Mar. 25, 2013; June 13, 2013; Nov. 7, 2013.
Sgt. Ken Ethier, May 13, 2011.
Spc4 John Ferrante, Oct. 2, 2010; Feb 7, 2011.
Spc4 Hank Fischer, Mar. 5, 2011; Mar. 21, 2013; Apr. 26, 2013; Jul 9, 2013.
Capt. Mike Hamer, Nov. 23, 2010; Feb. 10, 2011; Mar. 4, 2011; Sept. 14, 2011; Jan. 25, 2013; Apr. 16, 2013; June 29, 2013; July 8, 2013; Sept. 10, 2013.
Spc4 Mike Horan, Apr. 10 2011; June 6, 2013; June 11, 2013.
Sgt. Arthur Klassen, May 6, 2011; Mar. 4, 2013; Mar. 24, 2013; Aug. 4, 2013.
Spc4 Ralph Lent, May 25, 2011.
Sgt. Billy Lomnicki, Dec. 27, 2012; Apr. 13, 2013; June 24, 2013.
SSgt. Loya Mallory, May 19, 2013.
Spc4 Bob Masching, Mar. 21, 2011; Sept. 10, 2011.
Pfc. Eddie Meier, Mar. 1, 2011; Mar. 2, 2011; Apr. 3, 2013; May 21, 2013; June 18, 2013.
Spc4 Paul Modaferri, Mar. 23, 2011.
Spc4 Bill Moen, Mar. 26, 2011.
1st Lt. Steve Pestikas, Nov. 12, 2010; Nov. 28, 2010; Jan. 9, 2011; Jan. 18, 2011; Feb. 16, 2011; Jan. 24, 2012; Feb. 8, 2013; May 6, 2013.
Capt. Tom Pearson, May 23, 2011; May 27, 2011; Jan. 23, 2013; Aug. 12, 2013.
Sgt. Tom Radke, Mar. 10, 2011; Aug. 9, 2013.
Pfc. Rey Ramirez, Mar. 7, 2011; Apr. 1, 2013.
Sgt. Robert Ramirez, Feb. 10, 2011; Feb. 9, 2013; Feb. 17, 2013; Mar. 12, 2013; Apr. 27, 2013.
Spc4 Scott Reitenauer, June 5, 2011; Mar. 14, 2011; Apr. 14, 2013.
Pfc. Charles A. Richardson Jr., Feb. 15, 2011; May 4, 2013; June 18, 2013.
Spc4 Bob Rider, Dec. 19, 2013.
Sgt. Fred Roper, Dec.3, 2013.
Spc4 Larry Schindeldecker, Apr. 14, 2011.
Spc4 John Sobaski, Mar. 25, 2011.
Spc4 Gary Specht, Mar. 14, 2011.
Spc4 Roger Strand, Feb. 18, 2011; Sept. 26, 2013.
1st Lt. Doyle Volkmer, Jan. 14, 2011.
Lt. Col. John F. Vollmer, Oct. 27, 2010; Nov. 9, 2010; Feb. 1, 2011; Feb. 22, 2011.
Sgt. Wayne Watson, May 5, 2013; Sept. 12, 2013.

3rd of the 8th Infantry

Pfc. Russell Belden, July 2, 2013; July 3, 2013; Dec. 29, 2014.
Spc4 Jim Congrove, May 9, 2011.

Sgt. Richard Crooks, Mar. 24, 2014.

Spc4 Richard Elam, May 3, 2011; Mar. 12, 2014; Aug. 25, 2014; Sept. 13, 2014.

Pfc. Dave Fessler, Dec. 6, 2011; Mar. 10, 2014; Aug. 12, 2014; Aug. 23, 2014; Sept. 24, 2014; Oct. 29, 2014; Dec. 16, 2014.

Spc4 Bob Gamboa, May 8, 2011; Mar. 8, 2014; Mar. 28, 2014; Aug. 23, 2014; June 24, 2015.

Spc4 Ed Goehring, May 10, 2011; Mar. 19, 2014.

Spc4 Ken Irvin, May 11, 2011; Aug. 13, 2014.

Spc4 Ronyal Jacobs, Mar. 16, 2014.

Spc5 Richard Jackson, Apr. 26, 2011; Apr. 27, 2011; Apr. 2, 2014; May 30, 2014; Sept. 18, 2014; Nov. 17, 2014; Jan. 19, 2015.

Sgt. Larry Jumper, May 17, 2011; Mar. 11, 2014, Sept. 3, 2014; Sept. 22, 2014; Nov. 9, 2014.

Lt. Col. Tom Lynch, Oct. 23, 2010; Jan. 18, 2011.

1st Lt. Branko Marinovich, June 4, 2011; June 7, 2011; Mar. 24, 2014; Aug. 16, 2014; Oct. 15, 2014; Nov. 24, 2014.

1st Lt. Rick Nelson, Mar. 13, 2014; Aug. 16, 2014; Aug. 18, 2014; Sept. 10, 2014; Sept. 22, 2014; Oct. 9, 2014.

Pfc. Larry Orr, Mar. 14, 2014; Dec. 2, 2014.

Pfc. Bill Perkins, May 22, 2011.

Pfc. Gary Retana, July 1, 2011; July 2, 2011; Mar. 13, 2014; Aug 25, 2014; Oct. 5, 2014.

Pfc. Dan Shayotovich, Sept. 18, 2011; Dec. 7, 2011.

Sgt. Erin Stroh, Mar. 26, 2014; Mar. 27, 2014; May 7, 2014; May 11, 2014; Oct. 14, 2014; Nov. 3, 2014; Dec. 28, 2014; Jan. 9, 2015.

Spc4 Roger Tenbrink, Apr. 15, 2014; May 14, 2014.

Pfc. Don Tienhaara, Apr. 28, 2011; Apr. 29, 2011; July 29, 2014.

Spc4 Tom Thompson, April 25, 2014.

Friends and Relatives of 3-8 Inf. Veterans

Robert Childers (brother of 1st Sgt. Richard Childers), Apr. 11, 2014.

Charles Flood (author), Feb. 12, 2011.

Dan Mangas (friend of 1st Lt. Clayton Johnson), Mar. 9, 2014.

Dan Wilkins (brother of Richard Wilkins), May 25, 2014.

4th Aviation Battalion

WO1 Don Rawlinson, Dec. 8, 2011; Apr.16, 2012; June 9, 2013.

6th of the 29th Artillery

Pfc. Bill Avery, Feb. 25, 2011.

Capt. Ray Harton, Feb. 1, 2012; Feb. 2, 2012.

Sgt. Michael Scott, Aug. 25, 2014; Aug. 31, 2014; Nov. 25, 2014; Dec. 18, 2014; Feb. 23, 2015.

INDEX

Page numbers in *italics* indicate illustrations.